INVESTMENT PLANNING

FOR FINANCIAL PROFESSIONALS

Develope an Expected Return
    ↳ determine Standard Deviation based on market, economics
      etc.
    ↳ Review the relationship of the movement between 2
      securities or single security to the market Correlati
      Coefficent & Covariance
         ↳ Securities that tend to move in opposite directions
         (Negative correlation) do better in turbulant
         Markets. Prices move in opposite direction based
         on the Same financial event.

    ↳ R^2 Variation in the dependent variable that can be
      explained by the independent variable
         ↳ Ex- changes in Consumption are based on changes
         in income → consump being the dependent variable to
         income the independent variable.

INVESTMENT PLANNING
FOR FINANCIAL PROFESSIONALS

GEOFFREY A. HIRT

STANLEY B. BLOCK

SOMNATH BASU

McGraw-Hill

New York   Chicago   San Francisco   Lisbon   London   Madrid   Mexico City
Milan   New Delhi   San Juan   Seoul   Singapore   Sydney   Toronto

*The **McGraw·Hill** Companies*

Portions of this book have been previously published in *Fundamentals of Investment Management*, seventh edition, © 2003 and *Foundations of Financial Management*, eleventh edition, © 2004 by The McGraw-Hill Companies, Inc.

3 4 5 6 7 8 9 0 WCK/WCK 0 9

ISBN 0-07-132721-5

McGraw-Hill books are available at special quantity discounts to use as premiums and sales promotions, or for use in corporate training programs. For more information, please write to the Director of Special Sales, Professional Publishing, McGraw-Hill, Two Penn Plaza, New York, NY 10121-2298. Or contact your local bookstore.

Library of Congress Cataloging-in-Publication Data

Hirt, Geoffrey A.
Investment planning for financial professionals/by Geoffrey A. Hirt, Stanley B. Block, and Somnath Basu.
p. cm.
ISBN 0-07-132721-5 (hardcover: alk. paper)
1. Investments. 2. Finance, Personal. 3. Portfolio management. I. Block, Stanley B. II. Basu, Somnath. III. Title.

HG4521.H5792 2006
332.6–dc22   2005024463

To my mother, Aparna

SB

Contents

Preface

This first edition of *Investment Planning for Financial Professionals* has been primarily written for the many students and practitioners of financial planning and services. The Certified Financial Planner (CFP) Board of Standards has prescribed for many years what students must know about investment planning and management, through a list of investment topics. However, over all these years, there has never been a book that covered each and every one of these topics. As a result, financial planning educational programs were forced to use textbooks that were written for very different audiences. Further, as students turned into practitioners, they never had a reference text on their shelves that described what they had learnt and what they practiced. With the introduction of this book, all this has now changed. The reader will find that this textbook captures the excitement and enthusiasm that we feel for the topic of investment for financial planners.

For the first time, a sincere commitment has been made to provide the students and professionals of this vibrant and dynamic community with an investments planning textbook that they can truly call their own. Not only should it be the textbook of choice for all financial planning educational programs, but it is a "must have" library copy for all CFP practitioners and financial services professionals.

Throughout the book, we have attempted to establish the appropriate theoretical and practical base, while at the same time following through with real-world examples. Students learn not only about the theory but also about the practice of financial planning. The similarities, consistencies and differences between theory and practice are brought out explicitly in this book – a sentiment and a need that planners have expressed from the field for a long time.

The book is completely based on the Investment Planning Syllabus as created by the AFS–CFP Board of Standards Model Curriculum Committee in 2003. Hence, all the items in the syllabus topic list have been covered in great detail. Furthermore, the layout and flow of the textbook also reflects the Model Syllabus, which was developed by experts in the field of investments for financial planning. Since 2003, the CFP Board topic list has changed; however, the changes to the topic list are still perfectly consistent with the material presented in this book.

INVESTMENT PLANNING

FOR FINANCIAL PROFESSIONALS

Chapter 1

Investment Planning and the Financial Planning Process

INTRODUCTION

Investments and investment planning take on an extremely important role in the financial planning process. Without proper investment planning, it would be difficult for people to achieve financial goals. When people think of investing, they oftentimes only think of one aspect of investing, such as picking stocks or investing in mutual funds. Individuals can have false perceptions about investing because they may have lost or gained abnormal sums of money in the markets in the past. In such cases, their expectations about what their investments would yield obviously varied between their perception and the final investment outcome.

In the fourth quarter of 2002, stock market indices such as the Dow Jones Industrials, the Nasdaq Composite Index, and the S&P 500 all started to experience precipitous declines in the indices. These declines partially resulted especially from worse than expected performance from the technology industry, which ultimately resulted in declining revenues and profits, and eventually to major layoffs in the industry. This was also the era in which many publicly traded companies were caught illegally altering the accounting books. When the activities of companies such as Enron and MCI WorldCom were exposed, it became evident that profits within these companies were also less than previously stated. Major restructurings within these companies were necessary in order to ensure their long-term survival. As a result, these companies were forced to make vast reductions in capital expenditures and human capital. This resulted in more layoffs, depressed stock prices and an economy that quickly slid into a recession. The events of September 11, 2001, also played a large part in shaping the economic health of the economy for the next couple of years as the government diverted funds from the economy to building up the military and fighting the war on terror.

The government did not stand idle in these events. Academics and business people alike had different opinions about whether the government did enough to help the U.S. economy in such a time of universal need. In response to this recession, the U.S. government reacted by implementing a tax cut package. The Federal Reserve lowered interest rates in order to stimulate business and consumer spending. While these two actions probably helped the U.S. economy from sliding into a major depression, they were not immediately able to stimulate the economy so much as to help create jobs and increase business and consumer spending. The interest rate drops also had unintended outcomes, which we will discuss below.

It is not difficult to see that from an investor's standpoint then, that precipitous drops in stock price would affect the overall value of an investor's portfolio. Those who previously had invested in safe investments such as T-bills or money market funds clearly experienced lower overall returns due to the lower prevailing interest rates in the economy. Almost every investor in the economy was hurt by the economic and political events that our economy encountered in 2001 and the years following.

Many people had put their fortunes into the stock market. Millionaires became paupers overnight. Retirees living on variable interest rate investments also found themselves with less money to spend due to pitiful returns on their investments. It became impossible for many to live on these retirement savings. In these cases, clearly many people's portfolios were not built such that they could withstand the negative forces acting on them. It is possible, however, to build portfolios that they may be able to weather such tumultuous events. This is not to say that your clients will never lose money in the short run. With careful planning, however, and understanding of your clients' needs, it is possible to create portfolios that can weather the tests of time and get your clients to their ultimate end-game.

This chapter will provide an understanding of the steps and considerations of investment planning in the financial planning process. We will see what a pivotal role investing plays in the overall picture of financial planning. We will then discuss some of the main considerations in financial planning, insurance planning, retirement planning, education planning, estate planning, and tax planning. Finally, we will discuss the rules and regulations that govern investment advisors and will finish the chapter with ethical considerations for planners.

STEPS AND CONSIDERATIONS IN INVESTMENT PLANNING DURING THE FINANCIAL PLANNING PROCESS

The development of a sound investment strategy begins with the planner establishing and defining a relationship with the client. In order to understand the **goals**, high-level statements identifying short- and long-term financial requirements, and **objectives**, quantifiable, tactical statements that are in sync with the high level goals, it is first necessary to form a relationship with clients, learning about their general and specific attitudes toward their finances and toward the external factors that will ultimately affect their financial situation.

After the planner has established the client/planner relationship, the planner must assist the client in establishing short-term and long-term goals as they relate to insurance needs, retirement needs, estate needs, tax planning needs, educational funding needs, and any unique needs the client may have. Investment planning needs will be an outcome of this process since all goals will have a funding requirement and hence an investing component. After defining the goals, the planner must obtain all relevant, current financial data from the client. Such information includes checking and savings statements; portfolio, retirement and social security statements; employee benefit information; insurance information such as home, health, auto, long-term care and life policies; educational funds; estate information such as wills, living trusts or powers of attorney; and relevant tax documents. This list is by no means exhaustive but it gives an idea of the magnitude of the information required to implement a financial plan that inevitably has a central investment component.

When the data have been provided by the client, the data must be analyzed as it relates to the client's goals. Based upon the current financial situation of the client, the planner must develop and present a comprehensive plan that realistically addresses the client's short- and long-term goals. If the client accepts the planner's proposal, implementation of the plan can begin.

During the process of implementation, proper investment planning will now become a major factor in ensuring that the client has the best chance of success in maximizing the dollars committed to the financial plan. As such, the planner must fully consider the client's specific investment objectives and constraints. When we discuss investment objectives, we are talking about the client's **return requirements** and **risk tolerance** levels. Return requirements are the returns that the investor expects to receive on investments, usually expressed in percentage terms over the time frame of the investment. Risk tolerance refers to the level of risk that an investor is willing to undertake for an expected level of return. Higher risk investments are expected to yield higher returns over the investment period while lower risk investments are expected to yield lower returns over the investment period. Because all clients are individuals with unique experiences, backgrounds and attitudes, establishing an investor's risk tolerance level is a tricky business. In later chapters, we will discuss ways in which the planner can help the client to identify their relative risk tolerance. We will discuss risk and return objectives in detail in another chapter.

When we talk about constraints, we are identifying specific limitations in the investment plan such as **time horizon, liquidity,** and **tax factors.** Social, legal, regulatory, political, and economic considerations are additional external constraints that can interfere with an investment plan. Since both the individual investor and external forces contribute to the ultimate outcome of investment performance, it is clear that an investment plan is constrained by factors that make up these circumstances.

The time horizon of an investor involves identifying the time frame for which goals need to be met. Goals typically fall into **short-term, intermediate-term, and long-term** horizons. As human wants are limitless but funding is limited, it is imperative to have a priority of high or low assigned to each goal. Prioritizing goals helps to shape the investment policy as some goals have an ultimately low status in relation to other goals. Short-term goals are typically those goals that will take place in less than a few years. Some short-term goals might include establishing an emergency fund, purchasing a new car, or taking a summer vacation. Because the money will be required for use shortly, these types of investments will be in safe, highly liquid investments such as savings accounts, certificates of deposits, or money market accounts.

Long-term goals are typically those goals associated with time frames that are greater than five years. Some long-term goals may include the ability to achieve financial independence at a certain age, funding a child's education, or providing enough funds at death to ensure that estate taxes and expenses are taken care of. Because a long period of time exists between initial investment and the fund's requirement, the investor can consider a more aggressive investment approach. As such, a variety of stocks, bonds, mutual funds, or other investment alternatives should be evaluated as a means to accomplishing long-term goals.

Intermediate-term goals fall between the short- and long-term goals. Intermediate-term goals include goals that may include time horizons of 5 to 15 but could be shorter or longer depending on the specific nature of the goals. Some intermediate-term goals may include purchasing a home or an investment property. Other goals may include starting a business or investing in one. The investment strategies involved with these types of goals tend to be a mix of both conservative investments and higher risk investments. Investment time horizons and strategies will be discussed in subsequent chapters.

Liquidity is measured by the ability of the investor to convert an investment into cash within a relatively short time at its fair market value or with a minimum capital loss on the transaction. Most financial assets provide a high degree of liquidity. Stocks and bonds can generally be sold within a matter of minutes at a price reasonably close to the last traded value. Such may not be the case for real estate. Almost everyone has seen a house or piece of commercial real estate sit on the market for weeks, months, or years.

Liquidity can also be measured indirectly by the transaction costs or commissions involved in the transfer of ownership. Financial assets generally trade on a relatively low commission basis of perhaps 1 or 2 percent, whereas many real assets have transaction costs that run from 5 percent to 25 percent or more.

In many cases, the lack of immediate liquidity can be justified if there are unusual opportunities for gain. An investment in real estate or precious gems may provide sufficient return to more than compensate for the added transaction costs. Of course, a bad investment will be all the more difficult to unload.

Investors must carefully assess their own situation to determine the need for liquidity. If you are investing funds to be used for the next house payment or the coming semester's tuition, then immediate liquidity will be essential, and financial assets will be preferred. If funds can be tied up for long periods, bargain-buying opportunities of an unusual nature can also be evaluated.

Tax Factors

Investors in high tax brackets have different investment objectives than those in lower brackets or tax-exempt charities, foundations, or similar organizations. An investor in a high tax bracket may prefer municipal bonds (interest is not taxable), commercial real estate (with its depreciation and interest write-off), or investments that provide tax credits or tax shelters.

Though tax considerations should not be the primary consideration for investment decisions, all investors should seek to minimize the tax implications of investment outcomes through deferral or via favorable tax treatment (e.g. long-term capital gains tax rates vs. short-term capital gain tax treatment). Tax payers seek to defer gains during high income years and to accept deductions (losses) in these same years. Conversely, investors will capitalize on investment gains in otherwise lower income years and defer deductions (losses) if possible during these very same years.

The tax environment certainly changes as the U.S. government seeks to induce certain behaviors within the economy. For instance, the Economic Growth & Tax Relief Reconciliation Act (EGTRRA) of 2001 lowered the **long-term capital gains** rate for those in the highest income brackets (>15 percent tax bracket) from 28 percent to 20 percent. Long-term capital gains are those gains on the sale of investment assets that are held by the investor for one year or more. Likewise, EGTRRA reduced taxable dividends to 5 percent for taxpayers in the 10 percent and 15 percent tax brackets and to 15 percent for higher income tax payers, from their higher current rates. Both of these law changes were part of a comprehensive package through which the government is attempting to stimulate investments within the economy as well as restoring flailing faith for the investment climate within the U.S. economy at large.

The control that an investor exhibits over the tax consequences of certain types of investments is undoubtedly an important factor in the overall investment plan. In certain instances, the tax consequences of a particular, buy, sell, or hold strategy may not be clear to the investor or advisor. During these times, it may be necessary for outside tax counsel to provide advice on the various intricacies that will ultimately affect the outcome of the decision.

Once the constraints and objectives have been properly identified and discussed, the planner and client can implement investment strategies and contingency plans. Upon implementation, the plan must be monitored so that progress toward goals and objectives can be measured. If they are not being met, the planner and client should modify the plan as required. These issues will also be discussed in later chapters.

The Importance of Investment Planning in the Financial Planning Process

As we have already discussed, every aspect of the financial planning process depends upon appropriate investment planning. Consider the four main areas of the financial planning process: insurance, retirement, education, and estate planning. Tax planning also comes into consideration, and we have discussed the importance of its implications in a previous section. Without understanding how investment choices affect the financial planning process, a financial plan could be lacking in breadth and depth and therefore it could fall short of achieving the client's goals.

Investment planning seeks to accomplish two equally important goals that naturally conflict with each other. The first goal is to maximize returns on investments. The second is most often to minimize investment risk. Effective financial planning seeks to balance these two goals in all areas of the investment planning process so that the investor can achieve the desired outcomes.

Analyzing the other four aspects of the financial planning process—insurance, education, retirement, and estate planning—may help planners to understand why investment planning plays such a pivotal role in the financial planning process.

Investment Considerations in Life Insurance Planning

Insurance is purchased so that individuals and entities can safeguard themselves against financial loss. Typical types of insurance are auto, homeowner's, health, business liability, personal liability, and life insurance. Because insurance protects against loss, it is generally thought of as a protective vehicle rather than an investment vehicle. For the most part, this is true, except where some types of life insurance are considered.

At a very basic level, there are two types of life insurance: **term life insurance** and **permanent life insurance**. Term life insurance provides coverage against the pure risk of premature death for a set period of time (e.g. 5 years or 15 years) as long as the premiums are paid. If premature death occurs, the insurance policy pays the **beneficiary** the **face amount** of the policy. The beneficiary is one or more people named by the insured to collect the life insurance proceeds at death. The face amount is the amount of insurance that is paid out in the event of death. Amounts can be as little as $5,000 with ranges over $1 million. All else being equal, the greater the face amount of the policy, the greater will be the required premium payments. As the insured gets older, premiums increase at an exponential rate and, thus, the purchase of term life insurance is generally not suitable for these older individuals.

Oftentimes, a person buying a term life policy will experience a level term payment for the life of the insurance contract. However, this is not always the case and, therefore, it is important to read the terms of the policy very carefully. The only benefit that the term life insurance policy provides is for a face amount to be paid to beneficiaries at death. Otherwise these policies have no investment returns or other included benefits. Because these are often the cheapest type of life insurance, term policies are generally suitable for those families just starting out and for those who may have limited cash flow but who absolutely need life insurance coverage.

Permanent life insurance (sometimes called cash-value insurance) provides insurance for the entire life of the insured rather than for a specified term; provided premiums are paid. Premiums for permanent life insurance are generally higher than term life insurance premiums because permanent insurance is considered an investment vehicle designed to realize **cash value buildup** in addition to a face value on the policy. Like term life insurance, the insurance company will pay the face amount of the insurance policy in the event of premature death. The cash value buildup feature is an investment component whereby a portion of the monthly payment is contributed toward an investment fund for the policy holder.

This investment fund is a savings vehicle for the investor. In contributing a monthly amount toward this investment account, the investor expects to receive a rate of return on this investment. In early years, there will not be a lot of cash buildup since initial amounts invested are small. Over time, the investments can grow depending on the type of policy chosen and the rate of return earned on the cash buildup. Over time, the policy holder is achieving two objectives: financial protection in the event of premature death and a savings component that is coupled with a corresponding return objective.

There are several types of permanent life insurance. We will currently simplify the descriptions and explain them in more detail later. From an investment perspective, whole life and variable life insurance promise a minimum amount of return. Because of this, the insurance company directs the nature of the investment vehicles. With variable life products, the rate of return on the contributed capital is variable since the investment choices are driven by the investor. One important fact to note, however, is that even though the policy holder can choose among various investments, the insurance company will generally limit the quantity and quality of investments to the policy holder. This means that the investor cannot pick readily from the universe of products that currently exist in the broad marketplace.

Permanent life insurance policies have some features that may make them attractive to investors. All policies offer tax deferral on the cash buildup. Most policies allow the policy holder to borrow against the cash buildup via low interest rate loans (borrowing the insured's own money) in times of cash need.

One important thing to beware of in permanent policies is the fees that are associated with having the policy. Be sure to get a full understanding of all the fees in one of these policies. Additionally, even though there is a cash value buildup component to these policies, there is often a surrender value if the consumer wishes to close out or cancel the policy prior to death. The consumer could surrender as much as 40 percent of the cash buildup of the policy. Before purchasing one of these policies, it is important to ensure that it is being done for the right financial reasons.

Many individuals own term or permanent life policies. We will later discuss the detailed pros and cons of such policies. Depending on the final investment plan, life insurance policies can certainly be a significant portion of the investor's monthly income and can successfully be used in the overall financial planning process. While providing against financial loss due to the death of the policy holder and providing investment income from the cash buildup feature of permanent policies, life insurance can also be used in the estate planning process in order to provide consumption income to beneficiaries and to pay for estate taxes. One beneficial feature to all life insurance policies is that the payout to beneficiaries is not taxed by federal or state governments. For wealthy families who will inevitably be faced with estate taxes at death, life insurance provides a way for estate taxes to be paid without reducing the overall worth of the rest of the estate.

Investment Considerations in Retirement Planning

Investment strategy as it relates to retirement planning must be backed by a comprehensive plan in order to ensure that the client will be successful in reaching retirement objectives. The most important retirement objective is for the investor(s) to maintain a certain standard of living at retirement. In general, your clients will not want to accept a lower standard of living and may, in fact, want certain things that they did not have in their working years. For instance, many people will have postponed vacations or vacation homes during their working years because of work or child rearing. Retirement presents the time for them to participate in these types of activities.

Over the last two decades, the United States has seen a huge decline in pension income provided by employers. As such, retirement planning has become even more important for people. Social security is often not enough for most people to live on at retirement, so they must be dovetailed with other retirement planning strategies. There is also much speculation as to whether or not social security will be around in the coming years.

Some retirees will be forced to pay for health insurance if they retire prior to their Medicare age and if it is no longer provided by an employer upon retirement. Health insurance costs have been rising faster than inflation in recent years. Despite this fact, most people will not want to accept inferior healthcare and may have to pay for increased premiums. There will invariably be other retirement objectives that your clients will have. They will vary from client to client and will have to be incorporated into the overall investment strategy.

At all ages of life, but especially during old age, health insurance is one major aspect which needs to be considered. Costs of heart surgery, for instance, can cost tens of thousands of dollars. The medication requirements after heart surgery can pose ongoing budget constraints as well. Heart surgeries and treatments like it can wipe out savings and ultimately cause the liquidation of the home or other investments. Thus, it is necessary to place healthcare costs in the overall budgetary framework of the client such that other important investment objectives and contingency objectives can be thought of.

Several factors affect the investment strategies and tactics that a planner will employ in order to execute the retirement plan. Before deciding on any investment vehicles, the planner must first take into consideration the relative risk aversion of the clients. Consideration must be given to how much has been accumulated in retirement funds, the expected rates of return on investments in the future and the estimated funds that will be required for each of their retirement years. Depending on the amount that must be saved, the planner must consider the **Remaining Work Life Expectancy (RWLE)**, the number of years before the client expects to retire, of the client in order to assess the required savings amounts within the limited time available to the client.

The age of the client is also an important consideration since risk profiles will naturally change as the client gets closer to retirement. When an individual is closer to retirement, lower risk investments such as high quality bonds and money market funds will make up the bulk of the retirement portfolio. The converse is true when an individual has a long RWLE as the client can afford to have a higher percentage of the portfolio invested in more risky assets, such as stocks.

Investment Considerations in Education Planning

Educational planning is similar to retirement planning in that the planner must first consider how much has been accumulated to date, the time horizon that the funds will be required, the relative risk aversion of the investors, and the expected costs for funding the education over the period of education. All things being equal, the earlier in their children's life that parents begin to save for education, the closer they will be to achieving the funding requirements.

There are many important challenges in educational planning that compound the difficulty of the plan. Consider the list of unknown factors in educational planning. How much will tuition cost at the time the child starts college? Will the child be going to a community, a state, or a private college? Will the child eventually attend graduate school or doctorate school? How long will the child be in school? Will the child be living at home or in a residence hall? What are the expected costs for room and board, books and lab fees, and extracurricular activities? What type of investment plan should be chosen in order to maximize the savings and tax implications? What are the pros and cons of each type of investment scenario? Will the parents expect to save all the money prior to the college start date? Do they expect to use loans? Will the child be expected to contribute to the education? If so, at what percentage will the child contribute? Are they thinking of using the equity in their home to fund part of the expenditure? What if ultimately, the child decides not to go to college? What are the tax considerations of such an event?

As you can see, the unknown factors are endless. In using investment vehicles for educational funding, the planner must not only know the various types of education investment plans but must also have a clear understanding of the vision that the investors share for the child's education. In recent years it has become clear that college tuition rates are increasing faster than inflation. The U.S. Department of Education published a report in 2001 which found that both public and private four year colleges saw an increase in annual tuition in fees of approximately 4.3 percent in the late 1980s through the late 1990s.[1] To make

---

1. Study of College Costs and Prices, 1988–89 to 1997-98, Volume I, Statistical Analysis Report. Post Secondary Education Descriptive Analysis. Authors: Cunningham, Wellman, Clinedinst, Merisotis, Publication Date: 12/2001.

matters less complex, the planner must balance the relative risk aversion of the investors against these goals in order to make the most efficient plan possible.

Some investment vehicles such as educational IRAs and Section 529 plans allow the investments to accumulate interest on a tax-free basis. As long as withdrawals are used for qualified educational expenses, withdrawals may be tax-free. Contributions to an educational IRA may be tax deductible in the year that the contribution is made when the parents' incomes are below certain levels as deemed by the IRS. Contributions to 529 plans are not tax deductible though annual contributions are not as limited in the amount of annual contribution as IRAs. The other options for educational funding are endless and any number of investment vehicles can be used to achieve the goals. Of course, when an individual is closer to beginning college, lower risk investments such as high quality bonds and money market funds will make up the bulk of the educational portfolio. The converse is true when the student is expected to start college at a later date since the client can afford to have a higher percentage of the portfolio invested in more risky assets such as stocks.

Investment Considerations in Estate Planning

Clients often use **living trusts** that hold and manage investments during the life of the trust creator and after death. A living trust, a trust that is created during the life of the creator, is a legal entity which can store and manage the wealth of the creator. The creator of the trust assigns a **trustee**, an individual or a corporation whose responsibility it is to oversee the elements of the trust. When placing investments in the trust, the trustee then is responsible for overseeing the management of the investments. Since a living trust is creating during the creator's lifetime, the trust can be used to generate income to meet everyday needs for the creator. Upon death, the trustee will ensure that any assets retained in the trust are distributed from or retained in the trust according to the creator's wishes.

Individuals who have estates in excess of $1.5 million are currently subject to payment of estate taxes per current tax law. However, as we will see in our discussion in a later section, in the real world of investing, the estate taxation rules will become more beneficial for larger estates until 2010. Nonetheless, estate planning objectives must consider how to minimize taxes and maximize the funds left to beneficiaries. Though tax planning should not be the primary driver in estate planning, its effect for wealthy clients must be fully considered. More important estate/investment considerations include how much of the estate to leave to beneficiaries and the timing of such transfers; providing funding for transfer costs; providing for financial support for dependents; providing liquidity within the estate so that taxes can be paid without forcing liquidation of other assets; and planning for the management, accumulation or preservation of estate funds if certain beneficiaries are unwilling or unable to manage them on their own.

REGULATION OF ADVISORS

Now, we will switch gears to give an overview of the investment industry as a whole and why regulation of the industry came about. In this, we will discuss the important components of the laws for investment advisors as they pertain to the Securities Acts of 1933 and 1934, the Investment Company Act of 1940, and the Investment Advisor Act of 1940.

A Brief History in Regulation

The post-World War I environment was a high growth economic era in the United States. As such, there were plenty of investment opportunities that promised "get rich quick" schemes. Prior to the "Great Crash of 1929," there was no federal regulation of the securities markets. Companies that sold stock did not have to provide disclosure regarding the types of investments provided to the public, the quality of the investment, or any other financial information. The result was a stock market that was full of scams and deceitful security marketing practices. But when the stock market crashed in 1929, thousands of investors (individuals, companies, and banks) lost their fortunes overnight. In effect, the stock market crash had profound effects on the economy of the United States.

Over the next several years, public confidence in the economy and in the financial markets deteriorated. Investments were at an all-time low and economic progress was stagnated. Congress had many meetings to determine an appropriate course of action. And finally, they passed the Securities Act of 1933 and the Securities Exchange Act of 1934.

Securities Act of 1933

The Securities Act of 1933 was enacted after congressional investigations of the abuses in the securities markets during the 1929 crash and again in 1931. The act's primary purpose was to require full disclosure of all pertinent investment information whenever a corporation sold a new issue of securities. It is sometimes referred to as the "truth in securities" act. This act has several important features:

1. All offerings except government bonds and bank stocks that are to be sold in more than one state must be registered with the Securities Exchange Commission (SEC).

2. The registration statement must be filed 20 days in advance of the date of sale and include detailed corporate information. If the SEC finds the information misleading, incomplete, or inaccurate, it will delay the offering until the registration statement is corrected. The SEC in no way certifies that the security is fairly priced but that the information seems to be factual and accurate. Under certain circumstances, the previously mentioned shelf registration is used to modify the 20-day waiting period concept.

3. All new issues of securities must be accompanied by a **prospectus,** a detailed summary of the registration statement. Included in the prospectus is usually a list of directors and officers; their salaries, stock options, and shareholdings; financial reports certified by a certified public accountant (CPA); a list of the underwriters; the purpose and use for the funds to be provided from the sale of securities; and any other information that investors may need to know before they can wisely invest their money. A preliminary prospectus may be distributed to potential buyers before the offering date, but it will not contain the offering price or underwriting fees. It is called a red herring because stamped on the front in red letters are the words "Preliminary Prospectus."

4. Officers of the company and other experts preparing the prospectus or registration statement can be sued for penalties and recovery of realized losses if any information presented was fraudulent or factually wrong or if relevant information was omitted.

Securities Exchange Act of 1934

The Securities Exchange Act of 1934 created the Securities and Exchange Commission to enforce the securities laws. It was empowered to regulate the securities markets and those companies listed on the exchanges. Specifically, the major points of the 1934 act are[2] as follows:

---

2. Actually, the SEC did not come into existence until 1934. The Federal Trade Commission had many of these responsibilities before the formation of the SEC.

1. Guidelines for insider trading were established. Insiders must hold securities for at least six months before they can sell them. This is to prevent them from taking quick advantage of information that could result in a short-term profit. All short-term profits were payable to the corporation. Insiders were generally thought to be officers, directors, major stockholders, employees, or relatives of key employees. In the last two decades, the SEC widened its interpretation to include anyone having information that was not public knowledge. This could include security analysts, loan officers, large institutional holders, and many others who had business dealings with the firm.

2. The Federal Reserve Board of Governors became responsible for setting margin requirements to determine how much credit one had available to buy securities.

3. Manipulation of securities by conspiracies between investors was prohibited.

4. The SEC was given control over the proxy procedures of corporations. (A proxy is an absent stockholder vote.)

5. In its regulation of companies traded on the markets, it required certain reports to be filed periodically. Corporations must file quarterly financial statements with the SEC, send annual reports to the stockholders, and file 10-K reports with the SEC annually. The 10-K report has more financial data than the annual report and can be very useful to an investor or loan officer. Most companies will now send 10-K reports to stockholders on request. The SEC also has company filings available on the Internet under its retrieval system called EDGAR.

6. The act required all securities exchanges to register with the SEC. In this capacity, the SEC supervises and regulates many pertinent organizational aspects of exchanges such as listing and trading mechanics.

The Securities Acts Amendments of 1975

The major focus of the Securities Acts Amendments of 1975 was to direct the SEC to supervise the development of a national securities market. No exact structure was put forth, but the law did assume that any national market would make extensive use of computers and electronic communication devices. Additionally, the law prohibited fixed commissions on public transactions and also prohibited banks, insurance companies, and other financial institutions from buying stock exchange memberships to save commission costs for their own institutional transactions. This is a worthwhile addition to the securities laws since it fosters greater competition and more efficient prices.

Investment Company Act of 1940 and Investment Advisor Act of 1940

In addition to these three major pieces of legislation, a number of other acts deal directly with investor protection. For example, the Investment Advisor Act of 1940 is set up to protect the public from unethical investment advisors. Any advisor with more than 15 public clients (excluding tax accountants and lawyers) must register with the SEC and file semiannual reports. The Investment Company Act of 1940 provides similar oversight for mutual funds and investment companies dealing with small investors. The act was amended in 1970 and gave the National Association of Security Dealers (NASD) the authority to supervise and limit commissions and investment advisory fees on certain types of mutual funds.

The Investment Advisor Act of 1940 goes further to define who is considered an investment advisor. Investment advisor means any person who, for compensation, engages in the business of advising others, either directly or through publications or writings, as to the value of securities or as to the advisability of investing in, purchasing, or selling securities, or who, for compensation and as part of a regular business, issues or promulgates analyses or reports concerning securities.[3] Thus, advisors must register with the SEC. This applies to advisors who have more than $25 million in assets under management. Those advisors with less than $25 million in assets under management are not required by law to register with the SEC.

Another piece of legislation dealing directly with investor protection is the Securities Investor Protection Act of 1970. The **Securities Investor Protection Corporation (SIPC)** was established to oversee liquidation of brokerage firms and to insure investors' accounts to a maximum value of $500,000 in case of bankruptcy of a brokerage firm. It functions much the same as the Federal Deposit Insurance Corporation. SIPC resulted from the problems encountered on Wall Street from 1967 to 1970, when share volume surged to then all-time highs, and many firms were unable to process orders fast enough. A back-office paper crunch caused Wall Street to shorten the hours the exchanges were formally open for new business, but even this didn't help. Investors lost large sums, and for many months they were unable to use or get possession of securities held in their names. Even though SIPC insures these accounts, it still does not cover market value losses suffered while waiting to get securities from a bankrupt brokerage firm.

Insider Trading

The Securities Exchange Act of 1934 established the initial restrictions on insider trading. However, over the years, these restrictions have often proved to be inadequate. As previously indicated, the definition of *insider* may go beyond officers, directors, and major stockholders to include anyone with special insider knowledge. Both the Congress and the SEC are attempting to grapple with the issue of making punitive measures severe enough to discourage the illegal use of nonpublic information for profits. Future legislation is likely to include tougher civil penalties and stiffer criminal prosecution. Also, the penalties for improper action will expand beyond simple recovery of profits to a penalty three or more times the profits involved.

The 1980s saw a rash of insider trading scandals involving major investment banking houses, traders, analysts, and investors. Ivan Boesky and Dennis Levine were the first of the well-known investors to end up in jail, and Michael Milken was not far behind. These insider trading scandals have plagued Wall Street and tarnished its image, so it is no longer known as a place where investors can get a fair deal. On the other hand, all the legislation we have discussed has tended to increase the confidence of the investing public. In an industry where public trust is so critical, some form of supervision, whether public or private, is necessary and generally accepted.

Program Trading and Market Price Limits

Program trading is identified by some market analysts as the primary culprit behind the 508-point market crash on October 19, 1987. **Program trading** simply means that computer-based trigger points are established, in which large volume trades are initiated by institutional investors. For example, if the Dow Jones Industrial Average (or some other market measure) hits a certain point, a large sale or purchase may automatically occur. When many institutional investors are using program trading simultaneously, this process can have a major cumulative effect on the market. This was thought to be the case not only in the 1987 crash but also for many other highly volatile days in the market.[4]

After the crash of 1987, several studies of the role of program trading in creating market volatility were undertaken. In response to concerns that program trading might create

---

3. Investment Advisor Act of 1940.
4. Insiders, of course, may make proper long-term investments in a corporation.

market volatility, the NYSE instituted **Rule 80A.** Under Rule 80A, as amended by the SEC, all daily up or down movements in the Dow Jones Industrial Average (DJIA) of 50 points or more cause a tick test to go into effect.[5] In down markets, sell orders can only be executed on an increase in price (a plus tick) and buy orders can only be executed on a decrease in price (a minus tick).

In 1989, **circuit breakers** were also put in place; circuit breakers shut down the market for a period of time if there is a dramatic drop in stock prices. Under the initial provisions implemented by the NYSE, the exchange agreed to initiate a 30-minute halt in trading if the Dow Jones Industrial Average went down by 250 points during a given day as well as a one-hour halt in case of a 400-point decline.

As the market continued to go up during the 1990s, the circuit breakers were raised in February 1997 to a 30-minute halt for a 350-point decline and a one-hour break for a 550-point decline. Both circuit breakers were triggered by the 500-point-plus decline on October 27, 1997. The SEC has informed the New York Stock Exchange that it expects the exchange to continually evaluate the size of the circuit breakers as market conditions change.

Other markets, such as the Nasdaq, the American Stock Exchange, and the Chicago Board of Trade (for stock index futures) have also agreed to discontinue trading if there is a halt on the NYSE.

Ethical Considerations for Advisors

In light of the fact that there is so much federal regulation in the investment and financial planning environments, many professional organizations have taken it upon themselves to implement their own rules and codes of ethics. The Certified Financial Planner Board of Standards is one such organization. In addition to successfully completing the minimum education requirements to become a Certified Financial Planner™, completing the CFP Board's comprehensive exam, and possessing the appropriate amount of experience, any person wishing to be a member of the CFP Board must agree to abide by the CFP Board's Code of Ethics. The code of ethics pinpoints the responsibility that a financial planner has to the public at large, which includes clients, employers, and colleagues.

The Code of Ethics has seven self-explanatory principles that are further broken down into descriptive rules. The rules, being more specific than the principles, describe the standards of professional and ethical conduct expected from a Certified Financial Planner™.

The seven principles are (1) Integrity, (2) Objectivity, (3) Competence, (4) Fairness, (5) Confidentiality, (6) Professionalism, and (7) Diligence. Listed below are excerpts from the Financial Planning Association regarding the seven principles:

Integrity: "Integrity demands honesty and candor, which must not be subordinated to personal gain and advantage. Within the characteristic of integrity, allowance can be made for innocent error and legitimate difference of opinion; but integrity cannot co-exist with deceit or subordination of one's principles." *Objectivity:* "Regardless of the particular service rendered or the capacity in which an FPA member functions, an FPA member should protect the integrity of his or her work, maintain objectivity, and avoid subordination of his or her judgment that would be in violation of this Code." *Competence:* "One is competent only when he or she has attained and maintained an adequate level of knowledge and skill and applies that knowledge effectively in providing services to clients. Competence also includes the wisdom to recognize the limitations of that knowledge and when consultation or client referral is appropriate." *Fairness:* "Fairness requires impartiality, intellectual honesty, and disclosure of conflict(s) of interest(s). It involves a subordination of one's own

---

5. The rule specifically applies to stocks in the Standard & Poor's 500 Stock Index to protect against index arbitrage, that is, trading in stocks and stock index futures at the same time in order to profit from price differences between the two.

feelings, prejudices, and desires so as to achieve a proper balance of conflicting interests. Fairness is treating others in the same fashion that you would want to be treated and is an essential trait of any professional." ***Confidentiality:*** "A client, by seeking the services of an FPA member, may be interested in creating a relationship of personal trust and confidence with the FPA member. This type of relationship can only be built upon the understanding that information supplied to the FPA member or other information will be confidential." ***Professionalism:*** "An FPA member also has an obligation to cooperate with fellow FPA members to enhance and maintain the profession's public image and to work jointly with other FPA members to improve the quality of services." ***Diligence:*** "Diligence is the provision of services in a reasonably prompt and thorough manner. Diligence also includes proper planning for and supervision of the rendering of professional services." The end message regarding the code of ethics explains that the planner agrees to be a fiduciary to the client, and, as such, the client puts complete trust in the planner. It is, therefore, crucial for planners to act in accordance with these principles.

Summary

In this chapter, we saw how important the investment process is in the overall picture of financial planning. Every aspect of the process is tied to all of the others, making it a holistic process. Changing one part of the financial plan will invariably affect the other parts of the plan, so careful planning at all levels must be coordinated.

The investment industry is heavily regulated. Over the next decade, it is likely that it will be more regulated due to the changing complexity of the financial planning world. As we saw in 2002 to 2003, many investment firms were brought under scrutiny, and some of their officers were eventually brought to justice for practicing unscrupulous trading practices.

As regulation comes into the picture, there will be a call for investment advisors to seek more knowledge and education such that they can be of the best service to their clients. Belonging to organizations such as the Certified Financial Planner Board of Standards will give those in the financial services industry an edge up from other investment professionals. In addition, it gives some assurance to the public that a certain level of education has been met and that some code of ethics and procedure for filing complaints exists.

The Real World of Investing

Estate Planning: The Only Two Sure Things Are Death and Taxes!!

We know death is not going to go away (not even Elvis got out alive), but what about estate taxes, the taxes paid on your assets at time of death?

Fewer than 100,000 people pay the estate tax. The primary reason is that starting in 2002, you have to have an estate of at least $1 million to owe the tax (there is a $1 million exemption). Also, there are tax planning devices that help you avoid part of the tax (lifetime gifts, trusts, the marital deduction, etc.). Nevertheless, for those who pay the estate tax, it is indeed an onerous burden.

During his or her lifetime, a successful person tends to pay 50 percent of every dollar earned in federal and state income taxes, local property taxes, state sales taxes, and excise taxes on foreign imports, alcoholic beverages, etc.

Then, when he or she dies, an estate tax of up to 50 percent may be extracted. This double taxation may mean this person and his or her heirs may only get to keep

25 cents of each dollar earned; 75 cents could go to the government. Most people do not like that ratio.

To rectify this situation, the Bush Administration and Congress decided to eliminate the estate tax as one of the provisions of the newly enacted Economic Growth and Tax Reconciliation Act of 2001.

But wait a minute. Don't rush out to die just because of the legislation. First of all, the elimination is a slow process and is enacted by progressively larger estate tax exemptions. The tax table reads like this:

Years	Exemptions
2002–03	$1.0 million
2004–05	1.5 million
2006–08	2.0 million
2009	3.5 million
2010	Total exemption

Thus, a person who dies in 2004 will get a $1.5 million exemption and a death in 2006 will qualify for a $2 million exemption. The number goes up to $3.5 million in 2009, and finally there is no estate tax for those who die in 2010. If Bill Gates were to die in 2010 with an estate of $100 billion dollars, there would be no estate tax!

For those who wish to avoid the estate tax, this is all the good news. Now for the bad news. The Economic Growth and Tax Reconciliation Act of 2001 is automatically rescinded on January 1, 2011. This means the estate tax and all other provisions of the 2001 law are null and void unless a new Congress and president decide to re-pass it. We do not know what the politicians will do from one minute to the next, much less a decade from now. For estate tax planning purposes, you need to take care of business by 2010 (apply your own interpretation) or pay the consequences.

The Real World of Investing

The "See-Through" Wall between Security Analysts and Investment Bankers

The SEC and other related regulatory agencies have some of the toughest laws in the United States. Companies and executives that falsely report data can expect to face heavy penalties and even prison time. Just ask famed billionaire Michael Milken, who served a number of years in a federal jail for fraud and illegal insider trading. Much of the tough legislation dates back to the unregulated securities market abuses prior to the Great Market Crash of 1929 and the subsequent passage of the Securities Act of 1933 and the Securities Exchange Act of 1934. Before you get too satisfied with the thought that the stock market represents an appropriately regulated playing field, though, consider the fact that there is a new form of abuse that our legislative forefathers of the 1930s never even considered—the relationship between security analysts who supposedly analyze and evaluate companies and investment bankers who help sell stock to the public.

Whether it's at Merrill Lynch, Goldman Sachs, Lehman Brothers, or elsewhere, the security analysts who work for the firm are supposed to be free and independent of the investment bankers who also work for the firm. What this basically means is that the security analyst's responsibility is to provide an unbiased appraisal of the firm's operations and future outlook. Investors have a right to expect that analysts take a hard-nosed approach in "telling it like it is" and "letting the chips fall where they may." If the company is employing questionable accounting practices or failing to divulge problems in meeting debt obligations, it is up to the security analyst to bring this information to the public's attention, much as an investigative reporter for a newspaper would.

The investor banker, on the other hand, is supposed to bring new business and revenues to the firm. They are intended to be "homers" who root for and support the firm's clients. They are somewhat analogous to a major law firm that represents an important client. One of the investment banker's most important functions is to do initial public offerings (IPOs) for clients in which firms sell their stock to the public for the first time. The investment banker puts the deal together and promotes the issue, including doing "road shows" with the client. The abuse is that the security analyst has become more and more a part of the home team in promoting the new issue rather than analyzing the stock and giving an unbiased viewpoint.

In the wild dotcom IPO market of the late 1990s, security analysts often went so far as to take a piece of the action, thereby insuring a critical report on their part would put a hole in their own pocketbook. In an August 1, 2001, story in *The Wall Street Journal,* Laura Unger, the SEC's acting chairwoman, was quoted as saying: "Brokerage firms repeatedly obscured the supposed line that separates analysts, who work on behalf of investors, from investment bankers, who work to woo corporate clients." She further said, "Analysts routinely got involved in possible mergers, acquisitions and corporate-finance deals, and participated in corporate road shows. The firms also told the SEC that analysts' pay is largely based on the profitability of the investment-banking unit, and seven firms said that investment bankers provide input into the bonuses analysts receive."*

*Jeff D. Opdyke, "Many Analysts Found to Invest in Companies They Covered." *The Wall Street Journal,* August 1, 2001, pp. C1, C10.

Inflation was very tame from the mid-1980s through the late-1990s, growing at 2 to 3 percent per year. This was a far cry from the double-digit inflation of 11.4 percent in 1979 and 13.4 percent in 1980. Even these rates would have to be considered mild compared with the triple-digit (100 percent) inflation witnessed during the 1980s in such developing countries as Brazil, Israel, and Mexico.

As you plan your child's educational future, you might ask, "What effect could inflation have on tuition and room and board costs? The table gives the effect of 5 percent sustained inflation over a 18-year time period.

Impact of 5 Percent Inflation over 18 Years		
	2004	**18 Years**
Average Ivy League annual tuition and room and board	$39,000	$93,858
Average Private School annual tuition and room and board	$25,000	$60,165
Average State School annual tuition and room and board	$15,000	$36,099

Exploring the Web

http://www.cfp.net/	The main Web site for all of those interested in pursuing a CFP™ designation and other info.
http://www.sec.gov/	Provides information for obtaining all securities acts information as well as other educational information. Good site for individuals to lodge complaints about Investment Advisors.
http://finance.yahoo.com/?u	Provides data about stock market indices tracking as well as other stock and mutual fund pricing.
http://www.irs.gov	IRS Government Web site to download publications and forms used by tax professionals and individuals.
http://www.nasd.com/	Regulating body of investment advisors. Information on companies who are involved with NASD and other information
http://www.ssa.gov/	Provides information about Social Security benefits
http://www.medicare.gov	Provides information about Medicare benefits
http://www.napfa.org/	National Association of Fee Only Planners Career and planner information for planners who charge fees only rather than being commission based.
www.dol.gov	Summary laws for retirement laws
www.first.gov	Provides a portal into the U.S. government for all other Web sites

Chapter 2

Securities Markets

This chapter is primarily focused upon getting the reader familiar with the world of investments: it has a lot of information, most of which will be expanded upon in future chapters. You have probably heard many of the terms discussed below. The chapter will provide a general overview and then use this information to expand upon throughout the rest of the book.

The first half of the chapter is focused around market functions in the U.S. We will define what a generic market is, and then briefly discuss market efficiency. As market efficiency is a very important concept in investments, we will, in a later chapter, devote a significant amount of time to this topic.

We will then move on to a discussion of primary capital markets, secondary capital markets, and the organization of these markets within our economy. We will see that the primary markets use investment bankers as their main avenue for getting securities into the marketplace while the secondary markets have many avenues through which securities can flow.

We will have a brief discussion on the cost of trading, and then we will delve into a brief discussion of each security market. This will include a discussion of the money market, the bond market, and the equities market. Within each of these, we will talk about the types of securities that are included in each of these areas as well as taxation issues and other issues specific to these markets.

I will discuss derivatives: what they are, what their initial purpose is, and why investors use them today for investing purposes. We will then discuss a variety of investments such as Exchange Traded Funds, Index Funds, Real Estate Investment Trusts, and Mutual Funds, to name a few.

We will then end the chapter with a discussion of insurance-based products; annuities, and permanent life insurance.

MARKET FUNCTIONS

Many times people will call their stockbroker and ask, "How's the market?" What they are referring to is usually the market for common stocks as measured by the Dow Jones Industrial Average, the New York Stock Exchange Index, or some other measure of common stock performance. The stock market is not the only market. There are markets for each different kind of investment that can be made.

A **market** is simply a way of exchanging assets, usually cash, for something of value. It could be a used car, a government bond, gold, or diamonds. There doesn't have to be a central place where this transaction is consummated. As long as there can be communication between buyers and sellers, the exchange can occur. The offering party does not have to own what he sells but can be an agent acting for the owner in the transaction. For example, in the sale of real estate, the owner usually employs a real estate broker/agent who advertises and sells the property for a percentage commission. Not all markets have the same procedures, but certain trading characteristics are desirable for most markets.

Market Efficiency and Liquidity

In general, an **efficient market** occurs when prices respond quickly to new information, when each successive trade is made at a price close to the preceding price, and when the market can absorb large amounts of securities or assets without changing the price significantly. The more efficient the market, the faster prices react to new information, the closer in price is each successive trade, and the greater the amount of securities that can be sold without changing the price.

For markets to be efficient in this context, they must be liquid. Liquidity is a measure of the speed that an asset can be converted into cash at its fair market value. Liquid markets exist when continuous trading occurs, and as the number of participants in the market becomes larger, price continuity increases along with liquidity. Transaction costs also affect liquidity: the lower the cost of buying and selling, the more likely it is that people will be able to enter the market.

Competition and Allocation of Capital

An investor must realize that all markets compete for funds: stocks against bonds, mutual funds against real estate, government securities against corporate securities, and so on. The competitive comparisons are almost endless. Because markets set prices on assets, investors are able to compare the prices against their perceived risk and expected return and, thereby, choose assets that enable them to achieve their desired risk-return trade-offs. If the markets are efficient, prices adjust rapidly to new information, and this adjustment changes the expected rate of return and allows the investor to alter his or her investment strategy. Without efficient and liquid markets, the investor would be unable to do this. This allocation of capital occurs on both primary and secondary markets.

Secondary Markets

Secondary markets are markets for existing assets that are currently traded between investors. These markets create prices and allow for liquidity. If secondary markets did not exist, investors would have no place to sell their assets. Without liquidity, many people would not invest at all. Would you like to own $10,000 of Microsoft common stock but be unable to convert it into cash if needed? If there were no secondary markets, investors would expect a higher return to compensate for the increased risk of illiquidity and the inability to adjust their portfolios to new information.

Primary Markets

Primary markets are distinguished by the flow of funds between the market participants. Instead of trading between investors as in the secondary markets, participants in the primary market buy their assets directly from the source of the asset. A common example would be a new issue of corporate bonds sold by AT&T. You would buy the bonds through a brokerage firm, acting as an agent for AT&T's investment bankers. Your dollars would flow to AT&T rather than to another investor. The same would be true of buying a piece of art directly from the artist rather than from an art gallery.

Primary markets allow corporations, government units, and others to raise needed funds for expansion of their capital base. Once the assets or securities are sold in the primary market, they begin trading in the secondary market. Price competition in the secondary markets between different risk-return classes enables the primary markets to price new issues at fair prices to reflect existing risk/return relationships.

So far, our discussion of markets has been quite general but applicable to most free markets. In the following sections, we will deal with the organization and structure of specific markets.

ORGANIZATION OF THE PRIMARY MARKETS: THE INVESTMENT BANKER

The most active participant in the primary market is the investment banker. Since corporations, states, and local governments do not sell new securities daily, monthly, or even annually, they usually rely on the expertise of the investment banker when selling securities.

Underwriting Function

The **investment banker** acts as a middleman in the process of raising funds and, in most cases, takes a risk by underwriting an issue of securities. **Underwriting** refers to the guarantee the investment banking firm gives the selling firm to purchase its securities at a fixed price, thereby eliminating the risk of not selling the whole issue of securities and having less cash than desired. The investment banker may also sell the issue on a **best-efforts** basis where the issuing firm assumes the risk and simply takes back any securities not sold after a fixed period. A very limited number of securities are **sold directly** by the corporation to the public. Of the three methods of distribution, underwriting is far and away the most widely used.

With underwriting, once the security is sold, the investment banker will usually make a market in the security, which means active buying and selling to ensure a continuously liquid market and wider distribution. In the case of best efforts and for direct offerings by the issuer, which are even smaller than best efforts, the firm assumes the risk of not raising enough capital and has no guarantees that a continuous market will be made in the company's securities.

Corporations may also choose to raise capital through private placements rather than through a public offering. With a **private placement,** the company may sell its own securities to a financial institution such as an insurance company, a pension fund, or a mutual fund, or it can engage an investment banker to find an institution willing to buy a large block of stock or bonds. Most private placements involve bonds (debt issues) instead of common stock.

Distribution

In a public offering, the distribution process is extremely important, and on some large issues, an investment banker does not undertake this alone. Investment banking firms will share the risk and the burden of distribution by forming a group called a **syndicate**. The larger the offering in dollar terms, the more participants there generally are in the syndicate. For most original offerings, the investment banker is extremely important as a link between the original issuer and the security markets.

By taking much of the risk, the investment banker enables corporations and others to find needed capital and also allows investors an opportunity to participate in the ownership of securities through purchase in the secondary market.

ORGANIZATION OF THE SECONDARY MARKETS

Once the investment banker or the Federal Reserve (for U.S. government securities) has sold a new issue of securities, it begins trading in secondary markets that provide liquidity, efficiency, continuity, and competition. The **organized exchanges** fulfill this need in a central location where trading occurs between buyers and sellers. The **over-the-counter markets,** which provide customized products and services, also provide markets for exchange but not in a central location. A new type of market, which has developed in the last several years, is the **ECN** or **electronic communication network**.

Organized Exchanges

Organized exchanges are either national or regional, but both are organized in a similar fashion. Exchanges have a central trading location where securities are bought and sold in an auction market by brokers acting as agents for the buyer and seller. Stocks usually trade at various trading posts on the floor of the exchange. Brokers are registered members of the exchanges, and the total number of brokers is fixed by each exchange. The national exchanges are the New York Stock Exchange (NYSE) and the American Stock Exchange (AMEX). Both these exchanges are governed by a board of directors consisting of one half exchange members and one half public members.

The regional exchanges began by trading the securities of local firms. As the firms grew, they became listed on the national exchanges, but they also continued to trade on the regionals. Many cities, such as Chicago, Cincinnati, Philadelphia, and Boston, have regional exchanges. Today, most of the trading on these exchanges is done in nationally known companies. Trading in the same company in two exchanges is commonly conducted between the NYSE and such regionals as the Chicago Stock Exchange, the Pacific Coast Exchange (in San Francisco and Los Angeles), and the smaller regionals. More than 90 percent of the companies traded on the Chicago and Pacific Coast Exchanges are also listed on the NYSE. This is referred to as **dual trading**.

October 20, 1987, the day after the crash of '87, was the busiest day in the history of the New York Stock Exchange until October 28, 1997, the day after the next crash. On October 27, 1997, the stock market moved down significantly by about 25 percent on a single day and ranked as one of the 10 worst days in market history. What also made history was the 1.2 billion shares traded on the New York Stock Exchange the next day. This compares to 685 million shares on October 27, 1987. Perhaps the greatest triumph, however, was the record number of shares traded on the first day the New York Stock Exchange opened after being closed for almost one week after the attacks on the World Trade Center. The 2.368 billion shares set a record for the NYSE. The other markets (such as Chicago, Nasdaq, and Boston) also showed significant increases in volume from the previous record days. This data can be examined in Table 2–1.

Consolidated Tape

Although dual listing and trading have existed for some time, it was not until June 16, 1975, that a consolidated ticker tape was instituted. This allows brokers on the floor of one exchange to see prices of transactions on other exchanges in the dually listed stocks. Any time a transaction is made on a regional exchange or over-the-counter in a security listed on the NYSE, this transaction and any made on the floor of the NYSE are displayed on the composite tape. The composite price data keep markets more efficient and prices more competitive between exchanges at all times.

The NYSE and AMEX are both national exchanges and for years did not allow dual listing of companies traded on their exchanges, but as of August 1976, securities were able to be dually listed between these exchanges.

Listing Requirements for Firms

Securities can be traded on an exchange only if they have met the listing requirements of the exchange and have been approved by the board of governors of that exchange. All exchanges have minimum requirements that must be met before trading can occur in a company's

TABLE 2–1   Data on Trading Volume (Breakdown of Trading in NYSE Stocks)

By Market	Monday 27-Oct-87	Monday 28-Oct-97	Monday 17-Sep-01
New York	685,496,330	1,195,836,620	2,368,326,910
Chicago	28,857,300	40,187,200	95,613,840
CBOE	56,600	74,000	6,300
Pacific	20,331,100	20,001,000	8,512,700
NASD/Nasdaq Intermarket	59,636,200	85,585,150	157,846,400
Philadelphia	9,009,600	10,619,700	14,530,700
Boston	10,793,100	13,995,100	43,359,000
Cincinnati	9,605,000	8,432,100	10,205,400
Composite	823,785,230	1,374,731,570	2,698,401,250

Source: Various issues of *The Wall Street Journal*.

common stock. Since the NYSE is the biggest exchange and generates the most dollar volume in large, well-known companies, its listing requirements are the most restrictive.

Initial Listing: Although each case is decided on its own merits, there are minimum requirements that are specified by the exchanges. These requirements set minimums for the net income of the firm, the market value of publicly held shares, the number of shares publicly held, and the number of stockholders owning at least a round lot of 100 shares. Other exchanges, such as the Chicago Stock Exchange, have similar requirements, but the amounts are smaller. We have a Web exercise at the back of the chapter that takes you to the New York Stock Exchange Web site where you can look up the latest minimum standards for companies wanting to be listed on the NYSE.

Corporations desiring to be listed on exchanges have decided that public availability of the stock on an exchange will benefit their shareholders by providing liquidity to owners or by allowing the company a more viable means for raising external capital for growth and expansion. The company must pay annual listing fees to the exchange and additional fees based on the number of shares traded each year.

Delisting: The New York Stock Exchange also has the authority to remove (delist) a security from trading when the security fails to meet certain criteria. There is much latitude in these decisions, but generally, a company's security may be considered for delisting if there are fewer than 1,200 round-lots (100 shares).

OTHER ORGANIZED EXCHANGES

The American Stock Exchange

The American Stock Exchange trades in smaller companies than the NYSE, and except for one dually listed company on the NYSE in 1983, the stocks traded on the AMEX are different from those on any other exchange. Because many of the small companies on the AMEX do not meet the liquidity needs of large institutional investors, the AMEX has been primarily a market for individual investors. In an attempt to differentiate itself from the NYSE, the AMEX traded warrants in companies for many years before the NYSE allowed them.

Even now, the AMEX has warrants listed for stocks trading on the NYSE. The AMEX also trades put and call options on approximately 200 stocks, with most of the underlying common stocks being listed on the NYSE. This market has been a stabilizing force for the AMEX.

To become more innovative and to attract more business, the American Stock Exchange announced plans in 1991 to trade options in foreign stock indexes. By 1997 the AMEX was trading put and call options on the indexes of the stock markets of Mexico, Hong Kong, and Japan. Additionally, they also made markets in puts and calls for specific industry indexes such as computer technology, consumer companies, high tech Internet companies, and pharmaceutical companies. After merging with Nasdaq in the late 1990s, it appears that a divorce is on the horizon.

The Chicago Board Options Exchange

Trading in call options started on the Chicago Board Options Exchange (CBOE) in April 1973 and proved very successful. The number of call options listed grew from 16 in 1973 to more than 500 in 2000. A **call option** contract provides the owner the right to buy 100 shares of the underlying common stock at a set price for a certain period. The CBOE standardized call options into three-month, six-month, and nine-month expiration periods on a rotating monthly series. Other sequences have since been developed. The CBOE and the AMEX currently have many options that are dually listed, and the competition between them is fierce. The two exchanges also trade put options (options to sell). A number of smaller regional exchanges also provide for option trading, and the New York Stock Exchange sold its option business to the CBOE in 1997.

A new wrinkle in the options game has been options on stock market indexes, industry groupings (called subindexes). The CBOE offers puts and calls on the Standard & Poor's 500 Index and the Dow Jones Industrial Average; the AMEX has options on the AMEX Market Value Index, and so on.

Futures Markets

Futures markets have traditionally been associated with commodities and, more recently, also with financial instruments. Purchasers of commodity futures own the right to buy a certain amount of the commodity at a set price for a specified period. When the time runs out (expires), the futures contract will be delivered unless sold before expiration. One major futures market is the Chicago Board of Trade, which trades corn, oats, soybeans, wheat, silver, plywood, and Treasury bond futures. There are also other important futures markets in Chicago, Kansas City, Minneapolis, New York, and other cities. These markets are very important as hedging markets and help set commodity prices. They are also known for their wide price swings and volatile speculative nature.

In recent years, trading volume has increased in foreign exchange futures such as the Euro, Japanese Yen, and British Pound as well as in Treasury bill and Treasury bond futures. One important product having a direct effect in the stock market is the development of futures contracts on stock market indexes. The Chicago Mercantile Exchange, Chicago Board of Trade, New York Futures Exchanges (a division of the NYSE), and the Kansas City Board of Trade have all developed contracts in separate market indexes such as the Standard & Poor's 500, the Dow Jones Industrial Average, and the Value Line Index.

Over-the-Counter Markets

Unlike the organized exchanges, the over-the-counter (OTC) markets have no central location where securities are traded. Being traded over-the-counter implies the trade takes place by telephone or electronic device and dealers stand ready to buy or sell specific securities for their own accounts. These dealers will buy at a bid price and sell at an asked price that reflects the competitive market conditions. By contrast, brokers on the organized exchanges merely act as agents who process orders. The National Association of Securities Dealers

(NASD) a self-policing organization of dealers, requires at least two market makers (dealers) for each security, but often there are 5 or 10 or even 20 for government securities. As previously mentioned, the multiple-dealer function in the over-the-counter market is an attractive feature for many companies in comparison to the single specialist arrangement on the NYSE and other organized exchanges.

OTC markets exist for stocks, corporate bonds, mutual funds, federal government securities, state and local bonds, commercial paper, negotiable certificates of deposits, and various other securities. The trading in these securities make the OTC the largest of all markets in the United States in the amount of dollars traded each day.

In the OTC market, the difference between the bid and asked price is the **spread**; it represents the profit the dealer earns by making a market. For example, if common stock X is bid 10 and asked 10.50, this simply means the dealer will buy at least 100 shares at $10 per share or will sell 100 shares at $10.50 per share. If prices are too low, more buyers than sellers will appear, and the dealer will run out of inventory unless he raises prices to attract more sellers and balances the supply and demand. If his price is at equilibrium, he will match an equal number of shares bought and sold, and for his market-making activities, he will earn 50 cents per share traded.

Nasdaq

Nasdaq stands for the National Association of Securities Dealers Automated Quotations system. This system is linked by a computer network and provides up-to-the-minute quotations on approximately 6,000 of the OTC stocks traded on the Nasdaq system. These Nasdaq stocks are divided between national market issues and small cap issues. Each is presented separately in *The Wall Street Journal* and other newspapers.[1]

As the name implies, the national market issues represent larger Nasdaq companies that must meet higher listing standards than the small cap market. The standards are not as high as those on the NYSE but cover most of the same areas: net tangible assets, net income, pre-tax income, public float (shares outstanding in the hands of the public), operating history, market value of the float, a minimum share price, the number of shareholders, and the number of market makers.

Because the listing requirements are lower than those of the NYSE, many small public companies begin trading on the Nasdaq and many decide to stay there even after they far exceed the requirements for the NYSE. Companies such as Intel, Microsoft, Oracle, and Sun Microsystems trade on the Nasdaq Stock Market; this market is popular for listing technology stocks.

Nasdaq has made several significant transformations. It is changing its structure from a fully owned subsidiary of NASD (National Association of Security Dealers) to a privately held company. By August 2001, the NASD's stake in Nasdaq had been reduced to less than 30 percent. Nasdaq intends to eventually become a publicly traded company when market conditions are more stable. The Nasdaq Stock Market is also registering as a securities exchange under the federal securities laws, which is primarily a legal move. The actual operations of the market will stay the same.

Over the last decade, the Nasdaq Stock Market has taken its place in world equity markets based on its dollar volume of trading activity. The NYSE is first followed by Nasdaq, London, and then Tokyo. This is a dramatic change for a market that was in fifth place in 1990. The U.S. equity market for small-growth companies boomed in the 1990s, and this helped to increase Nasdaq's volume. Additionally, its multiple-dealer system, efficient computerized quotation systems, and enhanced reporting capability are other reasons for

---

1. Publicly traded firms that are not listed on organized exchanges or by the Nasdaq are normally not quoted in newspapers but may be shown on special pink sheets put out by investment houses.

the increased competitive nature. To add to its worldwide status, Nasdaq has begun to create Nasdaq stock markets in foreign cities such as Hong Kong.

Debt Securities Traded Over-the-Counter

Debt securities also trade over-the-counter. Actually, government securities of the U.S. Treasury provide the largest dollar volume of transactions on the OTC and account for billions of dollars in trades each week. These securities are traded by government securities dealers who are often associated with a division of a large financial institution, such as a New York, Chicago, or West Coast money market bank or a large brokerage house such as Merrill Lynch. These dealers make markets in government securities, such as Treasury bills and Treasury bonds, or federal agency securities such as Federal National Mortgage Association issues.

Municipal bonds of state and local governments are traded by specialized municipal bond dealers who, in most cases, work for large commercial banks. Commercial paper, representing unsecured, short-term corporate debt, is traded directly by finance companies, but a large portion of commercial paper sold by industrial companies is handled by OTC dealers specializing in this market. Every security has its own set of dealers and its own distribution system. On markets where large dollar trades occur, the spread between the bid and asked price could be as little as 1/16 or 1/32 of $1 per $1,000 of securities bought or sold.

The Third and Fourth Markets: Over-the-Counter Trading

Before the mid-1970s, commissions on the NYSE were fixed. This meant the same commission schedule applied to all transactions of a given size, and one broker could not undercut the other on the New York Stock Exchange. Several OTC dealers, most notably Weeden & Co., decided to make a market in about 200 of the most actively traded NYSE issues and to do this at a much smaller cost than the NYSE commission structure would allow. This trading in NYSE-listed securities in over-the-counter markets became known as the **third market.**

The third market diminished in importance for a while as the NYSE became more price competitive. However, in the 1980s and throughout the 1990s, this market has made a comeback. One advantage of the OTC market is that more than one specialist trades a security, making trading flexibility greater. For example, ITT Corporation reported a significant dividend cut and lower earnings after the NYSE was closed, but Jefferies Corporation, an over-the-counter trading firm, traded 3 million shares by the time the NYSE opened the next morning. Another example occurred when the Justice Department announced the breakup of AT&T on a Friday. MCI, a competitor in communications, traded OTC, while AT&T traded on the NYSE. AT&T trading was halted until Monday because the specialist was unable to stabilize the market, whereas the 29 market makers in MCI stock in the OTC market transacted more than $75 million of securities before AT&T opened on Monday morning. Still, much discussion is being held at the New York Stock Exchange about trading hours, revising rules, and ways of competing more effectively with the third market and the OTC.

The **fourth market** enables institutions to trade between themselves, bypassing the middleman broker (replacing the broker with a computer). Much of the trading in this market is done through Instinet (Institutional Networks Inc.). Instinet provides a low-cost, automated stock trading system, with transactions available on more than 3,500 securities, both listed and over-the-counter. The system allows banks, insurance companies, and mutual and pension funds to enter an order over a computer terminal. The computer searches a nationwide trading network until it finds the trader with the best price, then the computer holds the order 30 seconds so that another trader may offer a better price.

Cost of Trading

Nowhere has the field of investments changed more than in the means and cost of trading. A decade ago, the basic choice was between full-service brokerage firms such as Merrill

Lynch, PaineWebber (now UBS PaineWebber), and Dean Witter (now Morgan Stanley Dean Witter) and discount brokers such as Charles Schwab, Quick & Reilly, and Olde. The discount brokers provided bare-bones service and generally charged 25 to 75 percent of the commissions charged by full service brokers, and the discount brokers willingly provided research and stock analysis to clients, tax information, and help in establishing goals and objectives.

The nature of the landscape changed radically with the emergence of the Internet. Now, an investor can merely access an **online broker's** Web site to open an account, review the operating procedures and commission schedule, and initiate a trade. Confirmation of an electronic trade can take as little as 10 seconds and almost all trades are completed within a minute.

Online brokers such as Ameritrade and E*trade have become household names—and why not? A recent study by the American Association of Individual Investors indicated that for a 100-share trade, the average online broker charged $15. In comparison, the average discount broker charged $42, while a full-service broker charged $100.

To examine the effect of the pricing differential, assume 100 shares are traded at $40 per share for a total value of $4,000. Note the difference in percentage costs between the three types of brokers.

Because of the intense competition provided by online brokers in the late 1990s, many full-service and deep-discount brokers began offering their clients the alternative of online trading. Merrill Lynch was the first major full-service broker to go this route, and Charles Schwab led the way among discount brokers (over half of Schwab's trades are now online). All others in the industry have followed the same path, so the landscape is blurred between full-service and deep-discount brokers that offer an online alternative as well as pure online brokers. Even banks and mutual funds offer online trading through brokerage subsidiaries.

While online trading is a very attractive trading alternative because of the low commission rate, it is not for everyone. For the less technically competent investor or computer novice, full-service and discount brokers may be the way to go. The importance of explanations about capital gains, tax implications, potential merger tender offers, retirement and estate planning, etc., may outweigh savings in commissions. That is why most major traditional houses offer alternative ways to trade.

Nevertheless, for the sophisticated investor who knows what he or she wants, it is impractical to pay for additional unused and unnecessary services. While 10 to 15 percent of all trades are currently online, the number will undoubtedly double or triple in the next few years.

The Internet has not only influenced the way trades are executed, but has given the individual investor access to instant information that was once in the private domain of large institutional investors such as mutual funds or bank trust departments. Individual investors can download balance sheets, income statements, up-to-the-minute press releases, and so on. They can also participate with other investors in chat rooms and e-mail the company for immediate answers to questions.

All of these options certainly represent progress, with one caveat. The intoxication of it all has led to a new class of **day traders,** who attempt to beat the market on an hourly or by-the-minute basis. While some with exceptional skill have profited by this activity, many others were badly hurt, monetarily of course, when the ever-climbing bull market of CISCO Systems, Intel, and Microsoft came to an end. Surgeons and trial lawyers suddenly decided the market was not as easy as they once thought and returned to their "day jobs."

Financial Instruments & Specific Markets

In the previous section, the high level aspects of markets and the way markets work within the macroeconomy were covered. At this point, let us delve further into the types of investments that can be traded within these markets.

The Money Market

When you hear someone talk about money markets, they are primarily talking about investments that are short-term in nature: less than one year. Investors generally put up a fixed amount of cash and are promised a certain rate of return within the time frame. With all of these short-term investments, the interest income is taxed at the tax payer's ordinary income tax rate. Thus, it is advisable to consider whether investment in these types of funds is suitable for your client.

Money market investments then, tend to be comprised of debt-securities. For the typical investor, some of these types of investments may not be practical since they are traded in large blocks among large financial institutions. However, these types of investments may be made available to investors when large financial companies make portions available to individual investors. Of all the markets, money markets tend to provide safer investment vehicles due to the short-term nature of the promised return. The following money market instruments will be discussed below: **Certificates of Deposit**, **U.S. government Treasury bills** (T-bills), **Commercial Paper**, **Bankers Acceptances** and **Money Market Funds** and **Money Market Accounts**.

Certificates of Deposit (CDs)

The **certificates of deposit (CDs)** are provided by commercial banks and savings and loan institutions and other thrift institutions. They have traditionally been issued in small and large amounts ranging from approximately $1,000 to $100,000. The investor provides the funds and receives an interest-bearing certificate in return. The smaller CDs usually have a maturity of anywhere from six months to eight years, and the large $100,000 CDs mature at 30 to 90 days.

Large CDs are usually sold to corporate investors, money market funds, pension funds, and so on; small CDs are sold to individual investors. One main difference between the two CDs, besides the dollar amount, is that there may be a secondary market for the large CDs, which allows these investors to maintain their liquidity without suffering an interest penalty. Investors in small CDs have no such liquidity. Their only option when needing the money before maturity is to redeem the certificate to the borrowing institution and suffer an interest loss penalty.

Small CDs have been traditionally regulated by the government, with federal regulatory agencies specifying the maximum interest rate that can be paid and the life of the CD. In 1986, all such interest-rate regulations and ceilings were phased out, and the free market now determines return. Any financial institution is able to offer whatever it desires. Almost all CDs are federally insured for up to $100,000 in the event of the collapse of the financial institution offering the instrument. This feature became particularly important in the late 1980s and early 1990s as a result of the problems in the savings and loan and banking industries.

U.S. Government Treasury Bills

Treasury bills (T-bills) have maturities of 28, 91, 182 or 364 days. Treasury bills trade on a discount basis, meaning the yield the investor receives occurs as a result of the difference between the price paid and the maturity value, and no actual interest is paid. Treasury bills trade in minimum units of $1,000, and there is an extremely active secondary, or resale, market for these securities. Thus, an investor buying a Treasury bill from the government with an initial life of approximately six months would have no difficulty selling it to another investor after two or three weeks. Because the T-bill now has a shorter time to run, its market value would be a bit closer to par.

Treasury bills are not subject to state income tax but are still subject to federal income tax. Oftentimes, T-bills are carried in high proportions in an investor's retirement portfolio.

This is probably suitable for most retirees. Since interest from T-bills is taxed at ordinary rates, they may be suitable to carry in retirement accounts or other tax sheltered accounts.

Commercial Paper

Another form of a short-term credit instrument is **commercial paper**, which is issued by large business corporations to the public. Commercial paper usually comes in minimum denominations of $25,000 and represents an unsecured promissory note. Commercial paper carries a higher yield than small CDs or government Treasury bills and is in line with the yield on large CDs. The maturity is usually 30, 60, or 90 days, but up to six months is possible.

Bankers' Acceptance

This instrument often arises from foreign trade. A **bankers' acceptance** is a draft drawn on a bank for approval for future payment and is subsequently presented to the bank for payment. The investor buys the bankers' acceptance from an exporter (or other third party) at a discount with the intention of presenting it to the bank at face value at a future date. Bankers' acceptances provide yields comparable to commercial paper and large CDs and have an active secondary or resale market.

Money Market Funds

Money market funds represent a vehicle to buy short-term fixed-income securities through a mutual fund arrangement.[2] An individual with a small amount to invest may pool funds with others to buy higher-yielding large CDs and other similar instruments indirectly through the fund. There is a great deal of flexibility in withdrawing funds through check-writing privileges. These types of funds are excellent for ensuring that your clients can get at their funds cheaply and easily. Because of both the safe and liquid nature of money market funds, these types of funds are suitable for emergency fund and short-term cash needs. Retirees can also quickly convert their "current needs" portion of the annual income into money markets for use in the several months after investing.

Money Market Accounts

Money market accounts are similar to money market funds but are offered by financial institutions rather than mutual funds. Financial institutions, such as banks, mutual funds and other thrift institutions, introduced money market accounts in the 1980s to compete with money market funds. These accounts pay rates generally competitive with money market funds and normally allow up to three withdrawals (checks) a month without penalty. One advantage of a money market account over a money market fund is that it is normally insured by the federal government for up to $100,000. However, because of the high quality of investments of money market funds, this advantage is not particularly important in most cases.

Both money market funds and money market accounts normally have minimum balance requirements of $500 to $1,000. Minimum withdrawal provisions may also exist. Each fund or account must be examined for its rules. In any event, both provide much more flexibility than a certificate of deposit in terms of access to funds with only a slightly lower yield.

The Bond Market

The bond market is a market whereby investors put up a fixed amount of cash in return for an expected rate of return. A bond normally represents a long-term contractual obligation of

---

2. Most brokerage houses also offer money market fund options.

the firm to pay interest to the bondholder as well as the face value of the bond at maturity. The major provisions in a bond agreement are spelled out in the bond indenture, a complicated legal document often more than 100 pages long, administered by an independent trustee (usually a commercial bank). We shall examine some important terms and concepts associated with a bond issue.

The **par value** represents the face value of a bond. Most corporate bonds are traded in $1,000 units, while many federal, state, and local issues trade in units of $5,000 or $10,000.

Coupon rate refers to the actual interest rate on the bond, usually payable in semiannual installments. To the extent that interest rates in the market go above or below the coupon rate after the bond is issued, the market price of the bond will change from the par value. A bond initially issued at a rate of 8 percent will sell at a substantial discount from par value when 12 percent is the currently demanded rate of return. We will eventually examine how the investor makes and loses large amounts of money in the bond market with the swings in interest rates. A few corporate bonds are termed **variable-rate notes** or **floating-rate notes**, meaning the coupon rate is fixed for only a short period and then varies with a stipulated short-term rate such as the rate on U.S. Treasury bills. In this instance, the interest payment rather than the price of the bond varies up and down. Recently, **zero-coupon bonds** have also been issued at values substantially below maturity value. With zero-coupon bonds, the investor receives return in the form of capital appreciation over the life of the bond since no semiannual cash interest payments are received.

The **maturity date** is the date on which final payment is due at the stipulated par value.

Methods of bond repayment can occur under many different arrangements. Some bonds are never paid off, such as selected **perpetual bonds** issued by the Canadian and British governments, and have no maturity dates. A more normal procedure would simply call for a single-sum (lump) payment at the end of the obligation. Thus, the issuer may make 40 semiannual interest payments over the next 20 years plus one lump-sum payment of the par value of the bond at maturity.

There are also other significant means of repayment. The first is the **serial payment** in which bonds are paid off in installments over the life of the issue. Each serial bond has its own predetermined date of maturity and receives interest only to that point. Although the total bond issue may span more than 20 years, 15 to 20 maturity dates are assigned. Municipal bonds are often issued on this basis. Second, there may be a **sinking-fund provision** in which semiannual or annual contributions are made by a corporation into a fund administered by a trustee for purposes of debt retirement. The trustee takes the proceeds and goes into the market to purchase bonds from willing sellers. If no sellers are available, a lottery system may be used to repurchase the required number of bonds from among outstanding bondholders.

Third, debt may also be retired under a call provision. A **call provision** allows the corporation to call or force in all of the debt issue prior to maturity. The corporation usually pays a 3 to 5 percent premium over par value as part of the call provision arrangement. The ability to call is often *deferred* for the first 5 or 10 years of an issue and can only occur after this time period.

Debt may also be retired if it is a **convertible bond**. A convertible bond is one that can be converted into common stock at the option of the holder. Thus, the owner has the fixed income security that can be transferred to common stock if and when the performance of the firm indicates such a conversion is desirable.

Because bonds generally pay interest at some fixed interval such as annually or semiannually, they are usually not suitable for those investors in high tax brackets since they will have to pay income tax at ordinary rates. Investors should consider holding these types of bonds in retirement accounts or other tax sheltered accounts. We will see that in most cases, there is an exception to municipal bonds for federal taxes and state taxes.

U.S. TREASURY NOTES & BONDS, TREASURY STRIPS, AND INFLATION INDEXED TREASURY SECURITIES

T-Notes and T-Bonds

A **Treasury note** has an intermediate term and generally has a maturity of 1 to 10 years. **Treasury bonds** are long term in nature and mature in 10 to 30 years. T-bonds and T-bills are initially sold at auction and pay interest every six months to the bondholder. Even though U.S. T-bills and T-bonds have long maturities they are easy to sell in the secondary market due to the relative stability of the U.S. government. When you sell these securities, you are guaranteed to get the cash the next day.

Treasury notes and bonds are not subject to state income tax but are still subject to federal income tax. Thus they may be suitable to carry in retirement accounts or other tax sheltered accounts.

Treasury Strips

Treasury securities may also trade in the form of **Treasury strips** (strip-T's). Treasury strips pay no interest and all returns to the investor come in the form of increases in the value of the investment (as is true of Treasury bills also). Treasury strips are referred to as zero-coupon securities because they have no interest payments.

As an example, 25-year Treasury strips might initially sell for 19 percent of par value. You could buy a 25-year, $10,000 Treasury strip for $1,900.[3] All your return would come in the form of an increase in value. Of course, you could sell at the going market price before maturity should you so desire.

Actually, the U.S. Treasury does not offer Treasury strips directly. It allows government security dealers to strip off the interest payments and principal payment from regular Treasury notes and bonds and repackage them as Treasury strips. For example, on a 25-year Treasury bond, there would be 50 semiannual interest payments and one final principal payment. Each of these 51 payments could be stripped off and sold as a zero-coupon strip.[4] Those who desired short-term Treasury strips would buy into the early payments. The opposite would be true for an investor with a long-term orientation.

The Internal Revenue Service taxes zero-coupon bonds, such as Treasury strips, as if interest were paid annually even though no cash flow is received until maturity. The tax is based on amortizing the built-in gain over the life of the instrument. For tax reasons, zero coupons are usually only appropriate for tax-deferred accounts such as individual retirement accounts, 401(k) plans, or other nontaxable pension funds.

Inflation-Indexed Treasury Securities

In January 1997, the U.S. Treasury began offering 10-year notes that were intended to protect investors against the effects of inflation. The maturities were later expanded to include longer terms to maturity.

Here's how these inflation-indexed Treasury notes work. The investor receives two forms of return as a result of owning the security. The first is annual interest that is paid out semiannually, and the second is an automatic increase in the initial value of principal to account for inflation.

These securities are formally called **Treasury Inflation Protection Securities (TIPS).** TIPS might pay 3.5 percent in annual interest and, assuming a 3 percent rate of inflation, an

---

3. The yield is approximately $6\frac{3}{4}$ percent. Zero-coupon securities are also offered by corporations.
4. Any one payment, may be stripped from many hundreds of Treasury bonds at one time to provide a $10,000 Treasury strip.

additional 3 percent to compensate for inflation. As implied in the preceding paragraph, the 3 percent inflation adjustment is not paid in cash but is added on to the principal value of the bond. Assume the bond had an initial par value of $1,000. At the end of the first year, the principal value would go up to $1,030. Thus, during the first year, the investor would receive $35 (3.5 percent) in cash as interest payments, plus enjoy a $30 increase in principal. On a 10-year indexed Treasury security, this procedure continues for each of the remaining nine years and at maturity, the security is redeemed at the indexed value of the principal by the Treasury. If the investor needs to sell before the maturity date, he or she can sell it in the secondary market to other investors at a value approximating the appreciated principal value.[4]

The reader should be aware that the base against which the 3.5 percent annual interest is paid is the inflation-adjusted value of the security. Thus, in the second year, the interest payment would be $36.05 (3.5% of $1,030). In each subsequent year, there is a similar adjustment depending on the prior year's rate of inflation.

Assuming inflation remains at 3 percent over the 10-year time period, the inflation-adjusted value of the principal will increase to $1,344 (10 periods compounded at 3 percent). The investor is effectively getting a return of 6.5 percent in the form of interest and appreciation of principal. Of course, if inflation averages 6 percent over the life of the investment, the investor will get a return of 9.5 percent. The interest payment (real return) will remain at 3.5 percent, but the inflation adjustment will supply the extra return.

Through inflation-indexed Treasury notes, the investor is protected against the effect of inflation. This may be quite a benefit if inflation is high, but the security can provide an inferior return compared with other investments in a low inflation environment. (See the real world of investing section on TIPS—Flood Insurance During a Drought.)

Also, the investor should be aware that the annual adjustment in principal is treated as taxable income each year even though no cash is received until redemption at maturity. For this reason, inflation-indexed Treasury securities are more appropriate for tax-deferred or nontaxable accounts.

Corporate Securities

Corporate bonds are the dominant source of new financing for U.S. corporations. When issuing corporate securities, these companies borrow money from the general public or sometimes from large financial institutions. Corporate bonds differ from Treasury bonds in the amount of risk that they have. Treasury bonds are thought to have no default risk whereas corporate bonds do. Corporate bonds usually pay semiannual coupon rates but can pay annual coupon rates as well.

Corporate bonds of all types generally trade in units of $1,000, and this is a particularly attractive feature to the smaller investor who does not wish to purchase in units of $5,000 to $10,000 (which is necessary for many Treasury and federally sponsored credit agency issues). Because of the higher risk relative to government issues, the investor will generally receive higher yields on corporate bonds as well. All income from corporate bonds is taxable for federal, state, and local purposes. Finally, corporate issues have the disadvantage of being subject to calls. When buying a bond during a period of high interest rates, the call provision must be considered a negative feature because the high-yielding bonds may be called in for early retirement as interest rates go down.

Bond Ratings

Bond investors tend to place much more emphasis on an independent analysis of quality than do common stock investors. For this reason, both corporate financial management and institutional portfolio managers keep a close eye on bond rating procedures. The difference between an AA and an A rating may mean the corporation will have to pay one-fourth of a point more interest on the bond issue (perhaps 8.5 percent rather than 8.25 percent). On a $100 million, 20-year issue, this represents $250,000 per year (before tax), or a total of $5 million over the life of the bond.

The two major bond-rating agencies are Moody's Investors Service and Standard & Poor's (a subsidiary of McGraw-Hill, Inc.). They rank thousands of corporate and municipal issues as well as a limited number of private placements, commercial paper, preferred stock issues, and offerings of foreign companies and governments. U.S. government issues tend to be free of risk and therefore are given no attention by the bond-rating agencies. Moody's, founded in 1909, is the older of the two bond-rating agencies and covers twice as many securities as Standard & Poor's (particularly in the municipal bond area). Fitch Investors Service, Inc. Acquired Duff & Phelps, another rating agency, in an attempt to diversify and expand its rating coverage.

The bond ratings, often ranging from an AAA to a D category, are decided on a committee basis by both Moody's and Standard & Poor's. There are no fast and firm quantitative measures that specify the rating a new issue will receive. Nevertheless, measures pertaining to cash flow and earnings generation in relationship to debt obligations are given strong consideration. Of particular interest are coverage ratios that show the number of times interest payments, as well as all annual contractual obligations, are covered by earnings. A coverage ratio of 2 or 3 may contribute to a low rating, while a ratio of 5 to 10 may indicate the possibility of a strong rating. Operating margins, return on invested capital, and returns on total assets are also evaluated along with debt-to-equity ratios.[5] Financial ratio analysis makes up perhaps 50 percent of the evaluation. Other factors of importance are the nature of the industry in which the firm operates, the relative position of the firm within the industry, the pricing clout the firm has, and the quality of management. Decisions are not made in a sterile, isolated environment. Thus, it is not unusual for corporate management or the mayor to make a presentation to the rating agency, and on-sight visitations to plants or cities may occur.

The overall quality of the work done by the bond-rating agencies may be judged by the agencies' acceptance in the business and academic community. Their work is very well received. Although UBS PaineWebber and some other investment houses have established their own analysts to shadow the activities of the bond-rating agencies and look for imprecision in their classifications (and thus potential profits), the opportunities are not great. Academic researchers have generally found that accounting and financial data were well considered in the bond ratings and that rational evaluation appeared to exist.[6]

One item lending credibility to the bond-rating process is the frequency with which the two major rating agencies arrive at the same grade for a given issue (this occurs well over 50 percent of the time). When "split ratings" do occur (different ratings by different agencies), they are invariably of a small magnitude. A typical case might be AAA versus AA rather than AAA versus BBB. While one can question whether one agency is looking over the other's shoulder or "copying its homework," this is probably not the case in this skilled industry. Nevertheless, there is room for criticism. While initial evaluations are quite thorough and rational, the monitoring process may not be wholly satisfactory. Subsequent changes in corporate or municipal government events may not trigger a rating change quickly enough. One sure way a corporation or municipal government will get a reevaluation is for them to come out with a new issue. This tends to generate a review of all existing issues.

---

5. Similar appropriate measures can be applied to municipal bonds, such as debt per capita or income per capita within a governmental jurisdiction.

6. James O. Horrigan, "The Determination of Long-Term Credit Standing with Financial Ratios," *Empirical Research in Accounting: Selected Studies*, supplement to *Journal of Accounting Research* 4 (1966), pp. 44–62; Thomas F. Pogue and Robert M. Soldofsky, "What's in a Bond Rating?" *Journal of Financial and Quantitative Analysis*, June 1969, pp. 201–8; and George E. Pinches and Kent A. Mingo, "A Multivariate Analysis of Industrial Bond Ratings," *Journal of Finance*, March 1973, pp. 1–18.

ACTUAL RATING SYSTEM

Table 2-2 shows an actual listing of the designations used by Moody's and Standard & Poor's. Note that Moody's combines capital letters and small *a*'s, and Standard & Poor's uses all capital letters.

The first four categories are assumed to represent investment-grade quality. Large institutional investors (insurance companies, banks, pension funds) generally confine their activities to these four categories. Moody's also modifies its basic ratings with numerical values for categories Aa through B. The highest in a category is 1, 2 is the midrange, and 3 is the lowest. A rating of Aa2 means the bond is in the midrange of Aa. Standard & Poor's has a similar modification process with pluses and minuses applied. Thus, AA+ would be on the high end of an AA rating, AA would be in the middle, and AA− would be on the low end.

It is also possible for a corporation to have issues outstanding in more than one category. For example, highly secured mortgage bonds of a corporation may be rated AA, while unsecured issues carry an A rating.

The level of interest payment on a bond is the inverse of the quality rating. If a bond rated AAA by Standard & Poor's pays 7.5 percent, an A quality bond might pay 8.0 percent; a BB, 9.0 percent, and so on. The spread between these yields changes from time to time and is watched closely by the financial community as a barometer of future movements in the financial markets. A relatively small spread between two rating categories would indicate that investors generally have confidence in the economy. As the yield spread widens

TABLE 2–2   Description of Bond Ratings

Quality	Moody's	Standard & Poor's	Description
High grade	Aaa	AAA	Bonds that are judged to be of the best quality. They carry the smallest degree of investment risk and are generally referred to as "gilt edge." Interest payments are protected by a large or exceptionally stable margin, and principal is secured.
	Aa	AA	Bonds that are judged to be of high quality by all standards. Together with the first group, they comprise what are generally known as high-grade bonds. They are rated lower than the best bonds because margins of protection may not be as large.
Medium grade	A	A	Bonds that possess many favorable investment attributes and are to be considered as upper-medium-grade obligations. Factors giving security to principal and interest are considered adequate.
	Baa	BBB	Bonds that are considered as medium-grade obligations—they are neither highly protected nor poorly secured.
Speculative	Ba	BB	Bonds that are judged to have speculative elements; their future cannot be considered as well assured. Often the protection of interest and principal payments may be very moderate.
	B	B	Bonds that generally lack characteristics of the desirable investment. Assurance of interest and principal payments or of maintenance of other terms of the contract over any long period may be small.
Default	Caa	CCC	Bonds that are of poor standing. Such issues may be in default, or there may be elements of danger present with respect to principal or interest.
	Ca	CC	Bonds that represent obligations that are speculative to a high degree. Such issues are often in default or have other marked shortcomings.
	C		The lowest-rated class in Moody's designation. These bonds can be regarded as having extremely poor prospects of attaining any real investment standing.
		C	Rating given to income bonds on which interest is not currently being paid.
		D	Issues in default with arrears in interest and/or principal payments.

Sources: *Mergent Bond Record* (published by Mergent, Inc., New York, NY) and *Bond Guide* (Standard & Poor's).

between higher and lower rating categories, this may indicate loss of confidence. Investors are demanding increasingly higher yields for lower rated bonds. Their loss of confidence indicates they will demand progressively higher returns for taking risks.

High Yield Bonds

Lower quality bonds are sometimes referred to as **junk bonds** or high yield bonds. Any bond that is not considered to be of investment quality by Wall Street analysts is put in the junk bond category. As previously indicated, an investment is of high quality if the bond falls into one of the four top investment-grade categories established by Moody's and Standard & Poor's. This indicates investment-grade bonds extend down to Baa in Moody's and BBB in Standard & Poor's (Table 2–2). High yield bonds then, are bonds that promise a much higher yield than average. In general these types of bonds are much riskier than traditional bonds. Therefore, investors will require a greater rate of return for their investments for assuming the higher risk.

A wide range of quality is associated with junk bonds. Some are very close to investment quality (such as the Ba and BB bonds), while others carry ratings in the C and D category. Any bond that is not considered to be of investment quality by Wall Street analysts is put in the junk bond category. Bonds tend to fall into the junk bond category for a number of reasons. First, there are the so-called fallen angel bonds issued by companies that once had high credit rankings but now face hard times. Second, there are emerging growth companies or small firms that have not yet established an adequate record to justify an investment-quality rating. Finally, a major part of the junk bond market is made of companies undergoing a restructuring, either as a result of a leveraged buyout or as part of fending off an unfriendly takeover offer. In both these cases, equity capital tends to be replaced with debt, so a lower rating is assigned.

Distressed Debt

Distressed debt can be defined as debt from publicly traded companies, private placements or banks in which the issuer has defaulted or has filed for Chapter 11 under the U.S. bankruptcy laws. As a result, the debt notes get sold at a major discount in the market. Investors purchase the debt at lower than par value prices with the strategy that the company will eventually get back on its feet and continue paying the interest and eventually the face value of the bond.

This type of debt produces large opportunities for large institutional investors whereby they are able to purchase a significant amount of the outstanding debt. In turn, these investors assume some level of control within the company that is distressed and take the opportunity to turn the company around. However, such investments are only advisable for those seeking advanced returns from assuming higher risk.

State and Local Government Securities

Debt securities issued by state and local governments are referred to as **municipal bonds**. Examples of issuing agencies include states, cities, school districts, toll roads, or any other type of political subdivision. The most important feature of a municipal bond is the tax-exempt nature of the interest payment. Dating back to the U.S. Supreme Court opinion of 1819 in *McCullough v. Maryland*, it was ruled that the federal, state, and local governments do not possess the power to tax each other. An eventual by-product of the judicial ruling was that income from municipal bonds cannot be taxed by the IRS.

Furthermore, income from municipal bonds is also exempt from state and local taxes if bought within the locality in which one resides. Thus, a Californian buying municipal bonds in California would pay no state income tax on the issue. However, the same Californian would have to pay state or local income taxes if the originating agency were in Texas or New York.

We cannot overemphasize the importance of the federal tax exemption that municipal bonds enjoy. The consequences are twofold. First, individuals in high tax brackets may find highly attractive investment opportunities in municipal bonds.[7] The formula used to equate interest on municipal bonds to other taxable investments is:

$$Y = i / (1-T)$$

Y = Equivalent before-tax yield on a taxable investment
i = Yield on the municipal obligation
T = Marginal tax rate of the investor

If an investor has a marginal tax rate of 35 percent and is evaluating a municipal bond paying 6 percent interest, the equivalent before-tax yield on a taxable investment would be:

$$6\% / (1-0.35) = 6\% / 0.65 = 9.23\%$$

Thus, the investor could choose between a *non*-tax-exempt investment paying 9.23 percent and a tax-exempt municipal bond paying 6 percent and be indifferent between the two. We will get into a bit more detail in our taxation chapter regarding further outcomes for taxation of municipal bonds.

General Obligation versus Revenue Bonds

A **general obligation issue** is backed by the full faith, credit, and "taxing power" of the governmental unit. For a **revenue bond,** on the other hand, the repayment of the issue is fully dependent on the revenue-generating capability of a specific project or venture, such as a toll road, bridge, or municipal sports arena.

Because of the taxing power behind most general obligation (GO) issues, they tend to be of extremely high quality. Approximately three-fourths of all municipal bond issues are of the general obligation variety, and very few failures have occurred in the post-World War II era. Revenue bonds tend to be of more uneven quality, and the economic soundness of the underlying revenue-generating project must be carefully examined (though most projects are quite worthwhile).

Municipal Bond Guarantee. A growing factor in the municipal bond market is the third-party guarantee. Whether dealing with a general obligation or revenue bond, a fee may be paid by the originating governmental body to a third-party insurer to guarantee that all interest and principal payments will be made. There are four private insurance firms that guarantee municipal bonds, the largest are the Municipal Bond Investors Assurance (MBIA) and the American Municipal Bond Assurance Corporation (AMBAC). Municipal bonds that are guaranteed carry the highest rating possible (AAA) because all the guaranteeing insurance companies are rated AAA. Approximately 30 percent of municipal bond issues are guaranteed.

Promissory Note

A promissory note is a promise to repay a specific amount of money at a specified rate within a set period of time. In legal terms, the person who makes the promise is called the maker and the person/entity to whom the note is made is called the payee. An example of a promissory

---

7. It should be noted that any capital gain on a municipal bond is taxable as would be the case with any investment.

note is a student loan. Prior to receiving the funds, the student signs a note that promises to repay the note after he/she has completed school. Another example is when a home is purchased and money is borrowed in order to purchase the home. The purchaser of the home signs a promissory note to the lender, which agrees to pay back the loan amount for a specified rate of interest over a certain period of time (usually 15, 20 or 30 years).

Companies will sometimes issue promissory notes to an investor (a bank, individual, or institution) who agrees to lend the company money for a set period of time at a set rate of return.

Equity Markets

Equity markets are those markets in which purchasers can go to the primary or secondary market and purchase stocks and other equity-based investments. This market is the most well-known market to investors. The stock market gets much more hype than the bond markets and money markets because of the price volatility within this market relative to the others. An equity market is where many uneducated investors formulate "get rich quick" schemes. As we will see in subsequent chapters, there are many theories and beliefs on whether or not people can outsmart the market. But for now, we will focus on defining types of investments within the equity market. In the following sections, we will define **common stock**, **preferred stock**, and **warrants and rights**. In Chapter 3 we will discuss the types of orders one can expect to encounter when trading stocks, **derivatives** such as **options** and **futures**, **exchange-traded funds**, and **index securities**.

Common Stock

Common stock represents an ownership claim in a corporation. Common stock has voting rights at annual meetings and one share of stock gives the holder one vote. By voting, the shareholders elect the board of directors, who in turn hires managers to run the company. Shares of common stock can be bought by an Initial Public Offering (IPO) or can be purchased in the secondary markets on stock exchanges.

If you own a share of stock, you have a residual claim on the company's assets and earnings. This means that if the firm is going to be dissolved or liquidated, shareholders share the remaining assets and earnings after all of the firm's debt obligations have been paid to debtors. Another interesting feature of common stock is its limited liability. This means that shareholders can lose their initial investment in the event that a company fails. Shareholders will not be financially affected by lawsuits or other financial hardships otherwise incurred by the firm. However, the upside of owning common stock is unlimited. That is, the owners of common stock can share in the unlimited profits of the company as the stock price increases over time.

From a taxation standpoint, common stock presents an excellent investment vehicle when considered with other elements of risk and return. This is because there are no gains or losses on stock until it is sold. Thus, the investor can drive the timing and the tax consequences when owning a stock. For this reason owning equities can help in the overall tax planning context.

Preferred Stock

Preferred stock pays a stipulated annual dividend but does not include an ownership interest in the corporation. As such, preferred stockholders do not have voting rights. A $50 par value preferred stock issue paying $4.40 in annual dividends would provide an annual yield of 8.8 percent. Preferred stock as an investment, falls somewhere between bonds and common stock in so far as protective provisions are concerned for the investor.

In the case of debt, the bondholders have a contractual claim against the corporation and may force bankruptcy proceedings if interest payments are not forthcoming. Preferred

TABLE 2–3   Selected Warrants as of October 1, 2001

(1) Name of Firm, Place of Warrant Listing, and Stock Listing[a]	(2) Warrant Price	(3) Per Share Stock Price	(4) Per Share Option Price	(5) Intrinsic Value[b] [(3) − (4)]	(6) Speculative Premium [(2) − (5)]	(7) Shares per Warrant	(8) Due Date
ChinaB2BSourcing.com OTC, OTC	$ 1.63	$ 6.50	$ 5.00	$1.88[c]	−$ 0.25	1.250	4/23/2004
Micron Technology OTC, NYSE	17.25	22.30	56.00	0.00	17.25	26.163	5/15/2008
New Valley OTC, OTC	0.17	4.00	12.50	0.00	0.17	71.898	6/14/2004
Nexell Therapeutics OTC, OTC	0.20	1.13	5.42	0.00	0.20	2.399	6/20/2006
U.S. Laboratories OTC, OTC	1.88	8.75	7.80	0.95	0.93	1.000	2/23/2004
Video Network Communication OTC, OTC	0.18	0.54	4.00	0.00	0.18	4.000	6/15/2004

[a]OTC = over-the-counter; NYSE = New York Stock Exchange.

[b] When Column (4) is larger than Column (3), the intrinsic value will calculate as a negative number. Because the intrinsic value of a warrant cannot be less than zero (worthless), we put a zero in Column (5).

[c]Indicates that the warrants are offered at a conversion ratio of more than one share per warrant. The difference between the stock price and option price must be multiplied by Column (7) to get the intrinsic value.

Source: *The Value Line Convertibles Survey*, October 1, 2001.

stockholders, on the other hand, are entitled to receive a stipulated dividend and must receive the dividend before any payment to common stockholders. However, the payment of preferred stock dividends is not compelling to the corporation as is true in the case of debt. In bad times, preferred stock dividends may be omitted by the corporation. However, preferred dividends are cumulative, meaning that all arrearages of preferred dividends must be paid before common shareholders are entitled to receive dividends

While preferred stock dividends are not tax deductible to the corporation, as would be true with interest on bonds, they do offer certain investors unique tax advantages. The tax law provides that any corporation that receives preferred or common stock dividends from another corporation must add only 30 percent of such dividends to its taxable income. Thus, if a $5 dividend is received, only 30 percent of the $5, or $1.50, would be taxable to the corporate recipient. Because of this tax feature, preferred stock may carry a slightly lower yield than corporate bond issues of similar quality.

Preferred stock may carry a number of features that are similar to a debt issue. For example, a preferred stock issue may be *convertible* into common stock. Also, preferred stock may be *callable* by the corporation at a stipulated price, generally slightly above par. The call feature of a preferred stock issue may be of particular interest in that preferred stock has no maturity date as such. If the corporation wishes to take preferred stock off the books, it must call in the issue or purchase the shares in the open market at the going market price.

Stock Warrants

A **warrant** is an option to buy a stated number of shares of stock at a specified price over a given time period. The list of six warrants in Table 2-3 demonstrates the relationships discussed in the following sections. For example, U.S. Laboratories is a company specializing in quality control of building projects. It is a small company with a high stock price of $15 and a low stock price of $3.13 during the last 52 weeks. U.S. Laboratories has a warrant listed in Table 2-3 that allows the holder to buy one share of stock for $7.80 (Column 4) until February 23, 2004. The common stock (Column 3) is already selling above the option price and investors are willing to pay $1.88 (Column 2) for the warrant. Since investors have 2.5 years left to exercise their warrants at the time of this example, there is a possibility that the stock could rise back to its high of $15. If this were to happen the warrant would be worth at least $7.20 ($15 market price minus the $7.80 option price in Column 4). We will analyze this relationship after a few more examples.

Most warrants allow the holder to buy one share of common stock per warrant on the date of issue, but if the common stock performs well and stock splits occur, the warrant gets adjusted to reflect the stock splits. Five out of the six warrants listed in Table 2–3 have had stock splits, so the warrant carries with it the ability to buy more than one share. One of the most dynamic companies in the table is Micron Technology, a leading company in the computer memory-chip industry. This company has split so many times that its warrant allows the purchase of 26.163 shares (Column 7) of the underlying stock. If Micron common stock goes to $56 per share (option price), the intrinsic value will be zero, but if Micron common stock goes to $57 per share, the intrinsic value will be $26.163. Every dollar that the stock price is above $56 will generate one dollar of profit on 26.163 shares.

Warrants are usually issued as a sweetener to a bond offering, and they may enable the firm to issue debt when this would not be feasible otherwise. The warrants allow the bond issue to carry a lower coupon rate and are usually detachable from the bond after the issue date. After being separated from the bond, warrants have their own market price and may trade on a different market from the common stock. After the warrants are exercised, the initial debt with which they were sold remains in existence.

Because a warrant is dependent on the market movement of the underlying common stock and has no "security value" as such, it is highly speculative. If the common stock of the firm is volatile, the value of the warrants may change dramatically.

Chapter 3

Overview of Financial Instruments

TYPES OF ORDERS

When an investor places an order to establish a position, he or she has many different kinds of orders from which to choose. When the order is placed with the broker on an NYSE-listed stock, it is tele-typed to the exchange where it is executed by the company's floor broker in an auction market. Each stock is traded at a specific trading post on the floor of the exchange, so the floor broker knows exactly where to go to find other brokers buying and selling the same company's shares. Most orders placed will be straightforward market orders to buy or sell. The market order will be carried by the floor broker to the correct trading post and will usually trade close to the last price or within 0.25 of a point.[1] For example, if you want to sell 100 shares of AT&T at market, you would probably have no trouble finding a ready buyer since AT&T may be trading a few million shares per day. But, if you wanted to sell 100 shares of Bemis, as few as 1,000 shares might be traded in a day, and no other broker would be waiting at the Bemis post to make a transaction with the floor broker. If the broker finds no one else wishing to buy the shares, he will transact the sale with the specialist who is always at the post ready to buy and sell 100-share round lots. If the broker wants to sell, the specialist will either buy the shares for her own account at 0.125 or 0.25 less than the last trade or will buy out of her book in which special orders of others are kept.

Two basic special orders are the limit order and the stop order. A **limit order** limits the price at which you are willing to buy or sell and ensures you will pay no more than the limit price on a buy or receive no less than the limit price on a sell. Assume you are trying to buy a thinly traded stock that fluctuates in value and you are afraid that with a market order you might risk paying more than you want. So, you would place a limit order to buy 100 shares of Allied Waste Industries, as an example, at 16.50 or a better price. The order will go to the floor broker who goes to the post to check the price. The broker finds Allied Waste trading at its high for the day of 16.80, so he leaves the limit order with the specialist who records it in his book. The entry will record the price, date, time, and brokerage firm. There may be other orders in front of yours at 16.50, but once these are cleared, and assuming the stock stays in this range, your order will be executed at 16.50 or less. Limit orders are used by investors to buy or sell thinly traded stocks or to buy securities at prices thought to be at the low end of a price range and to sell securities at the high end of the price range. Investors who calculate fundamental values have a basic idea of what they think a stock is worth and will often set a limit to take advantage of what they view to be discrepancies in values.

---

1. Since the NYSE has gone to decimals the difference can be less.

Many traders are certain they want their order to be executed if a certain price is reached. A limit order does not guarantee execution if orders are ahead of you on the specialist's book. In cases where you want a guaranteed "fill" of the order, a stop order is placed. A **stop order** is a two-part mechanism. It is placed at a specific price like a limit order, but when the price is reached, the stop turns into a market order that will be executed at close to the stop price but not necessarily at the exact price specified. Often, many short-term traders will view a common stock price with optimism for a certain trading strategy. When the stock hits the price, it may pop up on an abundance of buy orders or decline sharply on a large volume of sell orders, and your "fill" could be several dollars away from the top price.

Assume AXE Corporation stock has been trading between $25 and $40 per share over the last six months, reaching both these prices three times. A trader may follow several strategies. One strategy would be to buy at $25 and sell at $40 using a stop buy and a stop sell order. Some traders may put in a stop buy at $41 thinking that if the stock breaks through its peak trading range it will go on to new highs, and finally some may put in a stop sell at $24 to either eliminate a long position or establish a short position with the assumption the stock has broken its support and will trend lower. When used to eliminate a long position, a stop order is often called a *stop-loss order*.

Limit orders and stop orders can be "day orders" that expire at the end of the day if not executed, or they can be GTC (good till canceled) orders. GTC orders will remain on the specialist's books until taken off by the brokerage house or executed. If the order remains unfilled for several months, most brokerage houses will send reminders that the order is still pending so that the client does not get caught buying stock for which he or she is unable to pay.

Market Strategies: Long/Short or Market Neutral

When investors establish a position in a security, they are said to have a **long position** if they purchase the security for their account. It is assumed the reason they purchased the security was to profit on an increase in price over time and/or to receive dividend income.

Sometimes, investors anticipate that the price of a security may drop in value. If they are long in the stock, some may sell out their position. Those who have no position at all may wish to take a **short position** to profit from the expected decline. When you short a security, you are borrowing the security from the broker and selling it with the obligation to replace the security in the future. How you can sell something you don't own is an obvious question. Your broker will simply lend you the security from the brokerage house inventory. If your brokerage house doesn't have an inventory of the particular stock you want to short, the firm will borrow the stock from another broker. Once you go short, you begin hoping and praying that the price of the security will go down so that you can buy it back and replace the security at a lower price. In a perverse way, bad news starts to become good news. When you read the morning paper, you look for signs of unemployment, high inflation, and rising interest rates in hopes of a stock market decline.

A short sale can only be made on a trade where the price of the stock advances (an uptick), or if there is no change in price, the prior trade must have been positive. These rules are intended to stop a snowballing decline in stock values caused by short sellers.

A market neutral strategy is action taken by an investor who takes both a long position and a short position in the market at the same time. An investor is seeking to benefit from perceived market inefficiencies by taking advantage of purchasing both an undervalued security (buying long) and an overvalued security (buying short). In the end, the investor hopes to gain on both transactions. This strategy is used as a tool to minimize risk to the investor and balance the portfolio.

Arbitrage Strategies

Arbitrage is defined as making profits without taking any risk. The classic example of arbitrage involves different prices that exist for the same security on two different exchanges. If shares of Microsoft are being sold on Nasdaq for $45 per share and the same shares are being sold on AMEX for $48 per share, then an arbitrager would buy shares of Microsoft on Nasdaq and sell them simultaneously on AMEX for a $3 profit. In the process of buying and selling the stock, arbitrageurs will bid up the price of stock on Nasdaq and will force the price of the stock on AMEX down until both prices in the market reach an equilibrium. The theory of arbitrage states that in an efficient market system, the profit will not be maintained for long periods of time since arbitrageurs will purchase and sell securities until the profit is completely eliminated, that is, when both market prices reach equilibrium.

Overview of Derivatives

Trading in stock index futures and options has had a tremendous impact on the financial markets in the United States. Stock index futures and options are sometimes referred to as **derivative products** because they derive their existence from actual market indexes but have no intrinsic characteristics of their own.[2] These derivative products are thought to make market movements more volatile. The primary reason is that enormous amounts of securities can be controlled by relatively small amounts of margin payments or option premiums. Also, these trades are initiated by institutional investors. Stock index futures and options facilitate program trading because a large volume of securities can be controlled. The presence of program trading, as supported by the use of stock index futures and options, was blamed by many for the 508-point market crash in the Dow Jones Industrial Average on October 19, 1987. It was thought that too many institutional investors were moving in the same direction (to sell) at one time. Increased stock price volatility since the market crash has also been blamed on program trading and the use of stock index futures and options.

Derivatives are somewhat controversial topics. A study by the Chicago Mercantile Exchange suggests program trading and the use of derivative products has no negative effect on the market volatility. These trading tools merely help the market reach a new equilibrium level (in terms of value) more quickly.[3]

Options

The word **option** has many different meanings, but most of them include the ability or right to choose a certain alternative. One definition provided by *Webster's Dictionary* is "the right, acquired for a consideration, to buy or sell something at a fixed price within a specified period of time." This definition is very general and applies to puts, calls, warrants, real estate options, or any other contract entered into between two parties where a choice of action or decision can be put off for a limited time at a cost. The person acquiring the option pays an agreed-upon sum to the person providing the option.

For example, someone may want to buy your house for its sale price of $100,000. The buyer does not have the money but will give you $2,000 in cash if you give him the right to buy the house at $100,000 for the next 60 days. If you accept, you have given the buyer an option and have agreed not to sell the house to anyone else for the next 60 days. If the buyer raises $100,000 within the 60-day limit, he may buy the house, giving you the $100,000.

---

2. Interest-rate futures and options are also considered to be derivative products.
3. *Report of the Committee of Inquiry Appointed by the Chicago Mercantile Exchange to Examine the Events Surrounding October 19, 1987* (Chicago: The Chicago Mercantile Exchange, December 17, 1987).

Perhaps he gets the $100,000 but also finds another house he likes better for $95,000. He will not buy your house, but you have a $2,000 option premium and must now find someone else to buy your house. By selling the option, you tied up the sale of your house for 60 days, and if the option is not exercised, you have forgone an opportunity to sell the house to someone else.

The most widely known options are puts and calls on common stock. A **put** is an option to sell 100 shares of common stock at a specified price for a given period. **Calls** are the opposite of puts and allow the owner the right to buy 100 shares of common stock from the option seller (writer). Contracts on listed puts and calls have been standardized and can be bought on several different exchanges. Options will be discussed in further detail in future chapters.

Futures

A **futures contract** is an agreement that provides for the delivery of a specific amount of a commodity at a designated time in the future at a given price. An example might be a contract to deliver 5,000 bushels of corn next September at $2.15 per bushel. The person who sells the contract does not need to have actual possession of the corn, nor does the purchaser of the contract need to plan on taking possession of the corn. Almost all commodities futures contracts are closed out or reversed before the actual transaction is to occur. Thus, the seller of a futures contract for the delivery of 5,000 bushels of corn may simply later buy back a similar contract for the purchase of 5,000 bushels and close out his position. The initial buyer also reverses his position. More than 97 percent of all contracts are closed out in this fashion rather than through actual delivery. The commodities futures market is similar to the options market in that there is a tremendous volume of activity, but very few actual items ever change hands.

The futures markets were originally set up to allow grain and livestock producers and processors to **hedge** (protect) their positions in a given commodity. For example, a wheat producer might have a five-month lead time between the planting of his crop and the actual harvesting and delivery to the market. While the current price of wheat might be $4 a bushel, there is a tremendous risk that the price might change before delivery to the market. The wheat farmer can hedge his position by offering to sell futures contracts for the delivery of wheat. Even though he will probably close out or reverse these futures contracts before the call for actual delivery, he will still have effectively hedged his position. For example, if the price of wheat goes down, he will have to sell his crop for less than he anticipated when he planted the wheat, but he will make up the difference on the wheat futures contracts. That is, he will be able to buy back the contracts for less than he sold them. Of course, if the price of the wheat goes up, the extra profit he makes on the crop will be lost on the futures contracts as he now has to buy back the contracts at a higher price.[4]

A miller who uses wheat as part of his processing faces the opposite dilemma in terms of pricing. The miller is afraid the price of wheat might go up and ultimately cut into his profit margin when he takes actual delivery of his product. He can hedge his position by buying futures contracts in wheat. If the actual price of wheat does go up, the extra cost of producing his product will be offset by the profits he makes on his futures contracts.

The commodities market allows the many parties in need of hedging opportunities to acquire contracts. Although some of this could be accomplished on a private basis (one party in Kansas City calls another party in Chicago on the advice of his banker), this would be virtually impossible to handle on a large-scale basis. Liquid, fluid markets such as those provided by the commodity exchanges are necessary to accomplish this function.

---

4. The hedger not only reduces risk of loss but also eliminates additional profit opportunities. This may be appropriate for farmers since they are not in the risk-taking business but rather in agriculture.

While the hedgers are the backbone and basic reason for the existence of commodity exchanges, they are not the only significant participants. We also have the speculators who take purely long or short positions without any intent to hedge actual ownership. Thus, there is the speculator in wheat or silver who believes that the next major price move can be predicted to such an extent that a substantial profit can be made. Because commodities are purchased on the basis of a small investment in the form of margin (usually running 2 to 10 percent of the value of the contract), there is substantial leverage on the investment, and percentage returns and losses are greatly magnified. The typical commodities trader often suffers many losses with the anticipation of a few very substantial gains. Commodities speculation, as opposed to hedging, represents somewhat of a gamble, and stories have been told of reformed commodities speculators who gave up the chase to spend the rest of their days merely playing the slot machines. Nevertheless, commodity speculators are quite important to the liquidity of the market. Futures contracts will be discussed further in another chapter.

Commodities

Commodities are physical substances such as grains, metals, livestock, oil, and coffee that investors buy or sell on organized commodities exchanges across the country. In general, they are purchased via future or forward contracts for investment purposes. They are generally purchased via these contracts in order to hedge inflationary pressures that an investor may perceive in the future. However, commodities are also purchased by speculative investors as discussed above.

Margin Requirements

Commodity trading is based on the use of margin rather than on actual cash dollars. Margin requirements are typically 2 to 10 percent of the value of the contract and may vary over time or even among exchanges for a given commodity. For our example, we will assume a $600 margin requirement on the $17,500 wheat contract.[5] That was the specified margin in 2001. The $600 would represent 3.4 percent of the value of the contract ($17,500).

Margin requirements on commodities contracts are much lower than those on common stock transactions, where 50 percent of the purchase price has been the requirement since 1974. Furthermore, in the commodities market, the margin payment is merely considered to be a good-faith payment against losses. There is no actual borrowing or interest to be paid.[6]

In addition to the initial margin requirements, **margin maintenance requirements** (minimum maintenance standards) run 60 to 80 percent of the value of the initial margin. In the case of the wheat contract, the margin maintenance requirement might be $400 (67% × $600). If our initial margin of $600 is reduced by $200 due to losses on our contract, we will be required to replace the $200 to cover our margin position. If we do not do so, our position will be closed out, and we will take our losses.

The margin requirement, relative to size, is even less for financial futures. For example, on a $1 million Treasury bill contract, the investor must post only an initial margin of $675. Similar requirements exist for other types of financial futures.

Note that the high risk inherent in a commodities contract is not so much a function of volatile price movements as it is the impact of high leverage made possible by the low initial margin requirements. A 5 percent price move may equal or exceed the size of our initial investment in the form of the margin deposit. The action in the commodities market is

---

5. The amount of margin required also differs between speculative and hedging activities. For example, $600 represents the margin for speculation. The margin for hedging is $400 in this case.
6. It should also be pointed out that a customer may need a minimum account balance of $5,000 or greater to open a commodity account.

much quicker. You can be asked to put up additional margin within hours after you establish your initial position.

OTHER TYPES OF SECURITIES

Exchange Traded Funds

A new wrinkle in closed-ended mutual funds is the concept of **exchange traded funds (ETFs)**. These are investment company shares that trade on stock exchanges, commonly the American Stock Exchange. The market determines the price of ETFs, and investors buy and sell them through brokers just like common stock. Exchange traded funds began in 1993.

Exchange traded funds are essentially index-based mutual funds that imitate a market index such as the Standard & Poor's 500 Index. The advantage of ETFs is that they allow the investor to buy "the market" or "an industry" just like a common stock.

In recent years, hundreds of ETFs have sprung up in the marketplace. Company names that are associated with ETFs are Diamonds, HOLDRs, iShares, QUBEs, SPDRs, StreetTracks, and VIPERS. Morningstar provides excellent information on these companies and their funds. You can also go to the individual sites of these companies to find out more about the funds.

Index Funds

Index funds are mutual funds that replicate a market index as closely as possible. Exchange traded closed-ended funds are index funds that trade on exchanges just like common stock. Conversely, index funds are open-ended and may be purchased directly from the fund sponsor. There are many indexes, including stock market indexes and bond market indexes as well as foreign and global indexes. If an investor truly believes that the market is efficient and that it is hard to outperform the market, he or she will try to reduce transaction costs and attempt to imitate the market. Index funds arose because of the efficient market hypothesis. Quite a bit of academic research indicates that it is difficult to outperform a market index unless you have superior information. Most investors do not have superior information and so index funds make sense.

Pooled Investments

A **pooled investment** allows an investor to contribute investment funds with other investors who have a similar investment strategy and a similar risk profile for a specific type of investment. The funds are similar to a mutual fund in that they are managed by a third party. However, under securities laws, pooled investments are not required to have a prospectus because, under the law, they are not considered to be public investments. Nevertheless, information regarding pooled funds must be reported to the SEC or applicable agency. Types of pooled investments include unit trusts, hedge funds, and Real Estate Investment Trusts (REITs).

Though being in a pooled fund is similar to investing in a mutual fund, management of a pooled fund tends to be less active than in mutual funds. Pooled funds draw investors with much larger investment amounts than mutual funds. As a result, there tends to be much less buying and selling in pooled funds than in mutual funds. Interest and dividend payments are passed on to investors at regular intervals. Fees charged can either come from within the fund or can be paid directly by the investors to fund managers.

Unit Investment Trusts

Unit investment trusts (UITs) are investment companies organized for the purpose of purchasing a pool of securities—usually tax-exempt municipal bonds. UITs issue units to investors, representing a proportionate interest in the assets of the trust. Investors also receive a proportionate share in the interest or dividends received by the trust. When the securities mature, the trust generally dissolves. In general, these funds are considered to be low risk and low return investments, which is why many unit trusts invest in tax-free securities. Individuals investing in these types of funds generally have a long-term, passive market strategy. Capital gains and dividends are paid out to members on a regularly scheduled basis. Unlike mutual funds, the strategy for these funds does not include active trading. Since these types of funds are not managed as aggressively as typical mutual funds, the expenses for these types of funds tend to be lower.

According to the Investment Company Institute, by the end of 2000 there were a total of 10,071 unit trusts with a market value of $88.75 billion. While this is not a lot of money compared with mutual funds, unit trusts do meet a market niche for specialized investors. Of the 10,000 trusts, more than 8,000 were tax-free bond trusts. While equity trusts only accounted for slightly more than 1,500 trusts, they made up the lion's share of the value with $62 billion. Unit investment trusts are passive investments. They normally purchase assets and hold them for the benefit of owners for a specified period.

Units of a trust are redeemable under terms set forth in the prospectus. In most cases, this means a unit holder can sell units back to the trust at their net asset value, which is the current market value of each trust unit.

A secondary market for unit trusts is evolving among broker-dealers. Investors seeking to acquire or sell units can sometimes find a better deal in this market. However, most investors in UITs do not intend to redeem early.

Investors in UITs benefit by professional selection of securities, by diversification, and by avoiding the housekeeping chores of collecting coupon payments. As a large buyer, a UIT can usually purchase securities at a better price than the individual who buys in small lots.

Open-Ended Mutual Funds and Closed-Ended Mutual Funds

Mutual funds offer an efficient way to diversify your investments. For many small investors, diversification may be difficult to achieve. The normal trading unit for listed stocks—the "round lot"—is 100 shares. If proper diversification required a portfolio of at least 10 different stocks, the investor should purchase 100 shares of each of them. If each stock had a market value of $30, the cost would be (excluding commission) $30,000 ($30 × 100 × 10). That's a big bite for most individuals just to get started.

With a mutual fund, you are also buying the expertise of the fund management. In many cases, fund managers have a long history of investment experience and may be specialists in certain areas such as international securities, gold stocks, or municipal bonds.

There are two types of mutual funds; open and closed. A **closed-ended fund** has a fixed number of shares, and purchasers and sellers of shares must trade with each other. You cannot buy the shares directly from the fund (except at the inception of the fund) because of the limitation of shares outstanding. Furthermore, the fund does not stand ready to buy the shares back from you. An open-ended fund represents exactly the opposite concept. The **open-ended fund** stands ready at all times to sell you new shares or buy back your old shares.

Real Estate Investment Trust (REIT)

A form of real estate investment is the **real estate investment trust (REIT)**. REITs are similar to mutual funds or investment companies and trade on organized exchanges or over the counter. Because of this, shares of REITs are highly liquid. They pool investor funds, along with borrowed funds, and invest them directly in real estate or use them to make construction or mortgage loans to investors.

The advantage to the investor of a REIT is that he or she can participate in the real estate market for as little as $10 to $20 per share. Furthermore, this is the most liquid type of real estate investment because of the large secondary market for the shares.

REITs were initiated under the Real Estate Investment Trust Act of 1960. Like other investment companies, they enjoy the privilege of single taxation of income (only the stockholder pays and not the trust). To qualify for the tax privilege of a REIT, a firm must receive at least 75 percent of its income from real estate (i.e., rents and interest on mortgage loans) and distribute at least 95 percent of its income as cash dividends. REITs may take any of three different forms or combinations thereof. **Equity trusts** buy, operate, and sell real estate as an investment; **mortgage trusts** make long-term loans to real estate investors; and **hybrid trusts** engage in the activities of both equity and mortgage trusts. REITs are generally formed and advised by affiliates of commercial banks, insurance companies, mortgage bankers, and other financial institutions. Representative issues include Bank America Realty, and Connecticut General Mortgage.

Hedge Funds

Hedge funds are products of the 1990s and became very popular in 2000–2002. Actually the name is somewhat misleading in that hedge funds do not restrict their activities to hedging or reducing risk. Rather, the term is a generic name for funds that engage in a wide range of activities at one time in an attempt to generate a superior return. Hedge funds pool investor money to engage in aggressive investment goals and use a variety of tactics in order to maximize returns. While some hedge funds do invest in traditional stocks and bonds, other tactics include short sales, market arbitrage, derivatives, and leverage, to name a few. The pay-offs can be extremely high, but, since the tactics employed are speculative in nature, belonging to a hedge fund is risky business.

Hedge funds help to diversify a portfolio by using various tactics in order to hedge against various economic factors such as inflation or currency exchange. In fact, hedge funds can be thought of as a hybrid to all of the other alternative investment types since all kinds of investments are bought and sold within these types of funds.

Alternative Investments

Alternative investments are those investments that do not follow typical risk and return patterns. Even though alternative investments tend to be riskier on average than traditional securities, the return opportunity is generally much greater. Those investing in alternatives are generally seeking to diversify the risk return ratio within their portfolio. There are many types of alternative investments: hedge funds, high yield bonds, long/short or market neutral strategies, arbitrage strategies, commodities, futures, venture capital, leveraged buyouts, energy, timber, etc.

Venture Capital

Venture capital is generally comprised of individuals or venture capital companies who invest money, generally by taking an equity position in a company that has a potential to yield a large return on investment. Venture capitalists are normally overwhelmed with potential proposals for funding. The acceptance rate is lower than 1 out of 100. The odds are long, but the potential payout is great. Not only do venture capitalists provide funding, but they also may share their expertise in management, marketing, finance, and so on.

Often, the financing takes place in sequential stages. This means that additional funding after the original funding will only take place if certain goals are met. These goals may relate to profitability ratios, new product development, market penetration, etc. The venture capitalist often provides relatively low-cost debt financing, but with the understanding that the funding carries with it the potential to participate in a major way in any successful public offering of stock in the future. Although the venture capitalist may not care about owning a direct equity interest in the company while it is private, he or she wants to participate in ownership when there is a public distribution of shares. Please see below, the Real World of Investing excerpt, "Venture Capitalists Love Convertibles and Warrants."

Insurance Based Investments

Insurance based investments are investment options offered to investors from insurance companies. Insurance companies use the investment funds to purchase various types of investments such as mutual funds, stocks, and bonds. Because many insurance based investments promise to pay a certain rate of return, many of these types of investments are for risk-averse investors. Be wary of the fees embedded in permanent life insurance policies.

Fixed and Variable Annuities

Fixed annuities are a series of fixed, equal payments that are paid to an investor over a fixed number of years such as 5, 10, 15, or 20 years. Other payment options are available and will be discussed below. The term and interval of payment of the annuity is designated in the fixed annuity contract. The contract is an agreement between an insurance company and the investor. Because the payment is fixed, the risk for investment performance is held by the insurance company. However, the return is generally not large.

A **variable annuity** is a contract between an insurance company and an individual. Like fixed annuities, variable annuities will make payments over the life of the annuity contract, but, unlike fixed annuities, variable annuities do not guarantee a fixed level of monthly payments. The reason for the differing dollar amount in payments is because the investments in the contract do not earn a fixed rate of interest. Rather, they earn a variable rate of interest. This is because the variable annuity investment portfolio may contain a variety of investment vehicles such as stocks, bonds, mutual funds, or money market funds. Having funds in these types of investments translates to rates of return that are variable. The contract then makes variable payments during the agreed upon intervals to the investor based upon the value of the investments in the annuity. Because of the nature of the investment risk, the risk for investment performance is borne by the investor.

Oftentimes, the funds that insurance companies choose as investment vehicles are long-term growth (or capital gain) funds. Since these types of funds would not trigger a taxable event unless sold, it is not necessarily the best use of the funds in terms of the tax deferral standpoint. Bonds, other fixed income securities and mutual funds which conduct a lot of trading due to the nature of the fund, are more suitable investments for this type of fund.

Variable annuities then, do not promise to preserve capital due to the fluctuating nature of the investments in the annuity. The insurance company, not the individual, picks from a limited universe of investment options, at which point the individual can choose some of the options.

Annuities are allowed to build up interest, tax-free until withdrawals begin. This is one of the major tenets upon which insurance agents rest when they are selling annuities to their clients. However, unlike retirement plans, the funds that the individual contributes to these accounts are not tax-deductible. Just like retirement plans, withdrawals are taxed according to Federal Tax Law rules for annuities. Section 72 of the IRS code includes a full description of the taxation of annuities. In short, however, the income made on investments is taxed when received. Since payments were made with after-tax dollars, the principal portion of the payment returned as part of the annuity payment is not taxed.

Generally, individuals can fund annuities all at once, say from a lump-sum pension pay out, or they can be funded over a period of time.

A major drawback to annuities is that there are often a lot of fees that the investor pays in order to have the insurance company manage the account for them. Additionally, since the investor has agreed to receive fixed, periodic payments, the insurance company generally imposes large fees, generally for the first 5 to 7 years on the individual should they wish to get all of their money out of the annuity.

Methods of Paying Annuity Premiums

Individuals can contribute annuity payments via Single Annuity Premium or Flexible Premium. Both of these are discussed below.

Single Premium Annuity

One way of purchasing an annuity is via a lump-sum payment, also called a **single premium annuity**. With a single premium annuity, the investor makes one payment in order to fund the entire annuity. Oftentimes, those participating in employer-sponsored retirement plans will receive a lump-sum distribution at retirement. These lump-sum payments are often rolled over into a fixed annuity in order to guarantee a stream of income over the life of the participant.

Flexible Premium Annuities

With **flexible premium annuities**, the investor makes a series of payments into the annuity prior to distribution. Oftentimes, the investor is allowed considerable leeway as to when he or she will make the contributions. Likewise, the investor is also able to change or discontinue the payments into the annuity. The investor decides when to begin receiving the payments from the annuity.

Types of Annuity Payments

Annuity payments can be received in several different ways. Options for distribution may include payments in the form of a life annuity, a joint and survivor annuity, a life annuity with guaranteed payments, and an annuity certain.

Life Annuity

A **life annuity** provides monthly payments for the investor over his or her lifetime. Upon death of the investor, payments are ceased, and therefore, beneficiaries have no claims. A life annuity is a suitable platform when there are no needs to provide annuity income to remaining beneficiaries.

Joint and Survivor Annuity

A **joint and survivor annuity** provides monthly payments to the investor over his or her lifetime. If, however, the investor dies, a living, designated beneficiary will be able to receive a portion of the remaining annuity over his or her lifetime. This option is a suitable platform when there is a need to provide income for living beneficiaries.

Life Annuity with Guaranteed Payments

A life **annuity with guaranteed payments** is an annuity that will guarantee annuity payments for the life of the investor. However, the guaranteed payment portion promises to make the payments for at least a specified period of time such as 5 years or 10 years. For example, if Joe chooses a life annuity with 10 year certain payments and dies after 5 years, then Joe's beneficiaries will receive the remaining 5 years of payments. Conversely, if Joe dies in 11 years, his beneficiaries will not be eligible to receive any payments. This payment option is generally chosen by those individuals who feel they have a shorter life expectancy.

Annuity Certain

An **annuity certain** provides the investor with a specified number of annuity payments after which time the payments cease. The annuity will be paid to beneficiaries for the length of time even if the investor dies. This option is a suitable platform when there is a need to provide income for living beneficiaries.

Life Insurance

Life insurance is purchased in order to protect against premature death. It is used as risk management tool in order to mitigate financial risks resulting from premature death.

Term Life Insurance

As discussed earlier, **term life insurance** provides protection for a specific period of time as long as premiums are paid on time. Typical **level terms** are 1-year, 5-year, 15-year, 20-year and 30-year terms. Term life policies can have small face values such as $10,000 or large face values in excess of $1 million. Recall that the face value is the amount that the insurance company will pay to beneficiaries in the event of premature death. Because term life policies do not have a cash value buildup or an investment component, the premiums are generally lower for same age individuals who participate in permanent life insurance policies.

It is cheaper for younger individuals to purchase term insurance since the expected mortality rates of younger people are much lower than those of elderly individuals. When purchasing level terms, the premium stays fixed until the end of the term at which point the insurance company will increase the policy premiums if the participant wishes to renew the term.

You may have heard the saying, "Buy term and invest the difference." This saying means that it is advisable to purchase term insurance, and invest the difference in premium that you would otherwise pay with a permanent insurance contract. The belief is that investment vehicles other than the permanent life policy will earn the insured a better rate of return. This belief is a function of the broad choices available to investors that are not otherwise offered through insurance companies.

Permanent Life Insurance

Permanent life insurance (sometimes called cash-value insurance) provides insurance for the entire life of the insured rather than for a specified term; provided premiums are paid timely. Premiums are generally higher than term life insurance premiums because permanent insurance is considered an investment vehicle designed to realize cash-value buildup in addition to a face value on the policy. Like term life insurance, the insurance company will pay the face amount of the insurance policy in the event of premature death. The **cash-value buildup** feature is an investment component whereby a portion of the monthly payment is contributed toward an investment fund for the policy holder. This investment fund is a savings vehicle for the investor. In contributing a monthly amount toward this investment account, the investor expects to receive a rate of return on this investment.

There are several types of permanent life insurance that allow an investor to accumulate cash in addition to funding a death benefit. Typical types of insurance purchased are whole life, universal life, variable life and variable universal life. All of these types of insurance have several elements of similarity between them. First of all, these types of insurance coverage promise life insurance protection for the life of the insured. Regardless of when the policy is purchased, the face value death benefit will be paid at the death of the insured.

One advantage touted by insurance agents is that the cash-value buildup is tax-deferred. While this is true, this is also for contributions to retirement plans. Contributions to retirement plans also enjoy tax deductible contribution status. Before your clients contribute to a permanent policy, you should consider the options in terms of the tax-deferral situation since term insurance can probably satisfy the same needs for far less cost.

Oftentimes, the funds that insurance companies choose as investment vehicles are long-term growth (or capital gain) funds. Since these types of funds would not trigger a taxable event unless sold, it is not necessarily the best use of the funds in terms of the tax deferral standpoint. Bonds, other fixed income securities and mutual funds which conduct a lot of trading due to the nature of the fund are more suitable investments for this type of fund.

Contributions to permanent life insurance policies are a long-term commitment. Once the cash-value buildup begins, it is difficult to withdraw the money without surrendering a large portion of the cash value. Therefore, it is wise to make sure that your client can be committed to making payments into this type of insurance.

Whole Life Insurance

Whole life insurance is the simplest of all the permanent life insurance policies. The premium payment and the death benefit are fixed for life. The rate of return earned on the investment portion of whole life insurance is also fixed for life. The investor has no control over the choice of investments since the insurance company promises a guaranteed rate of return.

Universal Life Insurance

Universal life policies have a premium that is subject to minimums that are set by the insurance company which can change over the life of the policy. The death benefit can also increase above the face amount depending upon the cash accumulation in the investment portion of the policy. Universal life insurance policies have a variable rate of return with a specified minimum. As such, the investor has no control over the investment choices since the insurance company promises a guaranteed rate of return.

Variable Life Insurance

Variable life insurance policies have fixed premium payments. The death benefit can also increase above the face amount depending upon the cash accumulation in the investment portion of the policy. The policy owner completely controls the investments, but a limited amount of investment choices are provided to the consumer by the insurance company. As a result, the investor is not promised a fixed rate of return. This is because the variable life investment portfolio may contain a variety of investment vehicles such as stocks, bonds, mutual funds, or money market funds. Having funds in these types of investments translates to rates of return that are variable.

Variable Universal Life Insurance

Variable universal life policies have a premium that is subject to minimums that are set by the insurance company which can change over the life of the policy. The death benefit can also increase above the face amount depending upon the cash accumulation in the investment portion of the policy. The policy owner completely controls the investments (though a limited amount of investment choices are provided to the consumer by the insurance company). As a result, the investor is not promised a fixed rate of return. This is because the variable life investment portfolio may contain a variety of investment vehicles such as stocks, bonds, mutual funds, or money market funds. Having funds in these types of investments translates to rates of return that are variable.

Summary

This chapter is an introductory chapter, meant to provide a broad overview of the world of investments including the markets in which we operate. Without knowledge of the types of investments, it will be difficult for you to choose which investments are suitable for your clients. At every consideration, there are multiple issues to consider, such as ease of trade, cost of trade, taxation issues, and risk and return issues. It is thus important to have a good theoretical background upon which to make these decisions.

The following chapters will allow us to do just that. Reading one book will not make you an expert overnight, but having a solid investments background will allow you to talk intelligently to your clients regarding their needs.

The Real World of Investing

Treasury Inflation Protection Securities (TIPS) are discussed in the main body of the chapter, so the basics will not be restated here. As the name implies, TIPS are a protection against the ravages of inflation, but absolutely no one was worried about inflation at the time they were introduced in January 1997. The years 1996–97 represented some of the lowest levels of inflation (about 2 percent) in the post–World War II period. Introducing TIPS at that point in time was like selling flood insurance to farmers who are suffering through a six month rain drought.

It's unlikely that private sector investment bankers such as Goldman Sachs or C.S. First Boston would have come out with a similar product at such an inopportune time, but keep in mind we are talking about the federal government. In fairness, it should also be pointed out that the majority of TIPS have an initial 10-year life, so even though there is no immediate threat of inflation, they could well prove to be important during the time period they are outstanding.

Furthermore, those who advocate the purchase of TIPS for a portfolio generally suggest that they represent a relatively small percentage of total holdings. The message is: "Bet on low inflation with 80 to 90 percent of your investments, but put the balance in inflation-protected securities."

Surprisingly, the first auction of TIPS went relatively well in January 1997, although subsequent auctions have seen less enthusiasm. This general lack of enthusiasm continued into 2001. However, among the more enthusiastic investors are foreigners from countries such as Great Britain, Canada, and Sweden, where inflation-indexed securities are more widely accepted. Eighteen percent of British government debt is actually financed by securities whose returns are tied to inflation.

The advantage to the federal government of offering TIPS is that they can be sold to the public at a slightly lower yield than conventional fixed-rate Treasury securities because the government is taking the risk of inflation going up (the amount the government will have to pay to redeem the securities will go up sharply if there is high inflation). In return for the government taking this risk, investors accept a slightly lower return.

Venture Capitalists Love Convertibles and Warrants

Venture capital is normally raised in the early stages of growth for a firm, well before the company has "gone public" (sold its shares in the public market). Even successful, rapidly developing young companies often have needs for capital that far outstrip their profit generating capability, their ability to borrow, or the resources of their owners. This is where the venture capitalist comes in. He or she provides funding (seed capital) with the hope that his or her capital will eventually be harvested in the form of a successful public offering of stock at some point in the future.

Venture capitalists (VC) are normally overwhelmed with potential proposals for funding. The acceptance rate is lower than 1 out of 100. When the Basses of Fort Worth, the Pritzkers of Chicago, or other venture capitalists see a deal, they always have their eye out for the next Microsoft or Intel. The odds that VCs take are long, but the potential payout is great. Not only do venture capitalists provide funding, but they also may share their expertise in management, marketing, finance, and so on. Some venture capitalists even specialize in certain areas such as biotechnology or computer software. Often, the financing takes place in sequential stages. This means that additional funding after the original funding will only take place if certain goals are met. These goals may relate to profitability ratios, new product development, market penetration, etc.

The venture capitalist often provides relatively low-cost debt financing, but with the understanding that the funding carries with it the potential to participate in a major way in any successful public offering of stock in the future. While the venture capitalist may not care about owning a direct equity interest in the company while it is private, he or she wants to participate in ownership when there is a public distribution of shares.

Convertibles and warrants fit very well into these investment parameters. With convertibles, the venture capitalist is able to receive interest income and enjoy a relatively high priority of claims among other suppliers of capital. At the time an equity position becomes desirable, he or she can merely convert the debt to common stock.

Another alternative is to provide the venture capitalist with warrants as part of the compensation package for extending debt financing. As incentive, the exercise price on the warrants may be set at one-fifth to one-tenth of the anticipated potential price for a public offering.

When convertibles or warrants are used in early stage financing, one can think of the interest payments on the related debt as providing singles or doubles to the venture capitalist. What he or she is really hoping for is a grand slam home run in the form of a successful public offering that is fully subscribed to and one in which the stock continues to go up in value after the offering.

THE REAL WORLD OF INVESTING

Variable Annuities—Are they Right for Your Client?

Many insurance agents are passionate about selling annuities to their clients. They will tout the fact that annuities promise a level of cash-value buildup, which is not taxed until withdrawal. While this is undoubtedly true, the planner needs to assess whether or not these kinds of products are right for his or her client.

One question to ask is: "Is my client already putting maximum contributions into his or her 401K or other retirement plan?" For people who are not putting the maximum amount into the retirement accounts, they are missing out on a twofold benefit: a tax deferred contribution and a tax deferred cash buildup. Both types of annuities have ongoing annual maintenance fees which can be significant depending on the type of annuity chosen.

In the late 1990s, many elderly people were sold variable annuity policies when they took retirement lump-sum distributions. This is because the stock market was doing so well.

As a result, many individuals chose aggressive funds in which to place their money. For a while, these individuals experienced great returns on their investments. But after the stock market declined in 2001, these very same people saw both a major drop in the value of their funds and precipitous drops in their monthly annuity payment. Because of surrender charges and fees that must be paid to the insurance company, many found themselves stuck between a rock and a hard place.

Of course the market will come back again, but in some cases these portfolios were not diversified enough and as such, it will be very difficult for these elderly to recover from such losses.

Annuities certainly do have a place in the market, but in general, they are for individuals who are already maxing out their other options with retirement plans and the like.

Individuals, with the help of an experienced investment advisor, can also create their own annuities such that they do not have to work with an insurance company. In this case, they will not necessarily be subject to the huge fees that insurance companies charge to maintain these, though they will be subject to fees if they pay someone to manage their portfolio. The benefit of this method is that individuals can still ensure annuity payments at a certain age, but can also have access to the funds in an emergency without ridiculous surrender charges. Lastly, the individual is able to pick from the universe of investments rather than the few that the insurance company may offer.

Exploring the Web

www.nasdaq.com	Link to Nasdaq site
www.nyse.com	Link to New York Stock Exchange. Information on regulations and market operations
www.investorwords.com	Definitions of investment terms
www.bondmarkets.com	Bond information and trading
www.moodys.com	Bond information; some is fee based
www.standardandpoors.com	Bond information; some is fee based
www.bondsonline.com	Bond information
www.morningstar.com	Mutual fund, EFT and other investment information; some information is free while other information must be paid for.

Chapter 4

Time Value of Money

In 1624 the Native Americans sold Manhattan Island at the ridiculously low figure of $24. But wait, was it really ridiculous? If they had merely taken the $24 and reinvested it at 6 percent annual interest up to 2004, they would have had $95 billion, an amount sufficient to repurchase part of New York City. If the Native Americans had invested the $24 at 7.5 percent compounded annually, they would now have over $14 trillion—and tribal chiefs would now rival oil sheiks and Bill Gates as the richest people in the world. Another popular example is that $1 received 2,004 years ago, invested at 6 percent, could now be used to purchase all the wealth in the world.

While not all examples are this dramatic, the time value of money applies to many day-to-day decisions. Understanding the effective rate on a business loan, the mortgage payment in a real estate transaction, or the true return on an investment depends on understanding the time value of money. As long as an investor can garner a positive return on idle dollars, distinctions must be made between money received today and money received in the future. The investor/lender essentially demands that a financial "rent" be paid on his or her funds as current dollars are set aside today in anticipation of higher returns in the future.

RELATIONSHIP TO THE CAPITAL OUTLAY DECISION

The decision to purchase new plant and equipment or to introduce a new product in the market requires using capital allocating or capital budgeting techniques. Essentially we must determine whether future benefits are sufficiently large to justify current outlays. It is important that we develop the mathematical tools of the time value of money as the first step toward making capital allocation decisions. Let us now examine the basic terminology of "time value of money."

Future Value—Single Amount

In determining the **future value**, we measure the value of an amount that is allowed to grow at a given interest rate over a period of time. Assume an investor has $1,000 and wishes to know its worth after four years if it grows at 10 percent per year. At the end of the first year, the investor will have $1,000 × 1.10, or $1,100. By the end of year two, the $1,100 will have grown to $1,210 ($1,100 × 1.10). The four-year pattern is indicated below.

1st year	$1,000 × 1.10 = $1,100
2nd year	$1,100 × 1.10 = $1,210
3rd year	$1,210 × 1.10 = $1,331
4th year	$1,331 × 1.10 = $1,464

After the fourth year, the investor has accumulated $1,464. Because compounding problems often cover a long period, a more generalized formula is necessary to describe the compounding procedure. We shall let:

TABLE 4–1   Future value of $1 (FV$_{IF}$)

Periods	1%	2%	3%	4%	6%	8%	10%
1	1.010	1.020	1.030	1.040	1.060	1.080	1.100
2	1.020	1.040	1.061	1.082	1.124	1.166	1.210
3	1.030	1.061	1.093	1.125	1.191	1.260	1.331
4	1.041	1.082	1.126	1.170	1.262	1.360	1.464
5	1.051	1.104	1.159	1.217	1.338	1.469	1.611
10	1.105	1.219	1.344	1.480	1.791	2.159	2.594
20	1.220	1.486	1.806	2.191	3.207	4.661	6.727

$$FV = \text{Future value}$$
$$PV = \text{Present value}$$
$$i = \text{Interest rate}$$
$$n = \text{Number of periods}$$

The simple formula is:

$$FV = PV(1 + i)^n$$

In this case, PV = $1,000, i = 10 percent, n = 4, so we have:

$$FV = \$1,000(1.10)^4, \text{ or } \$1,000 \times 1.464 = \$1,464$$

The term $(1.10)^4$ is found to equal 1.464 by multiplying 1.10 four times itself (the fourth power) or by using logarithms. An even quicker process is using an interest rate table, such as Table 4-1 for the future value of a dollar. With n = 4 and i = 10 percent, the value is also found to be 1.464.

The table tells us the amount that $1 would grow to if it were invested for any number of periods at a given interest rate. We multiply this factor times any other amount to determine the future value.

In determining the future value, we will change our formula from $FV = PV(1 + i)^n$ to:

$$FV = PV \times FV_{IF} \tag{4-1}$$

where FV$_{IF}$ equals the **interest factor** found in the table.

If $10,000 were invested for 10 years at 8 percent, the future value, based on Table 4-1, would be:

$$FV = PV \times FV_{IF} \ (n = 10, i = 8\%)$$
$$FV = \$10,000 \times 2.159 = \$21,590$$

Present Value—Single Amount

In recent years the sports pages have been filled with stories of athletes who receive multimillion-dollar contracts for signing with sports organizations. Perhaps you have wondered how the New York Yankees or Los Angeles Lakers can afford to pay such fantastic sums. The answer may lie in the concept of present value—a sum payable in the future is worth less today than the stated amount.

The **present value** is the exact opposite of the future value. For example, earlier we determined that the future value of $1,000 for four periods at 10 percent was $1,464. We could reverse the process to state that $1,464 received four years into the future, with a 10

FIGURE 4–1   Relationship of present value and future value

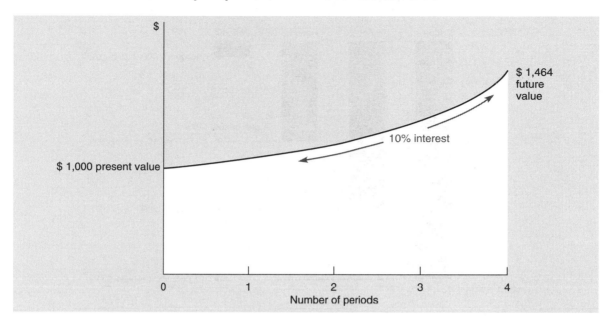

percent interest or **discount rate,** is worth only $1,000 today—its present value. The relationship is depicted in Figure 4-1.

The formula for present value is derived from the original formula for future value.

$$FV = PV(1 + i)^n \qquad \text{Future value}$$

$$PV = FV\left[\frac{1}{(1 + i)^n}\right] \quad \text{Present value}$$

The present value can be determined by solving for a mathematical solution to the formula above, or by using Table 4-2, the present value of a dollar. In the latter instance, we restate the formula for present value as:

$$PV = FV \times PV_{IF} \qquad\qquad\qquad (4\text{-}2)$$

Once again PV_{IF} represents the interest factor found in Table 4-2.

Let's demonstrate that the present value of $1,464, based on our assumptions, is $1,000 today.

$$PV = FV \times PV_{IF} \ (n = 4, i = 10\%) \ [\text{Table 4-2}]$$
$$PV = \$1,464 \times 0.683 = \$1,000$$

TABLE 4–2   Present value of $1 (PV$_{IF}$)

Periods	1%	2%	3%	4%	6%	8%	10%
1	0.990	0.980	0.971	0.962	0.943	0.926	0.909
2	0.980	0.961	0.943	0.925	0.890	0.857	0.826
3	0.971	0.942	0.915	0.889	0.840	0.794	0.751
4	0.961	0.924	0.888	0.855	0.792	0.735	0.683
5	0.951	0.906	0.863	0.822	0.747	0.681	0.621
10	0.905	0.820	0.744	0.676	0.558	0.463	0.386
20	0.820	0.673	0.554	0.456	0.312	0.215	0.149

FIGURE 4–2   Compounding process for annuity

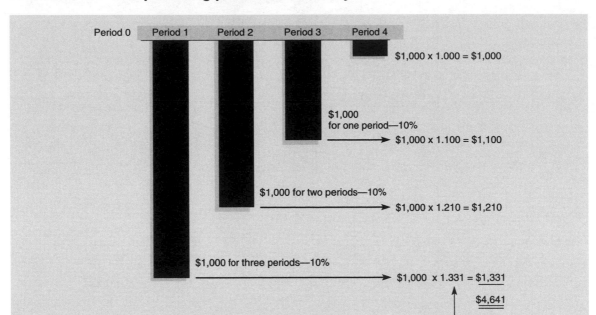

Future Value—Annuity

Our calculations up to now have dealt with single amounts rather than an **annuity**, which may be defined as a series of consecutive payments of receipts of equal amount. The annuity values are generally assumed to occur at the end of each period. If we invest $1,000 at the end of each year for four years and our funds grow at 10 percent, what is the future value of this annuity? We may find the future value for each payment and then total them to find the **future value of an annuity** (Figure 4-2).

The future value for the annuity in Figure 4-2 is $4,641. Although this is a four-period annuity, the first $1,000 comes at the *end* of the first period and has but three periods to run, the second $1,000 at the *end* of the second period, with two periods remaining—and so on down to the last $1,000 at the end of the fourth period. The final payment (period 4) is not compounded at all.

Because the process of compounding the individual values is tedious, special tables are also available for annuity computations. We shall refer to Table 4-3, the future value of an annuity of $1. Let us define A as the annuity value and use Formula 4-3 for the future value of an annuity.[1] Note that the A part of the subscript on both the left- and right-hand side of the formula below indicates we are dealing with tables for an annuity rather than a single amount. Using Table 4-3 for A = $1,000, n = 4, and i = 10%:

$$FV_A = A \times FV_{IFA} \ (n = 4, i = 10\%) \tag{4-3}$$
$$FV_A = \$1,000 \times 4.641 = \$4,641$$

---

1    $FV_A = A(1 + i)^{n-1} + A(1 + i)^{n-2} + \cdots A(1 + i)^{1} + A(1 + i)^{0}$

$$= A \left[\frac{(1 + i)^n - 1}{i} \right] = A \times FV_{IFA}$$

TABLE 4–3   Future value of an annuity of $1 (FV$_{IFA}$)

Periods	1%	2%	3%	4%	6%	8%	10%
1	1.000	1.000	1.000	1.000	1.000	1.000	1.000
2	2.010	2.020	2.030	2.040	2.060	2.080	2.100
3	3.030	3.060	3.091	3.122	3.184	3.246	3.310
4	4.060	4.122	4.184	4.246	4.375	4.506	4.641
5	5.101	5.204	5.309	5.416	5.637	5.867	6.105
10	10.462	10.950	11.464	12.006	13.181	14.487	15.937
20	22.019	24.297	26.870	29.778	36.786	45.762	57.275
30	34.785	40.588	47.575	56.085	79.058	113.280	164.490

STARTING SALARIES 50 YEARS FROM NOW—WILL $284,280 BE ENOUGH?

The answer is probably yes if inflation averages 4 percent a year for the next 50 years. Over the last 50 years the inflation rate was in the 3 to 4 percent range, so $284,280 might allow a college graduate to have enough money to pay his or her bills in 50 years if inflation rates stay about the same. The $284,280 is based on a starting salary of $40,000 today and the future value of a dollar for 50 periods at 4 percent. Of course, $40,000 may be too low for some majors, and too high for others.

Inflation in the United States actually was as high as 11.4 percent in 1979 and 13.4 percent in 1980. Conversely, there were declining prices during the depression of the 1930s. If inflation averages 6 percent over the next 50 years, it would require $736,800 to replace a $40,000 salary today. At a 10 percent rate of inflation, the college graduate in 50 years would need to ask an employer for a starting salary of $4,695,600 to be as well-off as his or her predecessor today. Those graduating in the more popular majors would certainly not take a penny under $5 million. While 10 percent inflation seems high for the United States, in countries such as Brazil, Israel, and Mexico, 10 percent inflation would be a welcome occurrence.

Returning to a more realistic 4 percent rate of inflation for the future, the college graduate in 50 years can expect to see his or her domestic airfare for a two-thousand mile round trip go from $750 to approximately $5,330 (only slightly more than the current rate if you don't stay over a Saturday night). Tuition at an average private university (over four years) will go from $64,000 to $455,000, and at an Ivy League School from $130,000 to $925,000. Save your money for that brilliant grandchild you're planning to have. Tickets for four persons to an NFL football game will increase from $160 to $1,123. But that might be a bargain to watch the descendants of Donovan McNabb and Chad Pennington play—quarter-backs who then will be paid $85 million a year. Actually, the salaries of pro football quarter-backs are growing at a rate of 20 percent a year, so a more realistic figure for their annual salary in 50 years might be $100 billion.

The intent of this discussion is to demonstrate the effects of the time value of money. So far, all of the discussion has been forward-looking. Now, let's look back. How much would one of your grandparents have had to make 50 years ago to equal a $40,000 salary today, assuming a 4 percent rate of inflation? The answer is $5,628.

If a wealthy relative offered to set aside $2,500 a year for you for the next 20 years, how much would you have in your account after 20 years if the funds grew at 8 percent? The answer is as follows:

$$FV_A = A \times FV_{IFA} \ (n = 20, i = 8\%)$$
$$FV_A = \$2,500 \times 45.762 = \$114,405$$

A rather tidy sum considering that only a total of $50,000 has been invested over the 20 years.

TABLE 4–4   Present value of an annuity of $1 (PV$_{IFA}$)

Periods	1%	2%	3%	4%	6%	8%	10%
1	0.990	0.980	0.971	0.962	0.943	0.926	0.909
2	1.970	1.942	1.913	1.886	1.833	1.783	1.736
3	2.941	2.884	2.829	2.775	2.673	2.577	2.487
4	3.902	3.808	3.717	3.630	3.465	3.312	3.170
5	4.853	4.713	4.580	4.452	4.212	3.993	3.791
8	7.652	7.325	7.020	6.773	6.210	5.747	5.335
10	9.471	8.983	8.530	8.111	7.360	6.710	6.145
20	18.046	16.351	14.877	13.590	11.470	9.818	8.514
30	25.808	22.396	19.600	17.292	13.765	11.258	9.427

Present Value—Annuity

To find the **present value of an annuity,** the process is reversed. In theory each individual payment is discounted back to the present and then all of the discounted payments are added up, yielding the present value of the annuity.

Table 4-4 allows us to eliminate extensive calculations and to find our answer directly. In Formula 4-4 the term PV$_A$ refers to the present value of the annuity.[2] Once again, assume A = $1,000, n = 4, and i = 10 percent—only now we want to know the present value of the annuity. Using Table 4-4:

$$PV_A = A \times PV_{IFA} \ (n = 4, i = 10\%) \tag{4-4}$$
$$PV_A = \$1,000 \times 3.170 = \$3,170$$

To reinforce your understanding of the material you have just covered, please proceed to the graphical presentation that follows.

GRAPHICAL PRESENTATION OF TIME VALUE RELATIONSHIPS

This section is designed to supplement the previous discussion of future value, present value, and annuities and to reinforce your understanding of these concepts before you continue into the next sections. This material is nonmathematical and focuses on time value concepts using a visual approach.

The Relationship between Present Value and Future Value

Earlier in this chapter we presented the future value of a single amount as well as the present value of a single amount and applied the concept of annuities to both future value and present value.

In Figures 4-3 and 4-4, we show how the future value and present value of a single amount are inversely related to each other. Future value takes a value today, for example

---

$$2 \quad PV_A = A\left[\frac{1}{(1+i)}\right]^1 + A\left[\frac{1}{(1+i)}\right]^2 + \ldots A\left[\frac{1}{(1+i)}\right]^n = A\left[\frac{1 - \frac{1}{(1+i)^n}}{i}\right]$$

$$= A \times PV_{IFA}$$

FIGURE 4–3   Future value of $.68 at 10%

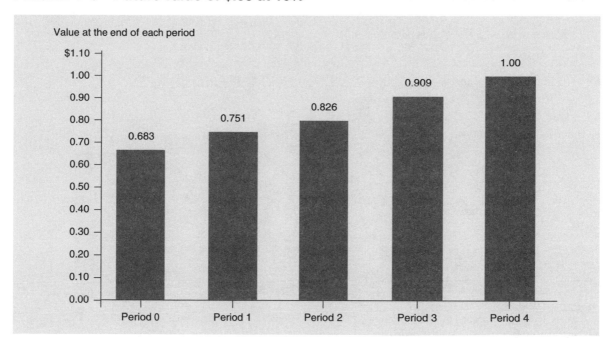

$.68, and computes its value in the future assuming that it earns a rate of return each period. In Figure 4-3, the $.68 is invested at 10 percent and grows to $1.00 at the end of period 4. Because we want to avoid large mathematical rounding errors, we actually carry the decimal points 3 places. The $.683 that we invest today (period 0), grows to $.751 after one period, $.826 after two periods, $.909 after three periods and $1.00 at the end of the fourth period. In this example, the $.68 is the present value and the $1.00 is the future value.

If you turn to Figure 4-4, you notice that the future value and present value graphs are the flip side of each other. In the present value table, it becomes clear that if I have $1.00 in period 0, it is worth its present value of $1.00. However, if I have to wait one period to receive my dollar, it is worth only $.909 if I can earn a 10 percent return on my money. You can see this by turning back to the future value graph. The $.909 at the end of period 3 will grow to $1.00 during period 4. Or by letting $.909 compound at a 10 percent rate for one period, you have $1.00.

Because you can earn a return on your money, $1.00 received in the future is worth less than $1.00 today, and the longer you have to wait to receive the dollar, the less it is worth. For example, if you are to receive $1.00 at the end of four periods, how much is its present value? Turn to Figure 4-4 and you see that the answer is $.68, the same value that we started with in period 0 in the future value graph in Figure 4-3. As you change the rate of return that can be earned, the values in Figures 4-3 and 4-4 will change, but the relationship will remain the same as presented in this example.

The Relationship between the Present Value of a Single Amount and the Present Value of an Annuity

Figure 4-5 shows the relationship between the present value of $1.00 and the present value of a $1.00 annuity. The assumption is that you will receive $1.00 at the end of each period. This is the same concept as a lottery, where you win $2 million over 20 years and receive $100,000 per year for 20 years. In this example we receive only four payments of $1.00 each and we use the transparency format to build up one year at a time.

FIGURE 4–4   Present value of $1.00 at 10%

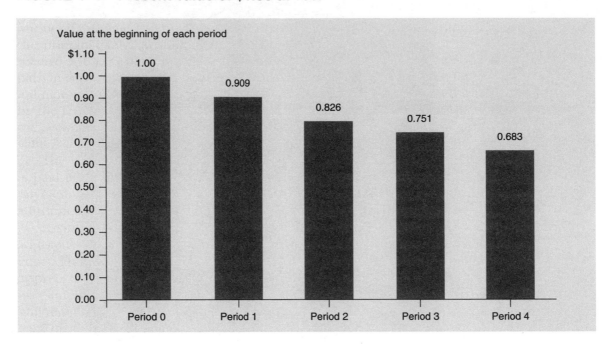

FIGURE 4–5   Present value of an annuity of $1.00 at 10%

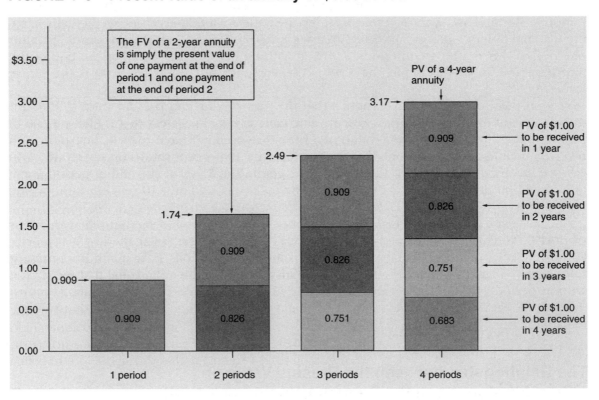

Looking at Figure 4-5 you see the present value of $1.00 to be received at the end of period 1 is $.909; $1.00 received at the end of period 2 is $.826; $1.00 received at the end of period 3 is $.751; and $1.00 received at the end of period 4 is $.683. These numbers should look very familiar. Figure 4-5 has the same values as Figure 4-4, except there is no period 0.

FIGURE 4–6   Future value of an annuity of $1.00 at 10%

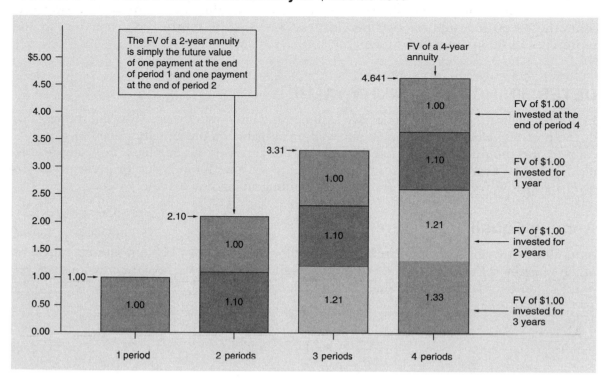

Turn to Figure 4–5. If you are to receive two $1.00 payments, the first at the end of period 1 and the second at the end of period 2, the total present value will simply be the sum of the present value of each $1.00 payment. You can see that the total present value of $1.74 represents the present value of $1.00 to be received at the end of the first period ($.909) and the present value of $1.00 to be received at the end of the second period.

This $3.17 is the sum of each present value. The top box is always $.909 and represents the present value of $1.00 received at the end of the first period; the second box from the top is always $.826 and is the present value of the $1.00 received at the end of the second year; the box third from the top is $.751 and is the present value of the $1.00 received at the end of the third year; and finally, the present value of the $1.00 received at the end of the fourth year is $.683.

Future Value Related to the Future Value of an Annuity

The next relationship is between the future value of a single sum and the future value of an annuity. We start with Figure 4–6, which graphically depicts the future value of $1.00 that is growing at a 10 percent rate of return each period. If we start with a present value of $1.00 today (period 0), at the end of period 1 we will have $1.10; at the end of period 2 we will have $1.21; and at the end of period 3 the $1.00 will have grown to $1.33.

One of the confusing features between the future value of $1.00 and the future value of a $1.00 annuity is that they have different assumptions concerning the timing of cash flows. The future value of $1.00 assumes the $1.00 is invested at the beginning of the period and grows to the end of the period. The future value of an annuity assumes $1.00 is invested at the end of the period and grows to the end of the next period. This means the last $1.00 invested has no time to increase its value by earning a return.

The calculation for the future value of a $1.00 annuity simply adds together the future value of a series of equal $1.00 investments. Since the last $1.00 invested does not have a chance to compound, the future value of a two-period annuity equals $2.10. This $2.10 comes from adding the $1.00 invested at the end of period 2 plus the first $1.00 that has grown to $1.10.

The $1.10 is always the second box from the top and represents the $1.00 that has been invested for only one period, while the $1.21 is always the third box from the top and represents the $1.00 invested for two periods. The $1.33 is the fourth box from the top and represents $1.00 invested for three periods.

DETERMINING THE ANNUITY VALUE

In our prior discussion of annuities, we assumed the unknown variable was the future value or the present value—with specific information available on the annuity value (A), the interest rate, and the number of periods or years. In certain cases our emphasis may shift to solving for one of these other values (on the assumption that future value or present value is given). For now, we will concentrate on determining an unknown annuity value.

Annuity Equaling a Future Value

Assuming we wish to accumulate $4,641 after four years at a 10 percent interest rate, how much must be set aside at the end of each of the four periods? We take the previously developed statement for the future value of an annuity and solve for A.

$$FV_A = A \times FV_{IFA}$$
$$A = \frac{FV_A}{FV_{IFA}} \qquad (4\text{-}5)$$

The future value of an annuity (FV_A) is given as $4,641, and FV_{IFA} may be determined from Table 4-3 (future value for an annuity). Whenever you are working with an annuity problem relating to future value, you employ Table 4-3 regardless of the variable that is unknown. For n = 4, and i = 10 percent, FV_{IFA} is 4.641. Thus A equals $1,000.

$$A = \frac{FV_A}{FV_{IFA}} = \frac{\$4,641}{4.641} = \$1,000$$

The solution is the exact reverse of that previously presented under the discussion of the future value of an annuity. As a second example, assume the director of the Women's Tennis Association must set aside an equal amount for each of the next 10 years to accumulate $1,000,000 in retirement funds and the return on deposited funds is 6 percent. Solve for the annual contribution, A, using Table 4-3.

$$A = \frac{FV_A}{FV_{IFA}} \quad (n = 10, \ i = 6\%)$$
$$A = \frac{\$1,000,000}{13.181} = \$75,867$$

Annuity Equaling a Present Value

In this instance, we assume you know the present value and you wish to determine what size annuity can be equated to that amount. Suppose your wealthy uncle presents you with $10,000 now to help you get through the next four years of college. If you are able to earn 6 percent on deposited funds, how many equal payments can you withdraw at the end of each year for four years? We need to know the value of an annuity equal to a given present value. We take the previously developed statement for the present value of an annuity and reverse it to solve for A.

$$PV_A = A \times PV_{IFA}$$
$$A = \frac{PV_A}{PV_{IFA}} \qquad (4\text{-}6)$$

The appropriate table is Table 4-4 (present value of an annuity). We determine an answer of $2,886.

$$A = \frac{PV_A}{PV_{IFA}} \quad (n = 4, \ i = 6\%)$$
$$A = \frac{\$100,000}{3.465} = \$2,886$$

The flow of funds would follow the pattern in Table 4-5. Annual interest is based on the beginning balance for each year.

The same process can be used to indicate necessary repayments on a loan. Suppose a homeowner signs a $40,000 mortgage to be repaid over 20 years at 8 percent interest. How much must he or she pay annually to eventually liquidate the loan? In other words, what annuity paid over 20 years is the equivalent of a $40,000 present value with an 8 percent interest rate?[3]

$$A = \frac{PV_A}{PV_{IFA}} \quad (n = 20, \ i = 8\%)$$
$$A = \frac{\$40,000}{9.818} = \$4,074$$

Part of the payments to the mortgage company will go toward the payment of interest, with the remainder applied to debt reduction, as indicated in Table 4-6.

If this same process is followed over 20 years, the balance will be reduced to zero. The student might note that the homeowner will pay over $41,000 of *interest* during the term of the loan, as indicated below.

Total payments ($4,074 for 20 years)	$81,480
Repayment of principal	−40,000
Payments applied to interest	$41,480

TABLE 4–5   Relationship of present value to annuity

Year	Beginning Balance	Annual Interest (6%)	Annual Withdrawal	Ending Balance
1	$10,000.00	$600.00	$2,886.00	$7,714.00
2	7,714.00	462.84	2,886.00	5,290.84
3	5,290.84	317.45	2,886.00	2,722.29
4	2,722.29	163.71	2,886.00	0

---

3   The actual mortgage could be further refined into monthly payments of approximately $340.

TABLE 4–6   Payoff table for loan (amortization table)

Period	Beginning Balance	Annual Payment	Annual Interest (8%)	Repayment or Principal	Ending Balance
1	$40,000	$4,074	$3,200	$ 874	$39,126
2	39,126	4,074	3,130	944	38,182
3	38,182	4,074	3,055	1,019	37,163

DETERMINING THE YIELD ON AN INVESTMENT

In our discussion thus far, we have considered the following time value of money problems.

		Formula	Table
Future value—single amount	(4-1)	$FV = PV \times FV_{IF}$	4-1
Present value—single amount	(4-2)	$PV = FV \times PV_{IF}$	4-2
Future value—annuity	(4-3)	$FV_A = A \times FV_{IFA}$	4-3
Present value—annuity	(4-4)	$PV_A = A \times PV_{IFA}$	4-4
Annuity equaling a future value	(4-5)	$A = \dfrac{FV_A}{FV_{IFA}}$	4-3
Annuity equaling a present value	(4-6)	$A = \dfrac{PV_A}{PV_{IFA}}$	4-4

In each case we knew three out of the four variables and solved for the fourth. We will follow the same procedure again, but now the unknown variable will be i, the interest rate, or yield on the investment.

Yield—Present Value of a Single Amount

An investment producing $1,464 after four years has a present value of $1,000. What is the interest rate, or **yield**, on the investment?

We take the basic formula for the present value of a single amount and rearrange the terms.

$$PV = FV \times PV_{IF}$$

$$PV_{IF} = \frac{PV}{FV} = \frac{\$1,000}{\$1,464} = 0.683 \tag{4-7}$$

The determination of PV_{IF} does not give us the final answer—but it scales down the problem so we may ascertain the answer from Table 4-2, the present value of $1. A portion of Table 4-2 is reproduced below.

Periods	1%	2%	3%	4%	5%	6%	8%	10%
2	0.980	0.961	0.943	0.925	0.907	0.890	0.857	0.826
3	0.971	0.942	0.915	0.889	0.864	0.840	0.794	0.751
4	0.961	0.924	0.888	0.855	0.823	0.792	0.735	0.683

Read down the left-hand column of the table above until you have located the number of periods in question (in this case n = 4), and read across the table for n = 4 until you have located the computed value of PV_{IF} from Formula 4-7. We see that for n = 4 and PV_{IF} equal to 0.683, the interest rate, or yield, is 10 percent. This is the rate that will equate $1,464 received in four years to $1,000 today.

If a PV_{IF} value does not fall under a given interest rate, an approximation is possible. For example, with n = 3 and PV_{IF} = 0.861, using Table 4-2, 5 percent may be suggested as an approximate answer.

Interpolation may also be used to find a more precise answer. In the above example, we write out the two PV_{IF} values that the designated PVIF (0.861) falls between and take the difference between the two.

PV_{IF} at 5%	0.864
PV_{IF} at 6%	0.840
	0.024

We then find the difference between the PV_{IF} value at the lowest interest rate and the designated PV_{IF} value.

PV_{IF} at 5%	0.864
PV_{IF} designated	0.861
	0.003

We next express this value (0.003) as a fraction of the preceding value (0.024) and multiply by the difference between the two interest rates (6 percent minus 5 percent). The value is added to the lower interest rate (5 percent) to get a more exact answer of 5.125 percent rather than the estimated 5 percent.

$$5\% + \frac{0.003}{0.024} \, (1\%) =$$
$$5\% + 0.125 \, (1\%) \; =$$
$$5\% + 0.125\% \quad\;\; = 5.125\%$$

Yield—Present Value of an Annuity

We may also find the yield related to any other problem. Let's look at the present value of an annuity. Take the basic formula for the present value of an annuity, and rearrange the terms.

$$PV_A = A \times PV_{IFA}$$
$$PV_{IFA} = \frac{PV_A}{A} \tag{4-8}$$

The appropriate table is Table 4-4 (the present value of an annuity of $1). Assuming a $10,000 investment will produce $1,490 a year for the next 10 years, what is the yield on the investment?

$$PV_{IFA} = \frac{PV_A}{A} = \frac{\$10,000}{\$1,490} = 6.710$$

If the student will flip back to Table 4-4 and read across the columns for n = 10 periods, he or she will see that the yield is 8 percent.

The same type of approximated or interpolated yield that applied to a single amount can also be applied to an annuity when necessary.

SPECIAL CONSIDERATIONS IN TIME VALUE ANALYSIS

We have assumed interest was compounded or discounted on an annual basis. This assumption will now be relaxed. Contractual arrangements, such as an installment purchase agreement or a corporate bond contract, may call for semiannual, quarterly, or monthly compounding periods. The adjustment to the normal formula is quite simple. To determine n, multiply the number of years by the number of compounding periods during the year. The factor for i is then determined by dividing the quoted annual interest rate by the number of compounding periods.

Case 1—Find the future value of a $1,000 investment after five years at 8 percent annual interest, **compounded semiannually.**

$$n = 5 \times 2 = 10 \qquad i = 8 \text{ percent} \div 2 = 4 \text{ percent}$$

Since the problem calls for the future value of a single amount, the formula is FV = $PV \times FV_{IF}$. Using Table 4-1 for n = 10 and i = 4 percent, the answer is $1,480.

$$FV = PV \times FV_{IF}$$
$$FV = \$1,000 \times 1.480 = \$1,480$$

Case 2—Find the present value of 20 quarterly payments of $2,000 each to be received over the next five years. The stated interest rate is 8 percent per annum. The problem calls for the present value of an annuity. We again follow the same procedure as in Case 1 in regard to n and i.

$$PV_A = A \times PV_{IFA} \qquad (n = 20, i = 2\%) \text{ [Table 4-4]}$$
$$PV_A = A \times \$2,000 \times 16.351 = \$32,702$$

Patterns of Payment

Time value of money problems may evolve around a number of different payment or receipt patterns. Not every situation will involve a single amount or an annuity. For example a contract may call for the payment of a different amount each year over a three-year period. To determine present value, each payment is discounted (Table 4-2) to the present and then summed.

(Assume 8% discount rate)

1. $1,000 \times 0.926 = \$\ 926$
2. $2,000 \times 0.857 = \ 1,714$
3. $3,000 \times 0.794 = \ \underline{2,382}$
$$\$5,022$$

A more involved problem might include a combination of single amounts and an annuity. If the annuity will be paid at some time in the future, it is referred to as a deferred annuity and it requires special treatment. Assume the same problem as above, but with an annuity of $1,000 that will be paid at the end of each year from the fourth through the eighth year. With a discount rate of 8 percent, what is the present value of the cash flows?

1. $1,000 ⎫
2.   2,000 ⎬ Present value = $5,022
3.   3,000 ⎭
4.   1,000 ⎫
5.   1,000 ⎪
6.   1,000 ⎬ Five-year annuity
7.   1,000 ⎪
8.   1,000 ⎭

We know the present value of the first three payments is $5,022, from our calculation above, but what about the annuity? Let's diagram the five annuity payments.

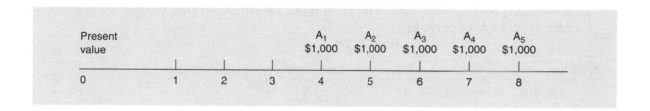

The information source is Table 4–4, the present value of an annuity of $1. For $n = 5, i = 8$ percent, the discount factor is 3.993—leaving a "present value" of the annuity of $3,993. However, tabular values only discount to the beginning of the first stated period of an annuity—in this case the beginning of the fourth year, as diagrammed below.

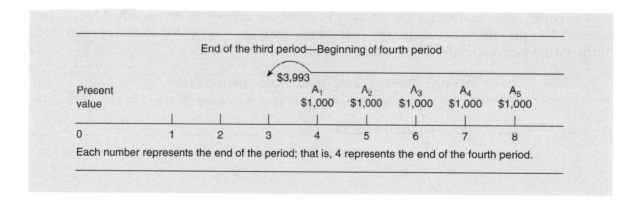

The $3,993 must finally be discounted back to the present. Since this single amount falls at the beginning of the fourth period—in effect, the equivalent of the end of the third period—we discount back for three periods at the stated 8 percent interest rate. Using Table 4–2, we have:

$$PV = FV \times PV_{IF} \qquad (n = 3, i = 8\%)$$
$$PV = \$3,993 \times 0.794 = \$3,170 \text{ (actual present value)}$$

The last step in the discounting process follows.

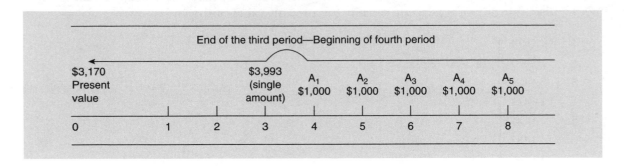

A *second method* for finding the present value of a deferred annuity is to:

1. Find the present value factor of an annuity for the total time period. In this case, where $n = 8$, $i = 8\%$, the PV_{IFA} is 5.747.

2. Find the present value factor of an annuity for the total time period (8) minus the deferred annuity period (5).

$$8 - 5 = 3$$
$$n = 3, i = 8\%$$

The PV_{IFA} value is 2.577.

3. Subtract the value in step 2 from the value in step 1, and multiply by A.

$$
\begin{array}{r}
5.747 \\
-2.577 \\
\hline
3.170
\end{array}
$$

$3.170 \times \$1,000 = \$3,170$ (present value of the annuity)

$3,170 is the same answer for the present value of the annuity as that reached by the first method. The present value of the five-year annuity may now be added to the present value of the inflows over the first three years to arrive at the total value.

$$
\begin{array}{ll}
\$5,022 & \text{Present value of first three period flows} \\
+3,170 & \text{Present value of five-year annuity} \\
\hline
\$8,192 & \text{Total present value}
\end{array}
$$

Chapter 5

Investment Return and Risk

Most, if not all, investors are familiar with the concept of investment risk. However, this understanding typically is a general one in the sense that investors do not recognize that the term "risk" can be broken down into many specifics. The beginning of this chapter examines the various forms in which risk may exist. This section is followed by a technical section of how risk is measured. Finally, these descriptions of risk and risk-measurement lead to equivalent determinations of measures of return which, like risk, have many forms.

While this chapter is of a descriptive and definitional nature, the planner should recognize that the concepts in this chapter are essentially the "tools and techniques" of investment planning. These tools and techniques are widely used in investments and will be used in many of the subsequent sections of investment analysis.

TYPES OF INVESTMENT RISK

The notion of risk is an integral and primary concept in the understanding of investments. Risk can be defined as the uncertainty of an outcome from an investment decision. In making an investment decision, an investor forms an expectation regarding that decision's outcome. Any departure from that expected outcome can be considered the risk of that decision. Thus, another way to consider risk is to consider the possibilities of unexpected outcomes. The outcome from an investment decision may *unexpectedly* increase or decrease the principal amount invested. While most people consider the decrease in value as the investment risk, we will observe that in measuring risk, both positive and negative unexpected outcomes must be considered. Before considering the issues regarding the measurement of risk let us begin by enumerating the different types of risk that may exist for an investment.

The issue of risk being incorporated in both positive and negative surprises can be explained with a simple example. Assume you are explaining the possible outcomes of an investment decision to a client where the client may receive a return of either 8% (poor outcome) or a 16% (good outcome). You also explain that the client may expect to receive a simple average of the two returns, or 12%, from the investment decision. Your client now states that she is averse to the 8% outcome and wants to know if the investment can yield 12% or better. That is, the client wishes to remove the poor outcome altogether. Notice that if this were possible, then the simple average of the new investment decision, or the expected outcome would now be 14% ((16% +12%)/2) and the new poor outcome would now be 12%. In other words, risk, or the unexpected outcomes, cannot go away. It is only meaningful in the context of an expected outcome and both positive and negative unexpected outcomes. There are many different ways in which the principal invested can be unexpectedly changed. We will now consider each of these types of risk.

Inflation Risk

Inflation risk is also known as **purchasing power** risk because the ability to purchase different quantities of goods and services is dependent upon the changing levels of prices of all items in an economy. For example, assume a client wishes to invest a sum of $19,000 which is expected to result in a certain outcome of $20,000. Now also consider that the client wishes to purchase a car, either today or one year from now and which is valued today also at $19,000. Suppose the price of this car increases to $21,000 over the year. In this case, the investor would have been better off if she had bought the car instead of investing the amount. Thus the investor has a choice in how the money may be used. If the money is invested then the client will need an additional $1,000 to purchase the car. In other words, the inflation in the car's price has eroded the purchasing power of the invested sum. If we consider that the increase in the price of the car was unexpected, then we can consider the effect of the outcome as arising out of inflation risk. Inflation risk is especially important to investment decisions where the financial securities being utilized are interest rate sensitive, such as bonds.

Interest Rate Risk

The values of all financial and real assets are in some part dependent on the general levels of interest rates in an economy. Therefore, any unexpected change in the general level of interest rates will also unexpectedly affect the values of all such assets. Financial assets such as bonds are especially affected by such changes. As we shall see later, the values of bonds and all other fixed income securities are inversely related to interest rates, i.e. when interest rates increase, these values decrease and vice versa. Values of stocks are also affected by changes in interest rates, though understanding the impact of interest rate changes on stock values is less straightforward than for bonds. Real assets such as real estate are also tremendously impacted by changes in interest rates. When changes in interest rates are unexpected, the uncertain changes in asset values are said to arise from interest rate risk. The reader can appreciate why participants in the financial markets are so engrossed in pending activities of the Federal Reserve Board, which through its policy-making decisions, has a considerable influence on interest rates.

Market Risk

A market is a place where goods and services are traded. Events occur within a market that similarly affect all the goods traded in that market. For example, when the Federal Reserve Board unexpectedly changes interest rates, most financial securities are affected similarly. Other examples of events that affect all securities are the possibilities of war, severe natural catastrophes, etc. When the unexpected change in values is *systematic* to the whole market, that risk is termed as market or **systematic risk**.

Business Risk

The risk associated with the changes in a firm's abilities to measure up to expectations is known as business risk or **unsystematic risk**. Business risk can be further segregated into operating risk and financial risk. The risk that a business may not be able to meet its fixed operating costs, such as rent, management salaries, etc., is known as operating risk. The risk that the firm may not be able to meet its fixed financial obligations, such as paying interest on its debt or lease payments, is known as financial risk. Financial risk is also known as **credit risk** since lenders or creditors of funds seek to assess the ability of the firm to meet its debt service obligations.

Liquidity Risk

Liquidity is concerned with the ability to convert the value of an asset into cash. Any event or condition that affects this ability is termed as liquidity risk. For example, an investor may wish to sell her holding in a stock. If the investor cannot find a buyer for the stock, then her position in that stock cannot be *liquidated*. Hence, in this example, she faces liquidity risk. Assets differ from each other by liquidity risk. Securities offered by the government (such as Treasury bills) are very liquid because there are many participants seeking to trade in these securities. Treasury bills can be sold almost instantaneously, and hence are considered to be highly liquid. At the other end of the spectrum, stocks of very small and little known companies are considered to contain high liquidity risk because they are *thinly* traded. When investors make purchase decisions that may require to be quickly converted to cash, they will always seek securities which have low liquidity risk. For example, firms that temporarily place excess cash in financial (marketable) securities in order to enhance yields will seek highly liquid securities that do not increase the firm's liquidity risk exposure.

Reinvestment Risk

The risk that future investment decisions cannot be made at current expected rates is termed reinvestment risk. In managing client portfolios, a planner often will encounter future cash flows from current and past investment decisions. A simple example is that of a client who owns a bond that is expected to produce future cash flows in the form of interest payments. If the client does not require those payments for consumption purposes but wishes to reinvest them, then the issue arises as to what the client may reasonably expect to earn on the reinvestment. Since future earning rates cannot be forecasted with any certainty, there exists a very strong likelihood that forecasted rates will not equate to prevailing actual rates. This uncertainty associated with reinvestment rates is thus termed reinvestment risk.

The notion of reinvestment rate risk is particularly easy to see in the retirement planning process. In assisting a client with a retirement plan, an assumed rate of return is built into the retirement forecast as to estimate the annual contributions the client will be required to make to the retirement plan. It is assumed that the funds will build at that rate of return until the client retires. What we see in reality is varying rates of return throughout the life of the portfolio. Some realized rates of return may be better than the forecast and some may be worse than the forecast. Either way, as the retirement plan grows, we will not see the steady, forecasted rate of return on the retirement portfolio. If the rates of return are consistently lower than the original forecast, the clients will not have enough funds at retirement to meet their needs. In this case, the reinvestment risk is the cause of the problem.

Political Risk

Many firms operate in foreign political climates that are more volatile than that of the United States. Firms can face the danger of the foreign operations being nationalized by the local government or can experience imposed restriction of capital flows from the foreign subsidiary to the parent. Danger from a violent overthrow of the political party in power can also have an effect on the rate of return investors receive on foreign investments. Many countries have also been unable to meet their foreign debt obligations to banks and other foreign institutions which contain important political and economic implications.

The informed investor must have some feel for the political/economic climate of the foreign country in which he or she invests. Political risk represents a potential deterrent to foreign investment. The best solution for the investor is to be sufficiently diversified around the world so that a political or economic development in one foreign country does not have a major impact on his or her portfolio.

The Real World of Investing

The Growth of American Depository Receipts

After years of going unnoticed, the benefits that American depository receipts (ADRs) offer American investors are better understood. To avoid investor difficulties in collecting dividends, receipts were created that provided proof of ownership of the shares held abroad. This made it is less expensive and less troublesome for shareholders to collect dividends on their own.

Many companies from around the world are scrambling to get their stocks traded on American exchanges. This move to Wall Street allows foreign companies to expand their capital while filling the growing demand for ADRs by American investors. Although ADRs are considered to be more liquid, less expensive, and easier to trade than buying foreign companies' stock directly on that country's exchange, there are some drawbacks.

ADRs are treated like domestic stock on the American front and are traded in dollars, but they are still traded in their local currencies on their home market. The gains or losses an investor can receive from changes in the currency exchange rate can also be offset by capital gains or losses on the investment itself. For those with short time horizons, this can be a serious problem, but for those with long-run interests, many experts argue that the dollar will usually even itself out, and high returns will win out.

There is still a lack of communication between companies and their shareholders abroad. It is difficult for individual investors to keep daily tabs on a foreign company without the aid of a broker.

Even though the SEC requires companies trading ADRs on American exchanges to use the U.S. standard of accounting, many "pink-sheet" ADRs not traded on an exchange are free from such restrictions. Pink sheets are price quotes for smaller or thinly traded over-the-counter companies. These companies are trying, however, to improve their accounting methods to catch the interests of foreign investors.

Politics can also be a disadvantage in ADRs. If a country is going through political turmoil, such unrest can send the stock price soaring or cause it to crash. The hefty taxes the foreign government takes out of the dividends can also be burdensome. To be reimbursed for the amount deducted, a U.S. investor has to request a credit by the Internal Revenue Service.

A final warning is to beware of management. History shows that in emerging economies, inexperienced companies often have tried to expand their business into markets in which they have little knowledge.

Exchange Rate Risk

The market for potential assets in which to invest spans the entire globe. Investors are not constrained to invest only in their home countries. However, when an investor purchases a security in a foreign country, it must be paid for in a foreign currency. At the time of the purchase, the value of the foreign security is derived from the current, or **spot**, exchange rate. The exchange rate that will prevail when the investor sells the security in the future cannot be predicted with any certainty, and hence, the conversion value becomes uncertain. This uncertainty can be considered as exchange rate risk. We illustrate this risk by a simple example. Assume an investment in Switzerland is expected to produce a 10 percent return.

Let's suppose that a U.S. investor invests $1,000 in Switzerland. The current spot rate for Swiss francs is SF1.40 per U.S. Dollar. The initial investment in Swiss francs is therefore, SF1,400. At the end of the year, assuming a 10 percent return, the U.S. investor will have realized a return of 10 percent, or SF1,540.

Initial U.S. Investment	$1,000
Exchange Rate, SF1.40 per dollar	SF.1.40
	SF.1,400
FV of 1400 at 10% for 1 year	SF.1,540

Let's assume that the investor would like to convert his or her dollars back into U.S. Dollars. At the same time, let us assume that during the year, the Swiss franc declines in value by 5 percent against the U.S. Dollar. When a currency declines in value against the dollar, it takes more of the foreign currency to buy one U.S. Dollar. In converting back to dollars, the investor will have to spend more Swiss francs in order to receive one U.S. Dollar. The spot exchange rate is now SF1.47 per U.S. Dollar (SF1.40 × 105 percent). This means that 10 percent gain is worth less in dollars than our initial expectation. Consider the profits if the exchange rate had not changed versus the decline in the exchange rate. The results are as follows:

	Value	Return
Exchange Rate, SF1.40 per dollar	$1,100	10.0%
Exchange Rate, SF1.47 per dollar	$1,048	4.8%

Assuming we want to exchange our money back into U.S. Dollars at the spot rate, we can see that a decline in the value of the Swiss currency has reduced our initial return from 10 percent to 4.8 percent.

Now let us assume that the Swiss franc increases in value by 5 percent against the U.S. Dollar. When a currency increases in value against the dollar, it takes less of the foreign currency to purchase one U.S. Dollar. In converting back to dollars, the investor will have to spend fewer Swiss francs in order to receive one U.S. Dollar. The spot exchange rate is now, SF1.33 per U.S. Dollar (SF1.40 × 95 percent). This means that the 10 percent gain is worth more in dollars than the initial 10% gain. If we compare the profits from the unchanged exchange rate with the appreciated exchange rate, the results are as follows:

	Value	Return
Exchange Rate, SF1.40 per dollar	$1,100	10.0%
Exchange Rate, SF1.33 per dollar	$1,158	15.8%

Assuming we want to exchange our money back into U.S. Dollars at the spot rate, we can see that an increase in the value of the Swiss currency has changed our initial return from 10 percent to 15.8 percent. The uncertain outcome is the result of exchange rate risk.

MEASURES OF INVESTMENT RISK

Assume it is 8:00 p.m. on Sunday evening, and you are watching a sporting event on ESPN. Commercials come on and, interspersed between the latest shiny BMW and Lexus commercials, there is an advertisement about mutual funds. We could take any mutual fund as an example, but in this particular case, we will use the Fidelity Blue Chip Growth Fund. The title of the fund is laden with upscale words. Fidelity is the best-known mutual fund company in the world (with scores of other funds besides this one). Blue chip implies high quality, and growth indicates that the fund manager invests in companies which have strong possibilities to enhance their value. The advertisement, as is true of most mutual fund advertisements, would show the fund return over the last decade. In this case the return was 22.40 percent per year. Thus an initial $10,000 investment would have grown to more than $70,000 during this time period (as opposed to $16,300 in a 5 percent money market fund). While Fidelity or any other mutual fund company is required to issue the caveat that past performance is no assurance of future performance, the warning is hardly adequate notice to the naïve investor and this message is somehow lost between the lines.

The real issue is how much risk or volatility the investor was exposed to in achieving this high return. There are two dimensions to any investment: risk and return. As usual, the advertisement has covered only one dimension; return. If the fund had to take an excessive amount of risk in order to achieve this result, the performance of the fund returns is certainly less commendable. The truth is that the fund did have a high degree of risk exposure, with 37.8 percent of its assets invested in technology stocks. As we saw in 2001 and 2002, the returns on the Magellan fund dropped significantly. In 2001, the annual returns were −11.65 percent and in 2002, the annual returns were −23.66 percent. These returns did not take front end load charges into consideration; therefore the returns would have been lower for investors in this fund during those years. These low returns were indicative of the abysmal performance of technology company stocks in these years.

We will now develop a more complete understanding of how the investor perceives risk and demands compensation for the associated risk. We will eventually build toward a theory of portfolio management that incorporates these concepts. The use of mathematical terms is an essential ingredient to a basic understanding of portfolio theory. As indicated previously, risk is generally associated with uncertainty about future outcomes. The greater the dispersion of possible outcomes, the greater the risk involved with an investment. Most investors tend to be risk-averse; that is, all things being equal, investors prefer less risk to more risk and will increase their risk-taking position only if a commensurate premium for risk is involved. Each investor has a different attitude toward risk. The inducement necessary to cause a given investor to withdraw funds from a money market account and to invest in the drilling of an oil well may be quite different from another's. For some, only a very small premium for risk is necessary, while others may not wish to participate unless there are exceptionally high rewards. We will now discuss a formal development of risk measures.

Formal Measurement of Risk

Having defined risk as uncertainty about future outcomes, how do we actually measure risk? The first task is to design a probability distribution of anticipated future outcomes. This is no small task. The possible outcomes and associated probabilities are likely to be based on economic projections, past experience, subjective judgments, as well as many other variables. In studying the behavior of a security under different economic conditions, we may be able to determine its return characteristics under different economic conditions. For example, a simple illustration of the expected economic conditions in the coming year will help us to understand the uncertainties related to future outcomes. An economy may experience a high level of growth, a normal level of growth, or may not experience any growth at all. Based upon these economic conditions, some securities may behave in a more predictable manner and which can assist the forecaster in assigning a probability to receiving an expected return from owning the security under these different possible outcomes. In doing this type of economic analysis, the analysis is generally based upon historical conditions in the economy and corresponding historical returns.

Economic projections are not the only way that an analyst can predict future outcomes of a security. One can include variables such as individual company information, growth or lack thereof in an industry or any other factor that the forecaster thinks may have an effect on the expected future outcome on a security's price. It is easy to see why predicting a security's price change is such a difficult process. In an economy such as the U.S., most

TABLE 5–1   Return and Probabilities for Investments *i* and *j*

Investment			Investment	
Return K_i	P_i (Probability of K_i Occurring)	Possible State of the Economy	Return K_j	P_j (Probability of K_j Occurring)
5%	0.20	Recession	20%	0.20
7	0.30	Slow growth	8	0.30
13	0.30	Moderate growth	8	0.30
15	0.20	Strong economy	6	0.20

projections will involve analysis of the interaction among multiple variables. The effects that each variable will have on other variables is difficult to project at best and near impossible at worst. But with careful analysis, an analyst will be able to assign intelligent probabilities with expected returns to a security and will therefore be able to build its corresponding probability distribution.

In the following section, we will define and show how to calculate the measures of an Expected Return of an investment. We will also discuss other statistics that will eventually help us to determine the risk and expected returns.

Expected Return

The **Expected Return** of an investment is defined as the sum of the possible outcome times the probability of occurrence. By calculating Expected Return, we are saying that given a set of probabilities and outcomes, we expect a certain return on our investment(s). Assume we are considering two investment proposals where K represents a possible outcome and P represents the probability of that outcome based on the state of the economy. If we were dealing with stocks, K would represent the price appreciation potential plus the dividend yield (total return). Table 5-1 presents the data for two investments, i and j.

We will say that K_i (the Expected Return of investment i) equals $\Sigma K_i P_i$. In this case, the answer would be 10.0 percent, as shown under Formula 5-1:

$$\bar{K}_i = \Sigma K_i P_i \qquad (5\text{-}1)$$

K_i	P_i	$K_i P_i$
5%	0.20	1.0%
7	0.30	2.1
13	0.30	3.9
15	0.20	3.0
		10.0% $= \Sigma K_i P_i$

In practice, expected return is an important concept to explain to clients. When building a portfolio for a client, a planner must be able to explain what the client can expect in terms of a return on the portfolio and then explain what parameters went into the analysis in order to derive the expected return. In later chapters we will elaborate more on constructing optimal portfolios where we minimize risk and maximize return for a given investor. In practice, most advisors will use computer software programs that are constantly being updated with new data on expected returns of certain security types. Given the widespread application of automated data, it is still crucial to understand the components of expected return and the assumptions that can cause the expected rate of return to vary.

Equally important to explaining the expected return from an investment is the explanation of the risk that is associated with that investment. Explaining to clients that actual returns can and very likely will vary from the expected return is an important step in setting proper client expectations.

Standard Deviation

A commonly used measure of risk is the **standard deviation**, which is a measure of the possible range of outcomes around the Expected Return. The formula for the standard deviation is:

$$\sigma_i = \sqrt{\Sigma(K_i - \bar{K}_i)^2 P_i} \qquad (5\text{-}2)$$

Let's determine the standard deviation for investment i around the Expected Return $\bar{K}_i$ of 10 percent.

K_i	$\bar{K}_i$	P_i	$(K_i - \bar{K}_i)$	$(K_i - \bar{K}_i)^2$	$(K_i - \bar{K}_i)^2 P_i$
5%	10%	0.20	−5%	25%	5.0%
7	10	0.30	−3	9	2.7
13	10	0.30	+3	9	2.7
15	10	0.20	+5	25	5.0
					15.4% $= \Sigma(K_i - \bar{K}_i)^2 P_i$

$$\sigma_i = \sqrt{\Sigma(K_i - \bar{K}_i)^2 P_i} = \sqrt{15.4\%} = 3.9\%$$

The standard deviation of investment i is 3.9 percent (rounded). To have some feel for the relative risk characteristics of this investment, we compare it with the second proposal, investment j.

Assume investment j is an investment that does well during a recession and poorly in a strong economy. Perhaps it represents a firm in the housing industry that is most profitable when the economy is sluggish and interest rates are low. Under these circumstances, people will avail themselves of low-cost financing to purchase a new home, and the stock of the firm will do well. In a booming economy, interest rates will advance rapidly, and the financing of housing will become expensive. Thus, we have a counter-cyclical investment. The outcomes and probabilities of outcomes for investment j are as follows:

The Expected Return for investment j is:

$$\bar{K}_j = \Sigma K_j P_j \qquad (5\text{-}3)$$

K_j	P_j	$K_j P_j$
20%	0.20	4.0%
8	0.30	2.4
8	0.30	2.4
6	0.20	1.2
		$\bar{K}_j = 10.0\%$

The standard deviation for investment j is:

$$\sigma_j = \sqrt{\Sigma(K_j - \bar{K}_j)^2 P_j} \qquad (5\text{-}4)$$

K_j	$\bar{K}_j$	P_j	$(K_j-\bar{K}_j)$	$(K_j-\bar{K}_j)^2$	$(K_j-\bar{K}_j)^2 P_j$
20%	10%	0.20	+10%	100%	20%
8	10	0.30	−2	4	1.2
8	10	0.30	−2	4	1.2
6	10	0.20	−4	16	3.2
					25.6% $= \Sigma(K_j-\bar{K}_j)^2 P_j$

We now see we have two investments, each with an Expected Return of 10 percent but with varying performances in different types of economies and different standard deviations ($\sigma_i = 3.9$ percent versus $\sigma_j = 5.1$ percent).[1]

Standard deviation of returns is a crucial concept in portfolio management. Investors need to understand how the variability in returns can affect the realized rate of return on their investments. For instance, if you explain to your client that a particular security has an expected return of 14 percent with a standard deviation of 17 percent, they must understand that the variability in their return can be 14 percent ± 17 percent. Therefore the actual rate of return will most likely be between −3 percent and +31 percent. A security with a standard deviation of 17 percent implies a much riskier investment than a security with a standard deviation of 5 percent. In the end, it is the investor who needs to accept or reject the risk associated with a particular investment. It is the planner's job to explain the forecasted outcomes to the client and guide them in a direction that will suit their overall objectives.

Covariance and Correlation Coefficient

The covariance and correlation coefficient measure the extent to which securities move together in the market. For instance, suppose you own Stock A and Stock B and both are high-tech stocks selling computer chips. Suppose that news breaks about Company A revealing a quality assurance issue with their computer chips and the announcement of a major recall. Stock A's price will probably decrease if the market had not expected such an announcement. Because Stock B is also in the computer chip industry, its stock may very well decrease as well since investors will respond adversely to the overall market for computer chips. The measure of Stock B's sensitivity to Stock A's stock price could be measured over time to see the extent to which they move together. We could use both the covariance and the correlation coefficient to track the movements.

Stock B could be measured relative to an overall stock market index as well in order to see how sensitive it is to that market's general movements. The relationship between the movements of two securities or between a single security and general market movements are critical observations. As we shall see in a later chapter, these observations and measures of co-movements provide the underpinning in constructing **efficient** portfolios that contain many securities. Securities that move together in the same direction to each other (positive correlation) tend to do very well in good times and very poorly in bad times. The opposite is true too in that securities which are negatively correlated balance each other out in good times and in bad times as well. Covariance and correlation coefficients are simple to calculate for two securities but become more complicated as the number of securities increases. That is why it is necessary to use computer programs to conduct such analysis.

---

1. Actually, rather than use the standard deviation, we can also use its squared value, termed the variance to describe risk. That is, we may use σ^2 (the standard deviation squared) to describe the risk in an individual security.

Covariance

Any two securities whose prices react to information similarly are said to have a positive covariance. Securities with a negative covariance have returns that vary inversely, or that their prices move in opposite directions as reactions to the same information event.

The covariance between two securities is calculated as follows:

$$\text{cov}_{ij} = \Sigma(K_i - \bar{K}_i)(K_j - \bar{K}_j)P \qquad (5\text{-}5)$$

Using our earlier example above we take our K and P values from investment i and investment j on page 77 to compute the following: **(use above example)**

K_i	$\bar{K}_i$	$(K_i-\bar{K}_i)$	K_j	$\bar{K}_j$	$(K_j-\bar{K}_j)$	$(K_i-\bar{K}_i)(K_j-\bar{K}_j)$	P	$(K_i-\bar{K}_i)(K_j-\bar{K}_j)P$
5%	10%	−5%	20%	10%	+10%	−50%	0.20	−10.0%
7	10	−3	8	10	−2	+6	0.30	+1.8
13	10	+3	8	10	−2	−6	0.30	−1.8
15	10	+5	6	10	−4	−20	0.20	−4.0
								−14.0%

$$\text{cov}_{ij} = \Sigma(K_i - \bar{K}_i)(K_j - \bar{K}_j)P = -14.0\%$$

As you can see, the covariance of these two securities is 0.14. This means that these two securities tend to move in opposite directions. Without calculating the correlation coefficient, it is difficult to determine the extent to which they move together. Since the covariance is calculated similar to the standard deviation, we know that this is an absolute number. That is why it is necessary to use the covariance to calculate the correlation coefficient.

Correlation Coefficient

The correlation coefficient measures the strength of the relationship between two securities and the coefficient is always a value between −1 and +1. If the value is −1, it can be said that the returns of the securities are perfectly negatively correlated, meaning that the prices change equally but in opposite directions, where direction implies increase and decrease. If the value is +1, the two securities are perfectly positively correlated and that the security prices change equally and in the same direction as well. If the correlation coefficient equals zero, it means that the two securities do not move together in any meaningful way.

The calculation for correlation coefficient is as follows:

$$r_{ij} = \frac{\text{cov}_{ij}}{\sigma_i \sigma_j} \qquad (5\text{-}6)$$

Continuing with our example from above, we can see that the correlation coefficient of securities i and j are as follows:

$$r_{ij} = \frac{\text{cov}_{ij}}{\sigma_i \sigma_j} = \frac{-14.0}{(3.9)(5.1)} = \frac{-14.0}{19.9} = -0.70$$

Thus we can see that the correlation coefficient is −0.70. This means that these two securities exhibit a strong negative movement in opposite directions. In this case, barring

FIGURE 5–1   Correlation Analysis

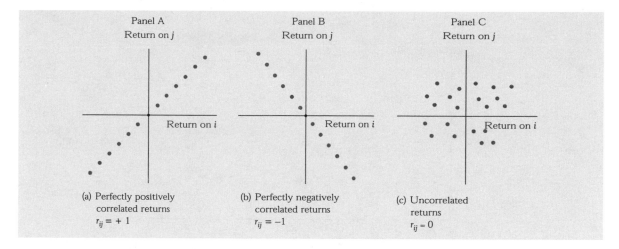

other issues, these two securities may be suitable to put in a portfolio in order to protect it from general stock market cycles.

Figure 5-1 demonstrates the concept of correlation. In Panel A, assets i and j are perfectly correlated, with r_{ij} equal to +1. As i increases in value, so does j in exact proportion to i. In Panel B, assets i and j exhibit a perfect negative correlation, with r_{ij} equal to −1. As i increases, j decreases in exact proportion to i. Panel C demonstrates assets i and j having no correlation at all, with r_{ij} equal to 0.

PORTFOLIO EFFECT

An investor who is holding only investment i may consider adding investment j in the portfolio. If equal amounts are invested in each stock, the new portfolio's Expected Return will be 10 percent. We define K_p as the Expected Return of the portfolio:

$$K_P = X_i \overline{K}_i + X_j \overline{K}_j \tag{5-7}$$

The X values represent the weights assigned by the investor to each component in the portfolio and are 50 percent for both investments in this example. The i and j values were previously determined to be 10 percent. Thus we have:

$$K_p - 0.5(10\%) + 0.5(10\%) = 5\% + 5\% = 10\%$$

What about the standard deviation (σ_p) for the total portfolio? If a weighted average were taken of the two investments, the new standard deviation would be 4.5 percent:

$$\sigma_i X_i + \sigma_j X_j$$
$$0.5(3.9\%) + 0.5(5.1\%) = 1.95\% + 2.55\% = 4.5\%$$

The interesting element is that the investor appears to be worse off from the combined investment. His Expected Return remains at 10 percent, but his standard deviation has increased from 3.9 to 4.5 percent. It appears that he is adding risk rather than reducing it by expanding his portfolio and without any change in return.

There is one fallacy in the analysis. *The standard deviation of a portfolio is not based on the simple weighted average of the individual standard deviations (as the Expected Return is).* Rather, it considers significant interaction between the investments. If one investment does well during a given economic condition while the other does poorly and vice

FIGURE 5–2   Investment Outcomes under Different Conditions

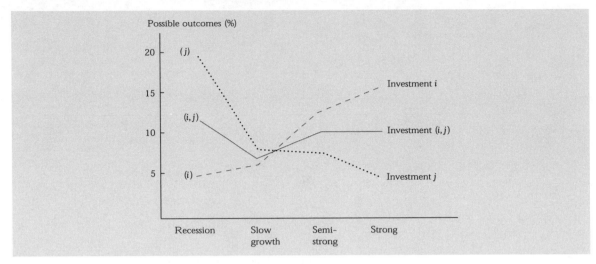

[handwritten margin note: STD Dev of Portfolio may be less than that of the individual Invest]

versa, there may be significant risk reduction from combining the two, and the standard deviation for the portfolio may be less than the standard deviation for either investment (this is the reason we do not simply take the weighted average of the two).

Note in Figure 5-2 the risk-reduction potential from combining the two investments under study. Investment i alone may produce outcomes anywhere from 5 to 15 percent, and investment j, from 6 to 20 percent. By combining the two, we narrow the range for investment (i, j) from 7.5 to 12.5 percent. Thus, we have reduced the risk while keeping the Expected Return constant at 10 percent. We now examine the appropriate standard deviation formula for the two investments.

Standard Deviation for a Two-Asset Portfolio

The reality of investing is that investors will most likely own more than one type of investment. Each investment generally has different risk and return characteristics. Combining different types of assets into the same portfolio can lead to varying amounts of risk and return for the portfolio. We are therefore interested in understanding how different asset combinations will affect our portfolio risk-return characteristics. We will start with a simple example of the two-asset portfolio. Specifically, we will be looking at how the portfolio risk changes as we combine two assets. The standard deviation for a two-asset portfolio is presented in Formula 5-8[2]:

$$\sigma_p = \sqrt{X_i^2\sigma_i^2 + X_j^2\sigma_j^2 + 2X_iX_jr_{ij}\sigma_i\sigma_j} \tag{5-8}$$

As noted in the above discussion, the correlation coefficient (r_{ij}) between investment i and investment j is -0.70. This indicates the two investments show a high degree of negative correlation. Plugging this value into equation 5-8, along with other previously determined values, the standard deviation (σ_p) for the two-asset portfolio can be computed[3]:

---

2. For a multiple asset portfolio, the expression is written as:

$$\sigma_p = \sqrt{\sum_{i=1}^{N} X_i^2\sigma_i^2 + 2\sum_{i=1}^{N-1}\sum_{j=i+1}^{N} X_iX_j\, r_{ij}\,\sigma_i\sigma_j}$$

N is the number of securities in the portfolio.

3. Note that the squared values, such as $(3.9)^2 = 15.4$, are the reverse of earlier computations. Previously we found the square root of 15.4 to be 3.9 (see computation following Formula 5-4). The use of rounding introduces slight discrepancies where we square numbers for which we previously found the square root.

$$\sigma_p = \sqrt{X_i^2 \sigma_i^2 + X_j^2 \sigma_j^2 + 2X_i \, X_j r_{ij} \, \sigma_i \, \sigma_j} \qquad (5\text{-}9)$$

where:

$X_i = 0.5, \quad \sigma_i = 3.9$

$X_j = 0.5, \quad \sigma_j = 5.1$

$r_{ij} = -0.70$

$\sigma_p = \sqrt{(0.5)^2(3.9)^2 + (0.5)^2(5.1)^2 + 2(0.5)(0.5)(-0.7)(3.9)(5.1)}$

$\quad = \sqrt{(0.25)(15.4) + (0.25)(25.6) + 2(0.35)(-0.7)(19.9)}$

$\quad = \sqrt{3.85 + 6.4 + (0.5)(-13.93)}$

$\quad = \sqrt{3.85 + 6.4 - 6.97}$

$\quad = \sqrt{3.28} = 1.8\%$

The standard deviation of the portfolio of 1.8 percent is less than the standard deviation of either investment i (3.9 percent) or j (5.1 percent). Any time two investments have a correlation coefficient (r_{ij}) less than 1 (perfect positive correlation), some risk reduction will result from combining the two assets in a portfolio. In the real world, most assets and securities are positively correlated; the extent that we can still get risk reduction from positively correlated items gives extra meaning to portfolio management. Note the impact of various assumed correlation coefficients for the two investments previously described in terms of individual standard deviations[4]:

Correlation Coefficient (r_{ij})	Portfolio Standard Deviation (σ_p)
+1.0	4.5
+0.5	3.9
0.0	3.2
−0.5	2.3
−0.7	1.8
−1.0	0.0

The conclusion to be drawn from our portfolio analysis discussion is that the most significant risk factor associated with an individual investment may not be its own standard deviation but how it affects the standard deviation of a portfolio through its correlation with other securities.

Coefficient of Determination

As we just saw, correlation and covariance are statistical measures that gauge the nature of the relationship between two random variables. Sometimes, the relationships between such variables may be one of dependence or causality. For example, when our income increases (decreases), our consumption of goods and services generally also increases (decreases). In this case, we can say that changes in consumption are caused (is dependent upon), to some extent, on changes in income. In this example, we can then classify consumption as the dependent variable and income as the independent variable. A common procedure to measure the extent of such a dependent relationship between two variables is known as simple regression analysis. Regression analysis provides us with many statistical gauges of the relationship which help us better understand the scope and nature of the relationship. One

---

4. Each is assumed to represent 50 percent of the portfolio.

such measure is a statistic known as the coefficient of determination, also known as R^2. This widely used statistic (R^2), represents the proportion of variation in the dependent variable that has been explained or accounted for by the independent variable. In the above example of income and consumption, the R^2 statistic from a simple regression analysis would tell us how much of changes in consumption are explained by changes in income.

What is interesting to note is that the coefficient of determination, when observed as a result of simple regression analysis, is also the square of the correlation coefficient, which was discussed previously. Since the correlation coefficient is commonly denoted by the symbol 'r', hence the R^2 for the determination coefficient. Also note that since correlation has a value between -1 and $+1$, its squared value must also necessarily be a value between 0 and 1. Continuing further, we consider the correlation value of -1 to represent a perfect negative relationship (each change in a variable being matched by an equal but directionally opposite change in the other) between two variables and a correlation value of $+1$ to represent a perfect positive relationship (each change in a variable being matched by an equal, in both magnitude and direction, change in the other) between two variables. Thus, the squared values in both these cases, or their R^2, would equal 1. We can say then that the value of R^2 being equal to 1 implies that the independent variable fully explains all changes in the dependent variable. When the value of R^2 is equal to zero, we can similarly say that there is absolutely no dependent relationship between the two variables.

In the case where multiple regression analysis is being used, i.e. relationships between and among more than two variables, the R^2 measure similarly interprets the depth of the relationship but is no more simply the squared correlation value.

Types of Returns

Investors use various methods by which they measure investment returns. We will discuss several types of returns; the nominal rate of return, the real rate of return, the real after tax rate of return, total return and risk adjusted return. We will briefly discuss each of these concepts but we will return to many of these return concepts in later chapters.

Nominal Rate of Return

The nominal rate of return is simply the return that one can earn on an investment. If for instance, you invest your money in a Certificate of Deposit that promises to pay 7 percent per year, a $100 investment will yield $107, one year later. In this example, the nominal rate of return is 7 percent, the rate you can earn before considering the effects of inflation or taxes on your investments.

Required Rate of Return

The required rate of return is a key concept in investment planning. However, it is also a difficult and complex concept to understand for reasons that require further discussion. Thus, it is worthwhile for us to spend some time on this issue.

When an investor assesses an investment opportunity, they may conduct much research and analysis to gauge the attractiveness of the investment. Ultimately, the investor will boil down the research and analysis to two factors: the risk of the investment opportunity and the return the investor expects to earn on this investment. The rate of return that an investor expects to earn on a risk-free security (e.g. A Treasury security) is the return that an investor expects to earn on a security that is free of default risk. All other securities contain the possibility of defaulting on their obligations. Hence, an investor will require returns in addition to the risk free rate as compensation for assuming the higher risk. We can think of this compensatory additional return as the security's **risk premium**. Thus we may express the **required rate of return,** as follows

$$\text{Required rate of return} = \text{risk-free return} + \text{risk premium}$$

What the planner needs to comprehend is that in arriving at a required rate of return, the primary assessment is the nature and extent of risk of an investment opportunity. The greater our understanding of the riskiness of a security, the more accurate our understanding of the risk premium we must receive, as compensation, in order to be induced to invest in that particular security. For example, suppose an investor, or planner, is considering an investment in two securities—a small cap stock and a highly rated bond. The planner will understand that the bond contains lower default risk than the small cap stock and will provide a greater assurance of an income stream and a redemption value at maturity. On the other hand, the small cap stock's price will most likely fluctuate greatly and a higher probability will exist that the firm may well go bankrupt. Thus, from the planner's or investor's perspective, the bond will be considered a much safer investment and the risk premium that the investor will require to invest in the bond will be much lower than what will be assessed for the stock. When these risk premiums are added to the risk free rate, the rate of return that the investor will require for the small cap stock will be much higher than the bond. In summary, the required rate of return may be considered as the gauge of the security's riskiness.

There are two other related return concepts that are also worth discussing briefly. Under various economic conditions, the performance of securities with varying characteristics will differ. For example, when the economy is in a recessionary stage, we expect most stocks to perform poorly, in terms of the returns they generate during this period. In this example, this rate would be the stock's **expected rate**. If the investor's required rate for this stock was higher than the expected rate, then the investor would not consider this investment, since the expected rate would not compensate the bearing of the risk of this particular security, as determined by the required rate. Similarly, in an economic growth cycle, the expected rate may equal or exceed the required rate and the investment would be made. Thus, we observe that both the required rate and the expected rate are assessed and compared and which lead to the eventual trading decision. Finally, note that the assessment of both the required rate and the expected rate begin before the investment decision and they continue to exist during the tenure of that decision, i.e. As long as the security is held. Once the investor sells the security, then the rate that was actually earned, or the **realized rate**, can be calculated. The realized rate may well be, and usually is, different from both the expected rate and the required rate.

The Real Rate of Return

The decision to invest is, in a sense, a decision not to consume. Alternately, an investment decision is a decision that implies a postponement of current consumption. To understand this further, consider this example: suppose you made a return of 12 percent in one year and 15 percent the following year, did you truly do better in the second year? The answer to this question depends on what your earnings could buy at the end of each of those years, or the purchasing power of your earnings. If the general level of prices, or inflation was very mild in the first year and severe in the second, your earnings would stretch further (purchase more) in the first year than in the second and hence you would have actually done better in the first year. Thus, the investment decision is related to the purchasing power of your earnings. This relationship, in turn, allows us to describe the concept of the real rate of return.

Consider another simple example. Suppose you have $100 that you are seeking to manage for one year and that you have two choices of how to use this money. The first choice is to invest the money in a savings account where you will earn a nominal rate of return of 3 percent/year. Thus, in this choice, if you decided to invest, you would have $103 at the end of the year. The second choice is to buy a watch, which you have always wanted, and which too costs $100, today. If you decided to invest the money, then you would buy the watch one year from today. However, due to the general increase in the level of prices, or inflation, you may find that at the end of the year, the price of the watch has increased to $104. In this case, you cannot buy the watch. Further, not having bought the watch before, you have also given up the enjoyment of possessing the watch for the entire year. Thus, at the beginning, if you feel that the price of the watch will increase to a level that is higher than what you would earn from your investment, you would be prone to not invest and buy the watch. The only way you would be inclined to invest instead would be if you were being provided with a nominal rate that was greater than what you would expect the price to be in a year's time. In the above example, you would invest only if the nominal rate was greater than 4%. Note that you would not be willing to invest if the nominal rate was just enough (equal to 4% in this example) to offset the cost increase. If that were so, you would rather buy the watch and get to enjoy it for the year.

There are two important observations that we can make from this example. First, the decision to invest is always in competition with the decision to consume. That is, the decision to invest can be considered as a decision to postpone consumption. Second, we will invest only when we expect not only to consume a similar product in the future but that we are also rewarded by a higher earning rate for postponing our consumption. If we are not offered this reward, we will always tend to consume and not invest.

In the above example, the rate we earn on the investment is the nominal rate, the rate at which the price of the product will rise is the inflation rate and the rate of the reward is the real rate of return. Thus in the above example, if the savings (nominal) rate was 6 percent and the inflation rate was 4 percent, the real rate of return would approximately be 2 percent. This approximate relationship can be expressed as follows:

$$\text{Nominal rate} = \text{real rate} + \text{inflation rate}$$

The exact relationship is given by the following equation:

$$(1 + \text{Nominal rate}) = (1 + \text{real rate}) \times (1 + \text{inflation rate})$$

or,

$$\text{The real rate} = [\,(1 + \text{Nominal rate})/(1 + \text{inflation rate})\,] - 1$$

Real After Tax Rate of Return

Many of the returns that investors earn are not tax-free. Short-term capital gains are taxed at the investor's marginal tax rate. Recall that short-term capital gains are those gains that are held for less than one year. Long-term capital gains are gains from increases in security prices where the security was held (owned) for one year or longer. Such gains are currently taxed at 20 percent for most individuals. (We will discuss both short-term and long-term gains in our chapter on Taxation.) In advising a client to sell a financial instrument, the real after tax rate of return must be taken into consideration in order to relay a true picture of return to the client. Taxes are relevant to all of us, but those clients in high income tax brackets are particularly affected by after tax returns.

The formula for the real after tax rate of return is:

$$r = (R)\,(1-t) - i$$

where r is the real after tax rate of return, R, is the nominal rate of interest, and t is the tax rate at which the investment will be taxed and i is the inflation rate for the period.

In this formula, we took the rate of inflation into consideration because it reduces the purchasing power of our returns. If the nominal rate of interest on a security is yielding 7.5 percent, the individual's tax rate is 40 percent and the inflation rate is equal to 1.4 percent, the real after tax rate of return is:

$$R = (0.075)\,(1 - 0.40) - 0.014$$
$$= 3.1\%$$

Total Return

The notion of total return centers on the total return that an investment yields. For example, when talking about stocks, the total return is equal to any dividends that the stock pays plus the capital gains or losses that the investor realizes on the sale of the stock. The same notion is true for mutual funds whereby the fund earns dividends and/or interest as well as capital gains or losses. Total returns are expressed in whole currency terms. For example, suppose an investor purchased Stock A for $15.00 per share. Over the next four years, Stock A paid annual dividends of $2.00 each year. At the end of the fourth year the investor decided to sell his stock at market for a price of $20.00 per share. Thus the gains are as follows:

Year 1	$2.00
Year 2	$2.00
Year 3	$2.00
Year 4	$2.00
Total Income	$8.00
Capital Gain:	$5.00
Total Gain:	$13.00

Thus, total return over the four years is $13/$15 = 86.67%

Risk Adjusted Return

A *risk premium* is a percentage return that an investment must expect to earn in order for an investor to assume a given level of risk. The *risk premium* will be different for each investment since all investments have different risk profiles and different expected returns. For example, for a federally insured certificate of deposit at a bank or for a U.S. Treasury bill, the risk premium approaches zero. For common stock, the investor's required return may carry a 6 or 7 percent risk premium in addition to the risk-free rate of return. If the *risk-free rate* were 5 percent, the investor might have an overall required return of 11 to 12 percent on common stock.

_ Real rate 2%
_ Anticipated inflation 3%
_ Risk-free rate 5%
_ Risk premium 6% or 7%
_ Required rate of return 11% to 12%

Corporate bonds fall somewhere between short-term government obligations (generally no risk) and common stock in terms of risk. Thus, for bonds, the risk premium may be 3 to 4 percent. Like the real rate of return and the inflation rate, the risk premium is not a constant but changes from time to time; for instance, if the issuing company's risk profile changes or if the macroeconomic outlook becomes more uncertain, then the risk premium too will change. If investors are very fearful about the economic outlook, the risk premium may be 8 to 10 percent as it was for junk bonds in 1990 and 1991.

Measuring Investment Returns

In order to begin to understand the various types of investment returns and their uses, we begin by considering a simple investment return for one time period. Recall, that when we discussed stocks, the total return was equal to any dividends that the stock paid plus the capital gains or losses that the investor realized on the sale of the stock. The same notion is true for mutual funds whereby the fund earns dividends and/or interest as well as capital gains or losses.

Suppose you purchase stock X, at a price of $25. During the year, the stock pays a dividend of $3. At the end of the year, you also sell the stock for $27 as it has increased in market value. Recall our formula for the Holding Period Return which is:

$$HPR = P_1 - P_0 + Dividends/P_0$$

The return on this investment is: $(27 - 25 + 3)/25 = 20\%$

Time Weighted Returns versus Dollar Weighted Returns

In reality we may want to consider investments over a period of time whereby we may have added to our investment positions or reduced our investment positions. If this is the case, measuring investment returns is a bit more difficult. With the basic concept of the holding period return, however, we measure investment returns where there are series of cash inflows and outflows.

Keeping with the example above, suppose that instead of selling the share of stock at the end of the year, we decide to purchase one more share of stock at the current market value of $27. At the end of the year, we collect our second $3 dividend, and subsequently sell both shares of our stock for $28 each.

The cash outflows for the purchase of stock are as follows:

T_0 — $25 to purchase first share of stock, where T_0 is our initial cash outflow at time zero
T_1 — $27 to purchase second share of stock

The cash inflows for the receipt of dividends are as follows:

T_1 — $3 dividend
T_2 — $3 dividend plus $56 for selling each share of stock at $28.

Using the discounted cash flow approach, we calculate the average return (r) over two years as follows:

$$-25 - 27/1 + r + 3/1 + r + 59/(1+r)^2 = 0$$

Solving for r, we get

$$r = 12.95\%$$

This value is known as the internal rate of return on the investment and is also known as the **dollar weighted rate of return** on the investment.

The time weighted rate of return is a formula which uses the holding period returns of an investment and averages them in order to yield an average rate of return. It is unlike the dollar weighted rate of return in that it ignores the number of shares held in each period. It does not take cash inflows/outflows into consideration during any period. Using the numbers from our previous examples, we find that the holding period return from at the end of period 1 was 20 percent. The return on the second share of stock was $28 - 27 + 3/27$ or 14.81 percent.

To calculate the average time weighted rate of return:

Time Weighted Rate of Return $= (20\% + 14.81\%)/2$
$$= 17.41\%$$

In this particular example, the dollar weighted return yielded less return than the time weighted rate of return. Depending upon the individual investment results either measurement could yield a result greater than the other. In general the results from these two measures will be different however.

Time weighted returns are generally used in order to measure results of money managers in their management of particular funds. Because money managers cannot control the timing or the amount of money coming into their funds, time weighted returns are used in order to measure results.

Since investors are particularly interested in the total amount of return that a portfolio or security yields over a period of time, the dollar weighted rate of return is generally considered to be the superior measure of return for this reason. This measure would thus be used by those wishing to know how investment returns fared within a particular portfolio or portfolios.

Arithmetic versus Geometric Averages

A separate set of measures arises from averaging returns on investments. The arithmetic and geometric weighted averages are examples of such returns. The time weighted return discussed in the previous section is also an example of **arithmetic average rate of return**. The **geometric rate of return** considers cash flows generated during the security's holding period to be reinvested at the security's required rate of return. Thus, this method includes the effect of compounding into consideration when calculating the return. The equation for the geometric return is as follows:

$$R_G = [(1 + HPR_{Year1}) \times (1 + HPR_{Year2}) \times (1 + HPR_{Year3}) + (1 + HPR_{Yearn})]^{1/n} - 1$$

where R_G is the geometric rate of return and n, stands for the nth period of investment.

The arithmetic rate of return is a simple average of annual returns. Using the same numbers from the previous example of calculating the time weighted rate of return, we calculate the geometric rate as follows:

$$R_G = [(1 + 0.2) \times (1 + 0.1481)]^{1/2} - 1$$
$$= 17.38\%$$

Notice that the geometric average return is 17.38% whereas the arithmetic rate of return is 17.41%. It will always be true that the geometric rate of return will yield a smaller number than the arithmetic rate of return. In general, the lower the returns, the greater is the disparity between the two averages.

Figure 5-3 shows the summary statistics of annual returns for various asset classes from 1926-2001. Note that in all cases, the arithmetic return is always greater than the geometric return.

Summary

This chapter began with a description of the different kinds of risk that accompany investments. It is useful to understand the nature and various types of risk since investors implicitly or explicitly price this risk in arriving at required returns investments. Therefore, the description of different types of risk is followed by explanations of how risk may be

FIGURE 5–3

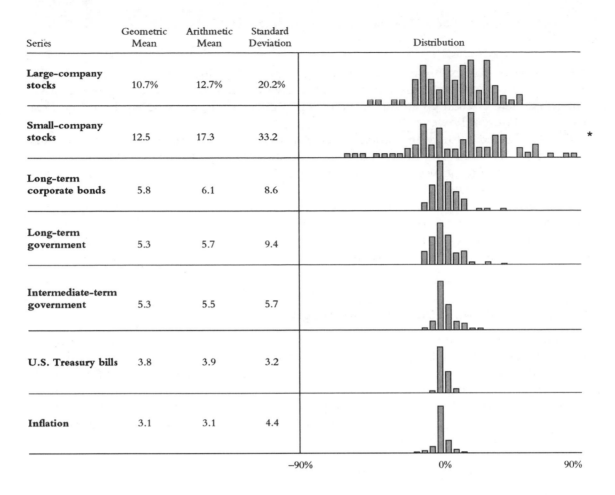

Series	Geometric Mean	Arithmetic Mean	Standard Deviation	Distribution
Large-company stocks	10.7%	12.7%	20.2%	
Small-company stocks	12.5	17.3	33.2	*
Long-term corporate bonds	5.8	6.1	8.6	
Long-term government	5.3	5.7	9.4	
Intermediate-term government	5.3	5.5	5.7	
U.S. Treasury bills	3.8	3.9	3.2	
Inflation	3.1	3.1	4.4	

−90%   0%   90%

measured. Once we can identify the types of risk in an investment and understand how to measure such risk, we can then proceed to identify what kinds of returns we may require from investing in different kinds of investment products.

"How much was the return on your investment?" Before having read this chapter, such a question may have been interpreted as a simple question. Not any more. In this chapter, we studied the many different forms that investment returns may take. Returns may be classified by inflation, as in the real rate return, or by the investment risk, as in the risk-free rate. Other return measures may incorporate taxes, the effect of time or the means of averaging. Even though the simplicity of the term is no more, the astute student should recognize that the various return definitions exist because they are all meaningful to investors under different investment circumstances and scenarios. These differing applications were explained in the context of defining each of the terms of returns. Armed with such knowledge, a financial planner can not only explain investment outcomes to clients more clearly but also help clients identify the misuse and abuse of these terms in the description of investment products.

Chapter 6

Portfolio Management

This chapter provides an overview of the Efficient Market Hypothesis (EMH) and discusses in some detail the implications of this hypothesis as well as the consequences of believing or disbelieving the hypothesis. The notion of informational efficiency is central to the proper functioning of a market oriented economy. However, for markets to be efficient, certain assumptions are required. These assumptions cannot be proved conclusively. Hence, the term "hypothesis" is used in describing EMH and not "theory." An implication of market efficiency is that active portfolio management will not lead to fruitful results. This implication implies that the charges (loads) many mutual funds impose on their buyers are uncalled for. This issue becomes contentious and the debate whether markets are efficient or not gets more heated. This chapter looks at the many different viewpoints that surround the issue of market efficiency, beginning with a clear description.

Efficient Market Hypothesis (EMH)

The debate, among academics and professionals, on the issue of whether markets are efficient or not is neither new nor will it end in the near future. Those who believe that markets are efficient maintain that financial markets reflect new information in the prices of securities, quickly, and accurately. Hence such believers claim that it is not possible to *consistently outperform* the market and that most analysis is futile. Hence, such people believe that investment managers should take a passive approach to investing and not try to engage in analysis of any sort. The opponents of this view think otherwise. Such viewers believe that the prices of securities do not reflect all information and hence securities may be trading at prices other than their implicit or fair market value. Thus, such people maintain that it is possible to analyze and predict the direction (and sometimes the magnitude) of price changes in securities, allowing people to consistently earn profits in excess of those an efficient market would allow. Such believers advocate an active approach to security analysis as a fruitful and desirable pursuit. Methods of security analysis include technical analysis (analysis of trends in securities) and fundamental analysis (economic, industry and company analysis). While the former method is discussed in greater detail at the end of this chapter, the latter method of analysis will be discussed in later chapters.

The following discussion will provide you with a more thorough understanding of the Efficient Market Hypothesis (EMH) and the reasons why the debate about it is a continuing one. In discussing the EMH we will observe the evidence forwarded to both support and refute the hypothesis. We begin with a general discussion of the EMH.

Overview of Efficient Market Hypothesis

Information is the basic component that determines security prices. Investors assess prices of stock based on both firm specific and market related information such as financial ratios, expected future cash flows, industry condition, company and market risk, etc. Based on this information and the resulting price expectations, investors trade in securities. The trading leads to security price adjustments and which adjustments incorporate the information sets upon which the trading is based. Because current security prices fully reflect all available information, it is referred to as informationally efficient market.

The importance of market efficiency in the context of a market-oriented economy is often misunderstood or not understood at all. Therefore, before we begin the discussion on market efficiency, we need to understand the reason why an informationally efficient market is desirable. An implication of market efficiency is that any analysis which uses past or current information may not lead to fruitful results if markets are efficient. Recall that in a perfectly efficient market, all information is fully reflected in all security prices. Therefore, it would be nearly impossible to achieve excess (or abnormal or unexpected) returns from trading based on past or current information. Under these circumstances, both fundamental and technical analysis would be somewhat redundant and many investment professionals would be engaged in activities that would not lead to any foreseeable benefit. Hence, it is worth exploring the issue of whether market efficiency is a desirable phenomenon, to begin with. While the answer and its proof are quite complicated technically, a short description to illustrate the reason is of merit.

The main reason why market efficiency is desirable is because it allows prices to accurately reflect the demand and supply forces in a market. This is especially true for demand, since this is more of an unseen force. When prices accurately portray demand and supply in a market, it facilitates the rational allocation of resources between competing markets. Higher prices in one market imply greater unsatiated demand; hence factors of production (land, labor, capital and technology) move to this market because the factors can receive higher compensation (rent, wages, returns, etc.) in these markets. When factors of production move from saturated markets to high-priced markets, a more desirable commodity is produced, prices fall and greater satisfaction is received by those who can now consume this more affordable product. Further, since factors of production also receive higher compensation, owners of such factors are also better off. Thus, rational allocation of resources leads to production or economic efficiency. This in turn increases the welfare level of a society. Rational allocation of resources and a higher level of welfare in society is an automatic process where the price in a market determines the movements of production factors. The price in turn reflects the unseen demand and observable supply conditions. As long as prices are accurate, market forces (especially the needs of people) determine what should or should not be produced. This automatic (market mechanism) process can be successful only if market prices are accurate. In other words we can say that informational efficiency is a pre-condition to production or economic efficiency.

Alternately, if prices were inaccurate (e.g. bubbles), then factors move to produce less desirable products. In such cases, the resulting production and resource allocation can be considered as an economically inefficiency which lowers social welfare standards. An example of this is the recent (early 2000s) debacle in the technology industry. High prices (for all factors) caused production factors to move into the technology market. When it was revealed that market prices of factors were overestimations, the market crashed. An effect of this crash was large layoffs, negative capital returns from stock price decreases and some downward adjustments to land value. All of the above outcomes were painful to the owners of these production factors.

Rational allocation and production efficiency provides us with the rationale for studying and analyzing the efficiency of capital markets. Efficient Market Hypothesis (EMH), the basic hypothesis of the behavior of efficient markets, makes certain assumptions as to the reasons why efficiency may exist in a market. They are as follows:

- Large numbers of investors actively analyze and value securities to maximize profits. All such investors may act independently on their information. Thus, no single investor can affect the price of any security.

- New information randomly enters the market, and it is freely available to all investors approximately at the same time, especially due to advances in computing and information technology. Information about labor strikes, new product development, currency values, global conflicts, etc. Are not predictable. They are freely available at the same time through mass media. Given that the arrival of such information is random and unpredictable, it follows that price responses are random as well and hence, cannot be accurately forecasted.

- Investors react quickly and accurately to new information causing security prices to quickly reflect new information. Resulting adjustments may be imperfect, unbiased, and may move independently in a random fashion. A price change today is based on the information that came to the market today. It need not be the equilibrium price, but an unbiased estimate of the final equilibrium price.

In an efficient market, security prices adjust quickly to all new information and therefore all available information is reflected in the price. Since new information in a market is unpredictable, price changes in securities are also unpredictable. As security prices move unpredictably and in tandem with all new information, price changes can be said to follow a random (walk) process over time. That is, price changes have no predictable pattern of change in response to new information in the market. If price changes are truly unpredictable, following trading rules and techniques to predict price movements will not be helpful. Therefore, investors cannot expect to consistently outperform the market, even if they decide to take additional risk. In this case, an investor can only expect to earn a return that is consistent with the amount of risk in a particular security. If, however, security prices are predictable, investors can outperform the market consistently with or without taking any additional risk.

Forms of Efficient Markets

Efficient market hypothesis indicates that the quality of information and the speed at which it is disseminated are the keys to produce informationally efficient markets. In a perfectly efficient market, security prices should reflect all available information making it equal to its intrinsic or fair market value. However, if markets are not perfectly efficient, many techniques may exist that can be used by investors to obtain superior results. Therefore, it is important to know the degree of efficiency in the market. The EMH is commonly considered to contain three cumulative categories or (efficient) forms of markets: The *weak, semi strong,* and *strong-form.*

Weak Form

This form of EMH holds that current stock prices contain all information which is included in past security prices. Thus, any technical analysis based on current and past price patterns or any trend analysis cannot help us predict future prices since the current price has already adjusted to all such information. If price changes only reflect randomly arriving information, price changes will also be random and unrelated to past data. The hypothesis therefore emphasizes that if current prices reflect all past price information, then that market can be considered to be of weak-form efficiency.

Semi-Strong Form

This form of EMH holds that the current price of a stock reflects all publicly available information about the security. This information includes all stock related data such as earnings information, dividend distributions, stock splits, all corporate and economic data such as inflation, new product developments, managerial competencies, etc. The semi-strong form hypothesis purports that investors cannot unearth and use any publicly available information for trading that would lead to earning superior and above normal returns. This is not surprising since we are assuming that all market participants have equal access to the same market information and process and act upon such information similarly as well. The resultant trading causes a speedy dissemination of such information in current prices. When stock prices reflect all currently available information the market is said to be semi-strong form efficient. Note that since past prices are contained in publicly available information, the weak form of efficiency is a perfect subset of the semi-strong form. In this way, the degrees of efficiency are cumulative.

Strong Form

This form holds that stock prices fully reflect all information, both public and private. Since all information includes publicly available information, the semi-strong form efficient market is a subset of the strong form efficient market. The main distinction between the semi-strong and strong form is that the latter also includes private or privileged inside information. In the strong form model of the EMH it is not possible for investors to consistently earn abnormal profits. However, since it is illegal in the U.S. To use insider information for trading purposes, the dissemination of private information into current stock prices becomes possible only when such information becomes public. The basic issue may then be the schedule by which private information becomes public.

Studies of Weak Form Efficiency

There are two major paths of studies conducted to test the weak form version of the EMH. The first series of studies focuses on statistical tests of independence between stock price movements and rates and return. The second path includes tests of specific trading rules against risk and return results of past market data.

Statistical Tests

Statistical studies have tested whether or not stock prices change independently as new information randomly enters the market. The two tests commonly used to measure this occurrence are *Serial Correlation Tests* and *Signs Tests.*

Serial correlation tests measures correlation between returns over time; to observe whether the return from a period to the next is correlated. If capital markets are truly efficient, there should not be any correlation in such combinations. Alternately, the existence of any significant serial correlation would imply that the known price today could be beneficially exploited. The general findings from such short-term analysis (both intra-day and inter-day) show insignificant or no correlation in stock returns. These findings generally support the weak form efficient market hypothesis. However, some results have suggested serial correlation exists for stocks of small size companies. We will discuss this observation in greater detail in a latter section on anomalies.

Sign Test or Runs

Tests designate each price change by a + or − sign to count the number of price changes with the same sign (runs) and compare it with the implication that if information arrived randomly, then there should not be any discernible runs. A run occurs when the same sign follows consecutively, and the run changes when the sign changes (e.g. plus to a minus). These runs are compared with known stock prices to confirm whether stock prices move randomly. Studies done on Dow Jones Industrial stocks have shown there are very little or no sustained runs that can be attributed to any pattern. Statistical runs tests indicate the same, i.e. stock price changes over time are independent (no discernible runs/patterns) implying that such runs can be identified from historical market data, that information events are speedily disseminated (no lingering effects) and thus can earn superior future rates of return.

Trading Rule Tests

Technical analysts believe prices tend to move in a trend over time and that statistical tests done are too rigid to detect these realistic price changes. To a technical analyst several plus or minus reactions do not signal any form of a stock movement. Rather they look for trend patterns over time. Studies conducted to test trading rules simulated various strategies and the results of such strategies were compared with the results from buy and hold strategies (passive investing) to test the validity of this argument.

The research indicated a few problems in interpreting the results of these strategies. First, it was observed that the results from different trading rules could be subjectively interpreted and thus could not be generalized. Second, there was such a profusion of rules that it was impossible to test all the rules and arrive at any supportable conclusions. Of the studies done the evidence does not indicate that following technical trading rules based on price and volume helps to outperform the market. These studies also generally agree that investors would be far more successful in a buy and hold strategy. It is more likely that inefficiencies can exist in small stock markets where fewer institutions hold ownership positions, very few analysts follow the stock and fewer trading activities take place. Therefore, because of the informational inefficiency that may exist in these markets, excess returns may be earned with some securities.

Evidence of Semi-Strong Form

This hypothesis asserts prices adjust quickly to publicly available information. To prove this argument, tests have been done to check how quickly prices adjust to publicly available information to earn excess returns. If security prices are influenced by the overall market, stocks rates of return should be equal to aggregate market return during a given period after adjusting for company specific information factors. To calculate excess returns, the expected rate of return should be subtracted from actual security returns to arrive at abnormal rate of returns, AR_{it} and

$$AR_{it} = R_{it} - E(R_{it})$$

where:

Ar_{it} = abnormal rate of return for security i during period i
R_{it} = actual rate of return on security i during period t
$E(R_{it})$ = expected rate of return for security i during period t based on the market rate of return or relationship with the market.

There are two ways to test the semi-strong form EMH. The first is an analysis of time series. Time series analysis estimates future rates of return based on long-run historical rates of publicly available information. Examples of publicly available information include changes in aggregate dividend yields, earnings yields, price to expected earning ratios, etc. Studies have indicated mixed results in predicting relationships. The second test of semi-strong EMH involves an event study. Event studies examine the impact of an event on gaining abnormal rate of return immediately after its announcement. Some examples of events are stock splits, initial public offerings, corporate finance events such as mergers, stock/bond issues, and unexpected world or economic events. These announcements are examined for the effect of stock price changes. The focus of event studies is twofold. First, it is concerned with assessing what kinds of events contain significant information. Another way to express this is to study the events that cause a statistically significant change in price where the change is sustained over a certain definite period of time (e.g. one month). The second issue in event studies is concerned with the speed of dissemination of information events. If a significant information event is not quickly and fully disseminated in the stock's price, then investors will have the ability to profit from trading in that stock once the information becomes public. In other words, the stock will continue to change in one direction long enough for investors to jump in at earlier points in order to gain abnormal profits. In this case, the price change will include a series of runs (same sign changes) for a significantly long period of time. The results from event studies are also mixed. While event studies help us to identify which events contain significant information and which do not (e.g. earnings surprises do contain significant information whereas stock splits do not), the studies do not agree on the speed at which such information is reflected in the stock's current price. While some studies show the information being integrated in the current price within 15 minutes, other studies show that information events take up to three days to be fully incorporated into the stock price.

An example of an event study is the issuance of IPOs (initial public offering) when a company goes public. IPO underwriters often tend to underprice new issues due to uncertainties of determining true price. Investors who buy underpriced IPO stocks expect to earn abnormal returns. In theory, if prices adjust quickly to available market information, IPOs should not create any excess returns. Results indicate investors benefit from underpriced stocks if they were able to buy it at the original issue price. Prices of IPOs have been found to adjust to their true values within a day of their issuance and investors who purchase after this time are not able to enjoy abnormal profits, which supports the semi-strong form EMH. Further, IPOs are not always underpriced and prices can adjust downward as well.

Studies also confirmed that prices adjusted quickly to unexpected economic events such as terrorist attacks and wars. On the other hand, economic news that involves money supply, inflation, interest rate changes by the Federal Reserve Boards had very little effect on prices beyond the day of announcement. Corporate finance events like mergers and acquisitions, stock and bond offerings have been examined for stock price reactions. Results have been mixed. All the above event studies generally support the semi-strong form of EMH. However, the time series analyses support the semi-strong form of EMH only on a long-term basis.

Evidence of Strong Form

This form states stock price adjusts to all forms of information including inside private information. Thus investors cannot obtain abnormal returns consistently even with availability of private information. Testing this form of EMH requires the study of investors who have access to true private information. Corporate insiders are required to report their monthly purchase or sale transactions to the Securities and Exchange Commission (SEC). This inside information is made public. Studies have shown that companies' insider buyers have enjoyed above average profits. Outsiders can also earn profits using publicly available information regarding inside transactions. Due to investor interest, Barron's and *Wall Street Journal* publishes insider trading data on a regular basis. The evidence on the strong form of EMH is mixed mainly due to the nature of regulations and difficulties in data reliability.

Implications of the Efficient Market Hypothesis

Given that some form of efficiency of the market is generally supported what are the implications of this to an investor, financial analyst, or to an institution? What can a portfolio manager do to earn excess returns if markets are efficient? If results support EMH, investors cannot believe in earning superior or abnormal returns and in this case a buy-and-hold strategy would seem to be the best tactic to assume. In contrast, if the evidence is mixed regarding the existence of efficient markets, how can superior results be achieved?

There is a wide disparity of views regarding EMH as it is a very controversial issue. At one side of the controversy are academics (professors of economics and finance, generally) who believe that markets are fairly efficient (somewhere between weak form and semi-strong form) and who forward especially the results from studies that seem to corroborate their views. On the other side are the professional analysts who too offer studies that show superior results from fundamental analysis are possible. Both sides also attempt to discredit the other. Thus, it is not surprising that a huge number of studies have been conducted to verify the nature and degree of market efficiency in order to validate the form or lack of, market efficiency. Generally, studies have supported the existence of a weak form of market efficiency. Some studies have also claimed to find the existence of a semi-strong form efficient market. However, other studies have revealed the existence of some other anomalies (exceptions) that refute the suggestion that markets are semi-strong or even weak form efficient. We will examine the issues of anomalies in a later section.

Let us first consider the implications of weak form efficiency. Since the information in past prices is assumed to be included in the current price, the use of past prices to forecast future price changes will not be fruitful. This implies that any attempt to extrapolate past price behavior into the future is of no use. The whole precept of technical analysis rests on the assumption of trends and patterns and their continuation and repetition, respectively. Whether we use regression and correlation techniques or whether we use observable patterns, all technical analysis presupposes that past (price) behavior will continue, or repeat itself, in the future. If markets are weak-form efficient, past prices will not help to predict future movements. This picture of the inadequacy of technical analysis is strongly connected with the randomness of the information flow. Technical analysts counter that stock prices do not only reflect fundamental information but that they also reflect the behavior of investors. If investors behave in a predictable way (herding behavior, for example) then identifiable and repeated patterns will result. The technical analysts continue by asserting that the pattern may disappear when the information is fully understood and disseminated, but that will occur only when the resulting pattern has already been exploited for abnormal profits. The study of investor behavior, or **behavioral finance**, is an emerging and exciting new field of study in finance and one which promises to enliven the debate on market efficiency in the years to come. A brief introduction to behavioral finance is provided in a following section in this chapter.

Technical analysis directly contradicts the EMH. It asserts that stock prices move in trends over a period of time; refuting the random walk notion. Technical analysts believe stock prices move to the equilibrium in a gradual movement, and investors do not act on information immediately. Although technical analysis cannot be fully refuted, since the evidence indicates the existence of the weak form of the EMH and which refutes technical analysis, the proper question to ask is why so many technical analysts and tools exist and what benefits do they provide? Moreover, if technical-trading rules cannot guarantee abnormal returns, then should not this information be also disseminated and such analysis eventually disappear?

The arguments for and against the semi-strong form is similar to the weak form except that it also includes the financial analysts who study the fundamental nature of information included in a stock's price. The basic approach to fundamental valuation lies in discounting the future expected cash flows of a company to the current value. The estimates of future cash flows are based on both the firm's overall current activities and plans for the future. The current and potential activities and plans incorporate both macroeconomic and microeconomic detail. The analyst studies the macroeconomic environment, the position of the firm's sector and industry within this environment as well as the micro-economic aspects of the firm's management, product and other competitive issues. The future cash flows are estimated and then discounted using a rate that is embedded in the general level of interest rates but which also adjusts this rate for firm specific risk considerations. Thus, fundamental analysis is an engaging task requiring the analysts to be thoroughly versed and knowledgeable about the firm and the economy. The analysts typically study the company's financial statements, assess the firm's industry and then value the firm on the overall basis. The analysts argue that their special skills and knowledge allow them to unlock value that is available in public information but which is not possible for the layperson since ordinary people do not possess their special skills. Proponents of semi-strong form efficient markets counter by showing that active fund managers (surrogate for people with special skills) do not outperform the market (proxy for passive investments) in returns and are definitely not capable of doing so in a consistent way. It is worthwhile for the student to note that the debate is live and promises to continue in its lively fashion for quite a while longer.

Fundamental analysts believe that the intrinsic value of a security depends on current market conditions which in turn reflect estimates of future cash flows. If the estimated present value is less (more) than the prevailing market price, investors can gain abnormal returns by buying (short selling) the securities. If the semi-strong form of EMH exists in markets then security analysis based on publicly available information will not be useful. Although analysts do outperform the market such outperformance cannot be truly relied upon if it is not consistently repeated.

Portfolio Management Implications

EMH suggest that an individual investor can earn returns consistent with the market just by randomly selecting a diversified portfolio. EMH also suggests that there are no superior analysts who can outperform a buy-and-hold policy on a risk-adjusted basis over a sustained period of time. Buy-and-hold strategies offer less transaction costs than an active strategy. Although an analyst can theoretically outperform the market, these returns can be quickly eliminated by excessive research and trading costs, making investing cost prohibitive. Thus proponents of EMH believe that in efficient markets, investment professionals should concentrate on structuring client portfolios to reflect the risk tolerances and tax needs of their clients.

Anomalies

An anomaly is an exception to a rule. The existence of an anomaly in any financial market is a contradiction to the hypothesis of an efficient market. Since such exceptions and their effects are known, then their effects should also be adjusted in current prices. Anomalies in financial markets exhibit two characteristics: (1) The anomaly can be structured into a trading rule to earn abnormal returns, and (2) The anomaly is recurring or that the trading rule can be repeatedly used. The basic contradiction in this context is that in an efficient market once such an anomaly is discovered, it should become integrated in that market so the opportunity should disappear. Since anomalies do not go away, by definition, and their persistence cannot be rationalized either, they imply that markets cannot integrate the informational content of anomalies and hence, are not efficient. However, the existence of anomalies does not directly refute market efficiency either.

There are a few anomalies that are known to exist in financial markets. For example, it is well tabulated that low P/E (or P/B) stocks outperform high P/E stocks on a regular basis. Since this knowledge should lead rational investors to bid up low P/E (P/B) stocks and bid down high P/E (P/B) stocks immediately, the disparity should be quickly removed. As stated above, this does not happen since abnormal returns generated in this manner occurs regularly. This contradicts the EMH as it implies investors can use publicly available information to predict abnormal returns.

Anomalies in the above example conform to a bigger set known as the mean reversion phenomenon. This phenomenon states that generally stocks which have characteristics of lower measures (e.g. small size, low P/E, low P/B, etc.) will over time increase and the opposite will happen for those with the higher measures. In other words, over time, all stocks will tend towards the average of the entire group of stocks, that is, revert to the mean. However, by this very definition, it implies that we can predict the behavior of groups of stocks from publicly available information—another contradiction to market efficiency. Another group of anomalies is related to calendar dates. For example, the January effect anomaly suggests that most of the abnormal returns earned from holding low capitalization stock occur in the first week of January. Many studies have tried to rationalize this phenomenon but none have been successful. Similarly it has been shown that there exists day-of-the-week (Monday) effect, holiday effect, etc. Again, the main point to note is that these anomalies provide abnormal returns and do not go away either.

Researchers have contended that the presence of transaction costs often reduce the abnormal returns to insignificant levels. However, other studies that factored both size and transaction cost over long periods have indicated that the abnormal profit may be reduced but not to insignificant levels.

Finally, opponents of market efficiency inevitably point to the event of Black Monday, the day in October 1987 when the market declined by 25 percent. These opponents point out that this very significant (statistical and otherwise) price decline happened without the existence of any negative news or information. Since market efficiency is a hypothesis of information dissemination in prices, they contend that this particular decline indicates that markets may move for reasons other than purely information reasons. Hence, it is quite likely that technical analysis may be picking up on such movements.

In conclusion, it is correct to say markets are generally efficient though it is difficult to pin down the exact degree of efficiency. Further, inefficiencies (anomalies) do exist and until they can be rationalized (and go away), market efficiency cannot be asserted in any way. Information is randomly received and generally adjusted quickly. Superior performance by any individual investor is difficult because information is available to all investors at the same time, and adjustments by all make the prices reflect such information quickly. EMH does not imply investment decisions are futile. Rather, it suggests that portfolios should be constructed to reflect the individual's objectives, risk tolerance, investment time horizon and tax requirements. Further, portfolios need ongoing management, albeit in a passive manner, to reflect changes in client needs, tolerances and life cycle factors.

The Scope of Rational Financial Behavior

The recent bestseller by Burton Malkiel, *A Random Walk Down Wall Street*, popularized the notion of irrational markets.[1] In the book, Malkiel argues that economists' portrait of people making rational financial decisions based on sufficient market information was simply a non-existent ideal. Malkiel offers as historical evidence such events as the Dutch Tulip craze of the 17th century and the Great Depression of 1929 to suggest that when it comes to investing, people generally follow their emotions, not their reason, their hearts, nor their minds.[2]

This line of argument has been gaining credibility over the last decade or so, not only among behavioral finance experts, but also economists themselves, as well as stock market pundits and the population at large.[3] There is a strong sense among all these groups that greed, exuberance, and herding behavior affect markets as much as or more than P/E ratios, profit projections, or market benchmarks. The stock market bubble of early 2000 only

---

1. Malkiel, Burton G. (1999) *A Random Walk Down Wall Street: The Best Investment Advice for the New Century* (Norton).

2. See also Landberg, W. (April 2003) "Fear, Greed and the Madness of Markets," *Journal of Accountancy*.

3. Minsky, R. (Spring 1999) "Fear and Greed in the 24-Hour Economy" (*Brown Economic Review*), Goetzmann, W.N. And Massa, M. (September 2002) "Daily Momentum and Contrarian Behavior of Index Fund Investors" (*Journal of Financial and Quantitative Analysis*) Vol. 37, No. 3.

confirmed these long-held suspicions.[4] As a result, such widely used economic models that are based on rational investor behavior as the CAPM have been reevaluated and found to be unreliable at best and irrelevant at worst.[5]

Using empirical evidence from the U.S. markets over the last decade, from January 1993 to May 2003 highlights the kinds of investor behavior that had such a large impact on equity and bond markets during the period. If we learn how investors act as a group this will help individual investors, money managers, academics, as well as casual observers of the market better understand what makes it tick. And understanding both the market and those who participate in it will also help financial planners better advise their clients about the risks and pitfalls of ignoring long-term strategies in favor of short-term phenomena and their own fears, concerns and biases.

Let us look, then, at the debate about rational investor behavior. The tenets of Modern Portfolio Theory (MPT) (covered in the next chapter) tell us that investors make rational decisions based on accurate information about the markets. In other words, we would not expect such investors to make the same mistake twice. The related notion of market efficiency suggests that past prices are not useful indicators of future prices.

But our evidence shows that investors actually behave differently than either MPT or the market efficiency theory would lead us to expect. Investors encounter a host of biases, fears and psychological pitfalls that lead them to act irrationally. For instance, our evidence suggests that investors evaluate and react to risk very differently when the market is up and when it is down. When the market is doing well, they tend to look quite risk-neutral. In other words, they chase returns because they underestimate the risk and overestimate the expected value of their investments. But their risk-aversion quickly kicks in, and rather than risking a downturn, they quickly sell in order to lock in their profits. However, if their investments start on a downward slide before they have a chance to sell, those same investors also often continue to hold out hope of a recovery as the value of their investments falls. Even though the market may be clearly signaling that it is on a downward trend, they hold out hope that their loss will prove to be otherwise. Overall, investors hold losers longer than they do winners—124 days for the losers, versus 102 days for the winners (Odean (2001)). This is a consistent phenomenon and goes against assumptions about rational choices and accurate information. It strongly suggests instead that investors are generally more loss-averse than they are risk-averse.

Behavioral biases also play a major role in investor behavior. A well-documented pattern suggests that many investors attribute good outcomes (i.e., gains) to skill while attributing bad outcomes (i.e., losses) to bad luck.[6] They are thus often overconfident, overestimating their chances of correctly predicting the direction of price changes. A study by Lichenstein and Fischoff (1977) found, for example, that 65 percent of interviewees expected their predictions regarding stock prices to be accurate, while only 47 percent of them were actually so.[7] Likewise, investors often overestimate their powers of discerning stock winners from losers. In order to use that power to its fullest, such investors (essentially, active traders) rapidly sell and buy back stocks, in order to capture expected gains. Evidence from the late 1990s provided by Odean (1998) shows that, had these investors held on to those stocks, instead of replacing them with stocks they thought would perform better, the resulting portfolio would have outperformed their active portfolio by an average of 3.4 percent a year over the span of the entire year.[8]

4. Payne, J. And Wood, A. (2002) "Individual Decision Making and Group Decision Processes" (*The Journal of Psychology and Financial Markets*) Vol. 3, No. 2, MacGregor, D.G., Slovic, P., Dreman, D., and Berry, M. (2002) "Imagery, Affect and Financial Judgment" (*The Journal of Psychology and Financial Markets*) Vol. 1, No. 2, Montier, J. (2002) *Behavioral Finance: Insights into Irrational Minds and Markets* (Wiley Finance).
5. Karceski, J. (December 2002) "Returns-Chasing Behavior, Mutual Funds, and Beta's Death" (*Journal of Financial and Quantitative Analysis*) Vol. 37, No. 4.
6. Cited by Montier (2002), p. 2.
7. Cited by Montier (2002), p. 2.
8. Cited by Montier (2002), p. 24.

Other behavioral biases include cognitive dissonance and confirmation bias. The former suggests that investors experience an internal conflict when a belief or assumption of theirs is proven wrong. The latter suggests that they then seek out information that will help confirm their existing views. Investors are also influenced by what is known as "anchoring," a phenomenon whereby people stay within range of what they already know in making guesses or estimates about what they do not know. Montier (2002) tested this hypothesis by incorporating a recent study.[9] In the study, Statman and Fisher (1998) point out that the value of the Dow Jones Industrial Average (DJIA), which grew from a value of 41 in 1896 to 9,181 in 1998, does not include dividends.[10] They then value the index in 1998, including dividends, at a whopping 652,230. When in that same year, Montier in turn asked investors to estimate what the value of the DJIA would be if dividends were included, all were way off the mark, keeping their answers close to its familiar value of 9,181. The highest guesses came in at under 30,000, less than 5 percent of the actual value.

Investors are also affected by what is known as the "representativeness heuristic," or an over-reliance on familiar clues, such as past performance. For instance, most investors assume that the stock of a company with strong earnings will perform well and that the stock of a company with weak earnings will perform poorly (Solt and Statman, 1989; Shefrin and Statman, 1995).[11] Mean reversion shows, however, that the exact opposite is true.[12] Finally, most investors exhibit what Tversky and Kahneman (1974) call "availability bias," or a strong tendency toward investing in what they know, such as companies based in their home countries.[13] Similarly, most investors associate high levels of press coverage about companies with continued strong performance. A study by Gadarowski (2001) shows, however, that within two years of such coverage, the stocks of most such companies are well underperforming other similar stocks.[14]

All in all, investors hardly ever behave the way that models of rational behavior would suggest. In fact, their behavior is often counter-intuitive, and therefore more often than not also counter-productive. They appear to be influenced by fads and are susceptible to market bubbles. Investors also exhibit herding and gambling behavior, both often related to over confidence. And as Malkiel and others have shown, this was no different even as far back as the 17th century.

Market Timing

Market timing refers to the ability of a planner to be able to position the portfolio of a client in such a way that the client can either profit, or prevent losses, from the subsequent movement of underlying securities and assets in a client's portfolio. Before exploring the concept of timing in further depth, the basic presumption in market timing, in the light of market efficiency needs to be examined. Market timing implies that it is possible for a planner to have some knowledge about the future direction of movement of asset and security prices. This, in turn, implies that the planner possesses some information regarding the securities and assets that are not currently incorporated in security and asset prices themselves. If this were true then an obvious conclusion must be that the markets for these assets and securities are to some extent, inefficient. This basic contradiction between the market efficiency level and the ability to time the market must be kept in mind in examining the different kinds of market timing that planners may engage in. Within this backdrop, market timing may now be examined.

---

9. Montier (2002), p. 5.
10. Cited by Montier (2002), p. 5.
11. Cited by Montier (2002), pp. 9–10.
12. Montier (2002), p. 10.
13. Cited by Montier (2002), p. 12.
14. Cited by Montier (2002), p. 12.

As mentioned earlier, market timing is the ability of a planner to predict, to some extent, the magnitude and direction of price changes and the duration of such movements. The timing of markets may take the following forms:

1. Changes (increase or decrease) in the prices of individual securities and in some cases, the duration over which these changes may occur.

2. Changes in the price levels, both in magnitude and direction, of broader market segments and the duration of such changes. Examples of broader segments include sectors such as defensive, cyclical and growth sector stocks. Included too among such segments are classifications of stocks by their industries such as technology, health, finance or foods. In the case of fixed income securities, bond ratings can be used to segment the market.

3. Finally, in timing markets, planners also consider price level changes of broad asset classes such as stocks, bonds, real estate, commodities, currencies, etc. As will be seen later, the change in price levels for asset classes forms the basis for **tactical asset allocation**.

Financial planners and advisors may attempt to time markets using two basic techniques: technical analysis and fundamental analysis. Typically, technical analysis, or "charting" is the methodology of predicting price movements in the *short term* by trying to identify price and volume patterns that may repeat themselves or by identifying price trends that may determine future price movements. Technical analysts look for price patterns (patterns with exotic names such as "head and shoulders" or "saucers") that are believed to repeat themselves over time. Such analysts will also look at price movement barriers such as resistance and support levels at which barriers prices reverse the direction of movement leading again to predictable price changes. Using smoothing techniques such as moving averages and exponential smoothing, analysts will try to capture price trends in order to predict future price movements. It is important to note that the basic assumption in technical analysis to use past prices in predicting future price movements implies that markets are not even "weak-form" efficient.

Technical analysts counter by arguing that their efforts at market timing are dictated by short-term trading, and whether markets are efficient in the short term is questionable or such efficiencies may not necessarily hold at all times. Technical analysis is examined in greater detail later in this chapter.

The second method of fundamental analysis used and justified by market timers is examined in greater detail in later chapters, and hence only a brief description follows. At the level of an individual security, fundamental analysis is concerned with evaluating the future prospects of a firm. Using various valuation techniques, planners assess whether the firm's current stock price is correctly valued or not. If this current market price is considered under or overvalued, then the planner advises the client to buy or sell the security, in the belief that the market will discover this valuation discrepancy, leading to greater buying and selling, until the price the planner believes to be correct is established. This subsequent market price discovery should lead to the profit or loss prevention for the planner's client. While the above example illustrates market timing considerations for individual securities, a similar type of fundamental analysis is also used to predict price movements in broader asset classes and over longer time periods. Macroeconomic analysis examines broad economic indicators such as gross domestic product, interest rates, unemployment, etc., to understand the economy's business cycle. The business cycle traces the changing fortune of the overall economy and is inclusive of changes in price levels for asset classes such as stocks and bonds.

Macroeconomic analysis attempts to predict both the direction and the magnitude of price level changes as well as the duration of such changes. Planners use such analysis and

FIGURE 6–1   Presentation of the Dow Theory

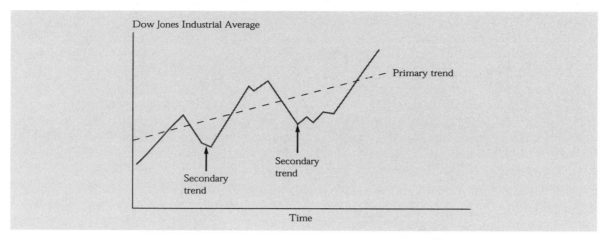

their predictions to position client portfolios to take advantage of the expected changes. Strategic asset allocation is concerned with allocating the wealth of a client among various asset classes, consistent with the clients' investment objectives, time horizons and risk preferences. Tactical asset allocation is concerned with shifting wealth between asset classes to take advantage of expected price levels changes (timing) arising from broad movements in the business cycle. Fundamental analysis, macroeconomic analysis and asset allocation techniques are all explored in greater detail in other chapters.

Technical Analysis

Technical analysis is based on a number of basic assumptions:

1. Market value is determined solely by the interaction of demand and supply.
2. It is assumed that though there are minor fluctuations in the market, stock prices tend to move in trends that persist for long periods.
3. Reversals of trends are caused by shifts in demand and supply.
4. Shifts in demand and supply can be detected sooner or later in charts.
5. Many chart patterns tend to repeat themselves.

For our purposes, the most significant items to note are the assumptions that stock prices tend to move in trends that persist for long periods, and these trends can be detected in charts. The basic premise is that past trends in market movements can be used to forecast or understand the future. The market technician generally assumes there is a lag between the time he perceives a change in the value of a security and when the investing public ultimately assesses this change.

In developing the tools of technical analysis, we shall divide our discussion between (a) the use of charting and (b) the key indicator series to project future market movements.

THE USE OF CHARTING

Charting is often linked to the development of the Dow theory in the late 1890s by Charles Dow. He was the founder of the Dow Jones Company and editor of *The Wall Street Journal.* Many of his early precepts were further refined by other market technicians, and it is generally believed the Dow theory was successful in signaling the market crash of 1929.

FIGURE 6–2   Market Reversal and Confirmation

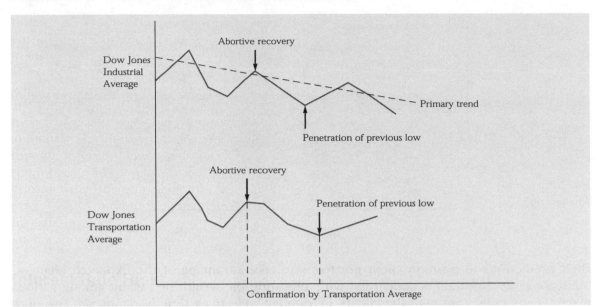

Essential Elements of the Dow Theory

The **Dow theory** maintains that there are three major movements in the market: daily fluctuations, secondary movements, and primary trends. According to the theory, daily fluctuations and secondary movements (covering two weeks to a month) are only important to the extent they reflect on the long-term primary trend in the market. Primary trends may be characterized as either bullish or bearish in nature.

In Figure 6-1, we look at the use of the Dow theory to analyze a market trend. Note that the primary movement in the market is positive despite two secondary movements that are downward. The important facet of the secondary movements is that each low is higher than the previous low and each high is higher than the previous high. This tends to confirm the primary trend, which is bullish.

Under the Dow theory, it is assumed that this pattern will continue for a long period, and the analyst should not be confused by secondary movements. However, the upward pattern must ultimately end. This is indicated by a new pattern in which a recovery fails to exceed the previous high (abortive recovery) and a new low penetrates a previous low as indicated in Figure 6-2. For a true turn in the market to occur, the new pattern of movement in the Dow Jones Industrial Average must also be confirmed by a subsequent movement in the Dow Jones Transportation Average as indicated on the bottom part of Figure 6-2.

A change from a bear to a bull market would require similar patterns of confirmation. While the Dow theory has proved helpful to market technicians, there is always the problem of false signals. For example, not every abortive recovery is certain to signal the end of a bull market. Furthermore, the investor may have to wait a long time to get full confirmation of a change in a primary trend. By the time the transportation average confirms the pattern in the industrial average, important market movements may have already occurred.

Support and Resistance Levels

Chartists attempt to define trading levels for individual securities (or the market) where there is a likelihood that price movements will be challenged. Thus, in the daily financial press or on television, the statement is often made that the next barrier to the current market move is at 11,000 (or some other level). This assumes the existence of support and

FIGURE 6–3   Support and Resistance

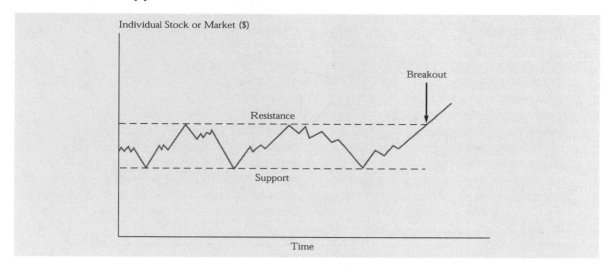

resistance levels. As indicated in Figure 6-3 a support level is associated with the lower end of a trading range and a resistance level with the upper end.

Support may develop each time a stock goes down to a lower level of trading because investors who previously passed up a purchase opportunity may now choose to act. It is a signal that new demand is coming into the market. When a stock reaches the high side of the normal trading range, **resistance** may develop because some investors who bought in on a previous wave of enthusiasm (on an earlier high) may now view this as a chance to get even. Others may simply see this as an opportunity to take a profit.

A breakout above a resistance point (as indicated in Figure 6-3) or below a support level is considered significant. The stock is assumed to be trading in a new range, and higher (lower) trading values may now be expected.

A good example of support and resistance levels can be found in the trading pattern of IBM in the 1990s. After trading in the $150 to $170 range in the early 1990s, the stock hit rock bottom in mid-1993 at $40 per share. Part of the decline was due to a loss in EPS in 1993 for the first time in decades. However, the stock did find support at $40 per share as investors began to purchase the stock in anticipation of a possible comeback. Lou Gerstner, Jr., a highly respected executive, had come on board as chairman and CEO. He immediately began eliminating redundant operations as well as implementing a strategic pattern for future growth. By 1996, the stock was in the 90s range and made a number of attempts to break through a resistance point of 100. After several tries, the stock finally crossed the 100 resistance barrier and then made an almost uninterrupted run up to $200 in mid-1997. The stock then split two for one. By March 2002 it was still in the post split $100 range. IBM will undoubtedly continue to face new support and resistance levels in the future.

Volume

The amount of volume supporting a given market movement is also considered significant. For example, if a stock (or the market in general) makes a new high on heavy trading volume, this is considered to be bullish. Conversely, a new high on light volume may indicate a temporary move that is likely to be reversed.

A new low on light volume is considered somewhat positive because of the lack of investor participation. When a new low is established on the basis of heavy trading volume, this is considered to be quite bearish.

In the early 2000s, the New York Stock Exchange averaged a volume of 900 million to 1 billion shares daily. When the volume jumped to 1.5 billion shares, analysts took a very strong interest in the trading pattern of the market.

FIGURE 6–4   Bar Chart

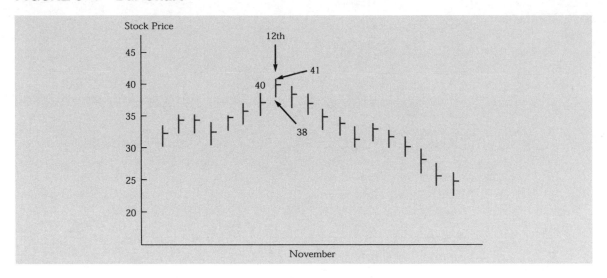

For an individual stock, the same principles also apply. In 2001, Intel normally traded 40 to 50 million shares daily. However, upward movements on volumes of 75 to 100 million shares or more were considered significant.

Types of Charts

Until now, we have been using typical line charts to indicate market patterns. Technicians also use bar charts and point and figure charts. We shall examine each.

Bar Chart   A bar chart shows the high and low price for a stock with a horizontal dash along the line to indicate the closing price. An example is shown in Figure 6-4.

We see on November 12 the stock traded between a high of 41 and a low of 38 and closed at 40. Daily information on the Dow Jones Industrial Average is usually presented in the form of a bar chart, with daily volume shown at the bottom as indicated in Figure 6-5.

Trendline, published through a division of Standard & Poor's, provides excellent charting information on a variety of securities traded on the major exchanges and is available at many libraries and brokerage houses. Market technicians carefully evaluate the charts, looking for what they perceive to be significant patterns of movement. For example, the pattern in Figure 6-4 might be interpreted as a head-and-shoulder pattern (note the head in the middle) with a lower penetration of the neckline to the right indicating a sell signal. In Figure 6-6 we show a series of the price-movement patterns presumably indicating market bottoms and tops.

Although it is beyond the scope of this book to go into interpretation of chart formations in great detail, special books on the subject are suggested at the end of our discussion of charting.

Point and Figure Chart   A point and figure chart (PFC) emphasizes significant price changes and the reversal of significant price changes. Unlike a line or bar chart, it has no time dimension. An example of a point and figure chart is presented in Figure 6-7.

The assumption is that the stock starts at 30. Only moves of two points or greater are plotted on the graph (some may prefer to use one point). Advances are indicated by Xs, and declines are shown by Os. A reversal from an advance to a decline or vice versa calls for a shift in columns. Thus, the stock initially goes from 30 to 42 and then shifts columns in its subsequent decline to 36 before moving up again in column 3. A similar pattern persists throughout the chart.

FIGURE 6–5   Bar Chart of Market Average

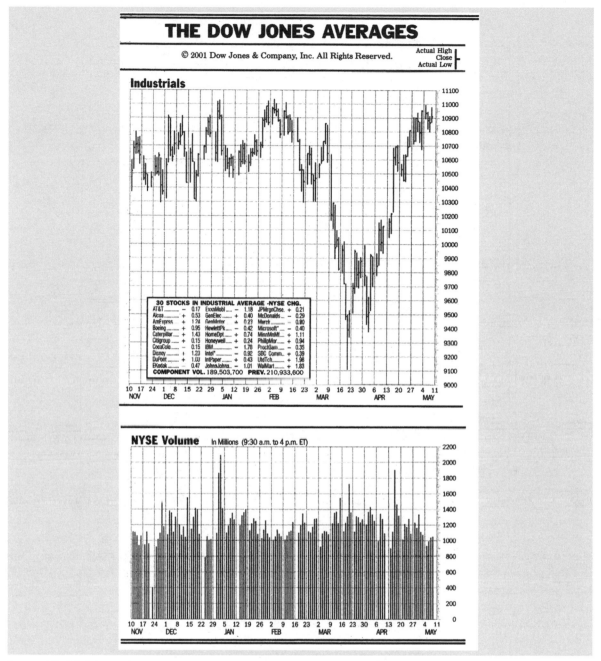

Source: *The Wall Street Journal*, May 11, 2001, p. C3. Reprinted by permission of *The Wall Street Journal*. © 2001 by Dow Jones & Company, Inc. All Rights Reserved Worldwide.

Chartists carefully read point and figure charts to observe market patterns (where there is support, resistance, breakouts, congestion, and so on). Students with a strong interest in charting may consult such books as Colby and Meyers, *The Encyclopedia of Technical Market Indicators*,[15] and DeMark, *The New Science of Technical Analysis*.[16] The problem in

---

15. Robert W. Colby and Thomas A. Meyers, T*he Encylopedia of Technical Market Indicators* (Homewood, IL: Business One Irwin, 1988).

16. Thomas R. DeMark, *The New Science of Technical Analysis* (New York: John Wiley & Sons, 1994).

FIGURE 6–6   Chart Representation of Market Bottoms and Tops

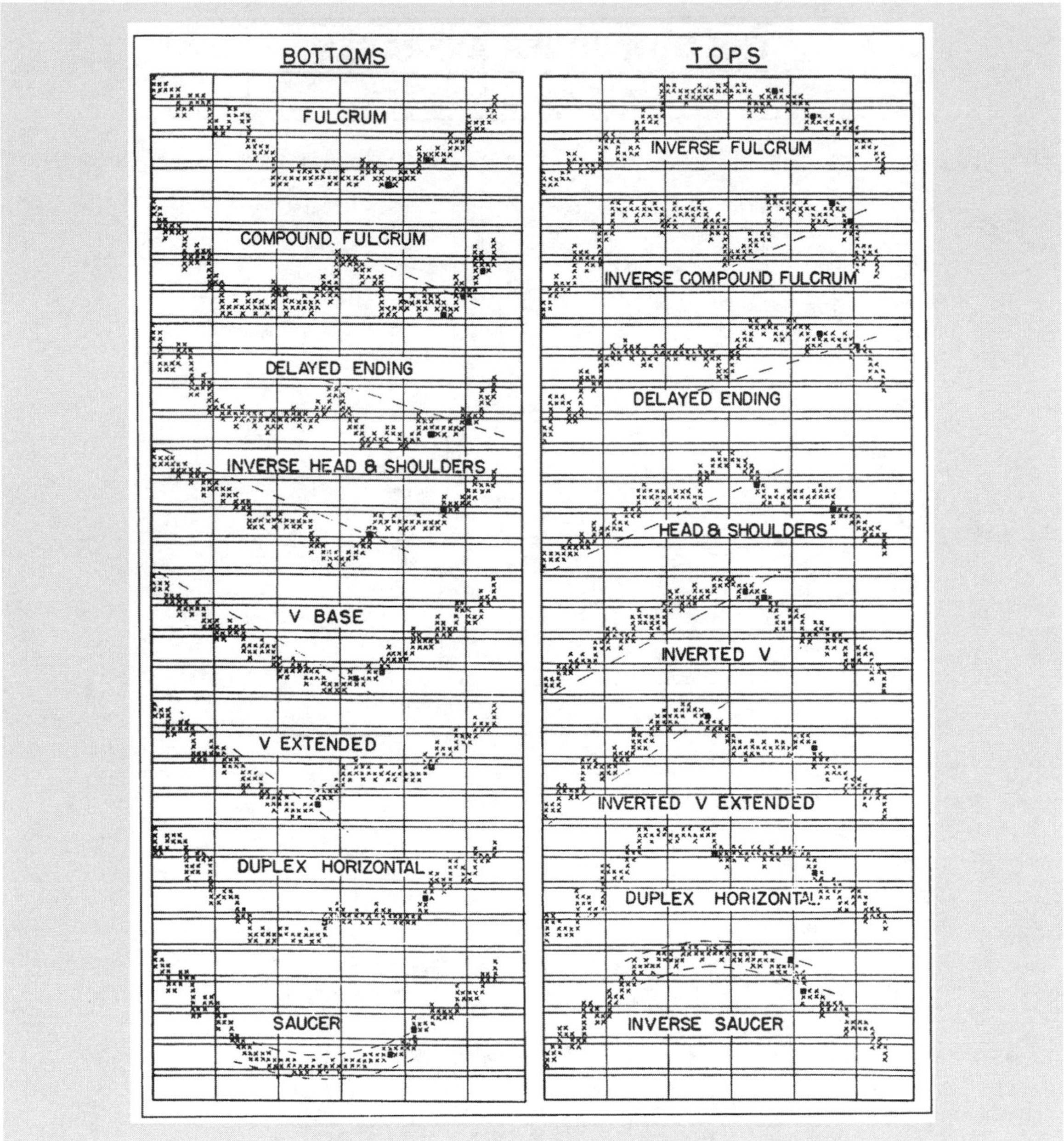

reading charts has always been to analyze patterns in such a fashion that they truly predict stock market movements before they unfold. To justify the effort, one must assume there are discernible trends over the long term.

KEY INDICATOR SERIES

In the television series "Wall Street Week," former host Louis Rukeyser traditionally watched a number of indicators on a weekly basis and compared the bullish and bearish indicators to determine what the next direction of the market might be.

In this section, we examine bullish and bearish technical indicator series. We first look at contrary opinion rules, then smart money rules, and finally, overall market indicators.

FIGURE 6–7   Point and Figure Chart

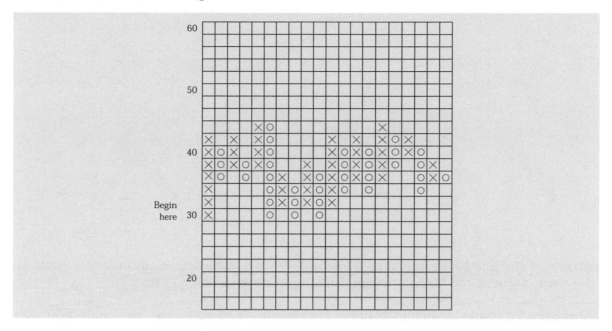

Contrary Opinion Rules

The essence of a **contrary opinion rule** is that it is easier to figure out who is wrong than who is right. If you know your neighbor has a terrible sense of direction and you spot him taking a left at the intersection, you automatically take a right. In the stock market there are similar guidelines.

Odd-Lot Theory   An odd-lot trade is one of less than 100 shares, and only small investors tend to engage in odd-lot transactions. The odd-lot theory suggests you watch very closely what the small investor is doing and then do the opposite. The weekly edition of *Barron's* breaks down odd-lot trading on a daily basis in its "Market Laboratory—Stocks" section. It is a simple matter to construct a ratio of odd-lot purchases to odd-lot sales. For example, on May 8, 2001, 7,034,000 odd-lot shares were purchased, and 8,604,300 shares were sold, indicating a ratio of 0.817. The ratio has historically fluctuated between 0.50 and 1.45.

The odd-lot theory actually suggests that the small trader does all right most of the time but badly misses on key market turns. As indicated in Figure 6–8, the odd-lot trader is on the correct path as the market is going up; that is, selling off part of the portfolio in an up market (the name of the game is to buy low and sell high). This net selling posture is reflected by a declining odd-lot index (purchase-to-sales ratio). However, as the market continues upward, the odd-lot trader suddenly thinks he or she sees an opportunity for a killing in the market and becomes a very strong net buyer. This precedes a fall in the market.

The odd-lot trader is also assumed to be a strong seller right before the bottom of a bear market. Presumably, when the small trader finally gets grandfather's 50 shares of AT&T out of the lockbox and sells them in disgust, it is time for the market to turn upward.

As if to add injury to insult, a corollary to the odd-lot theory says one should be particularly sensitive to what odd-lot traders do on Monday because odd-lotters tend to visit each other over the weekend, confirm each other's opinions or exchange hot tips, and then call their brokers on Monday morning. The assumption is that their chatter over the barbecue pit or in the bowling alley is even more suspect than their own individual opinions.

While the odd-lot theory appeared to have some validity in the 1950s and 1960s, it was not a particularly valuable tool in the last three decades. For one thing, the odd-lotters outguessed many of the professional money managers in selling off before the stock market

FIGURE 6–8   Comparing Standard & Poor's 500 Index and the Odd-Lot Index

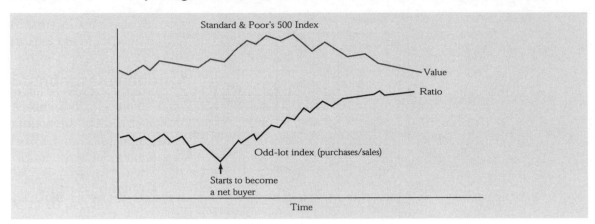

debacle of the mid-1970s and late 1980s, and they began buying in advance of a recovery. The same is true in the 500 plus point market decline of October 1997.

Short Sales Position   A second contrary opinion rule is based on the volume of short sales in the market. As you recall, a short sale represents the selling of a security you do not own with the anticipation of purchasing the security in the future to cover your short position. Investors would only engage in a short sale transaction if they believed the security would, in fact, be going down in price in the near future so they could buy back the security at a lower price to cover the short sale. When the aggregate number of short sellers is large (that is, they are bearish), this is thought to be a bullish signal.

The contrary opinion stems from two sources: first, short sellers are sometimes emotional and may overreact to the market; second and more important, there now is a built-in demand for stocks that have been sold short by investors who will have to repurchase the shares to cover their short positions.

Daily short sale totals for the New York Stock Exchange are recorded in *The Wall Street Journal*. Also once a month (around the 20th), *The Wall Street Journal* reports on total short sale figures for the two major exchanges as well as securities traded on those exchanges (based on midmonth data). This feature usually contains comments about current trends in the market.

Technical analysts compute a ratio of the total short sales positions on an exchange to average daily exchange volume for the month. The normal ratio is between 2.0 and 3.0. A ratio of 2.5 indicates that the current short sales position is equal to two and a half times the day's average trading volume.

As the short sales ratio (frequently called the short interest ratio) approaches the higher end of the normal trading range, this would be considered bullish (remember this is a contrary opinion trading rule). As is true with many other technical trading rules, its use in predicting future performance has produced mixed results.[17]

Applied to individual stocks, the same type of principles apply. If traders are aggressively short-telling MMM, CISCO systems, or Novell, it may be time to buy.

Investment Advisory Recommendations   A further contrary opinion rule states that you should watch the predictions of the investment advisory services and do the opposite. This has been formalized by Investors Intelligence (an investment advisory service itself) into the Index of Bearish Sentiment. When 60 percent or more of the advisory services are bearish,

---

17. Joseph Vu and Paul Caster, "Why All the Interest in Short Interest?" *Financial Analysts Journal*, July–August 1987, pp. 77–79.

FIGURE 6–9   Investor Sentiment Readings

<table>
<tr><th colspan="4">INVESTOR SENTIMENT READINGS</th></tr>
<tr><td colspan="4">In Investors Intelligence's poll, the correction figure represents advisers who are basically bullish, but are looking for some sort of short-term weakness. High bullish readings in that poll, in Consensus Inc., or in Market Vane's usually are signs of market tops; low ones, market bottoms.</td></tr>
<tr><td></td><th>Last Week</th><th>2 Weeks Ago</th><th>3 Weeks Ago</th></tr>
<tr><td colspan="4">Investors Intelligence</td></tr>
<tr><td>Bulls</td><td>47.9%</td><td>45.7%</td><td>43.9%</td></tr>
<tr><td>Bears</td><td>37.2</td><td>40.2</td><td>41.8</td></tr>
<tr><td>Correction</td><td>14.9</td><td>14.1</td><td>14.3</td></tr>
<tr><td colspan="4">Source: Investors Intelligence, 30 Church Street, New Rochelle, N.Y. 10801 (914) 632-0422.</td></tr>
<tr><td colspan="4">Consensus Index</td></tr>
<tr><td>Bullish Opinion</td><td>55%</td><td>52%</td><td>47%</td></tr>
<tr><td colspan="4">Source: Consensus Inc., P.O. Box 411128, Kansas City, Mo. 64141 (800) 383-1441.</td></tr>
<tr><td colspan="4">AAII Index</td></tr>
<tr><td>Bullish</td><td>53.3%</td><td>63.5%</td><td>46.6%</td></tr>
<tr><td>Bearish</td><td>17.8</td><td>21.6</td><td>31.0</td></tr>
<tr><td>Neutral</td><td>28.9</td><td>14.9</td><td>22.4</td></tr>
<tr><td colspan="4">Source: American Association of Individual Investors, 625 N. Michigan Ave., Chicago, Ill. 60611 (312) 280-0170.</td></tr>
<tr><td colspan="4">Market Vane</td></tr>
<tr><td>Bullish Consensus</td><td>38%</td><td>38%</td><td>32%</td></tr>
<tr><td colspan="4">Source: Market Vane, P.O. Box 90490, Pasadena, CA 91109 (626) 395-7436.</td></tr>
</table>

Source: *Barron's*, May 14, 2001, p. MW73. Reprinted by permission of *Barron's*. © 2001 by Dow Jones & Company. All Rights Reserved Worldwide.

you should expect a market upturn. Conversely, when only 15 percent or fewer are bearish, you should expect a decline.[18]

Figure 6-9 gives a summary of bullish and bearish sentiments as published in the "Market Laboratory—Economic Indicators" section of *Barron's*. Investors Intelligence as well as three other sources of sentiments are presented. Let's concentrate our attention on Investors Intelligence. Since the percentage of bears was declining in the "last week" to 37.2 percent "two weeks ago," this indicates a possible sell under contrary opinion rules.

Lest one take investment advisory services too lightly, however, observe the market impact of a recommendation by Joseph Granville, publisher of the *Granville Market Letter*. On Tuesday, January 6, 1981, Granville issued a late-evening warning to his subscribers to "sell everything." He helped cause a $40 billion decline in market values the next day. Although subsequent events proved Granville wrong in his prediction of an impending bear market, the fact that one man could trigger such a reaction is an indication of the number of people who are influenced by the suggestions of advisory services. Granville has been followed by many other so-called gurus in the 1980s and 1990s, most of whom have their day in the sun and then eventually fall into disrepute as they fail to call a major turn in the market or begin reversing their positions so often that investors lose confidence.

Put-Call Ratio   A final contrary opinion rule applies to the put-call ratio. Puts and calls represent options to sell or buy stock over a specified time period at a given price. A put is an option to sell, and a call is an option to buy. Options have become very popular since they

---

18. John R. Dortman, "The Stock Market Sign Often Points the Wrong Way," *The Wall Street Journal*, January 26, 1989, p. C1.

began trading actively on organized exchanges in 1973. As you will discover, there are many sophisticated uses for options to implement portfolio strategies (particularly to protect against losses). However, there is also a great deal of speculation by individual investors in the options market. Because some of this speculation is ill conceived, ratios based on options may tell you to do the opposite of what option traders are doing.

The ratio of put (sell) options to call (buy) options is normally about 0.60. There are generally fewer traders of put options than call options. However, when the ratio gets up to 0.65 to 0.70 or higher, this indicates increasing pessimism by option traders. Under a contrary opinion rule, this indicates a buy signal (he turned left so you turn right). If the put-call ratio goes down to 0.40, the decreasing pessimism (increasing optimism) of the option trader may indicate that it is time to sell if you are a contrarian. The put-call ratio has a better than average record for calling market turns. Put-call ratio data can be found in the "Market Week—Options" section of *Barron's*.

Smart Money Rules

Market technicians have long attempted to track the pattern of sophisticated traders in the hope that they might provide unusual insight into the future. We briefly observe theories related to bond market traders and stock exchange specialists.

***Barron's* Confidence Index**   The ***Barron's* Confidence Index** is used to observe the trading pattern of investors in the bond market. The theory is based on the premise that bond traders are more sophisticated than stock traders and pick up trends more quickly. The theory suggests that a person who can figure out what bond traders are doing today may be able to determine what stock market investors will be doing in the near future.

Barron's Confidence Index is actually computed by taking the yield on 10 top-grade corporate bonds, dividing by the yield on 40 intermediate-grade bonds,[19] and multiplying by 100:

$$\textit{Barron's } \text{Confidence Index} = \frac{\text{Yield on 10 top-grade corporate bonds}}{\text{Yield on 40 intermediate-grade bonds}} \times 100 \qquad (6-1)$$

The index is published weekly in the "Market Laboratory—Bonds" section of *Barron's*. What does it actually tell us? First, we can assume that the top-grade bonds in the numerator always have a smaller yield than the intermediate-grade bonds in the denominator. The reason is that the higher quality issues can satisfy investors with smaller returns. The bond market is very representative of a risk-return trade-off environment in which less risk requires less return and higher risk necessitates a higher return.

With top-grade bonds providing smaller yields than intermediate-grade bonds, the Confidence Index is always less than 100 (percent). The normal trading range is between 80 and 96, and it is within this range that technicians look for signals on the economy. If bond investors are bullish about future economic prosperity, they are rather indifferent between holding top-grade bonds and holding intermediate-grade bonds, and the yield differences between these two categories is relatively small. This would indicate the Confidence Index may be close to 96. An example is presented below in which top-grade bonds are providing 8.4 percent and intermediate-grade bonds are yielding 9.1 percent:

$$\textit{Barron's } \text{Confidence Index} = \frac{\text{Yield on 10 top-grade corporate bonds}}{\text{Yield on 40 intermediate-grade bonds}} \times 100$$

$$= \frac{8.4\%}{9.1\%} \times 100 = 92(\%)$$

---

19. The 40 bonds compose the Dow Jones 40 bond averages.

Now let us assume that investors become quite concerned about the outlook for the future health of the economy. If events go poorly, some weaker corporations may not be able to make their interest payments, and thus, bond market investors will have a strong preference for top-quality issues. Some investors continue to invest in intermediate- or lower-quality issues but only at a sufficiently high yield differential to justify the risk. We might assume that the *Barron's* Confidence Index will drop to 83 because of the increasing spread between the two yields in the formula:

$$Barron's \text{ Confidence Index} = \frac{\text{Yield on 10 top-grade corporate bonds}}{\text{Yield on 40 intermediate-grade bonds}} \times 100$$

$$= \frac{8.9\%}{10.7\%} \times 100 = 83(\%)$$

The yield on the intermediate-grade bonds is now 1.8 percentage points higher than that on the 10 top-grade bonds, and this is reflected in the lower Confidence Index reading. As confidence in the economy is once again regained, the yield spread differential narrows, and the Confidence Index goes up.

Market technicians assume there are a few months of lead time between what happens to the Confidence Index and what happens to the economy and stock market. As is true with other such indicators, it has a mixed record of predicting future events. One problem is that the Confidence Index is only assumed to consider the impact of investors' attitudes on yields (their demand pattern). We have seen in the 1980s and 1990s that the supply of new bond issues can also influence yields. Thus, a very large bond issue by General Electric or ExxonMobil may drive up high-grade bond yields even though investor attitudes indicate they should be going down.

Short Sales by Specialists   Another smart money index is based on the short sales positions of specialists. Recall that specialists make markets in various securities listed on the organized exchanges. Because of the uniquely close position of specialists to the action on Wall Street, market technicians ascribe unusual importance to their decisions. One measure of their activity that is frequently monitored is the ratio of specialists' short sales to the total amount of short sales on an exchange.

When we previously mentioned short sales in this chapter, we suggested that a high incidence of short selling might be considered bullish because short sellers often overreact to the market and provide future demand potential to cover their short position. In the case of market specialists, this is not necessarily true. These sophisticated traders keep a book of limit and stop orders on their securities so that they have a close feel for market activity at any given time, and their decisions are considered important.

The normal ratio of specialist short sales to short sales on an exchange is about 45 percent. When the ratio goes up to 50 percent or more, market technicians interpret this as a bearish signal. A ratio under 40 percent is considered bullish.

Overall Market Rules

Our discussion of key indicator series has centered on both contrary opinion rules and smart money rules. We now briefly examine two overall market indicators: the breadth of the market indicator series and the cash position of mutual funds.

Breadth of the Market   A breadth of the market indicator attempts to measure what a broad range of securities is doing as opposed to merely examining a market average. The theory is that market averages, such as the Dow Jones Industrial Average of 30 stocks or

TABLE 6–1   Comparing Advance-Decline Data and the Dow Jones Industrial Average (DJIA)

Day	(1) Advances	(2) Declines	(3) Unchanged	(4) Net Advances or Declines	(5) Cumulative Advances or Declines	(6) DJIA
1	1607	1507	201	+100	+100	+33.38
2	1550	1560	188	−10	+90	+20.51
3	1504	1602	194	−98	−8	+13.08
4	1499	1506	295	−7	−15	+35.21
5	1530	1573	208	−43	−58	−12.02
6	1550	1562	186	−12	−70	+50.43
7	1455	1650	200	−155	−225	+30.10
8	1285	1815	212	−530	−755	+21.30

the Standard & Poor's 500 Stock Average, are weighted toward large firms and may not be representative of the entire market. To get a broader perspective of the market, an analyst may examine all stocks on an exchange.

The technician often compares the advances-declines with the movement of a popular market average to determine if there is a divergence between the two. Advances and declines usually move in concert with the popular market averages but may move in the opposite direction at a market peak or bottom. One of the possible signals for the end of a bull market is when the Dow Jones Industrial Average is moving up but the number of daily declines consistently exceeds the number of daily advances on the New York Stock Exchange. This indicates that conservative investors are investing in blue-chip stocks but that there is a lack of broad-based confidence in the market. In Table 6-1, we look at an example of divergence between the advance-decline indicators on the New York Stock Exchange and the Dow Jones Industrial Average (DJIA).

In Column 4, we see the daily differences in advances and declines. In Column 5, we look at the cumulative pattern by adding or subtracting each new day's value from the previous total. We then compare the information in Column 4 and Column 5 to the Dow Jones Industrial Average (DJIA) in Column 6. Clearly, the strength in the Dow Jones Industrial Average is not reflected in the advance-decline data, and this may be interpreted as signaling future weakness in the market.

Breadth of the market data can also be used to analyze upturns in the market. When the Dow Jones Industrial Average is going down but advances consistently lead declines, the market may be positioned for a recovery. Some market technicians develop sophisticated weighted averages of the daily advances-declines to go along with the data in Table 6-1. Daily data on the Dow Jones Industrial Average and advancing and declining issues can be found in the "Stock Market Data Bank" section of *The Wall Street Journal*.

While a comparison of advance-decline data to market averages can provide important insights, there is also the danger of false signals. Not every divergence between the two signals a turn in the market, so analysts must be careful in their interpretation. The technical analyst must look at a wide range of variables. With the advent of decimalization of stock prices in 2001, many technicians think this indicator has lost some of its usefulness because now stocks only have to advance or decline a penny to make the list.

Mutual Fund Cash Position   Another overall market indicator is the cash position of mutual funds. This measure indicates the buying potential of mutual funds and is generally representative of the purchasing potential of other large institutional investors. The cash position of mutual funds, as a percentage of their total assets, generally varies between 5 and 20 percent [20]

At the lower end of the boundary, it would appear that mutual funds are fully invested and can provide little in the way of additional purchasing power. As their cash position goes to 15 percent or higher, market technicians assess this as representing significant purchasing power that may help to trigger a market upturn. While the overall premise is valid, there are problems in identifying just what is a significant cash position for mutual funds in a given market cycle. It may change in extreme market environments.

Summary

This chapter provides a comprehensive overview of the concept of the Efficient Market Hypothesis and all the issues that surround this contemporaneous and contentious issue. EMH is an important concept from the viewpoint of a rational resource allocation system. While proponents of the hypothesis forward evidence in support, sufficient evidence exists to cast doubts on the efficacy of the market. The theoretical assumption and the implications of irrational investment behavior are also examined within the context. The emerging role of behavioral finance is also briefly discussed.

---

20. The cash dollars are usually placed in short-term credit instruments as opposed to stocks and bonds.

Chapter 7

Modern Portfolio Theory

Various financial needs lead individuals to seek and make investment decisions. These investments are tempered both by the time horizon for the fulfillment of the objective and the investor's own sense or profile on risk assumption. The method of construction of investment portfolios that consider the individual investor's traits and finds a subjectively defined optimal solution is known as modern portfolio theory. This chapter begins by examining this method by which investor portfolios are constructed. Following the theoretical structure, the assessment of portfolio performances, by various techniques, are examined. The role of indexing in a buy-and-hold strategy is then considered. All these issues lead to an understanding of how money managers may be selected and the pitfalls in the selection choice.

MODERN PORTFOLIO THEORY

If we were to believe in the efficient market hypothesis then we would consider the activity to pick winners from individual stocks as not being very fruitful. The question then arises whether it is possible to earn high and superior returns from investing in the stock market. *Modern Portfolio Theory* (MPT) provides us with a basis in which an investor can realize returns on investment required to achieve investment objectives. Since investor objectives are different for each investor, the structure of each investor's portfolio should also differ. MPT is the methodology by which each investor's objectives and risk preferences are matched with sets of suitable investment opportunities. In doing so, MPT utilizes the interrelationships between different securities as well as the expected return and volatility of each of the individual securities. Recall our discussions in previous chapters on expected returns, standard deviations and correlation between security returns and the methods by which these statistical measures are calculated. In the following section we will discuss how MPT combines the statistical properties of securities with the subjective risk tolerance and investment objectives of an investor to arrive at a cohesive portfolio structure.

PORTFOLIO EFFECT

An investor who is holding only investment i may wish to consider bringing investment j into the portfolio. If the stocks are weighted evenly, the new portfolio's expected value will be 10 percent. We define K_p as the expected value of the portfolio:

$$K_p = X_i \bar{K}_i + X_j \bar{K}_j \tag{7-1}$$

The X values represent the weights assigned by the investor to each component in the portfolio and are 50 percent for both investments in this example. The $\bar{K}_i$ and $\bar{K}_j$ values were previously determined to be 10 percent. Thus we have

$$K_p = 0.5(10\%) + 0.5(10\%) = 5\% + 5\% = 10\%$$

What about the standard deviation for the combined portfolio (σ_p)? If a weighted average were taken of the two investments, the new standard deviation would be 4.5 percent:

$$X_i \sigma_i = X_j \sigma_j$$

$$0.5(3.9\%) + 0.5(5.1\%) = 1.95\% + 2.55\% = 4.5\%$$

The interesting element is that the investor in investment i would appear to be losing from the combined investment. His expected value remains at 10 percent, but his standard deviation has increased from 3.9 to 4.5 percent. Given that he is risk-averse, he appears to be getting more risk rather than less risk by expanding his portfolio.

There is one fallacy in the analysis. *The standard deviation of a portfolio is not based on the simple weighted average of the individual standard deviations (as the expected value is)*. Rather, it considers significant interaction between the investments. If one investment does well during a given economic condition while the other does poorly and vice versa, there may be significant risk reduction from combining the two, and the standard deviation for the portfolio may be less than the standard deviation for either investment (this is the reason we do not simply take the weighted average of the two).

Note in Figure 7-1 the risk-reduction potential from combining the two investments under study. Investment i alone may produce outcomes anywhere from 5 to 15 percent, and investment j, from 6 to 20 percent. By combining the two, we narrow the range for investment (i, j) to from 7.5 to 12.5 percent. Thus, we have reduced the risk while keeping the expected value constant at 10 percent. We now examine the appropriate standard deviation formula for the two investments.

Standard Deviation for a Two-Asset Portfolio

The standard deviation for a two-asset portfolio is presented in Formula 7-2[1]:

$$\sigma_p = \sqrt{X_i^2 \sigma_i^2 + X_j^2 \sigma_j^2 + 2X_i X_j r_{ij}\, \sigma_i\, \sigma_j} \tag{7-2}$$

The only new term in the expression is r_{ij}, the **correlation coefficient** or measurement of joint movement between the two variables. The value for r_{ij} can be from -1 to $+1$, although for most variables, the correlation coefficient falls somewhere in between these two values. Figure 7-2 demonstrates the concept of correlation. In Panel A, assets i and j are perfectly correlated, with r_{ij} equal to $+1$. As i increases in value, so does j in exact proportion to i. In Panel B, assets i and j exhibit a perfect negative correlation, with r_{ij} equal to -1. As i increases, j decreases in exact proportion to i. Panel C demonstrates assets i and j having no correlation at all, with r_{ij} equal to 0.

The correlation coefficient (r_{ij}) between our investment i and investment j is -0.70. This indicates the two investments show a high degree of negative correlation. Plugging this value into Formula 7-3, along with other previously determined values, the standard deviation (σ_p) for the two-asset portfolio can be computed:

$$\sigma_p = \sqrt{X_i^2 \sigma_i^2 + X_j^2 \sigma_j^2 + 2X_i X_j r_{ij}\sigma_i\sigma_j} \tag{7-3}$$

---

1. For a multiple asset portfolio, the expression is written as:

$$\sigma_p = \sqrt{\sum_{i=1}^{N} X_i^2 \sigma_i^2 + 2\sum_{i=1}^{N-1} \sum_{j=i+1}^{N} X_i X_j r_{ij}\sigma_i\sigma_j}$$

N is the number of securities in the portfolio.

FIGURE 7–1   Investment Outcomes under Different Conditions

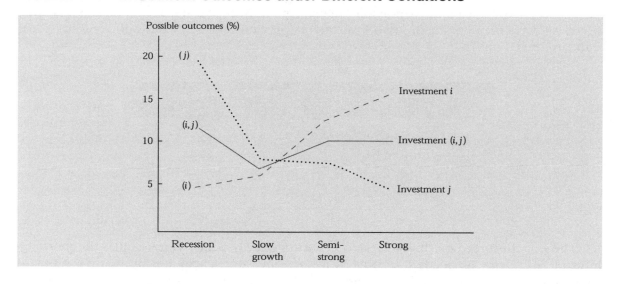

FIGURE 7–2   Correlation Analysis

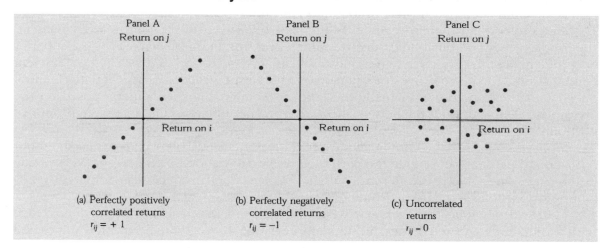

where:

$$X_i = 0.5, \sigma_i = 3.9$$
$$X_j = 0.5, \sigma_j = 5.1$$
$$r_{ij} = -0.70$$
$$\sigma_p = \sqrt{(0.5)^2(3.9)^2 + (0.5)^2(5.1)^2 + 2(0.5)(0.5)(-0.7)(3.9)(5.1)}$$
$$= \sqrt{(0.25)(15.4) + (0.25)(25.6) + 2(0.35)(-0.7)(19.9)}$$
$$= \sqrt{3.85 + 6.4 + (0.5)(-13.93)}$$
$$= \sqrt{3.85 + 6.4 - 6.97}$$
$$= \sqrt{3.28} = 1.8\%$$

The standard deviation of the portfolio of 1.8 percent is less than the standard deviation of either investment i (3.9 percent) or j (5.1 percent). Any time two investments have a correlation coefficient (r_{ij}) less than + 1 (perfect positive correlation), some risk reduction will be possible by combining the assets in a portfolio. In the real world, most items are positively correlated; the extent that we can still get risk reduction from positively correlated items gives extra meaning to portfolio management. Note the impact of various assumed correlation coefficients for the two investments previously described in terms of individual standard deviations:

Correlation Coefficient (r_{ij})	Portfolio Standard Deviation (σ_p)
+1.0	4.5
+0.5	3.9
0.0	3.2
−0.5	2.3
−0.7	1.8
−1.0	0.0

The conclusion to be drawn from our portfolio analysis discussion is that the most significant risk factor associated with an individual investment may not be its own standard deviation but how it affects the standard deviation of a portfolio through correlation. As we shall later observe in this chapter, there is not considered to be a risk premium for the total risk or standard deviation of an individual security, but only for that risk component that cannot be eliminated by various portfolio diversification techniques.

Modern portfolio theory begins by combinations of securities, or portfolios, which are superior to other combinations either from better returns and/or lower risk. These superior or "efficient" combinations are then plotted to determine a "frontier" of all such efficient combinations. Next, each investor's personal risk-return considerations or "utility" is introduced into the construction. Finally, the efficient combinations are superimposed on the investor's desired utilities, or benefits, to arrive at one efficient combination, an "optimal portfolio" for the stated investor.

We have seen how the combination of two investments has allowed us to maintain our return of 10 percent but reduce the portfolio standard deviation to 1.8 percent. We also saw in the preceding table that different coefficient correlations produce many different possibilities for portfolio standard deviations.

A shrewd portfolio manager may wish to consider a large number of portfolios, each with a different expected value and standard deviation, based on the expected values and standard deviations of the individual securities and, more importantly, on the correlations between the individual securities. Though we have been discussing a two-asset portfolio case, our example may be expanded to cover 5-, 10-, or even 100-asset portfolios.[2] The major tenets of portfolio theory that we are currently examining were developed by Professor Harry Markowitz in the 1950s, and so we refer to them as Markowitz portfolio theory. In 1990 Markowitz won the Nobel Prize in economics for this work.

Assume we have identified the following risk-return possibilities for eight different portfolios (there may also be many more, but we will restrict ourselves to this set for now).

In diagramming our various risk-return points in the table on page 121, we show the values in Figure 7–3.

Although we have only diagrammed eight possibilities, we see an efficient set of portfolios would lie along the ACFH line in Figure 7–3. This line is efficient because the portfolios on this line dominate all other attainable portfolios. This line is called the **efficient frontier** because the portfolios on the efficient frontier provide the best risk return trade-off.

---

2. The incremental benefit from reduction of the portfolio standard deviation through adding securities appears to diminish fairly sharply with a portfolio of 10 securities and is quite small with a portfolio as large as 20. A portfolio of 12 to 14 securities is generally thought to be of sufficient size to enjoy the majority of desirable portfolio effects. See W. H. Wagner and S. C. Lau, "The Effect of Diversification on Risk."

Portfolio	K_p	σ_p
A	10%	1.8%
B	10	2.1
C	12	3.0
D	13	4.2
E	13	5.0
F	14	5.0
G	14	5.8
H	15	7.2

FIGURE 7–3   Diagram of Risk-Return Trade-Offs

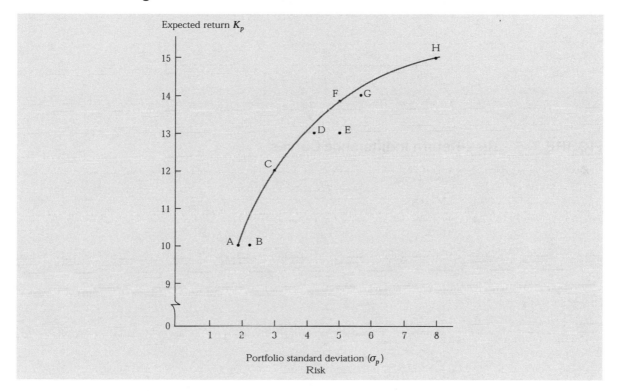

That is, along this efficient frontier we can receive a maximum return for a given level of risk or a minimum risk for a given level of return. Portfolios do not exist above the efficient frontier, and portfolios below this line do not offer acceptable alternatives to points along the line. As an example of *maximum return* for a given level of risk, consider point F. Along the efficient frontier, we are receiving a 14 percent return for a 5 percent risk level, whereas directly below point F, portfolio E provides a 13 percent return for the same 5 percent standard deviation.

To also demonstrate that we are getting *minimum risk* for a given return level, we can examine point A in which we receive a 10 percent return for a 1.8 percent risk level, whereas to the right of point A, we get the same 10 percent return from B, but a less desirable 2.1 percent risk level. One portfolio can consist of various proportions of two assets or two portfolios. For example, we can connect the points between A and C by generating portfolios that combine different percentages of portfolio A and portfolio C and so on between portfolios C and F and portfolios F and H. Although we have shown but eight points (portfolios), a fully developed efficient frontier may be based on a virtually unlimited number of observations as is presented in Figure 7–3.

In Figure 7–4, we once again view the efficient frontier in relationship to the feasible set and note that certain risk-return possibilities are not attainable (and should be disregarded).

FIGURE 7–4   Expanded View of Efficient Frontier

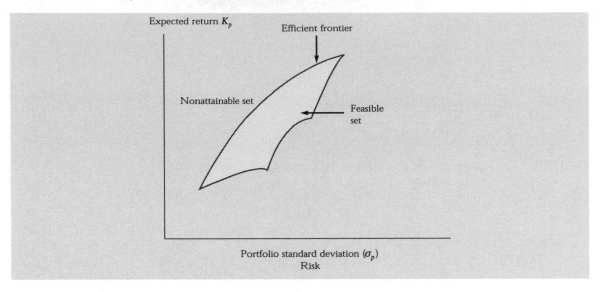

FIGURE 7–5   Risk-Return Indifference Curves

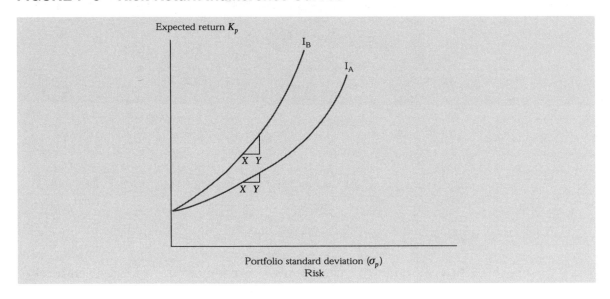

At this point in the analysis, we can stipulate that the various points along the efficient frontier are all considered potentially optimal and a given investor must choose the most appropriate single point based on individual risk-return trade-off desires. We would say that a low-risk-oriented investor might prefer point A in Figure 7–3, whereas a more-risk-oriented investor would prefer point F or H. At each of these points, the investor is getting the best risk-return trade-off for his or her own particular risk-taking propensity.

Risk-Return Indifference Curves

To actually pair an investor with an appropriate point along the efficient frontier, we look at his or her indifference curve as illustrated in Figure 7–5. The **indifference curves** show the investor's trade-off between risk and return. The steeper the slope of the curve, the more risk-averse the investor is. For example, in the case of Investor B (I_B in Figure 7–5), the

FIGURE 7–6   Indifference Curves for Investor A

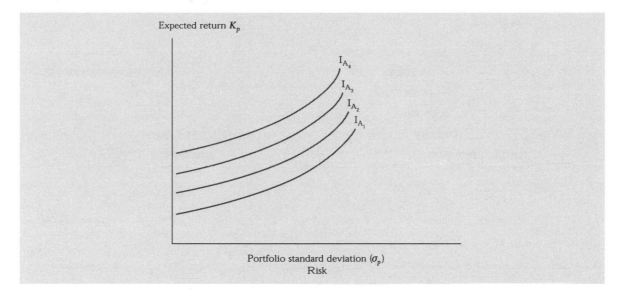

FIGURE 7–7   Combining the Efficient Frontier and Indifference Curves

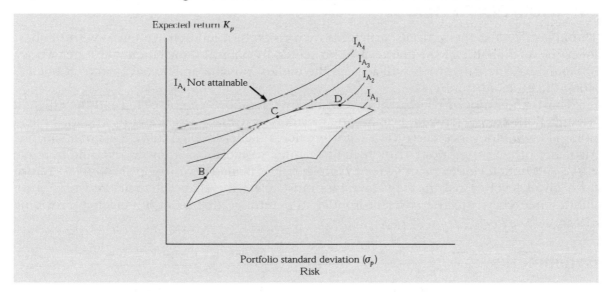

indifference curve has a steeper slope than for Investor A (I_A). This means Investor B will require more incremental return (more of a risk premium) for each additional unit of risk. Note that to take risks, Investor B requires approximately twice as much incremental return as Investor A between points X and Y. However, Investor A is still somewhat risk-averse and perhaps represents a typical investor in the capital markets. Once the shape of an investor's indifference curve is determined, a second objective can be established—to attain the highest curve possible. For example, Investor A, initially shown in Figure 7–5, would have a whole set of similarly shaped indifference curves as presented in Figure 7–6.

While he is indifferent to any point along a given curve (such as I_{A_4}), he is not indifferent to achieving the highest curve possible (I_{A_4} is clearly superior to I_{A_1}). I_{A_4} provides more return at all given risk levels. The only limitation to achieving the highest possible indifference curve is the feasible set of investments available.

FIGURE 7–8   Risk and Fund Objectives for 123 Mutual Funds

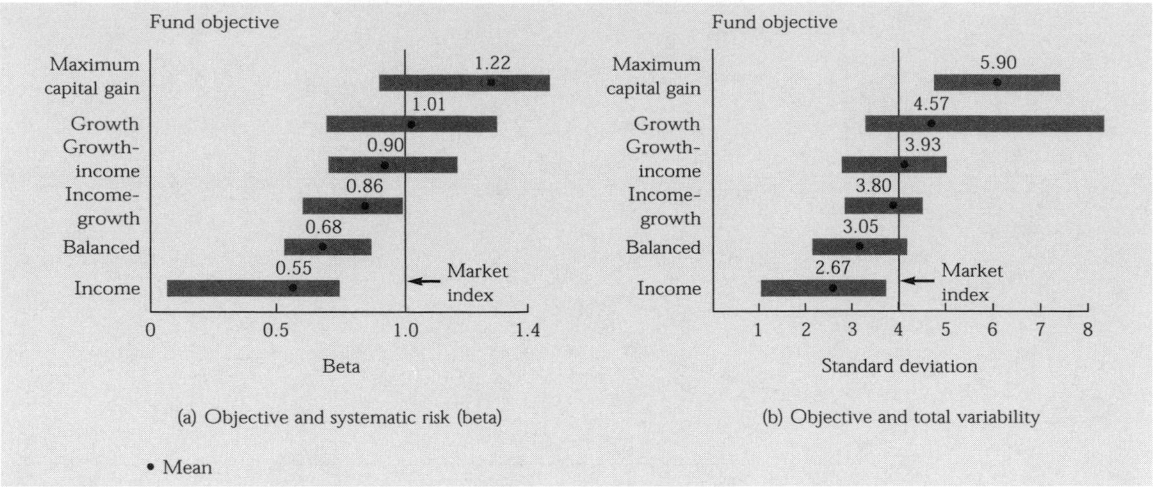

Source: John G. McDonald, "Objectives and Performance of Mutual Funds, 1960–1969," *Journal of Financial and Quantitative Analysis*, June 1974, p. 316.

OPTIMUM PORTFOLIO

The investor must theoretically match his own risk-return indifference curve with the best investments available in the market as represented by points on the efficient frontier. We see in Figure 7–7 that Investor A will achieve the highest possible indifference curve at point C along the efficient frontier.

This is the point of tangency between his own indifference curve (I_{A_3}) and the efficient frontier. Both curves have the same slope or risk-return characteristics at this point. While a point along indifference curve (I_{A_4}) might provide a higher level of utility, it is not attainable. Also, any other point along the efficient frontier would cross a lower level indifference curve and be inferior to point C. For example, points B and D cross I_{A_2}, providing less return for a given level of risk than I_{A_3}. Investors must relate the shape of their *own* risk-return indifference curves to the efficient frontier to determine that point of tangency providing maximum benefits.

Benchmarks

A first question to be posed to a professional money manager is: Have you followed the basic objectives that were established? These objectives might call for maximum capital gains, a combination of growth plus income, or simply income (with many variations in between). The objectives should be set with an eye toward the capabilities of the money managers and the financial needs of the investors. The best way to measure adherence to these objectives is to evaluate the risk exposure the fund manager has accepted. Anyone who aspires to maximize capital gains must, by nature, absorb more risk. An income-oriented fund should have a minimum risk exposure.

A classic study by John McDonald published in the *Journal of Financial and Quantitative Analysis* indicates that mutual fund managers generally follow the objectives they initially set. As indicated in Figure 7–8 he measured the betas and standard deviations for 123 mutual funds and compared these with the funds' stated objectives. In Panel a, we see the fund's beta dimension along the horizontal axis and the fund's stated objective along the vertical axis. Inside the panel, we see the association between the two. For example, funds with an objective of maximum capital gains had an average beta of 1.22. Those with a growth objective had an average beta of 1.01, and so on all the way down to an average beta of 0.55 for income-oriented funds. In Panel b of Figure 7–8, a similar approach was used to compare the fund's objective with the portfolio standard deviation.

In both cases of using betas and portfolio standard deviations, we see that the risk absorption was carefully tailored to the fund's stated objectives. Funds with aggressive capital gains and growth objectives had high betas and portfolio standard deviations, while the opposite was true of balanced and income-oriented funds. Other studies have continually reaffirmed the position established in this seminal study by McDonald.

Adherence to objectives as measured by risk exposure is important in evaluating a fund manager because risk is one of the variables a money manager can directly control. While short-run return performance can be greatly influenced by unpredictable changes in the economy, the fund manager has almost total control in setting the risk level. He can be held accountable for doing what was specified or promised in regard to risk. Most lawsuits brought against money managers are not for inferior profit performance but for failure to adhere to stated risk objectives. Although it may be appropriate to shift the risk level in anticipation of changing market conditions (lower the beta at a perceived peak in the market), long-run adherence to risk objectives is advisable.

Measurement of Return in Relation to Risk

In examining the performance of fund managers, the return measure commonly used is excess returns. Though the term **excess returns** has many definitions, the one most commonly used is total return on a portfolio (capital appreciation plus dividends) minus the risk-free rate:

$$\text{Excess returns} = \text{Total portfolio return} - \text{Risk-free rate}$$

Thus, excess returns represent returns over and above what could be earned on a riskless asset. The rate on U.S. government Treasury bills is often used to represent the risk-free rate of return in the financial markets (though other definitions are possible). Thus, a fund that earns 12 percent when the Treasury bill rate is 6 percent has excess returns of 6 percent.

Once computed, excess returns are then compared with risk. We look at three different approaches to comparing excess returns to risk: the **Sharpe approach,** the **Treynor approach**, and the **Jensen approach**.

Sharpe Approach

In the Sharpe approach, the excess returns on a portfolio are compared with the portfolio standard deviation:

$$\text{Sharpe measure} = \frac{\text{Total portfolio return} - \text{Risk-free rate}}{\text{Portfolio standard deviation}} \qquad (7\text{–}4)$$

The portfolio manager is thus able to view excess returns per unit of risk. If a portfolio has a return of 10 percent, the risk-free rate is 6 percent, and the portfolio standard deviation is 18 percent, the Sharpe measure is 0.22:

$$\text{Sharpe measure} = \frac{10\% - 6\%}{18\%} = \frac{4\%}{18\%} = 0.22$$

This measure can be compared with other portfolios or with the market in general to assess performance. If the market return per unit of risk is greater than 0.22, then the portfolio manager has turned in an inferior performance. Assume there is a 9 percent total market return, a 6 percent risk-free rate, and a market standard deviation of 12 percent. Then the Sharpe measure for the overall market is 0.25 or:

$$\frac{9\% - 6\%}{12\%} = \frac{3\%}{12\%} = 0.25$$

The portfolio measure of 0.22 is less than the market measure of 0.25 and represents an inferior performance. Of course, a portfolio measure above 0.25 would have represented a superior performance.

Treynor Approach

The formula for the second approach for comparing excess returns with risk (developed by Treynor) is:

$$\text{Treynor measure} = \frac{\text{Total portfolio return} - \text{Risk free rate}}{\text{Portfolio beta}} \qquad (7\text{-}5)$$

The only difference between the Sharpe and Treynor approaches is in the denominator. While Sharpe uses the portfolio standard deviation—Formula 7-4, Treynor uses the portfolio beta—Formula 7-5. Thus, one can say that Sharpe uses total risk, while Treynor uses only the systematic risk, or beta. Implicit in the Treynor approach is the assumption that portfolio managers can diversify away unsystematic risk, and only systematic risk remains.

If a portfolio has a total return of 10 percent, the risk-free rate is 6 percent, and the portfolio beta is 0.9, the Treynor measure would be 0.044.

$$\frac{10\% - 6\%}{0.9} = \frac{4\%}{0.9} = \frac{0.04}{0.9} = 0.044$$

This measure can be compared with other portfolios or with the market in general to determine whether there is a superior performance in terms of return per unit of risk. Assume the total market return is 9 percent, the risk-free rate is 6 percent, and the market beta (by definition) is 1; then the Treynor measure as applied to the market is 0.03:

$$\frac{9\% - 6\%}{1.0} = \frac{3\%}{1.0} = \frac{0.03}{1.0} = 0.030$$

This would imply the portfolio has turned in a superior return to the market (0.044 versus 0.030). Not only is the portfolio return higher than the market return (10 percent versus 9 percent), but the beta is less (0.9 versus 1.0). Clearly, there is more return per unit of risk.

Jensen Approach

In the third approach, Jensen emphasizes using certain aspects of the capital asset pricing model to evaluate portfolio managers. He compares their actual excess returns (total portfolio return–risk-free rate) with what should be required in the market, based on their portfolio beta.

The required rate of excess returns in the market for a given beta is shown in Figure 7-9 as the **market line**. If the beta is 0, the investor should expect to earn no more than the risk-free rate of return because there is no systematic risk. If the portfolio manager earns only the risk-free rate of return, the excess returns will be 0. Thus, with a beta of 0, the expected excess returns on the market line are 0. With a portfolio beta of 1, the portfolio has a systematic

FIGURE 7–9   Risk-Adjusted Portfolio Returns

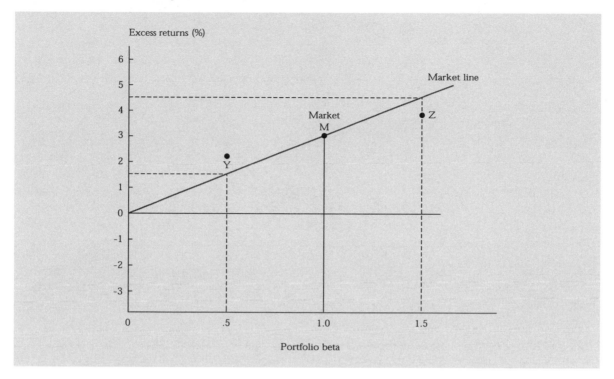

risk equal to market, and the expected portfolio excess returns should be equal to market excess returns. If the market return (KM) is 9 percent and the risk-free rate (RF) is 6 percent, the market excess returns are 3 percent. A portfolio with a beta of 1 should expect to earn the market rate of excess returns (KM–RF), equal to 3 percent. Other excess returns expectations are shown for betas ranging from 0 to 1.5. For example, a portfolio with a beta of 1.5 should provide excess returns of 4.5.

Adequacy of Performance

Using the Jensen approach, the adequacy of a portfolio manager's performance can be judged against the market line. Did he or she fall above or below the line?

While it would appear that portfolio manager Y in Figure 7–9 had inferior returns in comparison with portfolio manager Z (approximately 2.1 percent versus 3.9 percent), this notion is quickly dispelled when one considers risk. Actually, portfolio manager Y performed above risk-return expectations as indicated by the market line, while portfolio manager Z was below his risk-adjusted expected level. The vertical difference from a fund's performance point to the market line can be viewed as a measure of performance. This value, termed **alpha** or **average differential return,** indicates the difference between the return on the fund and a point on the market line that corresponds to a beta equal to the fund. In the case of fund Z, the beta of 1.5 indicated an excess return of 4.5 percent along the market line, and the actual excess return was only 3.9 percent. We thus have a negative alpha of 0.6 percent (3.9% to 4.5%). Clearly, a positive alpha indicates a superior performance, while a negative alpha leads to the opposite conclusion.

Key questions for portfolio managers in general include the following: Can they consistently perform at positive alpha levels? That is, can they generate returns better than those available along the market line, which are theoretically available to anyone? The results of the classic study conducted by John McDonald on 123 mutual funds are presented in Figure 7–10.

FIGURE 7–10   Empirical Study of Risk-Adjusted Portfolio Returns—Systematic Risk and Return

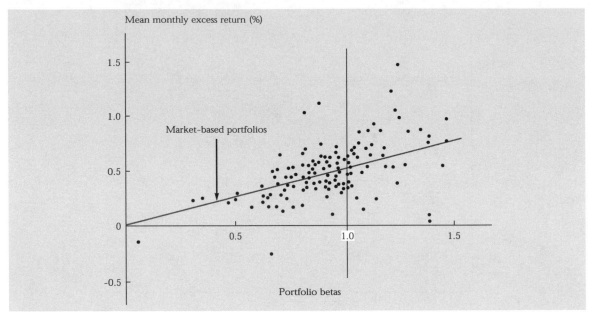

Source: John G. McDonald, "Objectives and Performance of Mutual Funds, 1950–1969," *Journal of Financial and Quantitative Analysis*, June 1974, p. 321.

The upward-sloping line is the market line, or anticipated level of performance based on risk. The small dots represent performance of the funds. About as many funds under-performed (negative alpha below the line) as overperformed (positive alpha above the line). Although a few high-beta funds had an unusually strong performance on a risk adjusted basis, there is no consistent pattern of superior performance.

Around this same time period (the 1960s), the studies by Sharpe and Jensen actually showed that mutual funds underperformed common stock indexes. Since then, there has been a raging debate about the adequacy of performance of mutual funds. In an excellent 1993 article in the *Financial Analysts Journal,* Richard Ippolito analyzed 21 major studies relating to mutual fund performance over the last four decades. In examining the Ippolito material, we are left with the impression that mutual fund managers are not inferior per-formers; however, we would be hard pressed to say that investing in mutual funds will pro-vide returns that are higher than those reported in the popular common stock market indexes such as the Standard & Poor's 500 Index or New York Stock Exchange Index (after adjustment for the fund's risk).

What the Ippolito article suggests is that mutual funds are efficient gatherers of informa-tion and that, on average, they use the information well in their investment activities. However, there are costs associated with acquiring this information, and wise use of the information covers the cost of its acquisition.

Another recent study was done by Thomas Goodwin, in which he breaks down excess returns (in this case relative to the standard deviation) for various types of investment styles as shown in Figure 7–11. The study is of 212 actively managed funds from 1986 to 1995 and uses the Frank Russell database. Risk-adjusted excess returns are shown on the x axis and the percent of time they occur is shown on the y axis. The important factor to note is that the pluses and minuses are pretty close to evening out. There is no statistically significant positive or negative excess returns for any of the six management styles.

Thus, we are left with the conclusion that after all factors are considered and after four decades of debate, mutual funds are neither superior nor inferior to the overall market in

FIGURE 7–11   Excess Returns: Based on Six Different Management Styles (1986–1995)

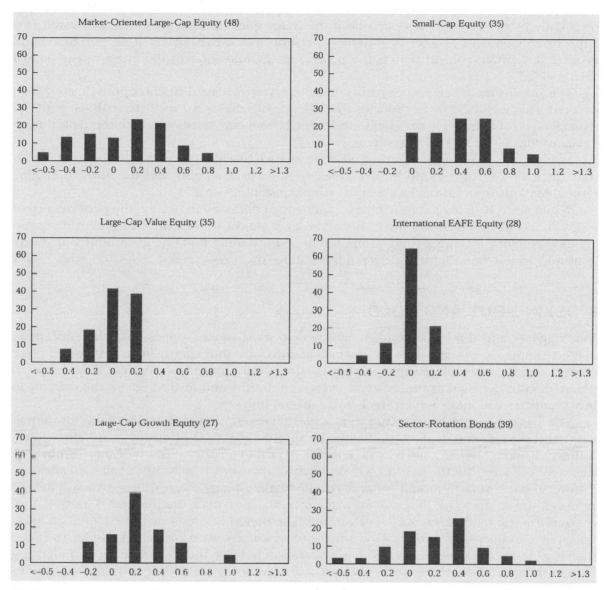

Note: Midpoints of ranges. Information ratios are on the *x* axes; relative frequencies, in percentages, are on the *y* axes. The number after the management style in the number of funds in that category.

Source: Thomas H. Goodwin, "The information Ratio," *Financial Analysts Journal*, July–August 1998, pp. 34–43.

terms of risk-adjusted returns. Studies of other types of money managers besides mutual funds, such as pension funds and endowment funds, have reached similar conclusions. Perhaps it is not surprising that more investors are shifting their assets to **index funds**, in which fund managers merely attempt to produce the same results as those that could be attained from investing in a market index, such as the Standard & Poor's 500 Stock Index.

An index fund is one that attempts to replicate the performance of a popular market average such as the Standard & Poor's 500 Index (www.standardandpoor.com). The largest index fund is the Vanguard Index 500 (www.vanguard.com) (based on the S&P500), which has tripled in the last decade.

Why all the growth? As pointed out in the chapter, it is somewhat difficult for mutual funds and other professional money managers to consistently beat the market averages. Between 1981 and 2000, the Standard & Poor's 500 Index went up at an 18 percent compound annual growth rate. A mutual fund, such as the Vanguard Index 500, that passively tracks that average is going to represent stiff competition for actively managed funds.

A passively managed stock fund invests in a portfolio that matches the S&P 500 Index on a daily basis. Thus if IBM's percent of the Index goes up on a given day as a result of a large price gain, and Procter & Gamble's percent goes down, IBM will be purchased and Procter & Gamble sold to match the percentage composition of the index at the end of the day.

The management fee and expenses for a passively managed fund is approximately 0.20 percent. This is quite low because of the absence of salaries for security analysts, portfolio managers, etc. For actively managed funds, which do incur the above costs, the typical management fee is 0.75 to 1.25 percent.

Index funds have also spread to other areas such as Fidelity's (www.fidelity.com) funds that track the Wilshire 5000 Equity Index (www.wilshire.com), and the Morgan Stanley Capital Markets International Index (www.morganstanley.com).

While actively managed funds have experienced difficulty in beating the performance of index funds, many optimistic investors consider it almost un-American to accept the "average performance" of index funds. Thus, the hope for finding that one great fund will always continue. Ninety percent of mutual funds are still actively managed.

INDEXING-BUY AND HOLD

Indexing-buy and hold is a concept which is, in most senses, opposite to the concept of market timing. In other words, planners who advocate indexing believe that future price changes or duration of changes cannot be predicted with any consistency. Hence, such planners consider market timing as an exercise in futility and instead, advise their clients to buy securities and funds which track broad market indexes.

The basic concept of indexing rests with the assumption that planners cannot outperform the performance of market indexes such as the S&P 500 Index, the Dow Jones Industrial Average (DJIA), on a *consistent* (i.e. year in, year out) basis. Indexers also believe that over the long run the market will generally outperform at least **50%** of all fund advisors. Further, the advisors who will outperform the market in any given year or two will in turn perform worse than the index in subsequent years. Moreover, the fund advisors who may outperform the market indexes over a **future time period** of time cannot be identified today with any certainty or reliability. Given these observations, such planners consider the alternative of investing in securities or funds that closely track the performance of underlying market indexes as desirable. Such planners also consider holding their investment positions for a longer time period, and hence, they will "buy and hold" their positions. The length of time over which a position is held depends primarily on the client particulars such as investment **objective, investment time** horizon and risk preferences and the macroeconomic conditions as reflected through the business cycle.

Mutual funds are most popular as securities that track the movement of market or securities indexes. Most large mutual fund companies, such as the Vanguard and the Fidelity group of funds, offer index mutual funds for investors. These funds provide the appropriate vehicles for both investors and financial planners to buy and hold a basket of securities, in the form of a single mutual fund, that track financial market indexes. Since indexers may choose to track a wide variety of indexes such as large and small cap indexes, broad and narrow market indexes, stock and bond market indexes, domestic and foreign market indexes, the fund companies offer numerous index funds that cover generally most indexing needs. Since the 1990s a new type of fund has appeared in the markets that also track indexes. These funds, known as **"Exchange Traded Funds"** or **ETFs**, have become very popular tracking tools in this decade, and the number of ETFs being offered in the market are increasing almost daily. The companies that offer ETFs claim that ETFs are much easier to trade since they are structured like common stocks, provide benefits in shielding against capital gains taxes and are generally cheaper than index mutual funds.

Indexers who follow a passive buy-and-hold strategy claim a number of benefits in their approach over a more active approach to investments. First, and as mentioned earlier, market indexes are generally expected to outperform most actively managed funds over longer time periods. This is because indexers believe the markets to be efficient and consistently picking winners near impossible. Second, passively investing through index tracking securities is considerably cheaper because the costs of researching to find winning investments are not expended. Further, since the compositions of indexes do not change very frequently, very little trading and transaction costs are incurred in managing index tracking funds.

On the other hand, funds that are actively managed charge high fees. These fees are paid because these fund managers consider their skills at investments to be superior and hence, require higher fees. Moreover, "active" managers continuously produce information about various securities that either indicates buying, selling or holding various investment positions. Since such an approach requires frequent alterations in portfolio structure, the costs involved in an active style also increase due to the much higher costs of transactions. The debate over which style is superior is considerably heated and acrimonious. Since the substance of the debate is continuous, it will be examined in greater detail in a later chapter.

MONEY MANAGER SELECTION AND MONITORING

The recent (2003–2004) turmoil in the mutual funds industry and the revelations of all the wrongdoings by mutual fund managers places an additional burden on the planner's attempt to select a money manager. Even without the recent upheaval, selecting a money manager from about 14,000 plus managers is as daunting a task as selecting a stock or a mutual fund. The problems encountered in the manager selection process are also similarly rooted in issues of information availability and authenticity as well as being able to gauge the abilities of managers from the wide plethora of indicators available for assessment purposes. In guiding this selection process, planners may consider following some simplifying criteria.

To begin with, the search process uses the same objectives used in the investment decision process itself. The first three questions to address, as in the investment decision process, are as follows:

1. What is the primary objective of the investment decision for which you need a money manager?

2. What are the risk/return preferences of the clients?

3. What is the investment time horizon?

Understanding the answers to these three questions thoroughly will considerably ease the burden of planners in selecting suitable money managers. We will return to the description of how the selection is made easy, but first let us evaluate each of these three questions in some detail.

There are many reasons to invest. Examples of reasons include savings and investments for retirement, for children's college education, to buy a house or car, to build wealth, etc. Along with each of these reasons is an associated objective. For example, in saving for retirement, an appropriate objective may be to maintain and/or increase the standard of living that pre-existed before retirement. Similarly, in providing for children's college education, provisions may be for public or private colleges and may include the financing of an auto for a child as well. The point being made here is that the need and the objectives help us determine certain aspects of the investment decision which in turn help us evaluate managers.

Consider the example of a parent who can afford to save a limited sum of money towards a child's education. Given this limitation (or budget constraint) the parent next has to consider the type of college (public or private) to fund for. Obviously, private colleges cost more and hence the future funding required for a private college education would require a higher rate of growth than the rate required for funding public college education. Thus, the choice of managers in this case would be determined by the style of the managers. A growth style manager would be desirable to grow money faster whereas a balanced fund manager may be considered for that same investment, if the objective were to fund the education at a public college. Being able to tie the objective (private or public education, in this example) allows us to narrow the manager selection criterion to only managers who practice/affirm a certain style of management. This inclusion reduces the universe of potential managers significantly. Similarly, for the need to fund for retirement, the objective may differ from maintaining living standards to improving them.

Continue with the example of funding for children's education. Assume that the limited funds that a parent can save towards this objective will require the fund to grow at a 12% rate in order to be sufficient to meet the funding need. This required rate of return of 12% would imply that most of the savings be invested in equity or other high-yielding instruments. An associated feature of such an investment would be a fairly significant amount of investment risk that the parent would be exposed to and which in turn would also imply that there would be a higher probability of accumulating insufficient funds. In this case, the risk preference of the client would become another input in the process of manager selection. The risk preference of the client would determine what styles of funds are chosen. The styles that were affirmed when the investment objective was considered may either be reinforced or rejected by including the risk preferences of clients. There is another important aspect of including the risk preferences of clients in selecting the fund manager. One of the important variables that enter the process of manager selection is the risk perspective of the manager themselves. It is a good idea to evaluate and match the risk preferences of the manager to those of the clients. Once the manager is selected and the investment process begins, the level of comfort, or discomfort, will considerably be influenced by the style of the chosen manager. In this case, matching the manager's risk preference with those of clients can considerably aid the planner in managing the client relationships.

Finally, the time horizon of the investment decisions must also be included in the selection process. In the college funding example, given some limited amount of funds and given a certain risk preference profile, the shorter the time available to accumulate the funds, the greater will be the need to find managers who pursue growth and aggressive growth styles, and vice versa. Another way to consider this is that if the planner can persuade a client to invest early, whatever the investment need be, then the planner can have more flexibility in choosing managers. The right choice of managers will ultimately lead to client satisfaction and retention.

The reader should note that the application of the basics of the investment process serves as screens in the manager selection process. They help us eliminate many managers from the selection process and isolate others. They help us narrow down the universe of managers to a level where the selection process is more manageable and where it is feasible to apply other subjective and objective criteria to further narrow the selection process. Finally, and most importantly, the inclusion of the client's basic inputs in the selection process should generally lead to a much greater level of client satisfaction. In the following sections, other selection criteria that need to be used on a smaller subset of managers are discussed.

Many planners tend to jump first on assessing the past performances of money managers in selecting a manager. The relationship between past performance and manager selection has been widely studied. Results of these studies generally support the notion that using past performance as the main criterion in the selection process is, at best, a very poor indicator of future performance potential. In a sense, manager performance should be the last screen in the selection process, the step that affirms a manager's choice. It is much more prudent to consider other facets of managers that reinforce the investment objectives, risk preferences and timing horizon decisions.

There are several subjective and objective criteria that may be applied to further narrow the selection process. Once the general fund style has been identified, managers within that style can be scrutinized further. The main objective at this stage is to identify inconsistencies and incongruencies between the stated style of the managers and the styles that they have actually implemented in their practices. The following are examples of questions that need to be assessed in determining the selection.

- Has the manager consistently selected securities that are compatible with the stated style?

- If not, how often have they strayed from their paths?

- Does the manager's trading activity (turnover) reflect the stated objective of the fund?

- Does the manager use risk management techniques that are consistent with the fund's stated objectives?

- How often have the fund's operating expenses exceeded both those stated and those that were expected?

- How often has the fund's risk exceeded the stated or expected risk?

- How long has a manager served for a fund?

- Is the manager known to have managed funds of many different styles or are their transitions been within similar styles?

- If the manager affirms a passive style, how often have they strayed from that style, and vice versa?

- How consistently does the manager apply security selection techniques, whether qualitative or quantitative or both?

- Has the manager ever violated or has not been in compliance with laws and regulations?

- Has the manager ever engaged in return chasing, risk maximizing or other practices that are inconsistent with the fund's stated objectives?

- Does the manager engage in "window dressing" types of activities that are harmful to clients?

- What are the answers to the above questions for the investment team members that the manager leads?

- How research oriented is the manager?

As the reader can observe, there are many questions that require to be evaluated in selecting a manager. However, it may be useful to categorize these questions along some common themes. Happily, such a categorization is possible. In using the above criteria, the selector is trying to assess two basic traits of a manager.

Perhaps the most important summation of these criteria is to understand how **consistent** a manager is and has been. The more consistent a manager has been towards her/his style, trading activity, security selection techniques, fund expense levels, etc. the better. Alternately, managers who change their operating activities often are much more likely to underperform against their expectations. Another way to consider the issue of consistency is that the manager's activities are as stable as the investment decision inputs of the clients. The clients' retirement objectives or their risk tolerances for those investments do not change on a weekly or monthly basis. The basic idea here is that neither should the manager's attitudes and perceptions change on those scales. In a sense, there is a direct relationship between consistency and competency.

The other important theme to assess is the ethical make-up of the manager. Managers (and funds) whose styles, trading, expenses, selection techniques, etc. change often are also much more likely to engage in activities that are undesirable or even in violation of investment rules and regulations. It is important to note that the manager's ethics is as important as his/her competency. Neither can be sacrificed at the expense of the other. Managers who rank high on both the scales are appropriate for further consideration in the selection process.

Finally, after the universe of managers has been whittled down to a few, the past performance of managers should be assessed. As has been noted before, past performance is not a reliable indicator of future performance. As it turns out, *given the considerations of consistency (competency) and ethics,* the issue of past performance in predicting future performance, is actually not that daunting a task. In assessing past performance, two observations need to be made. First, given the fund's objective and style, how close have the returns been to those that were expected and how different were they from their peers? Second, how widely did the past returns vary and in comparison to their peers? In other words, if a fund is expected to produce about 12 percent (e.g. growth fund) per year, how many times in the last 5 (or 10) years has the fund's returns been close to 12 percent? Further, if the average return over the past returns has indeed been around 12 percent, have the individual (annual) returns been widely divergent from the expected 12 percent, even though they average around 12 percent. As the reader can see, the main point being made here is that the *consistency and stability of performance and in accord with expectations* is a far more powerful tool in manager selection criteria than trying to find the superstars of yesterday.

It should be fairly clear to the reader that the selection criteria for a manager also define the monitoring criteria. Monitoring the performance of the manager is akin to ensuring that the manager does not change any facet of their behavior once they have been selected. Similarly, the planner must note that the very act of selecting a manager is also a reward for the past consistency, competency and the ethics of a manager. In the same vein, a planner should not seek to replace a manager whose performance in a certain year has not been up to par, especially if the manager has not strayed from the stated and expected objectives and behavior. The planner should note that in a longer framework of time, it is the consistent managers whose performances are most likely to satisfy the needs and objectives of their clients.

Modern portfolio theory is a method by which assets are selected to be included in a portfolio such that the expected portfolio outcome optimizes the individual's utility. The most powerful concept in this optimization process is the benefits of diversification across different asset classes. This benefit shows up primarily as both a reduction in risk and or an increase in return. This in turn leads to the optimal solution. The portfolio outcomes in turns of risk and return are used to assess the performance of portfolios both by comparisons with benchmarks and comparisons with peer group performances. The performance of portfolios and their managers is one of the criteria used in selecting money managers. Various money manager selection and monitoring criteria were examined and a set of guidelines were established for this very important task.

Chapter 8

Asset Allocation and Diversification

This chapter presents two key investment concepts: Investment Policy Statements (IPS) and Asset Allocation. The former concept is an essential part of any investment plan in that an IPS lays the framework and objectives of how an investment plan will be managed, why such a path is chosen and how it will serve the client. The asset allocation decision is the most notable decision managers have to make in managing client portfolios. Each of these two concepts are explained in detail, in this chapter. Managerial implications of these two concepts are also discussed in the latter sections of the chapter.

INVESTMENT POLICY STATEMENT

An **Investment Policy Statement** (IPS) serves as a plan that guides the investor and the planner in long-term financial and investment decisions. While investors may differ by type or form, each requires a clear investment policy statement in order to achieve long term goals and investment objectives.

Investors may be categorized as being either institutional investors or individual investors. Though financial planners will most often interact with individual investors, there will be occasions when an institutional investor may require the planner's service and advice. Hence, it is important for the planner to be able to understand the needs of both types of clients and articulate IPS's for both types. Of course, the obvious client for most financial advisors is the individual investor.

Generally, institutional investors differ from individuals in the amount and size of the portfolios under management. Within the institutional category of investors, there are sub-categories, each of which differs in their investment needs. Examples of such sub-categories of institutional investors include mutual funds, pension funds, endowment funds, insurance companies, etc.

To understand how these institutions differ in their investment needs, consider the example between the needs of a defined benefit pension plan and an endowment fund. The primary goal of pension plan managers is to ensure the availability of cash that requires to be distributed to plan beneficiaries every year. Thus, pension plan management and policy is integrally involved in investments that match cash outflows with inflows. In a pension plan, the amounts of distribution to be made are generally known in advance; this in turn, determines to a large extent the choice of investment vehicles required to meet those distribution needs. Thus, IPS's for pension funds are much more guided by regulatory and compliance needs, which in turn protect the interests of the plan beneficiaries.

Consider now the issues surrounding the management of investment assets for an endowment fund. An endowment fund is an accumulation of donations that are provided to a non-profit organization by its donors. Generally the investment objectives of endowment funds are much more attuned to the needs of the non-profit organization. Sometimes, the donors may impose managerial clauses themselves. Typically, endowment funds seek to produce a small stream of income to augment the operating budget of the organization and to grow the rest of the corpus at a very moderate rate, such that the income may take the form of a perpetual stream. Thus, the IPS of an endowment fund is generally very different from that of a pension fund.

Banks and insurance companies are other examples of institutional entities that need investment policies. Both these institutions are similar to pension funds in that their investment needs are dictated by those who lend them the investment funds. Insurance companies invest in order to ensure sufficient availabilities of future funds required to be distributed as payouts to policy holders. Banks invest in order to meet short- and long-term obligations that it promises to pay depositors on specific savings deposits. All types of investors, their needs and the appropriate investment policies, are discussed in the following sections.

INVESTMENT POLICIES FOR INDIVIDUAL INVESTORS

Life-Cycle Identification

Investment goals of the individual client naturally fall out of the financial planning process. It is important to note that the goals of an individual will change over time as the client progresses through various stages of his/her life. Thus, the investment objectives will also change over time as the client ages and succeeds at achieving previously set goals.

The investment goals that are generally associated with various stages of a client's life are known as the client's life-cycle needs. Generally, the needs of various individuals at certain stages of life tend to be similar. For example, early career individuals want to accumulate wealth, whereas in the late career stage individuals seek to protect wealth more. Thus, we can classify these typical investment needs at various life cycles. These classifications provide us with a tool to apply in the investment planning process.

The first stage of an individual's earning and career is considered as the accumulation phase. This phase begins when an individual first becomes gainfully employed and continues until the client is about 40 to 50 years of age. During this time period, investors are generally much more open to assuming greater investment risk to attain higher returns. Typically, such investors can shrug off losses on the assumption that they have sufficient time to earn and recoup their losses. Further, if the losses are in securities, they can understand that their investment time horizon permits them to wait out any temporary downturn in the economy and business cycle since they are expected to be followed by growth cycles that will eventually increase their wealth. Further, individuals progressing through their careers also observe increased incomes and savings; these savings augment the growth of their wealth. Essentially, individuals in this phase are the beneficiaries of the power of compounding in the value of their wealth. Common investment goals during this phase are the purchase of a house, saving for children's education and accumulating funds for retirement.

The next stage of the client life cycle is the conservation/protection phase. This stage begins seamlessly with the trailing off of the accumulation phase and remains as the dominant phase until the first few years of retired life. During this stage, the client seeks to consolidate the assets that have been accumulated. Individual earnings reach their peaks at this stage as does their savings. The aging of clients is reflected through their investments as they tend to lean toward a reduction in undertaking risk and are content to receive lesser returns. Unlike the accumulation phase, investors recognize the devastation that can be caused by significant losses of wealth to their well being. Further, they understand that the time they have left before retirement may not be sufficient to undo losses that result from excessive risk taking. Thus, at this stage, loss aversion becomes the dominating trait of the investment life cycle. Common investment goals during this time period are children's education, savings for retirement and the beginnings of the need to gift to their beneficiaries, charities and well wishers.

The last stage is known as the preservation and gifting stage. This stage tends to begin soon after retirement and continues through life expectancy. During this stage, the investor is primarily concerned with preserving capital rather than enhancing returns. The loss of earning power and the fixed expenses of retirement loom large during the early parts of this stage. Thus the investments in this stage of life tend to be more conservative relative to the other life-cycle stages. This is also the phase in which the client will most likely seek the planner's assistance in gifting income and property to desired beneficiaries.

The ages mentioned in the above life-cycle discussion are only benchmarks. Similarly, particular goals will vary by client, life-cycle stage, and age. For instance, over the last 100 years, the age at which individuals start families has considerably increased. This implies that the investment goal of saving for children's education has shifted along the entire life cycle. Thus, the educational savings requirements can be part of the life-cycle phase where the client is primarily interested in conservation and protection as compared to the traditional notion that this objective is mostly encountered in the accumulation phase. Similarly, emerging healthcare technologies are changing the needs of individuals in the latter stages. The growth of long-term care policies is a reflection of the impact of biotechnology on the longevity of life. The concept of life cycles is important for planners to understand, but care must be taken not to compartmentalize clients by age in order to impose life stage needs without considering the impact of the client's idiosyncratic or subjective attributes. Rather, careful discussion and analysis based upon client goals will yield a more accurate measure in which stage or stages the client resides.

Life-cycle planning is thus relevant in the investment processes because it allows the planner to identify with the client through the various time horizons for each goal within the financial plan. Without time horizons, an investment policy would not be whole. The client could be subject to too much risk and/or insufficient funds for current consumption (too much savings), etc. The policy then, would not accurately articulate the goals within the plan and thus would subject the achievement of goals to imminent failure.

Investment Objectives

Once the goals, life cycle, and time horizons for the goals have been identified, the investment objectives become easier to identify. Investment objectives identify the goals of the portfolio in relation to the reasons for the individual's financial needs. Investment objectives can be further classified into four types: current income, capital growth, total return, and preservation of capital.

Current income is a strategy whereby the main objective of the portfolio is to generate an immediate and ongoing flow of cash to the client. That is, the investor requires income generation from the principal balance of the portfolio via interest or dividend payments. An investor who relies on the portfolio for income in this way needs the cash for living purposes. Thus the investments tend to be conservative in nature. Common investment securities are corporate bonds, government bonds, government mortgage backed securities, preferred stocks and perhaps stable utility stocks that pay regular dividends.

Capital growth is a strategy whereby the portfolio funds are invested over the long term with the objective of capital appreciation in mind. Because the objective is growth over the long term, the riskiness of the portfolio tends to be higher. The most common securities for this type of approach are equities, particularly those in high growth companies or sectors. However, it is always a good idea to diversify the portfolio holdings among various sectors and industries. Further, stocks of very large companies that lead their industries (blue chip) in this case can help to diversify the portfolio while achieving some of the same growth objectives. Mutual funds, which invest in various sectors or industries, can also help to diversify a portfolio at a reasonable cost.

The total return approach is a strategy that melds the current income and capital growth approaches. Thus, the investor wants the portfolio to grow over time, but wishes to have income generated from it right away as well. Obviously having two objectives from the same portfolio can be challenging to manage, but it can be done if applied correctly. Thus, this strategy would use a blend of methods of the two strategies above.

Those investors interested in preservation of capital are most interested in ensuring that the amount of money invested in the portfolio does not decrease. Therefore, the investment choices are safe vehicles. Large returns are not important for these clients and types of investments are typically government bonds, certificates of deposit, money markets (funds), and fixed annuities.

Risk for Individual Investors

Although we may have determined the goals and the investment objectives of our client, we cannot seriously discuss the minute details of an investment policy without first assessing the risk tolerance of the client. Without a meaningful assessment of client risk attitudes, the investment policy will be useless.

Finance professionals often think of risk in terms of the standard deviation of returns and stock betas. In some cases, individual investors may understand these concepts but more often than not, most investors do not fully understand these concepts. After all, that is why they seek out investment advisors for such expertise. Since the client may not understand the intricacies of integrating investor risk preferences in financial applications, it is even more important for the advisor to determine the client's risk preference before structuring appropriate portfolios.

Many clients describe risk in terms of losing money so it may be a good starting point upon which to discuss the notion of risk. This notion of loss can be seen from several perspectives, so it can be helpful if the client can articulate risk to the planner in one of these ways. Loss to some individuals occurs when the original value of the portfolio has decreased in either absolute dollars or relative return percentages. For instance, suppose a client started with an initial investment of $250K and experienced a $50K decrease in value due to a general downturn in the market. Some investors feel that they have lost $50K and consider it a total loss. Similarly, they might say that they lost 20 percent of their portfolio.

Other investors who are investing for the long term may not be concerned if the value of the portfolio decreases for some period of time if they feel that the losses sustained are short term in nature. These types of investors often perceive a loss only when they sell assets from the portfolio and therefore have a realized loss.

Risk to clients may also appear in the form of the types of securities that they know of. Therefore suggesting new types of securities to these clients may appear to the client as a type of risk that they do not wish to engage in. It is a challenge of the advisor when these types of investments make sense to help the client understand why these types of investments are better for them. In the end, the advisor may or may not be successful in persuading the client.

Conversely, clients may have a notion of risk in areas where they have had previous investment losses. For instance, those who lost money in stock market crashes tend to be averse to investing in stocks in the future. It is up to the advisor to help clients understand why their investments failed in the first instance and the measures that the planner can put into place to minimize those types of losses in the future. Some investors may mimic the investment strategies of their peers while others may mimic investment activities which are popular or in vogue. Such practices can result in undesirable outcomes and result in large losses. Thus when an advisor advocates some technique or security as appropriate for the client, the client may consider this to be risky and very poor advice.

Risk is extremely difficult to define. The planner must initially spend a lot of time with the client to ascertain what risk means to that client. This can be accomplished through discussions with the client and is often done with questionnaires, which are used as complements to client/planner conversations. Since each investor is subjectively and idio-syncratically different, risk will have a different meaning to each investor. When implementing an investment policy, it is valuable to incorporate the risk characteristics into the plan. This should be done in such a way so that the investor and the planner can quantify the risk. Thus if certain events occur, such as a portfolio losing 10 percent of its value, the planner and investor will have identified, in advance, appropriate actions for that particular event. With such pre-planned and agreed upon actions, further risk to the portfolio value may be minimized.

Other Topical Considerations for Individual Investment Policies

Tax Considerations

Incorporating the notion of before- and after-tax investment returns on a portfolio is an important concept in portfolio planning. The after-tax considerations must effectively inte-grate with other portions of the financial plan so that taxes are minimized in years with high expected income. Recall that taxes can be deferred (paid at a later date when assets are sold at a profit), can be avoided through vehicles such as municipal bonds, or can be taxed at capital gains rates (investments held greater than one year) rather than at ordinary rates. It is useful to spell out the tax consequences in the investment policy. However, the advisor must discuss and incorporate into the plan the potentiality for changes in the tax law. Because laws change, tax planning relative to portfolio management can be a very challeng-ing aspect to the planner. When the client has a negative bias toward taxes or has compli-cated transactions, it may be useful to consult with tax counsel as to assist in decisions regarding the sale and purchase of assets to and from the portfolio. Tax considerations and goals should be spelled out in the investment policy as to assist the planner and the client in quantifying tax consequences of decisions.

Measurement of Returns and Successes of the Planner

The client and the planner should decide upon a method that measures the success of the advisor in picking investments. The time weighted rate of return (or the holding period return) is a method used for fund manager evaluation. This is so because a typical fund man-ager cannot control the amount of funds he or she has under management (in which case a geometric rate of return could be used). No matter what method is used, it should be spelled out in the investment policy so that both the planner and the investor have appro-priate expectations regarding what performance measures are going to be used to judge the advisor.

Macroeconomic Factors

A good planner is always aware of macroeconomic factors that can ultimately affect invest-ments. These factors should be integrated into the plan. For instance, historical inflation rates, which affect the real rate of return on assets, should be discussed in any plan in order to sustain the purchasing power of the client to the greatest extent possible. Other factors that should be taken into consideration are interest rates, economic growth or decline as a whole or in specific industries, unemployment, political stability, and the legal environment. While this list is not exhaustive, it is meant to give the advisor an appreciation of the areas that can affect the investment policy. As the planner gets to know the client, he or she can integrate those areas within the macroeconomic environment into the client's plan as they pertain to the client.

ASSET ALLOCATION STRATEGY

Asset allocation strategy is an extremely important concept to address in the IPS. We will discuss asset allocation strategy below, but in short, an asset allocation strategy considers the types and relative proportion of assets in the portfolio. Assets are considered in the broad classes, such as stocks, bonds, mutual funds, real assets, and commodities. As the portfolio experiences gains or losses, the asset allocations will change over time. They must, therefore, be reevaluated on an ongoing basis. Of course as the client passes through the various life- cycle states, the aversion to risk will increase and changes to the asset mix will necessarily have to be made. Asset allocation strategies should be reevaluated during major economic growth or decline as to maximize or minimize gains and losses.

The criteria for modifying the asset allocations within the policy should be stated clearly. This will help both the planner and the investor to have clear-cut decisions when there are changes in the portfolio value. This is useful when the portfolio has either sustained increases or decreases in value, causing rebalancing to be necessary. This will entitle the planner and investor to clear-cut rules for changing the asset mix and losses or gains in the portfolio will not have to be regarded subjectively.

From a practical standpoint, the IPS creates a clear commitment between the planner and the client/investor. A written plan often communicates difficult concepts in a more effective manner than verbal communication. It also serves as a reference that allows both the planner and the investor to invoke changes in the plan when certain criteria have been met. Lastly, the plan is an effective tool in protecting the planner in the case of investor disillusionment with investment results.

Institutional Investors

Investment Policies for Defined Benefit Pension Plans

Defined Benefit Pension Plans are plans whereby a company promises to pay employees an amount of money at retirement. The payout to the employee is generally based upon a specific formula. The most common formula used is called a unit benefit formula. An example of a unit benefit formula is that the plan promises to pay 2 percent of the final monthly average salary multiplied by years of service, which is limited to 25 years. An important point to make here is that the payout is based upon a final-average salary that is not yet known. Thus, companies that fund Defined Benefit Pension Plans bear the inflation risk for the payout to the employee.

Plan Life Cycle: The Business as a Going Concern versus Plan Termination

For purposes of this discussion, we will assume that the business is a going concern; the company is expected to make contributions for expected beneficiary payouts for an indeterminate amount of time. It is, however, possible in the course of a business that plans will terminate. There are several reasons for plan termination including insolvency of the business, termination by law, desire to implement a different kind of retirement plan, or major changes in the way a business currently operates, such as a merger with another company. The process for Plan Termination can be very long and is subject to many federal laws. If there are enough plan assets in the fund at the time of dissolution, the employer generally will purchase a single premium annuity contract from an insurance company who will then bear the risk for the remainder of the plan liabilities.

Assuming that a company that contributes to a defined benefit pension plan is a going concern, certain time-based characteristics must be taken into consideration. Unlike the individual investor who has a finite lifespan, the company that has a defined benefit pension plan has an indefinite lifespan. Therefore, capital market expectations cannot be ignored and long-run historical returns on valid asset classes should be considered. The time horizon is important because the plan will, in any given year, have to balance the estimated payouts to beneficiaries with the long-term goals of funding for beneficiaries who are expected to be paid out at later dates.

Investment and Asset Allocation Objectives

Because payout needs vary as the time horizon dictates, there will be varying investment objectives at any given point in time for a particular plan. The plan will have to balance the need for preservation of capital until payout begins against the growth requirements for benefits that are expected to be paid out at a later date. Asset mix may thus change from year to year since the liabilities may change from year to year. Please see the article on **The Impact of Investment Scandals on Defined Contribution Plans**.

THE IMPACT OF INVESTMENT SCANDALS ON DEFINED CONTRIBUTION PLANS

Anonymous. ***Pension Benefits***, New York: Feb. 2005. Vol. 14, Iss. 2, p. 6 (1 p.)

DEFINED CONTRIBUTION PLANS

PLANSPONSOR, December 2004

"During one of the more tumultuous years in the industry's history, plan sponsors—and the participants whose retirements they help support—are offering more than ever. On average, participants have access to more funds, more advice, more defined benefit plans, and more Internet services, and are more likely to have a larger company match than we found in last year's survey.

This year, of course, has been more than usually trying for plan sponsors but, for the industry overall, the heightened awareness and attention paid to fiduciary concerns is seen by most as a good, if stressful, turn of events. That heightened awareness also is borne out in a telling statistic among the participants in PLANSPONSOR's eighth annual defined contribution services survey.

Record Numbers Have Written Investment Policies

A record number (nearly 75%) of a record number (roughly 4,000 plan sponsor respondents) now have a written investment policy statement to guide their efforts. Larger plans continue to be more likely to have these than smaller programs but, incredibly, one in five of the largest plan respondents, those with more than $200 million in assets, apparently do not yet have one.

That statistic is particularly telling in times such as the year just past when events like the mutual fund trading scandal provide a unique impetus to reassess the actions appropriate to a process of prudence in evaluating plan options.

Most Have Not Changed Investment Policies

Still, it will be surprising to some to discover that the trading scandal has failed to push hordes of DC plans to the warm embrace of a nontainted provider. In fact, more than half the respondents to this year's survey, some 51%, said they had made no changes to investment policy, the way their plan chose funds, or the process for monitoring fund performance.

Even among those that made changes, the shift was largely toward information requests and heightened scrutiny, not provider terminations. Roughly a quarter had increased their oversight, for example, while a comparable number had sought the recommendation of either their advisor or provider on the matter. Less than 5% chose to select a new provider or a new advisor as a result of the trading scandal. So much for panic.

TABLE 6   Mutual Fund Scandal Resulted in Few Plan Changes

In light of the recent revelations about practices in the mutual fund industry, have you made any changes in your investment policy, the way you select funds, or the process for monitoring fund performance?

No changes made	51.4%
Increased fund oversight	24.4%
Selected new plan provider	2.7%
Selected new advisor	2.2%
Sought recommendation of advisor	19.5%
Sought recommendation of plan provider	13.4%
Increased investment information given to participants	11.8%
Added more investment options	11.4%
Other	5.0%

Source: PLANSPONSOR Magazine

Provider Information and Fund Options

About one in eight had increased the information provided to participants, while a nearly identical number had increased fund options. Of course, plan sponsors have been slowly, but surely, expanding their fund menu for years. In 2004, the average number of fund options was 18.6, up from 16.7 a year ago. Larger plans tended to have more options (28.7 versus 16.9 among plans with less than $5 million in assets) but, despite the larger menu, the average number of fund choices actually used by participants in the largest plans was a full fund choice less than those at smaller plans—just four funds, on average, versus five."

Risks for Defined Benefit Pension Plans

Although the benefit is defined as a percentage of final average salary, the expected payouts will be invariably unknown since the company can only estimate what an average salary will be at the time of retirement. Many other factors ultimately affect the payouts that a plan will have to make to its beneficiaries. Factors include the number of employees who will eventually be serviced by the plan, the final average salary for all employees, mortality rates, disability rates, turnover rates, length of benefit period for retirees, and investment returns from funding. Because of all these considerations and their relative unknown nature, pension plan managers must hire actuaries who calculate annual funding requirements for the plan.

Plan actuaries show that the plan is adequately funded according to IRS standards or the plan will be subject to harsh excise taxes. Interestingly, the actuary can choose from several funding methods that are approved by the IRS. The actuary also has discretion when determining the fund's annual contribution. In this way, tax objectives of the funding company can be met by contributing relatively higher amounts in high income years and relatively lower amounts in lower income years. Note that companies receive a tax deduction for the contributions that they make to defined benefit plans.

Income Tax Considerations

Beside the fact that companies receive income tax deductions for the amounts they contribute to plans, the funds in these types of plans are allowed to grow tax free. Taxes are realized by the beneficiary upon payout of benefits.

Endowment Funds

Endowment funds receive income from donors in order to achieve the objective of the endowment fund. Typically, endowment funds are established in organizations such as charitable or educational organizations and institutions which are also typically nontaxable organizations. Some examples of endowment funds are those that exist in colleges, private schools, museums, and hospitals. The objectives of endowment funds tend to be broad in nature. This is different from the pension plans where the objective is singular, i.e. investments are made to provide retirees with pensions.

Life Cycle, Investment Objectives, and Asset Allocation

The life cycle of an endowment fund is similar to that of a pension plan. Endowment funds are not individuals; rather, they are entities that can expect to operate for a long time in the foreseeable future. Endowment funds are invested to help institutions financially for both short-term and longer term needs. Thus there exists a demand that endowment funds balance the short-term goals with the long-term objectives. Endowment funds usually have a need for income today as well as income in the future in order to satisfy their many goals. This can be challenging for funds that do not have a regular flow of contributions from donors.

Funding of endowments can be sporadic since contributors may not maintain any regular routine of charitable donations. Contributed funds in any year may also be used to meet immediate payment obligations. Thus, endowment funds often forgo the growth in the fund from the effect of the compounded returns from investment, whenever contributions are used to meet current obligations. Further, since endowment funds have a need for both current income and long-term growth, investment objectives tend to often follow a total return approach. For those endowments with large amounts to invest, this objective can be much more easily reached than those funds with relatively small amounts of capital.

It is important for the advisor to work with the managers of the endowment fund to ascertain whether it is more important for them to have a current income or capital appreciation. While goals are often conflicting one approach generally takes precedence over another. Once the advisor understands the priorities of the managers, one investment objective will take the front seat to the others. For instance, if an endowment needs current income, the tendency will be toward long-term fixed-income securities. If the endowment has long-term goals, the tendency will be toward equity securities investments.

As long as endowments pay out a portion of their annual contributions to their beneficiaries, the endowment is not generally subject to income tax.

Macroeconomic Factors

The macroeconomic factors that affect individuals also affect any individual or entity and should be carefully examined when forming any investment policy. However, in the endowment, asset investment should carefully consider the effects of inflation. Both hospitals and educational institutions are good examples for consideration. In both cases, the costs in these areas have far exceeded the average annual inflation rate. Thus these types of organizations deserve special consideration when thinking about inflationary pressures.

Banks and Insurance Companies

Investment Policies for Banks and Insurance Companies

Banks and insurance companies are different from pension plans and endowment funds in that they operate in order to realize profits from their operations. The main goal for these types of entities is to make an adequate return while effectively balancing the assets and liabilities of the entities. Because of estimated liabilities (policy pay-outs for insurance companies and deposits for banks), risk control is a key component of investment policies for these types of entities. Investments for these entities are subject to the increasing role of the regulatory environment, inflationary risk, interest rate risk, macroeconomic factors, and investment risk. The life cycles for these entities is often considered to be ongoing or perpetual, that is, banks and insurance companies are expected to be engaged in their line of business indefinitely.

Investment and Asset Allocation Objectives

As mentioned above, the investment objectives of these entities are to match assets and liabilities of the institution at hand so that liabilities can be paid when expected. Insurance companies will have both short-term, intermediate-term, and long-term expected payouts due to the varying cycles of payout requirements. Banks, depending on their strategy, have liabilities from deposits (both short- and intermediate-term) and from loans that they make to customers. In both industries, the liabilities are more easily defined than they are with endowment funds and pension funds and are, therefore, easier to manage.

Risks

Because both banks and insurance companies will be required to pay out a portion of their assets to satisfy liabilities, the risk policies of these institutions have traditionally been conservative. That is not to say that a portion of the invested assets cannot be in the form of equities, but if such securities are used, they are generally of high quality.

Tax and Regulatory Considerations

Both banks and insurance companies are subject to income taxes and regulatory constraints. For the last 20 years, the environment has been characterized as having both a more difficult regulatory environment and tax environment. Unlike pension plans and endowment funds, banks and insurance companies must pay taxes on the earnings of their investments.

Macroeconomic Environment

The last 20 or so years also have been characterized by wide fluctuations within the macro-environment. Both banks and insurance companies have been at the whims of inflationary pressures during high inflation periods, causing them to change their asset mix and product offering in order to keep their customers happy. During times of economic downturns, these entities have also had to be wary of credit risk when investing in fixed-income securities such as bonds from both an interest rate perspective and a default perspective.

Strategic Asset Allocation

Asset allocation is the process of selecting generic asset combinations of equities, bonds, mutual funds or other investments so that the investment objectives of the investor can be met. The assets are considered in absolute proportions to other types of assets within the portfolio. The types of assets chosen for a particular strategy are chosen as they relate to the risk return objectives of the client. In creating an asset allocation for a particular client, the risk on correlation of investments must be carefully considered and explained to the client prior to finalizing any decision. Of course, well-designed portfolios are excellent at picking assets that have relatively low correlation to each other.

Strategic asset allocation, sometimes called fixed weightings allocation, is a form of asset allocation whereby the investor divides up the portfolio among major asset classes such as stocks, bonds, mutual funds, etc. This type of strategy uses asset mixes that are consistent with the investor's long-term financial goals. Although the asset mix will change over time as values in the portfolio increase and decrease, the objective is to keep the same proportions of securities in the portfolio. Thus, rebalancing will occur periodically based upon thresholds set by the advisor and the client. This strategy tends to be more of a passive strategy as the investor does not often shift the allocation of the assets.

Brinson, Hood, and Beebower (BHB) examined 91 large corporate pension plans from 1974 to 1983 and found that the average plan included investments in stocks, bonds, T-bills, and real estate.[1] The combined asset mix makes performance evaluation more complex than the Sharpe, Treynor, and Jensen measures discussed earlier which can be applied only to the stock portion of the portfolio.

BHB suggest that performance of portfolios diversified across asset classes be compared with a portfolio that consists of the pension plan's normal percentage distribution between asset classes. BHB use the Standard & Poor's 500 Index, the Shearson Lehman Government/ Corporate Bond Index, and 30-day Treasury bills as the measurement indicator for each of these asset classes. For an investment manager to generate superior performance, he or she would have to outperform a passively managed portfolio maintaining the plan's mix of asset classes.

Ignoring real estate and focusing on stocks, bonds, and T-bills, BHB found that, in general, the actual mean average total return on managed portfolios over the period was 9.01 percent versus 10.11 percent for the benchmark portfolio. In other words, active management cost the pension plans 1.10 percent per year. Of course, over other time periods the managed portfolios could reflect superior results. Stressed throughout the BHB analysis is also the fact that determining the appropriate asset allocation mix (stocks versus bonds versus T-bills) is much more important than simply picking winning or losing stocks.

Asset managers lose their jobs not so much because they picked stock A over stock B, but because they had a poorly allocated portfolio under a given market condition. For example, Table 8–1 shows a typical portfolio composition for large pension fund managers. Equities of all types make up 55 percent of the portfolio. If in a bull market, one is only 40 percent invested in equities, he or she could be in real trouble even if individual stock selection was great.

A Specific Example—Asset Allocation

Suppose a portfolio manager is charged with the responsibility of overseeing the performance of a $100 million portfolio. At the end of each quarter, she must report her performance to the plan sponsor, which we shall assume is a pension fund committee for a large corporation.

After intensive analysis of the economy, she decides to allocate her funds in the manner shown in column (1) of Table 8–2. The designation of funds into various categories of assets is called **asset allocation**. The second column represents her returns from each category during the course of the year. The third column shows the percentage invested (Column 1)

---

1. Gary P. Brinson, Randolph Hood, and Gilbert L. Beebower, "Determinants of Portfolio Performance," *Financial Analysts Journal*, July–August 1986, pp. 39–44.

TABLE 8–1 Typical Weighted Portfolio for Money Managers

Asset Class	Weight
Equities:	
Domestic large capitalization	30% ⎤
Domestic small capitalization	15 ⎥ 55%
International	10 ⎦
Venture capital	5
Fixed income:	
Domestic bonds	15
International dollar bonds	4
Nondollar bonds	6
Real estate	15
Cash equivalents	0
	100%

Source: Gary Brinson, Jeffrey J. Diermeier, and Gary C. Schlarbaum, "A Composite Portfolio Benchmark for Pension Plans," *Financial Analysts Journal*, March–April 1986, p. 15.

TABLE 8–2 Comparison of Managed and Benchmark Portfolios

Asset Class	Managed Portfolio			Benchmark Portfolio		
	(1) Asset Allocation	(2) Returns	(3) Weighted Returns	(4) Asset Allocation	(5) Returns	(6) Weighted Returns
Equities:						
Domestic large capitalization	30%	9%	2.70%	30%	10%	3.00%
Domestic small capitalization	20	15	3.00	15	13	1.95
International	20	18	3.60	10	14	1.40
Total equities	70%		9.30%	55%		6.35%
Fixed income:						
Domestic bonds	11%	8%	0.88%	15%	9%	1.35%
Foreign bonds	8	10	0.80	10	12	1.20
Total fixed income	19%		1.68%	25%		2.55%
Real estate	7	10%	0.70	15	11%	1.65
Cash equivalents	4	4	0.16	5	4	0.20
Total portfolio	100%		11.84%	100%		10.75%

times the returns (Column 2) and, in effect, represents her weighted return for each category and her total return for the year.

On the right side of the table, we see a representative benchmark portfolio that is the standard for measuring her performance. In Column 4, we observe the asset allocation; in Column 5, the return for each category; and in Column 6, the weighted returns for the benchmark portfolio.

For ease of presentation, we shall assume the risk associated with her portfolio is the same as that for the benchmark portfolio. Later we will consider the implications of different risk exposure.

In observing Table 8-2 note the overall results in Column 3 for the portfolio manager and those in Column 6 for the benchmark portfolio. The portfolio manager outperformed the benchmark portfolio by 1.09 percent; that is, her total return was 11.84 percent, while the benchmark portfolio had a 10.75 percent return.

The question is, How was this superior result achieved? In this particular case, she held a larger equity position (70 percent) than the benchmark portfolio (55 percent), which turned out to be fortunate because the stock market was moving up throughout the year (all categories of equities had strong positive returns).

We can further break down the performance of equities based on the three major categories of stock. Actually, for domestic, large capitalization stocks (those with $9 billion or more in market value), she slightly underperformed the market (9 percent versus 10 percent). An appropriate market measure for the benchmark portfolio of large capitalization stocks would be the Standard & Poor's 500 Index.[2] Notice that her performance on small capitalization stocks was 2 percent higher than the market portfolio (15 percent versus 13 percent). An appropriate market measure for the benchmark portfolio of small capitalization stocks would be the Russell 2000 Index.

Finally, she achieved a high rate of return on international equities, exceeding the benchmark return by a full 4 percent (18 percent versus 14 percent). The appropriate benchmark portfolio measure might be the Dow Jones World Stock Index. We might even decide to break down our international equity investments and the benchmark comparisons by different areas of the world such as Mexico, Europe, Asia/Pacific, and so on. Further comparisons can be made among investments in established markets and emerging markets. The effect that the changing value of the dollar had on returns could also be considered.

In moving to fixed-income securities, our portfolio manager underperformed the benchmark portfolio, both domestically (8 percent versus 9 percent) and internationally (10 percent versus 12 percent). The same slight underperformance can be found in real estate (10 percent versus 11 percent). However, with only 19 percent of assets allocated to fixed income and 7 percent to real estate in the managed portfolio, this underperformance is not a problem.

In summary, our portfolio manager had a strong performance because of an equity position (70 percent) that was much higher than the benchmark portfolio (55 percent); that is, she benefited from superior asset allocation. She also gained from superior stock selection in the small capitalization and international equity areas; these factors more than overcame the slightly inferior performance in other categories.

Earlier in the chapter, we talked about risk considerations in measuring performance. Although we will not make a formal evaluation of risk in this case, certain factors are worthy of note. To the extent that the managed portfolio is riskier than the benchmark portfolio, the superior return would have to be partially discounted. Of course, if it is less risky than the market, the superior performance becomes even more meaningful.

While the higher equity component in the managed portfolio might imply greater risk, the large degree of international diversification could easily compensate for this factor. International securities may offset shocks in the U.S. market, and vice versa. Also, the managed portfolio appears to be more liquid than the benchmark portfolio, with real estate representing 7 percent of the holdings versus 15 percent for the benchmark portfolio. This is true in spite of a slightly lower cash position in the managed portfolio.

One last factor is worthy of note in discussing the performance of the portfolio manager. The results presented in Table 8–2 represent annual data. As mentioned earlier, the portfolio manager will not only need to present annual information for evaluation but normally reports quarterly to the investor as well. Because there is always strong pressure for performance, short-term swings in the market can test a portfolio manager's convictions. For example, when the stock market is going down, a portfolio manager with a large equity position (perhaps 70 percent or greater) may be under pressure to lighten up on stocks because of negative returns. However, down markets are normally the best time to buy, not

---

2. We could also add another category of MidCap stocks, but we have omitted it to shorten the presentation.

to sell. This principle may be severely tested when a portfolio manager has to report a quarterly loss but, at the same time, suggests that unusually good buying opportunities now exist. While the stock market generally provides superior returns in comparison with other investments over the long term, such may not be the case over a short period of time. Well-informed portfolio managers, and those for whom they work, generally use a three- to five-year time horizon to determine whether performance is acceptable. However, in the world of money management, one or two bad quarters can sometimes mean the loss of an account.

Tactical Asset Allocation

The concept of strategic asset allocation is firmly rooted in Modern Portfolio Theory. It is worthwhile to note however, that the concept of tactical asset allocation, unlike strategic allocation, is derived more from the applications of practitioners and investment advisors. Thus, this practice of tactical allocation served as the lead in the development of the concept as described in practical textbooks. Tactical asset allocation begins where strategic allocation ends. Strategic allocation solves the problem of optimally allocating an individual's wealth among competing classes of assets. From the practitioners' viewpoint, the drawback of strategic asset allocation is that this solution for wealth distribution among asset classes is somewhat limited and inflexible.

To understand the practitioner's viewpoint further, consider this example. Assume that the strategic asset allocation solution for a client was to invest 60 percent of her wealth in stocks, 35 percent in bonds and 5 percent in cash. This solution is unique in the sense that all other possible wealth distributions would be suboptimal, given the inputs to this decision. Thus another distribution such as an allocation of 55 percent in stocks, 45 percent in bonds would not lead to the realization of the investment objective. Further, the optimal allocation would need to be maintained for at least some period of time for the results to bear. In a volatile and dynamic financial environment, being "stuck" in one portfolio position is a limitation. Given an unforeseen turn of events, a financial planner may assess the need to reallocate wealth among the asset classes and not be limited by the strict single solution from the strategic allocation model. This is why and how the need arose to modify the limitation of inflexibility in the strategic model. The solution forwarded by practitioners, known as tactical asset allocation, does not discard the strategic model but modifies the model by creating a range of allocation around the strategic solution. The following table describes this modification, using our earlier example.

Strategic Asset Allocation		
Stocks	Bonds	Cash
60%	35%	5%

Tactical Asset Allocation		
Stocks	Bonds	Cash
55–65%	30–40%	0–10%

With the additional flexibility, planners can now reallocate around the optimal solution to take advantage of opportunities arising from unexpected developments in the financial markets.

While the above rationale has some practical appeal, a more thorough examination of the idea leads us to some further questions. First, an implicit assumption being made is that a planner who adopts this strategy not only understands how to interpret a given turn of event, but also knows the resulting outcome from that event, in monetary terms. As the reader can follow, this takes us back to the question of whether we can forecast the future well enough to make claims about expected returns and justify a reallocation. If this were so and markets were inefficient, there would be no need for strategic asset allocation either, since expert managers could consistently find winners and losers and reap abnormal returns. Moreover, note that following a tactical asset allocation strategy may considerably increase the trading activity in a portfolio, as planners continually adjust allocation to market changes. Hence, the planner needs to perform at an even higher level in order to earn the stated excess returns after accounting for trading costs.

Second, the question arises as to whether there are any conditions that are more suitable for the application of tactical asset allocation for the benefit of clients. The answer to that is, yes. Tactical asset allocation can indeed aid the performance of portfolios. Changes in the stage of the business cycle can be used to make tactical shifts in assets. However, such allocation changes are much less frequent than what is currently practiced by the adherents of tactical allocation. This issue will be examined in greater detail in a later chapter on macroeconomic analysis.

PASSIVE VERSUS ACTIVE PORTFOLIO MANAGEMENT

In a previous chapter, we alluded to the concept of active versus passive management styles. Even though this concept is now being formally introduced, the idea contained within is not new. Simply put, an active manager believes that markets are **not** efficient while a passive manager does. Thus the issue of whether to manage actively or passively is simply the trading strategy perspective of opponents and proponents, respectively, of the efficient market hypothesis. While there are managers who may consider using management styles, the debate is straightforward to the extent that the debate over EMH is quite clear. That is, if EMH (in any of its forms) holds, it implies that **consistently** outperforming the market is not possible and vice versa.

Obviously, the primary claim of active managers is that EMH does not hold in financial markets. In other words, prices of securities do not accurately reflect information. In turn, this implies that active managers can **consistently** identify incorrectly valued securities, both real and financial securities, enabling them to earn profits greater than the market (or their benchmarks) managers base their superiority claim on two factors. First, they contend that given the resources at their command, they have access to better information than most, if not all, small investors, Second, given their training, specialization, experience and access to personnel of similar qualifications, they can also process the information better than all small or individual investors.

Active managers therefore contend that the above two factors allow them to conduct analysis, leading to superior stock selection. This analysis is termed as fundamental analysis. Fundamental analysis is the study of firm financial statements, valuation exercises to understand the firm's correct price, also known as **intrinsic value**, and an assessment of global macroeconomic conditions. Fundamental analysis, or the process of stock selection, is covered in detail in later chapters.

Active managers also contend that not only can they find mispriced securities, they can also assess when securities, they can also assess when securities should be bought or sold or how long a security should be held.

Active managers who claim such ability are said to understand **security timing** issues. To assess the timing criteria, managers may use either fundamental analysis or technical analysis. Recall that technical analysts look at past price patterns to predict the future. In this sense, technical analysis results in signals that supposedly allow the managers to enter or exit positions before some event occurs. For example, the signal indicates an exit strategy (sell a position) and then the security price goes down. Of course, and as noted in the previous chapter, a successful technical analysis also proves that markets couldn't even be weak form efficient. Security timing using fundamental analysis is concerned with the concept of **business cycles**. This topic will be covered in greater detail in a later chapter. Together, the analysis that leads to both security selection and timing is also considered as the outcome of **security analysis**.

Active managers attribute their ability to outperform their benchmarks for all the reasons discussed above. While superior performance is considered the benefit of active management, this performance is not without its costs. There are both direct and indirect costs associated with the services of active managers. The largest and most direct of all costs is the fee an active manager charges clients for his/her abilities, skills and talent. These fees, or **loads**, are often very high, costing clients large sums of money. The greater the reputation of an active manager, the higher the fee they charge. Loads of 4 to 6 percent are not unheard of, nor uncommon. Another way of thinking about these fees is that an active manager who charges a 5 percent fee must at least earn that much before the client can expect a profit. Alternately, if the benchmark is a tradable index, then the active manager must outperform the benchmark by at least 5 percent for it to be worthwhile for the investor to engage the services of this manager. This can prove to be a tall order. At the end of this section, we'll look at how active managers have *actually* performed in their practice. Other direct costs include management and sales fees which also increase the costs.

Besides direct costs, there are indirect costs as well. Since active managers claim the ability to know which securities to buy/sell and when, it must imply that they would trade more frequently than those who don't. Thus, the frequency of trades, or **turnover**, for active managers is also much higher than others. Since such trading is not costless, these transaction costs are also borne by the investors. It is thus straightforward to understand that all these loads, expenses and costs can and do sum up to a very tidy sum.

Passive managers are on the other end of the spectrum in every possible way. Passive managers begin by believing that markets are efficient and that security selection and timing exercises are not only futile but that the associated costs are unnecessary as well. Passive investors firmly believe that indexes and benchmarks will *consistently* outperform active managers.[3] Since they do not require any research and analysis, there are no costs associated with selection and timing related resource and analytical costs. Further, with no timing implication of which security is about to fall in or out of favor, trading needs and associated transaction costs are very low. Thus, passive investors are complacent in their knowledge about the performance of their benchmarks. Hence, they conduct very little analysis or trade, and are hence passive.

It is not that passive managers do not need to work at all, but it is in relation to active managers that they do not have to undertake all the activities their counterparts engage in; the work of passive managers is of another kind. First, passive managers construct portfolios that attempt to replicate the benchmark's performance. Examples of benchmarks include the S&P 500 as its benchmark index, the Russell 1000 index and the Wilshire 5000 index. There are many more indexes. A passive manager claiming to match the return performances of the stocks of larger firms may construct a portfolio using the S&P 500 as its benchmark or peer index. A manager offering to replicate returns similar to all exchange traded stocks may use the Wilshire 5000 as its benchmark index. Passive managers construct their fund portfolios in a way such that the performance of their fund is very closely correlated with the benchmark. In trying to closely track the index, passive managers also try to keep the number of securities required to track the index as low as possible. This in turn helps in keeping trading costs low as well. Passive managers use a variety of methods in constructing

---

3. Hence, passive investors simply replicate the holdings in their benchmarks.

replication funds methods; we will delve briefly into this in the next section. Thus, investors who subscribe to the services of passive managers are said to be "indexing." The final trait in passive management concerns the timing issue. A passive investor does have the choice of shifting wealth between various index funds. This is a hybrid investor or manager. Such a person may not believe in actively selecting securities but does think that different indexes will perform differently over time. There is no argument about the truth of this view since different indexes will perform differentially. What is questionable about such hybrid investors is that they believe they know when these shifts in index performance will happen. The immediately observe that such an investor is at least partially refuting EMH by accepting the ability to time the market. That leaves us with the passive manager or investor who is a complete believer in the EMH. This group will neither select nor time the trade. Such an investor will buy an index fund and hold it for a certain amount of time. These investors can be thought of as a *buy-and-hold* indexer, the most passive of all investors.

During the 1990s indexing and passive investing began increasing in popularity. The debacle in the stock market in early 2000 provided additional fuel for growth. Today, there are literally hundreds of index funds, tracking benchmarks of all possible hues and shapes. Funds track benchmarks for value, growth, sectors and industries (e.g. biotech index fund), precious metals, commodities, currencies and raw material besides the original benchmarks for the stock and bond markets. Further, while the replication funds in the 1990s were mostly structured as mutual funds, today there is a whole raft of funds, known as **Exchange Traded Funds** or **ETF's** that are structured and trade like individual stocks. All these innovations have simplified considerably the tasks of individual and small passive investors.

This discussion being over, we are now in a position to ask that 64 million dollar question. Which type of manager has **actually** performed better, historically? Unfortunately, for active managers, the evidence overwhelmingly supports a passive management approach. Numerous studies have been conducted, assessing the past performances of both managerial types, by all known methods. Nearly all these studies conclude similarly, in favor of passive management. The reader may ask the question as to why there are so many reports in the media about the superior performances of certain active managers. The answer is actually a caution to the readers that more often than not, such reports may be the outcome of (industry) sponsored research using techniques that may be questionable.

Instead, consider the studies, authenticated by publication, in noted (financial) scientific journals. Malkiel[4] for instance, examines the abnormal returns (**alpha**) of active managers on a risk adjusted basis, since this is what active managers promise. Alpha is equal to the actual return for active managers' fund minus the expected return (benchmark return), over a certain period of time, say one year. Each year, managers adhering to a certain benchmark or "style" are ranked by their performance in their category.[5] Studies of such rankings over time show that the performance of the benchmark index is superior to the performance of at least 50 percent of the active managers (the median ranking) in a majority of the years studied. Other studies also show that there are no superior managers who have *consistently* (over many years) outperformed their benchmarks. Similar studies in the bond market fund performances yield very similar results. Most studies indicate that active managers match their benchmark results at best, imposing the total charges for active management as a full cost (loss) on their clients. Ironically, this implies that the managers who charge the most are

---

4. In plotting the fund alphas for a large group of active managers over long periods of time, Malkiel found the alpha distribution to be normal and centered on zero. A conclusion of this observation is that active managers perform as well as their benchmarks. This in turn implies that the benchmark outperforms active managers after adjusting for the costs charged to their clients.

5. When the benchmark is introduced in these rankings, it places itself along with its active peers and shows how the benchmark performed in a certain year as compared to the managers in that category.

more likely to **consistently underperform** their benchmarks!! While consistent outperformance is not generally possible, consistent underperformance is not only possible but very likely for the most expensive active managers!!

What about the superstars of the fund industry, who are household names. Managers like Peter Lynch of Magellan Funds and Warren Buffett of Berkshire Hathaway. True, they did outperform the market consistently. Does it not imply the possibility that managers may exist who can select and time securities? The answer is yes, it is possible that such managers exist. An alternate question also arises: Given that there may be three or four such superstar managers and there are more than 15,000, total managers, what is the likelihood of finding them before they turn to superstars.

SECURITY SELECTION

The creation of an index meant for passive investors has already been discussed. The two main considerations in including or excluding a security are to identify securities for inclusion that will increase most the correlation between the index and the underlying basket it tracks and keeping the number of included securities as low as possible. A few methods exist in the selection process. The most common method for stock index funds is to use a weighted marker value method. In this technique, the stocks are ranked according to marker value after separating them along industry lines. Next, the largest stocks from each category are added into the fund. The track index being thus formed is back tested on correlation. As more stocks are added, the correlation begins to increase. When the correlation for the two approach some preset level, the inclusion of more stocks end. While this is a simple description, actual processes may employ other more sophisticated techniques. Similarly, bond index funds are often selected based on their **duration** or **coupon** rates, etc.

The selection of securities for passive indexes is more straightforward than for those constructed for active investors for obvious reasons. Since active managers claim this ability, they also use many different methods of security selection. It is useful to understand the various issues that are involved in these processes. Essentially there are two broad categories for security selection. These are technical and fundamental analysis. Technical analysis will be covered in great detail in later chapters; in this section we can consider some of the easy ways in which fundamental analysis leads to security selection.

The investment **style** of a fund is the process by which securities are included in various funds. In this section, we'll examine style issues for stocks. Bonds styles will be considered only briefly. Stocks are stratified first via different criteria. For example, stocks may be ranked by size where market value is the criterion used. All stocks having a market value of $5 billion or less are classified as small cap (capitalization) stocks. Stocks with market value of $20 billion are considered to be large cap stocks. Students should note that this nomenclature is not set in stone. Size structures may and can differ between funds, depending on how each fund considers the impact of size on fund performance. Once the size stratas have been established, second criteria may be applied across all stocks. Stocks may be classified as **value** stocks, **growth** stocks or as stocks with a blend of these attributes, like size. Various fund managers may use various criteria to separate stocks. Consider some of the ways in which value stocks may be identified. In the chapters on fundamental analysis, we'll learn techniques to value stocks. These valuation techniques use both qualitative and quantitative methods to assess what the value of a stock should truly be. This is called the stock's intrinsic value. If a stock trades in the market at a price higher or lower than its **intrinsic value**, then that stock is considered to be over and undervalued, respectively. Undervalued stocks get added to the value category with the understanding that undervalued stocks are expected to increase in value. Similarly growth stocks may be identified by criteria such as low or no dividend yield, small companies early in the company's life cycle, companies that have many high return (return **on equity** or ROE) projects, etc. Companies that fit neither

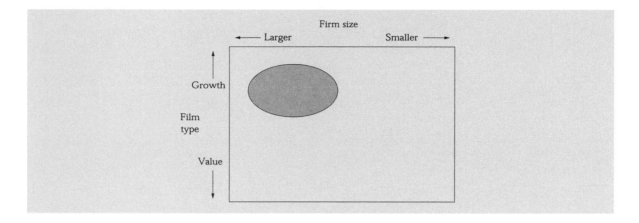

value nor growth are signed as being blend stocks. Some strategists use other methods to assign stocks to styles. For example, stocks can be ranked by their **price to earnings** (P/E) ratio or price to book ratio and then the stocks in the lower third are considered as value stocks, the middle third as blend stocks and the top third as growth stocks. There are many others. With both stock size and style identified, investors can then be presented a choice of funds which vary by both size and style. A fund may choose to position itself in any region of this grid, as shown above.

The shaded region represents a zone from which a fund picks its stocks. Such a fund expects a number of investors may be interested in this zone and expects to attract these investors. The method by which they arrive at these expectations is the subject of a different discussion.

Bonds are typically selected by various criteria as well. The coupon rate, its **yield to maturity**, duration, **bond quality**, etc. Are all used for this purpose. The conceptual methods and purposes are very similar to stocks. Commodity funds, real estate funds, such as **real estate investment trust** (funds) also follow the same guidelines.[6]

Some portfolios are constructed by imposing an alternate type of restriction. Inclusion of securities may be limited to a certain **industry** or **sector**. These portfolios are considered to be **concentrated** portfolios.

At this point, the reader should have a much clearer understanding of the integral issues of portfolio management along with the understanding of why various types of Investment Policy Statements are needed. The information provided in this chapter should also aid the advisor in crafting appropriate IPS's for different client types and in helping them understand how and to what degree asset allocation strategies are desirable for various clients. Finally, each advisor should also have an understanding of whether they want to follow an active or passive approach to portfolio management.

---

6. Stocks are also selected through screens; screens may rank and include stocks by many different criteria such as P/E and P/B ratio, dividend yield ratio, low price, etc. Other screens commonly used are criteria arising from anomalies. These screens can be automated which help to reduce costs.

Chapter 9

Asset Pricing Models

This chapter is devoted to the exploration of theoretical models that allow us to value or price securities, especially stocks. The first model examined is the now famous Capital Asset Pricing Model (CAPM) as developed by Professors Sharpe and Markowitz, who are both among the most notable pioneers in the field of modern finance. The CAPM (and the construct of the "Efficient Frontier") can be considered to be the first "truly" foundation models of finance. This model laid the path for many other advancements in the field. Today, the CAPM is a household word for all students of finance. The Arbitrage Pricing Theory (APT), another asset pricing model, is also examined in this chapter. The APT followed up on the CAPM. While the CAPM is considered to be path-breaking, the APT is considered as a much more sophisticated model, one that heralded that the science of finance had indeed become established as a modern science. Variants of other derived asset pricing models are also examined briefly at the end of the chapter.

CAPITAL ASSET PRICING MODEL

The development of the efficient frontier in the previous section gives insight into optimum portfolio mixes in an appropriate risk-return context. Nevertheless, the development of multiple portfolios is a rather difficult and tedious task. Professors Sharpe, Lintner, and others have allowed us to take the philosophy of efficient portfolios into a more generalized and meaningful context through the **capital asset pricing model**. Under this model, we examine the theoretical underpinnings through which assets are valued based on their risk characteristics.

The Real World of Investing

Students as Portfolio Managers—The Number of Programs Continues to Grow

It started at the University of Wisconsin more than 30 years ago. Now students manage part of the university endowment in more than 100 colleges and universities. This is no simulation.

The largest such program is at Ohio State University, where the students are enrolled in courses that allow them to manage more than $10 million of the permanent endowment of the university. Other schools such as UCLA, Indiana University, the University of Southern California, Southern Methodist University, Notre Dame, Gannon College, Virginia Military Institute, DePaul University, and Texas Christian University have similar programs. Professor Edward C. Lawrence of the University of Missouri–St. Louis tracks

---

all the programs across the country as to size, value, and source of funding.* Some schools operate with as little as a few thousand dollars, while the typical program size is $150,000 to $200,000.

The authors are most familiar with the student-managed fund at Texas Christian University, where they have both served as faculty advisors. The students manage $1.8 million in stocks and bonds and have power to make their own investment decisions. The faculty advisors do not even have veto power (don't ask if they swear a lot!). The students receive six hours of academic credit for their work and do intensive work to analyze securities and balance the portfolio. The students also have their own committees operating in such areas as economics and accounting.

As would be true of other professional money managers, they provide annual reports in which they compare their performance with their own goals as well as with the popular market averages.

*Edward C. Lawrence, "Financial Innovation: The Case of Student Investment Funds at United States Universities," *Financial Practice and Education*, Spring–Summer 1994, pp. 47–53.

The capital asset pricing model (CAPM) takes off where the efficient frontier concluded through the introduction of a new investment outlet, the risk-free asset (R_F). A risk-free asset has no risk of default and a standard deviation of 0 ($\sigma_{RF} = 0$) and is the lowest assumed safe return that can be earned. A U.S. Treasury bill or Treasury bond is often considered representative of a risk-free asset. Under the capital asset pricing model, we introduce the notion of combining the risk-free asset and the efficient frontier with the development of the R_FMZ line as indicated in Figure 9–1.

The R_FMZ line opens up the possibility of a whole new set of superior investment opportunities. That is, by combining some portion of the risk-free asset as represented by (R_F) with M (a point along the efficient frontier), we create new investment opportunities that will allow us to reach higher indifference curves than would be possible simply along the efficient frontier. The only point along the efficient frontier that now has significance is point M, where the straight line from R_F is tangent to the old efficient frontier. Let us further examine the R_FMZ line.

We can reach points along the R_FMZ line in a number of different ways. To be at point R_F, we would simply buy a risk-free asset. To be at a point between R_F and M, we would buy a combination of R_F and the M portfolio along the efficient frontier. To be at a point between M and Z, we buy M with our available funds and then borrow additional funds to further increase our purchase of the M portfolio (an example of this would be to be at point P in Figure 9–2). To the extent that M is higher than R_F and we can borrow at a rate equal to R_F or slightly higher, we can get larger returns with a combination of buying M and borrowing additional funds to buy M.

We also note that point M is considered the optimum "market basket" of investments available (although you may wish to combine this market basket with risk-free assets or borrowing). If you took all the possible investments that investors could acquire and determined the optimum basket of investments, you would come up with point M (because it is along the efficient frontier and tangent to the R_F line). Point M can be measured by the total return on the Standard & Poor's 500 Stock Average, the Dow Jones Industrial Average, the New York Stock Exchange Index, or similar measures. If point M or the market were not represented by the optimum risk-return portfolio for all investments at a point in time, then it is assumed there would be an instantaneous change, and the market measure (point M) would once again be in equilibrium (be optimal).

FIGURE 9–1   Basic Diagram of the Capital Asset Pricing Model

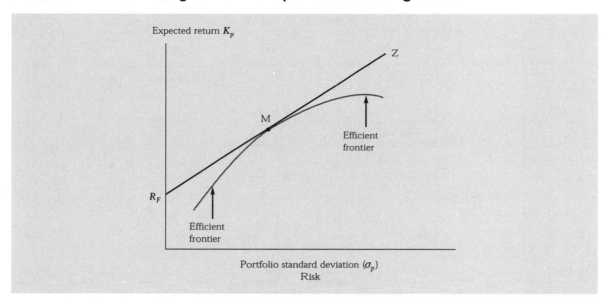

FIGURE 9–2   The CAPM and Indifference Curves

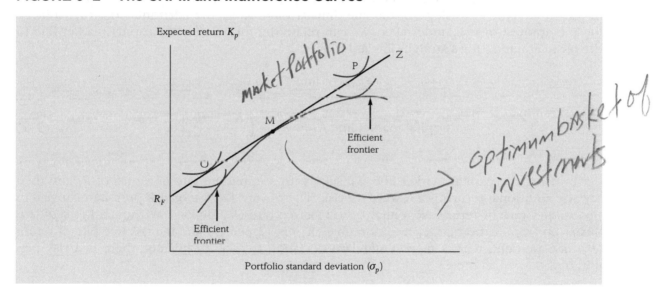

Capital Market Line

The previously discussed $R_F MZ$ line is called the **capital market line (CML)** and is once again presented in Figure 9–3.

The formula for the capital market line in Figure 9-3 may be written as:

$$
K_P = R_F + \left(\frac{K_M - R_F}{\sigma_M - 0} \right) \sigma_P
$$

FIGURE 9–3   Illustration of the Capital Market Line

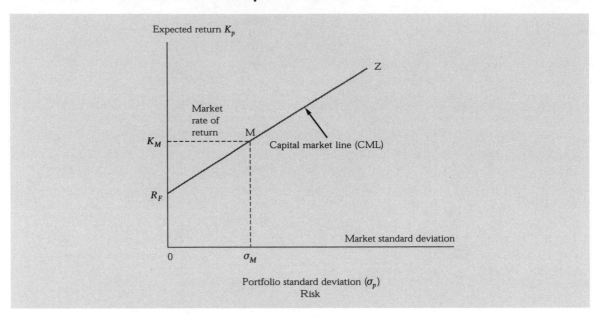

We indicate that the expected return on any portfolio (K_p) is equal to the risk-free rate of return (R_F) plus the slope of the line times a value along the horizontal axis (σ_p), indicating the amount of risk undertaken. We can relate the formula for the capital market line to the basic equation for a straight line as follows:

$$\text{Straight line } Y = a + bX$$

$$\text{Capital market line } K_P = R_F + \left(\frac{K_M - R_F}{\sigma_M} \right) \sigma_P \qquad (9\text{-}1)$$

In using the capital market line, we start with a minimum rate of return of R_F and then say any additional return is a reward for risk. The reward for risk or risk premium is equal to the market rate of return (K_M) minus the risk-free rate (R_F) divided by the market standard deviation (σ_M). If the market rate of return (K_M) is 12 percent and the risk-free rate of return (R_F) is 6 percent, with a market standard deviation (σ_M) of 20 percent, there is a risk premium of 0.3:

$$\frac{K_M - R_F}{\sigma_M} = \frac{12\% - 6\%}{20\%} = \frac{6\%}{20\%} = 0.3$$

Then, if the standard deviation of our portfolio (σ_p) is 22 percent, we can expect a return of 12.6 percent along the CML computed as follows:

$$K_P = R_F + \left(\frac{K_M - R_F}{\sigma_M} \right) \sigma_P$$

$$K_P = 6\% + \left(\frac{12\% - 6\%}{20\%} \right) 22\%$$

$$= 6\% + (0.3)22\%$$

$$= 6\% + 6.6\% = 12.6\%$$

The essence of the capital market line is that the way to get larger returns is to take increasingly higher risks. Thus, the only way to climb up the K_p *return* line in Figure 9–3 is to extend yourself out on the σ_p *risk* line. Portfolio managers who claim highly superior returns may have taken larger than normal risks and thus may not really be superior performers on a risk-adjusted basis; the best way to measure a portfolio manager is to evaluate his returns relative to the risks taken. Average to slightly above average returns based on low risk may be superior to high returns based on high risk. One does not easily exceed market-dictated constraints for risk and return.

RETURN ON AN INDIVIDUAL SECURITY

We have been examining return expectations for a portfolio; we now turn our attention to an individual security. Once again the return potential is closely tied to risk. However, when dealing with an individual security, the premium return for risk is not related to *all* the risk in the investment as measured by the standard deviation (σ). The reason for this is that the standard deviation includes two types of risk, but only one is accorded a premium return under the capital asset pricing model.

We now begin an analytical process that allows us to get at the two forms of risk in an individual security. The first form of risk is measured by the beta coefficient.

Beta Coefficient   In analyzing the performance of an individual security, it is first important to measure its relationship to the market through the **beta coefficient**. Let us lay the groundwork for understanding beta. In the case of a potential investment, stock i, we can observe its relationship to the market by tracing its total return performance relative to market total return over the last five years.[1]

Year	Stock i Return (K)	Market Return (K_M)
1	4.8%	6.5%
2	14.5	11.8
3	19.1	14.9
4	3.7	1.1
5	15.6	12.0

We see that stock i moves somewhat with the market. Plotting the values in Figure 9–4, we observe a line that is upward sloping at slightly above a 45-degree angle.

A straight line of best fit has been drawn through the various points representing the following formula:

$$K_i = a_i + b_i K_M + e_i \qquad (9\text{--}2)$$

K_i represents the anticipated stock return based on Formula 9–2 where: a_i (alpha) is the point at which the line crosses the vertical axis; b_i (beta) is the slope of the line; K_M is the independent variable of market return; and e_i is the random error term. The $a_i + b_i K_M$ portion of the formula describes a straight line, and e_i represents deviations or random, non-recurring movements away from the straight line. In the present example, the formula for the straight line is $K_i = 0.42 + 1.20\ K_M$ (indicating a beta or line slope of 1.2). These values

---

1. Although monthly calculations are often used, we can satisfy the same basic learning objectives with annual data, and the analysis is easier to follow.

FIGURE 9–4   Relationship of Individual Stock to the Market

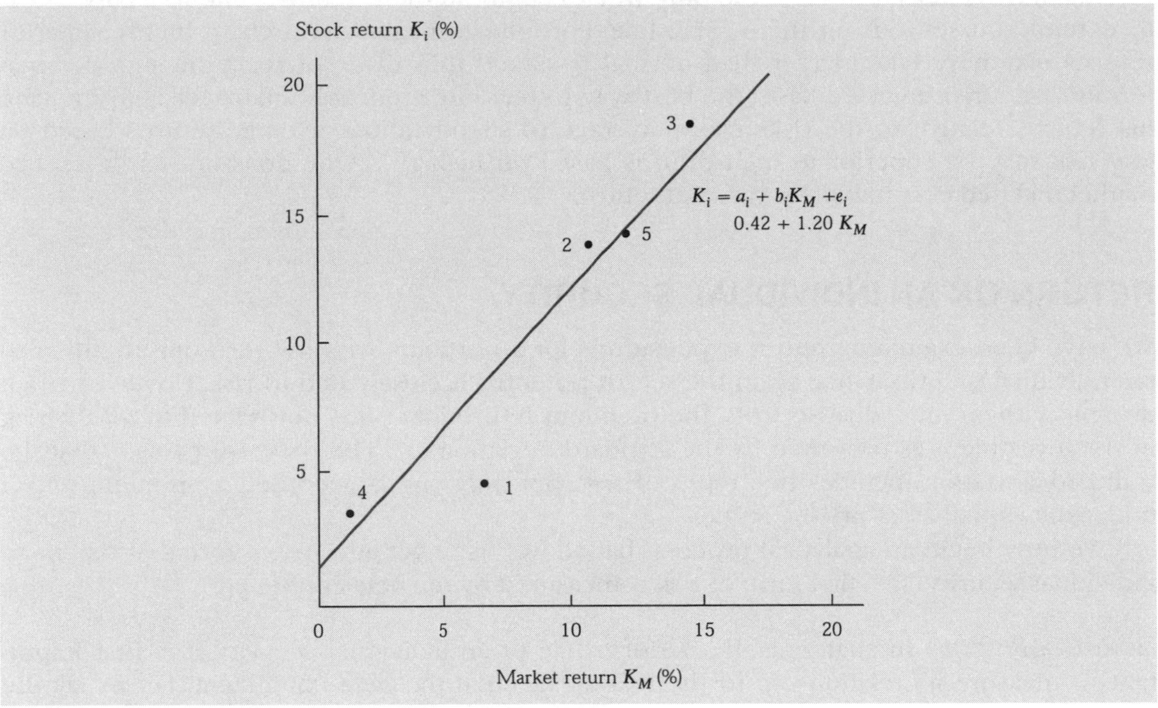

can be approximated by drawing a line of best fit as indicated in Figure 9-4. Basically, the equation tells us how volatile our stock is relative to the market through the beta coefficient. In the present case, if the market moves up or down by a given percent, our stock is assumed to move 1.2 times that amount.

Because beta measures the correlation of a stock's total return to a market index, the beta of the market when regressed on itself will always be 1.0. With a beta of 1.2, our stock is considered to be 20 percent more volatile than the market and therefore riskier. A stock with average volatility would have a beta of 1.0, the same beta as the market. A stock having a beta of less than 1.0 would have less risk than the market.

Systematic and Unsystematic Risk

Previously, we mentioned the two major types of risk associated with a stock. One is the market movement or beta (b_i) risk. If the market moves up or down, a stock is assumed to change in value. This type of risk is referred to as **systematic risk**. The second type of risk is represented by the error term (e_i) and indicates changes in value not associated with market movement. It may represent the temporary influence of a competitor's new product, changes in raw material prices, or unusual economic and government influences on a given firm. These changes are peculiar to an individual security or industry at a given point and are not directly correlated with the market. This second type of risk is referred to as **unsystematic risk**.

Because unsystematic risk is associated with an individual company or industry, it may be diversified away in a large portfolio and is not a risk inherent in investing in common stocks. Thus, by picking stocks that are less than perfectly correlated, unsystematic risk may be eliminated. For example, the inherent risks of investing in cyclical semiconductor stocks may be diversified away by investing in countercyclical housing stocks. Researchers have indicated that all but 15 percent of unsystematic risk may be eliminated with a carefully selected portfolio of 10 stocks, and all but 11 percent, with the portfolio of 20 stocks.[2]

---

2. Wagner and Lau, "The Effect of Diversification on Risk."

FIGURE 9–5   Illustration of the Security Market Line

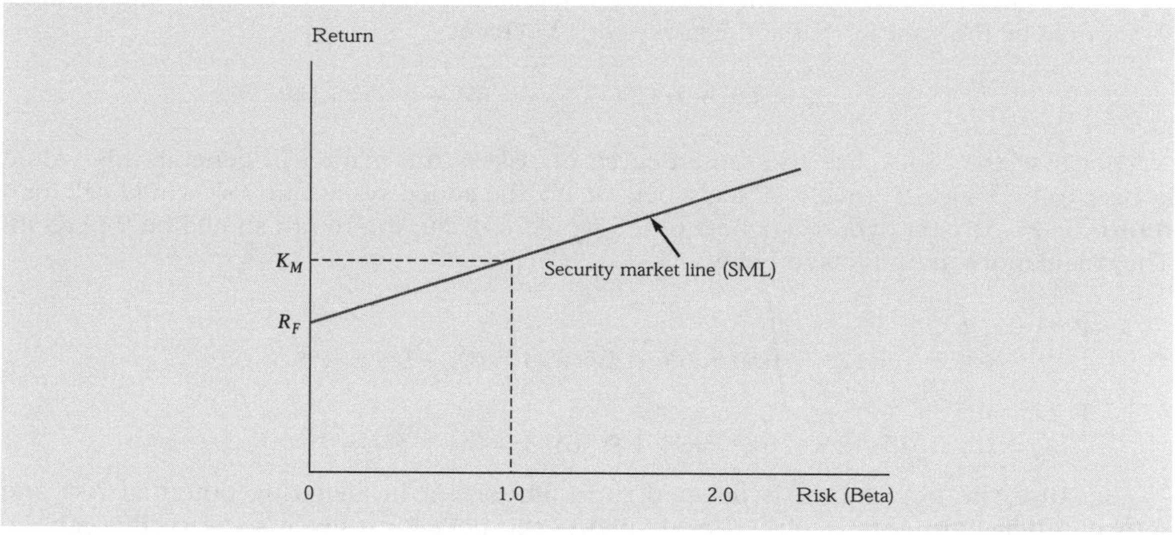

The systematic risk (beta) cannot be diversified away even in a large portfolio, and therefore, the market compensates an investor with a higher expected return when that investor buys securities with a high beta or a lower expected return than the market, when the investor buys securities with a beta less than the market. Using this method of risk adjustment, the capital asset pricing model creates a linear risk-return trade-off using the market as the reference point for risk and return.

Because unsystematic risk can be diversified away, systematic risk (b_i) is the only relevant risk under the capital asset pricing model. Thus, even though we can describe total risk as:

$$\text{Total risk} = \text{Systematic risk} + \text{Unsystematic risk}$$

in a diversified portfolio, unsystematic risk approaches 0.

Security Market Line

We actually express the trade-off between risk and return for an *individual stock* through the **security market line (SML)** in Figure 9–5. Whereas in Figure 9–4, we graphed the relationship that allowed us to compute the beta (b_i) for a security, in Figure 9–5 we now take that beta and show what the anticipated or required return in the marketplace is for a stock with that characteristic. The security market line (SML) shows the risk-return trade-off for an individual stock in Figure 9–5 just as the capital market line (CML) accomplished that same objective for a portfolio in Figure 9–3.

Once again, we stress that the return is not plotted against the total risk (σ) for the individual stock but only that part of the risk that cannot be diversified away, commonly referred to as the systematic or beta risk. The actual formula for the security market line (SML) is:

$$K_i = R_F + b_i(K_M - R_F) \tag{9-3}$$

As we did with the capital market line for portfolio returns, with the security market line we start out with a basic rate of return for a risk-free asset (R_F) and add a premium for risk. In this case, the premium is equal to the beta on the stock times the difference between the market rate of return (K_M) and the risk-free rate of return (R_F). If $R_F = 6\%$, $K_M = 12\%$, and the stock has a beta (b_i) of 1, the anticipated rate of return, using Formula 9-3, would be the same as that in the market, or 12 percent.

$$K_i = 6\% + 1(12\% - 6\%) = 6\% + 6\% = 12\%$$

Because the stock has the same degree of risk as the market in general, this would appear to be logical. If the stock has a beta of 1.5, the added systematic risk would call for a return of 15 percent, whereas a beta of 0.5 would indicate the return should be 9 percent. The calculations are indicated below:

Beta = 1.5
$$K_i = 6\% + 1.5(12\% - 6\%) = 6\% + 1.5(6\%) = 6\% + 9\% = 15\%$$

Beta = 0.5
$$K_i = 6\% + 0.5(12\% - 6\%) = 6\% + 0.5(6\%) = 6\% + 3\% = 9\%$$

Because the beta factor is deemed to be important in analyzing potential risk and return, much emphasis is placed on knowing the beta for a given security. Bloomberg, Value Line, Standard & Poor's, and various brokerage houses and investment services publish information on beta for a large number of securities. A representative list is presented in the table below:

Corporation	Beta (May 2001)
Merrill Lynch (**www.ml.com**)*	1.85
Novell, Inc. (**www.novell.com**)	1.40
Compaq Computer (**www.compaq.com**)	1.25
Southwest Airlines (**www.iflyswa.com**)	1.15
Du Pont (**www.dupont.com**)	1.00
Disney (Walt) (**www.disney.com**)	.90
Shell Transport (**www.shell.com**)	.80
Piedmont Natural Gas (**www.piedmontng.com**)	.60

* These Web sites will take you to the company homepage but not necessarily provide a beta.

ASSUMPTIONS OF THE CAPITAL ASSET PRICING MODEL

Having evaluated some of the implications of the CAPM, it is important that the student be aware of some of the assumptions that go into the model.

1. All investors can borrow or lend an unlimited amount of funds at a given risk-free rate.
2. All investors have the same one-period time horizon.
3. All investors wish to maximize their expected utility over this time horizon and evaluate investments on the basis of means and standard deviations of portfolio returns.
4. All investors have the same expectations—that is, all investors estimate identical probability distributions for rates of return.
5. All assets are perfectly divisible—it is possible to buy fractional shares of any asset or portfolio.
6. There are no taxes or transactions costs.
7. The market is efficient and in equilibrium or quickly adjusting to equilibrium.

FIGURE 9–6   Test of the Security Market Line

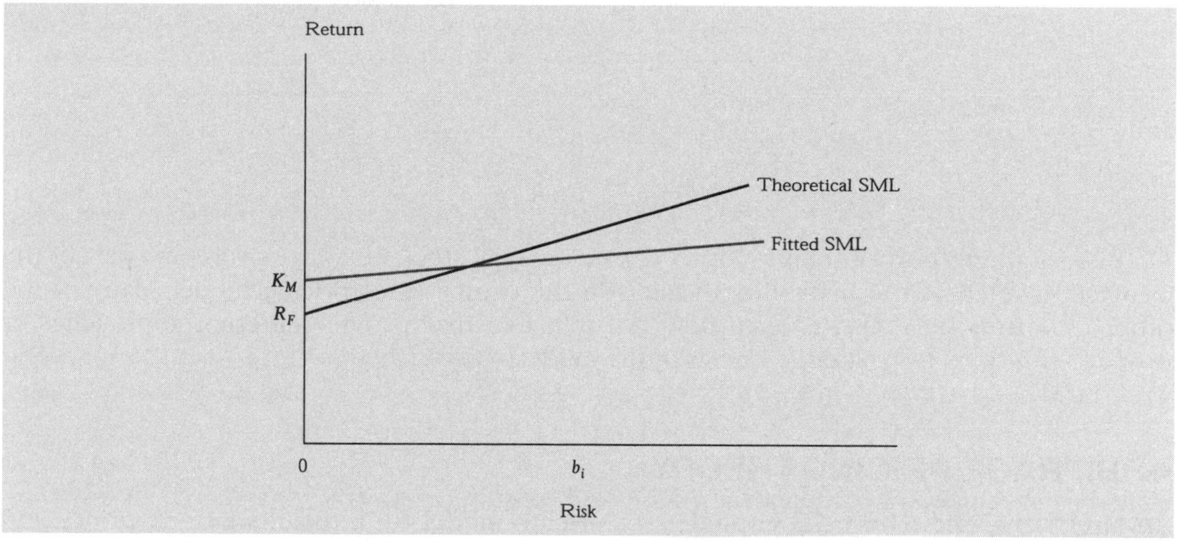

Listing these assumptions indicates some of the necessary conditions to create the CAPM. While at first they may appear to be severely limiting, they are similar to those often used in the standard economic theory of the firm and in other basic financial models.

The primary usefulness in examining this model or similar risk-return trade-off models is to provide some reasonable basis for relating return opportunity with risk on the invest ment. Portfolio managers find risk-return models helpful in explaining their performance or the performance of their competitors to clients. A competitor's portfolio that has unusually high returns may have been developed primarily on the basis of high-risk assets. To the extent that this can be explained on the basis of capital market theory, the competitor's per- formance may look less like superior money management and more like a product of high risk taking. Many of the techniques for assessing portfolio performance on Wall Street are explicitly or implicitly related to the risk return concepts discussed in this chapter.

Although empirical tests have somewhat supported the capital asset pricing model, a number of testing problems remain. To develop the SML in which stock returns (vertical axis) can be measured against beta (horizontal axis), an appropriate line must be drawn. Researchers have some disagreement about R_F. (Is it represented by short-term or long-term Treasury rates?) There is also debate about what is the approximate K_M, or market rate of return. Some suggest the market proxy variable will greatly influence the beta and that diffi- culties in dealing with this problem can bring the whole process under attack.[3]

When empirical data are compared with theoretical return expectations there is some discrepancy in that the theoretical SML may have a greater slope than the actual line fitted on the basis of real-world data as shown in Figure 9–6.[4]

There may also be a possible problem in that betas for individual securities are not necessarily stable over time (rather than remaining relatively constant at 1.3 or perhaps 0.7, they tend to approach 1 over time). Thus, a beta based on past risk may not always reflect current risk.[5] Because the beta for a portfolio may be more stable than an individual stock's

3. Richard Roll, "A Critique of the Asset Pricing Theory's Test," *Journal of Financial Economics*, March 1977, pp. 12–76. Also, "Ambiguity When Performance Is Measured by the Securities Market Line," *Journal of Finance*, September 1978, pp. 1051–69.
4. Franco Modigliani and Gerald A. Pogue, "An Introduction to Risk and Returns," *Financial Analysts Journal*, March–April 1974, pp. 68–86, and May–June 1974, pp. 69–86.
5. Robert A. Levy, "On the Short-Term Stationary of Beta Coefficients," *Financial Analysts Journal*, November–December 1971, pp. 55–62. Also, Marshall E. Blume, "Betas and Their Regression Tendencies," *Journal of Finance*, June 1975, pp. 785–95.

beta, portfolio betas are also used as a systematic risk variable. A portfolio beta is simply the weighted average of the betas of the individual stocks. We can say:

$$b_P \text{ (portfolio beta)} = \sum_{i=1}^{n} x_i b_i \qquad (9\text{-}4)$$

and

$$K_P = R_F + b_P(K_M - R_F) \qquad (9\text{-}5)$$

By examining portfolio betas rather than individual stock betas, we overcome part of the criticism leveled at the instability of betas in the capital asset pricing model. Many of the other criticisms have also evoked new research that may provide different approaches or possible solutions to past deficiencies in the model.

ARBITRAGE PRICING THEORY

An alternative theory to the capital asset pricing model for explaining stock prices and stock returns is the arbitrage pricing theory (APT). This is a fairly sophisticated theory and will be of interest to those who wish to learn more about asset pricing.

Arbitrage pricing theory assumes a linear return generating model that makes the return on an investment a function of more than one factor. The capital asset pricing model also uses a linear return generating model but assumes that returns are a function of a stock's sensitivity to the equity risk premium. APT acknowledges that a stock's return may be a function of many factors. The arbitrage pricing model is a more generalized model than the CAPM and less restrictive in its assumptions; it does not assume equilibrium markets or make assumptions about investor preferences. However, the concept of arbitrage behavior will drive markets to equilibrium as investors try to make risk-free profits.

Arbitrage behavior assumes one good should have the same price. If two different prices are found for gold in London and New York, an arbitrageur could sell short the high-priced gold and buy the low-priced gold. This behavior would drive the price of high-priced gold down and the price of low-priced gold up until the price of gold was the same. Theoretically, by selling short, the investor can use the proceeds from the short sale to buy long, and therefore, the transaction can be made without any investment. This makes the transaction a no-cost risk-less transaction. Arbitrage relies on the behavior of market participants to take advantage of prices in disequilibrium, and through this arbitrage mechanism, prices will move into equilibrium.

The arbitrage pricing model describes the expected return on a stock as a function of several factors. While there is no universal agreement on what factors have the greatest impact on stock returns, Chen[6] and Roll and Ross[7] suggest there are a few major factors. These are changes in expectations about:

1. Interest-rate risk.
2. Business-cycle risk.
3. Inflation.
4. The risk of changing risk premiums.

---

6. Nai-fu Chen, "Some Empirical Tests of the Theory of Arbitrage Pricing," *Journal of Finance*, December 1983, pp. 1393–1414.
7. Richard Roll and Stephen A. Ross, "An Empirical Investigation of the Arbitrage Pricing Theory," *Journal of Finance*, December 1980, pp. 1073–1103.

The return-generating process using the APT model appears in Formula 9-6. We have listed four factors here, but there could be as few as one factor or many other factors. Three or four factors probably capture the most significant return sensitivities.

$$K_{i,t} = a_i + b_{i,1} F_{1,t} + b_{i,2} F_{2,t} + b_{i,3} F_{3,t} + b_{i,4} F_{4,t} + e_{i,t} \qquad (9\text{-}6)$$

where:

$K_{i,t}$ = Return on stock i at time t
a_i = Expected return on stock i
$b_{i,j}$ = Sensitivity of stock i to factor j
$F_{j,t}$ = Value of factor j at time t
$e_{i,t}$ = Random term unique to stock i at time t

If a_i is the expected return on the stock, then the effect of the factors is expected to be zero (0). In other words, the market has already incorporated expectations about these factors into the stock's price. What will affect the actual return on stock i are any surprises in these factors that were not anticipated. For example, if factor 1 is changing real GDP and if real GDP goes up more than expected, stocks that are sensitive to changes in real GDP will go up, while those stocks that are not sensitive to the business cycle will be unaffected. Conversely, if inflation is factor 2 and if it increases more than expected, stocks that are subject to inflationary pressures will decline in price, while those that are not sensitive to changes in inflation will not be affected. The sensitivity to these various factors shows up in the b_i for each factor.

The random term e_i represents the unexpected portion of the return on security i, which is not explained by the factors. It captures unexpected events unique to firm i. For example, a new product announcement, a merger, or a takeover will affect firm i only. These unexpected events were not impounded into the stock's expected return, a_i.

The b_i's (factor sensitivities) reflect the sensitivity of the factor on the stock's return. Like the capital asset pricing model, the factor sensitivity for a portfolio is the sum of the weighted beta for each factor based on the percentage of market value that each stock contributes to the portfolio.

Let us take two stocks, x and y. Two factors affect the returns of both stocks, and the random variable e_i is eliminated because we assume that in a diversified portfolio, e_i approaches zero (0):

$$K_x = 12\% + 3F_{1,t} - 2F_{2,t}$$
$$K_y = 15\% + 1F_{1,t} - 6F_{2,t}$$

Each factor will have an impact on portfolio risk in proportion to the amount invested in each stock and the sensitivity of each factor on the stock's return. For example, if factor 1 represents the impact of changing real GDP (the business cycle risk), an unexpected increase in real GDP would increase the return on stock x by 3 percent. The same 1 percent unexpected change in GDP would increase the return on stock y by 1 percent. These effects show up in the factor sensitivities (b_i) of 3 for K_x and 1 for K_y.

If the second factor represents inflation, we can see that a 1 percent unexpected increase in inflation will cause a reduction in return of 2 percent for stock x and 6 percent for stock y. When we combine stocks x and y into a portfolio weighted 40 percent stock x and 60 percent stock y, we end up with portfolio risk dependent on the percentage of each stock in the portfolio and each stock's sensitivity to factors affecting risk. We multiply both sides of the return equations by the portfolio weights:

$$\begin{aligned}(0.4)\, K_x &= (0.40) \times 12\% + (0.40) \times (3)F_{1,t} - (0.40) \times (2)F_{2,t}\\ &= 4.8\% \qquad\quad + 1.2F_{1,t} \qquad\quad - 0.8F_{2,t}\end{aligned}$$

Forty percent of stock x will contribute 4.8 percent expected return to the portfolio and will have a factor sensitivity of 1.2 to the business-cycle risk and a negative factor sensitivity of 0.8 to the inflation risk:

$$(0.6)\,K_y = (0.60) \times 15\% + (0.60) \times (1)F_{1,t} - (0.60) \times (6)F_{2,t}$$
$$= 9.0\% \qquad\quad + 0.6F_{1,t} \qquad\quad - 3.6F_{2,t}$$

Sixty percent of stock y will contribute 9.0 percent expected return to the portfolio and will have a factor sensitivity of 0.6 to the business-cycle risk and a negative factor sensitivity of 3.6 to the inflation risk. When we combine the two stocks into a portfolio, we end up with a portfolio having an expected return of 13.8 percent and having a sensitivity to factor 1 (business-cycle risk) of 1.8 and a negative sensitivity to factor 2 (inflation risk) of 4.4:

$$\text{Portfolio return } K_P = (4.8\% + 9\%) + (1.2 + 0.6) - (0.8 + 3.6)$$
$$= 13.8\% \qquad\quad + 1.8F_{1,t} \qquad\quad - 4.4F_{2,t}$$

We have structured a portfolio that will be moderately sensitive to any unexpected events having to do with changes in real GDP and highly susceptible to unexpected changes in inflation.

It is important to understand that the sign in front of the factor sensitivity indicates whether the unexpected event is directly related to returns or inversely related to returns. For example, we assume unexpected increases in inflation reduce stock returns while unexpected decreases in inflation increase stock returns. Thus, we have a minus sign before the second factor.

Application to Portfolio Management

From the portfolio manager's point of view, the arbitrage pricing theory can help measure the sensitivity of a portfolio to various macro factors that could potentially affect the actual return on one stock or a portfolio. This model allows investment managers to structure portfolios that either are highly sensitive or insensitive to certain kinds of risk exposures. If a manager were concerned about a recession and this information were not yet factored into stock prices, he or she could create a portfolio that insulated the returns on the portfolio from unpleasant surprises. On the other hand, if the market had factored in expectations for a recession and the manager expected good business-cycle news, he or she could buy stocks sensitive to business-cycle news.

OTHER ASSET PRICING MODELS

The Capital Asset Pricing Model (CAPM) has had such a major impact on portfolio management mainly because it was viewed as a centerpiece in the foundation of modern finance. Previous to the CAPM, the subject of finance was not very well established as a discipline and a science. The advent of CAPM changed that perspective and for the first time, finance was being viewed as more of an exact science rather than a loosely defined social science or a derivative or form of applied economics. This is why the CAPM holds such a pride of place in the discipline.

What the CAPM essentially said was that the price or value of an equity security was commensurate with the risk of that security that could not be diversified away simply by adding more securities in the portfolio. Further, the price was also directly related to the amount of undiversifiable or the firm-specific market risk. Simply put, the returns that could be expected from holding a stock were directly commensurate with the firm's undiversifiable market risk. Thus, in an equation sense, we can express this (CAPM) relationship as follows:

Expected Return for firm's stock = constant + Beta (Market's risk premium)

If the firm's sensitivity to the market was zero, then the firm would be free of market risk and the stock would simply earn the risk free rate, which in this case would be the constant. If the firm was sensitive to the market's movements, as measured by its Beta, then the risk premium that one could earn from investing in the market would be adjusted by the firm's sensitivity index or Beta and added to the constant. The model is simple, easy to understand and hence elegant.

As the CAPM became familiar and the model came under greater scrutiny, academics and professionals alike started to ask the question as to whether a stock's price is valued only by its sensitivity to market movements or was it sensitive to other factors as well, factors that also could not be diversified away. For example, if the market conditions were healthy but the automobile industry was slipping, would a stock holding in the Ford Motor Company have no impact on the total portfolio returns? Further, could an industry risk premium exist that could be added to the above model that would enable portfolio managers to price stocks better? Thus came about the use of multi-factor models where additional factors that could be justified as having an undiversifiable impact on a security's valuation, started being added to the above model. The above equation was then re-expressed as follows:

$$\text{Expected Return for stock} = a + b_1 \text{(Index}_1) + b_2 \text{(Index}_2) + \ldots\ldots + b_n \text{(Index}_n)$$

Where a is the constant, b_1 the sensitivity to the first factor (in this case Index$_1$ could be a market index), Index$_1$ an industry index, Index$_2$ a sector index, or other firm specific measures such as the Price Earnings (P/E), Return on Equity (ROE), Price to Book ratio, etc. And there could be multiple (n) such indexes. One point to note is that including many indexes can also be counterproductive to pricing at some point since the impact of an index may already be quite fully integrated in other indexes included. For example, even if the market conditions are good, if the automobile industry does slip, that impact is included in the market conditions since the auto industry *is* a part of the total market.

Another common application along the same format was to include variables or factors that were more macroeconomic (or nonfirm specific) in nature, as indexes. For example, the effect of an inflationary environment may not be correctly priced in a stock simply by relating its return to market movements. In this case, including an index for inflation as an explanatory factor can be justified as incorporating greater information in the asset pricing model. Thus, there exists another set of pricing models which may include macroeconomic variables such as interest rates, growth rate in GDP, inflation, consumer confidence, etc.

It is important for the advisor to note that while all the models of asset pricing discussed in this chapter seem well founded, rational and well constructed, it does not mean that someone who uses such models to value stocks will arrive at correct valuations of security. Experience, and countless studies, has shown us that none of these models are capable of producing definitive and exact answers to asset pricing questions. The pricing models can be thought of as providing two major benefits. First, they at least provide us with a starting point for pricing a security. This initial price requires adjustments that can be derived from other qualitative and quantitative measures and sometimes even the "gut feelings" of a user. The models get us going in the business of portfolio management. Second, these models also provide us with a foundation to explore other techniques—they provide us with a platform to extend the body of knowledge of investments.

Chapter 10

Fundamental Analysis

Fundamental security analysis is concerned with finding the answers to two questions. They are 1. Which security to buy, sell or hold; and 2. When to buy, sell or how long to hold. Fundamental analysis is a three-step process. The analysis requires investigation at the macroeconomic level, at the level of industries and at the firm level. Some analysts prefer to start with the biggest picture (global macroeconomic analysis) first and then work their way to the individual security level. Such a method is known as a top-down approach to fundamental analysis. Its reverse, a bottom-up approach, begins at the firm (security level) and ends with the macroeconomy. An example of a bottom-up approach is the use of screens (anomalies, etc.) which was described in a previous chapter. In this chapter we will follow a top-down approach; though there is some debate as to which approach is superior. However, the reader should note that our adaptation of the top-down approach does not constitute evidence as to which approach is superior. It is simply the preference of the authors.

To determine the value of the firm, fundamental analysis relies on long-run forecasts of the economy, the industry, and the company's financial prospects. Short-run changes in business conditions are also important in that they influence investors' required rates of return and expectations of corporate earnings and dividends. This chapter presents the basic information for analysis of the economy, while some other chapters focus on industry analysis and the individual firm.

Figure 10–1 presents an overview of the top-down valuation process as an inverted triangle. The process starts with a macroanalysis of the economy and then moves into industry variables. Next, common stocks are individually screened according to expected risk-return characteristics, and finally the surviving stocks are combined into portfolios of assets. This figure is not inclusive of all variables considered by an analyst, but is intended to indicate representative areas applicable to most industries and companies.

ECONOMIC ACTIVITY AND THE BUSINESS CYCLE

An investor begins the valuation process with an economic analysis. The hope is that an accurate forecast and examination of economic activity will provide the basis for accurate stock market predictions and indicate which industries may prosper. The analyst needs information on present and expected interest rates, monetary and fiscal policy, government and consumer spending patterns, and other economic data. To be successful, investors must understand business cycles and be able to forecast accurately. Unfortunately, these are not easy tasks, but the rewards can be significant if the timing is right.

Whether analysts use statistical methods, such as regression analysis and probability theory, or simply seat-of-the-pants judgment, they are still basing their forecast on expectations related to past data and experiences. Past information usually is not extrapolated into the future without being adjusted to conform with the subjective beliefs of the decision

FIGURE 10–1   Top-Down Overview of the Valuation Process

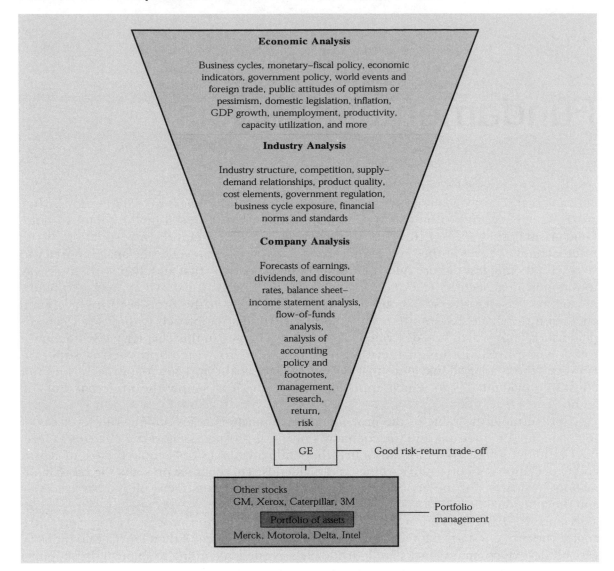

maker. Even when highly sophisticated statistical methods are used, subjectivity enters into the decision in some fashion.

Most likely, past knowledge will be helpful, but modifications for the present effects of worldwide currency fluctuations, international debt obligations, and other factors, which were not so important previously, need to be included in any forecast now. Since most companies are influenced to some degree by the general level of economic activity, a forecast will usually start with an analysis of the government's economic program.

Federal Government Economic Policy

Government economic policy is guided by the Employment Act of 1946 and subsequent position statements by the Federal Reserve Board, the President's Council of Economic Advisors, and other acts of Congress. The goals established by the Employment Act still hold and cover four broad areas. These goals, the focus of monetary and fiscal policy, are as follows with a second interpretation in parentheses:

1. Stable prices (a low inflation rate).

2. Business stability at high levels of production (low levels of unemployment).

3. Sustained real growth in gross domestic product (actual economic growth after deducting inflation).

4. A balance in international payments (primarily a balance of exports and imports but also including cash flows in and out of the United States).

These goals are often conflicting in that they do not all respond favorably to the same economic stimulus. Therefore, goal priorities and economic policies change to reflect current economic conditions. In the 1950s and early 1960s, the United States did not have an international trade problem or spiraling inflation, so economic policy focused on employment and economic growth. The economy grew rapidly between 1961 and 1969, and, because of the Vietnam War, unemployment reached very low levels. The demand for goods and competition for funds were very high during the war, and eventually war expenditures, large budget deficits, full employment, and large increases in the money supply caused many problems. Inflation accelerated to high levels, interest rates reached record heights, and an imbalance of international payments finally resulted in two devaluations of the U.S. dollar in the early 1970s.

By the time Jimmy Carter took office in January 1977, the primary goals were once again to reduce unemployment, control inflation, and create a moderate level of economic growth that could be sustained without causing more inflation (a very difficult task!). The achievement of these goals was thrown into the hands of the Federal Reserve Board. The Fed's tight money policy caused a rapid increase in interest rates to control inflation, and these high rates depressed common stock prices as the required rate of return by investors reached record levels.

Ronald Reagan inherited most of the problems Carter faced but tried new ways of reaching the goals. As the 1980s began, Reagan instituted a three-year tax cut to increase disposable income and stimulate consumption and thus economic growth, and, at the same time, he negotiated reductions in government spending. These policies were successful in sharply reducing inflation and creating strong growth in the gross domestic product (GDP), but they were accomplished with record government deficits. George H. Bush followed most of Reagan's domestic policies but focused more on international issues. In the middle of President Bush's term, the 90-month peacetime expansion came to an end with the start of a recession in July 1990. In looking back, the expansion that began in November 1982 created record employment, reduced unemployment percentages, and lowered interest rates and inflation from the high levels of 1980 and 1981. The stock market began a major bull market in 1982 in response to these improved conditions but also sustained the biggest one-day crash ever on October 19, 1987.

Unfortunately, the recession that began in July 1990 was extremely painful. Major companies such as IBM, AT&T, TRW, General Motors, and hundreds of others announced employee reductions totaling more than one-half million employees. In November 1992, President Clinton was elected to office on the promise of more jobs and universal health coverage. The economy was already benefiting from the recovery started in March 1991, and Clinton persuaded Congress to pass an increase in personal and corporate income taxes. Many economists thought the tax increase would create a "fiscal drag" on the economy by reducing spending. By the third quarter of 1992, the economy had slowed down considerably and stagnated at minimal real GDP growth. However, by year end 1993, real GDP growth in the fourth quarter was more than 7 percent, and by the end of 1994 had stabilized at between 3.0 and 3.5 percent real growth. A Republican Congress was elected in 1994 and came into office in January 1995. President Clinton was elected for a second term in 1996, and he and Congress went to work on a balanced budget proposal. Spending was held in check, and tax revenues rose to record levels as a result of the long-term healthy growth of the economy.

The combination of these factors created large surpluses and projections of even larger surpluses in the coming years. Between 1997 and 2001 the U.S. Treasury was able to retire several hundred billion dollars of government debt. One of the results of deficit reduction is the loss of a fiscal stimulus created by government spending, and this can cause a drag on the economy if consumers don't pick up the slack. Consumers were more than happy to spend, and the economy rolled along until about 2000 when it slowed a little. The stock market started to decline in April 2000, and when George W. Bush took office in January 2001, he inherited a crumbling economy that had run out of steam after years of exceptional growth. By summer 2001, the economy managed to squeeze out a 0.2 percent growth in second quarter GDP, and the surplus was shrinking fast due to declining tax revenues and the tax cuts passed in the early days of the Bush administration. The third quarter of 2001, punctuated by the September 11th terrorist attack, generated a negative growth rate and the NBER declared a recession with a starting date of March 2001. By the fourth quarter of 2001, the economy was once again growing but at a low rate.

Unfortunately, at the same time, Japan was still suffering from more than a decade of economic decline, and Europe (especially Germany) was also beginning to experience an economic slowdown. The new European currency, the Euro, was officially introduced in January 2002, but the economic impact of the 11 countries forming the European Monetary System was still in its early stages of economic transformation. Many former communist countries such as Russia, Poland, The Czech Republic, and Hungary were growing but still struggling to become capitalistic economies, and a slowdown in the industrialized world economies deprived them of investors and economic growth.

The international landscape is changing rapidly, and this includes economic changes in North America, South America, and Asia. As we enter this new era of the global economy, we cannot always rely on the past for indications about the future. The rising tide of capitalistic economies, China's emergence as an economic power, and world trade agreements will change the way the world's political and economic systems interact. The knowledge of economic theory and its applications will increase in importance to investors pursuing international strategies or to U.S. companies making foreign investments. The ability to interpret these events could have significant financial implications on investment returns for both investors and companies.

Fiscal Policy

Fiscal policy can be described as the government's taxing and spending policies. These policies can have a great impact on the direction of economic activity. One must realize at the outset that fiscal policy is cumbersome. It has a long implementation lag and is often motivated by political rather than economic considerations since Congress must approve budgets and develop tax laws. Figure 10-2 presents a historical picture of government income and expenditures. When the government spends more than it receives, it runs a **deficit** that must be financed by the Treasury.

A forecaster must pay attention to the size of the deficit and how it is financed to measure its expected impact on the economy. If the deficit is financed by the Treasury selling securities to the Federal Reserve, it is very expansive. The money supply will increase without having any significant short-run effects on interest rates. If the deficit is financed by selling securities to banks and individuals, there is not the same expansion in the money supply, and short-term interest rates will rise unless the Federal Reserve intervenes with open-market trading.

A look at Figure 10-2 shows that **surpluses**, in which revenues exceed expenditures, have been virtually nonexistent from 1966 to 1997, and the annual deficit increased dramatically during the 1980s. Surpluses tend to reduce economic growth as the government slows its demand for goods and services relative to its income. In an analysis of fiscal policy, the important consideration for the investor is the determination of the flow of funds. In a deficit economy, the government usually stimulates GDP by spending on socially productive

FIGURE 10–2   Federal Budget Seasonally Adjusted Annual Rates

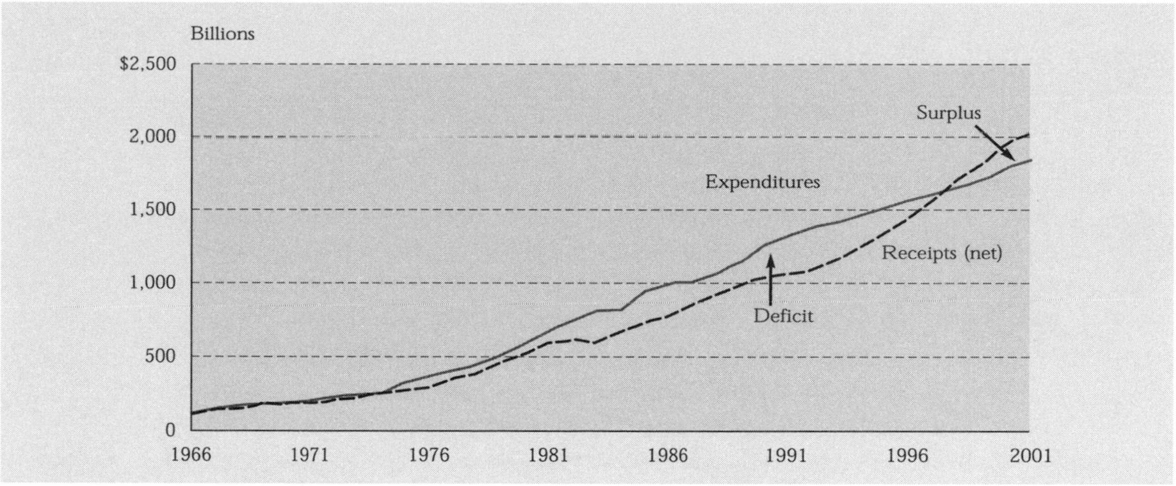

programs or by increasing spending on defense, education, highways, or other government programs. The Reagan administration instituted budget cuts in education and social programs at the same time it reduced tax revenues through tax cuts. This strategy was one that attempted to shift GDP growth from the government sector into the private sector. In the George H. Bush administration, there was inconsistent fiscal policy. Clinton made it clear with his new tax increases that he would use fiscal policy to increase tax revenues to help shrink the fiscal deficit. He instituted a more progressive tax policy in 1993 by raising rates and reducing deductions for high-income people. His hope was that the wealthy would not slow down their spending and that the increased tax revenues would help decrease the fiscal deficit. He was right. Although Clinton and the Republican Congress passed further legislation in 1997 to reduce the deficit, cut taxes, and reduce entitlements, the deficit was already well in check by then (and moving toward a surplus) because of greatly increased tax revenue in a prospering economy. The increasing surplus from 1997 to 2001 is quite visible in Figure 10-2. Unfortunately, the government expenditures following September 11th pushed the government into a deficit spending budget for fiscal year 2002.

One other area of fiscal policy deals with the government's ability to levy import taxes or tariffs on foreign goods. As a free market economy, we have fought for years with our trading partners to open their countries' markets to U.S. goods. Figure 10-3 depicts the annual trade deficits that started piling up beginning in 1982. This deficit occurred because U.S. consumers purchased more foreign goods than U.S. companies sold to foreigners. This occurred for several reasons; one was a lack of free markets with some of our trading partners, specifically Japan and the robust health of the U.S. economy. The United States has been trying to open markets for U.S. goods with Japan, China, and other countries for the last several decades. The World Trade Organization (WTO) and its round of tariff negotiations has been instrumental in breaking down trade barriers during the last half of the 1990s, and in 2001 China was approved for membership in the WTO, which should have long-term positive effects on world trade.

Countries can create trade barriers by either setting up import tariffs or taxes that raise the price of foreign goods and make them less competitive with domestic goods. This is a common way to protect domestic industries. The WTO deals with these issues through negotiations and if necessary through a world court to arbitrate complaints from one country against another.

As Figure 10-3 shows, the U.S. Trade deficit increased quite rapidly from 1996 to 2000, rising from a negative $89.4 billion in 1997 to a negative $364 billion in 2000. By 2001 the United States had the largest trading deficit with China, followed by Japan in second place.

FIGURE 10–3   Imports and Exports in Current Dollars

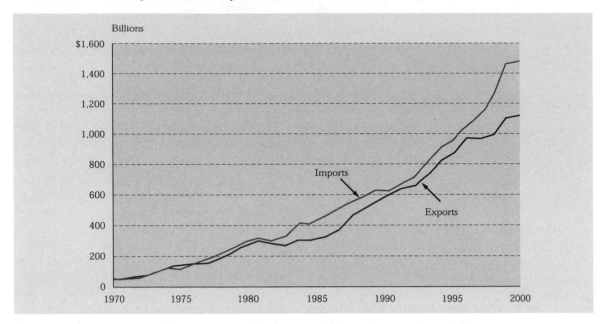

The rising trade deficit during this time period was a function of the healthy U.S. economy and a strong dollar. When a country's economy is healthy with high employment and income, its citizens spend more in general and import more goods (especially high-priced luxury goods) from other countries. When a recession is occurring, people spend less, look for less expensive items, and import fewer goods. The second factor is the exchange rate between two currencies. For example, if the U.S. dollar rises against the British pound, U.S. goods become more expensive for British citizens, and British goods become less expensive for U.S. citizens. If the dollar exchange rate stays high or continues to rise, eventually British citizens change their buying habits and buy fewer U.S. goods, and U.S. citizens buy more British goods. This effect can also be seen in the U.S.–Japanese automobile market. As the Japanese yen rose against the dollar, in the early 1990s, Americans bought fewer Japanese cars and more U.S. domestic cars. The Japanese consumer did the opposite. The pattern reversed itself in 1996–97 with an increase in the dollar versus the yen. Short-term swings in exchange rates have little effect on imports and exports, but changes in long-term currency relationships eventually change import–export balances between countries. It usually takes more than a year before the effects of exchange rates on prices show up at the retail level and influence the buying patterns of consumers. As world trade increases, exchange rates and economic trends around the world become more important. While exchange rates and economic activity are influenced by fiscal policy, they are also affected by monetary policy, as discussed in the next section.

Monetary Policy

Monetary policy determines the "appropriate" levels for the money supply and interest rates that accomplish the economic goals of the Employment Act of 1946. Monetary policy is determined by the Federal Open Market Committee (FOMC), which includes the Federal Reserve Board of Governors and the 12 Federal Reserve bank presidents. Monetary policy can be implemented very quickly to reinforce fiscal policy or, when necessary, to offset the effects of fiscal policy.

The Federal Reserve has several ways to influence economic activity. First, it can raise or lower the reserve requirements on commercial bank time deposits or demand deposits.

Reserve requirements represent the percent of total deposits that a bank must hold as cash in its vault or as deposits in Federal Reserve banks. An increase in reserve requirements contracts the money supply. The banking system has to hold larger reserves for each dollar deposited and is not able to lend as much money on the same deposit base. A reduction in reserve requirements has the opposite effect. The Fed also changes the discount rate periodically to reflect its attitude toward the economy. This **discount rate** is the interest rate the Federal Reserve charges commercial banks on very short-term loans. The Fed does not make a practice of lending funds to a single commercial bank for more than two or three weeks, and so this charge can influence an individual bank's willingness to borrow money for expansionary loans to industry. The Fed can also influence bank behavior by issuing policy statements, or jawboning.

Beyond these monetary measures, the tool most widely used is **open-market operations** in which the Fed buys and sells U.S. government securities for its own portfolio. When the Fed sells securities in the open market, purchasers write checks to pay for their securities, and demand deposits fall, causing a contraction in the money supply. At the same time, the increase in the supply of Treasury bills sold by the Fed forces prices down and interest rates up to entice buyers to part with their money. The Fed usually accomplishes its adjustments by selling securities to commercial banks, government securities dealers, or individuals.

If the Fed buys securities, the opposite occurs; the money supply increases, and interest rates go down. This tends to encourage economic expansion. The interest rate is extremely important in determining the required rate of return, or discount rate for a stock.

As chairman of the Federal Reserve, Alan Greenspan exercised unusual power over the economy in the last decade. The Fed not only carefully managed monetary policy, but his semiannual appearances before the House Banking Committee, as mandated by federal legislation, drew attention on Wall Street and throughout the world financial capitals. A good portion of the success of the U.S. economy during the 1990s is attributed to Greenspan and his carefully crafted economic policy. Whether future historians will be as generous only time will tell.

Government Policy, Real Growth, and Inflation

In November 1991, the U.S. Commerce Department's Economic Bureau of Analysis shifted from gross national product to gross domestic product as the measure of economic activity for the U.S. economy. The **gross domestic product (GDP)** measurement makes us more compatible with the rest of the world and measures only output from U.S. factories and consumption within the United States. Gross domestic product does not include products made by U.S. companies in foreign countries, but gross national product did. Other U.S. economic measures such as employment, production, and capacity are also measured within the boundaries of the United States, and, with the switch to GDP, we now measure economic output consistently with these other variables.

Figure 10-4 depicts 40 years of real gross domestic product (GDP) and the consumer price index. Real GDP reflects gross domestic product in constant dollars, which eliminates the effects of inflation from GDP expressed in current dollars. Real GDP measures output in physical terms rather than in dollars that are inflated by price increases.

This information in Figure 10-4 needs to be looked at in context with the annual percentage change in the consumer price index (CPI), which is used as a proxy for inflation. Notice the relationship between real GDP and the CPI. The change in real GDP is inversely related to the rate of inflation. As inflation rises, real GDP falls (as indicated in 1970, 1975, 1980–81, and 1989–90), and as inflation subsides, as in 1982–83 and 1985–86, real GDP rises. Because real GDP is the measure of economic output in real physical terms, it does not do any good to stimulate the economy only to have all the gains eroded by inflation.

To understand the major sectors of the economy and the relative influence of each sector, we divide gross domestic product into its four basic areas: personal consumption

FIGURE 10–4   Real Gross Domestic Product and the Consumer Price Index

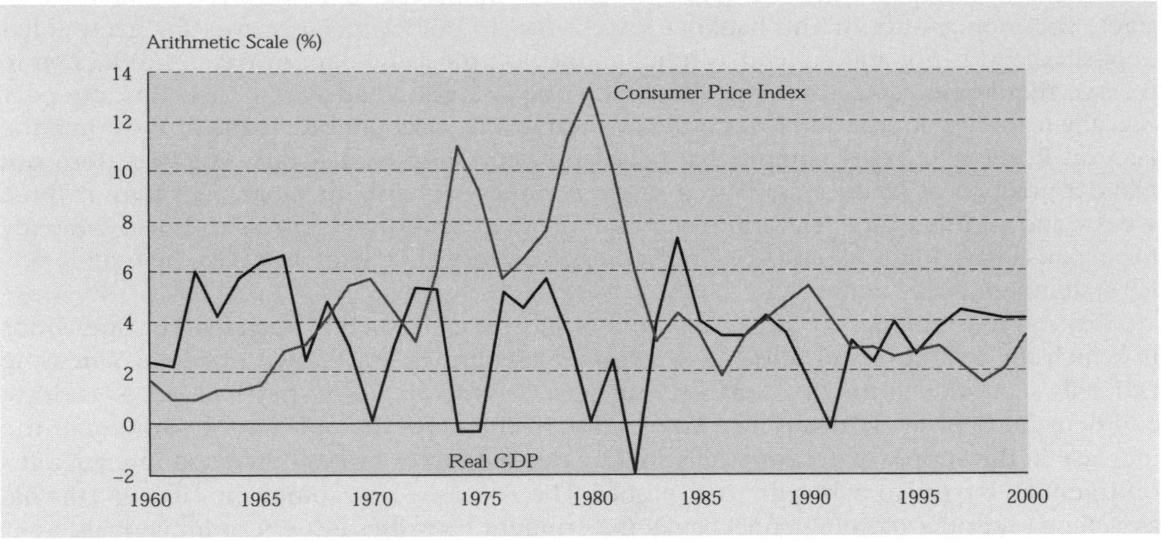

expenditures, government purchases, gross private investment, and net exports. Figure 10-5 shows the contribution of each one to the total GDP over the past four decades. It becomes clear from Figure 10-5 that personal consumption is growing faster than the other sectors and is the driving force behind economic growth. In fact consumer spending accounts for more than 60 percent of GDP. For this reason economic forecasters pay close attention to the mood of the consumer.

The University of Michigan surveys consumer expectations on a monthly basis and reports whether consumers are becoming more or less optimistic. Consumer expectation are a leading indicator of economic activity—when consumer confidence increases, this bodes well for spending; when consumer confidence decreases, this indicates a possible contraction in spending. Figure 10-6 presents a historical view of the index of consumer expectation. It is easy to spot the recessions of 1973-75, 1980-81, and 1990-91. In all cases consumer expectations turned down before the recession began. In looking at the period 1990-2001, we can see the large rise in confidence with many short-term reversals on the down-side. The index peaked in the first quarter of 2000, dropping from 111.3 to 92 by the first quarter of 2001. In the next section we look at the cyclical nature of gross domestic product.

BUSINESS CYCLES AND CYCLICAL INDICATORS

The economy expands and contracts through a **business cycle** process. By measuring GDP and other economic data, we can develop a statistical picture of the economic growth pattern. The National Bureau of Economic Research (NBER) is the final authority in documenting cyclical turning points. The NBER defines recessions as two or more quarters of negative real GDP growth and documents the beginning and end of a recession. Table 10-1 presents a historical picture of business cycle expansions and contractions in the United States. While the modern day data may be more relevant, it is interesting to see that economic cycles have existed and been defined for more than 140 years.

Table 10-1 measures each contraction and expansion and then presents summary data at the bottom of the table for all business cycles and for cycles in peacetime only. A **trough** represents the end of a recession and the beginning of an expansion, and a **peak** represents the end of an expansion and the beginning of a recession. In general, we see on the last line of Table 10-1 that during peacetime cycles between 1945 and 2001, contractions

FIGURE 10–5   Breakdown of Gross Domestic Product in Current Dollars

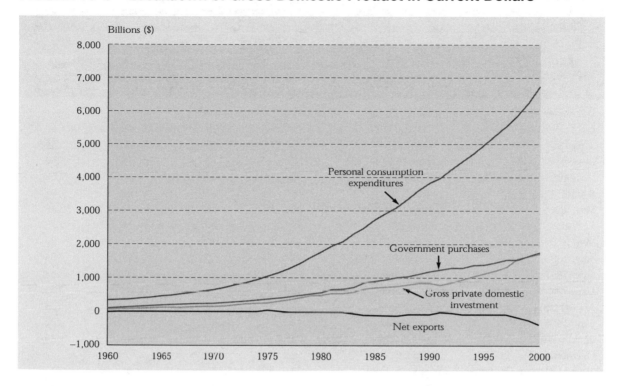

FIGURE 10–6   Consumer Expectations, University of Michigan (index: 1966: 1 = 100)

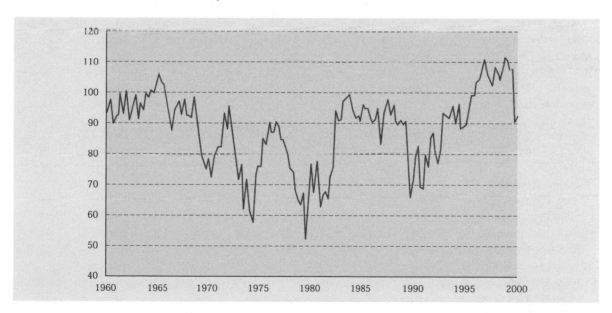

(recessions) lasted an average of 11 months, while expansions averaged 52 months.Thus, one *complete* business cycle during modern *peacetimes* lasts almost five and one-quarter years. The NBER declared that March 2001 was the beginning of a recession and the end of a 10 year expansion. This unusual dating of the recession occurred without two quarters of negative real GDP growth, but in the face of months of declining manufacturing output, declining employment, and sagging consumer confidence.

TABLE 10–1   Business Cycle Expansions and Contractions in the United States

Business Cycle Reference Dates		Duration in Months Cycle			
Trough	Peak	Contraction (Trough from previous peak)	Expansion (Trough to peak)	Trough from Previous Trough	Peak from Previous Peak
December 1854	June 1857	—	30	—	—
December 1858	October 1860	18	22	48	40
June 1861	April 1865	8	46	30	54
December 1867	June 1889	32	18	78	50
December 1870	October 1873	18	34	36	52
March 1879	March 1882	65	36	99	101
May 1885	March 1887	38	22	74	60
April 1888	June 1890	13	27	35	40
May 1891	January 1893	10	20	37	30
June 1894	December 1895	17	18	37	35
June 1897	June 1899	18	24	36	42
December 1900	September 1902	18	21	42	39
August 1904	May 1907	23	33	44	56
June 1908	January 1910	13	19	46	32
January 1912	January 1913	24	12	43	36
December 1914	August 1918	23	44	35	67
March 1919	January 1920	7	10	51	17
July 1921	May 1923	18	22	28	40
July 1924	October 1926	14	27	36	41
November 1927	August 1929	13	21	40	34
March 1933	May 1937	43	50	64	93
June 1938	February 1945	13	80	63	93
October 1945	November 1948	8	37	88	45
October 1949	July 1953	11	45	48	56
May 1954	August 1957	10	39	55	49
April 1958	April 1960	8	24	47	32
February 1961	December 1969	10	106	34	116
November 1970	November 1973	11	36	117	47
March 1975	January 1980	16	58	52	74
July 1980	July 1981	6	12	64	18
November 1982	July 1990	16	92	28	108
March 1991	March 2001	8	120	100	128
Average, all cycles:					
1854–1982 (30 cycles)		18	33	51	51[a]
1854–1919 (16 cycles)		22	27	48	49[b]
1919–1945 (6 cycles)		18	35	53	53
1945–2001 (10 cycles)		10	57	63	67
Average, peacetime cycles:					
1854–1982 (25 cycles)		19	27	46	46[c]
1854–1919 (14 cycles)		22	24	46	47[d]
1919–1945 (5 cycles)		20	26	46	45
1945–2001 (8 cycles)		11	52	53	63

Note: Underscored figures are the wartime expansions (Civil War, World Wars I and II, Korean War, and Vietnam War), the postwar contractions, and the full cycles that include the wartime expansions.

[a]29 cycles.   [b]15 cycles.   [c]24 cycles.   [d]13 cycles.

Source: *Business Conditions Digest* (U.S. Department of Commerce Bureau of Economic Analysis, July 1988, Nov. 1994).

Predicting business cycles is easier said than done. It is important to realize that each business cycle is unique; no two cycles are alike. Some cycles are related to monetary policy; some are demand related; some are inventory induced. The length and depth of each is also different—some are shallow, and others deep; some are short, while others are long.

Additionally, not all industries or segments of the economy are equally affected by business cycles. However, if investors can make some forecast concerning the beginning and ending of the business cycle, they will be better able to choose which types of investments to hold over the various phases of the cycle.

So far, we have discussed the government's impact on the economy. Fiscal policy and monetary policy both provide important clues to the direction and magnitude of economic expansions and contractions. Other measures are used to evaluate the direction of the business cycle. These measures, called economic indicators, are divided into leading, lagging, and roughly coincident indicators. The NBER classifies indicators relative to their performance at economic peaks and troughs. **Leading indicators** change direction in advance of general business conditions and are of prime importance to the investor who wants to anticipate rising corporate profits and possible price increases in the stock market. **Coincident indicators** move approximately with the general economy, and **lagging indicators** usually change directions after business conditions have turned around.

The leading, lagging, and coincident indicators of economic activity are published by the Conference Board in its publication called *Business Cycle Indicators*. This publication includes moving averages, turning dates for recessions and expansions, cyclical indicators, composite indexes and their components, diffusion indexes,[1] and information on rates of change. Many of the series are seasonally adjusted and are maintained on a monthly or quarterly basis. This information is also available on its Web site **www.conference-board.org** for a fee.

Table 10-2 presents a summary of cyclical indicators by cyclical timing with Part A of the table presenting timing at business cycle peaks and Part B showing timing at business cycle troughs. Thus, in the first part, we see the leading, coincident, and lagging indicators for business cycle peaks, and in the second part, similar indicators for the bottoming out of business cycles (troughs). While we would not expect you to study or learn all the leading or lagging indicators for a cyclical peak or trough, it is important that you know they are relied on by economists and financial analysts. Let's look more specifically at how they are used.

Economic Indicators

Of the 108 leading indicators shown in Parts A and B of Table 10-2, 61 lead at peaks and 47 lead at troughs. Of these, 10 basic indicators have been reasonably consistent in their relationship to the business cycle and are considered most important. These 10 leading indicators have been standardized and used to compute a composite index that is widely followed. It is a much smoother curve than each individual component since erratic changes in one indicator are offset by movements in other indicators. The same can be said for a similar index of four coincident indicators and six lagging indicators.

Figure 10-7 shows the performance of the composite index of leading, lagging, and coincident indicators over several past business cycles. The shaded areas are recessions as defined by the NBER. The minus figures indicate how many months the index preceded the economy. (Lagging indicators have plus signs.)

While the composite index of leading indicators (top of Figure 10-7) has been a better predictor than any single indicator, it has varied widely over time. Table 10-3 presents the components for the 10 leading, 4 roughly coincident, and 7 lagging indicators.

Studies have found that the 10 leading indicators do not exhibit the same notice at peaks as they do at troughs. The notice before peaks is quite long, but the warning before troughs is very short, which means it is very easy to miss a turnaround to the upside, but on

---

1. A diffusion index shows the pervasiveness of a given movement in a series. If 100 units are reported in a series, the diffusion index indicates what percentage followed a given pattern.

TABLE 10–2 Cross Classification of Cyclical Indicators by Economic Process and Cyclical Timing

A. Timing at Business Cycle Peaks

Economic Process / Cyclical Timing	I. Employment and Unemployment (15 series)	II. Production and Income (10 series)	III. Consumption, Trade Orders, and Deliveries (13 series)	IV. Fixed Capital Investment (19 series)	V. Inventories and Inventory Investment (9 series)	VI. Price, Costs, and Profits (18 series)	VII. Money and Credit (28 series)
Leading (L) Indicators (61 series)	Marginal employment adjustments (3 series) Job vacancies (2 series) Comprehensive employment (1 series) Comprehensive unemployment (3 series)	Capacity utilization (2 series)	Orders and deliveries (6 series) Consumption and trade (2 series)	Formation of business enterprises (2 series) Business investment commitments (5 series) Residential construction (3 series)	Inventory investment (4 series) Inventories on hand and on order (1 series)	Stock prices (1 series) Sensitive commodity prices (2 series) Prices and profit margins (7 series) Cash flows (2 series)	Money (5 series) Credit flows (5 series) Credit difficulties (2 series) Bank reserves (2 series) Interest rates (1 series)
Roughly Coincident (C) Indicators (24 series)	Comprehensive employment (1 series)	Comprehensive output and income (4 series) Industrial production (4 series)		Consumption and trade commitments (1 series) Business investment expenditures (6 series)	Business investment (4 series)		Velocity of money (2 series) Interest rate (2 series)
Lagging (Lg) Indicators (19 series)	Comprehensive unemployment (2 series)			Business investment expenditures (1 series)	Inventories on hand and on order (4 series)	Unit labor costs and labor share (4 series)	Interest rate (4 series) Outstanding debt (4 series)
Timing Unclassified (U) (8 series)	Comprehensive employment (3 series)		Consumption and trade (1 series)	Business investment commitments (1 series)		Sensitive commodity prices (1 series) Profits and profit margins (1 series)	Interest rates (1 series)
B. Timing at Business Cycle Troughs							
Leading (L) Indicators (47 series)	Marginal employment adjustments (1 series)	Industrial production (1 series)	Orders and deliveries (5 series) Consumption and trade (4 series)	Formation of business enterprises (2 series) Business investment commitments (4 series) Residential construction (3 series)	Inventory investment (4 series)	Stock prices (1 series) Sensitive commodity prices (3 series) Profit and profit margins (6 series) Cash flows (2 series)	Money (4 series) Credit flows (5 series) Credit difficulties (2 series)

(Continued)

TABLE 10–2 (Continued)

Cyclical Timing \ Economic Process	I. Employment and Unemployment (15 series)	II. Production and Income (10 series)	III. Consumption, Trade Orders, and Deliveries (13 series)	IV. Fixed Capital Investment (19 series)	V. Inventories and Inventory Investment (9 series)	VI. Price, Costs, and Profits (18 series)	VII. Money and Credit (28 series)
Roughly Coincident (C) Indicators (23 series)	Marginal employment adjustments (2 series) Comprehensive employment (4 series)	Comprehensive output and income (4 series) Industrial production (3 series) Capacity utilization (2 series)	Consumption and trade (3 series)	Business investment commitments (1 series)		Profits and profit margins (2 series)	Money (1 series) Velocity of money (1 series)
Lagging (Lg) Indicators (41 series)	Job vacancies (2 series) Comprehensive employment (1 series) Comprehensive unemployment (5 series)		Orders and deliveries (1 series)	Business investment commitments (2 series) Business investment expenditures (7 series)	Inventories on hand and on order (5 series)	Unit labor costs and labor share (4 series)	Velocity of money (1 series) Bank reserves (1 series) Interest rates (8 series) Outstanding debt (4 series)
Timing Unclassified (U) (1 series)							Bank reserves (1 series)

Source: *Business Conditions Digest* (U.S. Department of Commerce Bureau of Economic Analysis, July 1988).

FIGURE 10–7   Composite Indexes (Leading, Lagging, and Coincident Indexes)

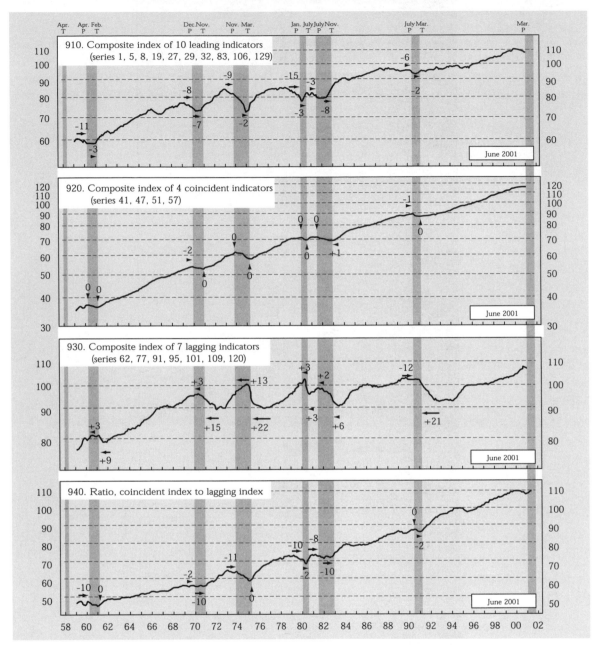

Source: *Business Cycle Indicators,* August 2001.

the downside you can be more patient waiting for confirmation from other indicators. Indicators occasionally give false signals. Sometimes the indicators give no clear signal, and with the large variability of leads and lags versus the average lead time, an investor is lucky to get close to predicting economic activity within three or four months of peaks and troughs.

Despite economic indicators and forecasting methods, investors cannot escape uncertainty in an attempt to manage their portfolios.

One very important fact is that the stock market is the most reliable and accurate of the 10 leading indicators. This presents a very real problem for us because our initial objective is to forecast (as well as we are able) changes in common stock prices. To do this, we are constrained by the fact that the stock market is anticipatory and, in fact, has worked on a lead time of nine months at peaks and five months at troughs.

TABLE 10–3   Components of the Leading, Coincident, and Lagging Indicators

BCI No.	Series
Leading index components:	
1.	Average weekly hours, manufacturing
5.	Initial claims for unemployment insurance, thousands
8.	Mfrs.' new orders, consumer goods and materials
32.	Vendor performance, slower deliveries diffusion index
27.	Mfrs.' new orders, nondefense capital goods
29.	Building permits, new private housing units
19.	Stock prices, 500 common stocks
106.	Money supply, M2
129.	Interest rate spread, 10-year Treasury bonds less federal funds
83.	Index of consumer expectations
Coincident index components:	
41.	Employees on nonagricultural payrolls
51.	Personal income less transfer payments
47.	Industrial production
57.	Manufacturing and trade sales
Lagging index components:	
91.	Average duration of unemployment, weeks
77.	Ratio, mfg. And trade inventories to sales
62.	Change in labor cost per unit of output, mfg
109.	Average prime rate charged by banks
101.	Commercial and industrial loans outstanding
95.	Ratio, consumer installment credit outstanding to personal income
120.	Changes in Consumer Price Index for services

Source: *Business Cycle Indicators,* August 2001.

MONEY SUPPLY AND STOCK PRICES

One variable that has been historically popular as an indicator of the stock market is the money supply. The money supply is supposed to influence stock prices in several ways. Studies of economic growth and the money supply by Milton Friedman and Anna Schwartz found a long-term relationship between these two variables.[2]

Why does money matter? If you are a **monetarist**, money explains much of economic behavior. The quantity theory of money holds that as the supply of money increases relative to the demand for money, people will make adjustments in their portfolios of assets. If they have too much money, they will first buy bonds (a modification of the theory would now include Treasury bills or other short-term monetary assets), stocks, and finally, real assets. This is the direct effect of money on stock prices sometimes referred to as the *liquidity effect.*

The indirect effect of money on stock prices would flow through the GDP's impact on corporate profits. As money influences economic activity, it will eventually influence corporate earnings and dividends and thus returns to the investors. Many studies have found that a significant relationship exists between the money supply variable and stock prices. However, even here, there have been some conflicting patterns in the last 10 to 20 years as shown in Figure 10–8. Note that in the first half of 1982, the money supply (M2) was increasing slightly while stock prices were declining sharply. This goes against the historical norm of comparable movements that can be seen in the same figure. Also note that from

2. Milton J. Friedman and Anna J. Schwartz, "Money and Business Cycles," *Review of Economics and Statistics,* Supplement, February 1963.

FIGURE 10–8   Relationship of Stock Prices to Money Supply

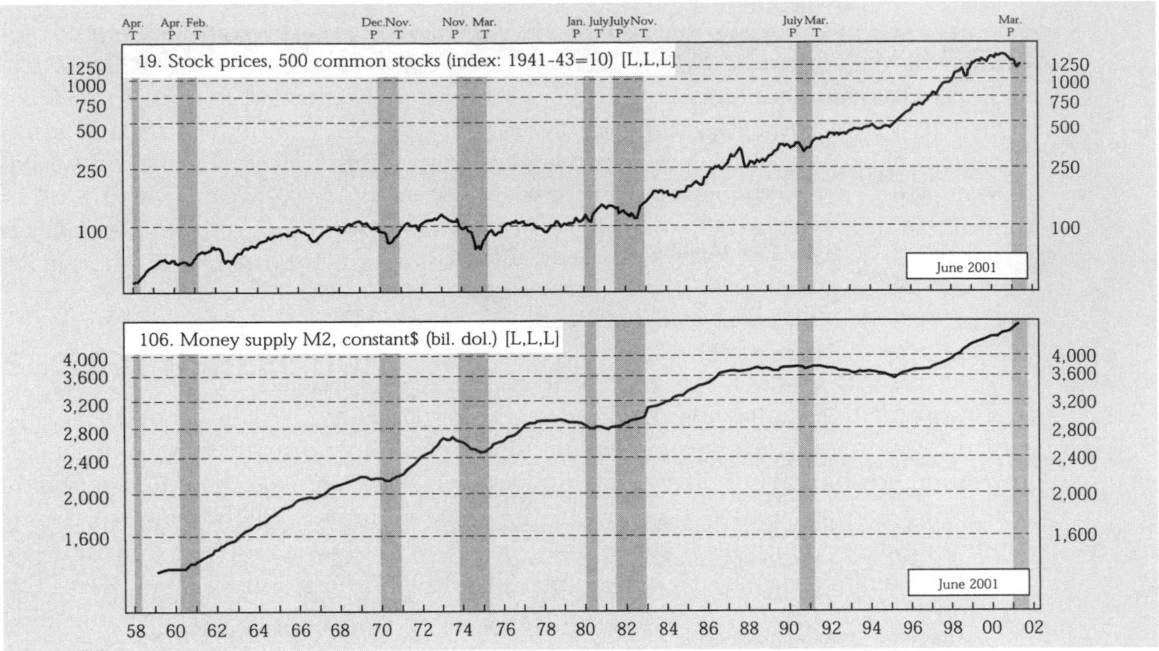

Source: *Business Cycle Indicators,* August 2001.

1987 to 1995, the money supply (M2) has been relatively flat and has not coincided with increasing stock prices. Since 1995, however, the trend on both has been up.

There are many important predictors of economic patterns and stock market movements, but an investor must be flexible and consider as many variables as possible rather than simply relying on one or two factors. You may wish to acquaint yourself with many of the leading, coincident, and lagging indicators presented previously in Table 10-3 as you become active in the stock market.

BUSINESS CYCLES AND INDUSTRY RELATIONSHIPS

Each industry may be affected by the business cycle differently. Industries where the underlying demand for the product is consumer oriented will quite likely be sensitive to short-term swings in the business cycle. These industries would include durable goods such as washers and dryers, refrigerators, electric and gas ranges, and automobiles. Changes in the automobile industry will also be felt in the tire and rubber industry as well as by auto glass and other automobile component suppliers.

Table 10-4 which appeared in the *Chicago Tribune*, demonstrates the impact of this ripple effect through many industries. The automobile industry purchases 77 percent of the output from the natural rubber industry (tires and bumpers), 67 percent of the output from the lead industry (batteries), and so on to 10 percent of the copper output (electrical and tubing). Additionally, the automobile industry accounts for more than 4 percent of the GDP. The U.S. Automobile industry employs 800,000 people, and one in seven workers (15 million) in America has a job in an industry somewhat dependent on the automobile industry.

The top of Figure 10-9 shows the automobile quarterly sales from 1967 to 2001 relative to GDP's growth rate (bottom of figure). Notice the similarity of the pattern. The peaks and troughs of economic activity mostly correspond with peaks in the auto industry. Perhaps the recessions of 1974–75 and 1981 are most easily identified as coinciding with auto sales. From about 1992, auto sales and GDP both maintained consistent performance.

The data do not include vehicles produced abroad but sales by foreign manufacturers such as Toyota, Honda, Volkswagen and BMW would also be influenced by the growth in

TABLE 10–4   Automobile Industry and Its Impact on Other Industries

The automotive industry purchases these percentages of the output of other U.S. industries.[a]		What's in a car
		A typical American car includes:[b]
Natural rubber	77%	1,774 pounds of steel
Lead	67	460 pounds of iron
Malleable iron	63	222 pounds of plastic
Synthetic rubber	50	183 pounds of fluids
Platinum	39	146 pounds of aluminum
Zinc	23	135 pounds of rubber
Aluminum	18	86 pounds of glass
Steel	12	25 pounds of copper
Copper	10	24 pounds of lead
		18 pounds of zinc

[a]Motor Vehicle Manufacturers Association.

[b]*World Book Encyclopedia.*

FIGURE 10–9   New Vehicle Sales and Real GNP Quarterly Percentage Change

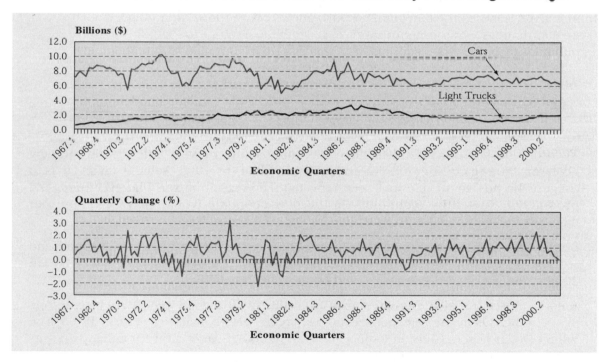

United States GDP, and additionally they would be affected by foreign currency exchange rates. When the U.S. dollar is strong against foreign currencies, foreign manufacturers have the ability to lower their prices and still maintain their profit margins relative to Ford and General Motors. When the U.S. dollar falls, the opposite effect is true, and foreign car sales suffer.

Not all industries are so closely related to the business cycle. Necessity-oriented industries, such as food and pharmaceuticals, are consistent performers since people have to eat, and illness is not dependent on the economy. Industries that have products with low price elasticities[3] that are habitual in nature, such as cigarettes and alcohol, do not seem to be

---

3. Price elasticity represents the sensitivity of quantity purchased to price.

much affected by business cycles either. In fact, some industries do better during a recession. The movie industry traditionally prospers during a recession as more people substitute low-cost entertainment for more expensive forms. This is one pattern that may not remain the same, however. As cable television, VCRs, and DVDs continue to come into their own, people may find it even more convenient to stay at home than to go to the movies when money is tight. This is one thing that makes investments exciting, the ever-changing environment.

Housing is another example of an industry that historically has done well in recessionary environments. As the economy comes to a standstill, interest rates tend to come down, and prospective home purchasers are once again able to afford mortgage rates on a home. After the period of extremely high mortgage rates in the early 1980s, a precipitous drop in mortgage rates helped to stimulate growth in the housing market. The Federal Reserve followed such a policy again in the early 1990s by pushing interest rates down to their lowest level in decades. This happened again in 2001. Sales of existing housing units picked up, and people refinanced their mortgages at lower rates, giving them more disposable income. As mortgage costs came down, housing became more affordable to more people. For example, if interest rates declined 3 percentage points on a $120,000 loan, the same priced house would now cost $300 per month less in interest expense.

Sensitivity to the business cycle may also be evident in industries that produce *capital* goods for other business firms (rather than consumer goods). Examples would be manufacturers of business plant and equipment, machine tools, or pollution-control equipment. A lag often exists between the recovery from a recession and the increased purchase of capital goods, so recoveries within these industries may be delayed.

The Real World of Investing

The New Economy: Going from Gain to Pain

According to some economists, there was supposed to be very little pain in the new economy. After a decade of uninterrrupted growth in the 1990s, some went so far as to suggest the business cycle had been repealed. The reasoning was that ever-increasing productivity fueled by technology in the new economy would increase output per man(woman)-hour to the point where growth could continue indefinitely.

But the 3 to 4 percent annual growth in GDP came to a halt in the new century, and so did the decade-long bull market. Many popular market indexes fell between 20 percent (S&P 500 Stock Index) and 60 percent (Nasdaq).

Among those to feel the greatest pain from the stock market decline were entrepreneurs and CEOs in the Internet/technology area. *Fortune* magazine actually listed "The Billion Dollar Losers Club" in its June 11, 2001, edition.* Among the 20 unhappy participants the top five losers were:

1. Michael Saylor, chair and CEO, MicroStrategy; lost $13.53 billion.
2. Jeffrey Bezos, chairman and CEO, Amazon.com; lost $10.80 billion.
3. David Filo, co-founder and chief, Yahoo; lost $10.31 billion.
4. Navaan Jain, chair and CEO, IntoSpace; lost $10.13 billion.
5. Jay Walker, founder, Pipeline.com; lost $7.51 billion.

Can you feel their pain?

---

* Julia Boorstein and Mathew Boyle, "The Billion Dollar Losers Club," *Forbes,* July 11, 2001, pp. 127–28.

Service industries have also become extremely important in our economy. While service-oriented business firms (doctors, lawyers, accountants) are generally less susceptible to the business cycle, there are exceptions. Examples of cyclically oriented service providers include architects, civil engineers, and auto repair shops.

One industry that has taken on increased importance is high technology. Companies in high technology generally include computer hardware and software producers; information technology, networking, database management firms; and other related fields. Examples of firms in these areas are Microsoft, Intel, CISCO, Oracle, IBM, and Sun Microsystems. These firms are also somewhat cyclical in that they depend on a high volume of business activity to continue an ever-expanding need for their products. Many of the newer high-tech firms are being severely tested in the economic slowdown of the early 2000s.

As a general statement, we do not mean to imply that cyclical industries are bad investments or that they should be avoided. We merely point out the cyclical influence of the economy. Often cyclical industries are excellent buys in the stock market because the market does not look far enough ahead to see a recovery and its impact on cyclical profits.

Exploring the Web

Web site Address	Comments
www.yardeni.com	Contains economic forecasts from private economist
www.economy.com	Provides access to economic data—some sources are fee based
finance.yahoo.com	Provides information about the economy
www.dismal.com	Contains articles on economies and tracks information from U.S. And global sources
www.fedstats.gov	Has links to economic data
www.freelunch.com	Has links to other economic sites, has listings of economic reports and news events, and provides access to economic data
www.smartmoney.com	Has information and news about U.S. economy
www.bea.doc.gov	Provides links to sources of U.S. government economic data
www.ny.frb.org	Contains links to New York Federal Reserve Bank analyses and data
www.stls.frg.org/fred	Contains historical interest rate, bond and economic data—site is free
www.mworld.com	Provides industry and economic data as well as data on money flows into stock funds
www.stat-usa.gov	Provides general information about the U.S. economy
www.bos.frb.org	Home page of the Federal Reserve of Boston providing economic information
www.ita.doc.gov	Provides access to U.S. government reports on international trade with reports being fee based

SUMMARY

The primary purpose of this chapter is to provide you with a process of valuation and an appreciation of some of the variables that should be considered. The valuation process is based on fundamental analysis of the economy, industry, and company. This method assumes decisions are made based on economic concepts of value over the long-term trend of the stock market. The purpose of the process is to eliminate losers from consideration in your portfolio and to thereby provide you with a good opportunity to build a sound portfolio.

The first step in the valuation process is an analysis of the economy and long-term economic trends. The difficulties of attaining government policy goals are discussed as trade-off between conflicting objectives (high growth versus low inflation). Fiscal and monetary policy are discussed as the primary tools used to stimulate economic activity. Interest rates are influenced by inflation, with the end result being a higher required rate of return for the investor.

Business cycles are short-term swings in economic activity; they affect stock prices because they change investor expectations of risk and return. To forecast economic activity, cyclical indicators are presented as leading, lagging, and coincident indexes. The one index potentially most valuable to an investor is the composite index of 10 leading indicators.

The sensitivity of various types of industries to the business cycle is also examined. Firms in consumer durable goods (automobiles), as well as those in heavy capital goods manufacturing (plant and equipment) are perhaps most vulnerable to the business cycle.

INDUSTRY LIFE CYCLE

Industry life cycles are created because of economic growth, competition, availability of resources, and the resultant market saturation by the particular goods and services offered. Life-cycle growth influences many variables considered in the valuation process. The particular phase in the life cycle of an industry or company determines the growth of earnings, dividends, capital expenditures, and market demand for products.

An analysis of industry financial data helps place an industry on the life-cycle curve and, in turn, guides the analyst toward decisions on industry growth, the duration of growth, profitability, and potential rates of return. The analyst can determine whether all companies in the industry are in the same stage of the life cycle and translate company differences into various assumptions that will affect their individual valuations.

Figure 10–10 shows a five-stage industry life cycle (although it could very well be a company life cycle) and the corresponding dividend policy most likely to be found at each stage. The vertical scale on this graph is logarithmic, which means that a straight line on this scale represents a constant growth rate. The steeper the line, the faster the growth rate, and the flatter the line, the smaller the growth rate. The slope of the line in the life-cycle curve and how it changes over time is very important in the analysis of growth and its duration. We will examine each stage separately and learn why the dividend policy is important in placing an industry or company in a particular stage.

Development—Stage I

The development stage includes companies that are getting started in business with a new idea, product, or production technique that makes them unique. Firms in this stage are usually privately owned and are financed with the owner's money as well as with capital from friends, family, and a bank. If the company has some success, there is a probability that outside money from a venture capital group may increase the financing available to the company. In this stage, the company is also the industry or a subset of an existing industry. For example, when Steve Jobs started Apple Computer in the early 1970s, it was a development startup company that created an entirely new industry. In the beginning, Apple was

FIGURE 10–10   Industry Life Cycle

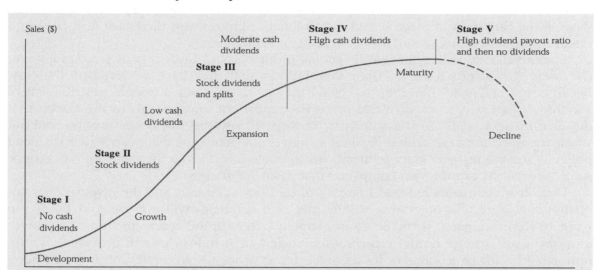

certainly not taken seriously by IBM, but by the early 2000s the personal computer (PC) industry and its related software products represented a sizable multibillion dollar industry much bigger than the old mainframe business of IBM and others.

The pharmaceutical industry has been around for a long time, but in the 1970s and 1980s many small biotechnology firms were founded that created drugs using different production and research techniques. Hundreds of small biotech firms using genetic techniques were created by entrepreneurs in medical research. This focus on medical research created a subset of the pharmaceutical industry, and, eventually, large companies such as Merck and Eli Lilly created joint partnerships with these companies. Some biotech firms such as Genentech eventually produced successful drugs and became large companies themselves.

One thing all these firms have in common is their need for capital. A small firm in the initial stages of development (Stage I) pays no dividends because it needs all of its profits (if there are any) for reinvestment in new productive assets. If the firm is successful in the marketplace, the demand for its products will create growth in sales, earnings, and assets, and the industry or company will move into Stage II.

Growth—Stage II

Stage II growth represents an industry or company that has achieved a degree of market acceptance for its products. At this stage, earnings will be retained for reinvestment, and sales and returns on assets will be growing at an increasing rate. The increasing growth can be seen from the increasing slope of the line in Figure 10-10.

By 1978 Apple Computer's PC was so successful that Apple needed more capital for expansion than could be generated internally, so it made an initial public offering of common stock to finance a major expansion. The success of the personal computer enticed IBM to enter this segment of the market, and, eventually, the IBM PC—with its open architecture—was copied and cloned by companies such as Compaq, Gateway, Dell, and Micron. All these firms are now publicly traded in U.S. markets and control more than 90 percent of the PC market.

Companies such as IBM entered the developing PC industry with a small amount of their total assets targeted at this market and were able to fund the move into this market with internal sources of capital. However, the other companies entering this market were "pure plays"; in other words, all they did was make personal computers. These companies were in the early part of Stage II, and they still needed to reinvest their cash flow back into research and development and into new plant and equipment.

In general, companies in Stage II become profitable, and, in their early stage of growth, they want to acknowledge to their shareholders that they have achieved profitability. Because they still need their internal capital, they often pay stock dividends (distributions of additional shares). A stock dividend preserves capital but often signals to the market that the firm made a profit. In the latter part of Stage II, low cash dividends may be paid out when the need for new capital declines as new sources of capital appear. A cash dividend policy is sometimes necessary to attract institutional investors to the company stock since some institutions cannot own companies that pay no dividends.

Obviously, industries in Stage I or early Stage II are very risky, and the investor does not really know if growth objectives will be met or if dividends will ever be paid. But if you want to have a chance to make an investment (after careful research) in a high-growth industry with large potential returns, then Stage I or II industries will provide you with opportunities for large gains or losses. Since actual dividends are irrelevant in these stages, an investor will be purchasing shares for capital gains based on expected growth rather than on current income.

Expansion—Stage III

In Stage III, sales expansion and earnings continue but at a decreasing rate. As the industry crosses from the growth stage to the expansion stage, the slope of the line in Figure 10-10 becomes less steep, signaling slower growth. It is this crossover point that is important to the analyst who will also be evaluating declining returns on investment as more competition enters the market and attempts to take away market share from existing firms. The industry has grown to the point where asset expansion slows in line with production needs, and the firms in the industry are more capable of paying cash dividends. Stock dividends and stock splits are still common in Stage III, and the dividend payout ratio usually increases from a low level of 5 to 15 percent of earnings to a moderate level of 25 to 30 percent of earnings by Stage III.

Because industries and companies do not grow in a nice smooth line, it is often difficult to tell when the industry or company has crossed from Stage II growth to Stage III expansion. Determining the crossover point is extremely important to investors who choose to invest in growth companies. Once investors recognize that the past growth rate will not be extrapolated and, instead, is in decline, stock prices can take a sizable tumble as price-earnings ratios collapse because of slower growth expectations. Figure 10-11 demonstrates this relationship.

Maturity—Stage IV

Maturity occurs when industry sales grow at a rate equal to the economy as measured by the long-term trend in gross domestic product (GDP). Some analysts like to use the growth rate of the Standard & Poor's 500 Index for comparison because the growth rate of these 500 large companies sets the norm for mature companies. Figure 10-12 graphs sales for the S&P Industrials and the GDP using a logarithmic graph. The use of a logarithmic graph (sometimes called a ratio scale) allows a comparison of growth rates between trend lines since a straight line on a vertical logarithmic scale represents a constant growth rate. The steeper the slope of the line, the faster the growth rate. Notice that on the graph, the S&P Industrials' sales and GDP seem to have similar long-term growth rates (slope).

Automobiles are a good example of a mature industry. Figure 10-13 shows the relationship between sales of the automobile industry and GDP in current dollars. While automobile

FIGURE 10–11   The Crossover Point

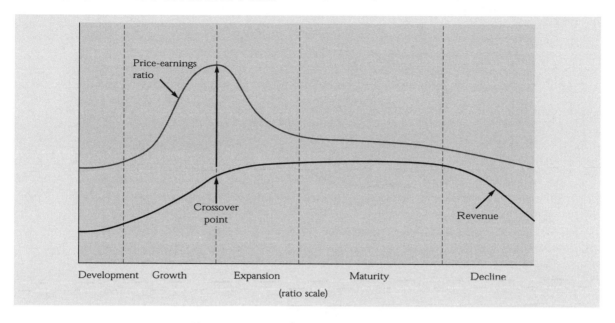

FIGURE 10–12   S&P Industrials versus GDP

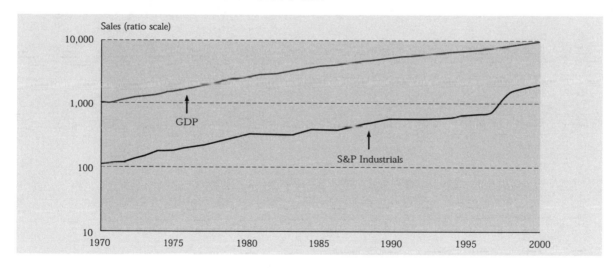

sales do not have the relatively smooth line of GDP, the slope of the two lines appears similar. Figure 10–14 plots sales for the auto industry against the GDP for the years 1970 through 2000. The scatter diagram again depicts the cyclical nature of automobile sales and a close relationship to that of GDP.

By the time an industry or firm reaches maturity, plant and equipment are in place, financing alternatives are available domestically and internationally, and the cash flow from operations is usually more than enough to meet the growth requirements of the firm. Under these conditions, dividends will usually range from 45 to 50 percent of earnings. These percentages will be different from industry to industry, depending on individual characteristics.

FIGURE 10–13   Automobile Industry versus GDP

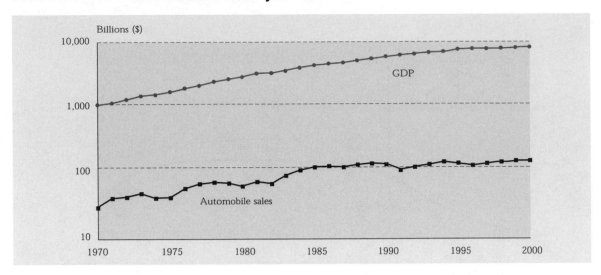

FIGURE 10–14   Automobile Sales versus GDP, 1965–2000

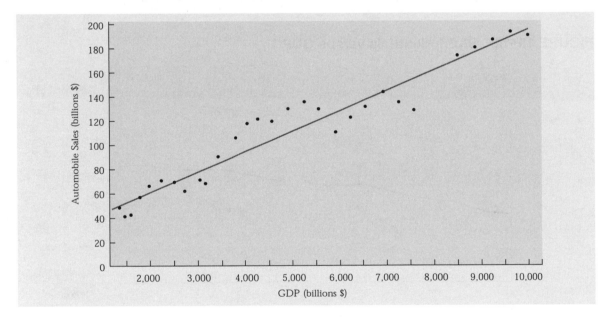

Decline—Stage V

In unfortunate cases, industries suffer declines in sales if product innovation has not increased the product base over the years. Declining industries may be specific to a country; passenger trains are such an example. In Europe, passenger trains are common forms of transportation, while in the United States, passenger trains have been in decline for many decades because competition from automobiles, buses, and airplanes has cut into the market. Besides the famous buggy whip example, black-and-white television, vacuum tubes, and transistor radios are examples of products within an industry that have been in decline. In some cases, the companies producing these products repositioned their resources into growth-oriented products, and, in other cases, the companies went out of business.

Often it is not a whole industry that goes into decline but the weakest company in the industry that cannot compete. Currently, industries such as banks, airlines, and breweries are undergoing consolidation. The number of banks has been declining, and this trend is expected to accelerate as national banking takes hold in the United States. The airline industry has been in consolidation for decades with famous names such as Braniff, Eastern, and Pan Am defunct and others such as TWA and Continental continually on the brink of bankruptcy. Apple Computer represents an extreme case of a leading company in the early stages of development that fell on hard times during the later stages because of intense competition and its inability to meet that competition in pricing and product development. Only time will tell whether its alliance with Microsoft will help save the company.

Dividend payout ratios of firms in decline often rise to 100 percent or more of earnings. Often, the firm does not want to signal stockholders that it is in trouble, so it maintains its dividends in the face of falling earnings. This causes the payout ratio to soar until management realizes that the firm is bleeding to death and needs to conserve cash. Then either drastic dividend cuts follow, or there is an elimination of dividends entirely.

Dividend Policy and the Life-Cycle Curve   The dividend payout ratio has an important effect on company growth. As previously pointed out, the more funds a firm retains—and, thus, the lower the dividend payout—the greater the opportunity for growth. The dividend policy followed by management often provides the analyst with management's view of the company's ability to grow and some indication of where the company is on the life-cycle curve. For example, a firm paying out 50 percent of earnings in dividends is probably not in Phase I, II, or III of the life-cycle curve.

Growth in Nongrowth Industries

It is also important to realize that growth companies can exist in a mature industry and that not all companies within an industry experience the same growth path in sales, earnings, and dividends. Some companies are simply better managed, have better people, have more efficient assets, and have put more money into productive research and development that has created new or improved products.

Many U.S. companies, such as Coca-Cola and McDonald's, have found growth by expansion abroad. While their domestic markets are saturated and growing at the rate of GDP or less, the international demand for their products in Asia, Europe, Eastern Europe, Russia, and China has allowed these two companies to maintain double-digit growth rates. This may also be true of other marketing-oriented companies with global trademarks such as Sony, Pepsi, Heineken, and Nike.

Electric utilities are generally considered mature, but utilities in states such as Florida, Arizona, and the Carolinas, which have undergone rapid population explosions over the last decade, would still have higher growth rates than the industry in general.

Computer companies such as IBM were fast approaching maturity until technical innovations created new markets. Unfortunately for IBM, demand for its mainframe computers declined worldwide as personal computers and local area networks increased in flexibility and power. To combat this decline in its major product line, IBM restructured in an effort to revive growth from its personal computer, software, and service divisions. Some analysts would place the PC industry in the expansion stage, but IBM as the dominant player in the computer industry is playing catchup to other PC makers who dominate the growth segments.

The warning to the investor is not to become enamored with a company just because it is in a "growth industry." Its time of glory may have passed. Other investors improperly ignore companies that are in the process of revitalization because they no longer carry the growth-stock tag.

INDUSTRY STRUCTURE

The structure of the industry is another area of importance for the analyst. Industry structure determines whether the companies in the industry are profitable, whether there are special considerations such as government regulations that positively or negatively affect the industry, and whether cost advantages and product quality create a dominant company within the industry.

A financial analyst may want to evaluate other significant factors for a given industry. For example, is the industry structure monopolistic like a regulated utility, oligopolistic like the automobile industry, partially competitive like the pharmaceutical industry, or very competitive like the industry for farm commodities? Questions of industry structure are very important in analyzing pricing structures and price elasticities that exist because of competition or the lack of it.

Economic Structure

We often look at the economic structure of an industry to determine how companies compete within the industry. **Monopolies** are generally not common in the United States because of our antitrust laws, but they have existed by government permission in the area of public utilities. In return for the monopoly, the government has the right to regulate rates of return on equity and assets and to approve customer fees. This sets the limits of growth and profitability and creates minimums and maximums for the analyst. Monopolies are almost always in mature industries, although the government may occasionally grant a monopoly on emerging technologies and even offer subsidies for the development of new technologies, especially in the defense industry.

Oligopolies have few competitors and are quite common in large mature U.S. industries such as automobiles, steel, oil, airlines, and aluminum to name a few. The competition between companies in an oligopoly can be intense, and profitability can suffer as a result of price wars and battles over market share. Increasingly, oligopolistic industries are facing international competition, which has altered their competitive strategies. Note that many of the industries mentioned earlier have competition from other industrial countries such as Japan, Germany, the Netherlands, Britain, and France.

Pure competition in manufacturing is not widely found in the United States. The food processing industry may be the closest example of this economic form. Generally, companies in pure competition do not have a differentiated product such as corn, soybeans, and other commodities. Firms will often compete by trying to create perceived differences in product quality or service.

Other Economic Factors to Consider   Questions of supply and demand relationships are very important because they affect the price structure of the industry and its ability to produce quality products at a reasonable cost. The cost variable can be affected by many factors. For example, high relative hourly wages in basic industries such as steel, autos, and rubber are somewhat responsible for the inability of the United States to compete in the world markets for these products. Availability of raw material is also an important cost factor. Industries such as aluminum and glass need to have an abundance of low-cost bauxite and silicon to produce their products. Unfortunately, the aluminum industry uses very large amounts of electricity in the production process, so the low cost of bauxite may be offset by the high cost of energy. Energy costs are of concern to all industries, but the availability of reasonably priced energy sources is particularly important to the airline and trucking industries. The list could go on and on, but as analysts become familiar with a specific industry, they learn the crucial variables.

Government Regulation   Most industries are also affected by government regulation. This applies to the automobile industry where safety and exhaust emissions are regulated and to all industries where air, water, and noise pollution are of concern. Many industries engaged in interstate commerce—such as utilities, railroads, and telephone companies—have been strongly regulated by the government, but even these have begun to feel the effects of deregulation and competition. The telephone companies have begun a global expansion with international partners that is changing the face of competition for long-distance calling worldwide. Industries such as airlines, trucking, and natural gas production have been deregulated and are still undergoing structural changes within the industry as new competitive forces emerge. Most industries are affected by government expenditures; this is especially true for industries involved in defense, education, health care, and transportation.

These are but a few examples to alert you to the importance of having a thorough understanding of your industry. This is why in many large investment firms, trust departments, and insurance companies, analysts are assigned to only one industry or to several related industries so that they may concentrate their attention on a given set of significant factors. Perhaps one of the most important aspects of industry analysis is the competitive structure of the industry.

Competitive Structure

Industries consist of competing firms; some industries have many firms, others have few. Nevertheless, the existing firms compete with each other and employ different strategies for success. Increasingly, the competition is among large international companies where cultural values and production processes are different. It becomes important for the investment analyst to know the attractiveness of industries for long-term profitability and what factors determine an industry's long-term outlook.

As we discussed previously, just because an industry as a whole is in a certain life-cycle stage, all companies within that industry may not be in the same position. An individual company within the industry may have chosen a poor competitive position or an excellent competitive position. While the industry outlook is important, a company may be able to create a competitive position that shapes the industry environment. There are profitable firms in poor industries and unprofitable firms in good industries.

Perhaps one of the most efficient ways to indicate competitive issues is to consider Michael Porter's elements of industry structure.[4]

Porter divides the competitive structure of an industry into five basic competitive forces: (1) threat of entry by new competitors, (2) threat of substitute goods, (3) bargaining power of buyers, (4) bargaining power of suppliers, and (5) rivalry among existing competitors. All affect price and profitability. The first is the threat of entry by new competitors. If competitors can easily enter the market, firms may have to construct barriers to entry that raise the cost to the firm. This threat places a limit on prices that can be charged and affects profitability. A second force, as we know from economics, is the threat of substitute goods. If we can easily substitute one good for another, this will again affect the price that can be charged and profit margins. An example of this would be in the beverage industry. We can drink water (tap or bottled), beer, soft drinks, fruit juice, and so on. If not for the tremendous advertising expenditures from companies trying to get us to drink their beverages, the cost would be considerably lower.

Two other competitive forces are the bargaining power of buyers and the bargaining power of suppliers. A large buyer of goods (Wal-Mart) can influence the price suppliers can charge for their goods. Firms such as McDonald's have stringent requirements for their suppliers, and, because it is a powerful buyer, McDonald's expects and gets cost-efficient service and quality control from its suppliers. This behavior restricts the prices that suppliers can charge. On the other hand, there are many powerful suppliers, such as the Middle East oil cartel or DeBeers, the company that controls more than 70 percent of the worldwide diamond market. These suppliers control the cost of raw materials to their customers, and their behavior determines a major part of their customers' profitability.

---

4. Professor Porter is a leading business strategist at Harvard University.

The Real World of Investing

In Analyzing an Industry or Company, What's a Brand Name Worth?

In our modern economy, a brand name is often worth as much as brick or mortar. In recognizing this fact, in August 2001, *Business Week* began publishing its ranking of the 100 most valuable brand names in the world and their value.*

The first question is, "How do you establish the value?" For this purpose *Business Week* engaged the services of Interbrand Corp., a pioneering brand consulting firm in New York. The value is based on the power to increase sales and earnings and is quantified through taking the present value of the future impact on these variables. While intangible assets such as brand name recognition are normally not quantified in the United States because of rulings by the Financial Accounting Standards Board, financial analysts recognize their essential nature in valuing a firm. The lack of inclusion of intangible assets on the balance sheet (with the exception of postmerger goodwill) is one reason firms in the S&P 500 Stock Index on average trade at five times their accounting determined book value. For companies in Great Britain and Australia, brand name value *must* be included on the balance sheet.

Having said all this, which U.S. company had the most valuable brand name recognition? The envelope please. And the answer is Coca-Cola with a value of $68.9 billion. The top 10 in the *Business Week* 2001 survey are:

	(in billions)		(in billions)
Coca-Cola	$68.9	Intel	$34.7
Microsoft	65.1	Disney	32.6
IBM	52.8	Ford	30.1
GE	42.4	McDonald's	25.3
Nokia	35.0	AT&T	22.8

Because this is chapter on industry analysis, we also show the top-ranked brand names in two industries where brand recognition is particularly important:

Automotive	(in billions)	Technology	(in billions)
Ford	$30.1	IBM	$52.8
Mercedes	21.7	Intel	34.7
Toyota	18.6	Hewlett-Packard	18.0
Honda	14.6	CISCO	17.2
BMW	13.9	Compaq	12.4
Volkswagen	7.3	Dell	8.3

The story is not positive for all companies. According to the survey, due to unfortunate events or poor performance, Xerox lost 38 percent of its brand name value in 2001, and Yahoo! and Amazon.com each lost 31 percent.

*"The Best Global Brands," *Business Week*, August 6, 2001, pp. 50–55.

The last competitive force is the rivalry among existing competitors. The extent of the rivalry affects the costs of competition—from the investment in plant and equipment, to advertising and product development. The automobile industry is a reasonable example of intense rivalry that eventually caused Japanese auto manufacturers, for political reasons, to limit their exports to the United States and instead start producing automobiles in the United States. Because the threat of entry was thought to be small, U.S. Automobile companies were complacent for years and did not modernize their production processes with new technology or work flow techniques. Once the Japanese took a large market share, the rivalry intensified and caused a restructuring of the whole U.S. Automobile industry. The impact of intense rivalry, therefore, has the same effect as the threat of new entrants.

These five forces vary from industry to industry and directly affect the return on assets and return on equity. The importance of each factor is a function of industry structure or the economic and technical characteristics of an industry. These forces affect prices, costs, and investment in plants, equipment, advertising, and research and development. While each industry has a set of competitive forces that are most important to it in terms of long-run profitability, competitors will devise strategies that may change the industry structure. Strategies that change the environment may improve or destroy the industry structure and profitability. Sometimes it takes several years to see the impact of competitive strategies.

INDUSTRY TREND ANALYSIS

In this section, we expand the horizon by shifting our attention to two industries—the pharmaceutical industry and the chemical industry. We look at their returns on equity and long-term debt-to-equity ratios over a 10-year period. By studying these important industries, the analyst develops a feel for comparative performance in our economy.

The return on equity (ROE) for the two industries shown in Table 10–5 indicates wide differences in profitability. These data are graphed in Figure 10–15 and the trends are more visible. The very strong economy of the mid-1990s has created a healthy earnings environment for both industries, and returns on equity are higher at the end of the period than at the beginning for both chemicals and pharmaceuticals. Since the 1996–97 period, however, the industry trend for ROE is up in the pharmaceutical industry, while the industry trend for ROE in the chemical industry is down.

The pharmaceutical industry is relatively stable as an industry, but individual companies go through cycles as their patents expire and popular drugs such as Prozac for Eli Lilly go off patent (August 2001). When a drug goes off patent and becomes manufactured by generic drug companies, profits plummet and returns on equity follow. The true test of sustainability

TABLE 10–5   Return on Equity

	1991	1992	1993	1994	1995	1996	1997	1998	1999	2000	2001
Pharmaceutical Industry	**27.2%**	**28.1%**	**26.7%**	**25.5%**	**25.3%**	**24.7%**	**28.5%**	**30.0%**	**31.9%**	**33.5%**	**35.0%**
Glaxo SmithKline	25.3	27.2	24.2	23.7	6.0	11.0	11.4	12.5	13.6	55.0	28.0
Eli Lilly	26.5	28.5	29.5	23.7	24.1	23.9	37.2	49.1	50.4	48.0	42.5
Merck & Co.	43.2	48.9	26.8	26.9	28.4	32.4	36.6	41.0	44.5	46.0	43.5
Pfizer	18.2	23.2	30.5	30.0	28.2	27.7	27.9	29.9	38.2	40.4	41.0
Schering-Plough	48.0	45.1	52.2	58.6	64.9	58.9	51.2	43.9	40.9	39.6	33.5
Chemical Industry	**12.7%**	**14.2%**	**12.4%**	**20.1%**	**33.3%**	**28.6%**	**31.2%**	**20.1%**	**19.1%**	**18.3%**	**21.5%**
Dow Chemical	10.2	7.1	6.9	13.2	28.8	23.9	23.6	18.4	16.7	16.5	8.5
Du Pont	10.3	14.4	14.8	21.6	40.4	34.0	36.3	20.9	22.1	21.5	12.5
Olin Corp.	10.7	7.4	6.7	12.1	16.6	18.3	17.4	9.9	5.5	24.6	8.5

FIGURE 10–15   Return on Equity—Pharmaceutical and Chemical Industries

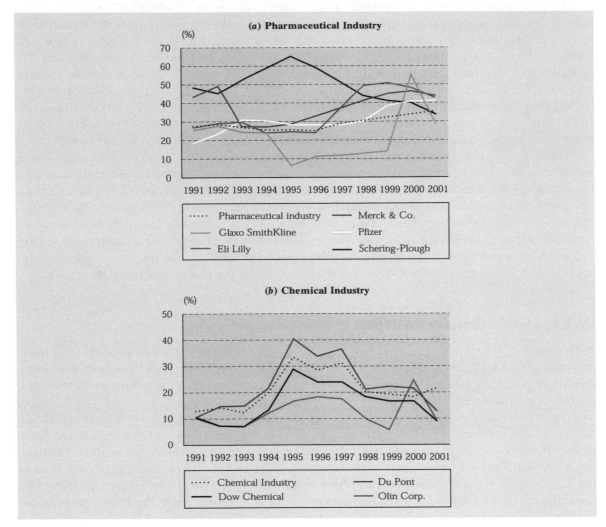

in the pharmaceutical industry is the ability of the company's research and development team to generate new products that solve medical problems and can get approved by the U.S. Food and Drug Administration.

The past decade has seen several major mergers in the pharmaceutical industry. Pfizer merged with Warner Lambert; Glaxo merged with Welcome and then several years later with SmithKline Beecham. A merger occurs in this industry for several reasons. The buying company needs a more comprehensive product line, or their pipeline of new drugs is rather bare and they need to buy research. In some cases, international companies are looking for better distribution because they are limited to one geographic area.

Some companies in this industry feel that they need to be very large to compete on an international playing field, and the pharmaceutical industry is truly a global industry. Often when mergers occur, profitability falls because of integration problems. If the merger occurred because of patent expirations, profits could decline until new drugs enter the market. Both these phenomenons were true of Glaxo SmithKline in 1995-96 when Glaxo bought Welcome and in 2000-01 when Glaxo bought SmithKline.

International regulation is also a problem for pharmaceutical companies. Government health care plans put tremendous pressure on drug companies to maintain prices at low levels, and many countries have price controls on prescription drugs. In the United States, large health maintenance organizations (HMOs) have very powerful buying power and can bargain for low prices with large quantity purchases.

TABLE 10–6   Long-Term Debt-to-Equity Ratios

	1991	1992	1993	1994	1995	1996	1997	1998	1999	2000	2001
Pharmaceutical Industry	**12.0%**	**12.0%**	**16.0%**	**32.0%**	**48.0%**	**40.0%**	**24.7%**	**26.6%**	**32.5%**	**28.5%**	**25.5%**
Glaxo SmithKline	4.2	3.7	4.5	5.1	17.9	20.8	23.4	22.2	16.9	22.7	23.9
Eli Lilly	8.0	11.9	18.3	39.7	47.7	41.3	50.1	49.3	56.1	43.6	35.0
Merck & Co.	10.0	9.9	11.2	10.3	11.7	9.7	10.7	25.2	23.7	24.3	21.2
Pfizer	7.9	12.1	14.8	14.0	15.1	9.9	9.2	6.0	5.9	7.0	7.3
Schering-Plough	56.0	11.5	11.5	11.8	5.4	2.3	1.6	0.1	0.0	0.0	0.0
Chemical Industry	**61.0%**	**82.0%**	**68.0%**	**58.0%**	**66.0%**	**57.0%**	**59.8%**	**67.0%**	**86.7%**	**85.2%**	**90.7%**
Dow Chemical	64.4	76.7	73.3	64.4	61.1	52.5	54.7	54.2	60.0	53.0	43.2
Du Pont	38.6	61.1	58.2	49.7	67.3	47.5	52.6	32.2	51.5	50.3	47.4
Olin Corp.	78.1	64.4	75.3	55.8	48.9	29.2	30.5	29.1	74.1	69.3	88.2

Traditionally pharmaceutical companies have relatively low long-term debt-to-equity ratios. Table 10–6 and Figure 10–16 show that the long-term debt-to-equity-ratios have fluctuated widely for the industry as well as for individual companies. Pfizer and Schering-Plough have very low debt-to-equity ratios, while Merck and Glaxo have ratios less than 30 percent. Eli Lilly's debt-to-equity ratio soared in 1995 because they spent many billions of dollars to purchase a pharmaceutical distribution business that in the end turned out to be a bad purchase. They divested this company several years later. Lilly has continued to spend large amounts of money on their research and development program in an effort to generate new drugs to replace Prozac. This is another reason for the increase in debt. However, since 1999 Lilly's debt-to-equity ratio has begun to approach the industry mean.

The basic chemical industry is cyclical in that it follows the ups and downs of the economy. Its returns are more cyclical than the pharmaceutical industry, and all companies in the industry seem to follow the same pattern even though not at the same level of profitability. We can see that this industry is very much influenced by the business cycle by looking at the low returns in 1991 (Figure 10–15b), during a time of economic recession. The good economic times in the 1990s raised the returns on equity for several years but eventually price competition in the late 1990s and the economic struggles of 2000–2001 caused another challenge to profitability.

Commodity prices greatly affect the profitability of the chemical industry worldwide. Many fibers and plastics are derived from petroleum and natural gas, and prices of these commodities have a big effect on their profits. The demand for the output produced by the chemical industry is influenced by the general level of economic activity, and companies in the industry seem to perform more efficiently when capacity is fully utilized.

This industry has gone through several mergers and restructuring in the last decade as pricing pressures have forced larger economies of scale on all companies. Du Pont sold off its ownership of Conoco Oil and used the funds from the sale to reduce debt, repurchase common stock, and make significant investments in pharmaceuticals and other higher growth industries. Dow Chemical bought Union Carbide and Monsanto, moved into biochemical agriculture, and moved out of basic chemicals.

Du Pont and Dow Chemical are the two dominant powerhouses in the basic chemical industry, and Olin is a much smaller player. Both Dow and Du Pont had peak ROEs in 1995 (Figure 10–15b). Declining earnings due to competitive pricing pressures, sagging demand, and rising oil prices have followed this robust period. As the economy struggles in 2001, all three companies exhibit significant declines in profitability. The pharmaceutical industry (except for Glaxo) will be much less affected by the sluggish economy.

Du Pont has traditionally had the lowest long-term debt-to-equity ratio in the chemical industry (Figure 10–16b), which is why it has been considered a blue chip. During the mid-1990s, however, Dow had a lower long-term debt-to-equity ratio than Du Pont, but its

FIGURE 10–16   Long-Term Debt-to-Equity Ratios—Pharmaceutical and Chemical Industries

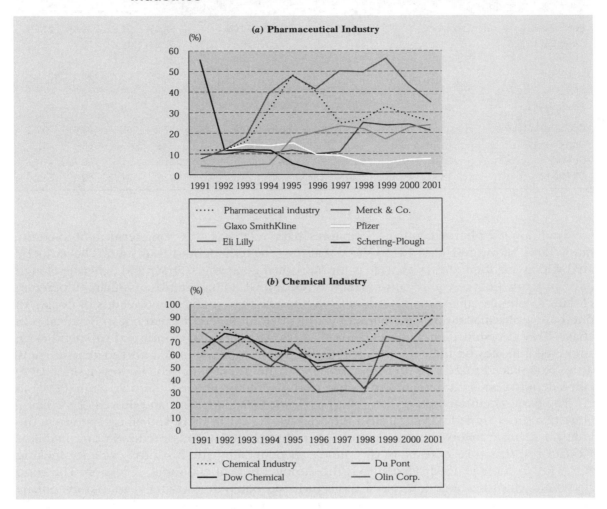

purchase of Union Carbide caused a significant increase in its debt. The irony of the debt ratios between the pharmaceutical industry and the chemical industry is that the pharmaceutical industry—because of its sales stability and higher profitability—can manage a higher debt-to-equity ratio than the chemical industry. The lower profitability and higher cost of plant and equipment in the chemical industry forces them to use more debt in their capital structure.

These tables and figures only cover two ratios, but they should show that industry comparisons allow one to pick the quality companies and find the potential losers. These two ratios (return on equity and long-term debt to equity) can be extremely important when making risk-return choices among common stocks. By comparing the two tables, we see a distinct relationship between the ratios. This trend analysis demonstrates that by analyzing just two ratios and looking across companies in the industry, an analyst can learn quite a bit about the structure of the industry and the competitive environment. A closer look at many other variables would add to the knowledge base.

INDUSTRY GROUPS AND ROTATIONAL INVESTING

One strategy of investment used by institutional investors and occasionally by individual investors is the concept of **rotational investing**. Rotational investing refers to the practice of moving in and out of various industries over the business cycle. As the business cycle moves

TABLE 10–7   Dow Jones Industry Groups

Basic Materials	Distillers and brewers	**Industrial**
Chemicals	Food products	Aerospace and defense
Chemicals, commodity	Soft drinks	Building materials
Chemicals, specialty	Food retailers and wholesalers	Heavy construction
Forest products	Consumer products	Containers and packaging
Paper products	Household products, durables	Industrial diversified
Aluminum	Household products, nondurables	Industrial equipment
Mining, diversified	Tobacco	Advanced industrial equipment
Other nonferrous (e.g., aluminum)	**Energy**	Electrical components and equipment
Precious metals	Coal	Factory equipment
Steel	Oil and gas	Heavy machinery
Consumer, Cyclical	Oil, drilling	Industrial services
Advertising	Oil, integrated majors	Pollution control and waste management
Broadcasting	Oil, secondary	Industrial transportation
Publishing	Oilfield equipment and services	Air freight and couriers
Auto manufacturers	Pipelines	Marine transportation
Auto parts	**Financial**	Railroads
Casinos	Banks	Trucking
Entertainment	Insurance, composite	Transportation equipment
Recreation products and services	Insurance, full line	**Technology**
Restaurants	Insurance, life	Hardware and equipment
Toys	Insurance, property and casualty	Communications technology
Home construction	Specialty finance	Computers
Furnishings	Real estate investment	Office equipment
Retailers	Financial services, diversified	Semiconductor and related
Retailers, apparel	Savings and loans	Software
Retailers, broadline	Securities brokers	**Telecommunications**
Retailers, drug-based	**Health Care**	Fixed line communications
Retailers, specialty	Health care providers	Wireless communications
(e.g., drug and apparel)	Medical products	**Utilities**
Clothing and fabrics	Advanced medical devices	Electric
Footwear	Medical supplies	Gas
Airlines	Pharmaceutical and biotech	Water
Lodging	Biotechnology	
Consumer, Noncyclical	Pharmaceuticals	
Consumer services		
Cosmetics and personal care		

from a trough to a peak, different industries benefit from the economic changes that accompany the cycle. Table 10-7 lists ten Dow Jones Industry Groups; industries are classified into groups that are related in some form and that may exhibit similar behavior during different phases of the business cycle.

For example, as interest rates bottom out, houses become more easily financed and cost less per month to purchase. Because of this, housing stocks, home builders, lumber, and housing-related industries such as household durable goods benefit from the lower interest rates. Earnings of companies in these fields are expected to rise, and investors start buying the common stocks of these companies before any profits are actually visible. The same could be said for the automobile industry because of the effect of low-cost financing.

Once an economic recovery is under way, the unemployment rate declines, personal income starts growing, and consumers start spending more. It may take six quarters or more of growth from the recessionary trough, but investors usually anticipate when the consumer will start spending again and bid prices of consumer cyclical stocks up before earnings increases appear. While automobiles are affected by the lower interest rates, they also get a second boost from healthier consumers.

When interest rates begin to rise, this is not good news for utility stocks. Utilities generate high dividend payouts and usually sell based on their dividend yield. As interest rates rise, utility stock prices fall along with prices of bonds. Another group that eventually loses favor after rates have risen somewhat from their bottom and are expected to continue rising is the banking sector. Rising rates eventually reduce bank lending and squeeze bank margins, which are small anyway.

Investors fearful of rising rates and a potential economic slowdown will often retreat into consumer noncyclical goods such as food, pharmaceuticals, beverages, and tobacco. A move into these industries is often considered defensive because the industries are not much influenced by economic downturns, so their earnings do not suffer nearly as much as cyclical industries.

Eventually, as the economy moves through its business cycle, inflation fears return as demand for products pushes up prices of goods. One possible move is into basic materials and energy. The pricing pressures in the economy spill over into rising prices for these commodities and rising profits for aluminum, oil, steel, and other companies in these industries. A move into these industry groups usually occurs later in the business cycle.

While we do not necessarily endorse buying and selling common stocks in a rotational manner throughout the business cycle, many investors follow this approach, and you should be well aware of this strategy.

Exploring the Web

Web site Address	Comments
www.hoovers.com	Provides limited free information about sectors and industries
cbs.marketwatch.com	Contains news and industry performance on daily basis
www.smartmoney.com	Provides sector and market performance—feature is map of market
www.wsj.com	Provides limited information about industry data; has searchable archive on articles about companies and industries
www.corporateinformation.com	Provides links to information on industries and by country
www.ita.doc.gov	Provides access to industry reports that are fee based
www.investorguide.com	Has links to sites providing sector and industry information

SUMMARY

This chapter presented a three-step model for stock valuation in Figure 10–1. Industry analysis as presented in this chapter is the second step in the top-down valuation process we use in the text. One of the most crucial issues in valuing a firm is its potential growth rate in sales, earnings, and cash flow. In order to have some idea of how fast a company can grow, we look at the underlying industry growth characteristics, especially its position on the life-cycle curve.

The industry life-cycle approach includes five stages: development, growth, expansion, maturity, and decline. The life-cycle process is depicted in Figures 10–10 and 10–11.

In addition to life-cycle analysis, the analyst must understand the importance of industry structure. Every industry has an economic structure, for example, monopoly, oligopoly, pure competition, or some other form of competition. The economic structure affects product pricing and returns Government regulation is another issue that affects many industries. The government regulates profits (utilities), product quality (U.S. Food and Drug Administration), energy consumption (automobile efficiency), and many other areas of commerce such as transportation and education. Other issues that need to be examined are international competition, supply and demand relationships, availability of raw materials, energy costs, and so on.

The analyst should study general industry trends. We present two industries for comparison: chemicals and pharmaceuticals. Competing firms are compared within each industry, and the industries are compared against each other. The comparisons are presented in Figures 10–15 and 10–16. Finally, the concept of rotational investing is discussed. This concept describes investors who move from one industry to another as business cycle conditions change.

TACTICAL ASSET ALLOCATION (TAA) REVISITED

At this point we're ready to revisit the concept of tactical asset allocation, in light of what has been described in this chapter. But before we examine further, one cautionary word about using business cycles and macroeconomics to select securities is necessary. By definition, a cycle is something that repeats itself. Further, cycles last for finite time periods (the span of the cycle) and they go up and down by certain amounts (the cycle's frequency). In the case of a business cycle, the high and low points are its peaks and troughs while the span is how long a growth or recession period lasts. Thus, growth periods are followed by recessions, etc. lasting for certain periods, and this process repeats itself over time. Hence, it is a cycle.

While the above seems self-explanatory and straightforward, consider the following implication: if the economic growth (recession) periods were cyclical then we should have a very good idea of what would be happening in the future and for how long that would last. That is, the future would be quite predictable. We know the fallacy of this latter statement. Even if the concept of using business cycles and the industry analysis to select securities and time their trades seems an attractive and rational proposition, in truth benefiting from such an approach does not happen quite that easily. Hence, any strategy based on business cycles, etc. should be taken with a grain of salt.

Now, let us return to the issue of tactical asset allocation and its use in portfolio management. There are two issues to consider. First, general interest rates increase as the economy grows, they peak together and recede together as well. Further, this co-movement lasts a fairly long time. That is, from trough to trough or peak to peak, a complete business cycle may well last seven to eight years. In this case, when we're at the trough of a cycle, we should be heavily invested in equities and should have sold much of our bond positions (buying equities low and selling bonds high, at the trough). Now as the economy grows, stocks should increase in price and bonds start decreasing in price, we should consider selling our equity positions and entering bond positions. A question commonly asked is how do we know when this should happen during the business cycle? Many advisors believe, mistakenly, that the indicators can be found among the numbers from the market. Not so. The timing should actually depend upon the client's return requirements and objectives. For example, if a client required an 8 percent rate of return and at some point during the economic growth phase, the portfolio showed a return of 10 percent, then that is the indicator that the timing was right to shift from stocks to bonds. By this method, the advisor not only locks in a higher rate than required, but can use this excess return to at least dampen partially the effects of the troughs that are also sure to follow. Further, at these times, buying into bonds also implies entering the market at cheaper prices. When the market starts receding and bonds are sold then they too should provide for a healthy return, besides of course their stability contributions to the portfolio.

Thus, we can see how TAA may be implemented. What is important to note is that such a TAA scheme would imply shifting assets every two or three years if the business cycle lasted seven to eight years. That is, in a complete business cycle, no more than two or three times should the need arise to change. Unfortunately, there are many advisors who may abuse TAA and trade much more frequently. Of course, frequent changes in allocation will wipe out most potential gains for the client while generating greater commissions for such advisors.

Similarly, industry analysis can also be used in TAA. In fact, advisors who claim the ability to time changes in sectors and who practice "**sector rotation**" strategies, do precisely that. They use a TAA model based upon both how the economy changes and how these changes lead to the peaking and troughing of different industries or sectors. These in turn can also be used (or abused) by advisors to move assets between sectors and industries in the equity section of the portfolio. However, again, frequent application of TAA is likely to be both futile and costly for clients.

The analysis of macroeconomic conditions, globally and nationally, is considered to be the first step in the process of fundamental analysis. Macroeconomic analysis provides us with the bigger pictures regarding individual stocks and bonds and how we may expect such securities to behave. Macroeconomic analysis also sets the stage for us to understand how different industries may behave and opens for us a path to analyze industries. The analysis of industries allows us to identify those industries which are more likely to contain the securities that a portfolio advisor may be interested in. For example, industries and sectors that contain growth or cyclical companies would be desirable to search during periods of economic growth. Alternately, if an advisor or money manager wanted to sell securities short then they would look at industries containing defensive companies. As can now be seen, the analysis of industries opens up the next path towards fundamental security analysis, that of security valuation. This is the subject of the following chapter.

Chapter 11

Equity Valuation

BASIC VALUATION CONCEPTS

The valuation of common stock can be approached in several ways. Some models rely solely on dividends expected to be received during the future, and these are usually referred to as **dividend valuation models**. A variation on the dividend model is the **earnings valuation model**, which substitutes earnings as the main income stream for valuation. Earnings valuation models may also call for the determination of a price-earnings ratio, or multiplier of earnings, to determine value. Some models rely on long-run historical relationships between market price and sales per share, or market price and book value per share. Other methods may include the market value of assets, such as cash and liquid assets, replacement value of plant and equipment, and other hidden assets, such as undervalued timber holdings. For the first part of our discussion, we develop the dividend valuation model and then go to earnings-related approaches.

REVIEW OF RISK AND REQUIRED RETURN CONCEPTS

Before moving to the valuation models, it would be helpful to review and consolidate the concepts of risk and required return presented earlier. Calculation of the required rate of return is extremely important because it is the rate at which future cash flows are discounted to reach a valuation. An investor needs to know the required rate of return on the various risk classes of assets to reach intelligent decisions to buy or sell.

The required return is a function of the risk-free rate plus a risk premium for a specific investment.

In this section, we develop a simple methodology based on the capital asset pricing model for determining a required rate of return when valuing common stocks in diversified portfolio. First, we determine the risk-free rate. The **risk-free rate** (R_F) is a function of the real rate of return and the expected rate of inflation. Some analysts express the risk-free rate as simply the addition of the real rate of return and the expected rate of inflation, while a more accurate answer is found as follows:

$$R_F \text{ (risk-free rate)} = (1 + \text{Real rate})(1 + \text{Expected rate of inflation}) - 1 \qquad (11\text{--}1)$$

We now add a risk component to the risk-free rate to determine K_e, the total **required rate of return.** We show the following relationships.

$$K_e = R_F + b(K_M - R_F) \qquad (11\text{--}2)$$

where:

$$
\begin{aligned}
K_e &= \text{Required rate of return} \\
R_F &= \text{Risk-free rate} \\
b &= \text{Beta coefficient} \\
K_M &= \text{Expected return for common stocks in the market} \\
(K_M - R_F) &= \text{Equity risk premium (ERP)}
\end{aligned}
$$

The risk-free rate, in practice, is normally assumed to be the return on U.S. Treasury securities. **Beta** measures individual company risk against the market risk (usually the S&P 500 Stock Index). Companies with betas greater than 1.00 have more risk than the market, companies with betas less than 1.00 have less risk than the market, and companies with betas equal to 1.00 have the same risk as the market. It stands to reason then that high beta stocks ($b > 1.00$) would have higher required returns than the market.

The last term ($K_M - R_F$) in Formula 11-2, the **equity risk premium (ERP)**, is not observable from current market information because it is based on investor expectations. The equity risk premium represents the extra return or premium the stock market must provide compared with the rate of return an investor can earn on U.S. Treasury securities.

Because K_M is not observable from the market, an analyst calculating K_e usually thinks of ($K_M - R_F$) as one number, which we express as the equity risk premium (ERP).

The raging bull market of the 1990s increased the equity risk premium from 6.5 percent in the period 1926–94 to 7.2 percent in six years' time. It takes a powerful bull market to raise 68 years of history by 0.7 percent over six years. If it were not for the stock market's negative returns in 2000, this equity risk premium would have risen even higher. We use a 7.0 percent equity risk premium in our calculations below but recognize that this risk premium for investing in common stocks instead of risk-free government securities is also dependent on perceptions of the future and an individual's propensity to accept risk. Let's compute a required rate of return for a sample company with a beta of 1.00 (beta equals the market risk) when the Treasury bill rate is 5.0 percent and the ERP is 7.0 percent. We should have a required return as follows:

$$
\begin{aligned}
K_e &= R_F + b(\text{ERP}) \\
&= 5.0\% + 1.00(7.0\%) \\
&= 12.00\%
\end{aligned}
$$

Now, K_e, the required rate of return, can be used as a discount rate for future cash flows from an investment. This methodology will be helpful as you work through the dividend valuation models and other valuation models for common stock.

DIVIDEND VALUATION MODELS

The value of a share of stock may be interpreted by the shareholder as the present value of an expected stream of future dividends. Although in the short run, stockholders may be influenced by a change in earnings or other variables, the ultimate value of any holding rests with the distribution of earnings in the form of dividend payments. Although the stockholder may benefit from the retention and reinvestment of earnings by the corporation, at some point, the earnings must generally be translated into cash flow for the stockholder.[1] While dividend valuation models are theoretical in nature and subject to many limitations, they are the most frequently used models in the literature of finance. Perhaps this is because they demonstrate so well the relationship between the major variables affecting common stock prices.

---

1. Some exceptions to this principle are noted later in the chapter.

General Dividend Model

A generalized stock valuation model based on future expected dividends can be stated as follows:

$$P_0 = \frac{D_1}{(1 + K_e)^1} + \frac{D_2}{(1 + K_e)^2} + \frac{D_3}{(1 + K_e)^3} + \cdots + \frac{D_\infty}{(1 + K_e)^\infty} \qquad (11\text{-}3)$$

where:

P_0 = Present value of the stock price
D_i = Dividend for each year, for example, $1, 2, 3 \ldots \infty$
K_e = Required rate of return (discount rate)

This model is very general and assumes the investor can determine the right dividend for each and every year as well as the annualized rate of return an investor requires.

Constant Growth Model

Rather than predict the actual dividend each year, a more widely used model includes an estimate of the growth rate in dividends. This model assumes a constant growth rate in dividends to infinity.

If a constant growth rate in dividends is assumed, Formula 11-3 can be re-written as:

$$P_0 = \frac{D_0(1 + g)^1}{(1 + K_e)^1} + \frac{D_0(1 + g)^2}{(1 + K_e)^2} + \frac{D_0(1 + g)^3}{(1 + K_e)^3} + \cdots + \frac{D_0(1 + g)^\infty}{(1 + K_e)^\infty} \qquad (11\text{-}4)$$

where:

$D_0(1 + g)^1$ = Dividends in the initial year
$D_0(1 + g)^2$ = Dividends in year 2, and so on
g = Constant growth rate in the dividend

The current price of the stock should equal the present value of the expected stream of dividends. If we can correctly predict the growth of future dividends and determine the discount rate, we can estimate the true value of the stock.

For example, assume we wanted to determine the present value of ABC Corporation common stock based on this model. We shall assume ABC anticipates an 8 percent growth rate in dividends per share, and we use a 12 percent discount rate as the required rate of return. The required rate of return is intended to provide the investor with a minimum real rate of return, compensation for expected inflation, and a risk premium. Twelve percent is sufficient to fulfill that function in this example.

Rather than project the dividends for an extremely long period and then discount them back to the present, we can reduce previously presented Formula 11-4 to a more usable form:

$$P_0 = D_1/(K_e - g) \qquad (11\text{-}5)$$

This formula is appropriate as long as two conditions are met. The first is that the growth rate must be constant. For the ABC Corporation, we are assuming that to be the case. It is a constant 8 percent. Second, K_e (the required rate of return) must exceed g (the growth rate). Since K_e is 12 percent and g is 8 percent for the ABC Corporation, this condition is also met. Let's further assume D_1 (the expected dividend at the end of period 1) is $3.38.

TABLE 11–1   Present Value Analysis of ABC Corporation

Year	Expected Dividends $g = 8\%$	Present Value Factor $K_e = 12\%$	Present Value of Dividends
2002	$ 3.38	0.893	$ 3.02
2003	3.65	0.797	2.91
2004	3.94	0.712	2.81
2005	4.26	0.636	2.71
2006	4.60	0.567	2.61
2007	4.97	0.507	2.52
2008	5.37	0.452	2.43
2009	5.80	0.404	2.34
2010	6.26	0.361	2.26
2011	6.76	0.322	2.18
2012	7.30	0.287	2.10
2013	7.88	0.257	2.03
2014	8.51	0.229	1.95
2015	9.19	0.205	1.87
2016	9.93	0.183	1.81
2017	10.72	0.163	1.75
2018	11.58	0.146	1.69
2019	12.51	0.130	1.63
2020	13.51	0.116	1.57
2021	14.59	0.104	1.52
PV of dividends for years 2002–2021			$43.71
PV of dividends for years 2022 to infinity			40.79
Total present value of ABC common stock			$84.50[a]

[a] Notice that this value is the same as that found below using Formula 11–5.

Using Formula 11-5, we determine a stock value of:

$$P_0 = D_1/(K_e - g)$$
$$= \$3.38/(0.12 - 0.08)$$
$$= \$3.38/0.04$$
$$= \$84.50$$

This value, in theory, represents the present value of all future dividends. The meaning is further illustrated in Table 11-1, in which we take the present value of the first 20 years of dividends ($43.71) and then add in a figure of $40.79 to arrive at the present value of all future dividends of $84.50 as previously determined by Formula 11-5. The $40.79 value represents the present value of dividends occurring between 2022 and infinity (i.e., after 2021).

We must be aware that several things could be wrong with our analysis. First, our expectations of dividend growth may be too high for an infinite period. Perhaps 6 percent is a more realistic estimate of expected dividend growth. If we substitute our new estimate into Formula 11-5, we can measure the price effect as dividend growth changes from an 8 percent rate to a 6 percent rate:

$$P_0 = \$3.38/(0.12 - 0.06)$$
$$= \$3.38/0.06$$
$$= \$56.33$$

FIGURE 11–1   JAYCAR Growth Pattern

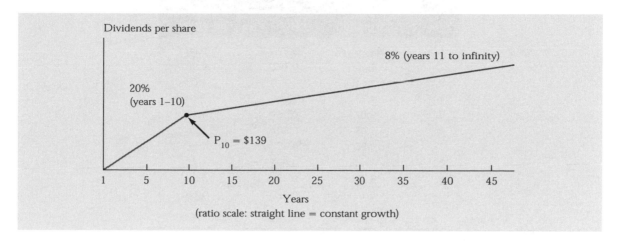

A 6 percent growth rate (a 2 percent change) cuts the present value down substantially from the prior value of $84.50.

We could also misjudge our required rate of return, K_e, which could be higher or lower. A lower K_e would increase the present value of ABC Corporation, whereas a higher K_e would reduce its value. We have made these points to show how sensitive stock prices are to the basic assumptions of the model. Even though you may go through the calculations, the final value is only as accurate as your inputs. This is where a security analyst's judgment and expertise are important—in justifying the growth rate and required rate of return.

A Nonconstant Growth Model

Many analysts do not accept the premise of a constant growth rate in dividends or earnings. Industries go through a life cycle in which growth is nonlinear. Growth is usually highest in the infancy and early phases of the life cycle, and as expansion is reached, the growth rate slows until the industry reaches maturity. At maturity, a constant, long-term growth rate that approximates the long-term growth of the macroeconomy may be appropriate for a particular industry.

Some companies in an industry may not behave like the industry in general. Companies constantly try to avoid maturity or decline, and so they strive to develop new products and markets to maintain growth.

In situations where the analyst wants to value a company without the constant-growth assumption, a variation of the constant-growth model is possible. Growth is simply divided into several periods with each period having a present value. The present value of each period is summed to attain the total value of the firm's share price. An example of a two-period model may illustrate the concept.

Assume that JAYCAR Corporation is expected to have the growth pattern shown in Figure 11–1.

It is assumed that JAYCAR will have a dividend growth rate of 20 percent for the next 10 years and an 8 percent perpetual growth rate after that. JAYCAR's dividend is expected to be $1 at the end of year one, and the appropriate required rate of return (discount rate) is 12 percent. Taking the present value for the first 10 years of dividends and then applying the constant dividend growth model for years 11 through infinity, we can arrive at an answer. First, we find the present value of the initial 10 years of dividends:

Year	Dividends (20% growth)	PV Factor (12%)	Present Value of Dividends First 10 Years
1	$1.00	0.893	$ 0.89
2	1.20	0.797	0.96
3	1.44	0.712	1.03
4	1.73	0.636	1.10
5	2.07	0.567	1.17
6	2.48	0.507	1.26
7	2.98	0.452	1.35
8	3.58	0.404	1.45
9	4.29	0.361	1.55
10	5.15	0.322	1.66
			$12.42

We then determine the present value of dividends after the 10th year. The dividend in year 11 is expected to be $5.56, or $5.15 (for year 10) compounded at the new, lower 8 percent growth rate ($5.15 × 1.08). Because the rest of the dividend stream will be infinite, Formula 11–5 can provide the value of JAYCAR at the end of year 10, based on a discount rate of 12 percent and an expected growth rate of 8 percent.

$$P_{10} = D_{11}/(K_e - g)$$
$$= \$5.56/(0.12 - 0.08)$$
$$= \$5.56/0.04$$
$$= \$139$$

An investor would pay $139 at the end of the 10th year for the future stream of dividends from year 11 to infinity. To get the present value of the 10th year price, the $139 must be discounted back to the present by the 10-year PV factor. This part of the answer is $139.00 × 0.322, or $44.76. The two parts of this analysis can be combined to get the current valuation per share of $57.18.

Present value of the dividends from years 1 to 10	$12.42
Present value of 10th year price ($139.00 × 0.322)	44.76
Total present value of JAYCAR common stock	$57.18

INTRINSIC VALUE

Prior to purchasing a stock, many analysts perform a fundamental analysis of the company which issued the stock. This fundamental analysis includes a dissection of the company from many aspects including its past and forecasted financial results, officers, product line, and product performance. From this analysis, an analyst or investor tries to determine whether a stock is undervalued or overvalued in the marketplace. The value used to determine under or over valuation as compared with the stock's current market value is known as the stock's intrinsic value.

By analyzing as much about the company as feasible, an analyst hopes to derive the future cash flows from the stock which include any estimated dividends and the future value of the stock at time of sale. Using a discount rate that reflects an equitable return relative to the risk for that type of investment, the analyst discounts the future cash flows to present value. The formula to calculate intrinsic value is as follows:

$$V_{IN} = P_n / (1 + k)^n + \text{Present Value } (D)$$

where V_{IN} is the intrinsic value of the stock, P_n is the forecasted value of the stock at the time of sale, D is the projected dividends over the holding period of the stock, and k is the discount rate that reflects the appropriate level of risk for that type of asset.

If V_{IN} is greater than the current market price of the stock, then the stock is undervalued. Therefore, an investor who feels confident in the analysis would buy the stock. Conversely, if the intrinsic value of the stock is less than the market value, the investor would not purchase the stock.

EARNINGS VALUATION MODELS

Dividend valuation models are best suited for companies in the expansion or maturity life-cycle phase. Dividends of these companies are more predictable and usually make up a larger percentage of the total return than capital gains. Earnings-per-share models are also used for valuation. For example, the investor may take the present value of all future earnings to determine a value. This might be appropriate where the firm pays no cash dividend and has no immediate intention of paying one.

The Combined Earnings and Dividend Model

Another, more comprehensive valuation model relies on earnings per share (EPS) and a price-earnings (P/E) ratio (earnings multiplier) combined with a finite dividend model. The value of common stock can be viewed as a dividend stream plus a market price at the end of the dividend stream. We have selected Johnson & Johnson from the health care and pharmaceutical industry as our sample company for the valuation models that follow. Assuming that we start our valuation at the beginning of 2002, we develop a present value for the common stock listed on the New York Stock Exchange. The numbers are shown in Table 11–2.

The present value of the common stock for Johnson & Johnson is shown at the bottom of Table 11-2 to be $55.26. Note that Part A of Table 11–2 calculates the present value of the future dividends, while Part B is used to determine the present value of the future stock price at the end of 2006. These are assumed to be the two variables that determine the current stock price under this model.

In Part A, earnings per share are first projected for the next five years. Johnson & Johnson's payout ratio fluctuated between 34 and 37 percent from 1992 to 2001 and averaged 35.74 percent over this 10-year period. Because we see no dramatic shift in the company's need for retained earnings, we estimate the pay-out ratio will average 36 percent over the next five years. The earnings are then multiplied by the company's estimated pay-out ratio of 36 percent to determine anticipated dividends per share for those five years. At the time of the analysis, Johnson & Johnson had a beta of 0.85, one-year U.S. government securities had a 3.62 percent yield, and we selected an equity risk premium $(K_M - R_F)$ of 7.5 percent for a total required rate of return of 10.00 percent. You need to recognize that this required rate of return changes continuously with changes in interest rates, betas, and equity risk premiums. The present value of dividends from 2002 through 2006 is shown in Column 5 of Part A to equal $3.84.

In Part B, we multiply estimated 2006 earnings per share of $3.67 by the P/E ratio (earnings multiplier) of 22.56 to arrive at an anticipated price of $82.80 five years into the future. The P/E ratio we used to determine the price is the average P/E over the last 10 years.

TABLE 11–2   Johnson & Johnson Combined Dividend and Earnings Present Value Analysis

	Part A: Present Value of Dividends for 5 Years				
Year	(1) Estimated EPS Growth = 13.61%	(2) Estimated Payout Ratio	(3) Estimated Dividends per Share	(4)* Present Value Factor at $K_e = 10.00\%$	(5) Present Value of Cash Flows
2002	$2.20	36%	$0.79	0.909	$ 0.72
2003	2.50	36	0.90	0.826	0.74
2004	2.84	36	1.02	0.751	0.77
2005	3.23	36	1.16	0.683	0.79
2006	3.67	36	1.32	0.621	0.82
				PV Dividends	$ 3.84

	Part B: Present Value of Johnson & Johnson's 2006 Common Stock Price				
	EPS	P/E	Price$_{2006}$	PV Factor	
2006	$3.67	22.56	$82.80	0.621	$51.42
A + B = Present Value of Johnson & Johnson at beginning of 2002					$55.26

$*K_e = R_F + b(K_M - R_F)$ $R_F = 3.62$ $b = 0.85$ $K_M - R_F = 7.5\%$ $K_e = 10.00\%$

Evidence over the last seven years indicates that Johnson & Johnson always reached a P/E of at least this number. The future P/E could be affected by higher or lower expected growth rates of earnings, the risk characteristics of the stock in 2006, and other variables. The future price of $82.80 is then discounted for five years at 10 percent to arrive at a present value of $51.42. The total present value of the stock is equal to the present value of the dividend stream for five years ($3.84) plus the present value of the future stock price ($51.42) for a total present value of $55.26 at the beginning of 2002. The common stock was trading in the $54 to $55 range at the time of analysis.

This model can be used with your choice of time periods. Five years is not a magic number. As the time period used increases, the estimate of earnings per share becomes more uncertain for cyclical companies, and the future stock price based on an earnings multiplier (P/E ratio) becomes a risky forecast. Some companies in industries such as utilities or food have more predictable earnings streams than those in consumer-sensitive markets such as automobiles and furniture, but they still may exhibit fluctuating P/E ratios. The next section develops the concept of the price-earnings ratio, which was used as the earnings multiplier in Table 11–2.

The Real World of Investing

EVA: The Hot New Valuation Term of the Current Decade: What Does It Mean?

There is a new valuation concept that has garnered attention at leading U.S. corporations such as Coca-Cola, AT&T, Eli Lilly, Merrill Lynch, and Monsanto. These firms are not nearly so interested at generating earnings per share as they are in maximizing economic value added (EVA).

Economic value added is based on the concept that decisions should be made or projects accepted only if net operating profit after taxes (NOPAT) exceeds the capital costs to finance the investment. If this rule is followed, then economic value will be added. To many readers, this may sound like the capital budgeting principle you learned in the first course in corporate finance, warmed over and served again as a hot new idea.

Not so, say the founders of the EVA concept at Stern Stewart & Co (**www.sternstewart. com**) in New York.* EVA is an overriding concept that is intended to be applied to every decision the corporation makes, from investing overseas to adding three more widgets in the stock room. The question repeatedly asked is, "Is the firm earning an adequate return on the money investors entrusted to it?" Even at the lowest levels of the organization, this question cannot be escaped.

Proponents of EVA say that all too often chief financial officers evaluate projects based on net present value, but they modify recommendations to meet earnings growth targets of the firm. Business unit evaluations may not be based on either parameter but rather on return on assets or some other unrelated profit goal set by top management. Bonuses for operating managers may be linked to demand–supply conditions within an industry. New-product introductions may be based on gross profit margin. Furthermore, the analysis for some decisions may be based on cash flow, while other decisions are linked to earnings per share. There is no coherent theme or goal, and stockholder wealth may be harmed in the process.

With EVA, the firm is assumed to always be working for the stockholder's benefit. Under the EVA concept, the firm will not accept a project or idea that does not earn back the cost of funds the stockholder provided. Economic value added is also intended to lead to market value added (MVA). MVA is another hot new topic and represents the total market value of the firm minus the total capital provided since day one (including the retained earnings). MVA requires a company's top managers to justify what they did with the money that was given to them. Did they increase the value and thereby produce a positive MVA, as expected, or did they destroy contributed capital and generate a negative MVA?

Based on the Stern Stewart & Co. report related to recent financial reports, Coca-Cola (**www.cocacola.com**) was the leading producer of market value over contributed capital with an MVA of $124.9 billion. General Motors (**www.gm.com**) was the largest destroyer of capital with a negative MVA of $20.7 billion.

MVA is thought to be linked to EVA because, according to Stern Stewart & Co., the way MVA increases is by consistently increasing EVA. In fact, MVA is intended to be the present value of all future EVAs.

Annual data on MVA and EVA for the 1,000 largest companies can be acquired directly from Stern Stewart & Co. of New York. *Fortune* magazine also publishes Stern Stewart & Co. data on the 200 top MVA creators toward the end of each year. (However, not all of these companies formally use EVA and MVA.)

Detractors of the EVA-MVA emphasis say it is not widely enough followed to truly affect value. They suggest that earnings per share is still the "king" on Wall Street. In spite of EVA, it is still quarterly earnings estimates that drive investors crazy. Only time will tell whether this hot new concept can permanently compete. Today, there are 300 to 350 firms that use EVA in their strategic development.

EVA, The Real Key to Creating Wealth (New York: Stern Stewart & Co., 1996–97).

THE PRICE-EARNINGS RATIO

Mathematically, the **price-earnings ratio** (P/E) is simply the price per share divided by earnings per share, and it is ultimately set by investors in the market as they bid the price of a stock up or down in relation to its earnings. Price-earnings ratios are often expressed in the financial press as historical numbers using today's price divided by the latest 12-month earnings.

For companies with cyclical earnings, a P/E using the latest 12-month earnings might be misleading because these earnings could be high. If investors expect earnings to fall back to a normal level, they will not bid the price up in relation to this short-term cyclical swing in earnings per share, and the P/E ratio will appear to be low. But if earnings are severely depressed, investors will expect a return to normal higher earnings, and the price will not fall an equal percentage with earnings, and the P/E will appear to be high.

In the Johnson & Johnson example in Table 11-2, we used a P/E of 22.56 in 2006. This P/E ratio of 22.56 is determined by historical analysis and by other factors such as expected growth in earnings per share. The P/E of a company is also affected by overall conditions in the stock market. At the time of this writing Johnson & Johnson had a P/E of 31, but its 5-year average P/E was 26.62. In our judgment, we choose to use the more conservative 10-year average of 22.56.

Even though the current P/E ratio for a stock is known, investors may not agree it is appropriate. Stock analysts and investors probably spend more time examining P/E ratios and assessing their appropriate level than any other variable. Although the use of P/E ratios in valuation approaches lacks the theoretical under-pinning of the present value-based valuation models previously discussed, P/E ratios are equally important. The well-informed student of investments should have a basic understanding of both the theoretically based present value approach and the more pragmatic, frequently used P/E ratio approach.

What determines whether a stock should have a high or low P/E ratio? Let's first talk about the market for stocks in general, and then we will look at individual securities.

Stocks generally trade at a relatively high P/E ratio (perhaps 20 or greater) when there are strong growth prospects in the economy. However, inflation also plays a key role in determining P/E ratios for the overall market.

To illustrate the latter point, Figure 11–2 presents the relationship between the year-end Standard & Poor's 500 composite P/E ratio and the annual rate of inflation measured by the change in the consumer price index (CPI). The graphical relationship between these two variables shows they are inversely related. The price-earnings ratio goes down when the change in the CPI goes up, and the reverse is also true.

The dramatic drop in the P/E ratio in 1973–74 can be attributed in large measure to the rate of inflation increasing from 3.4 percent in 1972 to 12.2 percent in 1974, or a change of more than three times its former level. For a brief period in 1976, inflation decreased to an annual rate of less than 5 percent, only to soar to 13.3 percent by 1979. The average rate of inflation for 1982 was reduced to 3.8 percent, and the market responded by paying higher share prices for one dollar of earnings (that is, higher P/E ratios).

From 1983 through 1985, the consumer price index hovered around 3 to 4 percent, but in 1986, inflation subsided to 1.1 percent, and the S&P price-earnings ratio soared. In 1987, the S&P 500 P/E ratio remained high until the crash of October 1987 brought stock prices down to lower levels. During the sobering and risk-averse period after the crash, market prices were fairly stable.

As fears of higher inflation rose during 1989, the S&P 500 P/E ratio came back to the low-midrange of its 40-year history shown in Figure 11–2. The higher price-earnings ratios in 1991–93 reflect both the impact of falling inflationary expectations and depressed earnings suffered by corporations during the recessionary period of 1990–91 and the slow recovery in 1992 and 1993. As earnings grew quickly in 1994, 1995, and 1996, the Standard & Poor's 500 P/E ratio fell below 20 again. The economy in 1997 saw low inflation, strong economic

FIGURE 11–2   Inflation and Price-Earnings Ratios

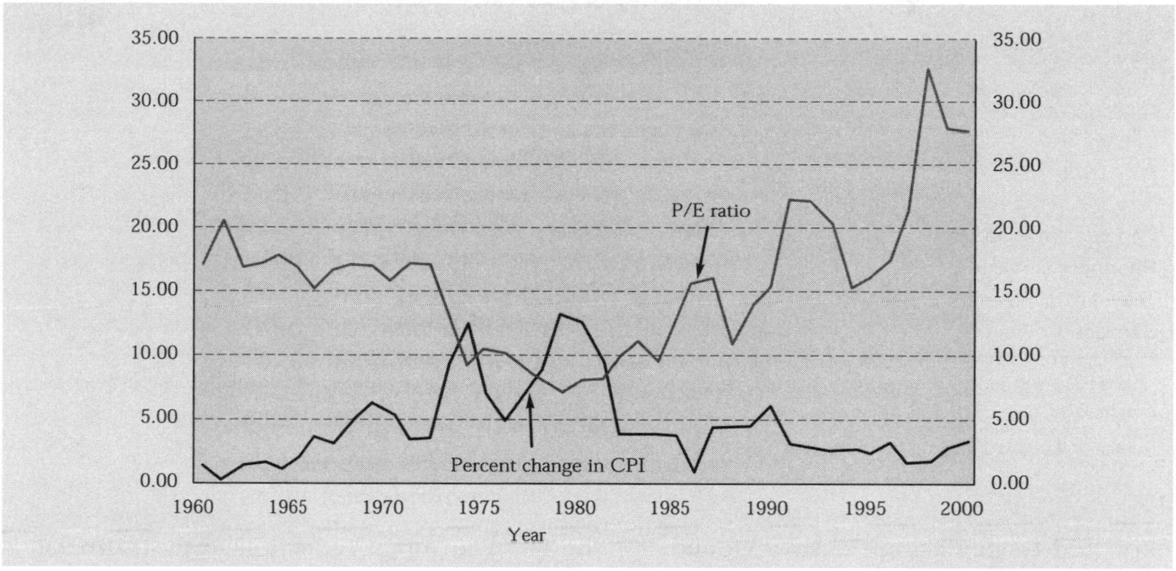

growth, low unemployment, and reduced government deficits. This economy was described as a dream economy, one that was perfectly balanced with GDP growth of 3.8 percent and inflation of 1.8 percent. In response, P/E ratios again soared above 21 times earnings, and the raging bull market, lasting through 1999, pushed P/E ratios over 30. Collapsing earnings in 2000 and 2001 kept P/E ratios higher than normal for an economic slowdown as the market waited for earnings to recover and hoped for a return to above-average GDP growth.

As was pointed out earlier, required rates of return are directly influenced by the rate of inflation. As inflation changes, the required rate of return on common stock, K_e, changes, and prices go up or down. This is the basic mechanism that causes inflation to influence P/E ratios.

Other factors besides inflationary consideration and growth factors influence the P/E ratio for the market in general. Federal Reserve policy and interest rates, federal deficits, the government's leading indicators, the political climate, the mood and confidence of the population, international considerations, and many other factors affect the P/E ratio for the overall market. The astute analyst is constantly studying a multitude of variables that could cause P/E ratios to move higher or lower.

The P/E Ratio for Individual Stocks

Although the overall market P/E ratio is the collective average of individual P/Es, those factors that influence the market P/E do not necessarily affect P/E ratios of individual companies consistency from one industry to another. An individual firm's P/E ratio is heavily influenced by its growth prospects and the risk associated with its future performance. Table 11–3 shows examples of growth rates and P/E ratios for different industries and firms. Generally, a strong expected future growth rate for 2001–2006 (Column 3) is associated with a reasonably high P/E for mid-2001 (Column 4) and vice versa.

In addition to the future growth of the firm and the risk associated with that growth, investors and analysts also consider a number of other factors that influence a firm's P/E ratio. These cannot be easily quantified, but they affect a broad range of stocks. Included in this category are the debt-to-equity ratio and the dividend policy of the firm. All things being equal, the less debt a firm has, the more likely it is to be highly valued in the marketplace.

The dividend policy is more elusive. For firms that show superior internal reinvestment opportunities, low cash dividends may be desired. But maturing companies may be

TABLE 11–3   P/E and Growth in EPS

(1) Industry	(2) Company	(3) Expected 5-year Growth in EPS 2001–2006	(4) P/E July 2001
Electric utility	First Energy	6.50%	11.1
Auto parts	Genuine Parts	7.50	13.6
Telecom services	Bell South	13.50	16.7
Paper/forest products	Weyerhauser	13.50	20.9
Pharmacy services	Walgreens	17.50	39.4
Telecom equipment	Qualcomm	29.00	52.4
Semiconductors	Intel*	9.00	51.0

*Intel's P/E is inflated because earnings declined faster than the stock price, and the market expects this high-quality technology company to eventually recover but grow at a slower rate.

Source: *Value Line Investment Survey*, selected issues (Value Line Inc.).

expected to pay a high cash dividend. For the latter group, a reduction in cash dividends may be associated with a lower P/E ratio if the dividend cut signals falling earnings per share.

Certain industries also traditionally command higher P/E ratios than others. Investors seem to prefer industries that have a high technology and research emphasis. Thus, firms in computers, medical research and health care, and sophisticated telecommunications often have higher P/E ratios than the market in general. This does not mean firms in these industries represent superior investments, but merely that investors value their earnings more highly.[2] Also, fads and other factors can cause a shift in industry popularity. For example, because Ronald Reagan emphasized military strength, defense-oriented stocks were popular during his administration. Jimmy Carter stressed the need for environmental control, and stocks dealing in air and water pollution traded at high P/E ratios during his tenure. Bill Clinton's health care proposals lowered P/Es of pharmaceutical stocks dramatically until a Republican Congress killed his proposals. Tobacco stocks rallied under George W. Bush.

The quality of management as perceived by those in the marketplace also influences a firm's P/E ratio. If management is viewed as being highly capable, clever, or innovative, the firm may carry a higher P/E ratio. Investors may look to magazines such as *Forbes* or *Business Week,* which highlight management strategies by various companies, or to management-oriented books. Of course, it is possible that today's trendsetters may represent tomorrow's failures.

Not only is the quality of management important to investors in determining the firm's P/E ratio, but the quality of earnings is also. There are many interpretations of a dollar's worth of earnings. Some companies choose to use very conservative accounting practices so their reported earnings can be interpreted as being very solid by investors (they may even be understated). Other companies use more liberal accounting interpretations to report maximum earnings to their shareholders, and they, at times, overstate their true performance (e.g. Enron). It is easy to see that a dollar's worth of conservatively reported earnings (high quality earnings) may be valued at a P/E ratio of 20 to 25 times, whereas a dollar's worth of liberally reported earnings (low quality earnings) should be valued at a much lower multiple.

All of these factors affect a firm's P/E ratio. Thus, investors will consider growth in sales and earnings, future risk, the debt position, the dividend policy, the quality of management

---

2. William Kittrell, Geoffrey A. Hirt, and Roger Potter, "Price-Earnings Multiples, Investors' Expectations, and Rates of Return: Some Analytical and Empirical Findings" (Paper presented at the 1984 Financial Management Association meeting).

and earnings, and a multitude of other factors in arriving at the P/E ratio. The P/E ratio, like the price of the stock, is set by the interaction of the forces of demand and supply. Those firms that are expected to provide returns greater than the overall economy, with equal or less risk, generally have superior P/E ratios.

The Pure, Short-Term Earnings Model

Often investors/speculators take a very short-term view of the market and ignore present value analysis with its associated long-term forecasts of dividends and earnings per share. Instead, they only use earnings per share and apply an appropriate multiplier to compute the estimated value.

Applying this approach to Johnson & Johnson's financial data initially presented in Table 11-2, we can arrive at a value of $58.58 based on an earnings per share estimate of $2.20 for 2002 and a P/E ratio of 26.62 reflecting the five-year average P/E from 1997 through 2001:

$$P_0 = \text{EPS}_{2002} \times \text{P/E}_{\text{5-year average}}$$
$$= \$2.20 \times 26.62$$
$$P_{2002} = \$58.56$$

Every valuation method has its limitations. Although this method is simplified by ignoring dividends and present value calculations, earnings need to be correctly estimated, and the appropriate price-earnings multiplier must be applied. Unfortunately, even if the estimated EPS is correct, you have no assurance that the market will agree with your P/E ratio.

Relating an Individual Stock's P/E Ratio to the Market

Johnson & Johnson is the leading producer of health care products and pharmaceuticals. Everyone has probably used at least one of their products, such as Band-Aids, Q-tips, baby oil, or Tylenol, but you may not be familiar with the financial data presented in Table 11-4. This table provides an historical summary and an estimate of sales per share (SPS), dividends per share (DPS), earnings per share (EPS), cash flow per share (CFPS), and book value per share (BVPS). It also indicates Johnson & Johnson's high and low stock prices and the high and low P/E ratios for the company and the Standard & Poor's 500 index.

In the last three columns, the high and low P/E ratios for Johnson & Johnson are compared with the high and low P/E ratio for the S&P 500. For example, in the first row for 1992, Johnson & Johnson's high P/E ratio was 23.71 and the S&P 500 high P/E was 23.40. When Johnson & Johnson's high P/E ratio is divided by the S&P 500 high P/E, a relative P/E of 1.01 is calculated in the high relative P/E column. This indicates that Johnson & Johnson's high P/E ratio was at 101 percent of the market or selling at a 1 percent premium to the S&P index. Over the 10 years listed we can see that Johnson & Johnson's high P/E relative to the S&P 500 sold as high as a 34 percent premium in 1995 (shown as 1.34) and as low as a 15 percent discount in 1993 when it sold at only 85 percent of the index.

For each year, a high and low relative was calculated for Johnson & Johnson with the 10-year average of the high and low shown on the last line. Over this time period, Johnson & Johnson's high relative P/E averaged 1.09 (a 9 percent premium to the market's high P/E) and its low relative P/E averages 0.93 (a 7 percent discount to the market's low P/E). When we add the high and low and divide by 2, we get an average of 1.01, which indicates that Johnson & Johnson historically sells at 101 percent of the S&P 500 P/E ratio.

Notice that Table 11-4 also gives us estimates for SPS, DPS, EPS, CFPS, and BVPS. We will use these estimates for our valuation models. Table 11-4 indicates that earnings per share (fourth column) for 2002 will be $2.20.

At the time of the analysis, the S&P 500 stock index was selling at a P/E ratio of 26.65 times earnings. In Table 11-5, the relative P/E model uses the high, low, and average P/E times

TABLE 11–4   Johnson & Johnson

Year	Sales per Share (SPS)	Dividends per Share (DPS)	Earnings per Share (EPS)	Cash Flow per Share (CFPS)	Book Value per Share (BVPS)	Stock Price High	Stock Price Low	P/E Ratio High	P/E Ratio Low	S&P 500 P/E Ratio High	S&P 500 P/E Ratio Low	Relative P/E Ratios High	Relative P/E Ratios Low
1992	$ 5.25	$0.22	$0.62	$0.85	$1.97	$14.70	$10.80	23.71	17.42	23.40	20.92	1.01	0.83
1993	5.50	0.25	0.69	0.93	2.17	12.60	8.90	18.26	12.90	21.55	19.64	0.85	0.66
1994	6.12	0.28	0.78	1.06	2.77	14.10	9.00	18.08	11.54	16.12	14.57	1.12	0.79
1995	7.27	0.32	0.93	1.26	3.49	23.10	13.40	24.84	14.41	18.50	13.66	1.34	1.05
1996	8.11	0.37	1.09	1.46	4.07	27.00	20.80	24.77	19.08	19.55	15.45	1.27	1.24
1997	8.41	0.43	1.21	1.62	4.59	33.70	24.30	27.85	20.08	24.77	18.56	1.12	1.08
1998	8.80	0.49	1.34	1.83	5.06	44.90	31.70	33.51	23.66	32.93	24.60	1.02	0.96
1999	9.88	0.55	1.49	2.03	5.83	53.40	38.50	35.84	25.84	30.50	25.16	1.18	1.03
2000	10.47	0.62	1.70	2.27	6.76	53.00	33.10	31.18	19.47	30.00	25.30	1.04	0.77
2001	11.40	0.70	1.95	2.55	7.70	54.98	40.30	28.19	20.67	30.10	24.10	0.94	0.86
10-year average	$ 8.12	$0.42	$1.18	$1.59	$4.44	$33.15	$23.08	26.62	18.51	24.74	20.20	1.09	0.93
2002 estimates	$12.55	$0.80	$2.20	$2.90	$8.55	$28.11 average stock price for 1992–2001							

TABLE 11–5   Projected Earnings and Relative P/E Valuation Model

	Relative P/E	S&P 500 Current P/E	Johnson & Johnson's Expected P/E	Johnson & Johnson's Estimated EPS$_{2002}$	Johnson & Johnson's Value in 2002 Based on Relative P/E
Average high P/E	1.09	26.65	29.05	$2.20	$63.91
Average low P/E	0.93	26.65	24.78	2.20	54.52
Average P/E	1.01	26.65	26.92	2.20	59.22

the S&P 500 P/E to calculate the appropriate price-earnings ratio for Johnson & Johnson based on its relationship to the current market level. When applied to the $2.20 EPS estimate, we find that Johnson & Johnson should be selling between $54.52 at its low price and $63.91 at its high price. This would indicate that at a market price in the range of $54 to $55, Johnson & Johnson is selling at the low end of its historical valuation relative to the S&P 500.

OTHER VALUATION MODELS USING AVERAGE PRICE RATIOS AND 10-YEAR AVERAGES

Using the 10-year averages for price and per share data from Table 11–4, we can use the average price of $28.11 (bottom line) as the average per-share data to determine the historical relationships. These models will simply determine whether the current stock price is selling above or below its historical valuation. It is up to the analyst to determine if the results are warranted by expectations.

Using the data in Table 11–4 we develop these five models in Table 11–6. In each case in Table 11–6, we calculate the historical price ratios and multiply the result times the value estimated for 2002. The answer provides an estimated value of the common stock based on history. For example in Part A of Table 11–6, Johnson & Johnson exhibits a price-to-sales ratio of 3.46, which indicates that over the 10 years covered, Johnson & Johnson stock sold at 346 percent of its sales per share. Multiplying this ratio times estimated sales per share of $12.55 for 2002 produces a value of $43.42. This is quite a bit below the current market price of $54 to $55. On the other hand the price-to-book value model in Part E generates a value of $54.12, almost identical to the current market price.

The analyst needs to look at the results of these models as information. In the case of Johnson & Johnson, all the models show that the current stock price of $54 to $55 is probably a fair value. Several models in the chapter indicate that the company could be slightly undervalued by $4 to $8 per share. It is the analyst's job to make a judgment based on experience, expectations, and an in-depth knowledge of the company. These models do not provide foolproof values, only information that can be used to make a financial judgment.

FORECASTING EARNINGS PER SHARE

The other side of choosing an appropriate P/E ratio is forecasting the earnings per share of a company with the proper growth rate. Investors can get earnings forecasts in several ways. They can rely on professional brokerage house research, investment advisory firms such as Value Line or Standard & Poor's, or financial magazines such as *Forbes, Business Week, Worth,* or *Money*, or they can do it themselves.

TABLE 11–6   Other Valuation Models Using Average Price Ratios and 10-Year Averages

A. Price to sales per share

Average Price	÷	Average Sales per Share	=	Price-to-SPS Ratio	×	Estimated 2002 SPS	=	Projected 2002 Price
$28.11		$8.12		3.46		$12.55		$43.42

B. Price to dividend per share

Average Price	÷	Average Dividends per Share	=	Price-to-DPS Ratio	×	Estimated 2002 DPS	=	Projected 2002 Price
$28.11		$0.42		66.93		$0.80		$53.54

C. Price to earnings per share

Average Price	÷	Average Earnings per Share	=	Price-to-SPS Ratio	×	Estimated 2002 EPS	=	Projected 2002 Price
$28.11		$1.18		23.82		$2.20		$52.40

D. Price to cash flow per share

Average Price	÷	Average Cash Flow per Share	=	Price-to-CFPS Ratio	×	Estimated 2002 CFPS	=	Projected 2002 Price
$28.11		$1.59		17.68		$2.90		$51.27

E. Price to book value per share

Average Price	÷	Average Book Value per Share	=	Price-to-BVPS Ratio	×	Estimated 2002 BVPS	=	Projected 2002 Price
$28.11		$4.44		6.33		$8.55		$54.12

The Real World of Investing

Valuing Companies without Earnings: EBITDA and Free Cash Flow

In the high-tech, "new economy" era of the late 1990s and early 2000s, many popular companies did not achieve consistent earnings (or earnings at all). Examples include Ebay, WorldCom, Oracle, and virtually every high-tech or telecommunications startup firm.

For a firm with negative earnings per share, the concept of a price-earnings ratio is hardly application. For example, a company that has a loss of $0.75 a share and is assigned a P/E ratio of 20 by analysts would have a negative value of $15. No such concept exists in finance. For that reason, analysts looked for other values to track besides earnings. Some developed stock price to revenue, stock price to Web site hits, stock price to actual Web site sales (as opposed to just hits), and so on. All of these were done on a per-share basis. While these new "metrics" were popular, sophisticated analysts looked for greater depth in their analysis.

The term EBITDA fits the bill. **EBITDA** stands for earnings before interest, taxes, depreciation, and amortization. Companies that have negative earnings may well have a positive EBITDA.

An example of computing EBITDA is shown here for a company with reported negative earnings of $5 million and 1 million shares outstanding:

Earnings	−$5,000,000
Amortization	1,000,000
Depreciation	6,000,000
Taxes	0
Interest	2,000,000
Earnings before interest, taxes, depreciation, and amortization (EBITDA)	$4,000,000
Shares outstanding	1,000,000
EBITDA per share	$4.00

Amortization (line 2) usually represents the write-off of intangible assets (perhaps goodwill), while depreciation represents the write-off of physical assets (such as plant and equipment). The other terms are self-explanatory. EBITDA per share is very close to the concept of cash flow per share, but in addition to depreciation and amortization, taxes and interest are added back to earnings. What the analyst ends up with is operating income per share. In other words, this tells the analyst how much the company is making purely from its operations out in the plant before financing charges and taxes as well as noncash charges. While the latter items are important in a traditional sense, the analyst needs to get a handle on something, and what better than how it's doing on its actual day-to-day operations.

Once EBITDA is determined for a firm in a given industry, analysts look to other companies in the same industry to determine their stock price to EBITDA multiplier. Because this often is not commonly available data, the analyst may have to do the work on his or her own. Assume in this example that the industry average stock price/EBITDA ratio was 12×, then the firm with $4 in EBITDA per share might be valued at $48. If the firm has unusually bright prospects, it might be higher and the opposite would also be true.

Analysts may also use a slightly different concept of **free cash flow** per share by adding depreciation and amortization to earnings and subtracting out necessary capital expenditures and dividends (and dividing by the number of shares outstanding). Once again, an industry multiplier of stock price to free cash flow is developed and applied to free cash flow per share.

Least Squares Trendline

One of the most common ways of forecasting earnings per share is to use regression or **least squares trend analysis.** The technique involves a statistical method whereby a trendline is

FIGURE 11–3   Least Squares Trendline for EPS of XYZ Corporation

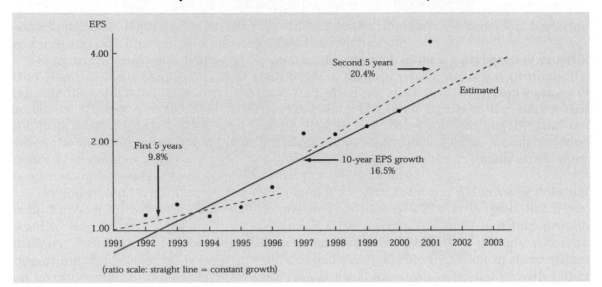

(ratio scale: straight line = constant growth)

fitted to a time series of historical earnings. This trendline, by definition, is a straight line that minimizes the distance of the individual observations from the line. Figure 11–3 depicts a scattergram for the earnings per share of XYZ Corporation. The earnings of this company have been fairly consistent, and so we get a good trendline with a minimum of variation. The compounded growth rate for the whole 10-year period was 16.5 percent, with 9.8 percent for the first 5 years and 20.4 percent for the second 5 years. This shows up in Figure 11-3 as two distinct five-year trendlines. There are many statistical programs on PCs and mainframes that run regression analysis, and even handheld calculators have the ability to compute a growth rate from raw data.

Whenever a mechanical forecast is made, subjectivity still enters the decision in choosing the data that will be considered in the regression plot. If we compare two companies, one with consistent growth and one with cyclical growth, we find that the cyclical companies (e.g., autos, chemicals, airlines, forest products) are much more difficult to forecast than the consistent growth companies (e.g., pharmaceuticals, food, beverages). Cyclical companies are much more sensitive to swings in the economy and are likely to be in industries with high-priced durable goods where consumers can postpone purchases or where the economy has a direct effect on their products. Do not confuse cyclical with seasonal. Seasonal companies show earnings variability because their products have seasonal demand, such as fuel oil for winter heating and electricity for summer air conditioning or snowmobiles for winter. Cyclical companies have earnings related to the economy and exhibit variability over many years rather than three-month seasons.

Consistently growing companies often have higher P/E ratios on average than cyclical companies because investors are more confident in their future earnings. We compare two growth trends in Figure 11–4.

With cyclical companies you have to be careful not to start your forecast at a peak or trough period because you will get either biased-downward or -upward forecasts. Instead it is important to forecast cyclical companies throughout several business cycles with several peaks and troughs. Often the forecast for cyclical firms will cover 10 to 15 years of historical data, while the forecast for consistently growing firms might be based on five years of data.

The Income Statement Method

A more process-oriented method of forecasting earnings per share is to start with a sales forecast and create a standardized set of financial statements based on historical relationships.

FIGURE 11–4   Trendlines for Cyclical and Consistent Growth Companies

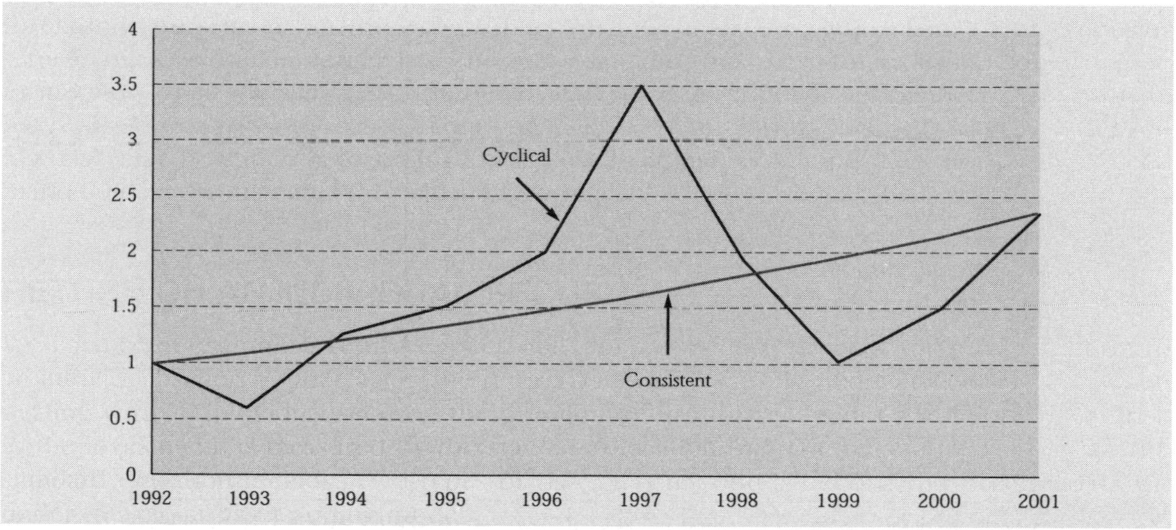

The sales forecast must be accurate if the earnings estimates are to have any significance. This method can be involved and provides a student with a very integrated understanding of the relationships that go into the creation of earnings.

Several important factors are included in this method of forecasting. The analyst is forced to examine profitability and the resultant fluctuations in profit margins before and after taxes. The impact of short-term interest expense and any new bond financing can be factored into the analysis as well as any increase in shares of common stock from new equity financing.

Some analysts use an abbreviated method of forecasting earnings per share. They use a sales forecast combined with after-tax profit margins. For example, let us assume the Hutchins Corporation has a sales and profit margin history as set forth in Table 11–7. The sales have been growing at a 10 percent growth rate, so the forecast is a simple extrapolation. However, the profit margin has fluctuated between 6.7 and 9.7 percent, with 8.2 percent being the average. Common stock outstanding has also grown by an average of 1.4 million shares per year. Given the cyclical nature of the profit margin, 8.2 percent was used for 2002, which is expected to be an average year. Nine percent was used for 2003, a year expected to be economically more robust for the firm. Multiplying the profit margin times the estimated sales produced an estimate of earnings that was divided by the number of shares outstanding to find the earnings per share. Once the EPS is found, it still must be plugged into an earnings valuation model to determine an appropriate value.

GROWTH STOCKS AND GROWTH COMPANIES

In assessing the worth of an investment, stockholders, analysts, and investors often make reference to such terms as growth stock and growth companies. As part of the process of improving your overall valuation skills, you should have some familiarity with these terms.

A **growth stock** may be defined as the common stock of a company generally growing faster than the economy or market norm. These companies are usually predictable in their earnings growth. Many of the more popular growth stocks, such as Disney, Coca-Cola, and McDonald's, are really in the middle-to-late stages of the expansion phase. They tend to be fully valued and recognized in the marketplace.

Growth companies, on the other hand, are those companies that exhibit rising returns on assets each year and sales that are growing at an increasing rate (growth phase of the life cycle curve). Growth companies are found in stage 1 and 2 of the life cycle curve. Growth

TABLE 11–7   Abbreviated Income Statement Method—Hutchins Corporation

Year	Sales ($000s) ×	After-Tax Profit Margin =	Earnings ($000s) −	Shares (000s) =	Earnings per Share
1996	$1,250,000	7.9%	$ 98,750	30,000	$3.29
1997	1,375,000	9.1	125,125	31,500	3.97
1998	1,512,500	8.5	128,562	33,200	3.87
1999	1,663,750	6.7	111,471	35,000	3.18
2000	1,830,125	8.3	151,900	35,200	4.31
2001	2,013,137	8.5	171,117	37,000	4.62
2002e	2,214,452	8.2	181,585	38,400	4.73
2003e	2,435,896	9.0	219,230	39,800	5.50

e = Estimated.

companies may not be as well-known or recognized as growth stocks. Companies that may be considered to be growth companies might be in such industries as computer networking, cable television, cellular telephones, biotechnology, medical electronics, and so on. These companies are growing very rapidly, and extrapolations of growth trends can be very dangerous if you guess incorrectly. Growth companies have many things in common. Usually, they have developed a proprietary product that is patented and protected from competition like the original Xerox process. This market protection allows a high rate of return and generates cash for new-product development.

There are also other indicators of growth potential. Companies should have sales growth greater than the economy by a reasonable margin. Increasing sales should be translated into similar earnings growth, which means consistently stable and high profit margins. Additionally, the earnings growth should show up in earnings per share growth (no dilution of earnings through unproductive stock offers). The firm should have a low labor cost as a percentage of total cost since wages are prone to be inflexible on the downside but difficult to control on the upside.

The biggest error made in searching for growth-oriented companies is that the price may already be too high. By the time you identify the company, so has everyone else, and the price is probably inflated. If the company has one quarter where earnings do not keep up with expectations, the stock price could tumble. The trick is to find growth companies before they are generally recognized in the market, and this requires taking more risk in small companies trading over-the-counter.

ASSETS AS A SOURCE OF STOCK VALUE

Until now, our emphasis has been primarily on earnings and dividends as the source of value. However, in certain industries, asset values may have considerable importance. These assets may take many forms—cash and marketable securities, buildings, land, timber, old movies, oil, and other natural resources. At times, any one of these assets may dominate a firm's value. Furthermore, companies with heavy cash positions are attractive merger and acquisition candidates because of the possibility that a firm with highly liquid assets could be taken over and its own cash used to pay back debt incurred in the takeover.

In the last two decades, natural resources also had an important influence on value. Let's briefly examine this topic.

Natural Resources

Natural resources such as timber, copper, gold, and oil often give a company value even if the assets are not producing an income stream. This is because of the present value of the future income stream that is expected as these resources are used up. Companies such as International Paper, Weyerhaeuser, and other forest product companies have timberlands with market values far in excess of their book values and, in some cases, in excess of their common stock prices.

Oil companies with large supplies of oil in the ground may have to wait 20 years before some of it is pumped, but there may be substantial value there. In the case of natural gas pipeline companies, increasing reserves have changed the way these companies are viewed by the market. They were previously considered similar to utilities because of their natural gas transmission system, but now they are also being valued based on their hidden assets (energy reserves). The term **hidden assets** refers to assets that are not readily apparent to investors in a traditional sense but that add substantial value to the firm.

Investors should not overlook hidden assets because of naive extrapolation of past data or failure to understand an industry or company. Furthermore, assets do not always show up on the books of a company. They may be fully depreciated, like the movies *Sound of Music*, *101 Dalmations*, or *Star Wars*, but still have substantial value in the television or VCR market.

Exploring the Web

Web site Address	Comments
my.yahoo.com	Provides portfolio and stock tracking and screening
cbs.marketwatch.com	Provides stock information, screening, and evaluation
www.quicken.com	Provides stock screening and analysis; has intrinsic value calculator
www.valuepro.net	Has free intrinsic value calculator—other services fee based
www.morningstar.com	Provides stock screening and detailed evaluation with Quick Quotes
www.fool.com	Contains stock evaluation and information from Motley Fool
www.wjs.com	Provides company information along with news
www.finportfolio.com	Has portfolio tracker
moneycentral.msn.com	Has portfolio tracker, company information, investment information
www.valuengine.com	Provides stock analyses and forecasts, mainly fee based
www.411stocks.com	Provides information on stocks and portfolio tracking
www.bestsignals.com	Provides stock research; has interactive research tools
www.pcquote.com	Provides stock quotes, portfolio tracking, and news
www.validea.com	Provides fee-based valuation of stocks
www.stockworm.com	Provides stock analysis and screening

SUMMARY

This chapter presents several common stock valuation models that rely on dividends and earnings per share. For the valuation to be accurate, the forecast of earnings and dividends needs to be correct.

Firms can be valued in many ways, and an analyst may use several methods to substantiate estimates. Valuation models based primarily on dividends look at future projections of dividends and the associated present values of the dividends. Assumptions must be made as to whether the dividend growth pattern is constant, accelerating, or decreasing.

Valuation using the earnings method requires that a price-earnings ratio be used as a multiplier of EPS. Price-earnings ratios are influenced by many variables such as growth, risk, capital structure, dividend policy, level of the market in general, industry factors, and more. A careful study of each situation must be concluded before choosing the appropriate P/E. The price-earnings ratio is a function of two fluctuating variables—earnings and price. The two variables combine to form a ratio that is primarily future oriented. High price-earnings ratios usually indicate positive expectations of the future, whereas low price-earnings ratios connote negative expectations.

To choose a P/E that is reasonable, the analyst must have some idea about the expected growth rate in earnings per share. Investors may find earnings estimates in investment advisory services, in statistical forecasts by brokerage houses, through their own time series statistical regression analysis, or by using the income statement method. Growth stocks were discussed more with the view of alerting the student to what to look for when trying to identify a growth stock or company than with the concept of valuation. The previously developed methods of valuation can be used on growth stocks as long as care is taken to evaluate the duration and level of growth.

We also presented some basic ideas about the value of companies based not on their earnings or dividend stream but on their assets such as cash or natural resources.

INVESTMENT FUNDS, LONG-TERM PLANNING, AND DOLLAR-COST AVERAGING

Perhaps more than anything else, the liquidity and conveniences inherent in mutual funds lend themselves best to financial planning activities. The most important of these is the gradual accumulation of capital assets.

Using the preauthorized check plan, investors can have fixed amounts regularly withdrawn from their checking accounts to purchase fund shares. Just as savers can have their banks channel a specific amount from their paychecks into savings accounts, so too can investors make regular, lump-sum fund share purchases on an "out of sight, out of mind" basis. Reinvestment of distributions enhances this strategy.

What distinguishes the mutual fund from the bank savings strategy is the fact that fund shares are purchased at different prices. The investor can even use a passive strategy known as dollar-cost averaging. Using **dollar-cost averaging**, the investor buys a fixed dollar's worth of a given security at regular intervals regardless of the security's price or the current market outlook. By using such a strategy, investors concede they cannot outsmart the market. The intent of dollar-cost averaging is to avoid the common practice of buying high and selling low. In fact, investors are forced to do the opposite. Why? They commit a fixed-dollar amount each month (or year) and buy shares at the current market price. When the price is high, they are buying relatively fewer shares; when the price is low, they are accumulating more shares. An example is presented in Table 11–8. Suppose we use the preauthorized check plan to channel $200 per month into a mutual fund. The price ranges from a low of $12 to a high of $19.

Note that when the share price is relatively low, such as in January, we purchased a larger number of shares than when the share prices were high, as in April. In this case, the share price ended in June at the same price it was in January ($12).

TABLE 11–8   Dollar-Cost Averaging

(1) Month	(2) Investment	(3) Share Price	(4) Shares Purchased
January	$ 200	$12	16.66
February	200	14	14.28
March	200	16	12.50
April	200	19	10.52
May	200	15	13.33
June	200	12	16.66
Totals	$1,200	$88	83.95 total shares
		Average price $14.67	Average cost $14.29

What would happen if the price merely ended up at the average price over the six-month period? The values in column (3) total $88, so the average price over six months is $14.67 ($88/6). Actually, we would still make money under this assumption because the average *cost* is less than this amount. Consider that we invested $1,200 and purchased 83.95 shares. This translates to an average cost of only $14.29:

$$\frac{\text{Investment}}{\text{Shares purchased}} = \frac{\$1,200}{83.95} = \$14.29$$

The average cost ($14.29) is less than the average price ($14.67) because we bought relatively more shares at the lower price levels, and they weighed more heavily in our calculations. Thus, under dollar-cost averaging, investors can come out ahead over a period of investing fixed amounts, even if the share price ends up less than the average price paid on each transaction.

The only time investors lose money is if the eventual price falls below the average cost ($14.29) and they sell at that point. While dollar-cost averaging has its advantages, it is not without criticism. Clearly, if the share price continues to go down over a long period, it is hard to make a case for continued purchases. However, the long-term performance of most diversified mutual funds has been positive, and long-term investors may find this strategy useful in accumulating capital assets for retirement, children's education funds, or other purposes.

DIVIDEND REINVESTMENT PLANS

Dividend reinvestment plans (also call DRIPs) are plans whereby shareholders of a corporation are given the option to reinvest the dividends of said corporation into additional shares of stock. DRIPs are regulated by the SEC. These types of plans can be suitable for investors who are taking a long-term view of the market and the companies they invest in. They are also suitable for investors who do not have large amounts of funds to invest into the market. Corporations will oftentimes be able to reinvest all of the dividends into their stock even if the shareholder can only purchase a fractional share of stock.

DRIPs are either managed directly by the issuing company or by a financial institution such as a bank that the corporation hires as its fiduciary. If it is managed directly by the company, the shareholder works directly with the company in order to purchase and sell shares of stock in addition to signing up for the dividend reinvestment plan. Those companies who hire a financial institution to manage the program, hire the institution as an intermediary who collects dividends for its stockholders and distributes them or reinvests them at the shareholder's request. In either case, the program may be set up to allow the shareholder to purchase additional shares of stock by investing new capital into the company either through open market purchase or the issue of new stock (Direct Stock Purchase discussed below).

There are several advantages to DRIPs. First, companies can either by self-management or through a financial fiduciary reduce overall transactions costs as there are few fees associated with these types of plans. Sometimes a financial fiduciary will charge a small fee for this service though oftentimes the corporation will split the fee with the investor. Generally corporations that manage these plans directly will only charge a small initial set-up fee. Many dividend reinvestment plans only require the purchase of one share of the stock before the company will allow the shareholder to invest in them. Some companies require somewhat more of a capital investment. In either case, even those with very low amounts of investment capital can invest in these types of plans for only a small amount of money. Additionally, for those investors who have a difficult time saving money, these types of plans offer a forced savings approach while realizing the beneficial effects of compounding. In most plans, once you are signed up, you can change your investment amounts as often as the plan allows (either monthly, quarterly or annually). Because a small investor can participate in DRIPs at a low cost, diversification of a portfolio is possible in a short amount of time.

For the firm, advantages come in the form of cost savings during new issues of stock where dividends are reinvested. These savings are primarily in the form of underwriting and advertising for new issues. Because the current shareholders may have the first option of purchasing new issues, this scenario creates goodwill between the shareholders and the company.

There are several ways to research and invest in companies who offer a DRIP. NetStock Direct (http://www3.netstockdirect.com) offers a list of companies and the minimum required investment amount in order to belong to a company DRIP plan. There are services that also allow investment in multiple DRIPs by requiring an investor to invest a small amount of dollars and a membership fee. Two Web sites are: http://www.firstshare.com/ and http://www.better-investing.org/.

Given the advantages of DRIPs, one must also consider the disadvantages of these plans. If working directly with a company, there is initially a lot of paperwork to complete. It will take several weeks for the initial transaction to occur. If an investor decides to purchase or sell a security, the requests are lumped together and are bought and sold at the same time. Therefore an investor has no control over the timing of the purchase or sale of the stock. In order to keep costs down, most companies generally do this once per month. Because correspondence is generally by mail, the investor must be sure to complete the paperwork and send it in by any deadline posted by the company.

Taxes on dividends whether received by the shareholder or reinvested into the corporation are still taxed. Favorable tax treatment which was enacted in the Jobs & Growth Tax Relief Reconciliation Act of 2001 reduced taxable dividends to 5 percent for taxpayers in the 10 percent and 15 percent tax brackets and to 15 percent for higher income tax payers. This provision applies to dividends received in taxable years 2003 through 2008.

There are many differences from DRIP to DRIP. Therefore, for those who are acting on their own accord and without an advisor, it is extremely important for the potential investor to read the particulars of the plan. It is tempting for those who have small amounts of investment capital to invest their money anywhere if given the choice. However, sound investment decisions must be considered when investing in any program. Since there are over 1,000 companies worldwide that offer a plan, the investor or advisor should match the goals of the client to the particular corporation.

DIRECT STOCK PURCHASE PLANS

Direct stock purchase plans (DSPs) are plans whereby an investor can purchase shares of stock directly from a corporation. These types of plans are similar in many respects to DRIPs discussed above. Some corporations that offer DSPs may also offer DRIPs. However, any combination of these types of plans may be found in a company. Like DRIPs, DSPs are also managed by the SEC.

Advantages as discussed above are the brokerage cost savings, low required investment amounts, and long-term investment strategy. The issuing corporation realizes the same benefits as discussed above.

Many of the disadvantages that apply are also relevant such as control over the timing of the sale or purchase and the amounts of initial paperwork required in signing up.

If belonging to a DRIP with a reinvestment plan, the same tax implications will apply. However, the investor controls when to sell and hence the nature of the capital gain of shares. An investor who works directly with a company on the purchase and sale of the funds will still be subject to the timing of when the company batches and sells/buys the securities. However, there are new services on the market such as http://www.share-builder.com and http://www.BuyAndHold.com whereby the investor can also participate in market sales for purchases of direct stock. These types of services offer multiple services whereby the investor can either participate in lump-sum purchasing with other investors or can execute direct market purchases or sales. The two sites mentioned above are geared towards those who want to invest regular amounts of funds at regular intervals. They are also geared towards those investors who have small amounts of capital to invest. Trades that are bundled are executed at approximately $4 or less. Thus for small investors, this fee can represent a larger percentage of cost to overall investment. However, there are no required minimums to set up an account with these services. Lastly in using these types of plans to invest, the investor can eliminate most of the paperwork of working directly with a corporation. Diversification can be had almost immediately.

Just like DRIPs, care should be taken when investing in DSPs. The merits of the company rather than the nature of the transaction should be highly considered before committing any funds to these types of plans. All plans have different requirements and are structured differently. Therefore care should be taken to read the plan details prior to investment. Additionally, the investor should be wary of how the purchased shares can be traded. If they can be traded on an organized exchange, it will probably not be difficult to sell shares if needed. However, if they are not traded on organized exchanges, it may be difficult for the investor to trade shares.

Chapter 12

Bond Valuation

THE BOND CONTRACT

A bond normally represents a long-term contractual obligation of the firm to pay interest to the bondholder as well as the face value of the bond at maturity. The major provisions in a bond agreement are spelled out in the **bond indenture**, a complicated legal document often more than 100 pages long, administered by an independent trustee (usually a commercial bank). We shall examine some important terms and concepts associated with a bond issue.

The **par value** represents the face value of a bond. Most corporate bonds are traded in $1,000 units, while many federal, state, and local issues trade in units of $5,000 or $10,000.

Coupon rate refers to the actual interest rate on the bond, usually payable in semiannual installments. To the extent that interest rates in the market go above or below the coupon rate after the bond is issued, the market price of the bond will change from the par value. A bond initially issued at a rate of 8 percent will sell at a substantial discount from par value when 12 percent is the currently demanded rate of return. We will eventually examine how the investor makes and loses large amounts of money in the bond market with the swings in interest rates. A few corporate bonds are termed **variable-rate notes** or **floating-rate notes**, meaning the coupon rate is fixed for only a short period and then varies with a stipulated short-term rate such as the rate on U.S. Treasury bills. In this instance, the interest payment rather than the price of the bond varies up and down. In recent times, zero-coupon bonds have also been issued at values substantially below maturity value. With **zero-coupon bonds**, the investor receives return in the form of capital appreciation over the life of the bond since no semiannual cash interest payments are received.

The **maturity date** is the date on which final payment is due at the stipulated par value.

Methods of bond repayment can occur under many different arrangements. Some bonds are never paid off, such as selected **perpetual bonds** issued by the Canadian and British governments, and have no maturity dates. A more normal procedure would simply call for a single-sum lump payment at the end of the obligation. Thus, the issuer may make 40 semiannual interest payments over the next 20 years plus one lump-sum payment of the par value of the bond at maturity. There are also other significant means of repayment.

The first is the **serial payment** in which bonds are paid off in installments over the life of the issue. Each serial bond has its own predetermined date of maturity and receives interest only to that point. Although the total bond issue may span more than 20 years, 15 to 20 maturity dates are assigned. Municipal bonds are often issued on this basis. Second, there may be a **sinking-fund provision** to which semiannual or annual contributions are made by a corporation into a fund administered by a trustee for purposes of debt retirement. The trustee takes the proceeds and goes into the market to purchase bonds from willing sellers.

If no sellers are available, a lottery system may be used to repurchase the required number of bonds from among outstanding bondholders.

Third, debt may also be retired under a call provision. A **call provision** allows the corporation to call or force in all of the debt issue prior to maturity. The corporation usually pays a 3 to 5 percent premium over par value as part of the call provision arrangement.The ability to call is often *deferred* for the first 5 or 10 years of an issue (it can only occur after this time period).

The opposite side of the coin for a bond investor is a put provision.The **put provision** enables the bondholder to have an option to sell a long-term bond back to the corporation at par value after a relatively short period (such as three to five years).This privilege can be particularly valuable if interest rates have gone up since the initial issuance and if the bond is currently trading at 75 to 80 percent of par. A put bond generally carries a lower interest rate than conventional bonds (perhaps 1 to 2 percent lower) because of this protective put privilege. If one buys a put bond and interest rates go down and bond prices up (perhaps to $1,200), the privilege is unnecessary and is merely ignored.

SECURED AND UNSECURED BONDS

We have discussed some of the important features related to interest payments and retirement of outstanding issues. At least of equal importance is the nature of the security provision for the issue. Bond market participants have a long-standing practice of describing certain issues by the nature of asset claims in liquidation. In actuality, pledged assets are sold and the proceeds distributed to bondholders only infrequently. Typically, the defaulting corporation is reorganized, and existing claims are partially satisfied by issuing new securities to the participating parties. Of course, the stronger and *better secured* the initial claim, the higher the quality of the security to be received in a reorganization.

A number of terms are used to denote **secured debt**, that is, debt backed by collateral. Under a **mortgage** agreement, real property (plant and equipment) is pledged as security for a loan. A mortgage may be senior or junior in nature, with the former requiring satisfaction of claims before payment is given to the latter. Bondholders may also attach an **after-acquired property clause** requiring that any new property be placed under the original mortgage.

A very special form of a mortgage or collateralized debt instrument is the **equipment trust certificate** used by firms in the transportation industry (railroads, airlines, etc.). Proceeds from the sale of the certificate are used to purchase new equipment, and this new equipment serves as collateral for the trust certificate.

Not all bond issues are secured or collateralized by assets. Most federal, state, and local government issues are unsecured. A wide range of corporate issues also are unsecured. There is a set of terminology referring to these unsecured issues. A corporate debt issue that is unsecured is referred to as a **debenture**. Even though the debenture is not secured by a specific pledge of assets, there may be priorities of claims among debenture holders. Thus, there are senior debentures and junior or subordinated debentures.

If liquidation becomes necessary because all other avenues for survival have failed, secured creditors are paid off first out of the disposition of the secured assets.The proceeds from the sale of the balance of the assets are then distributed among unsecured creditors, with those holding a senior ranking being satisfied before those holding a subordinate position (subordinated debenture holders).[1]

---

1. Those secured creditors who are not fully satisfied by the disposition of secured assets may also participate with the unsecured creditors in the remaining assets.

FIGURE 12–1   Long-Term Funds Raised by Business and Government

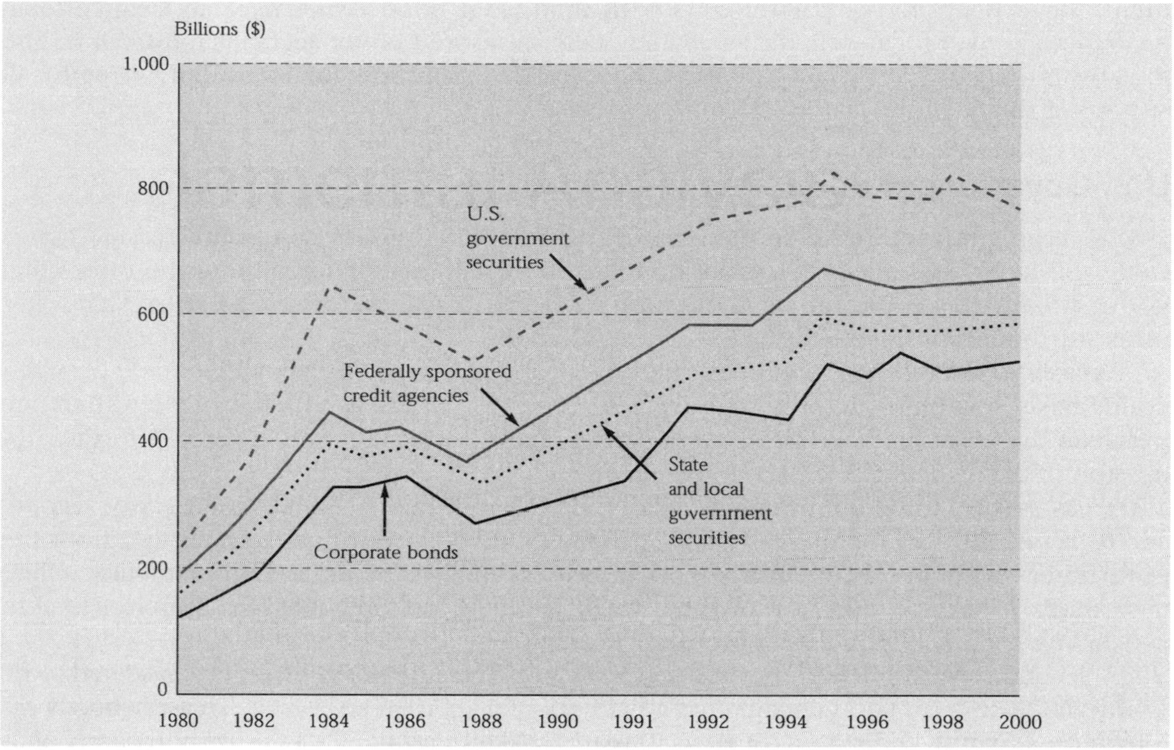

Unsecured corporate debt may provide slightly higher yields because of the greater suggested risk. However, this is partially offset by the fact that many unsecured debt issuers have such strong financial statements that security pledges may not be necessary.

Companies with less favorable prospects may issue income bonds. **Income bonds** specify that interest is to be paid only to the extent that it is earned as current income. There is no legally binding requirement to pay interest on a regular basis, and failure to make interest payments cannot trigger bankruptcy proceedings. These issues appear to offer the corporation the unusual advantage of paying interest as a tax-deductible expense (as opposed to dividends) combined with freedom from the binding contractual obligation of most debt issues. But any initial enthusiasm for these issues is quickly reduced by recognizing that they have very limited appeal to investors. The issuance of income bonds is usually restricted to circumstances where new corporate debt is issued to old bondholders or preferred stockholders to avoid bankruptcy or where a troubled corporation is being reorganized.

THE COMPOSITION OF THE BOND MARKET

Having established some of the basic terminology relating to the bond instrument, we are now in a position to take a more comprehensive look at the bond market. Corporate issues must vie with offerings from the U.S. Treasury, federally sponsored credit agencies, and state and local governments (municipal offerings). The relative importance of the four types of issues is indicated in Figure 12–1.

Over the 20-year period presented in Figure 12–1, the two fastest growing users of funds (borrowers) were the U.S. government and corporations. The former's needs can be attributed to persistent federal deficits that must be financed by increased borrowing. It should also be pointed out that as the government began running surpluses in the late 1990s to early 2000s, the need for such financing diminished.

In the case of corporations, strong growth combined with the need to finance mergers and leveraged buyouts has led to increased borrowing requirements. State and local governments have been active participants with municipal bond issues used to finance local growth and cover local deficits. Finally, federally sponsored credit agencies must call on the long-term funds market. Please observe the explosive growth in long-term borrowing by all sectors of the economy since 1980.

U.S. Government Securities

U.S. government securities take the form of Treasury bills, Treasury notes, and Treasury bonds (only the latter two are considered in Figure 12-1). The distinction among the three categories relates to the life of the obligation. A fourth category, termed Treasury strips, has other attributes and is also discussed.

Treasury bills (T-bills) have maturities of 91 and 182 days. Treasury bills trade on a discount basis, meaning the yield the investor receives occurs as a result of the difference between the price paid and the maturity value (and no actual interest is paid). A further discussion of this is presented later in the chapter.

Treasury bills trade in minimum units of $1,000, and there is an extremely active secondary, or resale, market for these securities. Thus, an investor buying a Treasury bill from the government with an initial life of approximately six months would have no difficulty selling it to another investor after two or three weeks. Because the T-bill now has a shorter time to run, its market value would be a bit closer to par.

A second type of U.S. government security is the **Treasury note**, which is considered to be of intermediate term and generally has a maturity of 1 to 10 years. Finally, **Treasury bonds** are long term in nature and mature in 10 to 30 years. Unlike Treasury bills, Treasury notes and bonds provide direct interest and trade in units of $1,000 and higher. Because there is no risk of default (unless the government stops printing money or the ultimate bomb explodes), U.S. government securities provide lower returns than other forms of credit obligations. Interest on U.S. government issues is fully taxable for IRS purposes but is exempt from state and local taxes.

Treasury securities may also trade in the form of **Treasury strips** (strip-T's). Treasury strips pay no interest, and all returns to the investor come in the form of increases in the value of the investment (as is true of Treasury bills also). Treasury strips are referred to as zero-coupon securities because of the absence of interest payments.

As an example, 25-year Treasury strips might initially sell for 19 percent of par value. You could buy a 25-year, $10,000 Treasury strip for $1,900.[2] All your return would come in the form of an increase in value. Of course, you could sell at the going market price before maturity should you so desire.

Actually the U.S. Treasury does not offer Treasury strips directly. It allows government security dealers to strip off the interest payments and principal payment from regular Treasury notes and bonds and repackage them as Treasury strips. For example, on a 25-year Treasury bond, there would be 50 semiannual interest payments and one final principal payment. Each of these 51 payments could be stripped off and sold as a zero-coupon strip.[3] Those who desired short-term Treasury strips would buy into the early payments. The opposite would be true for an investor with a long-term orientation.

The Internal Revenue Service taxes zero-coupon bonds, such as Treasury strips, as if interest were paid annually even though no cash flow is received until maturity. The tax is based on amortizing the built-in gain over the life of the instrument. For tax reasons, zero coupons are usually only appropriate for tax-deferred accounts such as individual retirement accounts, 401(k) plans, or other nontaxable pension funds.

---

2. The yield is approximately 6¾ percent. Zero-coupon securities are also offered by corporations.
3. Any one payment, such as the first, may be stripped from many hundreds of Treasury bonds at one time to provide a $10,000 Treasury strip.

Inflation—Indexed Treasury Securities   In January 1997, the U.S. Treasury began offering 10-year notes that were intended to protect investors against the effects of inflation. The maturities were later expanded to include longer terms to maturity.

Here's how these inflation-indexed Treasury notes work. The investor receives two forms of return as a result of owning the security. The first is annual interest that is paid out semi-annually, and the second is an automatic increase in the initial value of principal to account for inflation.

These securities are formally called **Treasury Inflation Protection Securities (TIPS)**. TIPS might pay 3.5 percent in annual interest and, assuming a 3 percent rate of inflation, an additional 3 percent to compensate for inflation. As implied in the preceding paragraph, the 3 percent inflation adjustment is not paid in cash but is added on to the principal value of the bond. Assume the bond had an initial par value of $1,000. At the end of the first year, the principal value would go up to $1,030, Thus, during the first year, the investor would receive $35 (3.5 percent) in cash as interest payments, plus enjoy a $30 increase in principal. On a 10-year indexed Treasury security, this procedure continues for each of the remaining nine years and at maturity, the security is redeemed at the indexed value of the principal by the Treasury. If the investor needs to sell before the maturity date, he or she can sell it in the secondary market to other investors at a value approximating the appreciated principal value.[4]

The Real World of Investing

TIPS—Flood Insurance During a Drought?

Treasury Inflation Protection Securities (TIPS) are discussed in the main body of the chapter, so the basics will not be restated here. As the name implies, TIPS are a protection against the ravages of inflation, but absolutely no one was worried about inflation at the time they were introduced in January 1997. The years 1996–97 represented some of the lowest levels of inflation (about 2 percent) in the post–World War II period. As the title of this box implies, introducing TIPS at that point in time was like selling flood insurance to farmers who are suffering through a six-month rain drought.

It's unlikely that private sector investment bankers such as Goldman Sachs or C.S. First Boston would have come out with a similar product at such an inopportune time, but keep in mind we are talking about the federal government. In fairness, it should also be pointed out that the majority of TIPS have an initial 10-year life, so even though there is no immediate threat of inflation, they could well prove to be important during the time period they are outstanding.

Furthermore, those who advocate the purchase of TIPS for a portfolio generally suggest that they represent a relatively small percentage of total holdings. The message is, "Bet on low inflation with 80 to 90 percent of your investments, but put the balance in inflation-protected securities."

Surprisingly, the first auction of TIPS went relatively well in January 1997, although subsequent auctions have seen less enthusiasm. This general lack of enthusiasm has continued into 2001. However, among the more enthusiastic investors are foreigners from countries such as Great Britain, Canada, and Sweden, where inflation-indexed

---

4. Other factors can come into play in pricing this security, but they unnecessarily complicate this basic example.

securities are more widely accepted. Eighteen percent of British government debt is actually financed by securities whose returns are tied to inflation.

The advantage to the federal government of offering TIPS is that they can be sold to the public at a slightly lower yield than conventional fixed-rate Treasury securities because the government is taking the risk of inflation going up (the amount the government will have to pay to redeem the securities will go up sharply if there is high inflation). In return for the government taking this risk, investors accept a slightly lower return.

The reader should be aware that the base against which the 3.5 percent annual interest is paid is the inflation-adjusted value of the security. Thus, in the second year, the interest payment would be $36.05 (3.5% × $1,030). In each subsequent year, there is a similar adjustment depending on the prior year's rate of inflation.

Assuming inflation remains at 3 percent over the 10-year time period, the inflation-adjusted value of the principal will increase to $1,344 (10 periods compounded at 3 percent). The investor is effectively getting a return of 6.5 percent in the form of interest and appreciation of principal. Of course, if inflation averages 6 percent over the life of the investment, the investor will get a return of 9.5 percent. The interest payment (real return) will remain at 3.5 percent, but inflation adjustment will supply the extra return.

Through inflation-indexed Treasury notes, the investor is protected against the effect of inflation. This may be quite a benefit if inflation is high, but the security can provide an inferior return compared with other investments in a low-inflation environment (the reader may wish to see the related box on the previous page for further discussion of this point).

Also, the investor should be aware that the annual adjustment in principal is treated as taxable income each year even though no cash is received until redemption at maturity. For this reason, inflation-indexed Treasury securities are more appropriate for tax-deferred or nontaxable accounts.

Federally Sponsored Credit Agency Issues

Referring back to Figure 12–1, the second category represents securities issued by federal agencies. The issues represent obligations of various agencies of the government such as the Federal National Mortgage Association and the Federal Home Loan Bank. Although these issues are authorized by an act of Congress and are used to finance federal projects, they are not direct obligations of the Treasury but rather of the agency itself.

Although the issues are essentially free of risk (there is always the implicit standby power of the government behind the issues), they carry a slightly higher yield than U.S. government securities simply because they are not directly issued by the Treasury. Agency issues have been particularly active as a support mechanism for the housing industry. The issues generally trade in denominations of $5,000 and up and have varying maturities of from 1 to 40 years, with an average life of approximately 15 years. Examples of some agency issues are presented below:

	Minimum Denomination	Life of Issue
Federal Home Loan Bank	$10,000	12–25 years
Federal Intermediate Credit Banks	5,000	Up to 4 years
Federal Farm Credit Bank	50,000	1–10 years
Export-Import Bank	5,000	Up to 7 years

Interest on agency issues is fully taxable for IRS purposes and is generally taxable for state and local purposes although there are exceptions. (For example, interest on obligations issued by the Federal Farm Credit Bank are subject to state and local taxes, but those of the Federal Home Loan Bank are not.)

One agency issue that is of particular interest to the investor because of its unique features is the **GNMA (Ginnie Mae) pass-through certificate**. These certificates represent an undivided interest in a pool of federally insured mortgages. Actually, GNMA, the Government National Mortgage Association, buys a pool of mortgages from various lenders at a discount and then issues securities to the public against these mortgages. Security holders in GNMA certificates receive monthly payments that essentially represent a pass through of interest and principal payments on the mortgages. These securities come in minimum denominations of $25,000, are long term, and are fully taxable for federal, state, and local income tax purposes. A major consideration in this investment is that the investor has fully consumed his or her capital at the end of the investment. (Not only has interest been received monthly but also all principal has been returned over the life of the certificate, and therefore, there is no lump-sum payment at maturity.)

Because mortgages that are part of GNMA pass-through certificates are often paid off early as a result of the sale of a home or refinancing at lower interest rates, the true life of a GNMA certificate tends to be much less than the quoted life. For example, a 25-year GNMA certificate may actually be paid off in 12 years. This feature can be a negative consideration because GNMA certificates are particularly likely to be paid off early when interest rates are going down and home owners are refinancing. The investor in the GNMA certificate is then forced to reinvest the proceeds in a low interest rate environment.

State and Local Government Securities

Debt securities issued by state and local governments are referred to as **municipal bonds**. Examples of issuing agencies include states, cities, school districts, toll roads, or any other type of political subdivision. The most important feature of a municipal bond is the tax-exempt nature of the interest payment. Dating back to the U.S. Supreme Court opinion of 1819 in *McCullough v. Maryland,* it was ruled that the federal government and state and local governments do not possess the power to tax each other. An eventual by-product of the judicial ruling was that income from municipal bonds cannot be taxed by the IRS. Furthermore, income from municipal bonds is also exempt from state and local taxes if bought within the locality in which one resides. Thus, a Californian buying municipal bonds in that state would pay no state income tax on the issue. However, the same Californian would have to pay state or local income taxes if the originating agency were in Texas or New York.

We cannot overemphasize the importance of the federal tax exemption that municipal bonds enjoy. The consequences are twofold. First, individuals in high tax brackets may find highly attractive investment opportunities in municipal bonds.[5] The formula used to equate interest on municipal bonds to other taxable investments is:

$$Y = \frac{i}{(1 - T)}$$

(12–1)

where:

Y = Equivalent before-tax yield on a taxable investment
i = Yield on the municipal obligation
T = Marginal tax rate of the investor

---

5. It should be noted that any capital gain on a municipal bond is taxable as would be the case with any investment.

If an investor has a marginal tax rate of 35 percent and is evaluating a municipal bond paying 6 percent interest, the equivalent before-tax yield on a taxable investment would be:

$$\frac{6\%}{(1 - 0.35)} = \frac{6\%}{0.65} = 9.23\%$$

Thus, the investor could choose between a *non*-tax-exempt investment paying 9.23 percent and a tax-exempt municipal bond paying 6 percent and be indifferent between the two. Table 12-1 presents examples of trade-offs between tax-exempt and non-tax-exempt (taxable) investments at various interest rates and marginal tax rates. Clearly, the higher the marginal tax rate, the greater the advantage of tax-exempt municipal bonds.

A second significant feature of municipal bonds is that the yield the issuing agency pays on municipal bonds is lower than the yield on taxable instruments. Of course, a municipal bond paying 6 percent may be quite competitive with taxable instruments paying more. Average differentials are presented in Table 12-2. You should notice in Table 12-2 that the yield differences between municipal bonds and corporate bonds was normally 2 to 4 percentage points. A major distinction that is also important to the bond issuer and investor is whether the bond is of a general obligation or revenue nature.

General Obligation versus Revenue Bonds   A **general obligation issue** is backed by the full faith, credit, and "taxing power" of the governmental unit. For a **revenue bond**, on the other hand, the repayment of the issue is fully dependent on the revenue-generating capability of a specific project or venture, such as a toll road, bridge, or municipal colosseum.

Because of the taxing power behind most general obligation (GO) issues, they tend to be of extremely high quality. Approximately three-fourths of all municipal bond issues are of the general obligation variety, and very few failures have occurred in the post-World War II era. Revenue bonds tend to be of more uneven quality, and the economic soundness of the underlying revenue-generating project must be carefully examined (though most projects are quite worthwhile).

Municipal Bond Guarantee   A growing factor in the municipal bond market is the third-party guarantee. Whether dealing with a general obligation or revenue bond, a fee may be paid by the originating governmental body to a third-party insurer to guarantee that all interest and principal payments will be made. There are four private insurance firms that guarantee municipal bonds, the largest of which are the Municipal Bond Investors Assurance (MBIA) and the American Municipal Bond Assurance Corporation (AMBAC). Municipal bonds that are guaranteed carry the highest rating possible (AAA) because all the guaranteeing insurance companies are rated AAA. Approximately 30 percent of municipal bond issues are guaranteed.

A municipal bond that is guaranteed will carry a lower yield and have a better secondary or resale market. This may be important because municipal bonds, in general, do not provide

Table 12–1   Marginal Tax Rates and Return Equivalents

Yield on Municipal	27% Bracket	35% Bracket	38.6% Bracket
5%	6.85%	7.69%	8.14%
6	8.22	9.23	9.77
7	9.59	10.77	11.40
8	10.96	12.31	13.03
9	12.32	13.85	14.66
10	13.70	15.38	16.28

Table 12–2 Comparable Yields on Long-Term Municipals and Taxable Corporates (Yearly Averages)

Year	Municipals Aa	Corporates Aa	Yield Difference
2001	5.80%	7.14%	1.34%
2000	6.01	7.80	1.79
1999	5.48	7.36	1.88
1998	5.13	6.80	1.67
1997	5.52	7.48	1.96
1996	5.90	7.72	1.82
1995	5.60	7.55	1.95
1994	6.40	8.60	2.20
1993	5.51	7.40	1.89
1992	6.30	8.46	2.16
1991	6.80	9.09	2.29
1990	7.15	9.56	2.41
1989	7.51	9.46	1.95
1988	8.38	9.66	1.28
1987	8.50	9.68	1.18
1986	7.35	9.47	2.12
1985	8.81	11.82	3.01
1984	9.95	12.25	2.30
1983	9.20	12.42	3.22
1982	11.39	14.41	3.02
1981	10.89	14.75	3.86
1980	8.06	12.50	4.44
1979	6.12	9.94	3.82
1978	5.68	8.92	3.24
1977	5.39	8.24	2.85
1976	6.12	8.75	2.63

Source: *Moody's Municipal & Government Manual, Moody's Industrial Manual,* and *Mergent Bond Record* (published by Mergent, Inc., New York, NY), selected issues.

as strong a secondary market as U.S. government issues. The market for a given municipal issue is often small and fragmented, and high indirect costs are associated with reselling the issue.

Corporate Securities

Corporate bonds are the dominant source of new financing for the U.S. corporation.

Bonds normally supply 80 to 85 percent of firms' external financial needs. Even during the great bull stock market of the 1990s, corporations looked as heavily as ever to the debt markets to provide financing (this was justified by the decreasing interest rates during this period).

The corporate market may be divided into a number of subunits, including *industrials, public utilities, rails and transportation,* and *financial issues* (banks, finance companies, etc.). The industrials are a catchall category that includes everything from high-technology companies to discount chain stores. Public utilities represent the largest segment of the market and have issues that run up to 40 years in maturity. Because public utilities are in constant need of funds to meet ever-expanding requirements for power generation, telephone services, and other essential services, they are always in the bond market to raise new funds. The needs associated with rails and transportation as well as financial issues

Table 12–3   Comparative Yields on Aa Bonds among Corporate Issuers

Year	Industrial	Public Utility
2001	7.14%	7.89%
2000	7.80	8.05
1999	7.36	7.92
1998	6.80	7.12
1997	7.48	8.00
1996	7.55	7.70
1995	7.72	7.84
1994	8.41	8.74
1993	7.05	7.19
1992	8.24	8.65
1991	9.01	9.25
1990	9.41	9.65
1989	9.35	9.55
1988	9.41	10.20
1987	9.73	9.83
1986	9.49	9.44
1985	11.57	12.02
1984	12.39	13.02
1983	11.94	12.74
1982	15.01	16.48
1981	13.01	14.03
1980	11.16	11.95
1979	9.24	9.70
1978	8.42	8.76
1977	7.90	8.41
1976	8.87	9.39

Source: *Mergent Bond Record* (published by Mergent, Inc., New York, NY), selected issues.

tend to be less than those associated with public utilities or industrials. Table 12–3 shows comparative yields for the two main categories.[6]

The higher yields on public utility issues represent a supply-demand phenomenon more than anything else. A constant stream of new issues to the market can only be absorbed by a higher yield pattern. In other cases, the higher required return may also be associated with quality deterioration as measured by profitability and interest coverage. During 1983–84, the default of the Washington State Power Authority on bonds issued to construct power-generating facilities sent waves through the bond market. Again in 1984, when Public Service of Indiana canceled construction of a partially complete nuclear power plant, nuclear utility issues (both stocks and bonds) suffered severe price erosion, and the bond market demanded high risk premiums on bonds of almost all nuclear utilities. In 2001, the public utility bond market was once again "spooked" by the energy crisis and blackouts in northern California.

Corporate bonds of all types generally trade in units of $1,000, and this is a particularly attractive feature to the smaller investor who does not wish to purchase in units of $5,000 to $10,000 (which is necessary for many Treasury and federally sponsored credit agency issues). Because of higher risk relative to government issues, the investor will generally receive higher yields on corporates as well. All income from corporates is taxable for

---

6. Financial and transportation issues are generally not broken out of the published data.

federal, state, and local purposes. Finally, corporate issues have the disadvantage of being subject to calls. When buying a bond during a period of high interest rates, the call provision must be considered a negative feature because the high-yielding bonds may be called in for early retirement as interest rates go down.

BOND MARKET INVESTORS

Having considered the issuer or supply side of the market, we now comment on the investor or demand side. The bond market is dominated by large institutional investors (insurance companies, banks, pension funds, mutual funds) even more than the stock market. Institutional investors account for 80 to 85 percent of the trading in key segments of the bond market. However, the presence of the individual investor is partially felt in the corporate and municipal bond market where the incentives of low denomination ($1,000) corporate bonds or tax-free municipal bonds have some attraction. Furthermore, in the last decade individual investors have made their presence felt in the bond market through buying mutual funds that specialize in bond portfolios.

Institutional investors' preferences for various sectors of the bond market are influenced by their tax status as well as by the nature of their obligations or liabilities to depositors, investors, or clients. For example, banks traditionally have been strong participants in the municipal bond market because of their substanial tax obligations. Their investments tend to be in short- to intermediate-term assets because of the short-term nature of their deposit obligations (the funds supplied to the banks). One problem that banks find in their bond portfolios is that such investments are often preferred over loans to customers when the economy is weak and loan demand is sluggish. Not so coincidentally, this happens to be the time period when interest rates are low. When the economy improves interest rates go up, and so does loan demand. To meet the loan demand of valued customers, banks liquidate portions of their bond portfolios. The problem with this recurring process is that banks are buying bonds when interest rates are *low* and selling them when interest rates are *high*. This can cause losses in the value of the bank portfolio.

The bond investor must be prepared to deal in a relatively strong primary market (new issues market) and a relatively weak secondary market (resale market). While the secondary market is active for many types of Treasury and agency issues, such is not the case for corporate and municipal issues. Thus, the investor must look well beyond the yield, maturity, and rating to determine if a purchase is acceptable. The question that must be considered is: How close to the going market price can I dispose of the issue if that should be necessary? If a 5 or 10 percent discount is involved, that might be unacceptable. Unlike the stock market, the secondary market in bonds tends to be dominated by over-the-counter transactions (although listed bonds are traded as well).

A significant development in the last decade has been the heavy participation of foreign investors in U.S. bond markets. Foreign investors now bankroll between 10 to 15 percent of the U.S. government's debt. While these investors have helped to finance the U.S. government's deficits, they can be a disruptive factor in the market when they decide to partially withdraw their funds. This happened in the mid-1990s when the declining value of the dollar and fear of inflation in the United States caused many foreign investors to temporarily cash in their investments. Because the U.S. government fears the flight of funds provided by foreign investors, it is sensitive to their needs and desires.

DISTRIBUTION PROCEDURES

In February 1982, the Securities and Exchange Commission began allowing a process called shelf registration under SEC Rule 415. **Shelf registration** permits large companies to file one comprehensive registration statement that outlines the firm's plans for future long-term financing. Then, when market conditions seem appropriate, the firm can issue the securities through an investment banker without further SEC approval. Future issues are said to be sitting on the shelf, waiting for the most advantageous time to appear. An issue may be on the shelf for up to two years.

Approximately half of the new public bond issues are distributed through the shelf registration process. The rest are issued under more traditional procedures in which the bonds are issued shortly after registration by a large syndicate of investment bankers in a highly structured process.

Private Placement

A number of bond offerings are sold to investors as a **private placement;** that is, they are sold privately to investors rather than through the public markets. Private placements are most popular with investors such as insurance companies and pension funds, and they are primarily offered in the corporate sector by industrial firms rather than public utilities. The lender can generally expect to receive a slightly higher yield than on public issues to compensate for the extremely limited or nonexistent secondary market and the generally smaller size of the borrowing firm in a private placement.

BOND RATINGS

Bond investors tend to place much more emphasis on independent analysis of quality than do common stock investors. For this reason, both corporate financial management and institutional portfolio managers keep a close eye on bond rating procedures. The difference between an AA and an A rating may mean the corporation will have to pay ¼ point more interest on the bond issue (perhaps 8½ percent rather than 8¼ percent). On a $100 million, 20-year issue, this represents $250,000 per year (before tax), or a total of $5 million over the life of the bond.

The two major bond-rating agencies are Moody's Investors Service and Standard & Poor's (a subsidiary of McGraw-Hill, Inc.). They rank thousands of corporate and municipal issues as well as a limited number of private placements commercial paper, preferred stock issues, and offerings of foreign companies and governments. U.S. government issues tend to be free of risk and therefore are given no attention by the bond-rating agencies. Moody's, founded in 1909, is the older of the two bond-rating agencies and covers twice as many securities as Standard & Poor's (particularly in the municipal bond area). Fitch Investors Service Inc., acquired Duff & Phelps, another rating agency, in an attempt to diversify and expand its rating coverage.

The bond ratings, generally ranging from an AAA to a D category, are decided on a committee basis at both Moody's and Standard & Poor's. There are no fast and firm quantitative measures that specify the rating a new issue will receive. Nevertheless, measures pertaining to cash flow and earnings generation in relationship to debt obligations are given strong consideration. Of particular interest are coverage ratios that show the number of times interest payments, as well as all annual contractual obligations, are covered by earnings. A coverage of 2 or 3 may contribute to a low rating, while a ratio of 5 to 10 may indicate the possibility of a strong rating. Operating margins, return on invested capital and returns on total assets are also evaluated along with debt-to-equity ratios.[7] Financial ratio analysis makes up perhaps 50 percent of the evaluation. Other factors of importance are the nature of the

---

7. Similar appropriate measures can be applied to municipal bonds, such as debt per capita or income per capita within a governmental jurisdiction.

industry in which the firm operates, the relative position of the firm within the industry, the pricing clout the firm has, and the quality of management. Decisions are not made in a sterile, isolated environment. Thus, it is not unusual for corporate management or the mayor to make a presentation to the rating agency, and on-sight visitations to plants or cities may occur.

The overall quality of the work done by the bond-rating agencies may be judged by the agencies' acceptance in the business and academic community. Their work is very well received. Although UBS PaineWebber and some other investment houses have established their own analysts to shadow the activities of the bond-rating agencies and look for imprecisions in their classifications (and thus potential profits), the opportunities are not great. Academic researchers have generally found that accounting and financial data were well considered in the bond ratings and that rational evaluation appeared to exist.[8]

One item lending credibility to the bond-rating process is the frequency with which the two major rating agencies arrive at the same grade for a given issue (this occurs well over 50 percent of the time). When "split ratings" do occur (different ratings by different agencies), they are invariably of a small magnitude. A typical case might be AAA versus AA rather than AAA versus BBB. While one can question whether one agency is looking over the other's shoulder or "copying its homework," this is probably not the case in this skilled industry.

The Real World of Investing

The Bond Rating Game: Who Really Runs the Corporation?

When Shell Canada (**www.shellcanada.com**), an integrated oil company with many U.S. investors, decided to sell its coal business, it called Moody's and Standard & Poor's first. Although its own financial analysis indicated the move was appropriate, it would not have made the decision without the blessings of the two major U.S. bond-rating agencies as well as similar rating agencies in Canada. The sell-off provided a $120 million write-off that could have caused a downgrading of Shell Canada's double. A rating, and the firm was not about to take a chance.

The firms concern was well justified. Its action was taken in June 1991 (a recession year). During the first six months of 1991, 422 corporations suffered a downgrading in ratings while only 88 had an increase. In the prior decade, the big causes for downgradings were the effects of acquisitions or attempts by corporations to defend themselves against takeovers. In the 1990s, these factors were less important, and the major concern was poor earnings performance.

Three good rules for firms to follow in dealing with bond-rating agencies is never surprise the agencies, tell all, and show good intent. A number of years ago, Manville Corporation (**www.jm.com**) was severely downgraded not for poor performance, but because it took Chapter 11 bankruptcy protection as a way to face asbestos damage litigation. The decision may have been right at the time, but the firm did not have the blessings of the bond-rating agencies.

---

8. James O. Horrigan, "The Determination of Long-Term Credit Standing with Financial Ratios," *Empirical Research in Accounting: Selected Studies*, supplement to *Journal of Accounting Research* 4 (1966), pp. 44–62; Thomas H. Pogue and Robert M. Soldofsky, "What's in a Bond Rating?" *Journal of Financial and Quantitative Analysis*, June 1969, pp. 201–8; and George E. Pinches and Kent A. Mingo, "A Multivariate Analysis of Industrial Bond Ratings," *Journal of Finance*, March 1973, pp. 1–18.

Table 12–4   Description of Bond Ratings

Quality	Moody's	Standard & Poor's	Description
High grade	Aaa	AAA	Bonds that are judged to be of the best quality. They carry the smallest degree of investment risk and are generally referred to as "gilt edge." Interest payments are protected by a large or exceptionally stable margin, and principal is secure.
	Aa	AA	Bonds that are judged to be of high quality by all standards. Together with the first group, they comprise what are generally known as high-grade bonds. They are rated lower than the best bonds because margins of protection may not be as large.
Medium grade	A	A	Bonds that possess many favorable investment attributes and are to be considered as upper-medium-grade obligations. Factors giving security to principal and interest are considered adequate.
	Baa	BBB	Bonds that are considered as medium-grade obligations—they are neither highly protected nor poorly secured.
Speculative	Ba	BB	Bonds that are judged to have speculative elements; their future cannot be considered as well assured. Often the protection of interest and principal payments may be very moderate.
	B	B	Bonds that generally lack characteristics of the desirable investment. Assurance of interest and principal payments or of maintenance of other terms of the contract over any long period may be small.
Default	Caa	CCC	Bonds that are of poor standing. Such issues may be in default, or there may be elements of danger present with respect to principal or interest.
	Ca	CC	Bonds that represent obligations that are speculative to a high degree. Such issues are often in default or have other marked shortcomings.
	C		The lowest-rated class in Moody's designation. These bonds can be regarded as having extremely poor prospects of attaining any real investment standing.
		C	Rating given to income bonds on which interest is not currently being paid.
		D	Issues in default with arrears in interest and/or principal payments.

Source: *Mergent Bond Record* (published by Mergent, Inc., New York, NY) and *Bond Guide* (Standard & Poor's).

Nevertheless, there is room for criticism. While initial evaluations are quite thorough and rational, the monitoring process may not be wholly satisfactory. Subsequent changes in corporate or municipal government events may not trigger a rating change quickly enough. One sure way a corporation or municipal government will get a reevaluation is for them to come out with a new issue. This tends to generate a review of all existing issues.

Actual Rating System

Table 12-4 shows an actual listing of the designations used by Moody's and Standard & Poor's. Note that Moody's combines capital letters and small *a*'s, and Standard & Poor's uses all capital letters.

The first four categories are assumed to represent investment-grade quality. Large institutional investors (insurance companies, banks, pension funds) generally confine their activities to these four categories. Moody's also modifies its basic ratings with numerical values for categories Aa through B. The highest in a category is 1, 2 is the midrange, and 3 is the lowest. A rating of Aa2 means the bond is in the midrange of Aa. Standard & Poor's has a similar modification process with pluses and minuses applied. Thus, AA+ would be on the high end of an AA rating, AA would be in the middle, and AA− would be on the low end.

It is also possible for a corporation to have issues outstanding in more than one category. For example, highly secured mortgage bonds of a corporation may be rated AA, while unsecured issues carry an A rating.

The level of interest payment on a bond is inverse to the quality rating. If a bond rated AAA by Standard & Poor's pays 7.5 percent, an A quality bond might pay 8.0 percent; a BB, 9.0 percent; and so on. The spread between these yields changes from time to time and is watched closely by the financial community as a barometer of future movements in the financial markets. A relatively small spread between two rating categories would indicate that investors generally have confidence in the economy. As the yield spread widens between higher and lower rating categories, this may indicate loss of confidence. Investors are demanding increasingly higher yields for lower rated bonds. Their loss of confidence indicates they will demand progressively higher returns for taking risks.

JUNK BONDS

Lower quality bonds are sometimes referred to as **junk bonds** or high yield bonds. Any bond that is not considered to be of investment quality by Wall Street analysts is put in the junk bond category. As previously indicated, investment quality means the bond falls into one of the four top investment-grade categories established by Moody's and Standard & Poor's. This indicates investment-grade bonds extend down to Baa in Moody's and BBB in Standard & Poor's (Table 12–4). A wide range of quality is associated with junk bonds. Some are very close to investment quality (such as the Ba and BB bonds), while others carry ratings in the C and D category.

Bonds tend to fall into the junk bond category for a number of reasons. First are the so-called fallen angel bonds issued by companies that once had high credit rankings but now face hard times. Second are emerging growth companies or small firms that have not yet established an adequate record to justify an investment-quality rating. Finally, a major part of the junk bond market is made of companies undergoing a restructuring either as a result of a leveraged buyout or as part of fending off an unfriendly takeover offer. In both these cases, equity capital tends to be replaced with debt and a lower rating is assigned.

Many junk bonds behave more like common stock than bonds and rally on good news, actual interest payments, or improving business conditions. Several institutions such as Merrill Lynch and Fidelity Investments manage mutual funds with a junk bond emphasis.

The main appeal of junk bonds historically is that they provided yields 300 to 800 basis points higher than that for AAA corporate bonds or U.S. Treasury securities. Also, until the recession of 1990–91, there were relatively few defaults by junk bond issuers. Thus, the investor got a substantially higher yield with only a small increase in risk.

However, in the 1990–91 recession, junk bond prices tumbled by 20 to 30 percent, while other bond values stayed firm. Examples of junk bond issues that dropped sharply in value included those issued by Rapid-American Corporation, Revco, Campeau Corporation, and Resorts International. Many of these declines were due to poor business conditions. However, the fall of Drexel Burnham Lambert, the leading underwriter of junk bond issues, also contributed to the difficulties in the market. That problem was further compounded when Michael Milken, the guru of junk bond dealers, was sentenced to 10 years in prison for illegal insider trading.

As the economy came out of the recession of 1990–91, junk bonds once again gained in popularity. Many of these issues had their prices battered down so low that they appeared to be bargains. As a result, junk bonds recovered and continued to perform exceptionally well throughout the 1990s—so much so that the spread between the yield on junk bonds and AAA corporates or U.S. Treasury securities was half of its historical spread in 1997. While these securities took a hit in 2001 as the economy slowed down, they still appear to have a place in the portfolio of investors with a higher than average risk tolerance. This is particularly true for bonds that are in the low- to mid-B rating categories.

DURATION

The concept of weighted average life of a bond falls under the general topic of duration. We shall first of all do a simple example of weighted average life and then more formally look at duration. Assume we have a five-year bond that provides $80 per year for the next five years plus $1,000 at the end of five years. For ease of calculation, we are using annual coupon payments in our analysis. Semiannual analysis would change the answer only slightly. An approach to computing weighted average life is presented in Table 12-5.

First, we see that the weighted average life of the bond, based on the annual cash flows, is 4.4290 years. Let's see how this is calculated. In column (1) is the year in which each cash flow falls, and in column (2) is the size of the cash flow for each year plus the total cash flow. Column (3) calls for dividing the annual cash flow in column (2) by the total cash flow at the bottom of column (2) to determine what percentage of the total it represents. For example, the annual cash flow of $80 on the first line of column (2) represents 0.0571 of the total cash flow of $1,400. ($80 ÷ $1,400 = 0.0571.) The same basic procedure is followed for all subsequent years. In column (4), each year is multiplied by the weights (percentages) developed in column (3). For example, year 1 is multiplied by 0.0571 to arrive at 0.0571 in column (4). Year 2 is multiplied by 0.0571 to arrive at 0.1142 in column (4). This procedure is followed for each year and each weight. The final answer is 4.4290 for the weighted average life of the bond.

If you can understand the approach presented in Table 12-5, you should have no difficulty following a more formal and appropriate definition of weighted average life called duration. **Duration** represents the weighted average life of a bond where the weights are based on the *present value* of the individual cash flows relative to *the present value* of the total cash flows. An example of duration is presented in Table 12-6. Present value calculations are based on the market rate of interest (yield to maturity) for the bond, which in this case, we shall assume to be 12 percent.

The only difference between Tables 12-5 and 12-6 is that in Table 12-6, the cash flows are present valued before the weights are determined. Thus, the cash flows (2) are multiplied by the present value factors at 12 percent (3) to arrive at the present value of cash flows (4). The total present value of cash flows at the bottom of column (4) is also the same as the price of the bond. In column (5), weights for each year are determined by dividing the present value of each annual cash flow (4) by the total present value of cash flows [bottom of column (4)] For example in year 1, the present value of the cash flow is $71.44, and this is divided by the total present value of cash flows of $855.40 to arrive at 0.0835 in column (5). Similarly, the weight in year 2, as shown in column (5), is determined by dividing $63.76 by $855.40 to arrive at 0.0745. In column (6), each year is multiplied by the weights developed in column (5). For example, year 1 is multiplied by 0.0835 to arrive at 0.0835 in column (6). Year 2 is multiplied by 0.0745 to arrive at 0.1490. This procedure is followed for each year, and the values are then summed.

Table 12–5   Simple Weighted Average Life

(1) Year, t	(2) Cash Flow	(3) Annual Cash Flow (2) ÷ by Total Cash Flow	(4) Year × Weight (1) × (3)
1	$ 80	0.0571	0.0571
2	80	0.0571	0.1142
3	80	0.0571	0.1713
4	80	0.0571	0.2284
5	80	0.0571	0.2855
5	1,000	0.7145	3.5725
Total cash flow →	$1,400	1.0000	4.4290

Table 12–6   Duration Concept of Weighted Average Life

(1) Year, t	(2) Cash Flow (CF)	(3) PV Factor at 12 Percent	(4) PV of Cash Flow (CF)	(5) PV of Annual Cash Flow (4) ÷ by Total PV of Cash Flows	(6) Year × Weight (1) × (5)
1	$ 80	0.893	$ 71.44	0.0835	0.0835
2	80	0.797	63.76	0.0745	0.1490
3	80	0.712	56.96	0.0666	0.1998
4	80	0.636	50.88	0.0595	0.2380
5	80	0.567	45.36	0.0530	0.2650
5	$1,000	0.567	567.00	0.6629	3.3145
	Total PV of cash flows (V) →		$855.40	1.0000	4.2498

Duration

The Real World of Investing

International Bond Managers—Changing Interest Rates and Bond Prices

International bond managers have their hands full managing interest rate risk around the globe. In addition to changing interest rates, these managers also have to pay attention to currency fluctuations, local economies, and government intervention into the money markets. During the last-half of 2000, long-term interest rates in the world's large economies all declined. Between June and December long-term U.S. Treasuries fell from 6.5 percent to 6.0 percent and similar patterns were present for the British gilts, German bonds, and other securities.

It is difficult to forecast changes in interest rates, and most bankers admit that any forecast of interest rates more than three months into the future is hazardous. There are always unexpected changes in inflation, GDP, central bank policy, etc.

All these factors can impact world bond prices and create price fluctuations. Given the sophistication of these international bond managers, let's give them the benefit of the doubt and assume they can actually forecast changing interest rates over the next three months. Let's also assume they can make money by shorting bonds whose prices will fall as interest rates rise and buying long those bonds whose prices will rise as interest rates fall.

How does a bond manager know whether an increase in rates by ¼ percent on a 1.8 percent Japanese bond will change the price more or less than a ½ percent increase on a 5.5 percent German bond? They will most likely have to use the concept of *duration* to calculate which bond is most price sensitive to a change in interest rates. Given that all international bonds will not have the same maturity may appear to complicate the decision, but duration measures bond price sensitivity and considers the current market interest rate, the maturity of the bond and the bond's coupon rate. This is just what the international trader needs to make decisions in this fast moving world of international interest rate movements.

The final answer for duration (the weighted average life based on present value) is 4.2498. This 4.2498 duration is referred to as **Macaulay duration,** named after Frederick Macaulay who developed this concept more than 100 years ago. Duration, once determined, is the most representative value for effective bond life and the measure against which bond price sensitivity should be evaluated.

The formula for duration can be formally stated as:

$$\text{Macaulay duration (D)} = \underbrace{\frac{CF\,PV}{V}}_{\uparrow\ \text{Weight}}\ \underbrace{(1)}_{\uparrow\ \text{Year}} + \underbrace{\frac{CF\,PV}{V}}_{\uparrow\ \text{Weight}}\ \underbrace{(2)}_{\uparrow\ \text{Year}} + \underbrace{\frac{CF\,PV}{V}}_{\uparrow\ \text{Weight}}\ \underbrace{(3)}_{\uparrow\ \text{Year}}$$

$$+\ \dots\ +\ \underbrace{\frac{CF\,PV}{V}}_{\uparrow\ \text{Weight}}\ \underbrace{(n)}_{\uparrow\ \text{Year}}$$

(12-2)

where:

CF = Yearly cash flow for each time period
PV = Present value factor for each time period
V = Total present value or market price of the bond
n = Number of periods to maturity[9]

In Table 12-7, we observe durations for an 8 percent coupon rate bond with maturities of 1, 5, and 10 years. The discount rate is 12 percent. The procedure used to compute duration in Table 12-7 is the same as that employed in Table 12-6. Although many calculations are involved, you should primarily direct your attention to the last value presented in column (6) for each of the three bonds. This value represents the duration of the issue.

We see in Table 12-7 that the duration for a one-year bond is 1.0. Since all cash flows are paid at the end of year 1, duration equals the maturity.[10] As maturity increases (to 5 and 10 years), duration increases but less than the maturity of the bond. With a 5-year bond, duration is 4.2498, and with a 10-year bond, duration is 6.8381. Duration is increasing at a decreasing rate because the principal repayment in the last year becomes a smaller percentage of the total present value of cash flow, and the annual coupon payments become more important.[11]

DURATION AND PRICE SENSITIVITY

Once duration is computed, its most important use is in determining the price sensitivity of a bond. In Table 12-8, we consider the maturity, duration, and percentage price change for

---

9. Using the symbols from Formula 12-1, duration can also be stated as:

$$\text{Duration} \sum_{t=1}^{n} \frac{C_t \dfrac{1}{(1+i)^t}}{V}(t) + \frac{P_n \dfrac{1}{(1+i)^n}}{V}(n)$$

If semiannual analysis is used throughout the calculation, the answer should be divided by two to convert the figure to annual terms.

10. If semiannual analysis were used, the duration would be slightly less than the maturity in the first year.

11. A sinking-fund provision can also have an effect on duration, causing the weighted average life of the bond to be shorter.

Table 12–7   Duration for an 8 Percent Coupon Rate Bond with Maturities of 1, 5, and 10 Years Discounted at 12 Percent

(1) Year, t	(2) Cash Flow (CF)	(3) PV Factor at 12 Percent	(4) PV of Cash Flow (CF)	(5) PV of Annual Cash Flow (4) ÷ by Total PV of Cash Flows	(6) Year × Weight (1) × (5)
1-Year Bond					
1	$ 80	0.893	$ 71.44	0.0741	0.0741
1	1,000	0.893	893.00	0.9259	0.9259
	Total PV of cash flows	→	$964.44	1.0000	1.0000 ↑ Duration
5-Year Bond					
1	$ 80	0.893	$ 71.44	0.0835	0.0835
2	80	0.797	63.76	0.0745	0.1490
3	80	0.712	56.96	0.0666	0.1998
4	80	0.636	50.88	0.0595	0.2380
5	80	0.507	45.36	0.0530	0.2650
5	1,000	0.567	567.00	0.6629	3.3145
	Total PV of cash flows	→	$855.40	1.0000	4.2498 ↑ Duration
10-Year Bond					
1	$ 80	0.893	$ 71.44	0.0923	0.0923
2	80	0.797	63.76	0.0824	0.1648
3	80	0.712	56.96	0.0736	0.2208
4	80	0.636	50.88	0.0657	0.2628
5	80	0.567	45.30	0.0586	0.2930
6	80	0.507	40.56	0.0524	0.3144
7	80	0.452	36.16	0.0467	0.3269
8	80	0.404	32.32	0.0418	0.3344
9	80	0.361	28.88	0.0373	0.3357
10	80	0.322	25.76	0.0330	0.3330
10	$1,000	0.322	322.00	0.4160	4.1600
	Total PV of cash flows	→	$774.08	1.0000	6.8381 ↑ Duration

an 8 percent coupon rate bond based on a 2 percent decrease and on a 2 percent increase in interest rates. The *market* rate of interest for computing duration in Table 12-8 is 8 percent. Duration is related not only to maturity but also to coupon rate and market rate of interest. For example, in Table 12-7, the coupon rate of interest was 8 percent, and the market rate of interest was 12 percent. In the calculations in Table 12-8, the coupon rate is 8 percent, and the initial market rate of interest is assumed to be 8 percent. Because of the different market rates of interest in Tables 12-7 and 12-8, the duration for a given maturity (such as 5 or 10 years) will be different. The point just discussed will be further clarified later in the chapter, so even if you do not fully understand it, you should still continue to read on.

We see in Table 12-8 that the longer the maturity or duration, the greater the impact of a 2 percent change in interest rates on price. However, we shall also observe how much more

TABLE 12–8   Duration and Price Sensitivity (8 Percent Coupon Rate Bond)

(1) Maturity	(2) Duration	(3) Impact of a 2 Percent Decline in Interest Rates on Price	(4) Impact of a 2 Percent Increase in Interest Rates on Price
1	1.0000	+1.89%	−1.81%
5	4.3121	+8.42	−7.58
10	7.2470	+14.72	−12.29
20	10.6038	+22.93	−17.03
25	11.5290	+25.57	−18.50
30	12.1585	+27.53	−18.85
40	12.8787	+30.09	−19.55
50	13.2123	+31.15	−19.83

closely the percentage change in price parallels the change in duration as compared with maturity. For example, between 25 and 50 years, duration increases very slowly [column (2)], and the same can be said for the increase in the percentage impact that a 2 percent decline in interest rates has on price [column (3)]. This is true despite the fact that the maturity period has increased by 100 percent, from 25 to 50 years.

As a rough measure of price sensitivity, one can multiply duration times the change in interest rates to determine the percentage change in the value of a bond.

$$\text{Percentage change in the value of a bond approximately equals} \rightarrow \text{Duration} \times \text{Change in interest rates} \qquad (12\text{--}3)$$

The sign in the final answer is reversed because interest-rate changes and bond prices move in opposite directions. For example, if a bond has a duration of 7.2470 years, and interest rates go down by 2 percent, a rough measure of bond value appreciation is +14.494 percent (7.2470 × 2). Columns (2) and (3) in Table 12–8, across from 10 years maturity, indicate this is a good approximation. That is, when duration was 7.2470, a 2 percent drop in interest rates actually produced a 14.72 percent increase in bond prices (not too many basis points away from our formula value of +14.494 percent).[12] The approximation gets progressively less accurate as the term of the bond is extended. It is also a less valid measure for interest-rate increases (and the associated price decline). Even with these qualifications, one can observe a more useful relationship between price changes and duration than between price changes and maturity.

It is for this reason that the analyst must have a reasonable feel for the factors that influence duration. The length of the bond affects duration, but as previously mentioned, it is not the only variable. Duration is also influenced by market rate of interest and the coupon rate on the bond. It is theoretically possible for these two factors to outweigh maturity in determining duration. That is to say, it is possible that a bond with a shorter maturity than another bond may actually have a longer duration and be more price sensitive to interest rate changes.

---

12. The approximation can be slightly improved by using modified duration instead of actual duration.

TABLE 12–9   Duration of an 8 Percent Coupon Rate Bond with a 16 Percent Market Rate of Interest

(1) Year, t	(2) Cash Flow (CF)	(3) PV Factor at 16 Percent	(4) PV of Cash Flow (CF)	(5) PV of Annual Cash Flow (4) ÷ by Total PV of Cash Flows	(6) Year × Weight (1) × (5)
1	$ 80	0.862	$ 68.96	0.0935	0.0935
2	80	0.743	59.44	0.0806	0.1612
3	80	0.641	51.28	0.0695	0.2085
4	80	0.552	44.16	0.0598	0.2392
5	80	0.476	38.08	0.0516	0.2580
5	1,000	0.476	476.00	0.6451	3.2255
		Total PV of → cash flows	$737.92	1.0000	4.1859 ↑ Duration

TABLE 12–10   Duration Values at Varying Market Rates of Interest (Based on 8 Percent Coupon Rate Bond)

Maturity (Years)	Market Rates of Interest				
	4 Percent	6 Percent	8 Percent	10 Percent	12 Percent
1	1.0000	1.0000	1.0000	1.0000	1.0000
5	4.3717	4.3423	4.3121	4.2814	4.2498
10	7.6372	7.4450	7.2470	7.0439	6.8381
20	12.3995	11.4950	10.6038	9.7460	8.9390
25	14.2265	12.8425	11.5290	10.3229	9.2475
30	15.7935	13.8893	12.1585	10.6472	9.3662
40	18.3274	15.3498	12.8787	10.9176	9.3972
50	20.2481	16.2494	13.2123	10.9896	9.3716

Duration and Market Rates

Market rates of interest (yield to maturity) and duration are inversely related. The higher the market rate of interest, the lower the duration. This is because of the present-value effect that is part of duration. Higher market rates of interest mean lower present values. For example, in Table 12–6, if the market rate of interest in column (3) had been 16 percent instead of 12 percent, the final answer for duration would have been 4.1859. The new value is computed in Table 12–9. Clearly, it is less than the 4.2498 duration value in Table 12–6.

To expand our analysis, in Table 12–10 we see the duration values for an 8 percent coupon rate bond at different market rates of interest. As market rates of interest increase, duration decreases. This can be easily seen in the 20-year row (reading across). At a 4 percent market rate of interest, duration for the 8 percent coupon rate bond is 12,3995. At 8 percent, it is 10.6038, and at 12 percent, 8.9390.

Also note in Table 12–10 that an equal change in market rates of interest will have a bigger impact on duration when rates move down than when they move up. For example, in the 50-year row, a 4 percentage point decrease in market rates of interest (say, from 8 percent

TABLE 12–11   Duration and Coupon Rates (25-Year Bonds)

Market Rate of Interest	Coupon Rates		
	4 Percent	8 Percent	12 Percent
4%	16.2470	14.2265	13.3278
6	14.7455	12.8425	12.0407
8	13.2459	11.5290	10.8396
10	11.8112	10.3229	9.7501
12	10.4912	9.2475	8.7844

to 4 percent) causes duration to increase by 7.0358 years, from 13.2123 to 20.2481 years. A similar increase from 8 percent to 12 percent would cause duration to decrease by only 3.8407 years, from 13.2123 to 9.3716 years.

Duration and Coupon Rates

In the previous section, we learned that duration is inversely related to the market rate of interest. We now look at the relationship between duration and the coupon rate on a bond. As the coupon rate rises, duration decreases. Why? The answer is that high coupon rate bonds tend to produce higher annual cash flows before maturity and thus tend to weight duration toward the earlier to middle years. On the other hand, low coupon rate bonds produce less annual cash flows before maturity and have less influence on duration. Duration is weighted more heavily toward the final payment at maturity, and duration tends to be somewhat closer to the actual maturity on the bond. At the extreme, a zero-coupon bond has the same maturity and duration.

The relationship between duration and coupon rates can be seen in Table 12–11. Here three different coupon rate bonds are presented. Each bond is assumed to have a maturity of 25 years. The best way to read the table is to pick a market rate of interest in the first column and then read across the table to determine the duration at various coupon rates. For example, at an 8 percent market rate of interest, duration is 13.2459 at a 4 percent coupon rate, 11.5290 at an 8 percent coupon rate, and 10.8396 at a 12 percent coupon rate. Clearly, the higher the coupon rate, the lower the duration (and vice versa).

The impact of coupon rates on duration is also demonstrated in Figure 12–2. Note that with a zero-coupon bond, the line is at a 45-degree angle; that is, duration and years to maturity are always the same value. There is only one payment, and it is at maturity.

You can also observe in Figure 12–2 that progressively higher coupon rates lead to a lower duration. As an example, go to point N on the horizontal axis and observe duration for 4 percent, 8 percent, and 12 percent interest. Clearly the higher the coupon rate, the lower the duration value.

Because the higher the duration, the greater the price sensitivity, it follows that an investor desiring maximum price movements will look toward lower coupon rate bonds. As previously demonstrated, low coupon rate and high duration go together, and high duration leads to maximum price sensitivity.

BRINGING TOGETHER THE INFLUENCES ON DURATION

The three factors that determine the value of duration are the maturity of the bond, the market rate of interest, and the coupon rate. Duration is positively correlated with maturity

FIGURE 12–2   The Effect of Coupon Rates on Duration

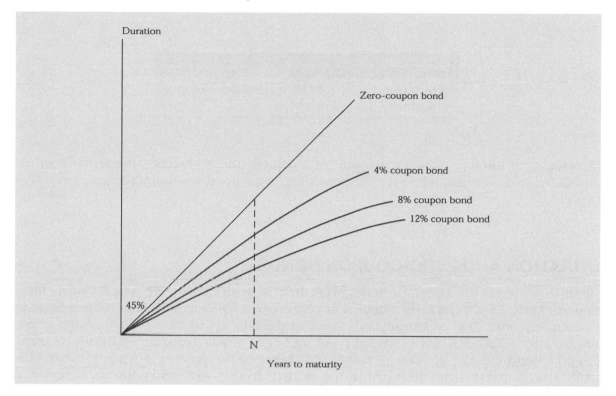

but moves in the opposite direction of market rates of interest and coupon rates; that is, the higher the market rate of interest or the coupon rate, the lower the duration. Earlier in this chapter, you were asked to consider whether you should invest in an 8 percent coupon rate, 20-year bond or a 12 percent coupon rate, 25-year bond. Since we were assuming interest rates were going to go down, you were looking for maximum price volatility. Had you not studied duration, you probably would have selected the bond with the longer maturity. This would generally be a valid assumption. However, the primary emphasis to the sophisticated bond investor when assessing price volatility, or sensitivity, is duration.

Note that the bond with the longer maturity (25 years versus 20 years) also has a higher coupon rate (12 percent versus 8 percent). The first factor (longer maturity) would indicate higher duration, but the second factor (higher coupon rate) would indicate a lower duration. What is the net effect? The answer can be found in earlier tables in this chapter. Let's assume that the *market rate* of interest is 12 percent for both bonds. Table 12–10 presented information on 8 percent coupon rate bonds for varying maturities and market rates of interest. To determine the duration on the 8 percent coupon rate, 20-year bond, assuming a 12 percent market rate of interest, we read across the 20-year row to the last column in the table and see the answer is 8.9390. (Note that all bonds in Table 12–10 have an 8 percent coupon rate, so we must identify the value associated with 20 years and a 12 percent market rate of interest.)

To determine the duration for the 12 percent coupon rate, 25-year bond with a 12 percent market rate of interest, we must go to Table 12–11. Note that all bonds in this table have a 25-year maturity, so read down to a market rate of interest of 12 percent and across to a coupon rate of 12 percent. The value for duration on this bond is 8.7844.

Based on this analysis, the answer to the question posed earlier in the chapter is that the bond with the shorter maturity (8 percent coupon rate for 20 years) has a higher duration than the bond with the greater maturity (12 percent for 25 years) and thus is the most price sensitive.[13]

Bond	Duration
8%, 20 years	8.9390 ← greater price sensitivity
12%, 25 years	8.7844

In actuality, if interest rates went down by 2 percent, the 8 percent, 20-year bond would go up by 18.5 percent, while the 12 percent, 25-year bond would increase by only 17.9 percent.

DURATION AND ZERO-COUPON BONDS

Characteristics of zero-coupon bonds were briefly described earlier. As previously mentioned, Figure 12–2 depicts the duration of zero-coupon bonds as a 45-degree line relative to years to maturity. This graphically indicates that the duration of a zero-coupon bond equals the number of years it has to maturity. For all bonds of equal risk and maturity, the zero-coupon bond has the greatest duration and therefore the greatest price sensitivity. This price risk is one that is often lost in the image of safety that zero-coupons have when backed by U.S. government securities.

A classic headline in *The Wall Street Journal* on June 1, 1984, appeared as follows: "Zero-Coupon Bonds' Price Swings Jolt Investors Looking for Security."[14] It was reported that between March 31, 1983 and March 31, 1984, Salomon Brothers' 30-year CATs declined 25 percent in price, while returns on conventional 30-year government bonds declined only a few percentage points. The article cited one client buying $100,000 of zero-coupons, thinking they were similar to short-term Treasury bill investments, only to find out four weeks later that his zero-coupon bonds had declined in value by $24,000.

To put the volatility of a zero-coupon bond into better perspective, we compare the duration of a zero-coupon bond to that of an 8 percent coupon bond for several maturities in Table 12–12.

The far right column in Table 12–12 indicates the ratio of duration between zero-coupon and 8 percent coupon rate bonds. As stressed throughout the chapter, duration represents a measure of price sensitivity. Thus, for a 10-year maturity period, a zero-coupon bond is almost $1\frac{1}{2}$ times as price sensitive as an 8 percent coupon rate bond (the ratio in the last column is 1.4625). For a 20-year maturity period, it is over two times more price sensitive (2.2374), and for 50 years the price sensitivity ratio is over five times greater (5.3353). This might explain why zero-coupons were much more sensitive to rising interest rates during 1983–84 as described in the story in *The Wall Street Journal*. Of course, tremendous profits can be made in zero-coupon bonds when there is a sharp drop in interest rates as in early 1985 and again in 1997 and early 1998.

---

13. As previously indicated, if we vary the market rate of interest, we can also influence the outcome to our question.

14. Randall Smith, "Zero-Coupon Bonds' Price Swings Jolt Investors Looking for Security," *The Wall Street Journal*, June 1, 1984, p. 19.

TABLE 12–12   Duration of Zero-Coupon versus 8 Percent Coupon Bonds (Market Rate of Interest Is 12 Percent)

(1) Years to Maturity	(2) Duration of Zero-Coupon Bond	(3) Duration of 8 Percent Coupon Bond	(4) Relative Duration of Zero-Coupon to 8 Percent Coupon Bonds (2) ÷ (3)
10	10	6.8374	1.4625
20	20	8.9390	2.2374
30	30	9.3662	3.2030
40	40	9.3972	4.2566
50	50	9.3716	5.3353

THE USES OF DURATION

Duration is primarily used as a measure to judge bond price sensitivity to interest rate changes. Because duration includes information on several variables (maturity, coupon rate, and market rate of interest), it captures more information than any one of them. It therefore allows more accurate decisions for complex bond strategies. One such strategy involves the timing of investment inflows to provide a needed cash outlay at a known future date. Perhaps $1 million is needed after five years. Everything is tailored to this five-year time horizon. If interest rates go up, there will be a decline in the value of the portfolio but a higher reinvestment rate opportunity for inflows. Similarly, if interest rates go down, there will be capital appreciation for the portfolio but a lower reinvestment rate opportunity. By tying all the investment decisions to a duration period, the portfolio manager can take advantage of these counter forces to ensure a necessary outcome. This strategy is called **immunization** and is used by insurance companies, pension funds, and other institutional money managers to protect their portfolios against swings in interest rates. For a more comprehensive discussion of immunization strategies, an article by Fisher and Weil is an appropriate source.[15] For an excellent criticism of duration and immunization strategy, see Yawitz and Marshall.[16] One of the problems with duration analysis is that it often assumes a parallel shift in yield curves. Although long-duration bonds are clearly more price sensitive than shorter-duration bonds, there is no assurance that long- and short-term interest rates will move by equal amounts.

BOND REINVESTMENT ASSUMPTIONS AND TERMINAL WEALTH ANALYSIS

Reinvestment Assumptions

As indicated in the previous section, one concern an investor may have when purchasing bonds is that the interest income will not be reinvested to earn the same return the coupon payment represents. This may not be a problem for an individual consuming the interest payments, but it could be a serious concern for individuals building a retirement portfolio or a pension fund manager accumulating funds for future payout to retirees. The crucial issue

---

15. Lawrence Fisher and Roman L. Weil, "Coping with Risk of Interest Rate Fluctuations: Returns to Bondholders from Naive and Optimal Strategies," *Journal of Business*, October 1971, pp. 408–31.
16. Jess B. Yawitz and William J. Marshall, "The Shortcomings of Duration as a Risk Measure for Bonds", *Journal of Financial Research*, Summer 1981, pp. 91–101.

is the amount of money accumulated at the time the retirement fund will be used to cover living expenses. One major determinant of the ending value of a retirement fund is the rate of return on coupon payments as they are reinvested.

Since the middle 1970s, interest rates have generally been more volatile than during previous periods. This has caused more emphasis on the management of fixed-income securities, not only in the selection of maturity but also in the switching from short- to long-term securities. These volatile rates have caused more emphasis on concepts such as duration to measure bond price sensitivity and on total return as a measure of bond management success. Given that interest rates change daily and by large amounts over a year, what impact would a lower or higher **reinvestment assumption** have on the outcome of your retirement nest egg?

First, let us look at the back of the text (partially reproduced Table 12–13). The material covers the compound sum of $1. Assume all interest is reinvested at the stated rate in order to find the ending value of $1 invested to maturity. For our current analysis, we are assuming annual interest (though the answer changes only slightly if we use semiannual interest).

The table values are given in $1 amounts, so for a $1,000 bond we would just move the decimal three places to the right. A $1,000 bond having a 12 percent coupon rate with interest being reinvested at 12 percent would compound to $93,051 over 40 years, while a 7 percent coupon bond reinvested at 7 percent would compound to only $14,974 over a similar period. A difference of 5 points in the rates creates a total difference of $78,077. This is quite a large difference. Notice that the longer the compounding period, the larger the amount. From further inspection of Table 12–13, other comparisons can be made between years and total ending values.

The importance of the reinvestment assumption can also be viewed from the perspective of its contribution to total wealth. For example, an investor owning a 40-year bond with a 12 percent coupon rate and an assumed reinvestment rate of 12 percent will have an accumulated value of $93,051. In terms of payout, $4,800 (40 × $120) comes directly from 40 years of 12 percent interest payments, $1,000 comes from principal, and the balance of $87,251 comes from interest that is earned on the annual interest payments. In this case, interest on interest represents 93.8 percent of the overall return ($87,251/$93,051).

Terminal Wealth Analysis

Now, we will assume a reinvestment assumption different from the coupon rate. Take the two extreme values from Table 12–13 of 12 percent and 7 percent. Assume you buy a bond having a 12 percent coupon rate, but the interest can only be reinvested at 7 percent. To find the ending value of this investment, we will need to use a **terminal wealth table**.

Table 12–14 is called a terminal wealth table because it generates the ending value of the investment at the end of each year, assuming the bond has a *maturity* date corresponding to that year. Let's use 10 years as an example in examining Table 12–14. If the bond matures in 10 years, the $1,000 principal in column (2) will be recovered. Also the investor will receive $120 in annual interest (12 percent of $1,000) in year 10 as indicated in column (3). In column (4), the accumulated interest up to the *beginning* of year 10 is shown. The reinvestment rate on this previously accumulated interest is a mere 7 percent as indicated in

TABLE 12–13   Compound Sum of $1.00

Period	7 Percent	8 Percent	9 Percent	10 Percent	11 Percent	12 Percent
10	$ 1.967	$ 2.159	$ 2.367	$ 2.594	$ 2.839	$ 3.106
20	3.870	4.661	5.604	6.727	8.062	9.646
30	7.612	10.063	13.268	17.449	22.892	29.960
40	14.974	21.725	31.409	45.259	65.001	93.051

Table 12–14   Terminal Wealth Table (12 Percent Coupon with 7 Percent Reinvestment Rate on Interest)

(1) Years to Maturity	(2) Principal	(3) Annual Coupon Interest	(4) Accumulated Interest[a]	(5) Reinvestment Rate on Interest	(6) Interest on Interest	(7) Total Annual Interest	(8) Portfolio Sum	(9) Compound Sum Factor	(10) Annual Percentage Return
0.0	$1,000.00								
1.0	1,000.00	$120.00	$ 0.00			$ 120.00	$ 1,120.00	1,12000	12.00%
2.0	1,000.00	120.00	120.00	0.07	$ 8.40	128.40	1,248.40	1.24840	11.73
3.0	1,000.00	120.00	248.40	0.07	17.39	137.39	1,385.79	1,38579	11.48
4.0	1,000.00	120.00	385.79	0.07	27.01	147.01	1,532.80	1,53280	11.26
5.0	1,000.00	120.00	532.80	0.07	37.30	157.30	1,690.10	1,69010	11.06
6.0	1,000.00	120.00	690.10	0.07	48.31	168.31	1,858.41	1,85841	10.86
7.0	1,000.00	120.00	858.41	0.07	60.90	180.09	2,038.50	2,03850	10.71
8.0	1,000.00	120.00	1,038.50	0.07	72.70	192.70	2,231.20	2,23120	10.55
9.0	1,000.00	120.00	1,231.20	0.07	86.18	206.18	2,437.38	2,43738	10.40
10.0	1,000.00	120.00	1,437.38	0.07	100.62	220.62	2,658.00	2,65800	10.26
11.0	1,000.00	120.00	1,658.00	0.07	116.06	236.06	2,894.06	2,89406	10.14
12.0	1,000.00	120.00	1,894.06	0.07	132.58	252.58	3,146.64	3,14664	10.02
13.0	1,000.00	120.00	2,146.64	0.07	150.26	270.26	3,416.90	3,41690	9.91
14.0	1,000.00	120.00	2,416.90	0.07	169.18	289.18	3,706.08	3,70608	9.80
15.0	1,000.00	120.00	2,706.08	0.07	189.43	309.43	4,015.51	4,01551	9.71
16.0	1,000.00	120.00	3,015.51	0.07	211.09	331.09	4,346.60	4,34660	9.61
17.0	1,000.00	120.00	3,346.60	0.07	234.26	354.26	4,700.86	4.70086	9.54
18.0	1,000.00	120.00	3,700.86	0.07	259.06	379.06	5,079.92	5,07992	9.44
19.0	1,000.00	120.00	4,079.92	0.07	285.59	405.59	5,485.51	5,48551	9.37
20.0	1,000.00	120.00	4,485.51	0.07	313.99	433.99	5,919.50	5,91950	9.29
21.0	1,000.00	120.00	4,919.50	0.07	344.37	464.37	6,383.87	6,38387	9.22
22.0	1,000.00	120.00	5,383.87	0.07	376.87	496.87	6,880.74	6,88074	9.16
23.0	1,000.00	120.00	5,880.74	0.07	411.65	531.65	7,412.39	7,41239	9.09
24.0	1,000.00	120.00	6,412.39	0.07	448.87	568.87	7,981.26	7,98126	9.04
25.0	1,000.00	120.00	6,981.26	0.07	488.69	608.69	8,589.95	8,58995	8.98
26.0	1,000.00	120.00	7,589.95	0.07	531.30	651.30	9,241.25	9,24125	8.92
27.0	1,000.00	120.00	8,241.25	0.07	576.89	696.89	9,938.14	9,93814	8.87
28.0	1,000.00	120.00	8.938.14	0.07	625.67	745.67	10,683.81	10,68381	8.82
29.0	1,000.00	120.00	9,683.81	0.07	677.87	797.87	11,481.68	11,48168	8.78
30.0	1,000.00	120.00	10,481.68	0.07	733.72	853.72	12,335.40	12,33540	8.73
31.0	1,000.00	120.00	11,335.40	0.07	793.48	913.48	13,248.88	13,24888	8.69
32.0	1,000.00	120.00	12,248.88	0.07	857.42	977.42	14,226.30	14,22630	8.65
33.0	1,000.00	120.00	13,226.30	0.07	925.84	1,045.84	15,272.14	15,27214	8.61
34.0	1,000.00	120.00	14,272.14	0.07	999.05	1,119.05	16,391.19	16,39119	8.57
35.0	1,000.00	120.00	15,391.19	0.07	1,077.38	1,197.38	17,588.57	17,58857	8.53
36.0	1,000.00	120.00	16,588.57	0.07	1,161.20	1,281.20	18,869.77	18,86977	8.50
37.0	1,000.00	120.00	17,869.77	0.07	1,250.88	1,370.88	20,240.65	20,24065	8.46
38.0	1,000.00	120.00	19,240.65	0.07	1,346.85	1,466.85	21,707.50	21,70750	8.43
39.0	1,000.00	120.00	20,707.50	0.07	1,449.53	1,569.53	23,277.03	23,27703	8.40
40.0	1,000.00	120.00	22.277.03	0.07	1,559.39	1,679.39	24,956.42	24,95642	8.37

[a] At beginning of year.

column (5). The interest on the previously accumulated interest is $100.62 (0.07 × $1,437.38). Finally, the total interest for year 10 is shown in column (7). This consists of the coupon interest of $120 and the interest on interest of $100.62 and totals to $220.62. The total ending value of the portfolio is shown in column (8). The ending value consists of the recovered principal of $1,000 plus the accumulated interest of $1,437.38 up to the beginning of year 10 plus the total interest paid in year 10 of $220.62. The ending wealth value (portfolio sum) thus shown in column (8) is $2,658.00. The value is summarized below:

Recovered principal	$1,000.00	Column (2)
Accumulated interest (beginning of year 10)	1,437.38	Column (4)
Total annual interest (during year 10)	220.62	Column (7)
Ending wealth value (portfolio sum)	$2,658.00	Column (8)

A $1,000 investment that grows to $2,658.00 after 10 years is the equivalent of a $1 investment that grows to 2.65800 as indicated in column (9). The annual percentage return for a $1 investment that grows to 2.65800 after 10 years is 10.26 percent as indicated in column (10).

A similar analysis can be done for all other maturity periods running from 1 to 40 years. One thing to notice from Table 12–14 is that the longer the maturity period of the bond, the greater the effect the low 7 percent reinvestment rate has on the bond. For 5 years, the annual percentage return [column (10)] is 11.06 percent; for 15 years, 9.71 percent; and for 40 years, 8.37 percent.

What is the actual difference between the ending value for a 40-year, 12 percent coupon rate bond assuming a *12 percent* reinvestment rate and the 40-year, 7 *percent* reinvestment rate just presented in Table 12–14? Earlier in this section, Table 12–13 demonstrated that a 12 percent coupon rate bond with an assumed 12 percent reinvestment rate for 40 years would grow to $93,051. In Table 12–14 we see that a 12 percent coupon rate bond with a 7 percent reinvestment rate will grow to only $24,956.42 after 40 years. It should be evident that it is not only the coupon rate that matters but the reinvestment rate as well.

If the bond were not held to maturity in our analysis, then we would have to rely on the realized rate of return analysis. The realized rate of return approach would assume that the bond is not held to maturity and that it is sold at either a gain or a loss. In the case of the bond analyzed in the terminal wealth table (Table 12–14), we know that since interest rates are assumed to decline, any sale of the bond before maturity should result in a capital gain. How large that capital gain would be will be dependent on its duration. Terminal wealth analysis is a way of analyzing the reinvestment assumption when bonds are held to maturity, while the realized yield approach assumes bonds are actively traded to take advantage of interest-rate swings.

Zero-Coupon Bonds and Terminal Wealth

One of the benefits of zero-coupon bonds is that they lock in a compound rate of return (or reinvestment rate) for the life of the bond *if held to maturity*. There are no coupon payments during the life of the bond to be reinvested, so the originally quoted rate holds throughout if held to maturity. If a $1,000 par value, 15-year zero-coupon bond is quoted at a price of $183 to yield 12 percent, you truly have locked in a 12 percent reinvestment rate. Some would say you have not only locked in 12 percent but have thrown away the key. In any event, zero-coupon bonds allow you to predetermine your reinvestment rate.

Of course, if a zero-coupon bond is sold before maturity, there could be large swings in the sales price of the bond because of its high duration characteristics. Under this circumstance, the locked-in reinvestment concept for the zero-coupon bond loses much of its meaning. It is valid only when the zero-coupon bond is held to maturity.

MODIFIED DURATION AND CONVEXITY
Modified Duration

If we want to more accurately measure bond price sensitivity resulting from the impact of a change in interest rates, we can use a term called **modified duration**, which is Macaulay duration divided by (1 plus the yield to maturity denoted as i). Macaulay duration is simply the duration value computed in the main body of the chapter:

$$\text{Modified duration } (D^*) = \text{Macaulay duration } (D)/(1 + i) \qquad (12\text{-}4)$$

For example, let's take the 10-year bond in Table 12–8 of the chapter with a duration of 7.2470. To get modified duration we use $7.2470 \div (1 + 0.08)$, where 0.08 represents the 8 percent yield to maturity. The modified duration for this 10-year bond equals 6.712. The basic reason for calculating a modified duration is that it is more accurate than Macaulay duration in measuring the change in the price of the bond for a given change in the interest rate:

Percentage change
in the value of a bond $\rightarrow$ Modified duration $\times$ Change in interest rates/$(1 + i)$ (12-5)
approximately equals

This equation is similar to Equation 12–3 in the chapter except that modified duration is used instead of normal or Macaulay duration and "change in interest rate divided by $(1 + i)$" is used instead of simply "change in interest rate." The term i represents initial yield to maturity.

For example, if interest rates in the market move from 8 to 10 percent on the 10-year bond described in Table 12–8 of the chapter, this equation would predict that the price of the bond would decrease by 12.42 percent. This is derived as follows using Equation 12–4:

Percentage change in the value of a bond approximately equals:
$$6.712 \times 2/1.08$$
$$6.712 \times 1.85 = 12.42 \text{ percent}$$

The sign in the final answer changes because interest rate changes and bond prices move in opposite directions. If we compare our example with the actual bond price change in Table 12–8, we see that the tabular value in column (4) of -12.29 percent is close to the more exacting value of 12.42 percent.

As was true of Macaulay duration, the value using modified duration gets less accurate as the term of the bond is extended. The reason for the loss of accuracy in predicting the change in the bond's price comes from the issue of convexity.

Convexity

The approximation formula used with the modified duration generates a linear relationship in bond price changes when in fact actual bond price changes are not linear. We can see from Table 12–8 that a 2 percent change in interest rates does not create equal percentage changes in bond prices for both increases and decreases in interest rates [columns (3) and (4)]. Table 12–8 demonstrates that a decrease in interest rates for a 10-year maturity bond causes a bigger increase in the bond price (14.72 percent) than the change in price caused by a 2 percent increase in rates (-12.29 percent).

Using Figure 12–3 to explain convexity, we start at point B where the bond price (V) and approximation price begin in equilibrium at the market interest rate i. An increase in interest rates $+i$, estimates that the price of the bond using modified duration estimates will fall to $-V_{D^*}$ while the actual price only falls to $-V$. The difference between the estimated price and the actual price is due to the convexity of bond prices. For a decrease in interest

FIGURE 12–3   Convexity

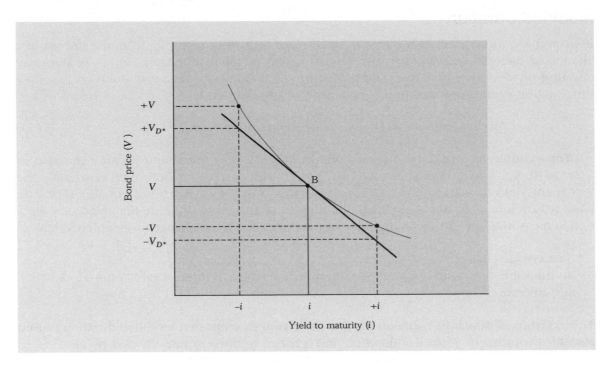

rates $-i$, the modified duration estimates a price of $+V_{D*}$ while the actual price is really $+V$. Looking at the differences between the estimates and reality, it can be observed that with a decline in interest rates, modified duration underestimates the bond price and that with an increase in interest rates, modified duration overestimates the bond price.

Convexity is only one of the issues that the analyst must understand in measuring the impact of bond price changes caused by interest rate fluctuations. While convexity makes duration a less than perfect measure for predicting bond price changes, it does not negate its value to the analyst in predicting bond price changes in individual bonds or bond portfolios.

INNOVATIONS IN THE BOND MARKETS

Bond innovations involve the creation of instruments that satisfy financial needs in the market and the development of these products are driven by such market needs. Financial product development is an engineering process. An example of a financially engineered product is a **pay in kind** bond. This bond provides a payment in kind (additional bonds) as opposed to cash. Such a payment is very similar to a stock dividend payment and pay in kind bonds help companies to facilitate their cash management functions. **Reverse floaters** are bonds that change coupon payments in reverse to the general level of market rates of interest. When interest rates are low they pay a high rate and vice versa. **Disaster bonds** pay a specified rate during normal times but pay a greater rate during a disaster. For example, there is an earthquake bond which pays a special rate in the event of an earthquake. This is an insurance type feature built into bond payments. **Asset backed** bonds pay interest based on the asset that backs the bond. An **indexed** bond has its interest payments tied to an index such as a commodity index, bond index, or oil. A bond issued by an oil company may tie the value to the oil price. The company will pay higher interest when oil prices are up and lower interest when oil prices drop. This way the oil company can match payments to their revenue stream. Another kind of indexed bond is the **Treasury Inflation protected**

Securities (TIPS). This is an index bond tied to the inflation rate in the economy. The interest payments on this bond reflect the real rate of return.

FORMULA INVESTING: LADDERS AND BARBELLS

Bond Ladder

A bond ladder is a strategy that seeks to manage the cash flow needs of a client while at the same time attempts to diversify the risks associated with interest rate movements. A bond ladder is a strategy where bonds are bought in different quantities with differing maturities. The underlying assumption is that the maturity amounts are required to fulfill cash needs at that point in time. For example, individuals in retirement may seek to ensure a certain amount of funding available every year to cover their basic expenses. These expenses typically are not discretionary and hence the client must ensure their availabilities. Similarly, pension fund managers know with a fair degree of certainty the amounts of payout they need to make at future points in time. The basic concept in using fixed-income securities in a portfolio is the higher degree of certainty in satisfying cash flow needs at future points in time. Thus, a laddered bond portfolio is one which has bonds maturing in successive (or specific) years and in specified amounts. For example, a bond portfolio may contain 250 zero coupon $1,000 par value bonds. Of these 250 bonds, 25 mature 10 years from now, the next 25 mature 11 years from now and so on with the last 25 maturing 20 years from now. In this case, the investor will receive a sum of $25,000 each year. This sum can be earmarked to cover non-discretionary expenses. By laddering the bonds, the investor receives the necessary assurance of being protected in the future years.

There is yet another benefit to laddering bonds. In the simple example above, the investor has bonds ranging in maturity from 10 to 20 years. The expected rate of return from the bonds for each year will almost certainly be different from each other. When the general level of interest rates change, they do not change uniformly over all future years. That is, for any given change, the expected rate for the 10 year maturity bond will change by a greater or lesser amount than all other maturities. Hence, by laddering the portfolio, the immediate effect of a rate change will lead to a diverse set of price changes for bonds in each maturity category. This will have the impact of cushioning adverse rate change effects and this diversification will help reduce the portfolio's volatility. Further, the effects of reinvestment rate risk will be similarly impacted. However, the main point to note is that if the investor maintains the hold on the bonds till maturity, the expected amounts of money will be realized. This is of course on the condition that the bond issuers themselves do not go into default on their debt service obligations.

Bond Barbell

A bond ladder reduces the risk of the portfolio by creating differential impacts on bond prices by having maturities stagger over time. This effect mainly happens since rate changes over the yield curve are not uniform. Observation from past changes in the yield curve indicate that there is significantly more volatility in yield changes in the long end of the yield curve over the short end. Further, yield curves are not always upward sloping. They are inverted often enough to indicate that an inverted yield curve is not an uncommon phenomenon. On an average, yield curves are more flat than anything else. These observations belie the fact that a term premia should exist for longer maturity fixed income securities. The reasons are complex and were discussed in the section on term structure.

Given the observation on yield curves, creating a portfolio with short and long maturity bonds implies that adverse changes in yields and interest rates can be diversified away by such a combination. Bond portfolios using this strategy are said to be using a barbell strategy. Barbells are not restricted to using long and short maturities only. In fact, barbells can be more effective if combinations of long and short bond durations are used instead of maturities. A simple example of the usefulness of a barbell can be provided by considering a situation when a normal sloping yield curve starts inverting, i.e. long-term rates begin decreasing as short-term rates increase. Short-term bonds will lose value from the decreases in prices while long-term values of bonds will increase. These value changes will tend to offset each other somewhat and reduce the portfolio volatility. Once the rates have changed and the barbell strategy is maintained, reinvestment effects of interim cash flows from long- and short-term bonds in the new interest rate regime will also tend to offset each other.

SUMMARY

Debt continues to play an important role in our economy from both the issuer's and investor's viewpoints. The primary fund raisers in the bond market are the U.S. Treasury, federally sponsored credit agencies, state and local governments, and corporations.

Bond instruments are evaluated on the basis of many factors, including yield, maturity, method of repayment, security provisions, and tax treatment. The greater the protection and privileges accorded the bondholder, the lower the yield.

A significant feature for a bond issue is the rating received by Moody's Investors Service or Standard & Poor's. The ratings generally range from AAA to D and determine the required yield to sell a security in the marketplace. Although there are no firm and fast rules to determine a rating, strong attention is given to such factors as cash flow and earnings generation in relation to interest and other obligations (coverage ratios) as well as to operating margins and return on invested capital and total assets. Qualitative factors are also considered.

The bond market appears to be reasonably efficient in terms of absorbing new information into the price of existing issues. Some researchers have suggested that the bond market may be slightly less efficient than the stock market in pricing outstanding issues because of the lack of a highly active secondary, or resale, market for certain issues. Insurance companies, pension funds, and bank trust departments are not normally active traders in their bond portfolios.

Short-term investors with a need for fixed income may look to certificates of deposit, commercial paper, bankers' acceptances, money market funds, money market accounts, and the previously discussed government securities as sources of investment. Such factors as maturity, yield, and minimum amount must be considered.

Finally, preferred stock may also be thought of as an alternative form of a fixed-income security. Although dividends on preferred stock do not represent a contractual obligation to the firm as would be true of interest on debt, they must be paid before common stockholders can receive any payment.

We have taken the concepts developed earlier and expanded on the principles of bond price volatility and total return. We developed the concept of duration so that the student has a basic understanding of its meaning and some of its applications. In general, we have shown that duration is the number of years, on a present-value basis, that it takes to recover an initial investment in a bond. More specifically, each year is weighted by the present value of the cash flow as a proportion of the present value of the bond and then summed. The higher the duration, the more sensitive the bond price is to a change in interest rates. Duration as one number captures the three variables—maturity, coupon rate, and market rate of interest—to indicate the price sensitivities of bonds with unequal characteristics. Generally, bond duration increases with the increase in number of years to maturity. Duration also increases as coupon rates decline to zero, and finally, duration declines as market interest rates increase.

Zero-coupon bonds are highlighted as the most price sensitive of bonds to a change in market interest rates, and comparisons are made between zero-coupon bonds and coupon bonds. Duration's primary use is in explaining price volatility, but it also has applications in the insurance industry and other areas of investments where interest-rate risk can be reduced by matching duration with predictable cash outflows in a process called immunization.

An important concept has to do with the reinvestment of interest at rates other than the coupon rate. The method used to explain the effect on the total return is terminal wealth analysis, which assumes that the investment is held to maturity and that all proceeds over the life of the bond are reinvested at the reinvestment rate. In general, the longer the maturity, the more total annualized return approaches the reinvestment rate. If the reinvestment rate is significantly different from the coupon rate, the annualized return can differ greatly from the coupon rate in as little as five years.

Chapter 13

Mutual Funds

Mutual funds have become a very important part of investing. According to the Investment Company Institute (**www.ici.org**), in the year 2001, mutual funds were owned by 54.8 million U.S. households, an increase from 23.4 million households in 1990. Figure 13–1 shows both the number and percentage of U.S. households owning mutual funds between 1980 and 2001. Another fact is that in 1990 U.S. based mutual fund assets were slightly less than $1 trillion but had grown to $6.4 trillion in September 2001.

Because many investors use mutual funds as an investment vehicle for retirement, they are long-term investors and not likely to abandon mutual funds in down markets. However, they may change their asset allocation between stocks, bonds, and international and short-term securities. At year-end 2000, mutual funds accounted for $2.5 trillion of U.S. retirement assets, or 20 percent of the $12.3 trillion earmarked for retirement. The other $9.8 trillion was held in accounts at insurance companies, brokerage firms, banks, and pension funds.

The concept of a mutual fund is best understood by an example. Suppose you and your friends are too busy to develop the expertise needed to manage your own assets. One of your neighbors, however, has had years of hands-on experience as a trustee of his company's pension fund. You and your friends decide to pool your money and have this experienced investor act as your investment advisor. He will be compensated by receiving a small percentage of the average amount of assets under his management during the forthcoming year.

By common agreement, the pooled money is to be invested in the common stock of large, stable companies with the objective of capital appreciation and moderate dividend income; funds not so invested are to be placed in short-term T-bills to earn interest. Group members collectively contribute $100,000 and decide to issue shares in the fund at a rate of one share for each $10 contributed—a total of 10,000 shares. Since you put in $10,000, you receive 1,000 shares of the fund—or 10 percent of the fund's shares. Over the next few weeks, your investment advisor uses $90,000 to purchase common stock in a number of companies representing several different industries and puts $10,000 in T-bills. The portfolio looks like this:

Companies grouped by different industries to get some diversification

Industries	Companies
Automobiles	General Motors
Banking	Citigroup
Chemicals	Du Pont
Computers	Gateway Computers
Financial services	Merrill Lynch
Oil	Exxon-Mobil
Pharmaceuticals	Eli Lilly
Semiconductors	Texas Instruments
Telecommunications	SBC
Treasury bills: $10,000	

FIGURE 13–1   U.S. Households Owning Mutual Funds, 1980–2001

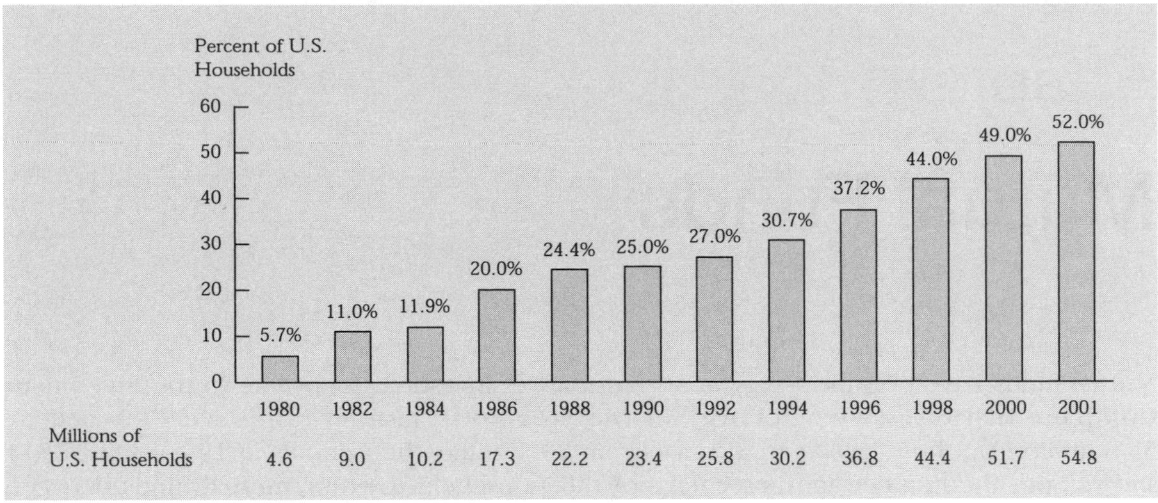

Source: *Fundamentals* (Washington, D.C.: Investment Company Institute, 2001).

Since you own 10 percent of this portfolio, you are entitled to 10 percent of all income paid out to shareholders and 10 percent of all realized capital gains or losses.

The initial value of the portfolio is $100,000, or $10 per share. Assume your investment manager picked some winning stocks, and the portfolio rises to $115,000. Now each share is worth $11.50.

Your group of investors has many characteristics of a mutual fund: ownership interest represented by shares, professional management, stated investment objectives, and a diversified portfolio of assets. A multibillion dollar mutual fund would operate with many of the same concepts and principles—only the magnitude of the operation would be thousands of times larger.

A mutual fund is a pool of money from many investors who have a common investment goal. Mutual fund pools are organized by companies who hire fund managers to manage the funds so as to achieve the investment goal of the fund. Mutual funds differ from stocks, bonds and other traditional securities in that they invest in multiple securities rather than a single security in order to meet investment objectives. Each year a mutual fund must have its prospectus updated so potential investors will have information on the fund and its investment objectives. Each fund has specific investment objectives such as growth, value, balanced equity-income and others which will be discussed below.

Because mutual funds invest in this manner, they offer several advantages that traditional types of investments do not. Investors are able to realize some diversification in their portfolios by simply investing in one mutual fund. This is particularly relevant for those investors who have limited funds to invest. This diversification can also be important for those investors who have large amounts of money to invest, who seek further diversification but are not well versed in certain types of investments.

Since many investors do not have large amounts of funds to invest, many mutual funds offer relatively low required initial investment amounts in order to participate in a fund. Most mutual funds offer the ability to redeem shares of the mutual funds with relative ease, thus offering the investor a high degree of liquidity. Selling or redeeming shares of mutual funds may, however, have tax implications so investors must weigh the consequences of selling or redeeming shares. Mutual funds are professionally managed. Most individuals do not have the time or the education to pick individual securities. Thus mutual funds offer professional investment advice for a nominal fee.

ADVANTAGES AND DISADVANTAGES OF MUTUAL FUNDS

Mutual funds offer an efficient way to diversify your investments. For many small investors, diversification may be difficult to achieve. The normal trading unit for listed stocks—the "round lot"—is 100 shares. If proper diversification required a portfolio of at least 10 different stocks, the investor should purchase 100 shares of each of them. If each stock had a market value of $30, the cost would be (excluding commission) $30,000 ($30 × 100 × 10). That's a big bite for most individuals just to get started.

With a mutual fund, you are also buying the expertise of the fund management. In many cases, fund managers have a long history of investment experience and may be specialists in certain areas such as international securities, gold stocks, or municipal bonds. By entrusting your funds to capable hands, you are freeing your time for other pursuits. This may be particularly important to people such as doctors or lawyers who may be capable of earning $200 to $300 an hour in their normal practice but are novices in the market.

As will be demonstrated throughout the chapter, you can choose from a multitude of funds to satisfy your investment objectives. Thus, another advantage of mutual funds is that they can be used to buy not only stocks but also U.S. government bonds, corporate bonds, municipal securities, and so on. Also, they represent an efficient way to invest in foreign securities. With many of these advantages in mind, it is not surprising that mutual funds have enjoyed enormous growth in the last decade.

Having stated some of the advantages of mutual funds, let's look at the drawbacks. First, mutual funds, on average, do not outperform the market. That is to say, over long periods, they do no better than the Standard & Poor's 500 Stock Index, the Dow Jones Industrial Average, and so on. Nevertheless, they provide an efficient means for diversifying your portfolio. Also, a minority of funds have had exceptional returns over time (many of these have had exposure to international investments).

Some mutual funds can be expensive to purchase. However, this factor should not overly concern you because a high commission can often be avoided. As you read further into the chapter, you will become very proficient at identifying the absence or presence of a commission and whether it is justified.

An investor in mutual funds must also be sensitive to the excessive claims sometimes made by mutual fund salespeople. Often, potential returns to the investor are emphasized without detailing the offsetting risks. The fact that a fund made 20 to 25 percent last year in no way ensures such a return in the future. Although the Securities and Exchange Commission has begun clamping down on false or overly enthusiastic advertising practices by members of the industry, the buyer still needs to be cautious. We will also help develop your skills in measuring actual performance as we progress through the chapter.

A final potential drawback to mutual funds is actually a reverse view of an advantage. With more than 8,100 mutual funds from which to choose, an investor has as much of a problem in selecting a mutual fund as a stock. For example, there are approximately 2,900 stocks on the New York Stock Exchange, considerably less than the number of mutual funds in existence. Nevertheless, if you sharpen your goals and objectives, you will be able to focus on a handful of funds that truly meet your needs.

Having discussed the general nature of mutual funds and some of the potential advantages and disadvantages, we now examine the actual mechanics. In the remainder of this chapter, we shall discuss closed-end versus open-end funds, load versus no-load funds, fund objectives, considerations in selecting a fund, and measuring the return on a fund. There is also a brief description of unit investment trusts (UITs) later in the chapter. UITs have some attributes similar to mutual funds.

Mutual funds also have some other disadvantages that should be considered prior to purchasing shares from a fund. Because funds are professionally managed by a fund manager, the individual does not have control over the portfolio's asset make-up. Regardless of whether a fund is realizing a positive or negative rate of return, the investor must still pay the fees and expenses associated with the fund. Depending on the fund, these fees can be sizable relative to the amounts invested. When purchasing a stock or bond, the investor knows with certainty what the price of the investment will be per share or per bond. However, mutual funds compute their Net Asset Value at the end of each day. Therefore, if one decides to purchase shares of a mutual fund, the investor will most likely have to wait until the beginning of the next business day to learn of the initial share price.

Mutual funds do not have a guaranteed rate of return, nor are they guaranteed by any federal agency. Many investors are unaware of this and therefore should be forewarned of these inherent risks. Mutual fund fees are not standardized. Depending on the fund, fees can be high. Therefore it is important for the investor to weigh the relative costs of the funds to the expected benefit by having the assets professionally managed. As assets under management in a fund grow, the relative ease to which fund managers can purchase and sell assets can be cumbersome. Oftentimes the fund manager will be required to pay additional fees to complete a transaction. As a result, the investor ends up bearing the cost of these transactions which cost more money than if purchased by an individual in isolation. As we mentioned, mutual funds offer diversification at a relatively low cost to most investors. However, many investors may be tricked into thinking they have diversified when they really have not. For instance, purchasing a fund with all high-tech firms' common stock is not really diversification since these types of stock tend to move in unison with changes in the market. Simply buying one fund does not necessarily offer diversification. This is an important point to make to clients when assisting them with the selection of funds.

Definitions

Fund Manager

A fund manager is an individual who oversees the allocation of funds within a mutual fund. The fund manager insures that the portfolio of the mutual fund is structured such that the risk return profile of the investment objective is being met.

Load Fund

A load is a commission fee that is charged to the consumer when initially investing in a mutual fund. This commission fee is paid to the brokerage firm or sales person.

Low Load Fund

A low load is a commission fee that is charged to the consumer when initially investing in a mutual fund. This commission fee is lower than in a traditional load fund but is still paid to the brokerage firm or sales person.

No Load

No load means that there is no commission to be paid by the consumer when investing, selling or redeeming shares in a particular mutual fund. However, it is important to note that all funds incur expenses, such as management and 12-b1 expenses (described below), in running the fund. These expenses are also borne by investors.

Back End Load

A back end load is a fee charged to a mutual fund investor for selling the shares of the fund earlier than a specified time, usually seven years. Fees levied for early withdrawal can be large.

Management Fee

A fee charged to the owner of a mutual fund for annual management of the mutual fund. It is a fee for the professional management of the fund. The management fee must be paid regardless of fund performance.

12b-1 Fees

12b-1 fees are fees charged by the mutual fund company for advertising and distribution expenses. 12b-1 fees have come under a lot of scrutiny over the past several years as several companies are using them to pay hidden costs such as commission to brokerage firms. These 12b-1 fees can sometimes charge as much as 1 percent to the investor.

MUTUAL FUND PROSPECTUS

The mutual fund prospectus provides a plethora of information that the financial planner should always read prior to suggesting investments for clients. A prospectus is a legal document that a company prepares in accordance with standards set by the Securities and Exchange Commission. All prospectuses must be updated annually and the date of update is printed on the front cover of the prospectus.

The first section of a prospectus generally contains the Investment Summary. The investment summary highlights the investment objectives (such as capital growth, income, etc.) and also contains the Principal Investment strategies which discuss the types of securities (common stock, bonds, international securities, etc.) that will be purchased into the fund. This summary also contains a discussion of the investment risks that are associated with the fund. This discussion is a valuable tool for the financial planner as it allows for a comparison of client objectives *vis-à-vis* the fund objectives. Based upon this analysis, a keen planner will be able to eliminate any funds that do not coincide with the client's objectives.

The prospectus must contain a section that discusses the performance of the fund. Included is a bar chart that spans the last ten years of returns. Additionally, the prospectus must have a calculation that includes the average after-tax annual returns. This calculation is based on average federal marginal tax rates with no inclusion of state tax rates (since taxes vary by state). When analyzing this, the financial planner must consider the tax implications that are specific to the individual client as the tax impact could be different from that quoted in the prospectus.

The document also contains a section that discusses the fees associated with investing in the fund. Such fees may or may not include load fees, management fees, distribution fees, 12b-1 advertising fees and miscellaneous fees.

Included in the prospectus is information regarding the minimum investment for the initial investment, and minimum amounts for subsequent investments. A fund will generally have a minimum amount that must be kept in the account. If an investor desires to sell or exchange shares in the mutual fund, the prospectus outlines how this can be accomplished by the investor and how and when the company will treat this transaction.

Other areas discussed in the prospectus are dividend and capital gain distributions. The tax consequences related to distributions and transactions are discussed as well. The main areas of the prospectus have been highlighted in this discussion. However, the prospectus does provide other relevant information for those interested in investing in a particular fund. Under no circumstances should an investor go into an investment without knowing as much about a fund as possible. Since there are so many excellent mutual fund choices in the marketplace today, with some diligence an investor should be able to find a fund suitable for achieving the investment goals.

While it is crucial to read and understand the prospectus, it is also of substance to remember that past returns do not evince future performance. The astute financial planner must therefore take other aspects in the external environment into consideration prior to recommending a particular mutual fund.

INVESTMENT OBJECTIVES

An investment objective is the desired result of an investment. We will discuss the objectives of growth funds, aggressive growth funds, value funds, balanced funds, equity-income funds, bond funds, and money market funds. We will also briefly touch upon other fund types.

Growth Fund

A growth fund is a fund whereby the fund manager purchases securities (generally common stock) in companies that have promising growth potential. Because these types of funds have volatile returns, these funds do not often pay dividends. As a result, this type of fund is for those investors who desire long-term growth investments and long-term capital gains. Because of the volatility of security prices within these funds, a growth fund is typically appropriate for an investor with a higher risk tolerance than average.

Aggressive Growth Fund

An aggressive growth fund is a fund whereby the fund manager purchases many types of risky securities such as stock from Initial Public Offerings, bonds from leverage buy-outs, small company stocks with expected large appreciation and various alternative investment vehicles such as derivatives, arbitrage strategies and futures. The primary investment objective of these funds is to achieve a high rate of return. It is not difficult to see that an investor's risk profile must be high in order to even consider one of these funds.

Value Fund

A value fund is a fund whereby the fund manager invests in funds that they perceive to be undervalued in the marketplace. That is, the security's intrinsic value exceeds its current market value. In general, fund managers are purchasing securities that they perceive to have moderate long-term growth potential. Additionally it is not uncommon for these types of company's to have low price/earnings ratios and higher than average dividend payouts. The objective of these types of funds is current income and conservative future long-term growth. This type of fund is a good choice for an investor with a moderate risk profile.

Balanced Funds

Balanced funds generally invest in a variety of common and preferred stocks and bonds. As its name implies, these types of funds tend to balance current income and long-term appreciation objectives by investing in common stocks for growth and in preferred stocks and bonds for current income. The funds can allocate the stocks and bonds in the percentage that is most apt to meet the fund objectives. Those funds with higher percentages of common stocks will have a higher risk and return profile with less current income. Conversely, those funds with greater percentages of preferred stocks and bonds will have a lower risk return profile with more current income and less long-term growth potential.

Equity-Income Funds

Equity-income funds are funds that invest the lion's share of the investment in stocks with high dividend payments. Stocks can consist of common stock, preferred stock or convertible stock. Because these funds seek to provide current income from dividends, the types of companies in the portfolio of these funds are generally blue chip and utility companies. These funds do however seek long-term capital appreciation but do not have as an aggressive stance as many of the growth funds. This type of fund is good for an investor with a low to moderate risk profile.

Bond Funds

Bond funds, as the name implies, are funds made up of bonds. Bond funds can satisfy investors with varying risk profiles. However, these types of funds generally satisfy those investors who have a need for current income and have low risk tolerance. There are various types of bond funds in the marketplace for those who are in a high income tax bracket and wish to avoid taxes. These funds are called municipal bond funds. Municipal bond funds are bonds issued by state and local governments. By federal statute interest earned on these funds is tax exempt at the federal level (though not necessarily at the state level). Additionally interest received on these types of funds may subject the individual to taxes on social security income or subject the taxpayer to Alternative Minimum Tax (AMT).

Since the real rate of return on bond funds is sensitive to changes in interest rate fluctuations within the economy, short-term bond funds are least sensitive to interest rate changes. In general they also provide lower rates of return than intermediate and long-term bond funds. These types of funds are good investment vehicles for funds that will be needed in the immediate future. While intermediate and long-term bond funds are more sensitive to the volatility in interest rate changes, they can generally offer a larger return over a longer time horizon.

Money Market Funds

Money market funds use the proceeds from investors to invest in short-term financial instruments such as bank certificate of deposits, Treasury bills and short-term corporate debt from companies with excellent credit ratings. These types of investments tend to be very safe and can yield investors somewhat more than they would receive in a passbook savings account. Money market funds are safer investments than other funds because the Securities and Exchange Commission allows money managers to invest in only credit worth short-term instruments (maturities of 90 days or less).

Money market funds are attractive to investors who are seeking higher yields than in general savings accounts. These funds generally offer additional flexibility such as check writing and ATM access to the fund.

Index Funds   **Index funds** are mutual funds that replicate a market index as closely as possible. It was pointed out earlier that exchange traded closed-end funds were index funds that traded on exchanges just like common stock. Conversely, index funds are open-end and may be purchased directly from the fund sponsor. As you may remember, there are many indexes, including stock market indexes and bond market indexes as well as foreign and global indexes. If an investor truly believes that the market is efficient and that it is hard to outperform the market, he or she will try to reduce transaction costs and attempt to imitate the market. Index funds arose because of the efficient market hypothesis. Quite a bit of academic research indicates that it is difficult to outperform a market index unless you have superior information. Most investors do not have superior information and so index funds make sense.

Sector Funds   Special funds have been created to invest in specific sectors of the economy. **Sector funds** exist for such areas as energy, medical technology, computer technology, leisure, and defense.

Because stock performance of companies within a particular industry, or sector, tend to be positively correlated, these funds offer investors less diversification potential.

Investors should be cautious with regard to the initial offering of new sector funds. An initial offering usually occurs after the sector has already been the subject of intense interest based on recent spectacular performance. As a result, stocks in that sector are often fully priced or overpriced.

Foreign Funds   Investors seeking participation in foreign markets and foreign securities confront a number of obstacles, but the rewards can be remarkable. The mutual fund industry has made overseas investing convenient by establishing **foreign funds** whose policies mandate investing on an international basis (Templeton World Fund), within the markets of a particular locale (Canadian Fund, Inc.), or within a region (Merrill Lynch Pacific). Some funds even specialize in Third World countries.

The mutual fund industry distinguishes between global and international funds. Global funds have foreign stocks plus U.S. stocks, while international have only foreign stocks.

Specialty Funds   Some mutual funds have specialized approaches that do not fit neatly into any of the preceding categories and so are called **specialty funds**. Their names are often indicative of their investment objectives or policies, the Phoenix Fund (rising from the ashes?), the Calvert Social Investment Fund, and United Services Gold Shares, to name just a few.

Other Funds

We have mentioned some of the most common types of funds though there are many types of other mutual funds. Some such funds are international funds, index funds, specialty sector funds (such as financial, healthcare, communication, and high-tech), and socially responsible. An investor can realize a multitude of risk and return profiles within all of these types of funds so that investment objectives are executed in accordance with the investor's plan.

Calculating Returns for Mutual Funds

Calculating returns on mutual funds is relatively straightforward and is similar to the holding period return calculation. The formula for calculating mutual fund returns is as follows:

$$k_{mf} = \frac{NAV_1 - NAV_0 + (\text{Dividends} + \text{Capital Gain Distributions})}{NAV_0}$$

Assume that Fund X had a beginning net asset value of $13.50 per share and an ending net asset value of $14.50. During the year dividend distributions were $0.50 per share and there were no capital gain distributions. The rate of return on this mutual fund is:

$$k_{mf} = \frac{\$14.50 - \$13.50 + \$0.50}{\$13.50}$$

$$= 11.11\%$$

Sources of Mutual Fund Information

There are many places where a prospective investor can access research information for mutual funds. As previously discussed, the prospectus provides a plethora of information about the fund. Most investment companies currently have the prospectuses for their funds on their company Web site. Fidelity Investments and Vanguard are two companies that provide excellent fund information on their Web sites, including prospectuses, annual reports, and holding and cost information.

Value Line and MorningStar are known in the investment industry to provide information on various stocks, bonds and mutual funds. MorningStar publishes the *Mutual Fund Source Book* each year. Investors can also purchase a subscription service to both Value Line and MorningStar.

There are a multitude of publications that provide information on mutual funds. *Barron's Magazine* is a publication that is specifically designed to analyze events in the financial services industry. Other valuable publications are *Kiplingers, Forbes, Money, The Wall Street Journal*, and *Financial Times* to name a few.

Selection of Mutual Funds

The vast number of funds available in the marketplace can be overwhelming for any investor. Therefore, when investing in mutual funds, it is important to narrow the playing field by matching appropriate funds with investment objectives. Many mutual funds will be able to be eliminated immediately since they will not concur with the client objectives.

Once the funds have been narrowed down, careful analysis must be performed comparing factors important to clients achieving their investment goals. As discussed above, a careful analysis of investment objectives, loads, management fees, 121-b fees, fund-management turnover, portfolio diversification, fund make-up, tax implications, past returns and expected future returns must be assessed in order to make the best possible investment choice.

CLOSED-END VERSUS OPEN-END FUNDS

There are basically two types of investment funds, the closed-end fund and the open-end fund. We shall briefly discuss the closed-end fund and then move on to the much more important type of arrangement, the open-end fund.

Actually, these terms refer to the manner in which shares are distributed and redeemed. A **closed-end fund** has a fixed number of shares, and purchasers and sellers of shares must trade with each other. You cannot buy the shares directly from the fund (except at the inception of the fund) because of the limitation on shares outstanding. Furthermore, the fund does not stand ready to buy the shares back from you.

As we shall eventually see, an open-end fund represents exactly the opposite concept. The **open-end fund** stands ready at all times to sell you new shares or buy back your old shares. Having made this distinction, let's stay with the closed-end fund for now. The shares of closed-end funds trade on security exchanges or over-the-counter just as any other stock might; but when you look for their prices in *The Wall Street Journal*, you will find closed-end funds listed under a separate heading as illustrated in Table 13-1. This makes them more easily identifiable, but you still buy and sell them through a broker and pay a commission. We have highlighted Royce Value Trust Fund, a closed-end fund specializing in equities.

One of the most important considerations in purchasing a closed-end fund is whether it is trading at a discount or premium from net asset value. First, let's look at the formula for net asset value.

$$\text{Net asset value (NAV)} = \frac{\text{Total value of securities} - \text{Liabilities}}{\text{Shares outstanding}} \tag{13-1}$$

The **net asset value (NAV)** is equal to the current value of the securities owned by the fund minus any liabilities divided by the number of shares outstanding. For example, assume a fund has securities worth $140 million, liabilities of $5 million, and 10 million shares outstanding. The NAV is $13.50:

$$\text{NAV} = \frac{\$140 \text{ million} - \$5 \text{ million}}{10 \text{ million shares}} = \frac{\$135 \text{ million}}{10 \text{ million}} = \$13.50$$

The NAV is computed at the end of each day for a fund.

Intuitively, one would expect a closed-end fund to sell at its net asset value, but that is not the case. Many funds trade at a discount from NAV because they have a poor record of prior performance, are heavily invested in an unpopular industry, or are thinly traded (illiquid). A few trade at a premium because of the known quality of their management, the nature of their investments, or the fact they have holdings in nonpublicly traded securities that are believed to be undervalued on their books. Note in Table 13-1 (third column from the right), the predominance of common stock funds trading at discounts from NAV in October 2001. This has normally been the case over the last decade. Some researchers even use the fact that closed-end funds do not sell for what they are worth (in terms of their holdings) as evidence that the market is something less than truly efficient in valuing securities.

Hedge Funds   **Hedge funds** are products of the 1990s and became very popular in 2000–2002. Actually the name is somewhat misleading in that hedge funds do not restrict their activities to hedging or reducing risk. Rather the term is a generic name for funds that

Table 13–1   Closed-End Funds

Closed-end funds sell a limited number of shares and invest the proceeds in securities. Unlike open-end funds, closed-ends generally do not buy their shares back from investors who wish to cash in their holdings. Instead, fund shares trade on a stock exchange.

Friday, October 26, 2001

STOCK (SYM)	EXCH	NAV	CLOSE	NET CHG	VOL 100s	PREM/ DISC	DIV	52 WK MKT RET
General Equity Funds								
♣AdamsExp **ADX**	N	17.25	15.35	0.10	583	−11.0	1.85e	−32.8
AllncAll **AMO**	N	20.94	20.65	0.00	83	−1.4	7.12e	−32.5
Avalon Capital **MIST**	O	15.70	15.00	NA	NA	−4.5	NA	15.4
BergstrmCap **BEM**	A	162.67	152.50	1.00	3	−6.3	11.25e	−31.2
♣BlueChipVal **BLU**	N	6.81	7.37	0.06	575	8.2	.81e	6.4
Bouldr TotR **BTF**	N	17.16	15.95	0.02	27	−7.1	.20	47.1
BrntlyCap **BBDC**	O	NA	9.00	0.25	67	NA	.62	16.1
CntlSec **CET**	A	27.68	24.40	0.00	87	−11.8	4.20e	−17.9
CrnstStratFd **CRF**	N	9.51	7.85	0.00	NA	−17.5	.01	−19.4
CornstnStrat **CLM**	N	8.82	7.36	0.04	52	−16.6	e	−30.7
Engex **EGX**	A	11.91	11.40	0.15	1	−4.3		−58.9
♣Equus II **EQS**	N	14.25	8.40	0.01	37	−41.1	60e	−10.1
GabelliTr **GAB b**	N	8.46	10.21	0.13	1091	20.7	1.08a	7.8
♣GenAminy **GAM**	N	35.24	35.06	0.16	273	−0.5	8.19e	5.1
♣LibtyASE **USA**	N	10.29	11.25	0.11	1059	9.3	1.31e	−3.6
♣LibtyASG **ASG**	N	7.62	7.80	0.11	619	2.4	1.06e	−22.1
MFS SpcVal **MFV**	N	8.64	14.10	−0.05	91	63.2	1.65a	24.4
MorgFnshr **MFUN** c	O	7.56	6.25	0.00	NA	−17.3		−19.3
NAIC Growth **GRF** c	C	11.27	10.60	NA	NA	−5.9	NA	−0.4
PrgrssvRetFd **PGF**	N	10.47	8.50	0.04	18	−18.8	e	−12.8
RoyceFocus **FUND**	O	6.59	5.62	0.13	262	−14.7	34e	8.3
RycMcroCap **OTCM**	O	11.14	9.40	−0.10	209	−15.6	1.72	10.2
RoyceValTr **RVT**	N	15.92	14.05	−0.25	2205	−11.7	1.57e	14.7
SalomonSBF **SBF** j	N	13.45	12.32	0.02	1036	−8.4	1.90e	−20.7
♣SmallCapFd **MGC**	N	11.29	10.21	0.04	20	−9.6	2.05e	−10.1
SourceCap **SOR**	N	50.52	58.75	1.25	39	16.3	4.60a	31.5
♣TriContl **TY**	N	22.16	19.55	−0.04	663	−11.8	3.13e	−10.6
♣ZweigFd **ZF**	N	7.59	8.06	0.01	933	6.2	.72	−12.4
Specialized Equity Funds								
♣ASA **ASA** c	N	21.74	18.30	0.05	334	−15.8	.60	32.2
♣CntlFdCan g **CEF**cl	A	3.40	3.46	−0.01	147	1.8	.01g	17.6
CohnStrsAdvtg **RLF**	N	12.95	14.85	0.90	521	14.7	1.26	NS
♣CohenStrsTR **RFI**	N	12.68	12.95	−0.10	113	2.1	.96a	18.8
Dundee Prec Mtls **DPMA** cy	T	13.23	9.05	NA	NA	−31.6	NA	NA
FstFntFd **FF**	N	14.07	11.87	0.03	70	−15.6	10	30.5
GabelliMlti **GGT**	N	9.37	8.27	−0.08	115	−11.7	1.56e	−21.6
GabelliUt **GUT**	N	7.34	9.06	0.05	78	23.4	72	29.4
♣H&Q Hlth **HCH**	N	30.88	24.72	0.42	193	−19.9	4.78e	−12.3
♣H&Q LifeSci **HQL**	N	26.08	20.80	0.40	429	−20.2	3.93e	−13.9
♣HocKJ BkOpp, **BTO**	N	10.00	7.98	0.05	899	−20.2	.77	16.4
♣JohnHanckFol **JHFT**	O	17.49	13.85	0.00	35	−19.4	2.64e	22.3
LCM Intrnt **FND**	A	2.92	2.53	0.07	11	−13.4	26e	−61.0
meVC DrprFshr **MVC**	N	15.42	9.27	0.09	523	−39.9	.34	−16.6
Munder @ Vantage	Z	6.83	NA	NA	NA	NA	NA	NA
♣PeteRes **PEO**	N	26.79	24.64	0.04	141	−8.0	1.74e	−5.4
Seligman New Tech	Z	11.24	NA	NA	NA	NA	NA	NA
Seligman New Tech II	Z	9.42	NA	NA	NA	NA	NA	NA
Tuxis **TUX**	A	11.42	11.85	−0.01	5	3.8	1.30e	19.8

Source: *The Wall Street Journal*, October 29, 2001, p. C18. Reprinted by permission of *The Wall Street Journal*, © 2001 by Dow Jones & Company, Inc. All Rights Reserved Worldwide.

engage in a wide range of activities at one time in an attempt to generate a superior return. They normally are neither bullish nor bearish, but engage in buying, short selling, and transacting in puts and calls at the same time in the attempt to gain an edge. They tend to be highly leveraged and are usually in the form of a limited partnership.

Hedge funds are those types of funds that seek to provide excess returns by using aggressive strategies. Among others, strategies include the use of derivatives, short sales, borrowing and leverage, swaps and arbitrage. Hedge funds are exempt from the rules and regulations that govern mutual funds. This circumvention is made possible by holding the number of investors to no more than 100 per fund, thereby sidestepping the rules. Due to this reason, the 100 included investors tend to be either very wealthy individuals to very large institutions.

All hedge funds are not the same in terms of returns and volatility of returns. These differences arise mainly from the flexibility of the funds in the way they strategize, structure and manage the funds. A strategy where a hedge portfolio contains both long and short securities can be expected to be more stable and less risky than another which may contain many naked options. As mentioned at the beginning of this section, the term "hedge" in this context is a misnomer since a hedge means to protect or insure whereas hedge funds as such may be extremely speculative. While some hedge fund strategies tend to hedge against downturns in the markets there are many others who seek to exploit marketwide movements.

While most hedge fund strategies have paid off handsomely of late, speculative hedge funds have been troubled as their risk exposures have finally caught up with them. We can expect more such problems soon as well.

Hedge funds are constructed to meet various investment goals; some of these goals are also popular among mutual funds while others are not. These newer goal oriented hedge funds are worth describing further after examining the more popular goal oriented funds.

Popular goals include aggressive growth, value, emerging markets or current income. The names of these funds suggest the activities for such strategies. More exotic funds also exist. Distressed security funds buy equity, debt, or other types of trade claims at deep discounts of companies in distress. If the underlying funds survive the distress, these securities provide large returns. Market neutral funds invest both long and short in securities and where the respective weights are manipulated for market exposure. Leveraged funds borrow to invest and hence attempt to exploit the benefits of financing risk. Multi-strategy funds combine various strategies. Many hedge funds use derivatives like options, futures and swaps for speculation as well.

Exchange Traded Funds

A new wrinkle in closed-end mutual funds is the concept of **exchange traded funds (ETFs)**. These are investment company shares that trade on stock exchanges (most commonly the American Stock Exchange). The market determines the price of ETFs, and investors buy and sell them through brokers just like common stock. Exchange traded funds began in 1993 and, according to the Investment Company Institute, numbered 92 ETFs by September 2001. Of these, 66 were domestic and 26 were international ETFs, and together all had a total value of $64.4 billion. This is a small percentage of total mutual fund assets but one that is expected to grow rapidly in future years.

Exchange traded funds are essentially index-based mutual funds that imitate a market index such as the Standard & Poor's 500 Index. Of the 66 domestic ETFs, 33 used broad-based market indexes and the other 33 used industry indices. The advantage of ETFs is that they allow the investor to buy "the market" or "an industry" just like a common stock.

Exchange Traded Funds (ETF) are security certificates and for most perspectives, have characteristics of and behave very similarly to individual stocks. However, as their name suggests, they also reflect underlying baskets of securities that reflect broad market-based indexes, much like index funds while being traded, like individual stocks, on an exchange.

Even though they perform the same function as regular open-ended index mutual funds, ETFs can be bought and sold throughout the trading day, requiring broker commissions and order placements, etc. Unlike mutual funds and like stocks of individual companies they can be sold short, bought on margin or any other action that can also be done by an individual stock.

An ETF begins when an issuing firm assembles a basket of stocks that are highly correlated with an index that is being replicated and holds these stocks in safe custody. The issuer can now issue certificates (ETFs) against this basket to customers. Since this transaction represents an in-kind trade of essentially equivalent items, capital gains are not triggered from the transaction. The ETFs now reflect the value of the underlying basket as a whole which in turn reflects the index. Since the value of the basket replicates the index, the fund manager monitoring the basket has little activity (passive management) except to monitor the correlation between the basket and the index. Occasional trades occur when the correlation drops below certain required threshold values. This is the primary reason why the ETF expense charges are so very low.

Just like stocks, the market price of an ETF is determined by forces of supply and demand for the shares, which in turn reflect the underlying indexes market forces. Besides these, there are other factors that can and do affect their market prices. Thus, the potential exists for ETFs to trade at premiums and discounts to their underlying net asset values. However, since arbitrageurs can replicate the underlying basket of securities and conduct arbitrage transactions if the ETF and the basket are not equal, the premiums and discounts are generally very low.

There are a number of different ETFs on the market currently, including those tracking the S&P 500 (SPDRs), the Nasdaq (Qubes), the Dow Jones (Diamond), sector SPDRs, the Russell Indexes, etc. All of them are passively managed, tracking a wide variety of sector-specific, country-specific, and broad-market indexes. All ETFs trade on the American Stock Exchange and already there are over 100 such ETFs.

The expenses involved in trading in ETFs include a very small (passive) fund management fee, custodial fee, brokerage commission (one time) and a bid-ask spread cost. These expenses when added up place ETF expenses in the *lowest* expense deciles when compared with mutual funds in its categories. Further, since they are like stocks, no capital gains are triggered since the issuer does not have to sell underlying shares due to redemption as it happens with mutual funds. Thus, given their diversification, low costs and tax advantages, using ETFs for portfolio construction and management has unparalleled benefits. It is almost assured that ETFs will grow by leaps and bounds and threaten the whole mutual fund industry one day. The following table shows the tax advantages of ETFs over traditional mutual funds. The data in the table portray a telling story and also one of the many good reasons.

Capital Gains Distributions as a Percentage of Assets, August 2000–August 2001		
Index tracked	ETF	Index Mutual Fund
S&P 500	0.05%	0.00%
S&P MidCap 400	0.30%	8.54%
Russell 2000	0.17%	13.64%
S&P 500/Barra Value	0.24%	6.53%
S&P SmallCap 600/Barra Value	0.44%	7.13%
S&P 500/Barra Growth	0.16%	0.00%
S&P SmallCap 600/Barra Growth	0.81%	5.24%
Average	0.31%	5.87%

Source: Bloomberg, from May, 2002 issue of *Financial Planning Magazine*.

UNIT INVESTMENT TRUSTS (UITS)

Unit investment trusts (UITs) are investment companies organized for the purpose of purchasing a pool of securities—usually tax-exempt municipal bonds. UITs issue units to investors, representing a proportionate interest in the assets of the trust. Investors also receive a proportionate share in the interest or dividends received by the trust.

According to the Investment Company Institute, by the end of 2000 there were a total of 10,071 unit trusts with a market value of $88.75 billion. While this is not a lot of money compared with mutual funds, unit trusts do meet a market niche for specialized investors. Of the 10,000 trusts, more than 8,000 were tax-free bond trusts. While equity trusts only accounted for slightly more than 1,500 trusts, they made up the lion's share of the value with $62 billion.

Unit investment trusts are passive investments. They normally purchase assets and hold them for the benefit of owners for a specified period.

To understand UITs better, consider the following hypothetical example. Nuveen, Inc.— a prominent firm in this field—announces the formation of the next in its series of tax-exempt unit trusts: Nuveen Series 200. Through advertising and selling agents, Nuveen will raise $4 million; investors will pay approximately $1,000 per unit. After deducting 2 to 3 percent for sales commissions, Nuveen will use the remaining cash to purchase large blocks of municipal securities from 10 to 20 different issuers. Once this diversified pool of bonds is acquired, Nuveen will play a passive role. It will collect and pass on to unit holders all interest payments received and all principal repayments resulting from maturing or recalled bonds. While UITs usually hold bonds until maturity, the trust custodian may sell off bonds whose future ability to pay interest and principal is altered by events.

Often, trusts are formed to purchase tax-exempt securities from issuers in specific, high-tax states, such as New York, Massachusetts, and Minnesota. Unit holders residing in these states expect to receive a stream of income exempt from federal, state, and local taxation.

Even unit investment trusts dedicated to tax-exempt bonds have different investment objectives. Some deal strictly in long-term, high-rated issues. Others seek higher yields by purchasing issues with low ratings.

Units of a trust are redeemable under terms set forth in the prospectus. In most cases, this means a unit holder can sell units back to the trust at their net asset value, which is the current market value of each trust unit.

A secondary market for unit trusts is evolving among broker-dealers. Investors seeking to acquire or sell units can sometimes find a better deal in this market. However, most investors in UITs do not intend to redeem early.

Investors in UITs benefit by professional selection of securities, by diversification, and by avoiding the housekeeping chores of collecting coupon payments. As a large buyer, a UIT can usually purchase securities at a better price than the individual who buys in small lots.

Essential Difference between a Unit Investment Trust and a Mutual Fund

There is an important difference between UITs and mutual funds. UITs are formed with the intention of keeping all the initially purchased assets until maturity. The investment strategy, as described above, is strictly passive. A UIT of $4 million with a 10-year life will draw interest over that time period, while only cashing in bonds as they mature and returning the funds to the investors. The UIT will cease to exist after 10 years. Because of the features just described, there is very little interest-rate risk associated with UITs. Since all bonds are intended to be held until maturity, the investor can be reasonably well assured of recovering his initial investment (plus interest). The fact that interest rates and bond prices are changing at any point in time during the life of the UIT makes little difference.[1]

---

1. Of course, if the investor needs to redeem shares before the end of the life of the trust, there will be fluctuations in value.

A bond-oriented mutual fund has no such assurance of recovering the initial investment. First, mutual funds have no stipulated life. Second, the bonds in the portfolio are actively managed and frequently sold off before their maturity dates at large profits or losses. Thus, the purchaser of a bond-oriented mutual fund may experience large capital gains or losses as well as receiving interest income.

The message is that if preservation of capital is of paramount importance to the investor, the UIT may be a better investment than a mutual fund. Of course, if one thinks interest rates are going down and bond prices up, the bond-oriented mutual fund would be a better investment.

THE REAL WORLD OF INVESTING

Are REITs Going through a Renaissance Period?

In an article in *Fortune* magazine, Ken Heebner, manager of the CGM funds in Boston, was quoted as saying, "When I buy REITs today, it reminds me of buying stocks in the 1970s, when the Dow was under 1,000. I think REITs represent the beginnings of a major new asset class for individuals."*

Actually, REITs have been around a long time but appear to be going through a current renaissance period. In the same article, Russell Platt, head of real estate securities at Morgan Stanley Asset Management (**www.morganstanley.com**), suggests that most office REITs have property priced $100 to $150 per square foot, but the equivalent replacement cost is $150 to $250 per square foot. This, of course, makes for an excellent investment opportunity.

REITs tend to specialize in various sectors of the real estate market such as apartments, hotels, health care facilities, shopping centers, and so on. The performance of a given sector tends to be derivative in nature; that is, if the hotel industry is in a boom period with high occupancy rates, hotel REITs will share the benefits in terms of market valuation. In the mid- to late 1990s, revenue per room was growing by 5 to 10 percent per year, and occupancy rates were approaching an historical high of 75 percent.

If you invest in REITs you need to become familiar with the term *FFO*. FFO stands for *funds from operations* and represents net income plus depreciation and amortization charges (and excluding gains or losses from debt restructuring and sales of property). You do not need to be an expert in computing FFO to use it in your analysis; it is enough to know that it is the accepted measure of return in the REIT industry and is generally used in place of earnings per share. Thus, instead of talking about P/E (price-to-earnings) ratios, REIT analysts frequently refer to P/FFO (price-to-funds-from-operations) ratios. The P/FFO ratio is normally at a level of 50 to 70 percent of the P/E ratio for a REIT. In May 2000, the average REIT had a mean P/FFO ratio of $11\times$ and a mean P/E ratio of $17\times$. As a further example, Federal Realty, a highly regarded shopping center REIT, had a P/E ratio of $18.5\times$ and a P/FFO ratio of $10.1\times$. You would normally compare other shopping center REITs with the P/FFO of $10.1\times$ of Federal Realty.

While REITs have generally performed well in the stock market during their recent recovery period, they are subject to the same ups and downs as other equity investments. They are particularly sensitive to interest rate changes because they borrow heavily and are frequently classified as high-yield securities, which means they go up in value when interest rates are going down and vice versa. If you are a potential REIT investor, make sure to study the outlook for interest rates before committing funds.

*Susan E. Kuhn, "Here Come the Good Years in Real Estate; From REITs to Vacation Condos, Good Deals Abound," *Fortune*, December 23, 1996, pp. 127–30.

Real Estate Investment Trust

Another form of real estate investment is the **real estate investment trust (REIT)**. REITs are similar to mutual funds or investment companies and trade on organized exchanges or over-the-counter. They pool investor funds, along with borrowed funds, and invest them directly in real estate or use them to make construction or mortgage loans to investors.

The advantage to the investor of a REIT is that he or she can participate in the real estate market for as little as $10 to $20 per share. Furthermore, this is the most liquid type of real estate investment because of the large secondary market for the shares.

REITs were initiated under the Real Estate Investment Trust Act of 1960. Like other investment companies, they enjoy the privilege of single taxation of income (only the stockholder pays and not the trust). To qualify for the tax privilege of a REIT, a firm must receive at least 75 percent of its income from real estate (i.e., rents and interest on mortgage loans) and distribute at least 95 percent of its income as cash dividends.

REITs may take any of three different forms or combinations thereof. **Equity trusts** buy, operate, and sell real estate as an investment; **mortgage trusts** make long-term loans to real estate investors; and **hybrid trusts** engage in the activities of both equity and mortgage trusts. REITs are generally formed and advised by affiliates of commercial banks, insurance companies, mortgage bankers, and other financial institutions. Representative issues include Bank America Realty, and Connecticut General Mortgage.

There are more than 400 REITs from which the investor may choose.

SUMMARY

Investment funds allow investors to pool their resources under the guidance of professional managers. Some funds are closed-end, which means there is a *fixed* number of shares, and purchasers and sellers of shares must deal with each other. They normally cannot buy new shares from the fund. Much more important is the open-end fund, which stands ready at all times to sell new shares or buy back old shares. Actually, it is the open-end investment fund that technically represents the term *mutual fund*.

An important consideration with an open-end fund is whether it is a load fund or a no-load fund. The former requires a commission that may run as high as 7.25 percent, while the latter has no such charge. Because there is no proof that load funds deliver better performance than no-load funds, the investor should think long and hard before paying a commission.

Mutual funds may take many different forms such as those emphasizing money market management, growth in common stocks, bond portfolio management, special sectors of the economy (such as energy or computers), or foreign investment. The funds with an international orientation have enjoyed strong popularity in the last decade.

Through examining a fund's prospectus, the investor can become familiar with the fund's investment objectives and policies, its portfolio holdings, its turnover rate, and the fund's management fees. The investor can also become aware of whether the fund offers such special services as automatic reinvestment of distributions (when desired), exchange privileges among different funds, systematic withdrawal plans, and check-writing privileges.

Return to fund holders may come in the form of capital appreciation or yield. Over the long term, mutual funds have not outperformed the popular market averages. However, they do offer an opportunity for low-cost, efficient diversification, and they normally have experienced management. Also, a minority of funds have turned in above-average performances.

Chapter 14

Derivative Instruments and Markets

The word **option** has many different meanings, but most of them include the ability or right to choose a certain alternative. One definition provided by *Webster's* is "the right, acquired for a consideration, to buy or sell something at a fixed price within a specified period of time." This definition is very general and applies to puts, calls, warrants, real estate options, or any other contract entered into between two parties where a choice of action or decision can be put off for a limited time at a cost. The person acquiring the option pays an agreed-upon sum to the person providing the option. For example, someone may want to buy your house for its sale price of $100,000. The buyer does not have the money but will give you $2,000 in cash if you give him the right to buy the house at $100,000 for the next 60 days. If you accept, you have given the buyer an option and have agreed not to sell the house to anyone else for the next 60 days. If the buyer raises $100,000 within the 60-day limit, he may buy the house, giving you the $100,000. Perhaps he gets the $100,000 but also finds another house he likes better for $95,000. He will not buy your house, but you have a $2,000 option premium and must now find someone else to buy your house. By selling the option, you tied up the sale of your house for 60 days, and if the option is not exercised, you have forgone an opportunity to sell the house to someone else.

The most widely known options are puts and calls on common stock. A **put** is an option to sell 100 shares of common stock at a specified price for a given period. **Calls** are the opposite of puts and allow the owner the right to buy 100 shares of common stock from the option seller (writer). Contracts on listed puts and calls have been standardized and can be bought on several different exchanges.

OPTIONS MARKETS

Before the days of options trading on exchanges, puts and calls were traded over-the-counter by the Put and Call Dealers Association. These dealers would buy and sell puts and calls for their own accounts for stocks traded on the New York Stock Exchange and then try to find an investor, hedger, or speculator to take the other side of the option. For example, if you owned 1,000 shares of Ford and you wanted to write a call option giving the buyer the right to buy 1,000 shares of Ford at $20 per share for six months, the dealer might buy the calls and look for someone who would be willing to buy them from him.

This system had several disadvantages. Dealers had to have contact with the buyers and sellers, and the financial stability of the option writer had to be endorsed (guaranteed) by a brokerage house. The option writer either had to keep the shares on deposit with the brokerage firm or put up a cash margin. Options in the same stock could exist in the market at various strike prices (price at which the option could be exercised) and scattered expiration

TABLE 14–1   Options Data, Options Clearing Corp.

	Equity Volume	Non-equity Volume	Total Volume	Average Daily Volume	Year-End Open Interest	Number of Equity Issues
2000	672,871,757	53,856,182	726,727,939	2,883,841	71,249,929	2,364
1999	444,765,224	63,126,259	507,891,483	2,015,442	56,907,365	2,579
1998	329,641,875	76,701,323	406,343,198	1,612,473	36,285,828	2,724
1997	272,998,701	80,824,417	353,823,118	1,398,510	28,677,748	2,400
1996	199,117,729	95,679,973	294,797,702	1,160,621	21,252,103	2,080
1995	174,380,236	112,916,673	287,296,909	1,140,068	18,836,632	1,720
1994	149,932,665	131,449,737	281,382,402	1,116,597	16,030,910	1,512
1993	131,726,101	100,935,994	232,662,095	919,614	14,778,179	1,294
1992	106,484,452	95,511,305	201,995,757	795,259	11,612,580	1,104
1991	104,850,686	93,950,914	198,801,600	785,777	9,311,298	937
1990	111,425,744	98,497,004	209,922,748	829,734	7,295,008	808
1989	141,839,748	85,176,912	227,016,660	900,860	9,013,121	701
1988	114,927,723	81,020,868	195,948,591	774,501	7,648,262	641
1987	164,431,851	140,737,084	305,168,935	1,206,201	8,073,498	590
1986	141,930,945	147,280,190	289,211,135	1,143,127	10,039,591	490
1985	118,555,989	114,354,558	232,910,547	924,248	10,443,038	462
1984	118,925,239	77,512,122	196,437,361	776,432	7,984,602	395
1983	135,658,976	14,397,099	150,056,075	593,107	12,499,329	936
1982	137,264,816	41,389	137,306,205	543,394	9,802,070	375
1981	109,405,782	0	109,405,782	432,434	9,495,497	354
1980	96,728,546	0	96,728,546	382,326	5,865,776	241
1979	64,264,863	0	64,264,863	254,011	4,199,696	220
1978	57,231,018	0	57,231,018	227,107	3,636,918	217
1977	39,637,328	0	39,637,328	157,291	3,343,185	222
1976	32,373,925	0	32,373,925	127,960	2,746,882	202
1975	18,103,018	0	18,103,018	71,553	1,109,227	44
1974	5,682,907	0	5,682,907	22,462	380,840	40
1973	1,119,245	0	1,119,245	6,470	242,825	32

Source: www.optionsclearing.com/press/vol num/volume_historical.isp, November 12, 2001.

dates. This meant that when an option buyer wanted to exercise or terminate the contract before expiration, he or she would have to deal directly with the option writer. This does not make for an efficient, liquid market. Unlisted options also reduced the striking price of a call by any dividends paid during the option period, which did not benefit the writer of the call.

Listed Options Exchanges

The Chicago Board Options Exchange was established in 1973 as the first exchange for call options. The market response was overwhelming, and within three years, the American, Pacific, and Philadelphia exchanges were also trading call options. By 2000 the list of options on equity issues had increased from the original list of 32 to 2,364 down from the peak of 2,724 in 1998. Nevertheless, the volume on the combined options exchanges set records in 2000 with average daily volume reaching 2,883,841 contracts each representing 100 shares of stock.

Table 14-1, from the Options Clearing Corporation's Web site (**www.options clearing.com**) shows the growth in options trading since 1973. Currently the American

Exchange (AMEX), the Philadelphia Exchange (PHLX), and the Pacific Coast Exchange (PSE) trade options in addition to the Chicago Board Options Exchange (CBOE), which is the dominant market participant. According to the CBOE's 2000 annual report, the CBOE holds a 45.5 percent market share based on average daily volume in 2000. The AMEX is in second place with 28.4 percent, followed by the PSE and the PHLX, with each having 10 to 15 percent of the volume.

One can now also buy a put or call option on *stock indexes* in addition to individual stock. For example, options on the Dow Jones Industrial Average and the Standard & Poor's 500 Stock Index are traded on the CBOE, and options on the New York Stock Exchange Index are traded on the NYSE.

There are several reasons the listed options markets are so desirable compared with the previous method of over-the-counter trading for options. The contract period was standardized with three-, six-, and nine-month expiration dates on three calendar cycles:

Cycle 1: January/April/July/October.
Cycle 2: February/May/August/November.
Cycle 3: March/June/September/December.

The use of three cycles spread out the expiration dates for the options so that not all contracts came due on the same day.[1] Each contract expires at 11:59 P.M. Eastern time on the Saturday immediately following the third Friday of the expiration month. For all practical purposes, any closing out of positions must be done on that last Friday while the markets are open.

In an attempt to satisfy demand for longer-term options, **long-term equity anticipation securities (LEAPS)** were added and provided options with up to two years of expiration. LEAPS have generally been limited to blue-chip stocks such as Coca-Cola, Dow Chemical, General Electric, IBM, and others. LEAPS have the same characteristics as the short-term options, but because of their length, they have higher prices.

Another important feature of option trading is the standardized **exercise price** (strike price). This is the price the contract specifies for a buy or sell. For all stocks over $25 per share, the striking price normally changes by $5 intervals, and for stocks selling under $25 per share, the strike price usually changes by $2.50 a share. As the underlying stocks change prices in the market, options with new striking prices are added. For example, a stock selling at $30 per share when the January option is added will have a striking price of 30, but if the stock gets to 32.50 (halfway to the next striking price), the exchange may add another option (to the class of options) with a 35 strike price.

This standardization of expiration dates and strike prices creates more certainty when buying and selling options in a changing market and allows more efficient trading strategies because of better coordination between stock prices, strike prices, and expiration dates. Dividends no longer affect the option contract as they did in the unlisted market. Transactions occur at arm's length between the buyer and seller without any direct matchmaking needed on the part of the broker. The ultimate result of these changes in the option market is a highly liquid, efficient market where speculators, hedgers, and arbitrageurs all operate together.

CISCO Systems call and put options are presented in Table 14–2 as an example of different strike prices (15, 17.50, 20, 22.50, 25) and expiration months of December, January, and April. Calls represent options to buy stock and puts represent options to sell stocks. CISCO Systems common stock closed at $18.93 on November 8, 2001, but during the last 52 weeks its price had fallen from a high of $57.63 to as low as $11.06. The values within Table 14–2, such as 4.20 and 4.50, reflect the price of the various options contracts. This information will take on greater meaning as we go through the chapter.

---

1. Additional cycles have also been added.

TABLE 14–2   CISCO Systems Prices on November 8, 2001

Closing Stock Price	Strike Price	Calls—Last			Puts—Last		
		December	January	April	December	January	April
$18.93	$15.00	$4.20	$4.50	n/a	$0.40	$0.65	n/a
18.93	17.50	2.40	2.80	n/a	1.05	1.40	n/a
18.93	20.00	1.10	1.50	$2.50	2.20	2.60	$3.40
18.93	22.50	0.40	0.70	1.60	3.70	4.20	5.00
18.93	25.00	n/a	0.30	1.10	n/a	6.30	7.10

Note: n/a indicates that the put or call was either not traded on that day or that the option was not offered.

THE OPTIONS CLEARING CORPORATION

Much of the liquidity and ease of operation of the option exchanges is due to the role of the **Options Clearing Corporation,** which functions as the issuer of all options listed on the four exchanges—the CBOE, the AMEX, the Philadelphia Exchange, and the Pacific Coast Exchange. Investors who want to trade puts and calls need to have an approved account with a member brokerage firm; on opening an account, they receive a prospectus from the Options Clearing Corporation detailing all aspects of option trading.

Options are bought and sold through a member broker the same as other securities. The exchanges allow special orders, such as limit, market, and stop orders, as well as orders used specifically in options trading, such as spread orders and straddle orders. The order process originates with the broker and is transacted on the floor of the exchange. Remember that for every order there must be a buyer and seller (writer) so that the orders can be "matched." Once the orders are matched, they are filed with the Options Clearing Corporation, which then issues the necessary options or closes the position.[2]

Option Premiums

Before investors or speculators can understand various option strategies, they must be able to comprehend what creates option premiums (prices). In Table 14–3, using CISCO Systems as an example, we can see that the common stock closed at $18.93 ($18^{93}$) per share and that calls and puts are available at a variety of strike prices ranging from $15 to $25. Calls allow the option holder to buy the stock at the strike price. The January 17.50 calls closed at 2.80 ($280 for one call on 100 shares), while the January 20 call closed at 1.50. The 15 and 17.50 call options are said to be **in the money** because the market price of $18.93 is above the **strike** (or purchase) **price** of 15 and 17.50. The 20, 22.50 and 25 calls **are out of the money** because the strike price is above the market price. If CISCO common were trading at 20, the calls with a strike price of 20 would be **at the money** because the stock price and the strike price are equal. In this example, the stock price of $18.93 is 1.07 away from the January 20 put and call. Puts are the opposite of calls. Because the put allows the holder to sell the stock at the strike price, in the money puts would have strike prices greater than $18.93 and out of the money puts would have strike prices less than $18.93.

Intrinsic Value

In the money *call* options have an **intrinsic value** equal to the market price minus the strike price. In the case of the CISCO January 17.50 call, the intrinsic value is 1.43 as indicated by Formula 14–1:

---

2. In a transaction, holders and writers of options are not contractually linked but are committed to the Options Clearing Corporation.

$$\text{Intrinsic value (call)} = \text{Market price} - \text{Strike price} \qquad (14\text{-}1)$$
$$= \$18.93 - \$17.50$$
$$= \$1.43 \text{ (CISCO January 17.50 call)}$$

Options that are out of the money have no positive intrinsic value. If we use Formula 14-1 for the CISCO January 20 call, we calculate a negative intrinsic value of 1.07. When the market price minus the strike price is negative, the negative value represents the amount the stock price must increase to have the option at the money where the strike price and market price are equal. In actual practice, an option cannot have a negative value.

The intrinsic value for the in the money put options equals the strike price minus the market price. In the case of the CISCO January 20 put, the intrinsic value is 1.07 as indicated by Formula 14-2. Notice that this in the money put has the opposite value from the call:

$$\text{Intrinsic value (put)} = \text{Strike price} - \text{Market price} \qquad (14\text{-}2)$$
$$= \$20.00 - \$18.93$$
$$= \$1.07 \text{ (CISCO January 20.00 put)}$$

Because puts allow the owner to sell stock at the strike price, in-the-money put options exist where the strike price is above the market price of the stock. Out-of-the money puts have market prices for common stock above the strike price.

Speculative Premium

Returning to the CISCO January 17.50 call, we see in Table 14-3 that the total premium is 2.80, while the previously computed intrinsic value is 1.43. This call option has an additional **speculative premium** of 1.37 due to other factors. The total premium (option price) is a combination of the intrinsic value plus a speculative premium. This relationship is indicated in Formula 14-3 and shown in Figure 14-1:

$$\text{Total premium} = \text{Intrinsic value} + \text{Speculative premium} \qquad (14\text{-}3)$$
$$= 1.43 + 1.37$$
$$= 2.80$$

Generally, the higher the volatility of the common stock—as measured by the stock price's standard deviation or by its beta—and the lower the dividend yield, the greater the speculative premium.[3] The longer the exercise period, the higher the speculative premium, especially if market expectations over the duration of the option are positive. Finally, the deeper the option is in the money, the smaller the leverage potential and therefore the smaller the speculative premium. Most often, we examine the speculative premium separately to see if it is a reasonable premium to pay for the possible benefits.

The speculative premium can be expressed in dollars or as a percentage of the common stock price. A speculative premium expressed in percent indicates the increase in the stock price needed for the purchaser of a call option to break even on the expiration date. Table 14-4 shows this point.[4] Notice that the CISCO January 15 call option, which is deep in the money, has the lowest speculative premium, while the 25 call option has the highest. Realize that the 25 call option has a cash value of only 0.30 (the total premium), and the other 6.07 represents the required increase in the stock price for the market price and the strike price to be equal. The 33.65 percent speculative premium for the January 25 call option represents the percentage movement in stock price by the expiration date for a break-even position. At expiration, there will be no speculative premium. The option will reflect only the intrinsic value and possibly even a discount because of commission expenses incurred on exercise.

---

3. Some people refer to the speculative premium as the time premium because time may be the overriding factor affecting the speculative premium.

4. As applied to put options, the speculative premium indicates the decrease in stock price needed for the purchaser of a put option to break even on the expiration date.

TABLE 14–3   Listed Options Quotations

OPTION/ STRIKE		EXP.	CALL VOL.	CALL LAST	PUT VOL.	PUT LAST
AmOnline	30	Jan	34	6^{40}	2060	1^{55}
34^{50}	30	Apr	5515	7^{90}	113	2^{65}
34^{50}	32^{50}	Nov	961	2^{60}	1994	0^{55}
34^{50}	35	Nov	1262	0^{95}	506	1^{30}
34^{50}	40	Dec	1942	0^{55}	2	5^{70}
34^{50}	40	Apr	11015	2^{50}	21	7^{40}
ATT Wrls	15	Jan	3654	1^{55}	…	…
15^{32}	20	Jan	1988	0^{20}	…	…
AT&T	15	Dec	1521	1^{90}	440	0^{60}
16^{05}	17^{50}	Nov	1624	0^{10}	21	1^{30}
Abbt L	45	Nov	3250	9	…	…
53^{77}	55	May	7002	3^{90}	…	…
Adelph	25	Apr	1000	3	1500	5^{20}
A M D	10	Jan	4261	4^{30}	350	0^{50}
13^{52}	12^{50}	Nov	2384	1^{25}	1134	0^{30}
13^{52}	15	Nov	2015	0^{20}	186	1^{55}
13^{52}	15	Jan	1651	1^{30}	190	2^{55}
Aetna	30	Nov	473	2^{60}	7183	0^{75}
Alcoa	40	Jan	2209	0^{60}	2	6^{50}
Altera	25	Nov	1699	1^{20}	1187	1^{58}
Amazon	7^{50}	Jan	4054	1^{45}	143	1^{45}
Amdocs	30	Nov	1806	0^{75}	351	2
AmExpr	30	Nov	1868	1^{80}	2093	0^{30}
31^{65}	32^{50}	Nov	2096	0^{40}	55	1^{95}
AmIntGp	85	Nov	3792	0^{30}	12	4^{30}
80^{97}	85	Feb	2950	3^{40}	…	…
Amercrd	30	Dec	1740	0^{45}	…	…
Amgen	60	Jan	285	4^{40}	4097	4^{30}
Analog	45	Dec	764	5^{30}	2777	5^{20}
45^{25}	55	Jun	1789	5^{90}	…	…
Aon Cp	37^{50}	Nov	75	0^{55}	1844	1^{80}
35^{95}	40	Nov	2640	0^{10}	112	3^{80}
ApdidMat	35	Nov	892	4^{08}	1688	0^{50}
39^{34}	37^{50}	Dec	170	4^{90}	1836	2^{60}
39^{34}	40	Nov	1964	1^{40}	611	2^{10}
39^{34}	40	Dec	403	3^{30}	2823	3^{70}
AMCC	12^{50}	Dec	1322	1^{90}	460	1^{95}
BEA Sys	15	Nov	10429	0^{80}	699	1^{05}
14^{71}	17^{50}	Nov	1310	0^{25}	117	2^{80}
Bk ofAm	65	Nov	1687	50	187	2^{70}
Baxter	47^{50}	Nov	1825	1^{50}	23	1^{10}
47^{85}	50	Nov	3272	0^{55}	621	2^{35}
BecDic	40	Dec	3070	1	20	3^{50}
BestBuy	55	Nov	22	6^{90}	1346	0^{50}
Biogen	55	Nov	66	3	2535	0^{55}
BiotechT	130	Nov	46	6^{70}	1583	2^{20}
Biovail	50	Nov	257	0^{25}	1526	4^{10}
45^{75}	50	Dec	2014	1^{85}	20	4
BrMySq	55	Nov	467	1	2347	1^{40}
54^{26}	55	Dec	2101	2^{50}	344	2^{45}
Broadcom	35	Nov	311	6^{50}	4513	0^{70}
40^{75}	40	Nov	1052	2^{95}	1401	2^{05}
Brocade	25	Nov	587	5^{90}	2098	0^{35}
30^{51}	30	Nov	2561	2	1216	1^{70}
30^{51}	30	Dec	5280	4^{60}	133	4^{10}
BurlRs	35	Dec	…	…	2403	1^{60}
Calpine	25	Jan	29	2^{80}	1620	3^{30}
24^{52}	30	Jan	1690	1^{20}	2	6^{40}
CaremkRx	12^{50}	Nov	1529	1	15	0^{35}
Caterp	50	May	3201	4^{10}	3000	6^{10}
Celestica	35	Mar	…	…	2616	4^{10}

OPTION/ STRIKE		EXP.	CALL VOL.	CALL LAST	PUT VOL.	PUT LAST
40^{28}	35	Jun	…	…	2500	5^{30}
ChkPoint	35	Nov	2515	1^{30}	781	2
Chiron	55	Nov	9	2^{60}	1252	1^{65}
55^{36}	60	Dec	2654	2^{40}	20	6^{70}
CienaCp	15	Nov	839	2^{50}	13249	0^{63}
17^{40}	17^{50}	Nov	17604	1^{20}	964	1^{53}
17^{40}	20	Nov	3487	0^{35}	71	3^{10}
17^{40}	20	Dec	1304	1^{70}	46	4^{70}
Cisco	15	Nov	2254	3^{80}	890	0^{95}
18^{93}	15	Dec	1018	4^{20}	1666	0^{40}
18^{93}	15	Jan	3227	4^{50}	1050	0^{83}
18^{33}	17^{50}	Nov	10143	1^{65}	3822	0^{30}
18^{93}	17^{50}	Dec	2400	2^{48}	1930	1^{05}
18^{93}	17^{50}	Jan	2184	2^{50}	1354	1^{40}
18^{93}	20	Nov	13943	0^{75}	3503	1^{40}
18^{93}	20	Dec	17538	1^{10}	866	2^{20}
18^{93}	20	Jan	23188	1^{50}	538	2^{50}
18^{93}	20	Apr	2578	2^{50}	453	3^{40}
18^{93}	22^{50}	Dec	1925	0^{40}	227	3^{70}
18^{93}	22^{50}	Jan	3508	0^{70}	191	4^{20}
18^{93}	22^{50}	Apr	1370	1^{60}	286	5
18^{93}	25	Jan	2359	0^{30}	216	6^{30}
18^{93}	25	Apr	4827	1^{10}	85	7^{10}
Citigrp	47^{50}	Nov	3439	1^{30}	982	0^{90}
48^{10}	47^{50}	Dec	1605	2^{60}	1530	2
48^{10}	50	Dec	1829	1^{35}	128	3^{40}
CirtixSy	25	Nov	2727	1^{50}	1310	1
Comeric	50	Jan	1500	2^{70}	1500	3^{60}
Compaq	5	Jan	224	3^{40}	7650	0^{15}
7^{99}	7^{50}	Nov	2006	0^{75}	1735	0^{20}
7^{99}	7^{50}	Dec	7929	1^{15}	2170	0^{65}
7^{99}	7^{50}	Jan	1954	1^{40}	8117	0^{85}
7^{99}	10	Jan	1328	0^{45}	123	2^{45}
CompAsc	30	Dec	1186	1^{90}	1525	2^{40}
ConAgr	25	Dec	2012	0^{70}	…	…
24^{70}	25	Mar	2009	1^{25}	…	…
Conexnt	10	Nov	1266	3^{30}	…	…
13^{19}	12^{50}	Nov	1512	1^{10}	164	040
CoAir B	20	Dec	1461	1^{15}	…	…
Cooper	30	Nov	…	…	1806	0^{45}
40	30	Dec	…	…	2900	1^{45}
40	45	Dec	1937	2^{40}	…	…
Corning	7^{50}	Dec	4099	1^{70}	10	0^{35}
8^{75}	10	Dec	1274	0^{50}	52	1^{75}
Dell Cptr	20	Feb	12	7^{70}	4053	0^{85}
26^{25}	22^{50}	Nov	586	3^{80}	3836	0^{15}
26^{25}	25	Nov	2131	1^{70}	2456	0^{50}
28^{25}	27^{50}	Nov	4424	0^{40}	807	1^{80}
26^{25}	27^{50}	Dec	6752	1^{40}	323	2^{70}
Dow Ch	35	Dec	3765	2^{50}	211	1^{25}
Dynegy	35	Nov	3245	1^{35}	2816	3^{50}
33	35	Dec	738	3^{20}	3901	5^{30}
33	40	Dec	3665	1^{20}	101	8^{20}
ETradeGr	5	Jan	54	3	3855	0^{15}
eBay	40	Nov	…	…	5075	0^{10}
56^{59}	50	Nov	141	7^{90}	1654	0^{75}
56^{59}	55	Nov	659	3^{20}	2772	1^{85}
56^{59}	60	Nov	2093	0^{90}	253	4^{50}
EMC	12^{50}	Nov	1899	2^{75}	721	0^{10}
15^{02}	12^{50}	Jan	1282	3^{50}	1678	0^{88}
15^{02}	12^{50}	Apr	3012	4^{50}	89	1^{50}

OPTION/ STRIKE		EXP.	CALL VOL.	CALL LAST	PUT VOL.	PUT LAST
15^{02}	15	Nov	5919	0^{75}	903	0^{70}
15^{02}	15	Dec	18892	1^{59}	506	1^{50}
15^{02}	15	Jan	2265	1^{95}	200	1^{85}
15^{02}	17^{80}	Jan	2973	0^{95}	7	3^{50}
EKodak	30	Nov	116	1^{45}	8122	5^{60}
EchoStr	25	Dec	2815	1^{11}	93	1^{95}
24^{53}	25	Mar	1500	2^{70}	…	…
Enron	5	Nov	795	4^{20}	9849	0^{15}
9^{05}	5	Dec	630	3^{40}	4872	0^{65}
9^{05}	5	Jan	359	5^{10}	6679	0^{80}
9^{05}	5	Apr	182	5^{10}	2738	1^{15}
9^{05}	7^{50}	Nov	17672	2^{30}	16933	0^{60}
9^{05}	7^{50}	Dec	5395	3^{10}	10832	1^{80}
9^{05}	7^{50}	Jan	2005	3^{30}	1890	1^{75}
9^{05}	10	Nov	30148	0^{95}	15170	2^{75}
9^{05}	10	Dec	8830	1^{90}	1149	2^{95}
9^{05}	10	Jan	6840	2^{20}	850	3^{10}
9^{05}	10	Apr	1944	2^{85}	1550	3^{50}
9^{05}	12^{50}	Nov	5980	0^{50}	1585	3^{80}
9^{05}	12^{50}	Dec	2254	1^{05}	407	4^{50}
9^{05}	12^{50}	Jan	3932	1^{45}	741	5^{40}
9^{05}	12^{50}	Apr	1388	2	56	5^{70}
9^{05}	15	Nov	4964	0^{20}	8050	6^{20}
9^{05}	15	Dec	4733	0^{50}	559	6^{50}
9^{05}	15	Jan	2490	0^{30}	367	7
9^{05}	15	Apr	2171	1^{35}	50	7^{50}
Enzon	60	Nov	21	3^{30}	1340	2^{05}
Eqty Resd	27^{50}	Jan	1614	0^{65}	…	…
ExtrNetw	12^{50}	Nov	1356	2^{50}	170	0^{55}
FleetBost	40	Dec	2722	0^{40}	…	…
Foundry	12^{50}	Dec	9446	1^{20}	…	…
FHLB	70	Apr	6032	5^{30}	1010	4^{50}
70^{79}	75	Apr	2510	2^{95}	…	…
Gap	15	Mar	3	1^{55}	1700	2^{45}
Gen El	40	Nov	1910	0^{65}	1398	1^{45}
39^{35}	40	Dec	1942	1^{85}	338	2^{25}
GoldmnS	85	Nov	2249	3^{50}	1953	1^{95}
87^{50}	90	Nov	1629	0^{80}	31	3^{50}
HarleyDav	45	Nov	30	2	2309	1^{20}
45^{94}	50	Dec	392	1^{40}	1667	5^{70}
45^{94}	55	Feb	3740	1^{45}	51	9^{60}
HewlettPk	20	Nov	1301	0^{45}	1264	1^{45}
19^{18}	20	Dec	2192	1^{20}	977	2^{10}
HomeDp	50	Nov	4478	0^{05}	2	7^{40}
Honwell Int	32^{50}	Mar	1805	2^{35}	2030	4^{10}
i2 Tech s	5	Nov	1915	1^{45}	65	0^{10}
6^{42}	7^{50}	Nov	1308	0^{20}	253	1^{10}
6^{42}	7^{50}	Dec	1657	0^{65}	…	…
Inktomi	5	Jan	2090	0^{95}	…	…
Intel	20	Jan	55	8^{80}	3765	0^{35}
28^{29}	20	Apr	6	9^{40}	5115	0^{80}
28^{29}	22^{50}	Nov	1706	5^{80}	412	0^{10}
28^{29}	25	Nov	3129	3^{50}	2206	0^{15}
28^{29}	25	Jan	1516	4^{60}	818	1^{25}
28^{29}	27^{50}	Nov	3425	1^{40}	2724	0^{70}
28^{29}	30	Nov	6312	0^{30}	2999	2
28^{29}	30	Dec	5176	1^{20}	139	2^{90}
28^{29}	30	Jan	8659	1^{80}	306	3^{60}
28^{29}	32^{50}	Jan	2006	0^{95}	…	…
I B M	100	Nov	6868	15^{20}	116	0^{10}
113^{85}	105	Nov	1695	10	553	0^{30}

FIGURE 14–1   Components of the Total Premium on a Call Option

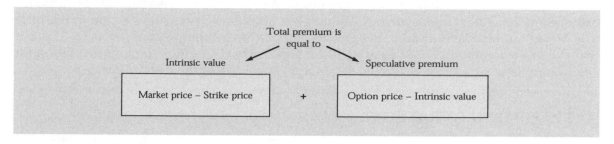

TABLE 14–4   Speculative Premiums on November 8, 2001 for CISCO Systems January Options

Market Price on November 8	Strike Price	Total Premium	−	Intrinsic Value	=	Speculative Premium	Speculative Premium as a Percentage of Stock Price
$18.93	$15.00 Jan Call	$4.50		$3.93		$0.57	3.01%
18.93	17.50 Jan Call	2.80		1.43		1.37	7.24
18.93	20.00 Jan Call	1.50		−1.07		2.57	13.58
18.93	22.50 Jan Call	0.70		−3.57		4.27	22.56
18.93	25.00 Jan Call	0.30		−6.07		6.37	33.65

Speculative Premiums and the Time Factor   Table 14–5 provides a look at premiums for the in the money and out of the money call options with varying times to expiration. Since the quotes are as of November, the December options will expire first, then the January options, and finally the April options. The option premiums increase with more time to expiration.

CISCO's speculative premiums in Table 14–5 demonstrate that percentage speculative premiums increase with time across all series of strike prices. The speculative premiums are lowest with the in-the-money 15 and 17.50 calls because of the low leverage potential and

TABLE 14–5   Speculative Premiums over Time (CISCO Call Options, November 8, 2001)

Market Price	Strike Price	December Total Premium Option (Price)	Speculative Dollars	Premium Percent	January Total Premium (Option Price)	Speculative Dollars	Premium Percent	April Total Premium (Option Price)	Speculative Dollars	Premium Percent
$18.93	$15.00	$4.20	$0.27	1.43%	$4.50	$0.57	3.01%	n/a	n/a	n/a
18.93	17.50	2.40	0.97	5.12	2.80	1.37	7.24	n/a	n/a	n/a
18.93	20.00	1.10	2.17	11.46	1.50	2.57	13.58	$2.50	$3.57	18.86%
18.93	22.50	0.40	3.97	20.97	0.70	4.27	22.56	1.60	5.17	27.31
18.93	25.00	n/a	n/a	n/a	0.30	6.37	33.65	1.10	7.17	37.88

CISCO's 52 Week High = 57.63; low 11.06.

Source: *The Wall Street Journal*, November 9, 2001.

the downside risk if the stock declines. The 25 call option has a high speculative premium, but an option writer (seller) *would not reap much cash inflow*. Generally, out-of-the-money call options have high speculative premiums, but little of the premium may be in the form of cash. As previously indicated, the January 25 call has a total premium of 0.30. The fact that the cash premium is only $0.30 ($30 on 100 shares) is an important consideration for an option writer. Commissions would eat up a good portion of the cash inflow.

BASIC OPTION STRATEGIES

Option strategies can be very aggressive and risky, or they can be quite conservative and used as a means of reducing risk. Option buyers and writers both attempt to take advantage of the option premiums discussed in the preceding section. In theory, many option strategies can be created, but in practice, the market must be liquid enough to execute these strategies. After a decade of explosive growth, option volume on individual common stocks has not expanded as much in the 1980s and 1990s as in the first years of the Chicago Board Options Exchange. Although volume on the underlying common stock has continued to increase, much of the option activity has been absorbed by options on the Standard & Poor's 100 and 500 Stock Indexes, where large institutional investors can transact portfolio strategies on the market rather than on individual stocks.

A reduction of individual option trading reduces the ability to create workable strategies for specific companies. For example, the lack of a liquid market can keep institutional investors from executing hedging strategies involving several hundred thousand shares. Even with these limitations in mind, the average investor can still find many opportunities for option strategies. In this section, we discuss the possible uses of calls and puts to achieve different investment goals. Table 14-6 provides option quotes as of three different dates for our examples. All the options expire in November 2001. We ignored commissions in most examples, but commissions can be a significant hidden cost in some types of option strategies.

Buying Call Options

The Leverage Strategy   Leverage is a very common reason for buying call options when the market is expected to rise during the exercise period. The use of calls in this way is similar to warrants discussed earlier, but calls have shorter lives. The call option is priced much lower than common stock, and the leverage is derived from a small percentage change in the price of the call option. For example, on September 28, 2001, CISCO Systems common stock closed at $12.18 per share and the November 15 call option closed at $0.40 (see Table 14-6).

About three weeks later, on October 19, 2001, the stock closed at $16.72 for a $4.54 gain on the stock or 37.27 percent ($4.54/$12.18). The November 15 call option closed at $2.35 on October 18, 2001, for a $1.95 gain of 487.5 percent ($1.95/$0.40). The call option increased by 13.1 times the percentage move of the common stock over this three-week span. The relationship is indicated below:

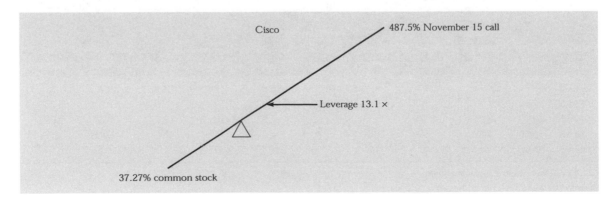

TABLE 14–6   November Call Option Quotes over Three Months

Company Name	Expiration Month	Strike Price	September 28, 2001 49 days to expiration		October 19, 2001 28 days to expiration		November 2, 2001 14 days to expiration	
			Option Price	Common Stock Price	Option Price	Common Stock Price	Option Price	Common Stock Price
America Online	November	$ 30.00	n/a	$33.10	$2.80	$ 31.17	$2.85	$ 32.01
America Online	November	32.50	n/a	33.10	1.60	31.17	1.35	32.01
America Online	November	35.00	$1.95	33.10	0.75	31.17	0.35	32.01
America Online	November	40.00	0.55	33.10	0.15	31.17	n/a	32.01
Boeing	November	35.00	2.00	33.50	1.25	33.45	0.95	34.35
CISCO	November	15.00	0.40	12.18	2.35	16.72	2.50	17.26
CISCO	November	17.50	0.15	12.18	1.00	16.72	0.90	17.26
CISCO	November	20.00	n/a	n/a	0.30	16.72	0.25	17.26
Dell	November	20.00	2.40	18.53	1.60	24.05	n/a	24.92
Dell	November	22.50	1.25	18.53	2.65	24.05	n/a	24.92
Dell	November	25.00	1.05	21.55	1.35	24.05	1.05	24.92
Hewlett-Packard	November	17.50	2.00	18.08	1.30	18.29	0.50	16.92
Home Depot	November	40.00	2.10	38.37	2.40	40.41	1.60	40.32
Home Depot	November	45.00	n/a	n/a	n/a	40.41	0.20	40.32
IBM	November	100.00	2.40	91.72	5.80	102.65	n/a	109.50
IBM	November	110.00	1.25	91.72	1.50	102.65	2.45	109.50
Intel	November	20.00	2.60	20.39	n/a	24.15	6.50	26.30
Intel	November	25.00	0.45	20.39	1.15	24.15	2.05	26.30
Oracle	November	12.50	1.35	12.58	n/a	14.54	2.05	14.45
Oracle	November	15.00	0.45	12.58	0.95	14.54	0.45	14.45
WorldCom	November	15.00	1.20	15.04	0.30	13.17	0.15	13.48

Note: n/a indicates that the quote was not available because the option did not trade on that date or was not yet listed because the stock price was too far below the strike price.

Source: *Barron's*, October 1, 2001; October 22, 2001; November 5, 2001.

Figure 14–2 depicts the relationship between profit and loss opportunities for the CISCO November 15 call option, assuming the option is held until the day of expiration (no speculative premium exists at expiration).

As long as the common stock closes under 15, the call buyer loses the whole premium of $0.40 (100 × $0.40 = $40). At a price of $15.40 the call buyer breaks even because the option is worth an intrinsic value of $0.40. As the stock increases past $15.40, the profit starts accumulating. At a price of $19.40, the profit equals $400 at expiration. If the option is sold before expiration, a speculative premium may increase the profit potential.

An investor striving for maximum leverage generally buys options that are out of the money or slightly in the money. Buying high-priced options for $10 or $15 that are well in the money limits the potential for leverage. You may have to invest almost as much in the options as you would in the stock.

Playing the leverage game doesn't always work. Let's once again look at Table 14–6. If, on September 28, 2001, a speculator assumed that Hewlett-Packard would go up and bought the November 17.50 call option for $2.00, approximately one month later, on November 2, 2001, the Hewlett-Packard call option would have been worth $0.50 per share. A $1.50 loss occurred in the option price. The decline in Hewlett-Packard stock from $18.08 to $16.92 was only $1.16, or a 6.4 percent loss, while at the same time the option lost 75 percent of its value, going from $2.00 to $0.50. A loss of $1.50 per share would equal a $150 loss on one call option. If the stock price stays below $17.50 until expiration, the owner of the

FIGURE 14–2   CISCO November 15 Call Option (excludes commissions)

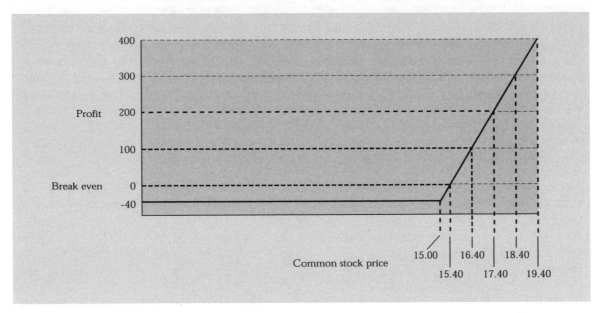

November 17.50 call can expect to lose the current call premium of $0.50. It is not hard to lose all your money under these circumstances—leverage works in reverse, too.

Call Options Instead of Stock   Many people do not like to risk large amounts of money and view call options as a way of controlling 100 shares of stock without a large dollar commitment. For example, assume you could buy 100 shares of common stock for $40 per share ($4,000) or a call option with a strike price of 40 at a cost of $4 or $400. You choose to spend the $400 and invest the $3,600 difference ($4,000 − $400) in short-term money market securities at 4 percent. The call option has six months to expiration. During the six months your common stock falls from $40 per share to $30 per share, and your call option is worthless at expiration. During this time your short-term money market securities have generated $72 of interest income[5] which helps offset your $400 loss on your call option. Your total loss on your call investment was $328 ($400 − $72) but if you had bought the common stock, you would have lost $1,000, or $10 per share on 100 shares. During much of 2000 and 2001 while stock prices were falling, this strategy would have reduced an investor's losses. This strategy worked to the investor's advantage because in the end the loss was less for owning the call option than it would have been for owning 100 shares of stock outright.[6] This will not always be the case.

Had your stock only declined in value by 1¢ to $39.99, you still would have lost $328 on your call option. If you had bought the stock you would have only lost $1.00 (1¢ × 100 shares). One thing to remember is that the purchaser of the call option cannot lose more than the initial purchase price of $400. This will be slightly offset by the $72 of interest earned. Of course, there is the possibility that the stock rises to $50 per share and both the stock purchaser and the option purchaser will show profits. Paying commissions to buy and sell will reduce profits.

---

5. The approximate calculation is $3,600 × 4% × 180/360 = $72.
6. It should be pointed out we are talking about absolute dollar losses. On a percentage basis, the options would be the bigger losers.

Protecting a Short Position   Calls are often used to cover a short sale against the risk of rising stock prices. This is called hedging your position. By purchasing a call, the short seller guarantees a loss of no more than a fixed amount while at the same time reducing any potential profit by the total premium paid for the call. Again refer to Table 14-6, and assume you sold 100 shares of Intel short at $20.39 on September 28, 2001, and bought a November 25 call for $0.45 as protection against a rise in the price of the stock. By November 2, 2001, the stock rises to $26.30 for a $591 loss on the short position [($26.30 − $20.39) × 100 shares]. This loss has been partially offset by an increase in the November 25 call option price from $0.45 to $2.05, or a $160 gain [($2.05 − $0.45) × 100 shares = $160]. The loss on the short sale has been cut from $591 to $431, or reduced by the $160 profit on the call option.

Reconsider the initial $0.45 call premium. If the stock goes up, the call limits your loss, but if the stock goes down as expected, your profit on the short position may be reduced by the call premium. If Intel had declined to $18 and generated a profit of $2.39 ($20.39 − $18) per share, this gain would have been reduced by the loss of $0.45 on the call option. Writing a call to protect a short sale is equivalent to buying an insurance policy that you hope you won't need.

Guaranteed Price   Often, an investor thinks a stock will rise over the long term but does not have cash currently available to purchase the stock. The important point for this strategy is that the investor wants to own this stock eventually but does not want to miss out on a good buying opportunity (based on expectations). Perhaps the oil stocks are depressed, or semiconductors have hit bottom. A call option can be utilized. The investor could be anticipating a cash inflow in the future when he or she plans to exercise the call option with a tax refund, a book royalty check, or even the annual bonus.

Please refer back to Table 14-6. On September 28, 2001, assume an investor buys an Oracle November 12.50 call option for $1.35. The intrinsic value for the November 12.50 call option is $0.08 because the stock is selling for $12.58 per share. The speculative premium is equal to the option price of $1.35 minus the intrinsic value of $0.08, or $1.27. By November 2, 2001, she has received her $1,250 royalty check and exercises the option to buy the stock at $12.50 when the stock is selling at $14.45. For tax purposes the cost or basis of these 100 shares of Oracle is the strike price of $12.50 plus the option premium of $1.35, or a total cost of $13.85 per share. If she had waited until November 2, 2001, to buy the stock she would have paid an extra $0.60 per share above $13.85, or $14.45. Her strategy locked in a guaranteed price just as it was supposed to. There is always the possibility that the stock price declines to below your strike price; in that case, you buy the stock in the market directly and consider your option premium an insurance policy.

Writing Call Options

Writers of call options take the opposite side of the market from buyers. The writer is similar to a short seller in that he or she expects the stock to decline or stay the same. For short sellers to profit, prices must decline, but because writers of call options receive a premium, they can make a profit if prices stay the same or even rise less than the speculative premium. Option writers can write **covered options**, meaning they own the underlying common stock, or they can write **naked options**, meaning they do not own the underlying stock.

Writing covered call options is often considered a hedged position because if the stock price declines, the writer's loss on the stock is partially offset by the option premium. A potential writer of a covered call must decide if he is willing to sell the underlying stock if it closes above the strike price. If not, the writer must repurchase the call option before the option is exercised by the owner.

Returning to Table 14-6 for another set of option quotes, find the Boeing November 35 call options on September 28, 2001. The market price of the common stock is $33.50 and the writer for a November 35 call option will receive $2.00 per share.

Remember, the writer agrees to sell 100 shares at the 35 strike price as the consideration for the premium. The 35 call option would be a good write if the stock closed at

FIGURE 14–3   Boeing 35 November Call, Payoff Graph for Writing One Naked Call

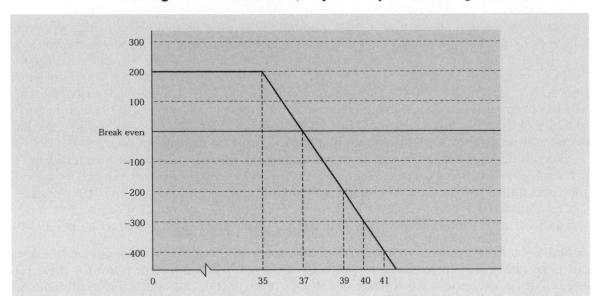

$35 per share or less because the call would not get exercised and the writer would keep the $2.00 premium. If the stock closed at $35 or higher, then the call could get exercised, and the writer would have to deliver 100 shares at $35. More likely, the option writer would buy back the option for its price in the market to avoid having the option exercised. If the ending value of the stock were 40, the option writer could buy back the 35 call for 5. The purchase at $5 would be offset by the initial receipt of the $2 premium and the total loss before commissions would be $3. Figure 14-3 shows this relationship between profit and loss and the common stock price in writing a naked option.

Let's now go to covered call options. Assume an investor bought 100 shares of Boeing at $33.50 on September 28, 2001. He also sold a November 35 call option for $2. If the stock ends up at $35, he will make a profit of $350. A $150 capital gain on the stock (100 shares × $1.50) plus the $200 option premium (100 × $2). Of course, if the stock really goes up in value, the covered call option writer will wish he had not written the call option. The increased cost to buy back the option will severely cut into the profit on the long position in the stock.

Let's look at what actually happened with Boeing. By November 2, 2001, Boeing stock closed at $34.35, and at that point, the cover call writer would make money, and a naked call writer would also make money. The covered call writer is assumed to have bought 100 shares at $33.50 per share at the time he or she wrote the option for $2.00 on September 28, 2001. The naked option writer merely sold the option for $2.00. It is further assumed the covered option writer would receive a $17 dividend during the period. Also note that the November 35 option is only worth $0.95 on November 2. The analysis is presented below:

Covered Writer		Naked Writer	
− Initial investment (100 × 33.50)	−$3,350.00	− Margin (30% × $3,350)	−$1,005.00
+ Option premium (100 × 2.00)	200.00	+ Option premium	200.00
+ Dividend	17.00	(no dividends received)	
+ Ending stock value (100 × 34.35)	3,435.00	+ Ending value margin	1,005.00
Gain	302.00	Gain	200.00
Investment = $3,350 − $200.00	$3,150.00	Investment	$1,005.00
Percent return on initial investment	9.6%	Return on investment	19.9%

Because the stock price ended at less than the strike price, neither the covered writer nor the naked writer needed to buy back their option as of November 2, 2001. They both had profits—with the covered writer ahead of the naked writer by $102 with $17 from the dividend and $85 from the capital gain on the stock, while the naked writer was ahead in percentage terms (19.9 percent versus 9.6 percent) because of a smaller initial investment. The naked writer was required to put up a margin on 30 percent of the value of the stock to ensure the ability to close out the option write if the stock should rise significantly. The capital was returned to the naked call writer when it was no longer needed as collateral. If the stock price had risen, the naked writer was exposed to unlimited risk because he either had to close out the position at a loss or purchase the stock above the strike price and deliver it at a loss. The covered writer had limited risk because she owned the stock and could deliver it or close out the position before it was called.

Another critical decision for a call writer is the choice of months. In the section on option premiums, we examined percentage premiums per day and found that the shortest expiration dates usually provided the highest daily speculative premium. In most cases, the call writer chooses the short-term options and as they expire, writes another short-term option. Annualized returns of 12 to 15 percent are not uncommon for continuously covered writing strategies.

Buying Put Options

The owner (buyer) of a put may sell 100 shares of stock to the put writer at the strike price. The strategy behind a put is similar to selling short or writing a call except losses are limited to the total investment (premium), and no more risk exposure is possible if the stock rises. Buying a put in anticipation of a price decline is one method of speculating on market price changes. The same factors influencing call premiums also apply to put premiums except that expectations for the direction for the market are the opposite.

Let's assume that the New Age Internet Co. was selling at $50 per share in July 2001, already down from its all-time high of $200 per share. You expected it to decline and possibly collapse as many other "new economy" companies had already done. You decided to buy a put rather than sell the stock short because you did not want to take the risk of unlimited loss if the stock should reverse and go back to $200. You found an at-the-money 50 put with an expiration date of April 2002 for an option premium of $7. This was a high premium, but New Age had been a quite volatile stock and often moved $4 or $5 per share in one day.

You bought the put for $700 and hoped that the stock fell. By April 2002, the company was almost bankrupt and the stock was selling at $5 per share, and at expiration your put option had an intrinsic value of $45 per share. For your $700 investment you received $4,500 when you sold the put for a profit of $3,800 on a $700 investment. These are stories that are nice to make up and in theory it would be nice if speculators who bought puts could profit as handily as this example. Puts make money in down markets.

Puts can also help an investor offset a potential decline in the price of common stock that you continue to hold for tax purposes. For example, assume you own ABZ Company at a gain and you would like to defer taking a profit until next year. You can protect yourself from a decline in the stock price by buying a put. If the stock falls, the put will make money as the stock loses money. In this case the put becomes an insurance policy against the potential decline in the stock. You can hold the put along with your stock and keep buying new puts if necessary until you are ready to sell your stock.

USING OPTIONS IN COMBINATIONS
Spreads

Now that you have studied puts and calls from both the buyer's and writer's perspectives, we briefly proceed with a discussion of spreads. Most combinations of options are called

spreads and consist of buying one option (going long) and writing an option (going short) on the same underlying stock. Spreads are for the sophisticated investor and involve many variations on a theme.

Straddles

A **straddle** is a combination of a put and call on the same stock with the same strike price and expiration date. It is used to play wide fluctuations in stock prices and is usually applied to individual stocks with high betas and a history of large, short-term fluctuations in price. The speculator using a straddle may be unsure of the direction of the price movement but may be able to make a large enough profit on one side of the straddle to cover the cost of both options even if one option expires worthless.

For example, assume a put and a call can be bought for $5 apiece on ABC October 50s when ABC Corporation is selling at 50 with six months to expiration. The total investment is 10 ($1,000). If the stock should rise from 50 to 65 at expiration, the call would provide a profit of 10 (15 value − 5 cost), and the put would be left to expire worthless for a loss of 5. This would provide a net gain of 5, or $500. The same type of example can be drawn if the price goes way down. Some who engage in spreads or straddles might attempt to close out one position before the other. This expands the profit potential but also increases the risk.

OTHER OPTION CONSIDERATIONS

Many factors have not been covered in detail because of their changing nature over time. Tax laws relating to options are constantly changing, and some items, such as capital gains, have been revised several times in the last few years. We do know that the tax laws have a significant impact on spread positions and also on the tax treatment where put options are involved. The recognition of the year in which a gain or loss is declared can still be affected by option strategies in combination with stock positions. The best advice we can give is to check the tax consequences of any option strategy with your accountant or stockbroker.

Commissions vary among brokerage houses and are not easy to pinpoint for option transactions since quantity discounts exist. Because many option positions involve small dollar investment outlays, commissions of $25 to $50 for buying and selling can significantly alter your returns and even create losses. Commissions on acquiring common stock through options are higher than the transaction costs of options, and this is a motivating force in closing out option transactions before expiration. Overall, commissions on options tend to be more significant than commissions on commodities or other highly leveraged investments.

Exploring the Web

Web site Address	Comment
www.cboe.com	Chicago Board Options Exchange Web site. A good source of education and data
www.amex.com	American Stock Exchange trades options and has a Web site section on options

SUMMARY

Put and call options are an exciting area of investment and speculation. We have discussed the past history of over-the-counter options trading and more recent trading of options on the listed options exchanges, such as the CBOE. The markets are more efficient, and the standardized practices of the listed exchanges have made options more usable for many investors and widened the number of option strategies that can be employed.

Option premiums (option prices) are affected by many variables such as time, market expectations, stock price volatility, dividend yields, and in-the-money/out-of-the-money relationships. The total premium consists of an intrinsic value plus a speculative premium that declines to zero by the expiration date. Calls are options to buy 100 shares of stock, while puts are options to sell 100 shares of stock.

Understanding the benefits and risks of trading options is complicated. Options can be risky or used to reduce risk. Calls can be bought for leverage, to cover a short position, or as an alternative to investing in the underlying common stock while buying time to purchase the stock (waiting for the financial resources to exercise the call). Calls are written either as a hedge on a long position in the underlying stock or to speculate on a price decline. Puts are bought to hedge a long position against a price decline or as an alternative to selling short. A writer of a put may speculate on a price increase or use the write as a hedge against a short position (if the price goes up, he will come out ahead on the writing of the put to partially offset the loss on the short sale).

Spreads are combinations of buying and writing the same options for an underlying common stock. In general, spreads reduce the risk of loss while limiting the gain. Straddles are a combination of a put and a call option in a stock at the same exercise date and strike price. They are used to profit from stocks showing large, short-term price fluctuations.

Other factors affect option profitability, such as taxes and commissions, and in general, each investor or speculator should check out his or her own situation and factor in the appropriate information with regard to taxes and commissions.

THE FUTURES MARKET FOR FINANCIAL INSTRUMENTS

The major event in the commodities markets for the last three decades has been the development of financial futures contracts. With the great volatility in the foreign exchange markets and in interest rates, corporate treasurers, investors, and others have felt a great need to hedge their positions. Financial futures also appeal to speculators because of their low margin requirements and wide swings in value.

Financial futures may be broken down into three major categories: currency futures, interest-rate futures, and stock index futures. Trading in currency futures began in May 1972 on the International Monetary Market (part of the Chicago Mercantile Exchange). Interest-rate futures started trading on the Chicago Board of Trade in October 1975 with the GNMA certificate. Trading in financial futures, regardless of whether they are currency or interest-rate futures, is very similar to trading in traditional commodities such as corn, wheat, copper, or pork bellies. There is a stipulated contract size, month of delivery, margin requirement, and so on. We will first look at currency futures and then shift our attention to interest-rate futures.

CURRENCY FUTURES

Futures are available in the currencies listed below:

Euro	Japanese yen
Australian dollar	Mexican peso
Canadian dollar	Russian ruble

The futures market in currencies provides many of the same functions as the older and less formalized market in foreign exchange operated by banks and specialized brokers, who maintain communication networks throughout the world. In either case, one can speculate or hedge. The currency futures market, however, is different in that it provides standardized contracts and a strong secondary market.

Let's examine how the currency futures market works. Assume you wish to purchase a currency futures contract in Mexican pesos. The standardized contract is 500,000 pesos. The value of the contract is quoted in cents per peso. Assume you purchase a December futures contract in May, and the price on the contract is $0.10850 per peso. The total value of the contract is $54,250 (500,000 × $0.10850). The typical margin on a peso contract is $1,500.

We also assume the peso strengthens relative to the dollar. This might happen because of decreasing U.S. interest rates, declining inflation in Mexico, or any number of other reasons. Under these circumstances, the currency might rise to $0.11000 (the peso is worth more cents than it was previously). The value of the contract has now risen to $55,000 (500,000 × $0.11000). This represents an increase in value of $750:

$55,000	Current value
−54,250	Original value
$750	Gain

With an original margin requirement of $1,500, this represents a return of 50 percent:

$$\frac{\$750}{\$1,500} \times 100 = 50\%$$

On an annualized basis, it could even be higher. Of course, the contract could produce a loss if the peso weakens against the dollar as a result of higher interest rates in the United States or increasing inflation in Mexico. With a normal margin maintenance requirement of $1,500, a $300 loss on the contract will call for additional margin.

Corporate treasurers often try to hedge an exposed position in their foreign exchange dealings through the currency futures market. Assume a treasurer closes a deal today to receive payment in two months in Japanese yen. If the yen goes down relative to the dollar, he will have less value than he anticipated. One solution would be to sell a yen futures contract (go short). If the value of the yen goes down, he will make money on his futures contract that will offset the loss on the receipt of the Japanese yen in two months.

Table 14–7 lists the typical size of contracts for four other foreign currencies that trade on the International Monetary Market.

INTEREST-RATE FUTURES

Since the inception of the interest-rate futures contract with GNMA certificates in October 1975, the market has been greatly expanded to include Treasury notes, Treasury bills, municipal bonds, federal funds, and Eurodollars. There is almost unlimited potential for futures contracts on interest-related items.

Interest-rate futures trade on a number of major exchanges, including the Chicago Board of Trade, the International Monetary Market of the Chicago Mercantile Exchange, and the New York Futures Exchange. There is strong competition between Chicago and New York City for dominance in this business, with Chicago being not only the historical leader but also the current leader.

Table 14–8 shows examples of quotes on interest-rate futures. Direct your attention to the first category, Treasury bonds (CBT), trading on the Chicago Board of Trade.

The bonds trade in units of $100,000, and the quotes are in percent of par value taken to 32nds of a percentage point. Although it is not shown in these data, the bonds on which

TABLE 14–7   Contracts in Currency Futures

Currency	Trading Units	Size of Contract Based on Mid-2001 Prices
Euro	125,000	$110,000
Canadian dollar	100,000	63,200
British pound	62,500	88,938
Japanese yen	12,500,000	103,750

the futures are based are assumed to be new, 15-year Treasury instruments paying 6 percent interest. In the first column for the June contract for Treasury bonds, we see an opening price of 99.16. This indicates a value of $99^{16}/_{32}$ percent times stated (par) value. We thus have a contract value of $99,500 ($99^{16}/_{32} \times \$100,000$). This represents the opening value. The entire line in Table 14–8 reads as follows:

	Open	High	Low	Settle	Change	Lifetime High	Lifetime Low	Open Interest
June	$99^{16}/_{33}$	$100^{6}/_{32}$	$99^{5}/_{32}$	$100^{3}/_{32}$	+21	$107^{8}/_{32}$	$96^{21}/_{32}$	428,317

The **settle price**, or closing price is $100^{3}/_{32}$, which represents a positive change of $^{21}/_{32}$ from the close of the previous day. The close for the previous day is not always the same as the open for the current day.[7] Since the value of the futures contract went up, we can assume interest rates declined. We can also observe the lifetime high and low for this contract. Finally, we see an open interest of 428,317, indicating the number of contracts outstanding for June.

Assume we buy a June futures contract for $100^{3}/_{32}$ or $100,094 ($100^{3}/_{32} \times \$100,000$). The margin requirement on the Chicago Board of Trade is $2,300 with a $1,750 margin maintenance requirement. In this case, it may be that we bought the futures contract because we anticipate easier monetary policy by the Federal Reserve, which will trigger a decline in interest rates and an increase in bond prices. If interest rates decline by 0.6 percent (60 basis points), Treasury bond prices will increase by approximately $1^{17}/_{32}$.[8] On a $100,000 par value futures contract, this would represent a gain of $1,531.25 as indicated below:

$$\begin{array}{r} \$100,000 \\ \times\ 1^{17}/_{32}\ \%\ \ (1.53125\%) \\ \hline \$1,531.25 \end{array}$$

With a $2,300 initial margin, the $1,531.25 profit represents an attractive return on our original $2,300 investment of 66.6 percent:

$$\frac{\$1,531.25}{\$2,300.00} = 66.6\%$$

---

7. A number of overnight events can cause the difference. In this case, we can assume the close for the previous day was $99^{14}/_{32}$.

8. This is derived from a standard bond table and not explicitly calculated in the example.

Table 14–8   Examples of Price Quotes on Interest-Rate Futures

	OPEN	HIGH	LOW	SETTLE	CHANGE	LIFETIME HIGH	LIFETIME LOW	OPEN INT.
INTEREST RATE								

Treasury Bonds (CBT)-$100,000: pts 32nds of 100%

	OPEN	HIGH	LOW	SETTLE	CHANGE	HIGH	LOW	OPEN INT.
June	99-16	100-06	99-05	100-03	+ 21	107-08	96-21	428,317
Sept	98-31	99-16	98-18	99-15	+ 22	106-25	96-22	82,147
Dec	...	...	...	98-26	+ 22	104-24	98-03	733

Est vol 331,000; vol Wed 320,081; open int 511,202 + 7,511

Treasury Notes (CBT)-$100,000; pts 32nds of 100%

	OPEN	HIGH	LOW	SETTLE	CHANGE	HIGH	LOW	OPEN INT.
June	03-055	03-115	102-22	03-095	+ 3.5	07-115	99-11	569,946
Sept	102-15	102-18	01-305	102-17	+ 3.5	106-28	01-305	83,704

Est vol 289.000; vol Wed 255,431; open int 653,650 + 16,056.

10 Yr Agency Notes (CBT)-$100,000; pts 32nds of 100%

	OPEN	HIGH	LOW	SETTLE	CHANGE	HIGH	LOW	OPEN INT.
June	98-26	98-27	98-08	98-24	+ 4.0	102-31	94-22	46,424

Est vol 4,200; vol Wed 6,502; open int 52,287 + 1,418

5 Yr Treasury Notes (CBT)-$100,000; pts 32nds of 100%

	OPEN	HIGH	LOW	SETTLE	CHANGE	HIGH	LOW	OPEN INT.
June	103-24	03-265	103-09	103-21	− 3.0	06-095	101-04	383,152
Sept	03-045	03-045	102-22	03-015	− 3.0	105-04	101-03	53,202

Est vol 167,000; vol Wed 130,535; open int 436,354 + 4,909

2 Yr Treasury Notes (CBT)-$200,000; pts 32nds of 100%

	OPEN	HIGH	LOW	SETTLE	CHANGE	HIGH	LOW	OPEN INT.
June	02.245	102-26	02-187	02-222	− 3.7	03-095	101-12	63,666

Est vol 5,800; vol Wed 6,129; open int 63,703, −1,835

30 Day Federal Funds (CBT)-$5 million; pts of 100%

	OPEN	HIGH	LOW	SETTLE	CHANGE	HIGH	LOW	OPEN INT.
May	95.780	95.785	95.780	95.780	− ...	95.785	94.020	33,697
June	96.02	96.02	96.01	96.01	− .01	96.03	94.10	40,577
July	96.17	96.18	96.13	96.14	− .04	96.20	95.02	10,729
Aug	96.18	96.21	96.14	96.17	− .05	96.24	94.18	3,587
Sept	96.17	96.17	96.16	96.17	− .06	96.26	95.50	5,765
Oct	96.16	96.18	96.14	96.17	− .07	96.35	95.62	2,732

Est vol 13,500; vol Wed 32,296; open int 97,737   −3,964

Mutual Bond Index (CBT)-$1,000; times Bond Buyer MBI

	OPEN	HIGH	LOW	SETTLE	CHANGE	HIGH	LOW	OPEN INT.
June	102.04	102-12	101-22	102-08	+ 13	105-11	100-18	11,914

Est vol 1,300, vol Wed 1,009; open int 12,255, + 65

Index Close 101-29; yield 5.70

	OPEN	HIGH	LOW	SETTLE	CHANGE	YIELD	CHANGE	OPEN INT.
Treasury Bills (CME)-$1 mil.; pts of 100%								
June	96.58	96.62	96.58	96.62	− .01	3.38	+.01	2,471

Est vol 4; vol Wed 7; open int 2,471, +2

Libor-1 Mo (CME)-$3,000,000; pts of 100%

	OPEN	HIGH	LOW	SETTLE	CHANGE	YIELD	CHANGE	OPEN INT.
June	95.99	96.00	95.96	95.97	− .03	4.03	+.03	12,812
July	96.08	96.08	96.04	96.05	− .05	3.95	+.05	7,286
Aug	96.07	96.07	96.05	96.06	− .04	3.94	+.04	1,206
Sept	96.06	96.06	96.04	96.04	− .07	3.96	+.07	165

Est vol 4, 228; vol Wed 4,299; open int 21,579, +496

Eurodollar (CME)-$1 Million; pts of 100%

	OPEN	HIGH	LOW	SETTLE	CHANGE	YIELD	CHANGE	OPEN INT.
June	96.02	96.02	95.97	95.98	− .04	4.02	+.04	632,399
July	96.04	96.04	95.99	96.00	− .05	4.00	+.05	17,969
Aug	95.98	95.99	95.97	95.97	− .08	4.03	+.08	755
Sept	96.04	96.04	95.94	95.96	− .08	4.04	+.08	657,139
Oct	...	...	...	95.72	− .11	4.28	+.11	100
Dec	95.70	95.71	95.59	95.61	− .12	4.39	+.12	541,255

(Continued)

Table 14–8 (Continued)

	OPEN	HIGH	LOW	SETTLE	CHANGE	YIELD	CHANGE	OPEN INT.
Mr02	95.47	95.48	95.34	95.37	− .13	4.63	+.13	425,476
June	95.12	95.13	95.00	95.02	− .11	4.98	+.11	406,127
Sept	95.78	94.80	94.68	94.71	− .08	5.29	+.08	297,958
Dec	94.43	94.43	94.34	94.37	− .06	5.63	+.06	223,373
Mr03	94.27	94.27	94.19	94.22	− .05	5.78	+.05	180,603
June	94.10	94.10	94.00	94.05	− .03	5.95	+.03	134,732
Sept	93.97	93.97	93.81	93.94	− .02	6.06	+.02	117,031
Dec	93.81	93.81	93.71	93.79	...	6.21	...	91,122
Mr04	93.81	93.81	93.69	93.79	...	6.21	...	89,771
June	93.71	93.73	93.64	93.71	+ .02	6.29	−.02	63,163
Sept	93.63	93.66	93.56	93.64	+ .03	6.36	−.03	58,960
Dec	93.46	93.54	93.43	93.52	+ .04	6.48	−.04	53,917
Mr05	93.53	93.55	93.44	93.54	+ .04	6.46	−.04	48,167
June	93.44	93.48	93.39	93.48	+ .05	6.52	−.05	40,864
Sopt	93.30	93.42	93.33	93.43	+ .06	6.57	−.06	40,429
Dec	93.27	93.32	93.22	93.32	+ .06	6.68	−.06	35,419
Mr06	93.30	93.36	93.24	93.35	+ .07	6.65	−.07	24,170
June	93.28	93.32	93.22	93.30	+ .08	6.70	−.08	20,085
Sept	93.24	93.28	93.18	93.26	+ .08	6.74	−.08	20,573
Dec	93.13	93.17	93.07	93.16	+ .09	6.84	−.09	15,299
Mr07	93.16	93.20	93.10	93.19	+ .09	6.81	−.09	12,042

Source: *The Wall Street Journal*, May 18, 2001. p. C12. Reprinted by permission of *The Wall Street Journal*,
© 2001 by Dow Jones & Company, Inc. All Rights Reserved Worldwide.

Note, however, that if interest rates go up by even a small amount, our Treasury bond futures contract value will fall, and there may be a margin call.

As is true of other commodities, when we trade in interest rate futures, we do not take actual title or possession of the commodity unless we fail to reverse our initial position. The contract merely represents a bet or hedge on the direction of future interest rates and bond prices.

THE CONCEPT OF DERIVATIVE PRODUCTS

Trading in stock index futures and options has had a tremendous impact on the financial markets in the United States. Stock index futures and options are sometimes referred to as **derivative products** because they derive their existence from actual market indexes but have no intrinsic characteristics of their own.[9] These derivative products are thought to make market movements more volatile. The primary reason is that enormous amounts of securities can be controlled by relatively small amounts of margin payments or option premiums. Also, these derivative products are often used as part of program trading. **Program trading** means that computer-based trigger points are established in which large volume trades are initiated by institutional investors. Stock index futures and options facilitate program trading because a large volume of securities can be controlled. The presence of program trading, as supported by the use of stock index futures and options, was blamed by many for the 508 point market crash in the Dow Jones Industrial Average on October 19, 1987. It was thought that too many institutional investors were moving in the same

---

9. Interest-rate futures and options are also considered to be derivative products.

direction (to sell) at one time. Increased stock price volatility since the market crash has also been blamed on program trading and the use of stock index futures and options.

Actually, these are somewhat controversial topics. A study by the Chicago Mercantile Exchange suggests program trading and the use of derivative products has no negative effect on the market volatility. These trading tools merely help the market reach a new equilibrium level (in terms of value) more quickly.[10]

It is the contention of the authors that stock index futures and options have many useful purposes, which we will cover throughout the chapter. We will also try to point out potential negatives where they exist.

TRADING STOCK INDEX FUTURES

There are major stock index futures contracts on the Dow Jones Industrial Average (Chicago Board of Trade), the S&P 500 Index (Chicago Mercantile Exchange), the S&P MidCap 400 (Chicago Mercantile Exchange), the Nikkei Stock Average (Chicago Mercantile Exchange), and the Nasdaq 100 Stock Index[11] (Chicago Mercantile Exchange).[12] An example of these stock index futures contracts is shown in Table 14-9.[13]

You will note in Table 14-9 that the title line for each contract (such as the DJ Industrial Average) indicates the appropriate multiple times the value in the table. For the DJ Industrial Average the multiplier is 10. For the S&P 500 Index, the multiplier is 250, and for the Mini S&P 500, it is 50 (the intent of the latter is to create a smaller contract based on the S&P 500 Index) and so on. Looking at the June settle price for each of the indexes, we see the value of the contracts in Table 14-10.

If the investor thinks the market is going up, he will purchase a futures contract. If he thinks the market is going down, he will sell a futures contract and hope the market will decline so that the contract can be closed out (repurchased) at a lower value than the sales price. Selling futures contracts can also be used to hedge a large stock portfolio. If the market goes down, what you lose on your portfolio you recoup in your futures contract.

In the example in Table 14-10, the investor has seven contracts from which to choose.

We shall direct our attention for now to the S&P 500 Index futures contract (although the same basic principles would apply to other contracts).

Part of the material from Table 14-9 that pertains to the S&P 500 Index futures contract is reproduced in Table 14-11 so we can examine a number of key features related to the contract.

Trading Cycle

The trading cycle in the table is made up of the four months of March, June, September, and December. The last day of trading for a contract is the third Thursday of the ending month.

Margin Requirement

As previously mentioned, the basic margin requirement for buying or selling an S&P 500 futures contract on the Chicago Mercantile Exchange was $21,500 in 2001. Based on the June

---

10. *Report of the Committee of Inquiry Appointed by the Chicago Mercantile Exchange to Examine the Events Surrounding October 19, 1987* (Chicago: The Chicago Mercantile Exchange, December 17, 1987).
11. The Nasdaq 100 is made up of the 100 largest companies on the Nasdaq.
12. There are also additional contracts on the Russell 2000 and other indexes.
13. An alternative way to trade the S&P 500 is through actual shares of QQQs; for the Dow Jones Industrial Average it is Diamonds. There are actual shares that trade on the American Stock Exchange and mimic the performance of the index. For example, Diamonds trade at 1/100th the value of the DJIA. If the Dow is at 11,000, a Diamond share of stock will trade for 110. If the DJIA increases to 12,000 over time, the Diamond shares will go up to 120. Diamonds fall under the topic of exchange traded funds.

TABLE 14–9 Stock Index Futures (May 17, 2001)

	OPEN	HIGH	LOW	SETTLE	CHANGE	LIFETIME HIGH	LIFETIME LOW	OPEN INT.
				INDEX				
DJ Industrial Average (CBOT)-$10 times average								
June	11280	11365	11216	11287	+ 35	11795	9148	32,974
Sept	11345	11425	11290	11365	+ 38	11425	9240	2,202
Dec	11395	11510	11380	11441	+ 36	12131	9360	182
Est vol 23,000; vol Wed 32,101; open int 35,361, + 2,446.								
Idx pri: Hi 11328.61; Lo 11181.91; Close 11248.58, + 32.66.								
S&P 500 Index (CME)-$250 times Index								
June	128900	129920	128450	129150	+ 310	166660	108850	417,757
Sept	129850	131050	129550	130200	+ 320	169060	110050	72,025
Dec	132000	132000	130730	131230	+ 350	171460	110900	2,579
Mr02	...	...	...	132260	+ 380	173860	111850	732
June	...	...	...	133510	+ 430	170550	112900	692
Est vol 81,049; vol Wed 92,052; open int 493,862, + 4,081.								
Idx pri: Hi 1296.48; Lo 1282.65; Close 1288.49, + 3.50.								
Mini S&P 500 (CME)-$50 times Index								
June	128900	129950	128475	129150	+ 300	140200	108800	122,168
Vol Wed 166,554; open int 122,193, + 10,804.								
S&P Midcap 400 (CME)-$500 times Index								
June	526.90	533.50	524.50	533.00	+ 6.75	571.00	435.50	15,343
Est vol 922; vol Wed 676; open int 15,404, + 70.								
Idx pri: Hi 532.83; Lo 523.75; Close 532.82, + 8.06.								
Nikkei 225 Stock Average (CME)-$5 times Index								
June	14090.	14100.	13925.	13955.	+ 10	17730.	11255.	20,804
Est vol 809, vol Wed 1,584, open int 20,887, + 327.								
Idx pri: Hi 13975.12; Lo 13725.25; Close 13910.67, + 216.40.								
Nasdaq 100 (CME)-$100 times Index								
June	189950	196500	189900	192550	+ 2850	396100	136000	48,189
Sept	...	...	...	194650	+ 2850	281500	139500	45
Est vol 22,380; vol Wed 30,654; open int 48,239, + 549.								
Idx pri: Hi 1955.77; Lo 1898.65; Close 1925.14, + 25.67.								
Mini Nasdaq 100 (CME)-$20 times Index								
June	1899.0	1965.0	1897.0	1925.5	+ 28.5	2791.5	1361.0	90,871
Vol Wed 165,897; open int 90,898, +6,867.								

2001 contract value (found on the second line in Table 14-10) this represents a margin requirement of 6.7 percent ($21,500/$322,875).

There is also a margin maintenance requirement of $17,250. Thus, if the initial margin or equity in the account falls to this level, the investor will be required to supply sufficient cash or securities to bring the account back up to $21,500. A drop from $21,500 to $17,250 represents $4,250. Because the contract trades at 250 times the index, a decline of 17 points in the S&P contract value would cause a loss of $4,250. The investor would be asked to put up that amount in new funds.

If the investor can prove he is hedging a long position, the margin requirement will be less. For example, if an investor owns a portfolio of stocks that roughly equals the value of the index futures contract ($322,875 in this case), the initial margin requirement is reduced.

TABLE 14–10   Value of Contracts

	June Settle Price	Multiplier	Contract Value
Dow Jones Industrial Average	11,287.00	10	$112,870
S&P 500 Index	1,291.50	250	322,875
Mini S&P 500	1,291.50	50	64,575
S&P MidCap 400	533.00	500	266,500
Nikkei 225	13,955.00	5	69,755
Nasdaq 100	1,922.50	100	192,250
Mini Nasdaq 100	1,922.50	20	38,450

TABLE 14–11   S&P Index Futures Contract (CME), 500 Multiplier (May 17, 2001)

	Open	High	Low	Settle	Change
June 2000	1,289.00*	1,299.20	1,284.50	1,291.50	3.10
September	1,298.50	1,310.50	1,295.50	1,302.00	3.20
December	1,320.00	1,320.00	1,307.30	1,312.30	3.80
March 2002	—	—	—	1,322.60	3.80

Value of S&P 500 Stock Index (May 17, 2001), 1, 288.49.

* Note the "assumed" decimal point in previously presented Table 14–9 for the S&P 500 Index is moved two places to the left.

Since a hedged position is not as risky as a speculative position, less initial margin is required?[14]

Cash Settlement

In traditional commodity futures markets, the potential for physical delivery exists. One who is trading in wheat could actually decide to deliver the commodity to close out the contract. As discussed earlier, this happens only a very small percentage of the time, but it is possible. The stock index futures market, on the other hand, is purely a **cash-settlement** market. There is never the implied potential for future delivery of the Standard & Poor's 500 Stock Index. An investor simply closes out (or reverses) his position before the settlement date. If he does not, his account is automatically credited with his gains or debited with his losses, and the transaction is completed.[15]

One of the advantages of a cash-settlement arrangement is that it makes it impossible for a "short squeeze" to develop. A short squeeze occurs when an investor attempts to corner a market in a commodity, such as silver, so that it is not possible for those who have short positions to make physical delivery. Clearly, with a cash-settlement position, this can never happen.

---

14. It should be mentioned that on a hedged position, the margin maintenance requirement is the same as the original margin.

15. Actually, the account is adjusted daily to reflect the gains and losses. This is known as marking the customer's position to market.

The Real World of Investing

The S&P Is Not Your Father's Index

Just as Buick and Chevrolet claim their latest models are not to be confused with "your father's car," similar claims are made for the Standard & Poor's 500 Index. This is of potential interest because the S&P 500 Index is the most popular venue on which to trade futures contracts.

Thomas McManus, U.S. investment strategist at NatWest Securities was quoted in *The Wall Street Journal* as saying, "The S&P 500 is higher growth, more global, less cyclical, and more diversified than it has ever been and therefore deserves a higher [price-to-earnings] multiple."* While the last point about higher multiple is subject to debate the changing characteristics of the Index are not.

The biggest change has been the inclusion of more technology and financial firms, industries that have shown particularly strong performance during the 1990s. Between 1989 and 2001, the two industries combined have grown from 14 percent of the S&P 500 index to 35 percent. While much of the growth can be attributed to market value gains that have outstripped the rest of the market, this is not the only explanation. For example, the number of financial firms represented in the S&P 500 has grown from 40 in the late 1980s to 70 in 2001. Furthermore, Microsoft was not added to the S&P 500 Index until 1994, but in mid-2001 represented 2.3 percent of the value of the Index.

The changes are not only in technology and finance, but in many other areas as well. Seventy-one changes in the Index have taken place since 1995. There has been a deemphasis on public utilities, energy, steel, and old-style retail establishments and a renewed emphasis on health care, multinationals, entertainment, as well as technology and finance.

The S&P 500 Index represents a slimmer, faster (in terms of growth) model than it was in your father's day. The same can also be said of the Dow Jones Industrial Average, which in early 2001 dropped Woolworth, Bethlehem Steel, Texaco, and Westinghouse Electric in favor of more widely traded stocks as represented by Hewlett-Packard, Johnson & Johnson, Travelers Group, and Wal-Mart Stores.

*Greg Ip, "S&P 500 Is Not Your Father's Index," *The Wall Street Journal*, July 29, 1997, pp. C1, C29.

Basis

The term basis represents the difference between the stock index futures price and the value of the actual underlying index.[16] We can now return to Table 14–11 to see a numerical example of basis. On the date of the table, the S&P 500 futures contract for June was quoted at a settle (closing) price of 1291.50 (second item from the right in the first row). The actual S&P 500 Stock Index, as shown at the bottom of Table 14–11, closed at 1288.49. The basis, or difference, between the futures price and the actual underlying index was 3.01:

$1291.50 Stock index futures price
−1288.49 Actual underlying index
$ 3.01 Basis

---

16. The same concept can be applied to other types of futures contracts.

Moving to the September 2001 contract in Table 14-11, the basis is the difference between the September contract settle value of 1302.00 and the value of the underlying index, which, of course, is still 1288.49. The difference is 13.51. For the data in Table 14-11, the basis indicates that a premium is being paid over the actual underlying index value, and furthermore, the premium expands with the passage of time. This is generally thought to be a positive sign. If the index futures price is below the actual underlying index, there is a negative basis.

An excellent discussion of the ability of stock index futures to forecast the actual underlying index is presented in an article by Zeckhauser and Niederhoffer in the *Financial Analysts Journal.*[17] A part of their thesis is that futures contracts move instantaneously to reflect market conditions, whereas the actual underlying index moves more slowly. If the market makes an important move, some of the stocks that are part of the actual underlying index will not yet have reacted. Thus, initial, significant, and potentially predictive information may be found in the futures market quotes.

Also, at times, futures or options markets stay open later or begin trading earlier than the actual underlying stock markets. This can be very beneficial not only in providing lead time information on market movements, but also in giving the trader an opportunity to take a position before the opening or after the closing of the stock market.

TRADING STOCK INDEX OPTIONS

Stock index options also allow the market participant to speculate or hedge against major market movements, although there is no opportunity for arbitraging. Stock index options are similar in many respects to the standard put and call options on individual stocks discussed earlier. The purchaser of an option pays an initial premium and then closes out the option at a given price in the future. One essential difference between stock index options and options on individual securities is that in the former case, there is only a cash settlement of the position, whereas in the latter case (individual securities), you can force the option writer to deliver the securities.

There are stock index options on the Dow Jones Industrial Average, the S&P 500, Nasdaq 100, Russell 2000, and other indices. They all trade on the Chicago Board Options Exchange. Examples of stock index options for the S&P Index are presented in Table 14-12.

In reading Table 14-12, you need to distinguish between put and call options. Read all the way down to the June 1285c and June I285p rows. The "c" after the strike price indicates it is a call option, while the "p" after the stock price indicates it is a put option.

Actual Trade in the S&P 500 index

We reproduce part of data covering the S&P 500 Index options in Table 14-13. For ease of presentation, we will reconstruct the data in columns for calls and columns for puts.

Note at the top of Table 14-13 that the S&P 500 Index closed on May 17, 2001, at 1288.49. With this value in mind, we can examine the strike prices and premiums for the various contracts. The premium in each case is multiplied by 100 to determine the total cash value involved. Let's read down to the 1285 strike price and across to the June call option (second row from the bottom). The premium is 32.50.

Assume an investor bought a June 1285 contract for a premium of 32.50 on May 17, 2001, and that when the June contract expired, the S&P 500 Index was 1340 under an optimistic assumption and 1240 under a pessimistic assumption. At an index value of 1340, the option value is 55 (1340 − 1285). The ending or expiration price is 55 points higher than the strike price. Also, keep in mind the option cost is 32.50. The profit is shown to be $2,250.

---

17. Richard Zeckhauser and Victor Niederhoffer, "The Performance of Market Index Futures Contracts," *Financial Analysts Journal,* January-February 1983, pp. 59-65.

Table 14–12 S&P 500 Stock Index Options (May 17, 2001 Closing Index = 1288.49)

STRIKE		VOL.	LAST S&P 500 (SPX)	NET CHG.		OPEN INT.
Jun	750 p	10	0^{45}	+	0^{25}	8,458
Jun	900 p	825	0^{15}	+	0^{05}	35,855
Jun	950 p	410	0^{20}		...	9,349
May	995 c	5	295	+	6	133
Jun	995 p	950	0^{35}	–	0^{15}	15,725
Jul	1005 p	6	1^{70}	–	0^{25}	308
Jun	1050 p	558	0^{75}	+	0^{25}	9,717
Jul	1050 p	850	2^{55}	–	0^{30}	1,829
May	1075 c	6	217	+	28	689
Jun	1075 p	85	0^{80}	–	0^{95}	9,333
Jul	1075 p	440	3^{80}	–	1^{70}	1,787
May	1100 p	4	0^{05}		...	13,347
Jun	1100 p	654	1^{10}	–	0^{45}	21,085
Jul	1100 c	10	199	+	35^{20}	240
Jul	1100 p	1,026	4^{50}	–	0^{50}	9,386
Jun	1105 p	30	1^{60}	–	2^{20}	27
Jun	1110 p	25	1^{65}	–	2^{30}	113
May	1125 c	25	167	+	9	2,711
May	1125 p	15	0^{05}	–	0^{05}	11,218
Jun	1125 p	75	2^{05}	+	0^{05}	11,724
Jul	1125 p	11	6^{10}	–	0^{30}	10,910
Jun	1130 p	80	2^{10}	+	0^{10}	2,708
Jun	1140 p	126	2^{20}	–	0^{80}	5,814
May	1150 c	16	139	+	24	5,204
May	1150 p	15	0^{10}	–	0^{20}	13,901
Jun	1150 c	79	143^{80}	+	5^{80}	10,426
Jun	1150 p	1,140	2^{20}	–	0^{80}	20,865
Jul	1150 p	153	8	–	0^{80}	803
Jun	1160 p	350	3^{20}	–	1^{30}	5,744
Jun	1170 p	1	0^{80}	–	5^{00}	5,210
May	1175 c	72	1^{16}	+	5	6,557
Jun	1175 c	76	120^{50}	+	2^{70}	11,074
Jun	1175 p	795	4	–	0^{50}	24,546
Jul	1175 p	6	10^{50}	–	1^{50}	1,822
Jun	1180 p	62	4^{70}	–	0^{30}	5,393
Jun	1190 c	1	1^{10}	+	62^{50}	2,802
Jun	1190 p	310	5	–	0^{40}	4,524
May	1200 c	177	90	+	6	8,940
May	1200 p	1,606	0^{06}	–	0^{15}	17,225
Jun	1200 c	126	99	+	8	28,909
Jun	1200 p	1,558	5^{40}	–	1^{40}	45,012
Jul	1200 c	22	103^{50}	+	14^{50}	1,605
Jul	1200 p	28	14	–	1^{70}	5,867
Jun	1210 p	7	7	–	3^{50}	1,683
Jun	1220 p	101	7^{50}	–	3	140
May	1225 c	4,556	65^{50}	+	6^{20}	11,166
May	1225 p	321	0^{05}	–	0^{20}	9,130
Jun	1225 c	117	75	+	3	18,860
Jun	1225 p	848	9	–	1^{10}	21,203
Jul	1225 p	33	18^{10}	–	1^{70}	2,591
May	1230 p	14	0^{30}	+	0^{05}	2,739
Jun	1230 c	2	75^{50}	+	36	293
Jun	1230 p	40	10	–	0^{70}	956
May	1235 c	66	54^{50}	+	22^{50}	889
May	1235 p	4	0^{05}	–	0^{20}	2,552
Jun	1235 c	2	69	+	32	911
Jun	1235 p	4,508	10^{50}	–	1	5,367
May	1250 c	3,978	39	+	3	21,859

(Continued)

Table 14–12   (Continued)

STRIKE		VOL	LAST	NET CHG.		OPEN INT.
			S&P 500 (SPX)			
May	1250 p	2,701	0^{20}	−	0^{60}	19,990
Jun	1250 c	886	54^{50}	+	1	46,801
Jun	1250 p	2,791	13^{80}	−	2^{20}	44,236
Jul	1250 c	8	69^{50}	+	9^{50}	2,350
Jul	1250 p	1,263	24	−	3^{50}	3,211
May	1260 c	234	32	+	4	1,045
May	1260 p	233	0^{25}	−	1^{25}	202
Jun	1260 c	102	47^{50}	+	15^{50}	2,356
Jun	1260 p	92	16^{70}	−	1^{30}	2,257
Jun	1270 c	50	43	+	5^{50}	488
Jun	1270 p	135	19	−	1^{50}	922
May	1275 c	11,329	14	−	1	10,582
May	1275 p	9,191	0^{90}	−	13^{60}	8,272
Jun	1275 c	8,672	38	+	8^{40}	12,828
Jun	1275 p	9,595	41	−	2^{60}	16,052
Jul	1275 c	2,426	57	+	9	232
Jul	1275 p	38	33^{90}	−	1^{10}	3,257
May	1280 c	447	9^{20}	−	0^{60}	445
May	1280 p	212	0^{85}	−	5^{15}	41
Jun	1280 c	72	35	+	4^{50}	629
Jun	1280 p	48	23	−	5	555
May	1285 c	723	4^{70}	−	3^{30}	765
May	1285 p	995	3	−	6	117
Jun	1285 c	5,204	32^{50}	+	1^{50}	1,483
Jun	1285 p	4,888	26	−	1	1,275
Jul	1285 c	1,814	49		...	...
Jul	1285 p	1	36^{50}	−	16	30
May	1300 c	10,215	1	−	1^{80}	11,037
May	1300 p	3,866	11^{50}	−	5^{50}	4,534
Jun	1300 c	6,135	23	−	0^{20}	19,589
Jun	1300 p	7,259	31	−	4	14,624
Jul	1300 c	472	41	+	2	962

Source: *The Wall Street Journal*, May 18, 2001, p. C16. Reprinted by permission of *The Wall Street Journal*, © 2001 by Dow Jones & Company, Inc. All Rights Reserved Worldwide.

TABLE 14–13   S&P 500 Index Options (May 17, 2001)

Strike Price	Calls			Puts		
	May	June	July	May	June	July
1275	14	38	57	0.90	21	33.90
1280	9.20	35	—	0.85	23	—
1285	4.70	32.50	49	3	26	36.50
1300	1	23	41	11.50	31	—

The multiplier times the premium is 100.

Value of the S&P 100 Index (May 17, 2001) = 1288.49.

	1340 Optimistic Assumption	1240 Pessimistic Assumption
Final value (100 × 55)	$5,500	$ 0
Purchase price (100 × 32)	−3,250	− 3,250
Profit or loss	$2,250	−$3,250

At an ending value of $1,240 (pessimistic assumption), the option is worthless, and there is a loss of $3,250. Remember these are 1,285 calls.

We have been working with 1285 call options. Let's shift our attention to put options. If a 1285 put option (the option to sell at 1285 rather than buy at 1285) had been acquired on May 17, 2001, we can see in Table 14–13 (June put column, second row from the bottom) that the price of our put option would be 26. Let's assume that when the June put option expired, the S&P 500 Index was 1340 under what is now the pessimistic assumption and 1240 under what is now the optimistic assumption.

At an index value of 1340, no value is associated with a put option that allows you to sell at 1285. No one would want to use the option to sell at 1285 if the index value is 1340. Because the put option cost is 26, there is a $2,600 loss. At a final value of 1240, the put option to sell at 1285 has a value of 45. With a cost of 26, a profit of $1,900 occurs. The profit and losses are indicated below:

	1340 Pessimistic Assumption	1240 Optimistic Assumption
Final value (100 × 55)	$ 0	$ 4,500
Purchase price (100 × 26)	2,600	2,600
Profit or loss	–$2,600	$1,900

HEDGING WITH STOCK INDEX OPTIONS

The discussion of stock index options thus far has pertained to speculation about market moves. Stock index options can also be used for hedging. Like stock index futures, stock index options can be utilized to protect a portfolio or for special purposes by underwriters, specialists, dealers, tax planners, and others.

At times, options may offer a hedging advantage over futures to investors who are limited by law from purchasing futures contracts. On the other hand, futures generally allow for a more efficient hedge than options. If the market goes down by 20 or 25 percent, chances are good that a completely hedged short futures position (selling futures contracts) will compensate for losses in a portfolio. An option write, used to hedge a portfolio, may be inadequate. Perhaps the option premium income represents 10 percent of the portfolio, but the market goes down by 25 percent. Fifteen percent of the loss will be unprotected. Buying a put option may overcome this problem, but the cash outflow to purchase the put option could involve substantial funds. Clearly, both futures and options have their advantages and disadvantages.

There are also options on industry indexes that can be used for hedging or speculation. For example, the American Stock Exchange has index options on high-tech and pharmaceutical companies, and the Philadelphia Exchange covers gold/silver, oil services, semiconductors, and public utilities. The trading in industry options is basically the same as trading in overall market options.

OPTIONS ON STOCK INDEX FUTURES

We have discussed *stock index futures* and *stock index options*, so a natural extension of our discussion is to consider the third form of stock index trading, *options on stock index futures*. The three forms of index trading are listed below for reference.

1. Stock index futures.
2. Stock index options.
3. Options on stock index futures.

An option on stock index futures (item 3 above) gives the holder the right to purchase the stock index *futures contract* at a specified price over a given period. This is slightly different from the stock index option (item 2) that gives the holder the right to purchase the *underlying index* at a specified price over a given time period.[18]

The primary topic for discussion in this section is represented by the left-hand column in Figure 14-4, an option on a stock index futures contract. The value of an option to purchase a stock index futures contract will depend on the outlook for the futures contract. Quotes on options to purchase stock index futures are shown in Table 14-14.

As indicated in Table 14-14, options on stock index futures are available for the Dow Jones Industrial Average and the S&P 500 Stock Index. A call option to buy a June DJIA futures contract at a strike price of 114 (representing 1140) has a premium of 18.05. On these option contracts, the premium is multiplied by 100 to get the value of the contract. Thus, the cost of the contract is $1,805 (100 × 18.05).

In examining Table 14-14, note that the premiums on the call options increase substantially with the passage of time from May to July. This gain in value is not only a function of the extended time period associated with the option but is also due to the fact that the DJIA futures contract normally has a higher value with the passage of time.[19] Thus, options on stock index futures not only have a time premium (all options do) but may also have an additional premium (or discount) depending on the relationship of the far-term futures market to the near-term futures market.

Options on stock index futures may be settled on a cash basis, or the holder of a call option may exercise the option and force the option writer to produce a specified futures contract. There are also puts for options on stock index futures.

Exploring the Web

Web site Address	Comments
www.cboe.com	Web site for major options exchange
www.schaeffersresearch.com	Offers technical analysis for options
www.cbs.marketwatch.com	Contains some information and tracking on stock options
www.888options.com	Educational site on options
www.cbot.com	Web site for the Chicago Board of Trade providing information, quotes, and educational features
www.pcquote.com	Provides research and quotes on options and commodities.
www.liffe.com	Home site for the London International Financial Futures and Options market
www.cme.com	Home site for the Chicago Mercantile Exchange containing quotes and information about futures
www.cftc.com	Home site for the future market regulator Commodities Futures Trading Commission

---

18. Because of cash-settlement procedures, the actual index will never actually be purchased, and the gain or loss will be settled for cash.

19. Of course, if the market outlook were highly pessimistic, there would be a decline in the S&P futures contract with the passage of time.

FIGURE 14–4   Comparison of Option Contracts

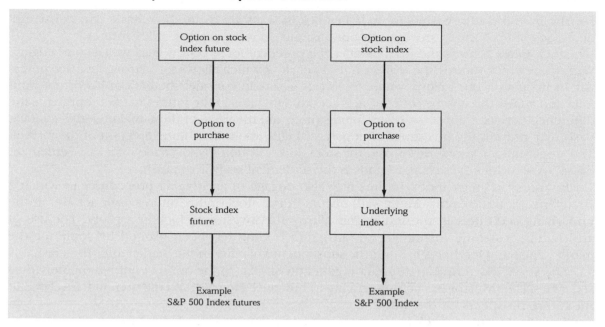

TABLE 14–14   Options on Stock Index Futures (May 17, 2001)

INDEX

DJ Industrial Avg (CBOT)
$100 times premium

	CALLS–SETTLE			PUTS–SETTLE		
STRIKE PRICE	**May**	**Jun**	**Jly**	**May**	**Jun**	**Jly**
111	19.50	35.00	...	1.00	16.40	...
112	11.00	28.70	...	2.50	20.05	28.50
113	4.50	23.05	...	6.00	24.35	...
114	1.00	18.05	33.50	12.50	29.30	...
115	0.55	13.70	28.50	...	34.95	...
116	0.20	9.95	23.50	...	41.75	...

For the DJIA, add two zeros to the strike price.

Est vol 3,100 Wd 438 calls 728 puts
Op int Wed 9,001 calls 28,845 puts

S & P 500 Stock Index (CME)
$250 times premium

	CALLS–SETTLE			PUTS–SETTLE		
STRIKE PRICE	**May**	**Jun**	**Jly**	**May**	**Jun**	**Jly**
1280	13.80	34.40	54.70	2.30	22.90	32.90
1285	10.00	31.40	...	3.50	24.90	...
1290	6.80	28.50	...	5.30	27.00	36.80
1295	4.40	25.80	...	7.90	29.30	38.90
1300	2.60	23.30	43.00	11.10	31.80	41.00
1305	1.40	21.00	...	...	34.40	...

Est vol 11,613 Wd 13,516 calls 11,690 puts
Op int Wed 73,715 calls 182,919 puts

Value of the DJIA (May 17, 2001) is 11,248.58.

Source: *The Wall Street Journal*, May 18, 2001, p. C18. Reprinted by permission of *The Wall Street Journal*, © 2001 by Dow Jones & Company, Inc. All Rights Reserved Worldwide.

SUMMARY

For the investor who wishes to trade in stock indexes, there are three basic types of securities: stock index futures, stock index options, and options on stock index futures.

Stock index futures and options offer the potential for speculation as well as for hedging. With stock index futures, the margin is relatively low, which allows for a strong leverage potential. In hedging a portfolio position, the investor should consider the beta of his or her portfolio and adjust the number of contracts accordingly. Basis in the futures market represents the difference between the stock index futures price and the value of the actual underlying index. Basis may present the investor with a potential clue about the future direction of the market. The stock index futures market and the stock index option market trade on a cash-settlement basis. No securities ever change hands as the settlement is always in cash.

Investors in stock index futures may also engage in arbitraging procedures in which a simultaneous trade (a buy and a sell) occurs in the stock index futures contract and in the underlying securities in the index. This allows the investor to lock in a profit. The use of arbitraging, portfolio insurance, and program trading has been blamed by some for the market crash in October 1987 and the subsequent volatility in the market after the crash.

The stock index option contract is generally similar to the option contract on individual securities. The investor has an opportunity to buy puts and calls, and the premium is related to the future prospects for the index.

The third form of stock index contracts, an option on stock index futures, combines the option concept with the futures market. Instead of an option on an actual index, you have an option on a stock index futures contract. The contract may be settled either with cash or with securities.

APPENDIX 14A

THE BLACK-SCHOLES OPTION PRICING MODEL*

Theory

In 1973, Fischer Black and Myron Scholes published their derivation of a theoretical option pricing model. They started with three securities: riskless bonds, shares of common stock, and call options. The shares of common stock and call options were combined to form a riskless hedge that, by definition, had to duplicate the return of a discount bond with the same maturity length as the option. Using the riskless-hedge concept as a basis, Black and Scholes then proceeded with their model derivation.

Black and Scholes made the following assumptions:

1. Markets are frictionless. This means there are no taxes or transactions costs; all securities are infinitely divisible; all market participants may borrow and lend at the known and constant riskless rate of interest; there are no penalties for short selling.

2. Stock prices are lognormally distributed, with a constant variance for the underlying returns.

3. The stock neither pays dividends nor makes any other distributions.

4. The option may be exercised only at maturity.

Given the above assumptions and the riskless hedging strategy, Black and Scholes derived a call option pricing model that may be expressed as:

$$c = (S)[N(d_1)] - (X)(e^{-rt})[N(d_2)] \qquad (14A\text{-}1)$$

*This appendix was developed by Professor Carl Luft of DePaul University in consultation with the authors.

where:

$$d_1 = \frac{\ln(S/X) + [r + (\sigma^2/2)](T)}{(\sigma)(\sqrt{T})} \tag{14A-2}$$

$$d_2 = d_1 - (\sigma)/(\sqrt{T}) \tag{14A-3}$$

The terms are defined as follows:

c = Price of the call option

S = Prevailing market price of a share of common stock on the date the call option is written

X = Call option's striking price (exercise price)

r = Annualized prevailing short-term riskless rate of interest

T = Length of the option's life expressed in annual terms

σ^2 = Annualized variance associated with the underlying security's price changes

$N(\cdot)$ = Cumulative normal density function

At maturity $(T = 0)$, the call option must sell for either its intrinsic value or zero, whichever is greater. This boundary condition may be expressed mathematically as:

$$c = \text{Max}(0, S - X) \tag{14A-4}$$

It can be shown that given a put option and a call option, with the same striking price, and one share of the underlying stock, one can form a portfolio that will earn an amount equal to the option's striking price no matter what value the stock takes at expiration. From this relationship, the value of a put option can be determined mathematically as:

$$p = (X)(e^{-rt}) - S + c \tag{14A-5}$$

with the boundary condition,

$$p = \text{Max}(0, X - S) \tag{14A-6}$$

Formula 14A–5 is known as the put-call parity relationship, and Formula 14A–6 shows that at maturity the put must sell for either its intrinsic value or zero.

Inspection of Formulas 14A–1 through 14A–6 reveals that both the call and put option prices are a function of only five variables: S, the underlying stock's market price; X, the striking price; T, the length of the option's life; σ^2, the volatility of the stock price changes; and r, the riskless rate of interest. All of these variables are easily observed or estimated. Previously developed option pricing models relied on variables that were based on individual investor risk preferences or on expected values of the stock price. Since the Black–Scholes model does not rely on such variables, it is superior to prior models.

To understand the behavior of options, it is necessary to examine the relationship of the option price to each of the five inputs. For call options, the price is positively related to the stock's price, the riskless rate of interest, the volatility, and the time to maturity; whereas an inverse relationship exists between the call option price and the striking price. Put options exhibit positive relationships with the striking price and volatility, negative relationships with the underlying stock price and riskless rate, and either a positive or negative relationship with time.

These relationships are easy to grasp if one realizes that options will not be exercised unless they have an intrinsic value. Consider first the price of the underlying stock. As it increases, calls go in the money and gain intrinsic value while puts fall out of the money and lose intrinsic value. If the stock price declines, then the reverse is true. This explains the positive relationship between the call price and the stock price and the inverse relationship between the put price and the stock price. Higher striking prices cause lower intrinsic values for call options but result in greater intrinsic values for put options. In this case, the loss of intrinsic value causes the inverse relationship between the call option and striking price, while the gain in intrinsic value causes the positive relationship between the put price and the striking price. The positive relationship of both put and call prices to the volatility can be explained by the fact that options written on higher volatility stocks have a relatively better chance of being in the money at expiration than do options written on lower volatility stocks. The positive relationship of the call price to the risk-free rate reflects the fact that the intrinsic value increases because the present value of the exercise price decreases as the risk-free rate rises. For put options, such rate increases and declining present values of exercise prices cause a loss of intrinsic value and account for the inverse relationship between the put option price and risk-free rate. Finally, the positive relationship of the call price to time is caused by an increasing intrinsic value due to lower present values of the exercise price for longer time periods. A more complex relationship exists for put options.

Intuitively, one might expect a strictly positive relationship between the put option price and time. Such a relationship will occur if the put is at the money or out of the money, while a negative relationship can exist for deep in-the-money puts. The reason for this inverse relationship lies embedded in the stock's price behavior. Since stock prices cannot be less than zero, the put option has a maximum value that equals the strike price. Investors who own deep in-the-money put options that are close to their maximum value because of extremely low stock prices are prohibited from exercising these options by assumption 4. Thus, time is working against these investors since they run the risk of losing intrinsic value if the stock price rises before expiration.

After deriving the model, Black and Scholes subjected it to empirical testing. They implemented the riskless-hedging strategy by combining options and stock in proportions dictated by the model and comparing these hedged returns to observed Treasury bill returns. They hypothesized that if the model provided equilibrium, or fair option prices, then the hedged returns should equal the returns generated by the investment in riskless securities. In effect, they attempted to create a synthetic Treasury bill by combining options and stock. If the returns from the option-stock hedge were not equal to the Treasury bill return, it meant the model was unable to provide equilibrium option prices. On the other hand, if there was no significant difference between the hedge and Treasury bill returns, then it could be concluded that the model provided equilibrium prices. The results of the Black–Scholes empirical test showed no significant difference between the option-stock hedged returns and the Treasury bill returns. Thus, Black and Scholes concluded the model did provide equilibrium prices.

The theoretical derivation and empirical justification of an option pricing model by Black and Scholes was an extremely important accomplishment with far-reaching implications. Basically, it meant that model-generated prices could be considered as the equilibrium, or correct, prices. Thus, an investor could use the model to determine whether the market had mispriced an option. Mispriced options spawn arbitrage opportunities. Given such an opportunity, the most obvious way to benefit is to form a riskless hedge by combining options and stock and then maintaining the hedge until the option's market price adjusts to the equilibrium model price. This strategy will provide arbitrage profits since the level of risk that is being assumed equals that of a Treasury bill, but the profits earned when the mispriced option adjusts to the equilibrium, or model price, will exceed the profits earned from investing in a Treasury bill.

Application

The data in Table 14A–1 illustrate the mechanics of the Black–Scholes option pricing model.

Column 1 simply denotes the stock's ticker symbol, while Columns 2 through 7 provide the required inputs for the model. Notice that the option maturity is expressed in calendar days and the volatility is given as the standard deviation of returns. The call and put option prices (for both stocks) implied by the data will not be computed.

When the values from Table 14A-1 for CFL stock are used in Formulas 14A-2 and 14A-3, we obtain the following answers for d_1 and d_2:

$$d_1 = \frac{\ln(33/35) + [0.09 + (0.04/2)][(0.4932)]}{(0.2)(\sqrt{0.4932})}$$

$$= \frac{-0.0588 + 0.0543}{0.1405}$$

$$= -0.032$$

$$d_2 = -0.032 - 0.1405$$

$$= -0.1725$$

To obtain values for $N(d_1)$ and $N(d_2)$, the Standard Normal Distribution Function Table (Table 14A-2) must be used. The $N(d_1)$ and $N(d_2)$ values are found by first locating the row and column entries in the table that correspond to the computed d_1 and d_2 values. For CFL stock, the row entry is -0.0, and the column entry is 3. This value of -0.03 approximates the computed d_1 value of -0.032. For d_2, the row entry is -0.1, and the column entry is 7, yielding a value of -0.17, approximating the computed value of -0.1725 for d_2.

Locating the d_1 and d_2 values yield the table entries that define the values of $N(d_1)$ and $N(d_2)$. For CFL stock, the $N(d_1)$ value is 0.4880, while the $N(d_2)$ value is 0.4325. In this example, these values are only approximations, since -0.03 and -0.17 are approximations. If one desires more precise $N(d_1)$ and $N(d_2)$ values, they can be obtained through interpolation. For these examples, the approximations are sufficient.

At this point, all the necessary values for computing the option price have been found. Determining the options' prices via Formulas 14A-1 and 14A-5 is all that remains to be done. Thus, the CFL call option price is:

$$c = (33)(0.4880) - (35)[e^{-(0.09)\,(0.4932)}](0.4325)$$

$$= 16.1040 - (35)(0.9566)(0.4325)$$

$$= 16.1040 - 14.4805$$

$$= 1.6235$$

and the CFL put option price is:

$$p = (35)[e^{-(0.09)(0.4932)}] - 33 + 1.6235$$

$$= (35)(0.9566) - 33 + 1.6235$$

$$= 2.1045$$

Since each option controls 100 shares of stock, the theoretical call price is $162.35, while the put's theoretical price is $210.45.

A second example (using GAH stock) again uses the variables from Table 14A-1 and substitutes them into Formulas 14A-2 and 14A-3 to derive d_1 and d_2 as follows:

$$d_1 = \frac{\ln(42/40) + [0.10 + (0.0529/2)](0.1370)}{(0.23)(\sqrt{0.1370})}$$

$$= \frac{0.0488 + 0.0173}{0.0851}$$

$$= 0.7767$$

$$d_2 = 0.7767 - 0.0851$$

$$= 0.6916$$

TABLE 14A–1   Illustrative Data for Black–Scholes Option Model

(1) Stock Symbol	(2) (S) Stock Price	(3) (X) Strike Price	(4) (T) Days to Maturity Dividend by Days in Year	(5) (r) Risk-Free Rate	(6) (σ) Standard Deviation of Returns	(7) (σ²) Variance of Stock Returns
CFL	33	35	180/365	0.09	0.20	0.04
GAH	42	40	50/365	0.10	0.23	0.0529

TABLE 14A–2   Standard Normal Distribution Function

t	0	1	2	3	4	5	6	7	8	9
−3.0	.0013									
−2.9	.0019	.0018	.0017	.0017	.0016	.0016	.0015	.0015	.0014	.0014
−2.8	.0026	.0025	.0024	.0023	.0023	.0022	.0021	.0021	.0020	.0019
−2.7	.0035	.0034	.0033	.0032	.0031	.0030	.0029	.0028	.0027	.0026
−2.6	.0047	.0045	.0044	.0043	.0041	.0040	.0039	.0038	.0037	.0036
−2.5	.0062	.0060	.0059	.0057	.0055	.0054	.0052	.0051	.0049	.0048
−2.4	.0082	.0080	.0078	.0075	.0073	.0071	.0069	.0068	.0066	.0064
−2.3	.0107	.0104	.0102	.0099	.0096	.0094	.0091	.0089	.0087	.0084
−2.2	.0139	.0136	.0132	.0129	.0125	.0122	.0119	.0116	.0113	.0110
−2.1	.0179	.0174	.0170	.0166	.0162	.0158	.0154	.0150	.0146	.0143
−2.0	.0227	.0222	.0217	.0212	.0207	.0202	.0197	.0192	.0188	.0183
−1.9	.0287	.0281	.0274	.0268	.0262	.0256	.0250	.0244	.0239	.0233
−1.8	.0359	.0351	.0344	.0336	.0329	.0322	.0314	.0307	.0300	.0294
−1.7	.0446	.0436	.0427	.0418	.0409	.0401	.0392	.0384	.0375	.0367
−1.6	.0548	.0537	.0526	.0516	.0505	.0495	.0485	.0475	.0465	.0455
−1.5	.0668	.0655	.0643	.0630	.0618	.0606	.0594	.0582	.0571	.0559
−1.4	.0808	.0793	.0778	.0764	.0749	.0735	.0721	.0708	.0694	.0681
−1.3	.0968	.0951	.0934	.0918	.0901	.0885	.0869	.0853	.0838	.0823
−1.2	.1151	.1131	.1112	.1093	.1075	.1056	.1038	.1020	.1003	.0985
−1.1	.1357	.1335	.1314	.1292	.1271	.1251	.1230	.1210	.1190	.1170
−1.0	.1587	.1562	.1539	.1515	.1492	.1469	.1446	.1423	.1401	.1379
−0.9	.1841	.1814	.1788	.1762	.1736	.1711	.1685	.1660	.1635	.1611
−0.8	.2119	.2090	.2061	.2033	.2005	.1977	.1949	.1921	.1894	.1867
−0.7	.2420	.2389	.2358	.2326	.2297	.2266	.2236	.2206	.2177	.2148
−0.6	.2743	.2709	.2676	.2643	.2611	.2578	.2546	.2514	.2483	.2451
−0.5	.3085	.3050	.3015	.2981	.2946	.2912	.2877	.2843	.2810	.2776
−0.4	.3446	.3409	.3372	.3336	.3300	.3264	.3228	.3192	.3156	.3121
−0.3	.3821	.3783	.3745	.3707	.3669	.3632	.3594	.3557	.3520	.3483
−0.2	.4207	.4168	.4129	.4090	.4052	.4013	.3974	.3936	.3897	.3859
−0.1	.4602	.4562	.4522	.4483	.4443	.4404	.4364	.4325	.4286	.4247
−0.0	.5000	.4960	.4920	.4880	.4840	.4801	.4761	.4721	.4681	.4641

(Continued)

TABLE 14A–2   Standard Normal Distribution Function—*(Continued)*

t	0	1	2	3	4	5	6	7	8	9
0.0	.5000	.5040	.5080	.5120	.5160	.5199	.5239	.5279	.5319	.5359
0.1	.5398	.5438	.5478	.5517	.5557	.5596	.5636	.5675	.5714	.5753
0.2	.5793	.5832	.5871	.5910	.5948	.5987	.6026	.6064	.6103	.6141
0.3	.6179	.6217	.6255	.6293	.6331	.6368	.6406	.6443	.6480	.6517
0.4	.6554	.6591	.6628	.6664	.6700	.6736	.6772	.6808	.6844	.6879
0.5	.6915	.6950	.6985	.7019	.7054	.7088	.7123	.7157	.7190	.7224
0.6	.7257	.7291	.7324	.7357	.7389	.7422	.7454	.7486	.7517	.7549
0.7	.7580	.7611	.7642	.7673	.7704	.7734	.7764	.7794	.7823	.7852
0.8	.7881	.7910	.7939	.7967	.7995	.8023	.8051	.8079	.8106	.8133
0.9	.8159	.8186	.8212	.8238	.8264	.8289	.8315	.8340	.8365	.8189
1.0	.8413	.8438	.8461	.8485	.8508	.8531	.8554	.8577	.8599	.8621
1.1	.8643	.8665	.8686	.8708	.8729	.8749	.8770	.8790	.8810	.8830
1.2	.8849	.8869	.8888	.8907	.8925	.8944	.8962	.8980	.8997	.9015
1.3	.9032	.9049	.9066	.9082	.9099	.9115	.9131	.9147	.9162	.9177
1.4	.9192	.9207	.9222	.9236	.9251	.9265	.9279	.9292	.9306	.9319
1.5	.9332	.9345	.9357	.9370	.9382	.9394	.9406	.9418	.9429	.9441
1.6	.9452	.9463	.9474	.9484	.9495	.9505	.9515	.9525	.9535	.9545
1.7	.9554	.9564	.9573	.9582	.9591	.9599	.9608	.9616	.9625	.9633
1.8	.9641	.9649	.9656	.9664	.9671	.9678	.9686	.9693	.9700	.9706
1.9	.9713	.9719	.9726	.9732	.9738	.9744	.9750	.9756	.9761	.9767
2.0	.9773	.9778	.9783	.9788	.9793	.9798	.9803	.9808	.9812	.9817
2.1	.9821	.9826	.9830	.9834	.9838	.9842	.9846	.9850	.9854	.9857
2.2	.9861	.9864	.9868	.9871	.9875	.9878	.9881	.9884	.9887	.9890
2.3	.9893	.9896	.9898	.9901	.9904	.9906	.9909	.9911	.9913	.9916
2.4	.9918	.9920	.9922	.9925	.9927	.9929	.9931	.9932	.9934	.9936
2.5	.9938	.9940	.9941	.9943	.9945	.9946	.9948	.9949	.9951	.9952
2.6	.9953	.9955	.9956	.9957	.9959	.9960	.9961	.9962	.9963	.9964
2.7	.9965	.9966	.9967	.9968	.9969	.9970	.9971	.9972	.9973	.9974
2.8	.9974	.9975	.9976	.9977	.9977	.9978	.9979	.9979	.9980	.9981
2.9	.9981	.9982	.9982	.9983	.9984	.9984	.9985	.9985	.9986	.9986
3.0	.9987									

The $N(d_1)$ and $N(d_2)$ values from the standard normal distribution table (Table 14A-2) are 0.7823 and 0.7549, respectively. As mentioned in the previous example, greater precision is possible through interpolation.

Given the above values, the GAH call and put prices are computed as:

$$c = (42)(0.7823) - (40)[e^{-(0.10)(0.1370)}]\,(0.7549)$$
$$= 32.8566 - (40)(0.9864)(0.7549)$$
$$= 32.8566 - 29.7853$$
$$= 3.0713$$
$$p = (40)[e^{-(0.10)(0.1370)}] - 42 + 3.0713$$
$$= (40)(0.9864) - 42 + 3.0713$$
$$= 0.5273$$

These calculations indicate the theoretically correct price (for 100 shares) for the call is $307.13 and that $52.73 is the theoretically correct price for the put.

Suppose the market had priced the GAH call at $262.50. How would you be able to earn arbitrage profits? According to Black and Scholes, you would buy the undervalued calls at $262.50 and sell shares of GAH stock at $42 per share to form a riskless hedge and thus obtain arbitrage profits when equilibrium is established. However, to implement such a strategy, an investor must know how many shares to combine with each option to form the riskless hedge. This information is provided by $N(d_1)$ and is known as the hedge ratio or delta.

Since each option controls 100 shares of stock, the appropriate arbitrage activity in this example is to sell 0.7823 shares of GAH stock for every option purchased. Practically speaking, one cannot buy and sell fractional shares. Thus, 78 shares should be sold for each option that is purchased. If the market had overpriced the option, then the arbitrageur would sell options and purchase 78 shares for each option sold. In either case, the hedge's risk level will equal that of a Treasury bill, but the hedge's returns will exceed the Treasury bill's return, thus generating arbitrage profits.

Chapter 15

Trading Strategies Using Derivatives

Hedging is the act of reducing or mitigating an economic risk. The word "hedge" evolved along with the usage of derivative securities for risk management and control. However, the concept of hedging is not new. Insurance is a prime example of a hedge. The act of buying a home-owner's policy is a hedge since it protects the policy owner from the risk of economic loss from potential damages to the house arising out of fire, burglary, etc. Similarly, a farmer who uses a drought-resistant seed is also a hedger who is protecting against the vagaries of weather. While both the homeowner and the farmer are hedgers, the usage of the word is more commonly applicable when a financial security is bought (or sold) to manage risk. Thus the home-owner's policy is closer to the concept of hedging than the example of the farmer's drought-resistant seeds.

In the first section of this chapter we will examine in some detail the usage of derivatives to hedge against economic loss. We will begin by a simple example of using a financial security to hedge. Assume that we are given the following information for a hypothetical investor.

> Amount to invest = $10,000
>
> Price per share of XYZ stock = $100
>
> 6-month yield on a T-bill = 4%/year or 2%/6 months
>
> Premium on an American call option on XYZ stock = $10/share
>
> The strike price of the option = $100
>
> The time to maturity of the option = 6 months

Let us assume that the investor wishes to buy 100 shares of the XYZ stock and holds the position for 6 months. If the price of the XYZ stock closes at $110 at the end of 6 months then the investor stands to make a profit of $1,000. Similarly, a closing price of $90 would result in a $1,000 loss. Table 15-1 shows some of the possible profit and loss positions at the end of the investment term.

The possible outcome from the above investment decision can also be depicted using a graph, as shown in Figure 15-1.

TABLE 15–1

Price of stock	70	80	90	100	110	120	130
Profit/Loss on stock	−3000	−2000	−1000	0	1000	2000	3000

FIGURE 15–1 Price of Stock vs. Profit/Loss on Stock

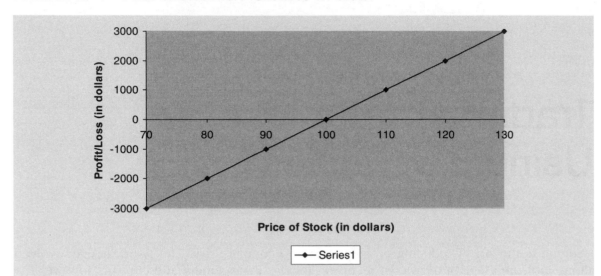

Figure 15-1 shows that the investor who buys the 100 shares of XYZ stock stands to gain large amounts of money if the stock price moves up but also is exposed to the potential of losing large sums if the price of XYZ stock declines. Under these conditions, and given that the investor has no way of knowing for certain which way the price will change, the investor may seek to reduce the exposure to the loss. Consider now this alternate investment decision.

In this alternate scenario the investor buys 1 call option contract (the right to buy 100 shares) for $1,000 (premium of $10/share × 100 shares) and invests the rest of the money in the risk-free Treasury bill for a six month period. The T-bill is expected to provide a guaranteed profit of $180 ($9,000 × 0.02) in six months' time. Table 15-2 shows the outcomes of this decision while Figure 15-2 plots the outcomes.

We can observe from Figure 15-2 that the alternate strategy also has a similar potential for profits if the stock price increases. We note that this alternate strategy underperforms strategy A by $820, i.e. if XYZ stock prices increased then holding stocks would be more profitable than strategy B by $820. However, if stock prices decreased, while holding stocks could lead to very large losses, the most one could lose by the alternate strategy would again be $820. Thus the alternate strategy contains all the upside potential of the first strategy with only a very limited and known loss amount. Further, as compared to strategy A, the maximum cost of strategy B is $820, which is the loss potential.

The reader will note from the earlier chapter on derivatives that the payoff depicted for strategy B is identical to the payoff depicted for a call option. That is, a call option on a stock hedges (or protects) the owner against declines but allows the owner to gain from price increases. This is how an option serves to hedge a position.

We will now examine several applications of options to hedge against economic risk.

Protective Put   Suppose you own a stock and you are bullish about the stock. However, given that you understand the uncertainties of stock prices, you are apprehensive that a near term and unexpected decline in the price of the stock would hurt your position and that it is worthwhile for you to hedge against this loss. You are also averse to selling the stock because you are ultimately bullish on the stock. Again, let us use an example to elucidate. We are given the following:

> Price of stock today = $100
> 6 month put premium = $10
> Exercise price = $100

TABLE 15–2

Price of stock	70	80	90	100	110	120	130
Value of option on expiration	0	0	0	0	1000	2000	3000
T bill	9180	9180	9180	9180	9180	9180	9180
Total	−820	−820	−820	−820	+180	+1180	+2180

FIGURE 15–2   Stock Price vs. P/L

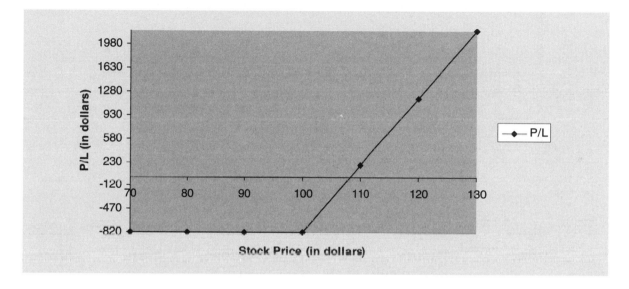

Table 15-3 shows the possible outcomes (payoffs) from this position while Figure 15-3 charts the payoffs on each of the securities and the protective put.

As can be seen again from Figure 15-3, a protective put has an outcome just like a call option, i.e. unlimited upside potential and a limit on losses. The investor is hedged against a downturn. However, it is important to note that a protective put is not the same as owning a call option. In the above example, if you owned a 6 month call, the call would expire at the end of 6 months and you would not have any position in that stock's market. On the other hand, at the end of 6 months, when the put expires, you still own the stock. This is consistent with your bullish expectation in the long run but apprehension about the near term. Thus, with an expectation of a near term price decline, you wouldn't want to own a call option.

The Covered Call   Assume you own a stock that you bought some time ago. Assume also that the stock's price has increased during this holding period and is currently at a price such that you desire to sell the stock to lock in the profit. The important issue in a covered call is this last concept: that you have decided to sell the stock. The question that arises is whether you can enhance your returns further even while you exit the position without jeopardizing the profit already earned. The answer is yes, and this is done through a covered call. The following example explains this concept.

TABLE 15–3

Value of stock	70	80	90	100	110	120	130
Value of put	+20	+10	0	−10	−10	−10	−10
Value of position	90	90	90	90	100	110	120

FIGURE 15–3   Price of Stock vs. Net Outcome

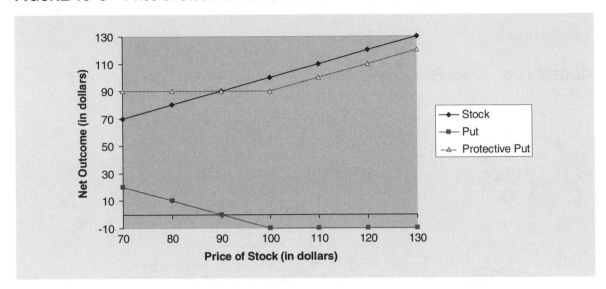

Current stock (exit) price = $100
3 month call option premium = $5
Exercise price = $100

In the example of covered call, you own the stock and *write* the call option. Table 15-4 shows the outcomes and Figure 15-4 charts the different securities.

In the case of the short call, the call won't be exercised if the price falls below $100 and you keep the $5 premium. If the price increases, the call is exercised and you sell your stock at $100 (as desired) but you get to keep the premium. Thus you exit your position at $105 instead of $100 (return enhancement). On the other hand if the stock prices decline in the next three months, you can still exit your position at $100 or more as long as the stock price does not go below $95. Thus you have a small cushion (hedge) if prices decline and have the opportunity to enhance returns if the stock price increases. As mentioned earlier and reiterated here again, a covered call is useful only when an investor has made up their mind to sell out of a position. In the following section on using puts and calls as part of a trading strategy, we will observe that the motivation of a certain trading activity is an important ingredient in trading strategies using puts and calls.

So far, we have been observing the activity of hedging from the perspective of the individual. We will now turn our attention to hedging by financial institutions. Consider the example of a small managed fund which has $2 million under management. Assume that the fund owns 15 different stocks in its portfolio and that the stocks are all large cap stocks, very similar to S&P 500 stocks. Suppose the manager expects a short-term decline in the market in the range of 5-10 percent within the next six months. The manager also feels that the decline will be temporary but is uncertain about both the duration and the magnitude of the downturn. Under these conditions, the manager considers hedging to be a prudent choice.

TABLE 15–4

Price of stock	70	80	90	100	110	120	130
Stock position	70	80	90	100	110	120	130
Written (short) call	+5	+5	+5	+5	−5	−15	−25
Covered call	75	85	95	105	105	105	105

FIGURE 15–4   Stock Price vs. Net Outcome

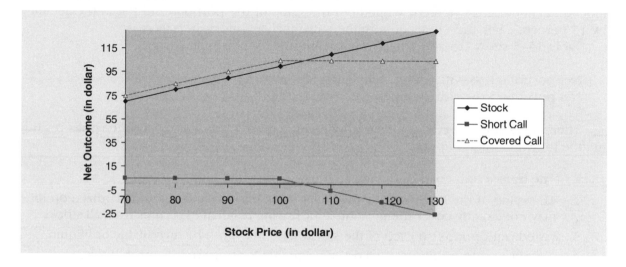

In protecting the fund's position, the first choice the manager faces is whether to sell all the stocks in the portfolio (liquidate all positions) or whether to use derivatives to hedge. Since the decision to liquidate the entire portfolio and convert it into cash is very expensive (both from transaction costs and the opportunity loss of not having an open position in the case of an unexpected market upturn), such a move would be warranted only when the manager was very reliably convinced of a deep and long downturn in the market. Since this is not the case in this example, we will assume that the manager will use derivatives to hedge.

Given this decision, the manager is now faced with two further choices. The manager could purchase puts on the 15 individual stocks (protective puts) to hedge. Alternately, the manager could use a put index option. Since the stocks in the portfolio were large cap stocks, the manager could use index options on the S&P 100 (OEX). We can use a numerical example to observe the impact of both strategies. Assume that we are given the following:

> Current value of portfolio of 15 stocks = $2 million
>
> Current value of the S&P 100 index = 1000
>
> Cost of buying individual options on the 15 stocks = $8,000
>
> The premium on one put option contract on the index = $6,000
>
> The exercise price of the above index put = 1,000
>
> Number of index puts needed to hedge position[1] = 20

---

[1] The number of puts required is calculated by dividing the portfolio value by the strike price times the OEX multiplier ($100), i.e. $2 million / $1000 × 100 = 20 contracts.

TABLE 15–5

	Portfolio	Individual Equity Put Options	S&P 100 Index	20 Index Put Options
Beginning value	$2 million	$80,000	1,000	$48,000
Ending value	$1.7 million	$264,000	850	$ 233,000
Change in value	($0.3 million)	+ $184,000	−15%	+$185,000

Let us assume that the manager's expectations were well founded and that the market indeed declines by 15 percent while both the value of the portfolio and the index declines by 15 percent each, the values of both the individual and index puts increase.

Table 15-5 shows the outcome from each of the two hedging strategies.

Net portfolio loss with individual puts = $116,000
Net portfolio loss with 20 index puts = $115,000

There are a few interesting observations to note. First, let us consider the issues regarding the individual Equity puts:

1. The transaction costs of buying 15 puts can be quite high.

2. The value of the holdings of a particular stock may be such that standardized options may not exactly cover the position held, leaving residual exposures from all stocks.

3. Listed put options on each of the stocks held may both be unavailable or illiquid.

4. If a put option is illiquid, the cost of using OTC options may be prohibitive.

5. There may be a potential mismatch between available maturities and the duration requirements of the fund.

6. A very important issue in holding individual equity options is that if the puts are in the money at expiration, an automatic exercise may be triggered, i.e. The underlying stocks may cause cash flow problems if any of the stocks sold implied capital gains and hence, taxes. Further, additional commissions would be charged on stock sales.

Let us now consider the advantages and disadvantages of using index put options. First, the advantages.

1. The cost to enter the position in index options is generally cheaper than the total position in individual equities. The reason why it is a bit cheaper is that buying an index option implies buying a blanket position in all the 100 stocks in the index—a volume discount is implied. An analogy is the case if insurance on home, car, earthquake, flood, etc. from the same carrier may be cheaper than buying from different carriers.

2. Since index options are settled on a cash basis, there are no cash flow issues as there are no automatic exercise needs requiring the delivery of securities.

3. Since the value of one contract on the index is generally much higher than any individual equity option value, the number of contracts required to hedge a portfolio is considerably lower for index options, resulting in lower transaction costs.

4. It is easier to match (come closer to) the value of the index put position to the fund's value than with individual equities.

There are a few major disadvantages of using index options for hedging. They are

1. Index options may turn out to be costlier when the market is very volatile.

2. The main problem in the above hedge example using index options is that we assumed that the portfolio's change in value would mimic the change in the S&P

100 index. The chances of such co-movements decrease as the number of individual stocks in a portfolio decrease. That is, the correlation between the fund's value and the index is an important determinant of how well the index puts hedge the funds. If the correlation is not high enough then individual puts may easily outperform index puts.

3. Another problem exists for fund managers when available indexes do not reflect the composition of a particular portfolio. In our example, we made a simplifying assumption that the stocks held mimicked the characteristics of the S&P 100 index. However, we can easily understand the problems that would arise in hedging where a portfolio was not comprised of equities of different characteristics but also contained securities from other asset classes.

Hedging a portfolio against downside risk using options is often termed as **portfolio insurance**. In the example above, both the individual puts and the index put applications were examples of portfolio insurance. Readers should note that most managed funds are large enough to warrant the use of index options both because of feasibility and because the disadvantages of index options are considerably mitigated for broad based funds.

Hedging stock positions are not the only application of options for hedging purposes. Options are used to hedge against interest rate risk, currency risk, commodity risk, etc. In fact, the development of options in the 1970s was in response to increased volatilities in all financial markets, especially currency markets; the development of options was principally for risk management purposes. However as is well known, options can be used for speculation. The use (abuse) of options to speculate, and resulting turmoil, has received much prominence through media coverage. Since it is important for students and practitioners to understand how options may be used to hedge in non-stock financial markets, we will now look at examples of such applications.

Interest Rate Risk Management   Let us assume that a firm needs to borrow $10 million at some time within the next quarter. Let us also assume that the loan will be pegged to the Euro$ LIBOR spot rate and the lender will charge 1 percent Euro$ LIBOR rate. The current Euro$ LIBOR rate is 4 percent/year for the appropriate loan term, so borrowing today would imply a cost of 5%. Let us assume that the borrower expects interest rates to decline in the near future but is concerned about the uncertainty of rates rising and having to borrow at a rate much higher than the current rate. In this case, the borrower might consider hedging the position by buying Euro$ LIBOR puts. Let us assume that a three month put on $1 million costs 0.30/$. Let us now consider what happens if the market interest rates rise or fall by 1% within the interim period. Also note that since rates are quoted on an annualized basis, the value of the puts needs to be adjusted for a quarter.

Scenario 1: Euro$ LIBOR increases to 5% and the annual interest cost for the borrower is at 6% (Euro$ LIBOR + 1). In this case, the quarterly interest expense for the borrower would be $10 million $\times$ 0.06 $\times$ 0.25 = $150,000. The cost of the put options is 0.30 $\times$ $10 million $\times$ 0.25 = $7,500. If interest rates rise by 1%, the gain on the put value would be equal to $25,000 (0.01 $\times$ $10 million $\times$ 0.25) resulting in a net profit of $17,500. Thus, the net cost to the borrower would be $132,500 ($150,000–$17,500) or an interest rate of 1.325%/qtr or 5.3%/year

Scenario 2: If the Euro$ LIBOR instead declined by 1%, the net effect to the borrower would be as follows:

Quarterly interest expense is $10 million $\times$ 0.25 $\times$ 0.04   = $100,000

Cost of put option, not exercised   = $+7,500

Net interest expense   = $107,500

In this case, the interest expense to the borrower would be 1.075%/qtr or 4.3%/yr.

In the above example, the borrower will benefit if the expectation of interest decline comes true. The borrower is also assured that they will not pay more than 5.3% if interest rates increase. The cost of this hedge is the slightly higher cost (4.3% instead of 4%) for an interest rate decrease.

Finally, let us examine the application of options by a firm which wants to buy back its stock. Assume that this company's stock is $48 and it wishes to buy back its stock at this price. Instead of buying the stock back outright, the company writes puts on the stock at an exercise price of $48 and receives a premium of $2/share.

If the price of the stock declines and the put is exercised, then the company buys back the stock at $46 ($48−$2). This is preferred to the current price. If the price increases and the put is not exercised then the company is assured of a buyback price of $48 or lower, as long as the stock price does not increase beyond $50. If the company feels that prices might increase beyond $50, then the company buys back the stock at the spot rate, closes out its naked put and reduces the buyback cost by the premium differential.

The last two examples of hedges were also strategies that companies can use to create value as hedge. In the next section we will examine how put and call options can be strategically used by individuals and institutions to create value.

FINANCIAL FUTURES: STOCK MARKET FUTURES, CURRENCY FUTURES & INTEREST FUTURES

Oftentimes, the owner of a portfolio of stocks will want to hedge against anticipated price declines or increases in the investment market. In the event of an anticipated decline in the market, the investor could sell all of his stocks, purchase put options or he could sell stock index futures. The first two options could be prohibitively expensive but, depending on the make-up of the portfolio, selling stock index futures could be effectively protective. By selling stock index futures, the investor is establishing a short position in the market. Thus if the market does go down during the prescribed period of the contract, the investor will have effectively hedged his loss.

Suppose an investor owns a portfolio with 50 stocks worth $150,000. In anticipation of a market decrease, the investor sells stock index futures. Suppose that Composite Index Futures Contracts have a value that is 500 times greater than the value of the stock index (such as the NYSE Index or the S&P 500 Index). Suppose the value of the stock index is currently 150. The investor would have to sell two Composite Index Futures Contracts in order to hedge the $150,000 portfolio (500 × 150 × 2 = $150,000). If the index drops 130, the investor will make a $6,000 profit (150 − 130) × 500. (Please note that the cost of the contract will reduce the profit.) Thus even though the market declines and the value of the portfolio declines, the hedge has allowed the investor to protect if not eliminate some of the loss. However, if the market increases to 160, the investor's portfolio has probably increased but the contract will lose $5,000 (150 − 160) × 500.

When investing in this sort of hedge, it is important for the investor to consider if the index matches the portfolio of stocks. If the portfolio and the market do not have a similar level of diversification, the investor may indeed lose value on the portfolio even though the hedge has realized a profit. It is therefore important to do research prior to entering into this kind of arrangement. These types of arrangements can be entered into via a margin payment. This makes the cost of the contract relatively cheap relative to the value of the portfolio.

Conversely, if an investor thinks that the market will increase, futures will be purchased instead of sold. The investor is establishing a long market position. The mechanism is the same as discussed above except the investor is betting that the index will increase rather than decrease and thus will be affected in the opposite way as the investor who is speculating that the market will decrease.

Currency Futures can be regarded in the same way as stock market futures. Suppose an American corporation invests in a Swiss money market account that guarantees a 3% return on funds invested for one year. Because yields on these accounts are 1% greater than U.S. money market funds a corporation would like to invest in this account. The company has $3.0 million to invest in this fund. At 3% interest, the company will have made $90,000 in one year. However, because of exchange rate fluctuations, the company wants to insure that the $90,000 does not get affected as it needs these funds in totality after one year.

Assume that it costs $0.7874 for one Swiss frank. The company will send 2,362,200 Swiss franks to the Swiss bank ($0.7874 × $3.0 million). In one year, the company requires its principal plus the $90,000 in interest. Therefore, in order to hedge the currency fluctuation, the company will sell a futures contract for the future delivery of Swiss francs and establish a short position so that they are able to purchase dollars at $1.27 ($1.00/$0.7874). If in one year the value of the dollar increases to $1.30, the hedge will have been effective since the Swiss frank is now worth $0.7692. If a hedge had not been purchased the value of the funds would only be $3,070,983 ((2,362,200 × 1.30)/$0.7692). If in one year the value of the dollar declines to $1.20, less profit will have been realized on the transaction.

Suppose an investor has a bond portfolio worth $1.0 million. Because of rumblings within the market regarding the Fed, the investor perceives that interest rates are going to be increased. The value of the investor's bonds will decrease if this case occurs. The investor could sell all of his bonds or purchase calls but this could be prohibitively expensive since he has a portfolio. Therefore, the investor will buy futures and establish a short position in the market. If interest rates do in fact increase, the portfolio is protected against loss. However, as we previously mentioned, the degree of the protection depends on how well the hedge matches the bond portfolio. If however, interest rates decrease, the investor will forgo potential profits as long as the hedge remains in place.

Swaps

A swap is an agreement to exchange a series of payments over a specified period of time. Most individual investors do not participate in swaps but corporations and financial institutions often do. These types of transactions are executed in order to perform portfolio rebalancing in order to mitigate risk. Swaps are relevant to individual investors because they must be disclosed in a publicly traded corporation's annual report or 10K. There are several kinds of swaps but two common types will be explained below. They are an interest rate swap and a currency swap.

An interest rate swap is generally structured such that one party agrees to pay a fixed amount of interest (based upon a principal amount) and the other party, in exchange pays an adjustable interest rate (based upon the same principal amount). These types of swaps are executed in order to match an institution's liabilities with its core of assets and also to increase or decrease exposure to interest rate changes in the market.

Exchange rate swaps are generally entered into by two corporations, each one from a different country in order to hedge against currency risk. For instance, suppose a U.S. firm has debt obligations payable in German marks, and a German company has U.S. debt obligations payable in U.S. dollars, both corporations may want to hedge against currency fluctuations. As we discussed above, each could sell currency futures. However, these two corporations could also trade payments with each other in order to alleviate exchange rate risk. Thus the U.S. firm would pay the German firm's debt obligations and the German firm would pay the U.S. firm's debt obligations.

Collars

A collar is an investment strategy whereby an investor will bind his gains or losses between two points. Investor's commonly use collars because the investor has a target gain amount that they would like to receive on a particular investment but are unwilling to sustain investment losses below a certain level. In this strategy, the investor will sell a call option and purchase a put option.

Suppose that an investor purchased 100 shares of Microsoft at $28.00 per share. In order to minimize loss, the investor will perhaps sell a call option at $23.00 per share and purchase a put option at $33.00. If the stock increases above $33.00 during the option period, the stock will be called away. The investor has thus made $5.00 per share on the transaction ($33.00–$28.00). If however, the price drops to $23.00, our investor will sell the shares of Microsoft stock and limit his loss to $5.00 per share ($28.00–$23.00). Of course in purchasing a put and selling a call, the investor will incur investment fees. These fees must be taken into consideration as well.

Commodities Hedges

In the first scenario we discussed a producer who wishes to protect against price deflation. In this case, the producer knows a couple of things. First, he knows what it will cost him to produce his corn. Second, he knows the current price of corn in the market. But he does not know what future prices of corn will be when he is ready to sell his corn in the market. Therefore he wishes to protect himself so that he can cover his costs and hopefully make a profit on his endeavors in the future. In this case, the farmer will sell a contract for future delivery. The hedge is created because the farmer/producer takes a long position (corn growing) and a short position (the futures contract).

Suppose corn is currently selling for $2.72 per bushel in March. The farmer will be selling his corn at market in July. His cost to produce corn is currently $2.25 per bushel. If he sells a future's contract where he is guaranteed to be able to sell his corn at $2.72, he will insure his profit of $0.47 per bushel ($2.72–$2.25). In July, suppose the market price of the corn is $2.50 per bushel. He has made an effective hedge by purchasing this contract. He has made $0.47 per bushel less any transaction costs of entering into the futures contract. Conversely, if the price of corn goes up to $2.80 per bushel, he will still only be able to get $2.72 per bushel. While he has still made a profit, he will not be able to realize the additional $0.08 per bushel. However, he has succeeded in effectively hedging himself against a major price decline.

In the case of a purchaser of corn, a contract will be purchased instead of sold. That is, the buyer of the corn will buy a contract for future delivery. A distiller needs to know the price of corn in the future so that he can prepare for production and sales to distributors. Thus in this case the long position is represented by the future delivery of corn and the short position is represented by future production of alcohol. If the purchaser of corn buys a contract at $2.72 per bushel, he will not be affected if the price of corn increases. However, if the price of corn decreases to $2.50, he will have missed out on a $0.22 per bushel decrease in price.

TRADING STRATEGIES USING PUTS AND CALLS

We will begin this section by first examining simple trading strategies using puts and calls for both individuals and institutions. Thereon, we will examine the engineering of financial products using options. This is a new and exciting area of development and students will gain a rudimentary understanding of strategic financial product development.

Before looking at examples, it is important to gain some insight about the objectives of such strategies. The main objective of using options is to affect the risks and returns of outcomes. A primary condition to ending a strategy is also the existence of an expectation regarding changes in the underlying assets. Finally, in applying the techniques, students need to understand the tools that may be used in strategies. Perhaps the simplest way to explain the above is by using the example of auto insurance, which most of us possess. In acquiring insurance the buyer considers first the various coverages that the policy contains. Thus, when a buyer chooses, for example, a certain collision coverage, it is to protect (hedge) against the costs of accidents. However, the buyer also considers the deductible on the collision coverage. The buyer can reduce the policy premium by increasing the size of the deductible. Clearly, this is a decision of the expectations about the possibility of an accident, its risk and the returns from having low premiums. The buyer can similarly decide on the term to change risk-return characteristics. Options are very similar in that the exercise (strike) prices perform the same function as the deductibles in the above example. Similarly, options are of varying maturities, which provide another different mechanism (tool) to strategize. We can now begin by examining some examples of strategic applications.

Example 1   Suppose an investor was bullish on a certain industry but the investor also felt that the increase in prices of companies in this industry would be short-lived and would last for about three to six months. The investor may buy the shares of stocks of some companies in the industry and await the price increase. Alternately, the investor could use call options. Table 15-6 shows the current and expected stock and call option hypothetical prices for five companies in some industry.

If the investor were to buy the stocks and sell them off at the expected price, on an initial investment of $232 they would have a profit of $13 or a return of 5.6%. Instead, the call strategy would require only $19 per unit stock/company and would return 52.6% over the same period. Of course this looks very attractive, but the investor could be wrong in their timing of the expectation. If the industry prices did not change as per expectation during the maturity of the options, the investor would also stand to lose the entire investment whereas owning the stocks would not have the same outcome.

Example 2   Assume a company deals in a commodity which currently sells at $150/unit. The company wishes to enhance its returns by writing a call option (covered call) for a premium of $4/unit. The company could also enhance this return further by writing a put option at the same strike price ($150) and maturity. Assume the put option has a premium of $5/unit. Table 15-7 shows the profits and losses from this strategy and Figure 15-5 charts the outcomes.

Note that on the covered call, as prices increase the company is forced to sell at the strike price but keeps the premium of $4 as revenue enhancement. The company will not suffer a loss as long as the price does not fall below $146 (cushion). In the case of the short put, if the price declines, the company buys at strike, sells as spot and nets with the put premium. Figure 15-5 shows how revenues are enhanced with a covered straddle but exposes to greater downside risk.

The above example provides us with a way of how options may be used in combination to arrive at desired outcomes, given some fundamental expectation about market movements. In the following section we will examine the strategies from the basic building blocks of put and call options.

Let us assume that a commodity currently trades at $50/unit and the premium a three month call option and put option with a $50 strike price is $5 and $4 respectively. Assume

TABLE 15–6

Company	Current price		Expected price		Expected Change	
	Stock	Call	Stock	Call	Stock	Call
1	80	6.00	100	20	+20	+14
2	48	5.00	40	0	−8	−5
3	23	4.00	15	0	−8	−4
4	18	2.00	22	4	+4	+2
5	63	2.00	68	5	+5	+3
Total	232	19.00	245	29	13	10

TABLE 15–7

Price of Commodity	144	145	146	147	148	149	150	151	152
P/L on Covered Call	−2	−1	0	1	2	3	4	4	4
P/L on Put	−1	0	1	2	3	4	5	5	5
Covered Straddle	−3	0	1	3	5	7	9	9	9

FIGURE 15–5 Price of Commodity vs. Profit/Loss

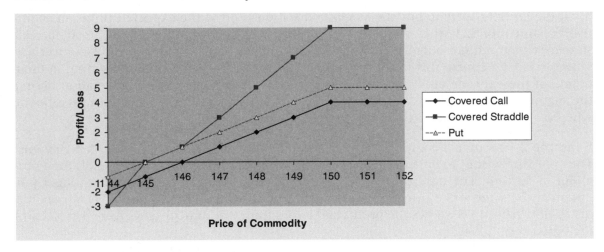

an investor buys one contract of each of the option. Table 15-8 shows the outcomes of each and in total while Figure 15-6 charts each individual outcome and Figure 15-7 charts the total position.

The above strategy is known as a **straddle**. In a straddle, the buyer profits if the price declines or increases beyond a certain point. Hence the buyer expects prices to change but does not know the direction of change, i.e. The buyer expects a volatile market and seeks to profit from this condition.

It is important to note that along traditional lines, most investors seek to profit from expectations of price increases. We observe that options allow us to profit from any change in direction (calls and puts) of prices or just changes in either direction (straddle). If our expectations are correct, then there is a strategy with puts and calls in combinations that will provide profits.

In the above example, the straddle buyer would lose the most if the price did not change at all. If the investor was more certain about the volatility and its magnitude and was averse to losing such a large amount if they were wrong in their expectation, then they could modify the straddle further. For example, the investor may buy a put and a call that were out of the money. This is much like the case of the collision deductible. In this case, the straddle holder would lose less if they were incorrect in their expectations and would profit only if the volatility was even greater. This is left as an exercise.

TABLE 15–8

Commodity price	35	40	45	50	55	60	65
Call	−5	−5	−5	−5	0	+5	+10
Put	+11	+6	+1	−4	−4	−4	−4
Total	+6	+1	−4	−9	−4	+1	+6

FIGURE 15–6   Price of Commodity vs. Profit/Loss

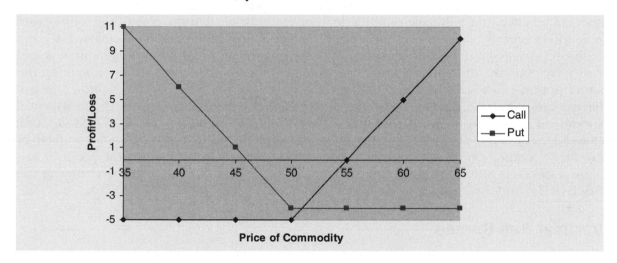

FIGURE 15–7   Price of Commodity vs. Profit/Loss

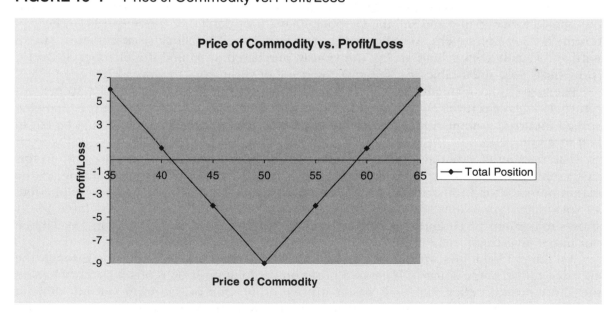

THE USE OF OPTION SPREADS AND STRADDLES

We will look at two primary types of option spreads: vertical spreads and horizontal spreads. Vertical spreads involve buying and writing two contracts at different striking prices with the same month of expiration. Horizontal spreads consist of buying and writing two options with the same strike price but different months, and a diagonal spread is a combination of the vertical and horizontal spread. Table 15-9 presents an example of XYZ Corporation demonstrating the options, months, and strike prices involved in each type of spread. There are more complicated spreads than these, such as the butterfly spread, variable spread, and domino spread. We cannot attempt to explain all of these spreads in the space available, so we will concentrate on vertical bull spreads and vertical bear spreads.

Because spreads require the purchase of one option and the sale of another option, a speculator's account will have either a debit or credit balance. If the cost of the long option position is greater than the revenue from the short option position, the speculator has a net cash outflow and a debit in his account. When your spread is put on with a debit, it is said you have "bought the spread." You have "sold the spread" if the receipt from writing the short option position is greater than the cost of buying the long option position and you have a credit balance. For example, the difference between the option prices for a vertical spread on XYZ Corporation in Table 15-9 with October strike prices of 35 and 40 is $2 ($4–$2). The $2 difference between these two option prices could be either a debit or credit, depending on whether a bull or bear spread is used. In either case, the profit or loss from a spread position results in the change between the two option prices over time as the price of the underlying stock goes up or down.

Vertical Bull Spread

In a bull spread, the expectation is that the common stock price will rise. The speculator can buy the common stock outright, or if he wants to profit from an expected price increase but reduce his risk of loss, he can enter into a bull spread. Vertical bull spreads limit both the maximum gain and maximum loss available. They are usually debit positions because the spreader buys the higher-priced, in-the-money option and shorts (writes) an inexpensive, out-of-the-money option. Using Table 15-9 for an XYZ October vertical bull spread, we would buy the October 35 at 4 and sell the October 40 at 2 for a debit of 2 (price spread). This represents a $200 investment. Assume that three weeks later, XYZ stock rises from $36\frac{3}{8}$ to 42 with the October 35 selling at $7\frac{1}{2}$ (previously purchased at 4) and the October 40 at $4\frac{1}{2}$ (previously sold at 2). Table 15-10 shows the result of closing out the spread.

Because the investment was only $200, the total return of $100 provided a 50 percent return. However, returns on spreads can be greatly altered by commissions. If the following spread incurred commissions of $25 in and $25 out, the percentage return could be cut in half to 25 percent.

The maximum profit at expiration is equal to the difference in strike prices ($5 in this case) minus the initial price spread ($2 in this case). For the XYZ vertical bull spread, the maximum profit is $300, and the maximum loss is the original debit of $200. At expiration, all speculative premiums are gone, and each option sells at its intrinsic value. Table 15-11 shows maximum profit and loss at various closing market prices at expiration. Remember, our initial investment is $200.

As Table 15-11 indicates, profit does not increase after the stock moves through the 40 price range. Every dollar of increased profit on the long position is offset by $1 of loss on the short position after the stock passes a price of 40. One of the important but difficult aspects of spreading is forecasting a range of prices rather than just the direction prices will move. If a speculator is bullish, he or she may buy a call instead of spreading. The potential loss is higher with the call but still limited, while the possible gain is unlimited. The relationship between long calls and bull spreads starts in the *bottom* of Figure 15-8. Note the

TABLE 15–9   Spreads (Call Options)

Vertical Spread				Option Prices	
	Market Price	Strike Price	(October)	January	April
XYZ	$36^3/_8$	(35)	(4)	6	$6^1/_2$
	$36^3/_8$	(40)	(2)	$3^3/_8$	4
	$36^3/_8$	45	$^{11}/_{16}$	$1^1/_2$	6

Horizontal Spread					
	Market Price	Strike Price	October	(January	April)
XYZ	$36^3/_8$	(35)	4	(6	$6^1/_2$)
	$36^3/_8$	40	2	$3^3/_8$	4
	$36^3/_8$	45	$^{11}/_{16}$	$1^1/_2$	6

Diagonal Spread					
	Market Price	Strike Price	(October)	January	(April)
XYZ	$36^3/_8$	(35)	(4)	6	$6^1/_2$
	$36^3/_8$	(40)	2	$3^3/_8$	(4)
	$36^3/_8$	45	$^{11}/_{16}$	$1^1/_2$	6

TABLE 15–10   Profit on Vertical Bull Spread

XYZ October 35		XYZ October 40		Price Spread
Bought at	4	Sold at	2	2
Sold at	$7^1/_2$	Bought at	$4^1/_2$	3
Gain	$3^1/_2$	(Loss)	$(2^1/_2)$	1
		Net gain	$100	
		Investment	$200	
		Return	50%	

Table 15–11   XYZ Vertical Bull Spread

XYZ Stock Price at Expiration 35				XYZ Stock Price at Expiration 40				XYZ Stock Price at Expiration 45			
October 35		October 40		October 35		October 40		October 35		October 40	
Bought at	4	Sold at	2	Bought at	4	Sold at	2	Bought at	4	Sold at	2
Expired at[a]	0	Expired at[a]	0	Sold at[a]	5	Expired at[a]	0	Sold at[a]	10	Bought at[a]	5
(Loss)	(4)	Gain	2	Gain	1	Gain	2	Gain	6	(Loss)	(3)
(Net loss) (2)				Net gain 3				Net gain 3			
(200) = 100 percent loss				$300 = 150 percent gain				$300 = 150 percent gain			

[a] All call options on date of expiration equal their intrinsic value.

maximum loss with the bull spread is $200 and $400 with a long call. The break-even point is also $2 less for the bull spread ($37 versus $39). However, the long call has unlimited profit potential, and the bull spread is locked in at $300 at a stock price of $40 or higher. The spread position lowers the break-even point by $2 per share but also limits potential returns—a classic case of risk-return trade-off.

FIGURE 15–8   Profit and Loss Relationships on Spreads and Calls

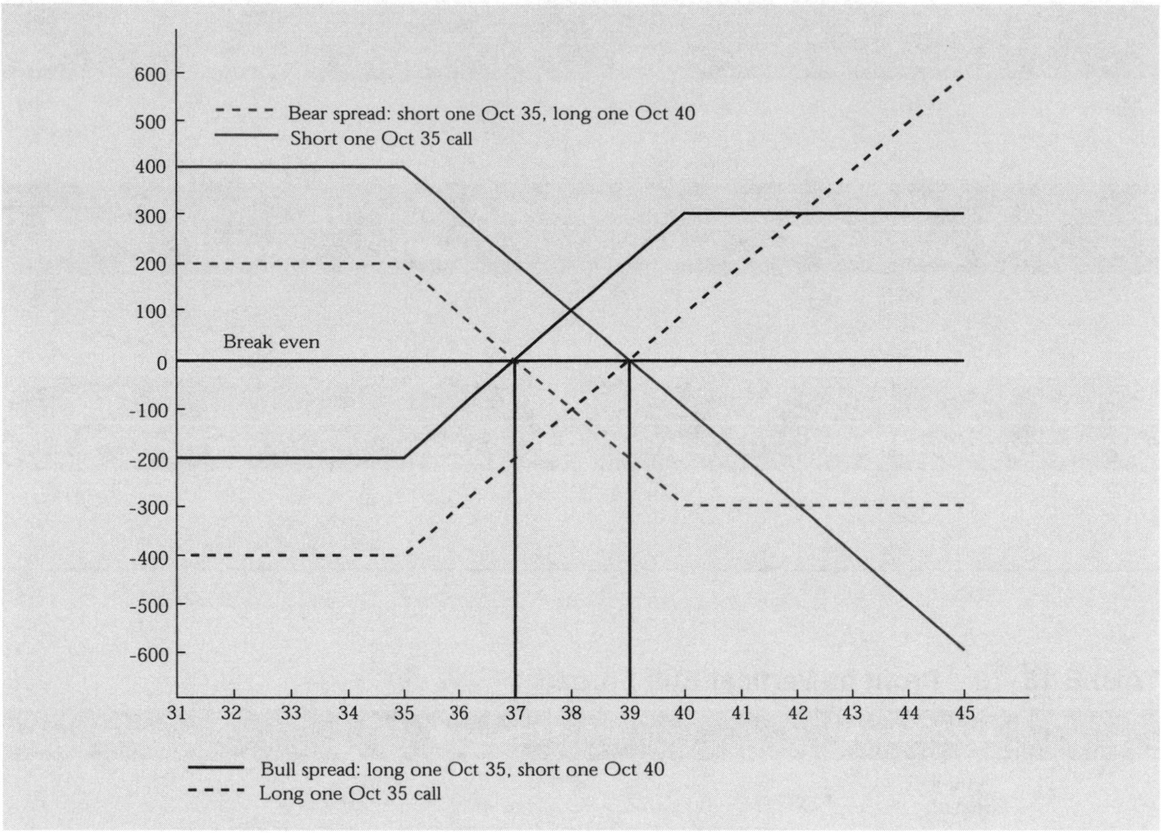

Vertical Bear Spread

The speculator enters a bear spread anticipating a decline in stock prices. Instead of selling short or writing a call with both having unlimited risk, he spreads by selling short the call with the lower strike price (highest premium) and covers the upside risk with the purchase of a call having a higher strike price. This creates a credit balance. In a sense, the bear spread does the opposite of the vertical bull spread as seen in Table 15-12 in which we show profits and losses from the strategy if XYZ ends up at 35 or at 40. With a bear spread, the price spread of 2 is the maximum gain if the stock closes at 35 or less at expiration, while the maximum loss equals 3, the difference between the exercise prices minus the price spread. The relationship between bear spreads and writing a call option is also demonstrated in Figure 15-8 (the comparison starts at the *top* of the figure).

There is yet another way to contain the risk of straddle. Let us assume we are given the following information.

Strike Price	Call Price
40	12
45	9
50	7

Assume an investor sells (writes) one option at $40, another at $50 and buys two calls at $45, i.e. writes a call each on the higher and lower prices and buys two calls in the mid-price. Table 15-13 shows the outcomes and Figures 15-9 and 15-10 chart this outcome. Note that the cost of this strategy is only $1/share ($-12 + 18 - 7$).

Table 15–12   XYZ Vertical Bear Spread

| XYZ Stock Price at Expiration 35 | | | | XYZ Stock Price at Expiration 40 | | | |
October 35		October 40		October 35		October 40	
Sold at	4	Bought at	2	Sold at	4	Bought at	2
Expired at	0	Expired at	0	Bought at	5	Expired at	0
Gain	4	(Loss)	(2)	(Loss)	1	(Loss)	2
	Net gain 2				Net loss (3)		
	$200				$(300)		

TABLE 15–13

Stock price	30	35	40	45	50	55	60
Call at $40	+12	+12	+12	+7	+2	−3	−8
2 × Calls at $45	−18	−18	−18	−18	−8	+2	+12
Call at $50	+7	+7	+7	+7	+7	+2	−3
Butterfly	+1	+1	+1	−4	+1	+1	+1

FIGURE 15–9   Stock Price vs. Profit/Loss

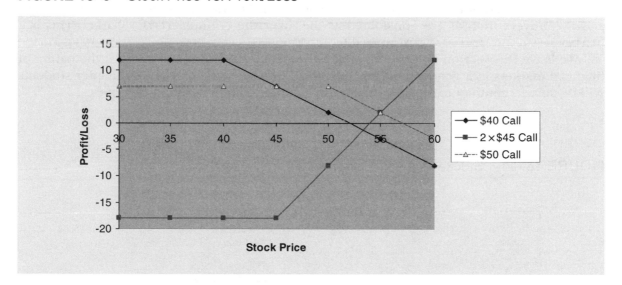

This example is the strategy of a **butterfly**. As can be seen, the holder of the butterfly will still profit even if volatility is low but will also not lose as much if the market was not volatile. In this way, the holder reduces both the risk and the return from the strategy. Thus, we can see that combinations of puts and calls not only allow us to profit from our expectations but also allow us to incorporate our risk tolerances in our strategies.

As the student can observe, there are an infinite number of strategies using different features. Combinations can vary by the number of puts and calls, the strike prices and the maturity dates. Further, each strategy has an inverse. For example, in a butterfly we could

FIGURE 15–10   Stock Price vs. Profit/Loss

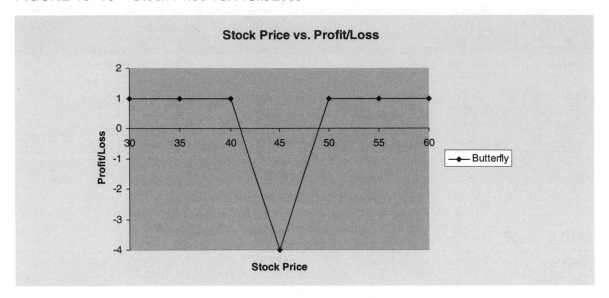

buy the two outlier calls and write the two mid-strike calls. In this case, we would profit if the market did not move but would limit our losses if it did. Figure 15–11 shows this inverse strategy, reflecting the opposite expectation but same risk tolerance.

In this world of financial engineering, if we are given an expectation, a risk tolerance and a profit level desired, then a product can be engineered (developed) to fit that need. Financial institutions that cater to the demands of the market by supplying such products and the buyers thereof are considered as the "over the counter" (OTC) market. This is a market where products are customized to needs.

We leave this section by observing that the advent of options has changed the nature of financial markets in a way that is quite historical. Finally, at the end of this chapter students will be able to conduct exercises that exemplify other common option strategies.

FIGURE 15–11   Stock Price vs. Profit/Loss

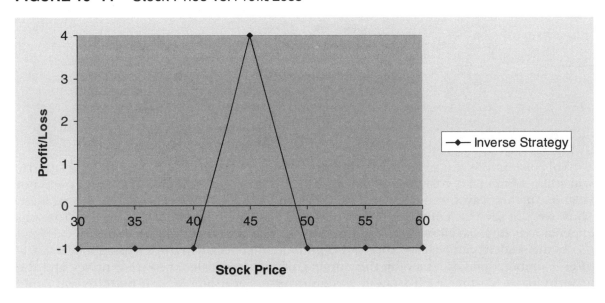

USE OF STOCK INDEX FUTURES

There are a number of actual and potential users of stock index futures. As is true of most commodity futures contracts, the motivation may be either speculation or the opportunity to hedge.

Speculation

The speculator may use stock index futures in an attempt to profit from major movements in the market. He or she may have developed a conviction about the next move in the market through fundamental or technical analysis. For example, those who utilize fundamental analysis may determine that P/E ratios are relatively low or that earnings performance should be extremely good in the next two quarters, so they wish to bet on the market moving upward. Market technicians might observe that a resistance or support position in the market is being penetrated and that it is time to take a position based on the anticipated consequences of that penetration.

While the market participant could put his or her money in individual stocks, it might be more efficient and less time consuming to simply invest in stock index futures. In buying futures on the S&P 500 Index, the investor is capturing the performance of 500 securities; with the S&P MidCap, 400 securities, and so on.

Two types of risks are associated with investments: systematic or market-related risks, and unsystematic or firm-related risks. Because many believe only systematic risk is assumed to be rewarded in an efficient capital market environment (unsystematic risk can be diversified away), the investor may wish to be exposed only to systematic risk. Stock index futures represent an efficient approach to only taking systematic, market-related risk.

Another advantage of stock index futures is that there is less manipulative action and insider trading than with individual securities. While it is possible (though not legal) for "informed" insider trading to cause an individual stock to move dramatically in the short term, such activity is not as likely for an entire index. This advantage, however, should not be overstated. Unusual trading activity of stock index futures comes under the scrutiny of federal regulators from time to time.

Stock index futures also offer leverage potential. A $322,875 S&P futures contract can be established for $21,500 in margin and with no interest on the balance.[2] If you were investing $322,875 in actual stocks through margin, you would have to put up a minimum of $161,437.50 (50 percent) in margin and pay interest on the balance. The margin requirement is still considerably lower than that on an outright stock purchase. Also, the commissions on a stock index futures contract are minuscule in comparison with commissions on securities of comparable value.

Volatility and Profits or Losses   Before the market crash of 1987, the average daily move on the S&P 500 Index was approximately 0.50 (one-half point per day). It has been moving up ever since. In the late 1990s and early 2000s, the daily move has been in the seven-point range. A seven-point upward move in an S&P 500 futures contract (say, from 1290 to 1297) means a daily gain of $1,750 (recall the contract has a multiplier of 250). With a margin requirement of $21,500, that is an 8.1 percent, one-day return on your money:

$ 7	Gain on futures contract
× 250	Multiplier
$ 1,750	Dollar gain
$21,500	Margin
8.1%	Percentage gain

---

2. As mentioned earlier margin on futures contracts merely represents good-faith money, and there is never any interest on the balance.

This translates into a 2,956.50 percent annualized return (8.1% × 365). By contrast, if the $21,500 were invested in a 5 percent certificate of deposit, only $2.94 in interest would accrue on a daily basis. The difference here, of course, is that the $1,750 average daily movement related to the index may be up or down, whereas the $2.94 is only up.

When a stock index futures contract starts to run against an investor, he or she can bail out and cut losses. If the contract value is going down rapidly, the investor will be continually called on to put up more margin as the margin position is being depleted. That puts tremendous pressure on the investor. He or she must decide whether to put up more margin and hold the position in hopes of a comeback or close out the position and take a loss.

Not all speculation in stock index futures must necessarily be based on the market going up. You can also speculate that the market will go down. You simply sell a contract with the anticipation of repurchasing it at a lower price later. Margin requirements are similar, and gains come from a declining market and losses from an increasing market. If the index goes up rapidly, the investor will be called on to put up more margin.[3]

Hedging

Up to now our discussion of stock index futures has mainly related to speculating (or anticipating the next major move in the market). Perhaps the most important use of stock index futures is for hedging purposes. An investor who has a large diversified portfolio may think the market is about to decline. A portfolio manager who suffers a 20 percent decline in his or her portfolio actually requires a 25 percent gain from the new lower base to break even.

A portfolio manager faced with the belief that a declining market is imminent may be inclined to sell part or all of the portfolio. The question becomes, is this realistic? First, large transaction costs are associated with selling part or all of a portfolio and then repurchasing it later. Second, it may be difficult to liquidate a position in certain securities that are thinly traded. For example, a mutual fund or pension fund that tries to sell 10,000 shares of a small over-the-counter stock may initially find a price quote of $25 but only be able to close out its relatively large position at $23.50. A $15,000 loss would be suffered. Furthermore, the fund might find the same type of problem in reacquiring the stock after the overall market decline is over. This problem could be multiplied by 25 or 50 times, depending on the number of securities in the portfolio. Although larger, more liquid holdings would be easier to trade, significant transactions costs are still involved.

A more easily executed defensive strategy would be to sell one or more stock index futures as a hedge against the portfolio. If the stock market does go down, the loss on the portfolio will be partially or fully offset by the profit on the stock index futures contract(s) because they are bought back at a lower price than the initial sales price.

As an example, assume a corporate pension fund has $20 million in stock holdings. The investment committee for the fund is very bearish in its outlook, fearing that the overall market could go down by 20 percent in the next few months and a $4 million loss would be suffered. The pension fund decides to fully hedge its position.

The fund is going to use S&P 500 Index futures for the hedge. We shall assume the futures can be sold for 1291.50, with a settlement date in three months. Before the number of contracts for execution is determined, the portfolio manager must consider the relative volatility of his portfolio. If the portfolio is more volatile than the market, this must be factored into the decision-making process. As discussed earlier, beta coefficient indicates how volatile a stock is relative to the market. If a stock has a beta of 1.20, it is 20 percent more volatile than the market. We shall assume the $20 million portfolio discussed above has a weighted average beta of 1.15 (that is, the portfolio is 15 percent more volatile than the market).

---

3. The margin maintenance requirements are similar to those on a long position.

To determine the number of contracts necessary to hedge the position, we use the following formula:

$$\frac{\$ \text{Value of portfolio}}{\$ \text{Value of contract}} \times \text{Weighted beta of portfolio} = \text{Number of contracts} \qquad (15\text{-}1)$$

In the example under discussion, we would show:

$$\frac{\$20,000,000}{1291.50 \times 250} \times 1.15 = \text{Number of contracts}$$

In the first term of the formula, the numerator is the size of the portfolio being hedged. The denominator is the size of each contract and, in this example, is found by multiplying the S&P futures contract value of 1291.50 by 250. The first term is then multiplied by the weighted beta value of 1.15. The answer works out as:

$$\frac{\$20,000,000}{\$322,875} \times 1.15 = 61.94 \times 1.15 = 71 \text{ contracts (rounded)}$$

The portfolio can be effectively hedged with 71 contracts.

Assume the market does go down but only by 10 percent instead of the 20 percent originally anticipated. Let's demonstrate that the hedge has worked. Since the portfolio has a beta of 1.15, its decline would be 11.5 percent (10% × 1.15). With a $20 million portfolio, the loss would be $2.3 million. To offset this loss, we will have a gain on 71 contracts. The gain is shown as follows:

$1,291.50 S&P Index futures contract (sales price)
− 129.15 Decline in price on the futures contract (10% × 950)
$1,162.35 Ending value (purchase price)

The 129.15 point decline on the index futures contract indicates the profit made on each contract.[4] They were sold for 1291.50 and repurchased for 1162.35. With 71 contracts, the profit on the stock index futures contracts comes out as $2,292,412.50:

$ 32,287.50 Profit per contract ($129.15 × $250)
× 71 Number of contracts
$2,292,412.50 Total profit

The gain of approximately $2.3 million on the stock index futures contracts offsets the loss of $2.3 million on the portfolio. The small difference between the two values represents the fact that we rounded values. Actually, executing a perfect hedge may be further complicated by a number of other factors such as the lack of an appropriate index to match against the portfolio and the change in basis over time. Also, the portfolio may not move exactly in accordance with the beta. No doubt, many real-world factors can complicate any hedge.

While a stock index futures hedge offers the advantage of protecting against losses, it takes away the upside potential. If the market goes up by 10 percent instead of down, the gain on the portfolio may be wiped out by the loss on the stock index futures contracts. The investor could be forced to buy back the futures contract for 10 percent more than the

---

4. Note that the futures contract is assumed to move on a one-to-one basis with the market. The actual relationship may not be this precise.

selling price. Because some portfolio managers are afraid of losing all their upside potential in a hedged position, they may wish to hedge less than 100 percent of their portfolio.

While the hedging procedure just described can be potentially beneficial to portfolio managers, it can be potentially detrimental to the market in general if overused. Actually, protecting a large portfolio against declines is sometimes referred to as **portfolio insurance**. It is potentially a good strategy, but what if many investors initiate their portfolio-insurance strategies at the same time? Perhaps they are worried because there has been an increase in the prime rate or a bad report on inflation. An overload of stock index futures sales hitting the market at the same time drives down not only stock index futures prices but the stocks in the indexes as well (such as those in the S&P 500 Stock Index). An overall panic can result. The chain reaction is that a whole new round of portfolio-insurance-induced sales is triggered.

Other Uses of Hedging   Hedging with stock index futures has a number of other uses besides attempting to protect the position of a long-term investment portfolio. These include the following.

Underwriter Hedge   As described earlier, the investment banker (underwriter) has a risk exposure from buying stock from the issuing corporation with the intention of reselling it in the public markets. If there is weakness during the distribution period, the potential resale price could fall below the purchase price, and the underwriter's profit would be wiped out. To protect against this market risk, the underwriter could sell stock index futures contracts. If the market goes down, presumably, the loss on the stock will be compensated for by the gain on the stock index futures contract as a result of being able to repurchase it at a lower price. This, of course, is not a perfect hedge. It is possible that the individual stock could go down while the market is going up, and losses on both the stock and stock index futures contract would occur (writing options directly against the stock might be more efficient, but in many cases such options are not available).

Specialist or Dealer Hedge   As indicated earlier, a specialist on an exchange or a dealer in the over-the-counter market buys and sells stocks for his own inventory for temporary holding. He may, at times, assume a larger temporary holding than desired, with all the risks associated with that exposure. Stock index futures can reduce the market (or systematic) risk, although the use of futures cannot reduce the specific risk associated with a security.

Retirement or Estate Hedge   As we move into the next two or three decades, large retirement funds will be accumulated from voluntary retirement plans. A retirement plan participant who has accumulated a large sum in an equity fund may feel a need to hedge his or her position in certain time periods in the economy (where liquidation is neither tax advantageous or possible). A futures contract may provide that hedge. Also, a person with responsibility for an estate may be locked into a portfolio during the period of probate (validation of the will process) and wish to hedge his or her position with a stock index futures contract.

Tax Hedge   An investor may have accumulated a large return on a diversified portfolio in a given year. To maintain the profitable position but defer the taxable gains until the next year, futures contracts may be employed.

Arbitraging

While stock index futures started out as a major tool for speculating and hedging, they are now also widely used for arbitraging. Basically, an **arbitrage** is set up when a simultaneous trade (a buy and a sell) occurs in two different markets and a profit is locked in. Assume the S&P 500 Stock Index has a value of 1288 based on the market value of all the stocks in the index. Also, assume the S&P 500 Stock Index futures contract, due to expire in two months, is selling for 1290. There is a two-point positive basis between the futures contract and the underlying index. A sophisticated institutional investor may decide to arbitrage based on this difference. He or she will simultaneously sell a futures contract for 1290 and buy a basket of stocks that matches[5] the S&P 500 Stock Index for 1288. Because at expiration, the futures contract and underlying index will have the same value, a two-point profit is locked in at the time of arbitraging. For example, if at expiration, the S&P 500 Stock Index has a value of 1286, a gain of four will occur on the sale, and a loss of two will be associated with the purchase for a net profit of two. If thousands of such contracts are involved, the profits can be substantial, and the potential for losses in a true arbitrage is nonexistent.

As you might assume, index arbitraging is in the exclusive providence of wealthy, sophisticated investors. For this reason, many smaller investors are somewhat resentful of the process and claim it tends to disrupt the normal operations of the marketplace. While there is nothing inherently wrong with arbitraging and it may even make the markets more efficient, it is sometimes a target for criticism by regulators. This is because it involves the process of program trading, discussed earlier in the chapter.

HEDGING WITH STOCK INDEX OPTIONS

The discussion of stock index options thus far has pertained to speculation about market moves. Stock index options can also be used for hedging. Like stock index futures, stock index options can be utilized to protect a portfolio or for special purposes by underwriters, specialists, dealers, tax planners, and others.

At times, options may offer a hedging advantage over futures to investors who are limited by law from purchasing futures contracts. On the other hand, futures generally allow for a more efficient hedge than options. If the market goes down by 20 or 25 percent, chances are good that a completely hedged short futures position (selling futures contracts) will compensate for losses in a portfolio. An option write, used to hedge a portfolio, may be inadequate. Perhaps the option premium income represents 10 percent of the portfolio, but the market goes down by 25 percent. Fifteen percent of the loss will be unprotected. Buying a put option may overcome this problem, but the cash outflow to purchase the put option could involve substantial funds. Clearly, both futures and options have their advantages and disadvantages.

There are also options on industry indexes that can be used for hedging or speculation. For example, the American Stock Exchange has index options on high-tech and pharmaceutical companies, and the Philadelphia Exchange covers gold/silver, oil services, semiconductors, and public utilities. The trading in industry options is basically the same as trading in overall market options.

OPTIONS ON STOCK INDEX FUTURES

We have discussed *stock index futures* and *stock index options,* so a natural extension of our discussion is to consider the third form of stock index trading, *options on stock index futures.* The three forms of index trading are listed below for reference.

1. Stock index futures.
2. Stock index options.
3. Options on stock index futures.

---

5. Actually, arbitraging has become sufficiently sophisticated through mathematics and computer analysis that all 500 stocks do not actually have to be purchased. Perhaps 10 or 15 key stocks bought in large quantities will be sufficient to adequately represent the S&P 500 Index. Commissions on such transactions tend to be extremely small. Mutual funds and exchange traded funds that replicate the S&P 500 Index can also be purchased.

FIGURE 15–12 Comparison of Option Contracts

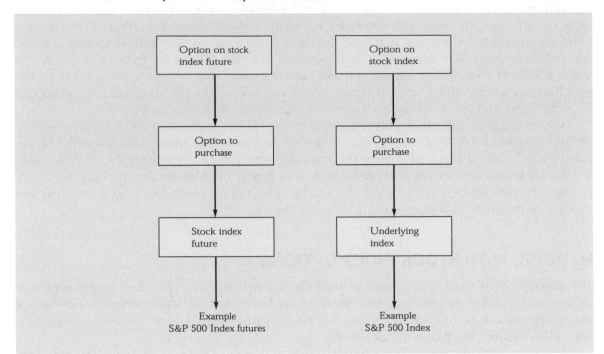

An option on stock index futures (item 3 above) gives the holder the right to purchase the stock index *futures contract* at a specified price over a given period. This is slightly different from the stock index option (item 2) that gives the holder the right to purchase the *underlying index* at a specified price over a given time period.[6]

The primary topic for discussion in this section is represented by the left-hand column in Figure 15–12, an option on a stock index futures contract. The value of an option to purchase a stock index futures contract will depend on the outlook for the futures contract. Quotes on options to purchase stock index futures are shown in Table 15–14.

As indicated in Table 15–14, options on stock index futures are available for the Dow Jones Industrial Average and the S&P 500 Stock Index. A call option to buy a June DJ1A futures contract at a strike price of 114 (representing 1140) has a premium of 18.05. On these option contracts, the premium is multiplied by 100 to get the value of the contract. Thus, the cost of the contract is $1,805 (100 × 18.05).

In examining Table 15–14, note that the premiums on the call options increase substantially with the passage of time from May to July. This gain in value is not only a function of the extended time period associated with the option but is also due to the fact that the DJIA futures contract normally has a higher value with the passage of time.[7] Thus, options on stock index futures not only have a time premium (all options do) but may also have an additional premium (or discount) depending on the relationship of the far-term futures market to the near-term futures market.

Options on stock index futures may be settled on a cash basis, or the holder of a call option may exercise the option and force the option writer to produce a specified futures contract. There are also puts for options on stock index futures.

---

6. Because of cash-settlement procedures, the actual index will never actually be purchased, and the gain or loss will be settled for cash.
7. Of course, if the market outlook were highly pessimistic, there would be a decline in the S&P futures contract with the passage of time.

TABLE 15–14 Options on Stock Index Futures (May 17, 2001)

INDEX

DJ Industrial Avg (CBOT)
$100 times premium

STRIKE PRICE	CALLS-SETTLE			PUTS-SETTLE		
	May	Jun	Jly	May	Jun	Jly
111	19.50	35.00	...	1.00	16.40	...
112	11.00	28.70	...	2.50	20.05	28.50
113	4.50	23.05	...	6.00	24.35	...
114	1.00	18.06	33.50	12.50	29.30	...
115	0.55	13.70	28.50	...	34.95	...
116	0.20	9.95	23.50	...	41.75	...

For the DJIA, add two zeros to the strike price

Est vol 3,100 Wd 438 calls 728 puts
Op int Wed 9,001 calls 28,845 puts

S&P 500 Stock Index (CME)
$250 times premium

STRIKE PRICE	CALLS-SETTLE			PUTS-SETTLE		
	May	Jun	Jly	May	Jun	Jly
1280	13.80	34.40	54.70	2.30	22.90	32.90
1285	10.00	31.40	...	3.50	24.90	...
1290	6.80	28.50	...	5.30	27.00	36.80
1295	4.40	25.80	...	7.90	29.30	38.90
1300	2.60	23.30	43.00	11.10	31.80	41.00
1305	1.40	21.00	...	...	34.40	...

Est vol 11,613 Wd 13,516 calls 11,690 puts
Op int Wed 73,715 calls 182,919 puts

Value of the DJIA (May 17, 2001) is 11,248.58.

Source: *The Wall Street Journal*, May 18, 2001, p. C18. Reprinted by permission of *The Wall Street Journal*, © 2001 by Dow Jones & Company, Inc. All Rights Reserved Worldwide.

Exploring the Web

Web site Address	Comments
www.cboe.com	Web site for major options exchange
www.schaeffersresearch.com	Offers technical analysis for options
www.cbs.marketwatch.com	Contains some information and tracking on stock options
www.888options.com	Educational site on options
www.cbot.com	Web site for the Chicago Board of Trade providing information, quotes, and educational features
www.pcquote.com	Provides research and quotes on options and commodities.

www.liffe.com   Home site for the London International Financial
                                           Futures and Options market

www.cme.com   Home site for the Chicago Mercantile Exchange
                                           containing quotes and information about futures

www.cftc.com   Home site for the future market regulator
                                           Commodities Futures Trading Commission

---

SUMMARY

For the investor who wishes to trade in stock indexes, there are three basic types of securities: stock index futures, stock index options, and options on stock index futures.

Stock index futures and options offer the potential for speculation as well as for hedging. With stock index futures, the margin is relatively low, which allows for a strong leverage potential. In hedging a portfolio position, the investor should consider the beta of his or her portfolio and adjust the number of contracts accordingly. Basis in the futures market represents the difference between the stock index futures price and the value of the actual underlying index. Basis may present the investor with a potential clue about the future direction of the market. The stock index futures market and the stock index option market trade on a cash-settlement basis. No securities ever change hands as the settlement is always in cash.

Investors in stock index futures may also engage in arbitraging procedures in which a simultaneous trade (a buy and a sell) occurs in the stock index futures contract and in the underlying securities in the index. This allows the investor to lock in a profit. The use of arbitraging, portfolio insurance, and program trading has been blamed by some for the market crash in October 1987 and the subsequent volatility in the market after the crash.

The stock index option contract is generally similar to the option contract on individual securities. The investor has an opportunity to buy puts and calls, and the premium is related to the future prospects for the index.

The third form of stock index contracts, an option on stock index futures, combines the option concept with the futures market. Instead of an option on an actual index, you have an option on a stock index futures contract. The contract may be settled either with cash or with securities.

Chapter 16

Taxation and Tax Strategies

TAX EFFICIENCY

When we talk about tax efficiency as it relates to investments, we are talking about the degree to which certain investments generate taxable income, whether we choose them to or not. Taxable income is generated in several different ways. For example, taxable interest income, capital gains income, and dividend income trigger tax consequence for most investors. For individuals in high income tax brackets, investments that generate low taxable interest income, low dividend income and low capital gain income are desirable since they are considered to be **tax efficient** investments. Conversely, those investments that generated high taxable interest income, high capital gains and high dividend are said to be **tax inefficient** and may not be desirable for those in high income tax brackets. Tax inefficient investments, however, may be excellent choices for those who are in lower income brackets and have a need for the current income that these investments provide for them. We will touch on these issues throughout the chapter.

We will first begin this chapter by discussing the tax treatment of the various types of investment income including ordinary income, capital gains, and capital losses. We will briefly discuss the implications of how capital gains and capital losses affect the income taxes of the investor. We will then explain what basis means and will discuss reasons for changes in the basis of investments. We will include a small section on how investment expenses can be used on the tax return as an expense to minimize income.

We will end this chapter by first discussing the tax efficiency of the three most common types of investments, mutual funds, stocks, and bonds. We will discuss the nuances of these investment vehicles as they relate to tax efficiency and basis calculations. We will then identify appropriate uses for these investments for the tax efficient portfolio. We will conclude this chapter with a short discussion of some other well-known investments and their tax efficiency such as annuities, limited partnerships, and unit investment trusts.

MUTUAL FUNDS

As we saw in Chapter 13, mutual funds are a type of pooled investment whereby individuals pool their money for investment purposes and pay fees to a professional fund manager to manage their funds. Because of this professional management, individual mutual fund holders put their trust in the fund manager to act on their behalf and therefore, do not exercise any discretion over when investments within the fund are bought and sold. Additionally, fund holders do not have control over when dividend and interest disbursements are made to the fund. If an investor is concerned about paying taxes on interest or dividends, he or she should not choose a mutual fund that disperses these types of payments regularly. As we discussed in Chapter 13, this information can be gleaned from the prospectus.

The degree to which assets are bought and sold within a fund is called **turnover**. Those funds that have high turnover will yield greater capital gain distributions for its shareholders than those with low turnover. One way to calculate turnover is to find the smaller of the fund's total asset sales or the fund's total asset purchases and divide it by the fund's average monthly assets. A small ratio indicates a relatively tax efficient fund for that last 12 months. For instance, if a fund has a turnover of 5 percent, it means that it has replaced only 5 percent of its value over the last 12 months. Conversely, if a fund has turnover of 80 percent, the fund has replaced 80 percent of its value over the last 12 months. This fund would be tax inefficient, and, as we will see below, investors in this fund would incur tax liabilities in the tax year of the distribution.

Unless a fund has the specific goal of tax efficiency, measuring turnover in one year does not mean that a fund manager will follow the same policy in future years. Therefore, past purchase and sales patterns of the fund manager may not be an indicator of turnover in the future. If tax efficiency is a goal for the investor, and a mutual fund is the desired investment vehicle, search out funds that are specifically geared toward tax efficiency.

TAXATION OF MUTUAL FUNDS

Types of Mutual Fund Distributions

Mutual funds are pass-through entities. As such, all of the income, dividends and capital gains/losses incurred as a result of operating the mutual fund are passed-through to the individual shareholders. Earnings are passed-through to shareholders in the form of dividends. As we discussed above, the actions of the fund manager as it relates to the purchase and sale of assets to and from the fund will have an impact on the taxation of the individual holding shares of a mutual fund. Additionally, the types of investments that are held within a mutual fund can have an impact on the taxation of the individual holding a mutual fund. For instance, income from bonds will generate dividend distributions and will impact the tax liability of the investors in the form of ordinary dividends. Conversely, stocks held within a fund that does not pay dividends, will not have a tax impact if there is no sale of that stock within that fund in a particular tax year.

Distributions from a mutual fund are called dividends no matter what form they come in. There are several forms of distributions from a mutual fund which we will discuss below. They are ordinary dividends which break down into qualified and non-qualified dividends, federal interest dividends, tax-exempt interest dividends, and capital gain dividends/distributions. To the extent that there are expenses associated with mutual funds, these will be offset by the gains. Thus the investor will pay tax only on the net gain.

Mutual funds may also have capital gains allocations and foreign tax allocations. While these are not distributions *per se*, they do have a tax impact on the investor. These distributions will also be discussed below.

Ordinary Dividends

Ordinary dividends are paid to fund shareholders when interest from money market funds, bond interest, dividends from common and preferred stock and short-term capital gains are earned by the fund and paid out to investors. These are called ordinary dividends but, depending on the type of distribution, they can be taxed at different rates. Dividends from money market funds, bond interest, some company dividends, and short-term capital gains are always taxed at ordinary income rates. Short-term gains are a result of the fund holding assets for less than one year which result in a net short-term gain to the fund. The tax treatment of these items is no different than if an individual held these same assets individually. All of these gains are called **non-qualified dividends** and therefore are taxed at ordinary rates. When the investor receives the 1099-DIV after the end of the tax year, these non-qualified, ordinary dividends will show up in Box 1a of the form.

In the past, the IRS required that dividends received from common and preferred stock be taxed at ordinary rates. With the passage of the Economic Growth & Tax Reconciliation Act of 2001, the new law allowed for **qualified dividends** to be taxed at 5 percent (for the 10 percent and 15 percent tax brackets) or 15 percent (for all other tax brackets). Because of this new law passage in 2001, all qualified dividends are taxed at these rates. When the investor receives the 1099-DIV form, qualified dividends will show up in Box 1b of the form.

There are some exceptions to those dividends that qualify within mutual funds for qualified treatment, however. In order to be considered a qualified dividend, the dividend must be paid by a qualified U.S. or foreign corporation and cannot be of the type excluded by law. For a more complete definition of these qualifications, IRS Publication 550 provides insight. Those seeking to use dividends as qualified must meet certain holding period requirements. This rule is the same for both individuals who hold stocks that pay dividends and for mutual funds which hold stocks that pay dividends. The law does not distinguish between either. The stock must be held for greater than 60 days during the 121-day period that begins 60 days before the **ex-dividend date**. The ex-dividend date is the date after which the dividend has been declared that will grant the dividend to the seller instead of the buyer of the stock. The fund cannot treat them as qualified dividends and its investors will not qualify for the favorable tax treatment. Another nuance of the tax law states that if the shareholder of the mutual fund owns shares for less than 61 days, the investor is technically not allowed to use the dividends as qualified and must therefore identify the dividends as ordinary. This is true even if the mutual fund can legally call the dividends qualified; the individual investor cannot.

Mutual funds oftentimes have plans whereby the investor can either reinvest the interest or dividends back into the fund or take them as a cash disbursement. In either case, the investor must still pay the appropriate income tax as determined by its qualified or non-qualified status. Funds with high non-qualified dividend disbursements are not appropriate investment vehicles for those investors who are already in high income tax brackets. These types of funds may be appropriate to hold in tax-deferred accounts such as retirement accounts or annuities since the investor is allowed a tax deferred cash build-up until distribution begins. With these investments, the investor begins taking disbursements from the account when he will presumably be in a lower tax bracket.

Federal Interest Dividends

Mutual funds exist that invest primarily in securities offered by the United States Government. For example, many mutual funds invest government securities such as Treasury bills and notes, U.S. Savings Bonds, Treasury strips and Treasury Inflation Indexed Securities (TIPS). Recall from our discussion of federal bonds, that the investor of these bonds must pay federal income tax at the ordinary from interest on these bonds. However, for those investors who live in states where there is a state tax, they are exempt from state income tax on these bonds. It is for this reason that these bonds may provide a tax benefit for those investors in high tax brackets in high income tax states.

The dividends for these investments will show up on the 1099-DIV in box 1a of the form. For federal income tax purposes the investor should treat the dividends from these funds just as any other ordinary dividend. However, the investor must follow the rules for each particular state to determine how to report these dividends on the state income tax form.

Tax-Exempt Interest Dividends

There are mutual funds which invest primarily in tax-exempt securities in order to provide its investors with tax-exempt interest income. Although these investments generally offer lower rates than other investments, the interest from these investments is generally exempt from federal taxes and some state taxes. For example, a mutual fund which provides tax exempt state of California municipal bonds will provide a source of tax exempt state and federal interest to an investor living in California. However, because the source of the interest income comes from a California state municipality, the interest may not be exempt from state income tax for an investor in another state such as Idaho or Texas. It will still be exempt from federal interest however.

The exempt interest income from these types of investments is not reported on the 1099-DIV. Rather, it will be reported to the investor on another type of form which varies from company to company. Even though this income is not taxable for federal purposes, it must be reported on the 1040(A) form on line 8b. Depending on the income level and other tax factors of the investor, exempt interest income could have Alternative Minimum Tax (AMT) implications for the investor. AMT was enacted to ward off concerns by Congress that those who were in substantially higher income tax brackets could legally avoid taxes by participating in economic activities that allowed taxpayers to avoid taxes on certain types of income. A discussion of AMT is beyond the scope of this text, but suffice it to say, that those investors who are in high income tax brackets have a chance of being affected by AMT. AMT has the direct effect of increasing the tax liability of the investor and is shown on line 42 of the 1040 and line 48 on the 1040A and is added directly to the tax liability of the taxpayer shown on line 41 on the 1040 and line 27 on the 1040A. In order to calculate AMT, form 6251, Alternative Minimum Tax must be completed.

Capital Gain Dividends/Distributions

Mutual funds can pay dividends to investors in the form of **capital gain dividends**. This occurs when mutual funds sell securities that they have held in the portfolio for over a year at a profit and distributes the gains to the shareholders. Recall that whether the funds are reinvested in the mutual fund or distributed to the shareholder, a long-term capital gain tax must still be paid by the investor. Currently, long-term capital gains are taxed at 5 percent (for the 10 percent and 15 percent tax brackets) or 15 percent (for all other tax brackets).

At the end of the year, the tax payer will receive form 1099-DIV. Box 2a shows the amount the investor must report on the annual tax return. The gains can be treated as long-term capital gains regardless of how long the investor owned shares in the mutual fund. The only requirement is that the mutual fund held the shares for greater than one year.

CAPITAL GAINS ALLOCATIONS

Although mutual funds experience capital gains, sometimes the fund may decide to retain these gains inside the fund rather than distribute them to the shareholders. Since there is not a distribution of funds, these types of transactions are called **capital gains allocations**. Even though mutual funds are pass-through entities, in this case, the mutual fund must pay a tax on the portion of the undistributed funds. The mutual fund must pay 35 percent tax on the undistributed capital gain. The difference between the gross gain and the amount of tax paid by the mutual fund is still subject to a long-term capital gain tax which is borne by the investor.

Capital Gains Allocations are reported to the investor on Form 2439 rather than the 1099-DIV form. Box 1a shows the investor's portion of the undistributed gain and box 2 shows the tax paid by the mutual fund. While the investor still needs to report the gain on Schedule D of the individual 1040, the investor also is allowed to receive a tax credit for the amount of tax paid by the mutual fund on behalf of the investor. The tax paid as a result of this transaction is allowed to be deducted from the total tax owed by the investor on form 1040 or 1040A. This directly reduces the net tax liability of the investor. A copy of Form 2439 must be attached to the tax return.

TABLE 16–1   Marginal Tax Rates and Return Equivalents

	Yield on Municipal	27% Bracket	35% Bracket	38.6% Bracket
	5%	6.85%	7.69%	8.14%
	6	8.22	9.23	9.77
	7	9.59	10.77	11.40
	8	10.96	12.31	13.03
	9	12.32	13.85	14.66
	10	13.70	15.38	16.28

Because monies are retained within the fund rather than being distributed to shareholders, the investor's basis in the shares increases by the amount of capital gains. We will discuss various adjustments that can be made to basis below. However, it is important to note that capital gains allocations will result in an increase in the basis of the shares of the mutual fund. This increase in basis should be kept for tax purposes in the future as understating the basis will result in larger than necessary capital gains.

Table 16-1 presents examples of trade-offs between tax-exempt and non-tax-exempt (taxable) investments at various interest rates and marginal tax rates. Clearly, the higher the marginal tax rate, the greater the advantage of tax-exempt municipal bonds.

A second significant feature of municipal bonds is that the yield the issuing agency pays on municipal bonds is lower than the yield on taxable instruments. Of course, a municipal bond paying 6 percent may be quite competitive with taxable instruments paying more. Average differentials are presented in Table 16-2. You should notice in Table 16-2 that the yield differences between municipal bonds and corporate bonds were normally 2 to 4 percentage points. A major distinction that is also important to the bond issuer and investor is whether the bond is of a general obligation or revenue nature.

STOCKS

Dividends

For tax purposes a dividend is a distribution of cash or property, made by a corporation to its shareholders out of present or past earnings. It is distributed as a result of the ownership by a shareholder of a corporation's common or preferred stock. A dividend is treated as ordinary income for tax purposes and not as capital gains.

In addition, there can be dividends paid to a shareholder that are not from present or past earnings which are referred to as a Return of Capital Distribution. Since these dividends are not paid out of earnings they are treated as a return of basis and thus they are not subject to income tax and the taxpayer's basis is reduced by the amount of the dividends received.

Do not confuse dividends with stock or other compensation for services rendered or goods provided or in payment of debt even though it may be made to a stockholder.

Qualified dividends are the dividends that are subject to the same 5 percent or 15 percent maximum tax rate that applies to net capital gain and mutual funds as earlier discussed. Qualified dividends are subject to the 15% rate if the regular tax rate that would apply is 25 percent or higher. If the regular tax that would be applied is lower than 25 percent, qualified dividend is subject to the 5 percent rate. To be a qualified dividend, the dividends must have been paid by a U.S. corporation or a qualified foreign corporation.

TABLE 16–2   Comparable Yields on Long-Term Municipals and Taxable Corporates (Yearly Averages)

Year	Municipals Aa	Corporates Aa	Yield Difference
2001	5.80%	7.14%	1.34%
2000	6.01	7.80	1.79
1999	5.48	7.36	1.88
1998	5.13	6.80	1.67
1997	5.52	7.48	1.96
1996	5.90	7.72	1.82
1995	5.60	7.55	1.95
1994	6.40	8.60	2.20
1993	5.51	7.40	1.89
1992	6.30	8.46	2.16
1991	6.80	9.09	2.29
1990	7.15	9.56	2.41
1989	7.51	9.46	1.95
1988	8.38	9.66	1.28
1987	8.50	9.68	1.18
1986	7.35	9.47	2.12
1985	8.81	11.82	3.01
1984	9.95	12.25	2.30
1983	9.20	12.42	3.22
1982	11.39	14.41	3.02
1981	10.89	14.75	3.86
1980	8.06	12.50	4.44
1979	6.12%	9.94	3.82
1978	5.68	8.92	3.24
1977	5.39	8.24	2.85
1976	6.12	8.75	2.63

Source: *Moody's Municipal & Government Manual, Moody's Industrial Manual,* and *Mergent Bond Record* (published by Mergent, Inc., New York, NY), selected issues.

The dividends must not be of a type that is not qualified such as capital gain distributions, payments made in lieu of dividends and several other dividends or payments restricted by the Tax Code. Finally the taxpayer must have held the common stock for more than 60 days during the 121 day period that begins 60 days before the ex-dividend date. In the case of preferred stock, the taxpayer must have held the stock more than 90 days during the 181 day period that begins 90 days before the ex-dividend date if the dividends are due to periods totaling more than 366 days. If the preferred dividends are due to periods totaling less than 367 days, the same rules applying to common stock holding period applies.

Ordinary cash dividends, whether paid on common or preferred stock, are generally included in the shareholder's gross income for the year in which they are actually or constructively received, regardless of the period(s) for which they are paid. For example, cumulative preferred stock may be making accumulated dividends covering several prior years. For example, preferred stock dividends that have accumulated prior to an individual's purchase of the cumulative preferred stock are taxed to the purchaser as dividends when actually or constructively received. Accumulated dividends therefore are not considered to be a return of a portion of the purchase price and thus do not reduce the tax basis.

A common issue occurs when a stock is sold around the time that a dividend is being declared or paid. If a stock is sold and a dividend is both declared and paid after the sale, the dividend is included in the purchaser's and not the seller's income. Likewise, when a stock is sold after the dividend is declared but before payment is made, it is generally taxed to the purchaser. If the sale occurred before the record date or the date the stock begins selling ex-dividend, it is generally taxed to the seller. But if the sale occurred after the record date, it is taxed to the purchaser. Note that the price of the sale should reflect who is going to be taxed.

A dividend can be paid in property, other than stock or stock rights of the distributing corporation and it is taxed in the same manner as a cash dividend. A dividend paid in property other than cash is often referred to as a dividend "in kind." For tax purposes, the amount of a dividend paid in kind is generally the fair market value of the property on the date of distribution. Therefore, a dividend paid in bonds, notes or other obligations of the distributing corporation will be treated as a dividend "in kind" and the obligations are treated as property received in a dividend distribution.

Stripped Preferred Stocks

Stripped preferred stock is stock where there has been a separation of ownership between the stock and any dividend on it that has not become payable. It applies, according to the IRS, when the stock is limited and preferred as to dividends, does not participate in corporate growth to any significant extent and has a fixed redemption price.

An individual who purchases stripped preferred stock generally must treat the stock as though it were a bond issued on the purchase date with an original issue discount (OID) equal to the excess, if any, of the redemption price over the price at which he purchased the stock. (OID's will be discussed later.) This tax treatment also applies with respect to any holder of stock whose basis is determined by reference to the basis in the hands of the purchaser, e.g. received as a gift.

An individual who strips the rights to one or more dividends from the stocks described above and disposes of those dividend rights generally will be treated as having purchased the stripped preferred stock on the date of the disposition for a purchase price equal to his adjusted basis in the stripped preferred stock.

The amount is included in gross income under these provisions. It is treated as ordinary income, and the stock basis will be adjusted accordingly.

Stock Dividend

A stock dividend is a dividend paid in shares of stocks of the distributing corporation to its shareholders with respect to its outstanding stock. Similar to cash dividends, a distribution of stock to compensate the individual for services rendered, goods provided, etc. Are not made with respect to the distributing of a corporation's outstanding stock and therefore, would not be a stock dividend.

Generally stock dividends are not taxed. But if any shareholder has an election or option to choose to receive the dividend in cash or property other than stock or stock rights of the distributing corporation, then the dividend is taxable with respect to all shareholders. The Tax Court has held that such an "election or option" did not exist where certain shareholders had the ability to request redemption of a portion of their stock for cash subsequent to the distribution, and where the issuer retained complete discretion as to whether it would redeem the shares, however, the court added that under different factual circumstances, a discretionary act of the board of directors of a shareholder corporation to redeem stock dividends might constitute an "option" that arises after the distribution.

Therefore, a stock dividend or dividend paid in stock rights would be taxable if the dividend distribution results in the receipt by some shareholders of cash or property other than stock or stock rights of the corporation and in an increase for other shareholders in their proportionate interests in the assets or earnings and profits of the corporation.

Similar situation exists if a stock dividend or dividend paid in stock rights of the distribution corporation results in the receipt of preferred stock by some common stock shareholders and the receipt of common stock by other common stock shareholders.

If there is any question regarding the ability of any of the shareholders to obtain anything other than stock of the same type in a stock dividend, the taxpayer should consult their tax preparer.

Stock Splits

A stock split is treated basically in the same manner as a stock dividend. Therefore, a stock split is generally a nontaxable event for the shareholder. The tax basis and holding period of the "New" stock received in a stock split is determined by a pro rata allocation of the basis of the original stock to the new stock and uses the holding period of the original stock.

Return of Capital Distributions

As mentioned under dividends above, to the extent that a distribution paid with respect to its stock exceeds the corporation's current and past earnings, the shareholders will be deemed to have received a "return of capital."

When a shareholder receives a "return of capital" distribution, the tax basis in the stock is reduced by the amount of the distribution. There is no tax to the extent that his basis is reduced. Any excess of "return of capital" over the shareholder's tax basis in the stock is generally treated as capital gain.

Dividend Re-investment Plans

Although dividends received or credited under a dividend reinvestment plan, commonly referred to as DRIPS, will be taxed as dividend income, the specifics depend on which of the two basic types of re-investment plans is involved.

In method one, the corporation may allow the shareholder to use dividends to buy more shares of stock in the corporation instead of receiving dividends in cash. The taxpayer must still report the dividends as income.

The second method offers participating shareholders an option to invest additional cash to purchase at a discount limited quantities of the corporation's stock. If a shareholder so elects, it must be treated as dividend income for income tax purposes with the difference being the fair market value of the stock on the dividend payment date and the optional payment made. A shareholder's tax basis in the shares purchased under this type of option is generally the fair market value on the dividend payment due. The holding period of stock purchased under the optional aspect of a dividend reinvestment plan begins on the day following the date the shares are purchased.

Sale or Exchange

Generally, a shareholder who sells or exchanges his stock for other property realizes a capital gain or loss. Whether such gain or loss is short-term or long-term usually depends on how long the shareholder held the stock before selling it. Stocks held for one year or less are short term and if over one year, they are long term.

However, one must look at the specific circumstances involved when there is a conversion of what appears to be a change from a long-term capital gain status to short-term gain, short-term capital loss to long-term loss, capital gain to ordinary income, etc. Also, certain derivative securities transactions may result in constructive sale with respect to an appreciated stock position, which may result in immediate recognition of gain and the start of a new holding period.

A taxpayer is treated as having made a constructive sale of an appreciated financial position if the taxpayer enters into a short sale of the same or substantially identical property; enters into an offsetting notional principal contract relating to the same or substantially identical property, enters into a futures or forward contract to deliver the same or substantially identical property or acquires the same or substantially identical property (if the appreciated financial position is a short sale, an offsetting notional principal contract or a futures or forward contract). A major exception to the constructive sale rules is a contract for any stock, debt instrument or partnership interest that is not a marketable security if it sells within one year of the date entered into. Competent tax advice is required when conversions or constructive sales are apparent.

Short Sales

In a "short sale" an individual contracts to sell stock or securities that the individual does not own, owns but does not wish to sell, or the certificates for which are not within his control so as to be available for delivery when, under the rules of the particular Exchange, delivery must be made, with the most common not under shareholder control being margin stock. Thus in a short sale, the seller usually borrows the stock (usually through a broker) for delivery to the buyer. At a later date, the short seller will repay the borrowed stock to the lender with shares he held at the time of the short sale or with shares he purchases in the market, whichever he chooses.

The act of delivering stock to the lender in repayment for the borrowed shares is referred to as "closing" the short sale. The date sales agreement is made is considered to be the "date of the short sale." In a **covered sale** the shorted seller already owns shares of stock that are identical to those sold short, but chooses to borrow the necessary shares rather than deliver his own.

As a general rule, the determination of whether it is a short-term or long-term capital gain or loss on a short sale is the amount of time the taxpayer held the property eventually delivered to the lender to close the short sale.

Note that borrowing the stock from another lender to close the sale does not meet the short sale closing. The taxpayer does not have a gain or loss until delivery of the property to close the short sale. If the property used to close the short sale is a capital asset based on the amount of time the taxpayer actually held the property eventually delivered to the lender to close the short sale, the taxpayer will have a capital gain or loss.

A contract to sell stock or securities on a "when issued" basis is also considered a short sale and the performance of the contract is considered to be the "closing" of that short sale. Likewise, a transaction in which a taxpayer purchases convertible bonds and as nearly simultaneously as possible sells the stock into which the bonds are convertible at a price relatively higher than the price of the bonds, then converts the bonds and uses the stock received to close the stock sale is a short sale.

In applying the short sale rules, a securities futures contract (which will be described later) to acquire property will be treated in a manner similar to the property itself.

The timing of the taxable event depends on when the short sale occurs and whether it constitutes a constructive sale of an appreciated financial position. Special tax rules also govern the determination of the holding period of property subject to a short sale. Under provisions predating the constructive sale rules, to prevent individuals from using short sales to convert short-term gains to long-term gains or long-term losses to short-term losses and to prevent the creation of artificial losses the IRC and regulations provide special rules.

If a taxpayer enters into a short sale of property and the property becomes worthless, a special rule requires that the taxpayer recognize gain in the same manner as if the short sale were closed when the property became worthless.

Wash Sales

A "wash sale" is a sale or other disposition of stock or securities at a loss and in which a seller, within a 30 day period, before or after the transaction, replaces the stock or securities by acquiring or entering a contract or option to acquire substantially identical stocks or securities. Typically the objective of a wash sale would be to take advantage of the deduction for any capital losses, and then repurchase the shares immediately thereafter. However, the IRS does not allow the deduction of losses from sales or trades of stock or securities if it is determined to be a wash sale under the wash sale rules. If the loss is disallowed because of the wash sale rules, the taxpayer must add the disallowed loss to the cost of the new stock or securities. The result thereof is the basis in the new stock or securities. This adjustment postpones the loss deduction until the disposition of the new stock or securities. The holding period for the new stock or securities begins on the same day as the holding period of the stock or securities sold.

Worthless Securities

When an investor's securities become worthless at any time during a year, the loss is treated as a capital loss realized in a sale or exchange of the worthless security on the last day of that year thus affecting whether the loss is long or short term. The determination as to when the security becomes worthless is often very difficult and has been the subject of an extensive amount of disputes between the IRS and taxpayers. The investor must be able to show that an identifiable event resulting in the worthlessness occurred in the year in which the claim the loss occurred. One must also be able to show that the security had some intrinsic or potential value at the close of the prior year. In determining whether a security is, in fact, worthless, any potential future value as well as any present value must be considered.

Incentive Stock Options

An incentive stock option (ISO) is an option granted to an individual in connection with his employment by the employer corporation to purchase stock of the corporation, if all of the requirements are met:

1. The option is granted pursuant to a plan that specifies the aggregate number of shares that may be issued and the employees or class of employees eligible to receive the option.

2. The option is granted within the earlier of 10 years of the date of the plan is adopted or approved by the shareholders.

3. The option must, by its terms, be exercisable within not more than 10 years of the date it is granted.

4. The exercise price of the option is not less than the fair market value of the stock at the time it is granted.

5. The option is nontransferable and exercisable only by the transferee except in the case of death.

6. The grantee of the option may not own stock representing more than 10 percent of the combined voting power of all classes of stock of the employer corporation, or its parent or subsidiary corporation.

Only up to $100,000 of options, determined by the fair market value on the date of grant, which are exercisable for the first time by any individual during any calendar year are considered ISO's.

Stock acquired under an ISO plan receives the most beneficial tax treatment for, if the holding periods are met, the entire gain from the sale of stock may be treated at the more favorable capital gain rate even if the stock was acquired at a cost of less than fair market value.

Options

An option is a contract in which an individual or an entity, in return for consideration, grants for a specified time to the purchaser of the option the right to purchase from the grantor certain specified property at a fixed price. Under an option contract, only the grantor is obligated to perform, the purchaser may choose to exercise the option or may allow it to lapse.

The term "Equity Option" is any option to buy or sell stock whose value is determined directly or indirectly by reference to any stock or any narrow-based security index. Thus single stock futures and narrow-based stock index futures are classified as equity options. Single stock futures and narrow-based stock index futures are subject to the joint jurisdiction of the Commodity Futures Trading Commission (CFTC) and the Securities Exchange Commission (SEC).

In the case of options on individual stocks, a **call option** is an option contract giving the owner thereof the right to purchase from the writer (grantor) of the call, at anytime before a specified future date and time, a stated number of shares of a particular stock at a specified price for a cash premium.

A **put option** on the other hand is an option contract giving the owner thereof the right to sell to the writer (grantor) of the put, at anytime before a specified future date and time, a stated number of shares of a particular stock at a specified price for a cash premium.

In any case only the grantor of the option is obligated to perform on it, the purchase or subsequent owner of the call or put may choose to dispose of it or allow it to expire. The owner of an option is referred to as holding a "long" position; the writer of an option is referred to as holding a "short" position. Thus it is always the holder of the short position who is obligated to perform on the contract and the holder of the long position who may choose to exercise the contract or permit it to lapse.

If a taxpayer buys a call or a put, the taxpayer may not deduct the cost thereof as a capital expenditure. If the taxpayer sells the call or the put before it is exercised, the difference between its cost and the amount the taxpayer receives for it is either a long-term or short-term capital gain or loss depending on how long it is held. If the option expires, its cost is either a long-term or short-term capital loss depending on the taxpayer's holding period which ended on the expiration date. If the call is exercised, its cost is added to the basis of the stock that was bought. If the exercise is of a put, reduce the amount realized on the sale of the underlying stock by the cost of the put when figuring the gain or loss.

For federal income tax purposes, a non-equity option is any option traded on a national securities exchange or commodity futures exchange that is not an equity option. Thus options on regulated futures contracts (to be discussed under "Futures" below) are non-equity options. In addition the term non-equity includes any option traded on a national securities exchange whose value is determined directly or indirectly by reference to broad-based groups of stocks and broad-based stock indexes. Non-equity options are taxed under the mark-to-market rules that apply to regulated futures contracts.

Spread Transactions

A "spread" is a position consisting of both long and short options of the same underlying security. The options may have different exercise prices and exercise dates. The basic purpose of the various types of spread transactions is to limit or define the risks of the options transactions. The "spread" is the actual dollar difference between the buy premiums and sell premiums.

The three basic types of spreads are vertical (or price), horizontal (time), and diagonal (combo of vertical and horizontal) referred to either credit, debit or even respectively.

Vertical spread is the simultaneous purchase and sale of puts or calls with the same underlying security and expiration date with different strike prices. An investment in a vertical spread is based upon the expectation that the option purchased is undervalued relative to the options sold.

Horizontal spread is simultaneous purchase and sale of puts or calls with same underlying security and strike price, but with different expiration dates. Horizontal spreads are purchased in anticipation that over time the spread will widen.

Diagonal spread is a combination of vertical and horizontal spread, thus it is the simultaneous purchase and sale of puts and calls with the same underlying security but with different strike prices and expiration dates.

Generally the spread transactions are taxed based on the straddle rules to the extent that the positions in the spread are offsetting. Consequently, certain spreads will apparently be subject to constructive sale treatment.

Securities Future Contracts

The IRS defines **securities futures contracts** As a contract of sale for future delivery of a single security or a narrow-based security index. A security futures contract will generally not be treated as a commodity futures contract for the purposes of taxation. Therefore, gain or loss on securities futures contracts will be treated under the rules relating to the disposition of the underlying property. The tax code provides that gain or loss from the sale, exchange, or termination of property that has the same character as the property to which the contract relates has is in the hands of the taxpayer. Thus if the underlying security would be a capital asset in the taxpayer's hands, then the gain or loss from the sale or exchange of the securities futures contract would be capital gain or loss.

Stock Warrants

A stock warrant is an instrument issued by a corporation granting the owner thereof the right to buy a specific amount of stock at a specified price, usually for a limited time. In the case of the holder, a stock warrant is treated like an option. If a warrant to acquire stock in the distributing corporation is acquired in a dividend distribution, taxation to the recipient-shareholder depends on whether the dividend is taxable or not. If it is a nontaxable stock dividend, there is no immediate income taxation. If the dividend is taxable, it is treated as a dividend "in kind," so that the amount that generally must be included in the recipient-shareholder's income is the fair market value of the warrant on the date of distribution.

A distribution of stock warrants is treated in the same manner as a stock dividend, discussed above, so long as the distribution of such warrants is made with respect to the corporation's outstanding stock. A distribution of stock of the distributing corporation made with respect to outstanding stock rights or convertible securities of that corporation to the owners thereof will also qualify as a stock dividend.

Futures

A future is a contract to purchase or sell a particular commodity or financial instrument at a specified price at a specified future date. A future is classified as either a "futures contract" or a "forward contract."

Futures contracts are bought and sold on at least one of the various commodities or futures exchanges. All terms and provisions of a futures contract, except price and delivery month are fixed by the bylaws and rules of the exchange, price and delivery month are agreed to when the trade is made on the floor of the exchange. Although all futures contracts originate between a buyer and seller, the exchange's clearing organization, at the end of business day, substitutes itself as the "other party" of each contract written that day.

Regulated Futures Contract is a futures contract that is traded on a domestic or foreign exchange that employs a cash flow system similar to the variations margin system and is designated by the U.S. government. Regulated Future Contracts generally call for the delivery of many types of property; however, they may cover things not generally thought of as property and may call for settlement in cash rather than delivery of the property.

Forward contracts, in contrast to futures, will deliver a substantially fixed amount of property (including cash) for a substantially fixed price. Forward contracts are not subject to CFTC regulation, are not standardized as to terms and provisions and do not involve a variations margin. All terms and provisions of a forward contract are subject to negotiation between the buyer and the seller. A taxpayer who enters into a forward contract to deliver property that is the same as or substantially identical to an appreciated financial position that he holds will generally be treated as having made a constructive sale of that position.

Tax Straddles

A "tax straddle" is the simultaneous ownership of offsetting interests in actively traded personal property. It includes stock options and contracts to buy stock but generally does not include stock. For this purpose, an interest may be ownership of the property itself or may be a regulated futures contract, a futures contract other than regulated futures contract, or an option. Interests owned by an investor's spouse, partnership, S corporation or a trust of which the investor is a deemed owner are treated as owned by the investor for purposes of determining whether a tax straddle exists.

Stock can be a straddle (see "Spread Transactions" above) if the stock is of a type which is actively traded and at least one of the offsetting positions is a position on that stock or substantially similar or related property or the stock is in a corporation formed or availed of to take positions in personal property that offset positions taken by any shareholder. Offsetting position is defined by the IRS as a position that substantially reduces any risk of loss one might have from holding another position. However, if a position is part of a straddle that is not an identified straddle, do not treat it as offsetting to a position that is part of an identified straddle. Position is defined by the IRS as an interest in personal property. It can be a forward or futures contract, or an option. A straddle is identified if the taxpayer identified the straddle on his/her records before the close of the day on which it was acquired and the straddle is not part of a larger straddle.

Conversion Transactions

A "conversion transaction" is a transaction from which substantially all of the taxpayer's expected return is attributable to the time value of the taxpayer's net investment in the transaction and the transaction is one of the following:

1. A straddle including any set of offsetting positions on stock.

2. Any transaction in which the taxpayer acquires property (whether or not actively traded) at substantially the same time that the taxpayer contracted to sell the same property or substantially identical property at a price set in the contract.

3. Any transaction that is marketed or sold as producing capital gains from a transaction from which substantially all of the taxpayer's expected returns is attributable to the time value of money invested in transaction.

The amount of gain treated as ordinary income is the smaller of the gain recognized on the disposition or other termination of the position, or the "applicable imputed income amount."

BONDS

Treasury bills are obligations of the United States government, generally issued with 4 weeks, 13 weeks and 26 weeks maturity periods. Treasury bills are issued in minimum denominations of $1,000 with $1,000 increments thereafter. Treasury bills are issued without interest and on a discount basis. The price is determined at auction. Treasury bills are capital assets and on sale or maturity of the bill, the seller recovers his tax basis tax free. Any gain realized over his tax basis must be treated as ordinary income to the extent it represents recovery discount. Any excess over that is capital gain.

The gain or loss on the sale or redemption of **short term corporate obligations** is ordinary income up to the portion of the OID (discussed below) allocable to the time the obligation was held by the taxpayer.

The share of original discount allocable to the taxpayer is the amount that bears the same ratio to the total discount as the number of days he held the obligation bears to the number of days after the issue date up to and including the date of maturity of the obligation. An irrevocable election may be made, on an obligation-by-obligation basis, to determine the amount using the daily compounding at a constant interest rate.

Treasury bonds and notes are obligations of the federal government. They are essentially similar, except that bonds mature in more than 10 years while Treasury notes have maturity dates ranging from one to 10 years. They are issued in denominations from $1,000 to $1,000,000. Bonds issued after September 3, 1982 and notes issued after 1982 must be registered in form; however bearer bonds and notes issued before registration requirement date may continue to be sought and sold in bearer form. Bearer notes and bonds have coupons attached that are cut off and redeemed, generally through a commercial bank or the Federal Reserve Bank.

Corporate bonds with interest accrued, but not yet due, before the date of a gift is included as ordinary income in the donor's income for the taxable year during which the bond interest is actually or constructively received by the donee. Therefore, the donor will not necessarily be taxed on such income in the year in which the gift is made. Amounts received from interest accruing after the transfer date are includable in the gross income of the donee.

Treasury Inflation Protection Securities are obligations of the federal government whose principal value is adjusted for inflation and deflation based on monthly changes in the non-seasonally adjusted U.S. City Average All Items Consumer Price Index for All Urban Consumers.

This security also provides for an additional payment at maturity if the security inflation-adjusted principal amount for the maturity date is less than the security's principal amount at issuance. The additional amount payable will equal the excess of the security's principal amount at issuance over the security's inflation-adjusted principal amount for the maturity date.

A bond is considered **inflation-indexed** for federal income tax purposes if it was issued for U.S. dollars and all payments on the instrument are denominated in U.S dollars; each payment on the debt instrument is indexed for inflation and deflation except for a minimum guarantee payment; and no payment on the debt instrument is subject to a contingency other the inflation contingency, a minimum guarantee payment, or certain inflation-indexed payments under one or more alternate schedules.

Market Discounts

Bond prices on the market fluctuate as interest rates change and as the borrower's credit rating changes. Thus, bonds may be bought at a discount because of a decline in value of the obligation after issue. A bond acquired at a discount on the market is called a market discount bond. For tax purposes the market discount bond does not include short-term obligations with fixed maturity dates of up to one year from the date of issue, tax exempt obligations that were purchased by the taxpayer before May 1, 1993, U.S. savings bonds, and certain installment obligations.

Market discount is the amount by which the stated redemption price exceeds the taxpayer's basis in the bond immediately after its acquisition, if the bond was originally issued on par.

When a cash basis taxpayer sells a market discount bond issued after July 18, 1984 or issued before July 19, 1984 and purchased after April 30, 1993 or if the taxpayer sells a tax exempt bond purchased on the market before May 1, 1993 at a discount, his gain is generally treated as ordinary interest income up to the instrument's accrued market discount.

Original Issue Discount (OID)

Original Issue Discount (OID) is a form of interest and is the amount by which the stated redemption price at maturity of a debt instrument is more than its issue price. The taxpayer includes OID in his/her income as it accrues over the term of the debt instrument, irrespective if the taxpayer receives any payments from the issuer. If a bond is issued at a price that is less than its stated redemption price at maturity, the difference is original issue discount. However, if the discount at which the bond was issued is less than ¼ of 1 percent (referred to as de minimis OID) of the stated redemption price multiplied by the number of complete years to maturity, the bond is treated as if it were issued without a discount.

If the bond is issued for the property and either the bond or the property is traded on an established market, the issue price of the bond is considered to be fair market value of the property.

The amount of original issue discount is included in income as it accrues over the life of the bond. For bonds issued after April 4, 1994, OID must be accrued at a constant rate. The holder of a bond may use accrual periods of different lengths provided that no accrual period is longer than one year. Payment may either occur on the first day or final day of the accrual period.

Bond Premiums

Bond premium is the amount by which the cost or other basis in the bond right after purchase is more than the total of all amounts payable on the bond other than payments of qualified stated interest. An individual who purchased a taxable bond at a premium, whether or not on original issue, may elect to amortize the premium over the remaining life of the bond by reducing the amount of interest included in the taxpayer's income. However, if the bond yields tax exempt interest, the taxpayer is required to amortize the premium and this amortized amount is not deductible in determining taxable income.

The term "bond" to which the election applies is quite broad and includes any taxable bond, debentures, certificate or other evidence of indebtedness issued by any corporation, government or political subdivision. However, the taxpayer is not required to amortize premiums on taxable bonds just because there are tax-exempt bonds that are being amortized.

State and Local Government Securities

Debt securities issued by state and local governments are referred to as **municipal bonds**. Examples of issuing agencies include states, cities, school districts, toll roads, or any other type of political subdivision. The most important feature of a municipal bond is the tax-exempt nature of the interest payment. Dating back to the U.S. Supreme Court opinion of 1819 in *McCullough v. Maryland*, it was ruled that the federal government and state and local governments do not possess the power to tax each other. An eventual by-product of the judicial ruling was that income from municipal bonds cannot be taxed by the IRS. Furthermore, income from municipal bonds is also exempt from state and local taxes if bought within the locality in which one resides. Thus, a Californian buying municipal bonds in that state would pay no state income tax on the issue. However, the same Californian would have to pay state or local income taxes if the originating agency were in Texas or New York.

We cannot overemphasize the importance of the federal tax exemption that municipal bonds enjoy. The consequences are twofold. First, individuals in high tax brackets may find highly attractive investment opportunities in municipal bonds.[1] The formula used to equate interest on municipal bonds to other taxable investments is:

$$Y = \frac{i}{(1 - T)} \qquad (16\text{--}1)$$

where:

Y = Equivalent before-tax yield on a taxable investment
i = Yield on the municipal obligation
T = Marginal tax rate of the investor

If an investor has a marginal tax rate of 35 percent and is evaluating a municipal bond paying 6 percent interest, the equivalent before-tax yield on a taxable investment would be:

$$\frac{6\%}{(1 - 0.35)} = \frac{6\%}{0.65} = 9.23\%$$

Thus, the investor could choose between a *non*-tax-exempt investment paying 9.23 percent and a tax-exempt municipal bond paying 6 percent and be indifferent between the two.

General Obligation versus Revenue Bonds   A **general obligation issue** is backed by the full faith, credit, and "taxing power" of the governmental unit. For a **revenue bond**, on the other hand, the repayment of the issue is fully dependent on the revenue-generating capability of a specific project or venture, such as a toll road, bridge, or municipal colosseum.

Because of the taxing power behind most general obligation (GO) issues, they tend to be of extremely high quality. Approximately three-fourths of all municipal bond issues are of the general obligation variety, and very few failures have occurred in the post–World War II era. Revenue bonds tend to be of more uneven quality, and the economic soundness of the underlying revenue-generating project must be carefully examined (though most projects are quite worthwhile).

Municipal Bond Guarantee   A growing factor in the municipal bond market is the third-party guarantee. Whether dealing with a general obligation or revenue bond, a fee may be paid by the originating governmental body to a third-party insurer to guarantee that all interest and principal payments will be made. There are four private insurance firms that guarantee municipal bonds, the largest of which are the Municipal Bond Investors Assurance (MBIA) and the American Municipal Bond Assurance Corporation (AMBAC). Municipal bonds that are guaranteed carry the highest rating possible (AAA) because all the guaranteeing insurance companies are rated AAA. Approximately 30 percent of municipal bond issues are guaranteed.

A municipal bond that is guaranteed will carry a lower yield and have a better secondary or resale market. This may be important because municipal bonds, in general, do not provide as strong a secondary market as U.S. government issues. The market for a given municipal issue is often small and fragmented, and high indirect costs are associated with reselling the issue.

---

1. It should be noted that any capital gain on a municipal bond is taxable as would be the case with any investment.

Index